Lecture ... ce   2305

Edited by ... Leeuwen

31.00

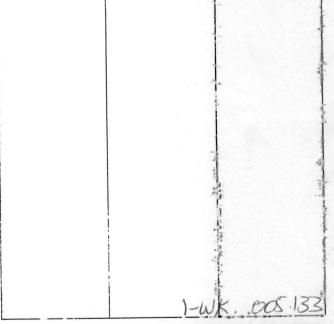

Springer
Berlin
Heidelberg
New York
Barcelona
Hong Kong
London
Milan
Paris
Tokyo

Daniel Le Métayer (Ed.)

Programming Languages and Systems

11th European Symposium on Programming, ESOP 2002
Held as Part of the Joint European Conferences
on Theory and Practice of Software, ETAPS 2002
Grenoble, France, April 8-12, 2002
Proceedings

 Springer

Series Editors

Gerhard Goos, Karlsruhe University, Germany
Juris Hartmanis, Cornell University, NY, USA
Jan van Leeuwen, Utrecht University, The Netherlands

Volume Editor

Daniel Le Métayer
Trusted Logic
5 rue du Bailliage, 78000 Versailles, France

Cataloging-in-Publication Data applied for

Die Deutsche Bibliothek - CIP-Einheitsaufnahme

Programming languages and systems : proceedings / 11th European Symposium on
Programming, ESOP 2001, held as part of the Joint European Conferences on
Theory and Practice of Software, ETAPS 2002, Grenoble, France, April 8 - 12,
2002. Daniel Le Métayer (ed.). - Berlin ; Heidelberg ; New York ; Barcelona ;
Hong Kong ; London ; Milan ; Paris ; Tokyo : Springer, 2002
  (Lecture notes in computer science ; Vol. 2305)
  ISBN 3-540-43363-5

CR Subject Classification (1998): D.3, D.1-2, F.3-4, E.1

ISSN 0302-9743
ISBN 3-540-43363-5 Springer-Verlag Berlin Heidelberg New York

Springer-Verlag Berlin Heidelberg New York
a member of BertelsmannSpringer Science+Business Media GmbH

http://www.springer.de

© Springer-Verlag Berlin Heidelberg 2002
Printed in Germany

Typesetting: Camera-ready by author, data conversion by Markus Richter, Heidelberg
Printed on acid-free paper   SPIN 10846513   06/3142   5 4 3 2 1 0

Foreword

ETAPS 2002 was the fifth instance of the European Joint Conferences on Theory and Practice of Software. ETAPS is an annual federated conference that was established in 1998 by combining a number of existing and new conferences. This year it comprised 5 conferences (FOSSACS, FASE, ESOP, CC, TACAS), 13 satellite workshops (ACL2, AGT, CMCS, COCV, DCC, INT, LDTA, SC, SFEDL, SLAP, SPIN, TPTS, and VISS), 8 invited lectures (not including those specific to the satellite events), and several tutorials.

The events that comprise ETAPS address various aspects of the system development process, including specification, design, implementation, analysis, and improvement. The languages, methodologies, and tools which support these activities are all well within its scope. Different blends of theory and practice are represented, with an inclination towards theory with a practical motivation on one hand and soundly-based practice on the other. Many of the issues involved in software design apply to systems in general, including hardware systems, and the emphasis on software is not intended to be exclusive.

ETAPS is a loose confederation in which each event retains its own identity, with a separate program committee and independent proceedings. Its format is open-ended, allowing it to grow and evolve as time goes by. Contributed talks and system demonstrations are in synchronized parallel sessions, with invited lectures in plenary sessions. Two of the invited lectures are reserved for "unifying" talks on topics of interest to the whole range of ETAPS attendees. The aim of cramming all this activity into a single one-week meeting is to create a strong magnet for academic and industrial researchers working on topics within its scope, giving them the opportunity to learn about research in related areas, and thereby to foster new and existing links between work in areas that were formerly addressed in separate meetings.

ETAPS 2002 was organized by the Laboratoire Verimag in cooperation with

Centre National de la Recherche Scientifique (CNRS)
Institut de Mathématiques Appliquées de Grenoble (IMAG)
Institut National Polytechnique de Grenoble (INPG)
Université Joseph Fourier (UJF)
European Association for Theoretical Computer Science (EATCS)
European Association for Programming Languages and Systems (EAPLS)
European Association of Software Science and Technology (EASST)
ACM SIGACT, SIGSOFT, and SIGPLAN

The organizing team comprised

Susanne Graf - General Chair
Saddek Bensalem - Tutorials
Rachid Echahed - Workshop Chair
Jean-Claude Fernandez - Organization

Alain Girault - Publicity
Yassine Lakhnech - Industrial Relations
Florence Maraninchi - Budget
Laurent Mounier - Organization

Overall planning for ETAPS conferences is the responsibility of its Steering Committee, whose current membership is:

Egidio Astesiano (Genova), Ed Brinksma (Twente), Pierpaolo Degano (Pisa), Hartmut Ehrig (Berlin), José Fiadeiro (Lisbon), Marie-Claude Gaudel (Paris), Andy Gordon (Microsoft Research, Cambridge), Roberto Gorrieri (Bologna), Susanne Graf (Grenoble), John Hatcliff (Kansas), Görel Hedin (Lund), Furio Honsell (Udine), Nigel Horspool (Victoria), Heinrich Hußmann (Dresden), Joost-Pieter Katoen (Twente), Paul Klint (Amsterdam), Daniel Le Métayer (Trusted Logic, Versailles), Ugo Montanari (Pisa), Mogens Nielsen (Aarhus), Hanne Riis Nielson (Copenhagen), Mauro Pezzè (Milan), Andreas Podelski (Saarbrücken), Don Sannella (Edinburgh), Andrzej Tarlecki (Warsaw), Herbert Weber (Berlin), Reinhard Wilhelm (Saarbrücken)

I would like to express my sincere gratitude to all of these people and organizations, the program committee chairs and PC members of the ETAPS conferences, the organizers of the satellite events, the speakers themselves, and finally Springer-Verlag for agreeing to publish the ETAPS proceedings. As organizer of ETAPS'98, I know that there is one person that deserves a special applause: Susanne Graf. Her energy and organizational skills have more than compensated for my slow start in stepping into Don Sannella's enormous shoes as ETAPS Steering Committee chairman. Yes, it is now a year since I took over the role, and I would like my final words to transmit to Don all the gratitude and admiration that is felt by all of us who enjoy coming to ETAPS year after year knowing that we will meet old friends, make new ones, plan new projects and be challenged by a new culture! Thank you Don!

January 2002   José Luiz Fiadeiro

Preface

This volume contains the papers selected for presentation at the 11th European Symposium on Programming (ESOP 2002), which took place in Grenoble, France, April 8-10, 2002. ESOP is an annual conference devoted to the design, specification, and analysis of programming languages and programming systems. Special emphasis was placed on research that bridges the gap between theory and practice.

The contributions of ESOP 2002 can be classified in three main categories:

- Typing and modularity.
- Programming paradigms (including distributed programming, lambda calculus, and domain specific languages).
- Program analysis (principles and applications) and program verification.

The volume begins with an invited contribution by Greg Morrisett. The remaining 21 papers were selected by the program committee from 73 submissions, and include one short paper which accompanied a tool demonstration.

Each submission was reviewed by at least three referees, and papers were selected during the latter stage of a two-week discussion phase. I would like to express my gratitude to the program committee and their referees (see below) for their care in reviewing and selecting the submitted papers. I am also very grateful to Tiziana Margaria, Martin Karusseit, and the Metaframe team for their support of the conference management software. Last but not least, many thanks to José Luiz Fiadeiro, Susanne Graf, and the ETAPS team for providing a well-organized framework for the conference.

January 2002   Daniel Le Métayer

Organization

Program Chair

Daniel Le Métayer   Trusted Logic, France

Program Committee

Charles Consel   LaBRI/ENSERB, France
Roberto Gorrieri   University of Bologna, Italy
Pieter Hartel   University of Twente, The Netherlands
Thomas Jensen   Irisa/CNRS, France
Julia Lawall   DIKU, Denmark
Florence Maraninchi   INPG/Verimag, France
John Mitchell   Stanford University, USA
Joachim Posegga   SAP AG, Germany
Didier Remy   INRIA-Rocquencourt, France
Mooly Sagiv   Tel-Aviv University, Israel
David Sands   Chalmers and Göteborg University, Sweden
David Schmidt   Kansas State University, USA
Jan Vitek   Purdue University, USA
Dennis Volpano   Naval Postgraduate School, USA

Additional Referees

Alessandro Aldini
Lorenzo Bettini
Stefano Bistarelli
Lydie du Bousquet
Mario Bravetti
Nadia Busi
Bogdan Carbunar
Jordan Chong
Catarina Coquand
Radhia Cousot
Olivier Danvy
Xavier Delord
Nurit Dor
Benoît Escrig
Sandro Etalle
Andrej Felinski
Jean-Claude Fernandez
Riccardo Focardi
Pascal Fradet
Carl C. Frederiksen
Thomas Genet
Rosella Gennari
Rajeev Goré
Christian Grothoff
Jörgen Gustavsson
Jochen Haller
Chris Hankin
Ferdy Hanssen
Jaap-Henk Hoepman
Bertrand Jeannet

Günter Karjoth
Jan Kuper
Marta Z. Kwiatkowska
Yassine Lakhnech
Cosimo Laneve
Peeter Laud
Didier Le Botlan
Chin Soon Lee
James Leifer
Xavier Leroy
Francesca Levi
Luis Lopez
Roberto Lucchi
Ian Mackie
Angelika Mader
Heiko Mantel
Fabio Martinelli
Ricardo Massa
Fabio Massacci
Bret Michael
Jon Millen
David Monniaux
Ugo Montanari
Alberto Montresor
Laurent Mounier
Jon Mountjoy
Gilles Muller
Xavier Nicollin
Lasse Neilsen
Karol Ostrovsky

Jens Palsberg
Lawrence C. Paulson
Luciano Porto Barreto
François Pottier
Morten Rhiger
Olivier Ridoux
Jon Riecke
Hanne Riss Nielson
Francesca Rossi
Vlad Rusu
Marie-France Sagot
Ivano Salvo
Alan Schmitt
Peter Schmitt
Ran Shaham
Gerard Smit
Geoffrey Smith
Scott Smolka
Axel Spriestersbach
Charles Stewart
Scott Stoller
Stavros Tripakis
Pim van den Broek
Harald Vogt
Eran Yahav
Francesco Zappa Nardelli
Gianluigi Zavattaro
Elena Zinovieva

Table of Contents

Invited Paper

Type Checking Systems Code 1
  Greg Morrisett (Cornell University, USA)

Typing and Modularity

Mixin Modules in a Call-by-Value Setting 6
  Tom Hirschowitz and Xavier Leroy (Inria Rocquencourt, France)

Existential Types for Imperative Languages 21
  Dan Grossman (Cornell University, USA)

Another Type System for In-Place Update 36
  David Aspinall (LFCS, Edinburgh, UK) and Martin Hofmann (University of Munich, Germany)

Programming Paradigms

Soft Concurrent Constraint Programming 53
  Stefano Bistarelli (CNR Pisa, Italy), Ugo Montanari (Università di Pisa, Italy), and Francesca Rossi (Università di Padova, Italy)

Programming Languages for Compressing Graphics 68
  Morgan McGuire, Shriram Krishnamurthi, and John F. Hughes (Brown University, USA)

An Accumulative Parallel Skeleton for All 83
  Zhenjiang Hu (University of Tokyo, Japan), Hideya Iwasaki (University of Electro-Communications, Japan), and Masato Takeichi (Japan Science and Technology Corporation)

Higher-Order Intensional Type Analysis 98
  Stephanie Weirich (Cornell University, USA)

Lambda Calculus

Branching Types 115
  Joe Wells and Christian Haack (Heriot-Watt University, UK)

Exceptions, Continuations and Macro-expressiveness 133
  James Laird (University of Sussex, UK)

A Theory of Second-Order Trees 147
    Neal Glew

Program Analysis: Applications

Tool Support for Improving Test Coverage 162
    Susan Horwitz (University of Wisconsin and GrammaTech, USA)

Data Space Oriented Tiling 178
    Mahmut Kandemir (Pennsylvania State University, USA)

Propagation of Roundoff Errors in Finite Precision Computations: A Semantics Approach... 194
    Matthieu Martel (CEA, France)

Asserting the Precision of Floating-Point Computations: A Simple Abstract Interpreter (demo paper) 209
    Eric Goubault, Matthieu Martel, and Sylvie Putot (CEA, France)

Program Analysis: Principles

A Modular, Extensible Proof Method for Small-Step Flow Analyses 213
    *Mitchell Wand and Galen B. Williamson (Northeastern University,
    USA)*

A Prototype Dependency Calculus 228
    Peter Thiemann (Universität Freiburg, Germany)

Automatic Complexity Analysis 243
    *Flemming Nielson, Hanne Riis Nielson (The Technical University of
    Denmark, Lyngby), and Helmut Seidl (Universität Trier)*

Distributed Programs: Verification and Analysis

Thread-Modular Verification for Shared-Memory Programs.............. 262
    *Cormac Flanagan, Stephen N. Freund, and Shaz Qadeer (Compaq Sys-
    tems Research Center, Palo Alto, USA)*

Timing UDP: Mechanized Semantics for Sockets, Threads and Failures ... 278
    *Keith Wansbrough, Michael Norrish, Peter Sewell, and Andrei Serjan-
    tov (University of Cambridge, UK)*

Finite-Control Mobile Ambients 295
    *Witold Charatonik (Max-Planck Institut für Informatik, Germany and
    University of Wroclaw, Poland), Andrew D. Gordon (Microsoft Re-
    search, UK), and Jean-Marc Talbot (LIFL, France)*

Dependency Analysis of Mobile Systems 314
    Jérôme Feret (ENS, Paris, France)

Author Index 331

Type Checking Systems Code

Greg Morrisett

Cornell University

Abstract. Our critical computing systems are coded in low-level, type-unsafe languages such as C, and it is unlikely that they will be re-coded in a high-level, type-safe language such as Java. This invited talk discusses some approaches that show promise in achieving type safety for legacy C code.

1 Motivation

Our society is increasingly dependent upon its computing and communications infrastructure. That infrastructure includes the operating systems, device drivers, libraries and applications that we use on our desktops, as well as the file servers, databases, web servers, and switches that we use to store and communicate data. Today, that infrastructure is built using unsafe, error-prone languages such as C or C++ where buffer overruns, format string errors, and space leaks are not only possible, but frighteningly common.

In contrast, type-safe languages, such as Java, Scheme, and ML, ensure that such errors either cannot happen (through static type-checking and automatic memory management) or are at least caught at the point of failure (through dynamic type and bound checks.) This fail-stop guarantee is not a total solution, but it does isolate the effects of failures, facilitates testing and determination of the true source of failures, and enables tools and methodologies for achieving greater levels of assurance. Therefore, the obvious question is:

Why don't we re-code our infrastructure using type-safe languages?

Though such a technical solution looks good on paper and is ultimately the "right thing", there are a number of economic and practical issues that prevent it from happening.

First, our infrastructure is *large*. Today's operating systems consist of tens of millions of lines of code. Throwing away all of that C code and reimplementing it in, say Java, is simply too expensive, just as throwing out old Cobol code was too difficult for Year 2000 bugs.

Second, though C and C++ have many faults, they also have some virtues—especially when it comes to building the low-level pieces of infrastructure. In particular, C provides a great deal of transparency and control over data representations which is precisely what is needed to build services such as memory-mapped device drivers, page-table routines, communication buffer management, real-time schedulers, and garbage collectors. It is difficult if not impossible to realize these services in today's type-safe languages simply because they force one

D. Le Métayer (Ed.): ESOP 2002, LNCS 2305, pp. 1–5, 2002.

to buy into the "high-level language assumption" in order to realize the benefits of type-safety.

2   Alternatives to High-Level Languages

An alternative to re-coding our infrastructure in a safe language is to change C and C++ compilers to do more run-time checking to ensure fail-stop behavior. For instance, the CCured project [6] at Berkeley has recently shown how to automatically compile C code so that we can ensure memory safety. The approach is based on dynamically tracking the types and sizes of the sequence of elements that a pointer might reference, and ensuring that upon dereference, a pointer is valid. In this respect, CCured is much like Scheme because it relies upon dynamic type tags, dynamic type tests, and a (conservative) garbage collector to recycle memory. And, like a good Scheme compiler, CCured attempts to minimize the dynamic tests and type tags that are necessary to ensure memory safety. Consequently, the resulting code tends to run with relatively little overhead (around 50%), especially when compared to previous research [2, 1] or commercial tools such as Purify where overheads of 10x are not uncommon.

But just as with Scheme or any other high-level language, CCured is less than ideal for building low-level infrastructure because control over data representations and memory management have been taken from the programmer. Depending upon the analysis performed by the CCured compiler, a pointer value may take up one word or two, and data values may be augmented with type tags and array bounds. The programmer has no idea what her data look like and thus interfacing to legacy code requires the wrappers and marshallers of a traditional foreign function interface. Garbage collection may introduce long pauses and space overheads. And finally, errors are detected at run-time instead of compile time. Nonetheless, CCured shows that we can achieve fail-stop behavior in a completely automatic fashion for legacy infrastructure that *should* be written in a higher-level language.

Another approach is to throw static analysis at the problem. However, there are serious tradeoffs in statically analyzing large systems and most current analyses fail in one respect or another. A critical issue is minimizing false positives (i.e., reporting a potential problem when there is none) else programmers will not use the tools. One way to achieve this is to sacrifice soundness (i.e., fail to report some bugs) by choosing careful abstractions that make it easier to find common mistakes. For example, Engler has recently used very simple flow analyses to catch bugs in operating systems [5]. The flow analysis is unsound because, for instance, it does not accurately track alias relationships. Though there is much merit in tools that identify the *presence* of bugs, in contexts where security is a concern, we need assurance of the *absence* of bugs. Otherwise, an attacker will simply exploit the bugs that the tools do not find. At a minimum, we ought to ensure fail-stop behavior so as to contain the damage.

An alternative way to minimize false positives in analysis is to increase the accuracy. Such accuracy often requires global, context-sensitive, flow-sensitive analyses that are difficult to scale to millions of lines of code. Few of these analyses work at all in the presence of features such as threads, asynchronous interrupts, or dynamic linking—features that are crucial for building modern systems.

3   Cyclone

Porting code to high-level languages, using compilers that automatically insert dynamic checks, and using tools to statically analyze programs for bugs each have their drawbacks and merits. The ideal solution is one that combines their benefits and minimizes their drawbacks. In particular, the ideal solution should:

- catch most errors at compile time,
- give a fail-stop guarantee at run time, and
- scale to millions of lines of code

while simultaneously:

- minimizing the cost of porting the code from C/C++,
- interoperating with legacy code,
- giving programmers control over low-level details needed to build systems.

For the past two years, Trevor Jim of AT&T and my group at Cornell have been working towards such a solution in the context of a project called Cyclone [4]. Cyclone is a type-safe programming language that can be roughly characterized as a "superset of a subset of C." The type system of Cyclone accepts many C functions without change, and uses the same data representations and calling conventions as C for a given type constructor. The type system of Cyclone also rejects many C programs to ensure safety. For instance, it rejects programs that perform (potentially) unsafe casts, that use unions of incompatible types, that (might) fail to initialize a location before using it, that use certain forms of pointer arithmetic, or that attempt to do certain forms of memory management.

Of course, once you rule out these potential errors, you are left with an essentially useless subset of the language. Therefore, we augmented the language with new type constructors and new terms adapted from high-level languages. For instance, Cyclone provides support for parametric polymorphism, subtyping, and tagged unions so that programmers can code around unsafe casts. We use a combination of default type parameters and local type inference to minimize the changes needed to use these features effectively. The treatment of polymorphism is particularly novel because, unlike C++, we achieve separate compilation of generic definitions from their uses. To achieve this, we must place restrictions on type abstraction that correspond to machine-level polymorphism. These restrictions are realized by a novel kind system which distinguishes those types whose values may be manipulated parametrically, while retaining control over data representations and calling conventions.

Cyclone also supports a number of different pointer types that are similar to those used in the internal language of CCured. These pointer types can be used to tradeoff flexibility (e.g., arbitrary pointer arithmetic) with the need for bounds information and/or run-time tests. The difference with CCured is that Cyclone requires the programmer to make the choice of representation explicit. This is crucial for building systems that must interoperate with legacy code and to achieve separate compilation in dynamically linked settings. A combination of overloading, subtyping, and local type inference helps to minimize the programmer's burden.

Cyclone also incorporates a region type system in the style of Tofte and Talpin [8, 7, 3]. The region type system is used to track the lifetimes of objects and ensure that dangling pointers to stack allocated objects are not dereferenced. The region type system can also be used with arena-style allocators to give the programmer real-time control over heap-allocated storage. Finally, programmers can optionally use a conservative collector if they are uninterested in the details of managing memory.

The Cyclone region system is particularly novel in that it provides a smooth integration of stack allocation, arena allocation, and garbage-collected heap allocation. The support for region polymorphism and region subtyping ensures that library routines can safely manipulate pointers regardless of the kind of object they reference. Finally, we use a novel combination of default regions and effects on function prototypes, combined with local inference to minimize the burden of porting C code.

All of the analyses used by Cyclone are local (i.e., intra-procedural) so that we can ensure scalability and separate compilation. The analyses have also been carefully constructed to avoid unsoundness in the presence of threads. The price paid is that programmers must sometimes change type definitions or prototypes of functions, and occasionally rewrite code.

4   Status and Future Work

Currently, we find that programmers must touch about 10% of the code when porting from C to Cyclone. Most of the changes involve choosing pointer representations and only a very few involve region annotations (around 0.6 % of the total changes.) In the future, we hope to minimize this burden by providing a porting tool which, like CCured, uses a more global analysis to guess the appropriate representation but unlike CCured, produces a residual program that can be modified and maintained by the programmer so that they retain control over representations.

The performance overhead of the dynamic checks depends upon the application. For systems applications, such as a simple web server, we see no overhead at all. This is not surprising as these applications tend to be I/O-bound. For scientific applications, we see a much larger overhead (around 5x for a naive port, and 3x with an experienced programmer). We belive much of this overhead is due to bounds and null pointer checks on array access. We have incorporated a simple, intra-procedural analysis to eliminate many of those checks and indeed, this results in a marked improvement. However, some of the overhead is also due to the use of "fat pointers" and the fact that GCC does not always optimize struct manipulation. By unboxing the structs into variables, we may find a marked improvement.

We are currently working to expand the region type and effects system to support (a) early reclamation of regions and (b) first-class regions in a style similar to what Walker and Watkins suggest [9]. We are also working on limited support for dependent types in the style of Hongwei Xi's Xanadu [10] so that programmers may better control the placement of bounds information or dynamic type tags.

References

[1] Todd M. Austin, Scott E. Breach, and Gurindar S. Sohi. Efficient detection of all pointer and array access errors. Technical Report 1197, University of Wisconsin - Madison, December 1993.

[2] Todd M. Austin, Scott E. Breach, and Gurindar S. Sohi. Efficient detection of all pointer and array access errors. In *ACM Conference on Programming Language Design and Implementation*, pages 290–301, June 1994.

[3] Lars Birkedal, Mads Tofte, and Magnus Vejlstrup. From region inference to von Neumann machines via region representation inference. In *Twenty-Third ACM Symposium on Principles of Programming Languages*, pages 171–183, St. Petersburg Beach, FL, January 1996.

[4] *Cyclone User's Manual*, 2001. http://www.cs.cornell.edu/projects/cyclone/.

[5] D. Engler, B. Chelf, A. Chou, and S. Hallem. Checking system rules using system-specific, programmer-written compiler extensions. In *Proceedings of the Fourth Symposium on Operating Systems Design and Implementation*, San Diego, California, October 2000.

[6] George C. Necula, Scott McPeak, and Westley Weimer. CCured: Type-safe retrofitting of legacy code. In *Twenty-Ninth ACM Symposium on Principles of Programming Languages*, pages 128–139, Portland, OR, January 2002.

[7] Mads Tofte and Jean-Pierre Talpin. Implementing the call-by-value lambda-calculus using a stack of regions. In *Twenty-First ACM Symposium on Principles of Programming Languages*, pages 188–201, January 1994.

[8] Mads Tofte and Jean-Pierre Talpin. Region-based memory management. *Information and Computation*, 132(2):109–176, 1997.

[9] David Walker and Kevin Watkins. On regions and linear types. In *ACM International Conference on Functional Programming*, pages 181–192, September 2001.

[10] Hongwei Xi. Imperative programming with dependent types. In *Proceedings of 15th IEEE Symposium on Logic in Computer Science*, pages 375–387, Santa Barbara, June 2000.

Mixin Modules in a Call-by-Value Setting

Tom Hirschowitz and Xavier Leroy

INRIA Rocquencourt
Domaine de Voluceau, B.P. 105, 78153 Le Chesnay, France
{Tom.Hirschowitz,Xavier.Leroy}@inria.fr

Abstract. The ML module system provides powerful parameterization facilities, but lacks the ability to split mutually recursive definitions across modules, and does not provide enough facilities for incremental programming. A promising approach to solve these issues is Ancona and Zucca's mixin modules calculus *CMS*. However, the straightforward way to adapt it to ML fails, because it allows arbitrary recursive definitions to appear at any time, which ML does not support. In this paper, we enrich *CMS* with a refined type system that controls recursive definitions through the use of dependency graphs. We then develop a separate compilation scheme, directed by dependency graphs, that translate mixin modules down to a CBV λ-calculus extended with a non-standard `let rec` construct.

1 Introduction

Modular programming and code reuse are easier if the programming language provides adequate features to support them. Three important such features are (1) *parameterization*, which allows reusing a module in different contexts; (2) *overriding and late binding*, which supports incremental programming by refinements of existing modules; and (3) *cross-module recursion*, which allows definitions to be spread across several modules, even if they mutually refer to each other. Many programming languages provide two of these features, but not all three: class-based object-oriented languages provide (2) and (3), but are weak on parameterization (1); conventional linkers, as well as linking calculi [9], have cross-module recursion built in, and sometimes provide facilities for overriding, but lack parameterization; finally, ML functors and Ada generics provide powerful parameterization mechanisms, but prohibit cross-module recursion and offer no direct support for late binding.

The concept of *mixins*, first introduced as a generalization of inheritance in class-based OO languages [8], then extended to a family of module systems [13, 3, 15, 21], offers a promising and elegant solution to this problem. A mixin is a collection of named components, either defined (bound to a definition) or deferred (declared without definition). The basic operation on mixins is the sum, which takes two mixins and connects the defined components of one with the similarly-named deferred components of the other; this provides natural support for cross-mixin recursion. A mixin is named and can be summed several times with different mixins; this allows powerful parameterization, including but not restricted to an encoding of ML functors. Finally, the mixin calculus of Ancona

D. Le Métayer (Ed.): ESOP 2002, LNCS 2305, pp. 6–20, 2002.

and Zucca [3] supports both late binding and early binding of defined components, along with deleting and renaming operations, thus providing excellent support for incremental programming.

Our long-term goal is to extend the ML module system with mixins, taking Ancona and Zucca's *CMS* calculus [3] as a starting point. There are two main issues: one, which we leave for future work, is to support type components in mixins; the other, which we address in this paper, is to equip *CMS* with a call-by-value semantics consistent with that of the core ML language. Shifting *CMS* from its original call-by-name semantics to a call-by-value semantics requires a precise control of recursive definitions created by mixin composition. The call-by-name semantics of *CMS* puts no restrictions on recursive definitions, allowing ill-founded ones such as `let rec x = 2 * y and y = x + 1`, causing the program to diverge when x or y is selected. In an ML-like, call-by-value setting, recursive definitions are statically restricted to syntactic values, *e.g.* `let rec f = λx...` `and g = λy...` This provides stronger guarantees (ill-founded recursions are detected at compile-time rather than at run-time), and supports more efficient compilation of recursive definitions. Extending these two desirable properties to mixin modules in the presence of separate compilation [9, 18] is challenging: illegal recursive definitions can appear a posteriori when we take the sum `A + B` of two mixin modules, at a time where only the signatures of A and B are known, but not their implementations.

The solution we develop here is to enrich the *CMS* type system, adding graphs in mixin signatures to represent the dependencies between the components. The resulting typed calculus, called CMS_v, guarantees that recursive definitions created by mixin composition evaluate correctly under a call-by-value regime, yet leaves considerable flexibility in composing mixins. We then provide a type-directed, separate compilation scheme for CMS_v. The target of this compositional translation is λ_B, a simple call-by-value λ-calculus with a non-standard `let rec` construct in the style of Boudol [6]. Finally, we prove that the compilation of a type-correct CMS_v mixin is well typed in a sound, non-standard type system for λ_B that generalizes that of [6], thus establishing the soundness of our approach.

The remainder of the paper is organized as follows. Section 2 gives a high-level overview of the *CMS* and CMS_v mixin calculi, and explains the recursion problem. Section 3 defines the syntax and typing rules for CMS_v, our call-by-value mixin module calculus. The compilation scheme (from CMS_v to λ_B) is presented in section 4. Section 5 outlines a proof of correctness of the compilation scheme. We review related work in section 6, and conclude in section 7. Proofs are omitted, but can be found in the long version of this paper [17].

2 Overview

2.1 The *CMS* Calculus of Mixins

We start this paper by an overview of the *CMS* module calculus of [3], using an ML-like syntax for readability. A basic mixin module is similar to an ML structure, but may contain "holes":

```
mixin Even =  mix
  ? val odd: int -> bool              (* odd is deferred *)
  let even = λx. x = 0 or odd(x-1)   (* even is defined  *)
end
```

In other terms, a mixin module consists of defined components, `let`-bound to an expression, and deferred components, declared but not yet defined. The fundamental operator on mixin modules is the sum, which combines the components of two mixins, connecting defined and deferred components having the same names. For example, if we define `Odd` as

```
mixin Odd = mix
  ? val even: int -> bool
  let odd = λx. x > 0 and even(x-1)
end
```

the result of `mixin Nat = Even + Odd` is equivalent to writing

```
mixin Nat = mix
  let even = λx. x = 0 or odd(x-1)
  let odd  = λx. x > 0 and even(x-1)
end
```

As in class-based languages, all defined components of a mixin are mutually recursive by default; thus, the above should be read as the ML structure

```
module Nat = struct
  let rec even = λx. x = 0 or odd(x-1)
      and odd  = λx. x > 0 and even(x-1)
end
```

Another commonality with classes is that defined components are late bound by default: the definition of a component can be overridden later, and other definitions that refer to this component will "see" the new definition. The overriding is achieved in two steps: first, deleting the component via the \ operator, then redefining it via a sum. For instance,

`mixin Nat' = (Nat \ even) + (mixin let even = λx. x mod 2 = 0 end)`

is equivalent to the direct definition

```
mixin Nat' = mix
  let even = λx. x mod 2 = 0
  let odd  = λx. x > 0 and even(x-1)
end
```

Early binding (definite binding of a defined name to an expression in all other components that refer to this name) can be achieved via the freeze operator !. For instance, `Nat ! odd` is equivalent to

```
mix
  let even = let odd = λx. x > 0 and even(x-1) in
                 λx. x = 0 or odd(x-1)
  let odd  = λx. x > 0 and even(x-1)
end
```

For convenience, our CMS_v calculus also provides a `close` operator that freezes all components of a mixin in one step. Projections (extracting the value of a mixin component) are restricted to closed mixins – for the same reasons that in class-based languages, one cannot invoke a method directly from a class: an instance of the class must first be taken using the "new" operator.

A component of a mixin can itself be a mixin module. Not only does this provide ML-style nested mixins, but it also supports a general encoding of ML functors, as shown in [2].

2.2 Controlling Recursive Definitions

As recalled in introduction, call-by-value evaluation of recursive definitions is usually allowed only if the right-hand sides are syntactic values (*e.g.* λ-abstractions or constants). This semantic issue is exacerbated by mixin modules, which are in essence big mutual `let rec` definitions. Worse, ill-founded recursive definitions can appear not only when defining a basic mixin such as

```
mixin Bad = close(mix  let x = y + 1    let y = x * 2   end)
```

but also *a posteriori* when combining two innocuous-looking mixins:

```
mixin OK1 = mix  ? val y : int    let x = y + 1   end
mixin OK2 = mix  ? val x : int    let y = x * 2   end
mixin Bad = close(OK1 + OK2)
```

Although OK1 and OK2 contain no ill-founded recursions, the sum OK1 + OK2 contains one. If the definitions of OK1 and OK2 are known when we type-check and compile their sum, we can simply expand OK1 + OK2 into an equivalent monolithic mixin and reject the faulty recursion. But in a separate compilation setting, OK1 + OK2 can be compiled in a context where the definitions of OK1 and OK2 are not known, but only their signatures are. Then, the ill-founded recursion cannot be detected. This is the major problem we face in extending ML with mixin modules.

One partial solution, that we find unsatisfactory, is to rely on lazy evaluation to implement a call-by-name semantics for modules, evaluating components only at selection or when the module is closed. (This is the approach followed by the Moscow ML recursive modules [20], and also by class initialization in Java.) This would have several drawbacks. Besides potential efficiency problems, lazy evaluation does not mix well with ML, which is a call-by-value imperative language. For instance, ML modules may contain side-effecting initialization code that must be evaluated at predictable program points; that would not be the case with lazy evaluation of modules. The second drawback is that ill-founded recursive definitions (as in the Bad example above) would not be detected statically, but cause the program to loop or fail at run-time. We believe this seriously decreases program safety: compile-time detection of ill-founded recursive definitions is much preferable.

Our approach consists in enriching mixin signatures with graphs representing the dependencies between components of a mixin module, and rely on these

graphs to detect statically ill-founded recursive definitions. For example, the
Nat and Bad mixins shown above have the following dependency graphs:

$$\text{Nat:} \quad \text{even} \xrightleftharpoons[1]{1} \text{odd} \qquad\qquad \text{Bad:} \quad x \xrightleftharpoons[0]{0} y$$

Edges labeled 0 represent an immediate dependency: the value of the source
node is needed to compute that of the target node. Edges labeled 1 represent a
delayed dependency, occurring under at least one λ-abstraction; thus, the value
of the target node can be computed without knowing that of the source node.
Ill-founded recursions manifest themselves as cycles in the dependency graph
involving at least one "0" edge. Thus, the correctness criterion for a mixin is,
simply: all cycles in its dependency graph must be composed of "1" edges only.
Hence, Nat is correct, while Bad is rejected.

The power of dependency graphs becomes more apparent when we consider
mixins that combine recursive definitions of functions and immediate computations that sit outside the recursion:

```
mixin M1 = mix              mixin M2 = mix
  ? val g : ...               ? val f : ...
  let f = λx. ...g...         let g = λx. ...f...
  let u = f 0                 let v = g 1
end                         end
```

The dependency graph for the sum M1 + M2 is:

$$u \xleftarrow{0} f \xrightleftharpoons[1]{1} g \xrightarrow{0} v$$

It satisfies the correctness criterion, thus accepting this definition; other systems
that record a global "valuability" flag on each signature, such as the recursive
modules of [11], would reject this definition.

3   The CMS_v Calculus

We now define formally the syntax and typing rules of CMS_v, our call-by-value
variant of CMS.

3.1   Syntax

The syntax of CMS_v terms and types is defined in figure 1. Here, x ranges over a
countable set *Vars* of (α-convertible) variables, while X ranges over a countable
set *Names* of (non-convertible) names used to identify mixin components.

Although our module system is largely independent of the core language, for
the sake of specificity we use a standard simply-typed λ-calculus with constants
as core language. Core terms can refer by name to a (core) component of a mixin
structure, via the notation $E.X$.

Core terms:	$C ::= x \mid cst$	variable, constant
	$\mid \lambda x.C \mid C_1\ C_2$	abstraction, application
	$\mid E.X$	component projection
Mixin terms:	$E ::= C$	core term
	$\mid \langle \iota; o \rangle$	mixin structure
	$\mid E_1 + E_2$	sum
	$\mid E[X \leftarrow Y]$	rename X to Y
	$\mid E\ !\ X$	freeze X
	$\mid E \setminus X$	delete X
	$\mid \mathtt{close}(E)$	close
Input assignments:	$\iota ::= x_i \overset{i \in I}{\mapsto} X_i$	ι injective
Output assignments:	$o ::= X_i \overset{i \in I}{\mapsto} E_i$	
Core types:	$\tau ::= \mathtt{int} \mid \mathtt{bool} \mid \tau \to \tau$	
Mixin types:	$T ::= \tau$	core type
	$\mid \{\mathcal{I}; \mathcal{O}; \mathcal{D}\}$	mixin signature
Type assignments:	$\mathcal{I}, \mathcal{O} ::= X_i \overset{i \in I}{\mapsto} T_i$	
Dependency graphs:	$\mathcal{D}$ (see section 3.2)	

Fig. 1. Syntax of CMS_v

Mixin terms include core terms (proper stratification of the language is enforced by the typing rules), structure expressions building a mixin from a collection of components, and the various mixin operators mentioned in section 2: sum, rename, freeze, delete and close.

A mixin structure $\langle \iota; o \rangle$ is composed of an *input assignment* ι and an *output assignment* o. The input assignment associates internal variables to names of imported components, while the output assignment associates expressions to names of exported components. These expressions can refer to imported components via their associated internal variables. This explicit distinction between names and internal variables allows internal variables to be renamed by α-conversion, while external names remain immutable, thus making projection by name unambiguous [19, 2, 21].

Due to late binding, a virtual (defined but not frozen) component of a mixin is both imported and exported by the mixin: it is exported with its current definition, but is also imported so that other exported components refer to its final value at the time the component is frozen or the mixin is closed, rather than to its current value. In other terms, component X of $\langle \iota; o \rangle$ is deferred when $X \in cod(\iota) \setminus dom(o)$, virtual when $X \in cod(\iota) \cap dom(o)$, and frozen when $X \in dom(o) \setminus cod(\iota)$.

For example, consider the following mixin, expressed in the ML-like syntax of section 2: mix ?val x: int let y = x + 2 let z = y + 1   end. It is expressed in CMS_v syntax as the structure $\langle \iota; o \rangle$, where $\iota = [x \mapsto X;\ y \mapsto$

Y; $z \mapsto Z$] and $o = [Y \mapsto x + 2; \ Z \mapsto y + 1]$. The names X, Y, Z correspond to the variables in the ML-like syntax, while the variables x, y, z bind them locally. Here, X is only an input, but Y and Z are both input and output, since these components are virtual. The definition of Z refers to the imported value of Y, thus allowing later redefinition of Y to affect Z.

3.2   Types and Dependency Graphs

Types $\mathcal{T}$ are either core types (those of the simply-typed λ-calculus) or mixin signatures $\{\mathcal{I}; \mathcal{O}; \mathcal{D}\}$. The latter are composed of two mappings $\mathcal{I}$ and $\mathcal{O}$ from names to types, one for input components, the other for output components; and a safe dependency graph $\mathcal{D}$.

A dependency graph $\mathcal{D}$ is a directed multi-graph whose nodes are external names of imported or exported components, and whose edges carry a valuation $\chi \in \{0, 1\}$. An edge $X \xrightarrow{1} Y$ means that the term E defining Y refers to the value of X, but in such a way that it is safe to put E in a recursive definition that simultaneously defines X in terms of Y. An edge $X \xrightarrow{0} Y$ means that the term E defining Y cannot be put in such a recursive definition: the value of X must be entirely computed before E is evaluated. It is generally undecidable whether a dependency is of the 0 or 1 kind, so we take the following conservative approximation: if E is an abstraction $\lambda x.C$, then all dependencies for Y are labeled 1; in all other cases, they are all labeled 0. (Other, more precise approximations are possible, but this one works well enough and is consistent with core ML.)

More formally, for $x \in FV(E)$, we define $\nu(x, E) = 1$ if $E = \lambda y.C$ and $\nu(x, E) = 0$ otherwise. Given the mixin structure $s = \langle \iota; o \rangle$, we then define its dependency graph $\mathcal{D}(s)$ as follows: its nodes are the names of all components of s, and it contains an edge $X \xrightarrow{\chi} Y$ if and only if there exist E and x such that $o(Y) = E$ and $\iota(x) = X$ and $x \in FV(E)$ and $\chi = \nu(x, E)$. We then say that a dependency graph $\mathcal{D}$ is *safe*, and write $\vdash \mathcal{D}$, if all cycles of $\mathcal{D}$ are composed of edges labeled 1. This captures the idea that only dependencies of the "1" kind are allowed inside a mutually recursive definition.

In order to type-check mixin operators, we must be able to compute the dependency graph for the result of the operator given the dependency graphs for its operands. We now define the graph-level operators corresponding to the mixin operators.

Sum: the sum $\mathcal{D}_1 + \mathcal{D}_2$ of two dependency graphs is simply their union:

$$\mathcal{D}_1 + \mathcal{D}_2 = \{X \xrightarrow{\chi} Y \mid (X \xrightarrow{\chi} Y) \in \mathcal{D}_1 \text{ or } (X \xrightarrow{\chi} Y) \in \mathcal{D}_2\}$$

Rename: assuming Y is not mentioned in $\mathcal{D}$, the graph $\mathcal{D}[X \leftarrow Y]$ is the graph $\mathcal{D}$ where the node X, if any, is renamed Y, keeping all edges unchanged.

$$\mathcal{D}[X \leftarrow Y] = \{A\{X \leftarrow Y\} \xrightarrow{\chi} B\{X \leftarrow Y\} \mid (A \xrightarrow{\chi} B) \in \mathcal{D}\}$$

Delete: the graph $\mathcal{D}\backslash X$ is the graph $\mathcal{D}$ where we remove all edges leading to X.

$$\mathcal{D}\backslash X = \mathcal{D} \setminus \{Y \xrightarrow{\chi} X \mid Y \in \mathit{Names}, \chi \in \{0, 1\}\}$$

Freeze: operationally, the effect of freezing the component X in a mixin structure is to replace X by its current definition E in all definitions of other exported components. At the dependency level, this causes all components Y that previously depended on X to now depend on the names on which E depends. Thus, paths $Y \xrightarrow{\chi_1} X \xrightarrow{\chi_2} Z$ in the original graph become edges $Y \xrightarrow{\min(\chi_1,\chi_2)} Z$ in the result graph.

$$\mathcal{D}!X = (\mathcal{D} \cup \mathcal{D}_{around}) \setminus \mathcal{D}_{remove}$$

where $\mathcal{D}_{around} = \{Y \xrightarrow{\min(\chi_1,\chi_2)} Z \mid (Y \xrightarrow{\chi_1} X) \in \mathcal{D},\ (X \xrightarrow{\chi_2} Z) \in \mathcal{D}\}$

and $\quad \mathcal{D}_{remove} = \{X \xrightarrow{\chi} Y \mid Y \in \textit{Names},\ \chi \in \{0,1\}\}$

The sum of two safe graphs is not necessarily safe (unsafe cycles may appear); thus, the typing rules explicitly check the safety of the sum. However, it is interesting to note that the other graph operations preserve safety:

Lemma 1 *If $\mathcal{D}$ is a safe dependency graph, then the graphs $\mathcal{D}[X \leftarrow Y]$, $\mathcal{D} \setminus X$ and $\mathcal{D}!X$ are safe.*

3.3   Typing Rules

The typing rules for CMS_v are shown in figure 2. The typing environment Γ is a finite map from variables to types. We assume given a mapping TC from constants to core types. All dependency graphs appearing in the typing environment and in input signatures are assumed to be safe.

The rules resemble those of [3], with additional manipulations of dependency graphs. Projection of a structure component requires that the structure has no input components. Structure construction type-checks every output component in an environment enriched with the types assigned to the input components; it also checks that the corresponding dependency graph is safe. For the sum operator, both mixins must agree on the types of common input components, and must have no output components in common; again, we need to check that the dependency graph of the sum is safe, to make sure that the sum introduces no illegal recursive definitions. Freezing a component requires that its type in the input signature and in the output signature of the structure are identical, then removes it from the input signature. In contrast, deleting a component removes it from the output signature. Finally, closing a mixin is equivalent to freezing all its input components, and results in an empty input signature and dependency graph.

4   Compilation

We now present a compilation scheme translating CMS_v terms into call-by-value λ-calculus extended with records and a `let rec` binding. This compilation scheme is compositional, and type-directed, thus supporting separate compilation.

$$\Gamma \vdash x : \Gamma(x) \text{ (var)} \qquad \Gamma \vdash c : TC(c) \text{ (const)} \qquad \frac{\Gamma + \{x : \tau_1\} \vdash C : \tau_2}{\Gamma \vdash \lambda x.C : \tau_1 \to \tau_2} \text{ (abstr)}$$

$$\frac{\Gamma \vdash C_1 : \tau' \to \tau \quad \Gamma \vdash C_2 : \tau'}{\Gamma \vdash C_1 \, C_2 : \tau} \text{ (app)} \qquad \frac{\Gamma \vdash E : \{\emptyset; \mathcal{O}; \emptyset\}}{\Gamma \vdash E.X : \mathcal{O}(X)} \text{ (select)}$$

$$\frac{\vdash \mathcal{D}\langle \iota; o \rangle \quad dom(o) = dom(\mathcal{O})}{\Gamma + \{x : \mathcal{I}(\iota(x))\} \mid x \in dom(\iota)\} \vdash o(X) : \mathcal{O}(X) \text{ for } X \in dom(o)}{\Gamma \vdash \langle \iota; o \rangle : \{\mathcal{I}; \mathcal{O}; \mathcal{D}\langle \iota; o \rangle\}} \text{ (struct)}$$

$$\frac{\Gamma \vdash E_1 : \{\mathcal{I}_1; \mathcal{O}_1; \mathcal{D}_1\} \quad \Gamma \vdash E_2 : \{\mathcal{I}_2; \mathcal{O}_2; \mathcal{D}_2\} \quad \vdash \mathcal{D}_1 + \mathcal{D}_2}{dom(\mathcal{O}_1) \cap dom(\mathcal{O}_2) = \emptyset \quad \mathcal{I}_1(X) = \mathcal{I}_2(X) \text{ for all } X \in dom(\mathcal{I}_1) \cap dom(\mathcal{I}_2)}{\Gamma \vdash E_1 + E_2 : \{\mathcal{I}_1 + \mathcal{I}_2; \mathcal{O}_1 + \mathcal{O}_2; \mathcal{D}_1 + \mathcal{D}_2\}} \text{ (sum)}$$

$$\frac{\Gamma \vdash E : \{\mathcal{I}; \mathcal{O}; \mathcal{D}\} \quad \mathcal{I}(X) = \mathcal{O}(X)}{\Gamma \vdash E \, ! \, X : \{\mathcal{I}_{\backslash X}; \mathcal{O}; \mathcal{D} ! X\}} \text{ (freeze)}$$

$$\frac{\Gamma \vdash E : \{\mathcal{I}; \mathcal{O}; \mathcal{D}\} \quad X \in dom(\mathcal{O})}{\Gamma \vdash E \backslash X : \{\mathcal{I}; \mathcal{O}_{\backslash X}; \mathcal{D} \backslash X\}} \text{ (delete)}$$

$$\frac{\Gamma \vdash E : \{\mathcal{I}; \mathcal{O}; \mathcal{D}\} \quad Y \notin dom(\mathcal{I}) \cup dom(\mathcal{O})}{\Gamma \vdash E[X \leftarrow Y] : \{\mathcal{I} \circ [Y \mapsto X]; \mathcal{O} \circ [Y \mapsto X]; \mathcal{D}[X \leftarrow Y]\}} \text{ (rename)}$$

$$\frac{\Gamma \vdash E : \{\mathcal{I}; \mathcal{O}; \mathcal{D}\} \quad dom(\mathcal{I}) \subseteq dom(\mathcal{O}) \quad \mathcal{I}(X) = \mathcal{O}(X) \text{ for all } X \in dom(\mathcal{I})}{\Gamma \vdash \texttt{close}(E) : \{\emptyset; \mathcal{O}; \emptyset\}} \text{ (close)}$$

Fig. 2. Typing rules

4.1   Intuitions

A mixin structure is translated into a record, with one field per output component of the structure. Each field corresponds to the expression defining the output component, but λ-abstracts all input components on which it depends, that is, all its direct predecessors in the dependency graph. These extra parameters account for the late binding semantics of virtual components. Consider again the M1 and M2 example at the end of section 2. These two structures are translated to:

```
m1 = { f = λg.λx. ...g...;  u = λf. f 0 }
m2 = { g = λf.λx. ...f...;  v = λg. g 1 }
```

The sum M = M1 + M2 is then translated into a record that takes the union of the two records m1 and m2:

```
m = { f = m1.f; u = m1.u; g = m2.g; v = m2.v }
```

Later, we close M. This requires connecting the formal parameters representing input components with the record fields corresponding to the output components. To do this, we examine the dependency graph of M, identifying the strongly connected components and performing a topological sort. We thus see that we must first take a fixpoint over the f and g components, then compute u and v sequentially. Thus, we obtain the following code for close(M):

```
let rec f = m.f g and g = m.g f in
let u = m.u f in
let v = m.v g in
{ f = f; g = g; u = u; v = v }
```

Notice that the let rec definition we generate is unusual: it involves function applications in the right-hand sides, which is usually not supported in call-by-value λ-calculi. Fortunately, Boudol [6] has already developed a non-standard call-by-value calculus that supports such let rec definitions; we adopt a variant of his calculus as our target language.

4.2   The Target Language

The target language for our translation is the λ_B calculus, a variant of the λ-calculus with records and recursive definitions studied in [6]. Its syntax is as follows:

$$M ::= x \mid cst \mid \lambda x.M \mid M_1\ M_2$$
$$\mid \langle X_1 = M_1; \ldots; X_n = M_n \rangle \mid M.X$$
$$\mid \textbf{let } x = M_1 \textbf{ in } M$$
$$\mid \textbf{let rec } x_1 = M_1 \textbf{ and } \ldots \textbf{ and } x_n = M_n \textbf{ in } M$$

4.3   The Translation

The translation scheme for our language is defined in figure 3. The translation is type-directed and operates on terms annotated by their types. For the core language constructs (variables, constants, abstractions, applications), the translation is a simple morphism; the corresponding cases are omitted from figure 3.

Access to a structure component $E.X$ is translated into an access to field X of the record obtained by translating E. Conversely, a structure $\langle \iota; o \rangle$ is translated into a record construction. The resulting record has one field for each exported name $X \in dom(o)$, and this field is associated to $o(X)$ where all input parameters on which X depends are λ-abstracted. Some notation is required here. We write $\mathcal{D}^{-1}(X)$ for the list of immediate predecessors of node X in the dependency graph $\mathcal{D}$, ordered lexicographically. (The ordering is needed to ensure that values for these predecessors are provided in the correct order later; any fixed total ordering will do.) If $(X_1, \ldots, X_n) = \mathcal{D}^{-1}(X)$ is such a list, we write $\iota^{-1}(\mathcal{D}^{-1}(X))$ for the list $(x_1, \ldots, x_n)$ of variables associated to the names $(X_1, \ldots, X_n)$ by the input mapping ι. Finally, we write $\boldsymbol{\lambda}(x_1, \ldots, x_n).M$ as shorthand for $\lambda x_1 \ldots \lambda x_n.M$. With all this notation, the field X in the record translating $\langle \iota; o \rangle$ is bound to $\boldsymbol{\lambda}\iota^{-1}(\mathcal{D}^{-1}(X)).[\![o(X) : \mathcal{O}(X)]\!]$.

The sum of two mixins $E_1 + E_2$ is translated by building a record containing the union of the fields of the translations of E_1 and E_2. For the delete operator

$$[\![(E : T').X : T]\!] = [\![E : T']\!].X$$

$$[\![\langle \iota; o \rangle : \{\mathcal{I}; \mathcal{O}; \mathcal{D}\}]\!] =$$
$$\quad \langle X = \lambda \iota^{-1}(\mathcal{D}^{-1}(X)).[\![o(X) : \mathcal{O}(X)]\!] \mid X \in dom(\mathcal{O}) \rangle$$

$$[\![(E_1 : \{\mathcal{I}_1; \mathcal{O}_1; \mathcal{D}_1\}) + (E_2 : \{\mathcal{I}_2; \mathcal{O}_2; \mathcal{D}_2\}) : \{\mathcal{I}; \mathcal{O}; \mathcal{D}\}]\!] =$$
$$\quad \textbf{let } e_1 = [\![E_1 : \{\mathcal{I}_1; \mathcal{O}_1; \mathcal{D}_1\}]\!] \textbf{ in let } e_2 = [\![E_2 : \{\mathcal{I}_2; \mathcal{O}_2; \mathcal{D}_2\}]\!] \textbf{ in}$$
$$\quad \langle X = e_1.X \mid X \in dom(\mathcal{O}_1);$$
$$\qquad Y = e_2.Y \mid Y \in dom(\mathcal{O}_2) \rangle$$

$$[\![(E : \{\mathcal{I}'; \mathcal{O}'; \mathcal{D}'\}) \setminus X : \{\mathcal{I}; \mathcal{O}; \mathcal{D}\}]\!] =$$
$$\quad \textbf{let } e = [\![E : \{\mathcal{I}'; \mathcal{O}'; \mathcal{D}'\}]\!] \textbf{ in } \langle Y = e.Y \mid Y \in dom(\mathcal{O}) \rangle$$

$$[\![(E : \{\mathcal{I}'; \mathcal{O}'; \mathcal{D}'\})[X \leftarrow Y] : \{\mathcal{I}; \mathcal{O}; \mathcal{D}\}]\!] =$$
$$\quad \textbf{let } e = [\![E : \{\mathcal{I}'; \mathcal{O}'; \mathcal{D}'\}]\!] \textbf{ in}$$
$$\quad \langle Z\{X \leftarrow Y\} = \lambda \overline{\mathcal{D}^{-1}(Z\{X \leftarrow Y\})}.(e.Z \ \overline{\mathcal{D}'^{-1}(Z)})\{\overline{X} \leftarrow \overline{Y}\} \mid Z \in dom(\mathcal{O}') \rangle$$

$$[\![(E : \{\mathcal{I}'; \mathcal{O}'; \mathcal{D}'\}) \, ! \, X : \{\mathcal{I}; \mathcal{O}; \mathcal{D}\}]\!] =$$
$$\quad \textbf{let } e = [\![E : \{\mathcal{I}'; \mathcal{O}'; \mathcal{D}'\}]\!] \textbf{ in}$$
$$\quad \langle Z = e.Z \mid Z \in dom(\mathcal{O}), \ X \notin \mathcal{D}'^{-1}(Z);$$
$$\qquad Y = \lambda \overline{\mathcal{D}^{-1}(Y)}.\textbf{let rec } \overline{X} = e.X \ \overline{\mathcal{D}'^{-1}(X)} \textbf{ in } e.Y \ \overline{\mathcal{D}'^{-1}(Y)} \mid X \in \mathcal{D}'^{-1}(Y) \rangle$$

$$[\![\textbf{close}(E : \{\mathcal{I}'; \mathcal{O}'; \mathcal{D}'\}) : \{\emptyset; \mathcal{O}; \emptyset\}]\!] =$$
$$\quad \textbf{let } e = [\![E : \{\mathcal{I}'; \mathcal{O}'; \mathcal{D}'\}]\!] \textbf{ in}$$
$$\quad \textbf{let rec } \overline{X_1^1} = e.X_1^1 \ \overline{\mathcal{D}'^{-1}(X_1^1)} \textbf{ and } \ldots \textbf{ and } \overline{X_{n_1}^1} = e.X_{n_1}^1 \ \overline{\mathcal{D}'^{-1}(X_{n_1}^1)} \textbf{ in}$$
$$\quad \ldots$$
$$\quad \textbf{let rec } \overline{X_1^p} = e.X_1^p \ \overline{\mathcal{D}'^{-1}(X_1^p)} \textbf{ and } \ldots \textbf{ and } \overline{X_{n_p}^p} = e.X_{n_p}^p \ \overline{\mathcal{D}'^{-1}(X_{n_p}^p)} \textbf{ in}$$
$$\quad \langle X = \overline{X} \mid X \in dom(\mathcal{O}) \rangle$$
$$\quad \text{where } (\{X_1^1 \ldots X_{n_1}^1\}, \ldots, \{X_1^p \ldots X_{n_p}^p\}) \text{ is a serialization of } dom(\mathcal{O}') \text{ against } \mathcal{D}'$$

Fig. 3. The translation scheme

$E \setminus X$, we return a copy of the record representing E in which the field X is omitted. Renaming $E[X \leftarrow Y]$ is harder: not only do we need to rename the field X of the record representing E into Y, but the renaming of X to Y in the input parameters can cause the order of the implicit arguments of the record fields to change. Thus, we need to abstract again over these parameters in the correct order after the renaming, then apply the corresponding field of $[\![E]\!]$ to these parameters in the correct order before the renaming. Again, some notation is in order: to each name X we associate a fresh variable written $\overline{X}$, and similarly for lists of names, which become lists of variables. Moreover, we write $M \, (x_1, \ldots, x_n)$ as shorthand for $M \, x_1 \, \ldots \, x_n$.

The freeze operation $E \, ! \, X$ is perhaps the hardest to compile. Output components Z that do not depend on X are simply re-exported from $[\![E]\!]$. For the other output components, consider a component Y of E that depends on

$Y_1, \ldots, Y_n$, and assume that one of these dependencies is X, which itself depends on $X_1, \ldots, X_p$. In $E \, ! \, X$, the Y component depends on $(\{Y_i\} \cup \{X_j\}) \setminus \{X\}$. Thus, we λ-abstract on the corresponding variables, then compute X by applying $[\![E]\!].X$ to the parameters $\overline{X_j}$. Since X can depend on itself, this application must be done in a **let rec** binding over $\overline{X}$. Then, we apply $[\![E]\!].Y$ to the parameters that it expects, namely $\overline{Y_i}$, which include $\overline{X}$.

The only operator that remains to be explained is $\texttt{close}(E)$. Here, we take advantage of the fact that $\texttt{close}$ removes all input dependencies to generate code that is more efficient than a sequence of freeze operations. We first *serialize* the set of names exported by E against its dependency graph $\mathcal{D}$. That is, we identify strongly connected components of $\mathcal{D}$, then sort them in topological order. The result is an enumeration $(\{X_1^1 \ldots X_{n_1}^1\}, \ldots, \{X_1^p \ldots X_{n_p}^p\})$ of the exported names where each cluster $\{X_1^i \ldots X_{n_i}^i\}$ represents mutually recursive definitions, and the clusters are listed in an order such that each cluster depends only on the preceding ones. We then generate a sequence of **let rec** bindings, one for each cluster, in the order above. In the end, all output components are bound to values with no dependencies, and can be grouped together in a record.

5   Type Soundness of the Translation

The translation scheme defined above can generate recursive definitions of the form **let rec** $x = M\,x$ **in** N. In λ_B, these definitions can either evaluate to a fixpoint (*i.e.* $M = \lambda x.\lambda y.y$), or get stuck (*i.e.* $M = \lambda x.x + 1$). In the full paper, we prove that no term generated by the translation of a well-typed mixin can get stuck. To this end, we equip λ_B with a sound type system that guarantees that all recursive definitions are correct. Boudol [6] gave such a type system, using function types of the form $\tau_1 \xrightarrow{0} \tau_2$ or $\tau_1 \xrightarrow{1} \tau_2$ to denote functions that respectively do or do not inspect the value of their argument immediately when applied. However, this type system does not type-check curried function applications with sufficient precision for our purposes. Therefore, we developed a refinement of this type system based on function types of the form $\tau_1 \xrightarrow{n} \tau_2$, where n is an integer indicating the number of applications that can be performed without inspecting the value of the first argument. In the full paper [17], we formally define this type system, show its soundness (well-typed terms do not get stuck), and prove that λ_B terms produced by the compilation scheme applied to well-typed mixins are well typed.

6   Related Work

Bracha [8, 7] introduced the concept of mixin as a generalization of (multiple) inheritance in class-based OO languages, allowing more freedom in deferring the definition of a method in a class and implementing it later in another class than is normally possible with inheritance and overriding.

Duggan and Sourelis [13, 14] were the first to transpose Bracha's mixin concept to the ML module system. Their mixin module system supports extensible functions and datatypes: a function defined by cases can be split across several mixins, each mixin defining only certain cases, and similarly a datatype (sum type) can be split across several mixins, each mixin defining only certain constructors; a composition operator then stitches together these cases and constructors. The problem with ill-founded recursions is avoided by allowing only functions (λ-abstractions) in the combinable parts of mixins, while initialization code goes into a separate, non-combinable part of mixins. Their compilation scheme (into ML modules) is less efficient than ours, since the fixpoint defining a function is computed at each call, rather than only once at mixin combination time as in our system.

The *units* of Flatt and Felleisen [15] are a module system for Scheme. The basic program units import names and export definitions, much like in Ancona and Zucca's *CMS* calculus. The recursion problem is solved as in [13] by separating initialization from component definition.

Ancona and Zucca [1–3] develop a theory of mixins, abstracting over much of the core language, and show that it can encode the pure λ-calculus, as well as Abadi and Cardelli's object calculus. The emphasis is on providing a calculus, with reduction rules but no fixed reduction strategy, and nice confluence properties. Another calculus of mixins is Vestergaard and Wells' m-calculus [21], which is very similar to *CMS* in many points, but is not based on any core language, using only variables instead. The emphasis is put on the equational theory, allowing for example to replace some variables with their definition inside a structure, or to garbage collect unused components, yielding a powerful theory. Neither Ancona-Zucca nor Vestergaard-Wells attempt to control recursive definitions statically, performing on-demand unwinding instead. Still, some care is required when unwinding definitions inside a structure, because of confluence problems [4].

Crary *et al* [11, 12] and Russo [20] extend the Standard ML module system with mutually recursive structures via a `structure rec` binding. Like mixins, this construct addresses ML's cross-module recursion problem; unlike mixins, it does not support late binding and incremental programming. The `structure rec` binding does not lend itself directly to separate compilation (the definitions of all mutually recursive modules must reside in the same source file), although some amount of separate compilation can be achieved by functorizing each recursive module over the others. ML structures contain type components in addition to value components, and this raises delicate static typing issues that we have not yet addressed within our CMS_v framework. Crary *et al* formalize static typing of recursive structure using recursively-defined signatures and the phase distinction calculus, while Russo remains closer to Standard ML's static semantics. Concerning ill-founded recursive value definitions, Russo does not attempt to detect them statically, relying on lazy evaluation to catch them at run-time. Crary *et al* statically require that all components of recursive structures are syntactic values. This is safe, but less flexible than our component-per-component dependency analysis.

Bono *et al* [5] use a notion of dependency graph in the context of a type system for extensible and incomplete objects. However, they do not distinguish between "0" and "1" dependencies.

7   Conclusions and Future Work

As a first step towards a full mixin module system for ML, we have developed a call-by-value variant of Ancona and Zucca's calculus of mixins. The main technical innovation of our work is the use of dependency graphs in mixin signatures, statically guaranteeing that cross-module recursive definitions are well founded, yet leaving maximal flexibility in mixing recursive function definitions and non-recursive computations within a single mixin. Dependency graphs also allow a separate compilation scheme for mixins where fixpoints are taken as early as possible, *i.e.* during mixin initialization rather than at each component access.

A drawback of dependency graphs is that programmers must (in principle) provide them explicitly when declaring a mixin signature, *e.g.* for a deferred sub-mixin component. This could make programs quite verbose. Future work includes the design of a concrete syntax for mixin signatures that alleviate this problem in the most common cases.

Our λ_B target calculus can be compiled efficiently down to machine code, using the "in-place updating" trick described in [10] to implement the non-standard `let rec` construct. However, this trick assumes constant-sized function closures; some work is needed to accommodate variable-sized closures as used in the OCaml compiler among others.

The next step towards mixin modules for ML is to support type definitions and declarations as components of mixins. While these type components account for most of the complexity of ML module typing, we are confident that we can extend to mixins the considerable body of type-theoretic work already done for ML modules [16, 18] and recursive modules [11, 12].

Acknowledgements. We thank Elena Zucca and Davide Ancona for discussions, and Vincent Simonet for his technical advice on the typing rules for λ_B.

References

1. D. Ancona. *Modular formal frameworks for module systems.* PhD thesis, Universita di Pisa, 1998.
2. D. Ancona and E. Zucca. A primitive calculus for module systems. In G. Nadathur, editor, *Princ. and Practice of Decl. Prog.*, volume 1702 of *LNCS*, pages 62–79. Springer-Verlag, 1999.
3. D. Ancona and E. Zucca. A calculus of module systems. *Journal of functional programming*, 2001. To appear.
4. Z. Ariola and S. Blom. Skew confluence and the lambda calculus with letrec. *Annals of pure and applied logic*, 2001. To appear.
5. V. Bono, M. Bugliesi, M. Dezani-Ciancaglini, and L. Liquori. Subtyping for extensible, incomplete objects. *Fundamenta Informaticae*, 38(4):325–364, 1999.
6. G. Boudol. The recursive record semantics of objects revisited. Research report 4199, INRIA, 2001. Preliminary version presented at ESOP'01, LNCS 2028.
7. G. Bracha. *The programming language Jigsaw: mixins, modularity and multiple inheritance.* PhD thesis, University of Utah, 1992.

8. G. Bracha and W. Cook. Mixin-based inheritance. In *OOPSLA90*, volume 25(10) of *SIGPLAN Notices*, pages 303–311. ACM Press, 1990.
9. L. Cardelli. Program fragments, linking, and modularization. In *24th symp. Principles of Progr. Lang*, pages 266–277. ACM Press, 1997.
10. G. Cousineau, P.-L. Curien, and M. Mauny. The categorical abstract machine. *Science of Computer Programming*, 8(2):173–202, 1987.
11. K. Crary, R. Harper, and S. Puri. What is a recursive module? In *Prog. Lang. Design and Impl. 1999*, pages 50–63. ACM Press, 1999.
12. D. Dreyer, K. Crary, and R. Harper. Toward a practical type theory for recursive modules. Technical Report CMU-CS-01-112, Carnegie Mellon University, 2001.
13. D. Duggan and C. Sourelis. Mixin modules. In *Int. Conf. on Functional Progr. 96*, pages 262–273. ACM Press, 1996.
14. D. Duggan and C. Sourelis. Recursive modules and mixin-based inheritance. Unpublished draft, 2001.
15. M. Flatt and M. Felleisen. Units: cool modules for HOT languages. In *Prog. Lang. Design and Impl. 1998*, pages 236–248. ACM Press, 1998.
16. R. Harper and M. Lillibridge. A type-theoretic approach to higher-order modules with sharing. In *21st symp. Principles of Progr. Lang*, pages 123–137. ACM Press, 1994.
17. T. Hirschowitz and X. Leroy. Mixin modules in a call-by-value setting (long version). Available at `http://pauillac.inria.fr/~hirschow`, 2001.
18. X. Leroy. Manifest types, modules, and separate compilation. In *21st symp. Principles of Progr. Lang*, pages 109–122. ACM Press, 1994.
19. M. Lillibridge. *Translucent sums : a foundation for higher-order module systems*. PhD thesis, School of Computer Science, Carnegie Mellon University, 1997.
20. C. Russo. Recursive structures for Standard ML. In *Int. Conf. on Functional Progr. 01*, pages 50–61, 2001.
21. J. Wells and R. Vestergaard. Equational reasoning for linking with first-class primitive modules. In *Programming Languages and Systems, 9th European Symp. Programming*, volume 1782 of *LNCS*, pages 412–428. Springer-Verlag, 2000.

Existential Types for Imperative Languages*

Dan Grossman

Cornell University
danieljg@cs.cornell.edu

Abstract. We integrate existential types into a strongly typed C-like language. In particular, we show how a bad combination of existential types, mutation, and aliasing can cause a subtle violation of type safety. We explore two independent ways to strengthen the type system to restore safety. One restricts the mutation of existential packages. The other restricts the types of aliases of existential packages. We use our framework to explain why other languages with existential types are safe.

1 Introduction

Strongly typed programming languages prevent certain programming errors and provide a foundation on which the user can enforce strong abstractions. High-level languages usually have primitive support for data hiding (e.g., closures, objects), which mitigate the burden of strong typing. At lower levels of abstraction, such as in C, exposed data representation and a rich set of primitive operations make it difficult to provide strong typing without unduly restricting the set of legal programs. A powerful technique is to provide a rich type system that the programmer can use to express invariants that ensure a program's safety.

In particular, *existential types* (often written $\exists \alpha.\tau$ where τ is a type) are a well-known device for permitting consistent manipulation of data containing values of unknown types. Indeed, they have become the standard tool for modeling the data-hiding constructs of high-level languages. Mitchell and Plotkin's seminal work [11] explains how constructs for abstract types, such as the rep types in CLU clusters [8] and the abstype declarations in Standard ML [9], are really existential types. For example, an abstraction for the natural numbers could have the type $\exists \alpha\{\texttt{zero}:\alpha;\ \texttt{succ}:\alpha \to \alpha\}$. As desired, if we had two such abstractions, we could not apply one's succ function to the other's zero value.

Existential types also serve an essential role in many encodings of objects [1] and closures [10]. For example, we can represent a closure as a record of values for the original code's free variables (its environment) and a closed code pointer taking the environment as an extra parameter. By abstracting the environment's type with an existential type, source functions with the same type but different environments continue to have the same type after this encoding.

* This material is based on work supported in part by AFOSR under grant F49620-00-1-0198. Any opinions, findings, and conclusions or recommendations expressed in this publications are those of the author and do not reflect the view of this agency.

D. Le Métayer (Ed.): ESOP 2002, LNCS 2305, pp. 21–35, 2002.

More recently, existential types have also proven useful in safe *low-level* languages [12, 3]. For example, many low-level interfaces let a client register a call-back with a server along with data to pass to the call-back when it is invoked. If the server specifies the data's type, then the interface is too restrictive. This idiom bears an uncanny resemblance to the closure encoding: A record holding the call-back and the data should have an existential type. Essentially, low-level languages do not provide data-hiding constructs directly, so it is sensible for the type system to be rich enough for programs to create them. Existential quantification has also been used to express connections beyond simple types. For example, Xanadu [20] lets programmers express that an integer holds the length of a particular array. An existential type lets us pack an array with its length.

In C, we must resort to `void*` and unchecked casts when existential types would be appropriate. For example, using the aforementioned encoding, a function closure that consumes an `int` and returns `void` could have the type `struct T {void (*f)(int,void*); void* env;};`. If x had this type, we could write `x.f(37,x.env)`, but nothing enforces that `x.env` has the type that `x.f` expects, nor can we prevent calling `x.f` with any other pointer. With existential types, we can enforce the intended usage by declaring `struct T` $\exists \alpha.${`void (*f)(int,`α`);` α `env;};`. For this reason, Cyclone [2, 6], a safe C-like language developed by Trevor Jim, Greg Morrisett, the author, and others, allows `struct` declarations to have existential type variables.

However, it does not appear that the interaction of existential types with features like mutation and C's address-of (&) operator has been carefully studied. Orthogonality suggests that existential types in a C-like language should permit mutation and acquiring the address of fields, just as ordinary `struct` types do. Moreover, such abilities are genuinely useful. For example, a server accepting call-backs can use mutation to reuse the same memory for different call-backs that expect data of different types. Using & to introduce aliasing is also useful. As a small example, given a value v of type `struct T` $\exists \alpha.${α `x;` α `y;};` and a polymorphic function $\forall \beta.$ `void swap(`β`*,` β`*)` for swapping the contents of two locations, we would like to permit a call like `swap(&v.x, &v.y)`.

Unfortunately, a subtle interaction among all these features can violate type safety. Somewhat embarrassingly, Cyclone was unsafe for several months before the problem was discovered. In order to expose the problem's essential source and provide guidelines for using existential types in low-level languages, this paper explains the unsoundness, describes two independent solutions, proves the solutions are correct, and explores why this problem did not arise previously.

In the next section, we present a full example exploiting the unsoundness that assignment, aliasing, and existential types can produce. We use this example to explain how we restore soundness. Section 3 presents a small formal language suitable for arguing rigorously that we have, in fact, restored soundness. Section 4 describes the soundness proof for the formal language; the excruciating details appear in a companion technical report [4]. Section 5 discusses related work. In particular, it uses the insights of the preceding sections to explain why other languages with existential types are safe.

2 Violating Type Safety

In this section, we present a violation of type safety discovered in Cyclone [2, 6] (a safe C-like language) and how we fixed the problem. We describe only the Cyclone features necessary for our present purposes, and we take the liberty of using prettier syntax (e.g., Greek letters) than the actual language.

A struct declaration may declare *existentially-bound type variables* and use them in the types of fields. Repeating an earlier example, a value of the type

$$\text{struct T } \exists \alpha.\{\text{void } (*f)(\text{int}, \alpha); \ \alpha \text{ env};\};$$

contains a function pointer in the f field that can be applied to an int and the env field *of the same value.*

Different values of type struct T can instantiate α with different types. Here is a program exploiting this feature. (The form T(e1,e2) is just a convenient way to create a struct T object with fields initialized to e1 and e2.)

```
void ignore(int x, int y) {}
void assign(int x, int *y) { *y = x; }
void f(int* ptr) {
  struct T p1 = T(ignore, 0xabcd);
  struct T p2 = T(assign, ptr);
  /* use p1 and p2 ... */
}
```

The type-checker infers that in T(ignore,0xabcd), for example, α is int. We call int the *witness type* for the *existential package* T(ignore,0xabcd). The type-checker would reject T(assign,0xabcd) because there is no appropriate witness type. Witness types are not present at run time.

Because p1 and p2 have the same type, we could assign one to the other with p2=p1. As in C, this assignment *copies* the fields of p1 into the fields of p2. Note that the assignment *changes* p2's witness type.

We cannot access fields of existential packages with the "." or "→" opera-tors.[1] Instead, Cyclone provides *pattern-matching* to bind variables to parts of aggregate objects. For existential packages, the pattern also *opens* (sometimes called "unpacking") the package by giving an abstract name to the witness type. For example, the function f could continue with

$$\text{let T}(g,\text{arg})<\beta> = \text{p2} \quad \text{in} \quad g(37,\text{arg});$$

The pattern binds g to (a copy of) p2.f and arg to (a copy of) p2.env. It also makes β a type. The scope of g, arg, and β is the statement after in. The types of g and arg are void (*f)(int,β) and β, respectively, so the function call is well-typed.

It is well-known that the typing rule for opening an existential package must forbid the introduced type variable (β) from occurring in the type assigned to

---

[1] struct declarations without existential type variables permit these operators.

the term in which β is in scope. In our case, this term is a statement, which has no type (or a unit type if you prefer), so this condition is trivially satisfied. Our unsoundness results from a different problem.

Another pattern form, which we call a *reference pattern*, is *id; it binds id to *the address of* part of a value. (So *id has the same type as that part of the value.) We need this feature for the swap example from the previous section. We can modify our previous example to use this feature gratuitously:

```
let T(g,*arg)<β> = p2  in  g(37,*arg);
```

Here arg is an alias for &p2.env, but arg has the *opened type*, in this case $\beta*$.

At this point, we have seen how to create existential packages, use assignment to modify memory that has an existential type, and use reference patterns to get aliases of existential-package fields. It appears that we have a smooth integration of several features that are natural for a language at the C level of abstraction. Unfortunately, these features conspire to violate type safety:

```
void f(int* ptr) {
  struct T p1 = T(ignore, 0xabcd);
  struct T p2 = T(assign, ptr);
  let T(g,*arg)<β> = p2  in  { p2 = p1; g(37,*arg); }
}
```

The call g(37,*arg) executes assign with 37 and 0xabcd—we are passing an int where we expect an int*, allowing us to write to an arbitrary address.

What went wrong in the type system? We used β to express an equality between one of g's parameter types and the type of value at which arg points. But after the assignment, which changes p2's witness type, this equality is false.

We have developed two solutions. The first solution forbids using reference patterns to match against fields of existential packages. Other uses of reference patterns are sound because assignment to a package mutates only the fields of the package. We call this solution, "no aliases at the opened type." The second solution forbids assigning to an existential package (or an aggregate value that has an existential package as a field). We call this solution, "no witness changes."

These solutions are *independent*: Either suffices and we could use different solutions for different existential packages. That is, for each existential-type declaration we could let the programmer decide which restriction the compiler enforces. Our current implementation supports only "no aliases at the opened type" because we believe it is more useful, but both solutions are easy to enforce.

To emphasize the exact source of the problem, we mention some aspects that are not problematic. First, pointers to witness types are not a problem. For example, given struct T2 $\exists\alpha.\{$void f(int, α); $\alpha*$ env;$\}$; and the pattern T2(g,arg)<β>, an intervening assignment changes a package's witness type but does *not* change the type of the value at which arg points. Second, assignment to a *pointer to* an existential package is not a problem because it changes which package a pointer refers to, but does *not* change any package's witness type.

Witness changes are more difficult with multithreading: A similar unsoundness results if the witness can change in-between the binding of g and arg. We would need some mechanism for excluding a mutation while binding a package's fields. If we restricted (shared, witness-changeable) packages to a single field (a pointer), atomic reads and writes of a single word would suffice.

3 Sound Language

To investigate the essential source of the unsoundness described in Section 2, we present a small formal language with the same potential problem. Instead of type definitions, we use "anonymous" product types (pairs) and existential types. Instead of pattern-matching, we use **open** statements for destructing existential packages. We omit many features that have no relevance to our investigation, including loops and function calls. Such features can be added in typical fashion.

3.1 Syntax

Figure 1 presents the language's syntax. Types include a base type (int), products ($\tau_1 \times \tau_2$), pointers ($\tau *$), existentials ($\exists^\phi \alpha.\tau$), and type variables (α). Because aliasing is relevant, all uses of pointers are explicitly noted. In particular, a value of a product type is a record, not a pointer to a record.[2] To distinguish our two solutions to restoring soundness, we annotate existential types with δ (the witness type can change) or & (aliases at the opened type are allowed).

$$\ell \in \text{Lab} \qquad c \in \text{Int} \qquad x \in \text{Var} \qquad \alpha \in \text{Tyvar} \qquad H : \text{Lab} \rightharpoonup \text{Value}$$

$$
\begin{aligned}
\text{Type } \tau &::= \text{ int } \mid \alpha \mid \tau * \mid \tau_1 \times \tau_2 \mid \exists^\phi \alpha.\tau \\
\text{Exp } e &::= c \mid x \mid \ell p \mid (e_1, e_2) \mid e.i \mid \&e \mid *e \mid \textbf{pack } \tau', e \textbf{ as } \exists^\phi \alpha.\tau \\
\text{Stmt } s &::= \textbf{skip} \mid e_1 := e_2 \mid s_1; s_2 \mid \textbf{let } x : \tau = e \textbf{ in } s \\
&\quad \mid \textbf{open } e \textbf{ as } \alpha, x \textbf{ in } s \mid \textbf{open } e \textbf{ as } \alpha, *x \textbf{ in } s \\
\text{Path } p &::= \cdot \mid i p \mid \textbf{u} p \\
\text{Field } i &::= 0 \mid 1 \\
\text{Style } \phi &::= \delta \mid \& \\
\\
\text{Value } v &::= c \mid \&\ell p \mid \textbf{pack } \tau', v \textbf{ as } \exists^\phi \alpha.\tau \mid (v_1, v_2)
\end{aligned}
$$

Fig. 1. Syntax

Expressions include variables (x), constants (c), pairs ((e_1, e_2)), field accesses ($e.i$), pointer creations ($\&e$), pointer dereferences ($*e$), and existential packages (**pack** τ', e **as** $\exists^\phi \alpha.\tau$). In the last form, τ' is the witness type; its explicit mention is just a technical convenience. We distinguish locations ("lvalues") from values ("rvalues"). Locations have the form ℓp where ℓ is a label (an address) for a heap

---

[2] Hence we could allow casts between $\tau_1 \times (\tau_2 \times \tau_3)$ and $(\tau_1 \times \tau_2) \times \tau_3$, but we have no reason to add this feature.

record and p is a path that identifies a subrecord. Locations do not appear in source programs, but we use them in the dynamic semantics, as described below.

Statements include doing nothing (**skip**), assignment—altering the contents of a heap record ($e_1 := e_2$), and local bindings—extending the heap (**let** $x : \tau = e$ **in** s). Because memory management is not our present concern, the dynamic semantics never contracts the heap. There are two forms for destructing existential packages. The form **open** e **as** α, x **in** s binds x to a *copy* of the contents of the evaluation of e, whereas **open** e **as** $\alpha, *x$ **in** s binds x to a *pointer* to the contents of the evaluation of e. The latter form corresponds to the previous section's reference patterns, but for simplicity it produces a pointer to the entire contents, not a particular field.

3.2   Dynamic Semantics

A heap (H) maps labels (ℓ) to values. We write $H[\ell \mapsto v]$ for the heap that is like H except that ℓ maps to v, and we write $\cdot$ for the empty heap. Because values may be pairs or packages, we use paths (p) to specify parts of values. A path is just a sequence of 0, 1, and u (explained below) where $\cdot$ denotes the empty sequence. We write $p_1 p_2$ for the sequence that is p_1 followed by p_2. We blur the distinction between sequences and sequence elements as convenient. So $0p$ means the path beginning with 0 and continuing with p and $p0$ means the path ending with 0 after p.

The get relation defines the use of paths to destruct values. As examples, $\text{get}((v_0, v_1), 1, v_1)$ and $\text{get}(\textbf{pack } \tau', v \textbf{ as } \exists^\phi \alpha.\tau, \text{u}, v)$. That is, we use u to get a package's contents. The set relation defines the use of paths to update parts of values: $\text{set}(v_1, p, v_2, v_3)$ means updating the part of v_1 corresponding to p with v_2 produces v_3. For example, $\text{set}((v_1, ((v_2, v_3), v_4)), 10, (v_5, v_6), (v_1, ((v_5, v_6), v_4)))$. Figure 2 defines both relations.

Unlike C, expression evaluation in our core language has no side effects, so we have chosen a large-step semantics. Given a heap, we use the $\Downarrow_L$ relation to evaluate expressions to locations and the $\Downarrow_R$ relation to evaluate expressions to values. The two relations are interdependent (see the $\Downarrow_L$ rule for $*e$ and the $\Downarrow_R$ rule for $\&e$). For many expressions there are no H, ℓ, and p such that $H \vdash e \Downarrow_L \ell p$ (for example, $e = (e_1, e_2)$). Only a few rules merit further discussion: The $\Downarrow_L$ rule for projection puts the field number on the right of a path. The $\Downarrow_R$ rules for ℓp and $*e$ use the heap H and the get relation. Figure 3 defines $\Downarrow_L$ and $\Downarrow_R$.

Statements operate on heaps; we define a small-step semantics in which $(H, s) \rightarrow (H', s')$ means, "under heap H, statement s produces H' and becomes s'." The meaning of a program s is H where $(\cdot, s) \rightarrow^* (H, \textbf{skip})$ (where $\rightarrow^*$ is the reflexive transitive closure of $\rightarrow$). We write $s\{\ell p/x\}$ for the substitution of ℓp for x in s and $s\{\tau/\alpha\}$ for the capture-avoiding substitution of τ for α in s. We omit the straightforward but tedious definitions of substitution.

We now describe the interesting rules for evaluating statements. (All rules are in Figure 4.) The interesting part for assignment is in the set judgment. For **let**, we map a fresh label ℓ in the heap to (a copy of) the value and substitute that location (that is, the label and path $\cdot$) for the binding variable in the body

$$\overline{\mathrm{get}(v, \cdot, v)} \qquad \frac{\mathrm{get}(v_0, p, v)}{\mathrm{get}((v_0, v_1), 0p, v)} \qquad \frac{\mathrm{get}(v_1, p, v)}{\mathrm{get}((v_0, v_1), 1p, v)}$$

$$\frac{\mathrm{get}(v_1, p, v)}{\mathrm{get}(\mathbf{pack}\ \tau', v_1\ \mathbf{as}\ \exists^{\&}\alpha.\tau, \mathbf{u}p, v)}$$

$$\overline{\mathrm{set}(v_{old}, \cdot, v, v)} \qquad \frac{\mathrm{set}(v_0, p, v, v')}{\mathrm{set}((v_0, v_1), 0p, v, (v', v_1))} \qquad \frac{\mathrm{set}(v_1, p, v, v')}{\mathrm{set}((v_0, v_1), 1p, v, (v_0, v'))}$$

$$\frac{\mathrm{set}(v_1, p, v, v')}{\mathrm{set}(\mathbf{pack}\ \tau', v_1\ \mathbf{as}\ \exists^{\phi}\alpha.\tau,\ \mathbf{u}p,\ v,\ \mathbf{pack}\ \tau', v'\ \mathbf{as}\ \exists^{\phi}\alpha.\tau)}$$

Fig. 2. Dynamic Semantics: Heap Objects

$$\overline{H \vdash \ell p \Downarrow_{\mathrm{L}} \ell p} \qquad \frac{H \vdash e \Downarrow_{\mathrm{L}} \ell p}{H \vdash e.i \Downarrow_{\mathrm{L}} \ell pi} \qquad \frac{H \vdash e \Downarrow_{\mathrm{R}} \&\ell p}{H \vdash *e \Downarrow_{\mathrm{L}} \ell p}$$

$$\overline{H \vdash c \Downarrow_{\mathrm{R}} c} \qquad \frac{\mathrm{get}(H(\ell), p, v)}{H \vdash \ell p \Downarrow_{\mathrm{R}} v} \qquad \frac{H \vdash e \Downarrow_{\mathrm{R}} (v_0, v_1)}{H \vdash e.0 \Downarrow_{\mathrm{R}} v_0} \qquad \frac{H \vdash e \Downarrow_{\mathrm{R}} (v_0, v_1)}{H \vdash e.1 \Downarrow_{\mathrm{R}} v_1}$$

$$\frac{H \vdash e_0 \Downarrow_{\mathrm{R}} v_0 \quad H \vdash e_1 \Downarrow_{\mathrm{R}} v_1}{H \vdash (e_0, e_1) \Downarrow_{\mathrm{R}} (v_0, v_1)} \qquad \frac{H \vdash e \Downarrow_{\mathrm{L}} \ell p}{H \vdash \&e \Downarrow_{\mathrm{R}} \&\ell p} \qquad \frac{H \vdash e \Downarrow_{\mathrm{R}} \&\ell p \quad \mathrm{get}(H(\ell), p, v)}{H \vdash *e \Downarrow_{\mathrm{R}} v}$$

$$\frac{H \vdash e \Downarrow_{\mathrm{R}} v}{H \vdash \mathbf{pack}\ \tau', e\ \mathbf{as}\ \exists^{\phi}\alpha.\tau \Downarrow_{\mathrm{R}} \mathbf{pack}\ \tau', v\ \mathbf{as}\ \exists^{\phi}\alpha.\tau}$$

Fig. 3. Dynamic Semantics: Expressions

$$\frac{H \vdash e_1 \Downarrow_{\mathrm{L}} \ell p \quad H \vdash e_2 \Downarrow_{\mathrm{R}} v \quad \mathrm{set}(H(\ell), p, v, v')}{(H, e_1 := e_2) \to (H[\ell \mapsto v'], \mathbf{skip})}$$

$$\overline{(H, \mathbf{skip}; s) \to (H, s)} \qquad \frac{(H, s_1) \to (H', s_1')}{(H, s_1; s_2) \to (H', s_1'; s_2)}$$

$$\frac{H \vdash e \Downarrow_{\mathrm{R}} v \quad \ell \notin \mathrm{dom}(H)}{(H, \mathbf{let}\ x : \tau = e\ \mathbf{in}\ s) \to (H[\ell \mapsto v], s\{\ell \cdot /x\})}$$

$$\frac{H \vdash e \Downarrow_{\mathrm{R}} \mathbf{pack}\ \tau', v\ \mathbf{as}\ \exists^{\phi}\alpha.\tau \quad \ell \notin \mathrm{dom}(H)}{(H, \mathbf{open}\ e\ \mathbf{as}\ \alpha, x\ \mathbf{in}\ s) \to (H[\ell \mapsto v], s\{\tau'/\alpha\}\{\ell \cdot /x\})}$$

$$\frac{H \vdash e \Downarrow_{\mathrm{L}} \ell' p \quad \mathrm{get}(H(\ell'), p, \mathbf{pack}\ \tau', v\ \mathbf{as}\ \exists^{\phi}\alpha.\tau) \quad \ell \notin \mathrm{dom}(H)}{(H, \mathbf{open}\ e\ \mathbf{as}\ \alpha, *x\ \mathbf{in}\ s) \to (H[\ell \mapsto \&\ell' p\mathbf{u}], s\{\tau'/\alpha\}\{\ell \cdot /x\})}$$

Fig. 4. Dynamic Semantics: Statements

of the statement. The rule for **open** e **as** α, x **in** s is similar; we also substitute τ' for α, where τ' is the witness type in the package to which e evaluates. The rule for **open** e **as** $\alpha, *x$ **in** s is like the rule for **open** e **as** α, x **in** s except that we use $\Downarrow_L$ to evaluate e to a location $\ell'p$ and we map ℓ to $\&\ell'p$u.

As an example, here is a variation of the previous unsoundness example. Instead of using function pointers, we use assignment, but the idea is the same. For now, we do not specify the style of the existential types.

(1) **let** $zero$: int $= 0$ **in**
(2) **let** $pzero$: int$* = \&zero$ **in**
(3) **let** pkg : $\exists^\phi \alpha.\alpha* \times \alpha = $ **pack** int$*, (\&pzero, pzero)$ **as** $\exists^\phi \alpha.\alpha* \times \alpha$ **in**
(4) **open** pkg **as** $\beta, *pr$ **in**
(5) **let** fst : $\beta* = (*pr).0$ **in**
(6) $pkg := $ **pack** int, $(pzero, zero)$ **as** $\exists^\phi \alpha.\alpha* \times \alpha$;
(7) $*fst := (*pr).1$;
(8) $*pzero := zero$

In describing the example, we assume that when binding a variable x, we choose ℓ_x as the fresh location. Hence line (3) substitutes $\ell_{pkg}\cdot$ for pkg and line (4) substitutes int$*$ for β and $\ell_{pr}\cdot$ for pr. Furthermore, after line (4), ℓ_{pkg} contains **pack** int$*, (\&\ell_{pzero}\cdot, \&\ell_{zero}\cdot)$ **as** $\exists^\phi \alpha.\alpha* \times \alpha$ and ℓ_{pr} contains $\&\ell_{pkg}$u. After line (6), ℓ_{fst} contains $\&\ell_{pzero}\cdot$ and ℓ_{pkg} contains **pack** int, $(pzero, 0)$ **as** $\exists^\phi \alpha.\alpha* \times \alpha$. Hence line (7) assigns 0 to ℓ_{pzero}, which causes line (8) to be stuck because there is no ℓp to which $\Downarrow_L$ can evaluate $*0$.

To complete the example, we need to choose δ or $\&$ for each ϕ. Fortunately, as the next section explains, no choice produces a well-typed program.

Note that the type information associated with packages and paths is just to keep type-checking syntax-directed. We can define an erasure function over heaps that replaces **pack** τ', v **as** $\exists^\phi \alpha.\tau$ with v and removes u from paths. Although we have not formally done so, it should be straightforward to prove that erasure and evaluation commute. That is, we do not need type information at run time.

3.3 Static Semantics

We now present a type system for source (label-free) programs. Section 4 extends the system to heaps and locations in order to prove type safety.

We use two auxiliary judgments on types. We allow **pack** τ', v **as** $\exists^\phi \alpha.\tau$ only if $\vdash \tau'$ packable. Assuming constants and pointers have the same run-time representation, this restriction ensures that code manipulating a package need not depend on the witness type, as it would if $\tau_1 \times \tau_2$ could be a witness type. We allow $e_1 := e_2$ only if e_1 has a type τ such that $\vdash \tau$ assignable. This judgment requires that any type of the form $\exists^\& \alpha.\tau'$ occurring in τ occurs in a pointer type. As a result, the witness type of a location holding **pack** τ_1, v **as** $\exists^\& \alpha.\tau_2$ never changes. A judgment on expressions, $\vdash e$ lval, defines the terms that are sensible for $\&e$ and $e := e'$. Figure 5 defines these auxiliary judgments.

With these auxiliary judgments, the rules for expressions and statements (Figure 6) are mostly straightforward. The context includes the type variables

$$\overline{\vdash \text{int packable}} \qquad \overline{\vdash \alpha \text{ packable}} \qquad \overline{\vdash \tau* \text{ packable}}$$

$$\frac{\vdash \tau \text{ packable}}{\vdash \tau \text{ assignable}} \qquad \frac{\vdash \tau_0 \text{ assignable} \quad \vdash \tau_1 \text{ assignable}}{\vdash \tau_0 \times \tau_1 \text{ assignable}} \qquad \frac{\vdash \tau \text{ assignable}}{\vdash \exists^\delta \alpha.\tau \text{ assignable}}$$

$$\overline{\vdash x \text{ lval}} \qquad \overline{\vdash \ell p \text{ lval}} \qquad \overline{\vdash *e \text{ lval}} \qquad \frac{\vdash e \text{ lval}}{\vdash e.i \text{ lval}}$$

Fig. 5. Static Semantics: Auxiliary Judgments

and term variables that are in scope. Term variables map to types. The rule for package expressions requires that the witness type is packable. The rules for **let** and **open** extend the context appropriately. The rule for assignment requires that the expressions' type is assignable. Most importantly, the rule for **open** e **as** $\alpha, *x$ **in** s requires that e has the form $\exists^\& \alpha.\tau$. (The repetition of α is not a restriction because $\exists^\& \alpha.\tau$ is α-convertible.) In other words, you cannot use this statement form to get an alias to a value of type $\exists^\delta \alpha.\tau$.

$$\begin{array}{l} \Delta \subset \text{Tyvar} \\ \Gamma : \text{Var} \rightharpoonup \text{Type} \end{array} \qquad \frac{\tau \text{ is closed under } \Delta}{\Delta \vdash \tau} \qquad \frac{\text{for all } \tau \in \text{rng}(\Gamma),\ \Delta \vdash \tau}{\Delta \vdash \Gamma}$$

$$\frac{\Delta \vdash \Gamma}{\Delta; \Gamma \vdash c : \text{int}} \qquad \frac{\Delta \vdash \Gamma}{\Delta; \Gamma \vdash x : \Gamma(x)} \qquad \frac{\Delta; \Gamma \vdash e : \tau_0 \times \tau_1}{\Delta; \Gamma \vdash e_i : \tau_i} \qquad \frac{\Delta; \Gamma \vdash e_0 : \tau_0 \quad \Delta; \Gamma \vdash e_1 : \tau_1}{\Delta; \Gamma \vdash (e_0, e_1) : \tau_0 \times \tau_1}$$

$$\frac{\Delta; \Gamma \vdash e : \tau\{\tau'/\alpha\} \quad \vdash \tau' \text{ packable}}{\Delta; \Gamma \vdash \textbf{pack } \tau', e \textbf{ as } \exists^\phi \alpha.\tau : \exists^\phi \alpha.\tau} \qquad \frac{\Delta; \Gamma \vdash e : \tau \quad \vdash e \text{ lval}}{\Delta; \Gamma \vdash \&e : \tau*} \qquad \frac{\Delta; \Gamma \vdash e : \tau*}{\Delta; \Gamma \vdash *e : \tau}$$

$$\frac{\Delta \vdash \Gamma}{\Delta; \Gamma \vdash \textbf{skip}} \qquad \frac{\Delta; \Gamma \vdash s_1 \quad \Delta; \Gamma \vdash s_2}{\Delta; \Gamma \vdash s_1; s_2} \qquad \frac{\Delta; \Gamma[x \mapsto \tau] \vdash s \quad \Delta; \Gamma \vdash e : \tau \quad x \notin \text{dom}(\Gamma)}{\Delta; \Gamma \vdash \textbf{let } x : \tau = e \textbf{ in } s}$$

$$\frac{\Delta; \Gamma \vdash e_1 : \tau \quad \Delta; \Gamma \vdash e_2 : \tau \quad \vdash e_1 \text{ lval} \quad \vdash \tau \text{ assignable}}{\Delta; \Gamma \vdash e_1 := e_2}$$

$$\frac{\Delta, \alpha; \Gamma[x \mapsto \tau] \vdash s \quad \Delta; \Gamma \vdash e : \exists^\phi \alpha.\tau \quad \alpha \notin \Delta \quad x \notin \text{dom}(\Gamma)}{\Delta; \Gamma \vdash \textbf{open } e \textbf{ as } \alpha, x \textbf{ in } s}$$

$$\frac{\Delta, \alpha; \Gamma[x \mapsto \tau*] \vdash s \quad \Delta; \Gamma \vdash e : \exists^\& \alpha.\tau \quad \alpha \notin \Delta \quad x \notin \text{dom}(\Gamma)}{\Delta; \Gamma \vdash \textbf{open } e \textbf{ as } \alpha, *x \textbf{ in } s}$$

Fig. 6. Static Semantics: Source Programs

In short, the static semantics ensures that "δ-packages" are not aliased except with existential types and that "&-packages" are not mutated. The next section shows that these restrictions suffice for type soundness.

Returning to the example from Section 3.2, we can show why this program is not well-typed: First, the rules for packages and assignment ensure that the three ϕ in the program (lines 3 and 6) must be the same. If they are δ, then line 4 is not well-typed because pkg's type does not have the form $\exists^{\&}\alpha.\tau$. If they are $\&$, then line 6 is not well-typed because we cannot derive $\vdash \exists^{\&}\alpha.\alpha* \times \alpha$ assignable.

4   Soundness Proof

In this section, we show how to extend the type system from the previous section in order to attain a syntactic [19] proof of type soundness. We then describe the proof, the details of which we relegate to a technical report [4].

For the most part, the extensions are the conventional ones for a heap and references [5], with several tedious complications that paths introduce. The basic idea is to prove that the types of labels are invariant. (That is, the value to which the heap maps a label may change, but only to a value of the same type.) However, we also need to prove an additional heap invariant for packages that have been opened with the **open** e **as** $\alpha, *x$ **in** s form. Such a package has the form **pack** τ', v **as** $\exists^{\&}\alpha.\tau$; its type does not mention τ', but τ' must not change. As explained below, we prove this invariant by explicitly preserving a partial map from locations to the witness types of "&-packages" at those locations.

4.1   Heap Static Semantics

For heap well-formedness, we introduce the judgment $H \vdash \Psi; \Upsilon$, where Ψ maps labels to types and Υ maps locations (labels and paths) to types. Intuitively, Ψ gives the type of each heap location, whereas Υ gives the witness types of the "&-packages" at some locations. Ψ is a conventional device; the use of Υ is novel. Every label in the heap must be in the domain of Ψ, but not every location containing an "&-package" needs to be in the domain of Υ. The location ℓp must be in the domain of Υ only if there is a value in the heap or program of the form $\ell p \mathbf{u} p'$. We say that Ψ' *extends* Ψ (similarly, Υ' *extends* Υ) if the domain of Ψ' contains the domain of Ψ and the two maps agree on their intersection.

The rule for type-checking locations, described below, needs a Ψ and Υ in its context. Hence we add a Ψ and Υ to the context for type-checking expressions and statements. Each rule in Figure 6 must be modified accordingly. A program state is well-typed if its heap and statement are well-typed and type-closed using the same Ψ and Υ. All of the above considerations are summarized in Figure 7.

What remains is type-checking expressions of the form ℓp. Intuitively, we start with the type $\Psi(\ell)$ and destruct it using p. However, when $p = \mathbf{u} p'$ we require that the type has the form $\exists^{\&}\alpha.\tau$ *and* the current location is in the domain of Υ. The resulting type uses Υ to substitute the witness type for α in τ. This operation is very similar to the way the dynamic semantics for **open** substitutes the witness type for the binding type variable. Υ has the correct witness type because $\vdash H : \Psi; \Upsilon$. We formalize these considerations with the auxiliary gettype relation in Figure 8. Using this relation, the rule for type-checking locations is:

$$\frac{\Upsilon; \ell \vdash \text{gettype}(\cdot, \Psi(\ell), p, \tau) \quad \Delta \vdash \Gamma}{\Psi; \Upsilon; \Delta; \Gamma \vdash \ell p : \tau}$$

$$\Psi : \text{Lab} \rightarrow \text{Type}$$
$$\Upsilon : \text{Lab} \times \text{Path} \rightarrow \text{Type}$$

$$\frac{\vdash H : \Psi; \Upsilon \qquad \Psi; \Upsilon; \emptyset; \emptyset \vdash s}{\text{for all } \tau \in \text{rng}(\Psi) \cup \text{rng}(\Upsilon), \ \tau \text{ is closed}}{\vdash (H, s)}$$

$$\frac{\text{dom}(H) = \text{dom}(\Psi)}{\text{for all } \ell \in \text{dom}(H), \ \Psi; \Upsilon; \emptyset; \emptyset \vdash H(\ell) : \Psi(\ell)}{\text{for all } (\ell, p) \in \text{dom}(\Upsilon), \ \text{get}(H(\ell), p, \textbf{pack } \Upsilon(\ell, p), v \textbf{ as } \exists^{\&}\alpha.\tau)}{\vdash H : \Psi; \Upsilon}$$

Fig. 7. Static Semantics: States and Heaps

$$\frac{}{\Upsilon; \ell \vdash \text{gettype}(p, \tau, \cdot, \tau)} \qquad \frac{\Upsilon; \ell \vdash \text{gettype}(pu, \tau'\{\Upsilon(\ell, p)/\alpha\}, p', \tau)}{\Upsilon; \ell \vdash \text{gettype}(p, \exists^{\&}\alpha.\tau', up', \tau)}$$

$$\frac{\Upsilon; \ell \vdash \text{gettype}(p0, \tau_0, p', \tau)}{\Upsilon; \ell \vdash \text{gettype}(p, \tau_0 \times \tau_1, 0p', \tau)} \qquad \frac{\Upsilon; \ell \vdash \text{gettype}(p1, \tau_1, p', \tau)}{\Upsilon; \ell \vdash \text{gettype}(p, \tau_0 \times \tau_1, 1p', \tau)}$$

Fig. 8. Static Semantics: Heap Objects

4.2 Proving Type Safety

We now summarize our proof of type safety. As usual with syntactic approaches, our formulation indicates that a well-typed program state (a heap and a statement) is either a terminal configuration (the statement is **skip**) or there is a step permitted by the dynamic semantics and all such steps produce well-typed program states.[3] Type safety is a corollary of preservation (subject-reduction) and progress lemmas, which we formally state as follows:

Lemma 1 (Preservation). *If* $\vdash (H, s)$ *and* $(H, s) \rightarrow (H', s')$, *then* $\vdash (H', s')$.

Lemma 2 (Progress). *If* $\vdash (H, s)$, *then either* $s = \textbf{skip}$ *or there exist* H' *and* s' *such that* $(H, s) \rightarrow (H', s')$.

Proving these lemmas requires analogous lemmas for expressions:

Lemma 3 (Expression Preservation). *Suppose* $\vdash H : \Psi; \Upsilon$ *and* $\Psi; \Upsilon; \emptyset; \emptyset \vdash e : \tau$. *If* $H \vdash e \Downarrow_{\text{L}} \ell p$, *then* $\Psi; \Upsilon; \emptyset; \emptyset \vdash \ell p : \tau$. *If* $H \vdash e \Downarrow_{\text{R}} v$, *then* $\Psi; \Upsilon; \emptyset; \emptyset \vdash v : \tau$.

Lemma 4 (Expression Progress). *If* $\vdash H : \Psi; \Upsilon$ *and* $\Psi; \Upsilon; \emptyset; \emptyset \vdash e : \tau$, *then there exists a* v *such that* $H \vdash e \Downarrow_{\text{R}} v$. *If we further assume* $\vdash e$ *lval, then there exist* ℓ *and* p *such that* $H \vdash e \Downarrow_{\text{L}} \ell p$.

We prove the progress lemmas by induction on the structure of terms, using the preservation lemmas and a canonical-forms lemma (which describes the form of values of particular types) as necessary.

---

[3] For our formal language, it is also the case that the dynamic semantics cannot diverge, but we do not use this fact.

For example, if $s = $ **open** e **as** α, x **in** s', we argue as follows: By assumption, there must be a Ψ and Υ such that $\Psi; \Upsilon; \emptyset; \emptyset \vdash s$, which means there is a τ such that $\Psi; \Upsilon; \emptyset; \emptyset \vdash e : \exists^\phi \alpha.\tau$. So by the expression-progress lemma, there is a v such that $H \vdash e \Downarrow_R v$. By the expression-preservation lemma, $\Psi; \Upsilon; \emptyset; \emptyset \vdash v : \exists^\phi \alpha.\tau$. By the canonical-forms lemma, $v = $ **pack** τ', v' **as** $\exists^\phi \alpha.\tau$ for some τ' and v'. So for any $\ell \notin \text{dom}(H)$, we can derive $(H, $ **open** e **as** α, x **in** $s) \rightarrow (H[\ell \mapsto v], s\{\tau'/\alpha\}\{\ell\cdot/x\})$.

The proof cases involving explicit heap references (such as $s = e_1 := e_2$ because $H \vdash e_1 \Downarrow_L \ell p$) require a lemma relating the get, set, and gettype relations:

Lemma 5 (Heap-Record Type Safety). *Suppose* $\vdash H : \Psi; \Upsilon$ *and* $\Upsilon; \ell \vdash \text{gettype}(\cdot, \Psi(\ell), p, \tau)$. *Then there is a* v' *such that* $\text{get}(H(\ell), p, v')$ *and* $\Psi; \Upsilon; \emptyset; \emptyset \vdash v' : \tau$. *Also, for all* v_1 *there is a* v_2 *such that* $\text{set}(v, p, v_1, v_2)$.

This lemma's proof requires a stronger hypothesis: We assume $\text{get}(H(\ell), p_1, v'')$, $\Upsilon; \ell \vdash \text{gettype}(p_1, \tau'', p_2, \tau)$, and $\Psi; \Upsilon; \emptyset; \emptyset \vdash v'' : \tau''$ to prove $\text{get}(H(\ell), p_1 p_2, v')$ (and analogues of the other conclusions), by induction on the length of p_2. The interesting case is when $p_2 = up'$ because its proof requires the heap invariant that the map Υ imposes. In this case, the gettype assumption implies that $(\ell, p_1) \in \text{dom}(\Upsilon)$, which means we know $\text{get}(H(\ell), p_1, $ **pack** $\Upsilon(\ell, p_1), v_p$ **as** $\exists^\& \alpha.\tau')$. Without Υ and heap well-formedness, a type other than $\Upsilon(\ell, p_1)$ could be in the package. We then could not invoke the induction hypothesis—there would be no suitable τ'' when using v_p for v''.

We prove the preservation lemmas by induction on the evaluation (dynamic semantics) derivation, proceeding by cases on the last rule used in the derivation. We need auxiliary lemmas for substitution and heap extension:

Lemma 6 (Substitution).

- If $\Psi; \Upsilon; \Delta, \alpha; \Gamma \vdash s$, $\Delta \vdash \tau'$, and $\vdash \tau'$ packable, then $\Psi; \Upsilon; \Delta; \Gamma\{\tau'/\alpha\} \vdash s\{\tau'/\alpha\}$.
- If $\Psi; \Upsilon; \Delta; \Gamma[x \mapsto \tau'] \vdash s$ and $\Psi; \Upsilon; \Delta; \Gamma \vdash \ell p : \tau'$, then $\Psi; \Upsilon; \Delta; \Gamma \vdash s\{\ell p/x\}$.

Lemma 7 (Heap Extension). *Suppose* Υ' *and* Ψ' *are well-formed extensions of well-formed* Υ *and* Ψ, *respectively.*

- If $\Psi; \Upsilon; \Delta; \Gamma \vdash e : \tau$, then $\Psi'; \Upsilon'; \Delta; \Gamma \vdash e : \tau$.
- If $\Psi; \Upsilon; \Delta; \Gamma \vdash s$, then $\Psi'; \Upsilon'; \Delta; \Gamma \vdash s$.

With these lemmas, most of the proof cases are straightforward arguments: Rules using substitution use the substitution lemma. Rules extending the heap use the heap-extension lemma for the unchanged heap values and the resulting statement. Rules using the get relation use the heap-record type-safety lemma.

The most interesting cases are for $e_1 := e_2$ (proving the invariant Υ imposes still holds) and **open** e **as** $\alpha, *x$ **in** s' (extending Υ in the necessary way).[4]

---

[4] The $H \vdash e.i \Downarrow_L \ell p i$ case is also "interesting" in that it extends the path on the *right* whereas the gettype relation destructs paths from the *left*. The **open** e **as** $\alpha, *x$ **in** s' case has an analogous complication because it adds u on the right.

We prove the case $e_1 := e_2$ as follows: By the assumed derivations and the expression-preservation lemma, there are ℓ, p, v, v', and τ such that we have $\Psi; \Upsilon; \emptyset; \emptyset \vdash \ell p : \tau$, $\Psi; \Upsilon; \emptyset; \emptyset \vdash v : \tau$, $\vdash \tau$ assignable, and $\mathrm{set}(H(\ell), p, v, v')$. Letting $\Psi' = \Psi$ and $\Upsilon' = \Upsilon$, we need to show $\vdash H[\ell \mapsto v'] : \Psi; \Upsilon$. The technical difficulties are showing $\Psi; \Upsilon; \emptyset; \emptyset \vdash v' : \Psi(\ell)$ and for all p such that $(\ell, p) \in \mathrm{dom}(\Upsilon)$, $\mathrm{get}(v', p, \mathbf{pack}\ \Upsilon(\ell, p), v''\ \mathbf{as}\ \exists^{\&}\alpha.\tau)$. The proofs are quite technical, but the intuition is straightforward: The typing judgment holds because v has type τ. The other requirement holds because the part of the old $H(\ell)$ replaced by v has no terms of the form $\mathbf{pack}\ \Upsilon(\ell, p), v\ \mathbf{as}\ \exists^{\&}\alpha.\tau$ (because $\vdash \tau$ assignable) and the rest of the old $H(\ell)$ is unchanged.

We prove the case $\mathbf{open}\ e\ \mathbf{as}\ \alpha, *x\ \mathbf{in}\ s'$ as follows: By the assumed derivations, the expression-preservation lemma, and the induction hypothesis, there are ℓ', p, τ', v, and τ such that $H \vdash e \Downarrow_{\mathrm{L}} \ell' p$, $\mathrm{get}(H(\ell'), p, \mathbf{pack}\ \tau', v\ \mathbf{as}\ \exists^{\&}\alpha.\tau)$, and $\Psi; \Upsilon; \alpha; [x \mapsto \tau*] \vdash s'$. Heap well-formedness ensures $\vdash \tau'$ packable. Letting $\Psi' = \Psi[\ell \mapsto \tau\{\tau'/\alpha\}*]$ and $\Upsilon' = \Upsilon[(\ell', p) \mapsto \tau']$, we must show $\vdash H[\ell \mapsto \&\ell' p\mathrm{u}]$ and $\Psi; \Upsilon; \emptyset; \emptyset \vdash s'\{\tau'/\alpha\}\{\ell'/x\}$.[5] The latter follows from the heap-extension and substitution lemmas. For the former, we need a technical lemma to conclude that $\Upsilon'; \ell' \vdash \mathrm{gettype}(\cdot, \Psi(\ell'), p\mathrm{u}, \tau\{\tau'/\alpha\})$. The difficulty comes from appending u to the right of the path. From this fact, we can derive $\Psi'; \Upsilon'; \emptyset; \emptyset \vdash \&\ell' p\mathrm{u} : \tau\{\tau'/\alpha\}*$. The heap-extension lemma suffices for showing the rest of the heap is well-typed.

5   Related Work

It does not appear that previous work has combined existential types with C-style aliasing and assignment.

Mitchell and Plotkin's original work [11] used existential types to model "second-class" abstraction constructs, so mutation of existential packages was impossible. Similarly, encodings using existentials, such as objects [1] and closures [10], have not needed to mutate a witness type. Current Haskell implementations [16,15] include existential types for "first-class" values, as suggested by Läufer [7]. Of course, these systems' existential packages are also immutable.

More relevant are low-level languages with existential types. For example, Typed Assembly Language [12] does not allow aliases at the opened type. There is also no way to change the type of a value in the heap—assigning to an existential package means making a *pointer* refer to a different heap record. Xanadu [20], a C-like language with compile-time reasoning about integer values, also does not have aliases at the opened type. Roughly, int is elaborated to $\exists \alpha \in \mathcal{Z}.\alpha$ and uses of int values are wrapped by the necessary **open** expressions. This expression *copies* the value, so aliasing is not a problem. It appears that witnesses can change: this change would happen when an int in the heap is mutated.

Languages with *linear* existential types can provide a solution different than the ones presented in this work. In these systems, there is only one reference to an existential package, so *a fortiori* there are no aliases at the opened type.

---

[5] Note that $\mathrm{get}(H(\ell'), p, \mathbf{pack}\ \tau', v\ \mathbf{as}\ \exists^{\&}\alpha.\tau)$ ensures Υ' is an extension of Υ.

Walker and Morrisett [18] exploit this invariant to define a version of **open** that does not introduce any new bindings. Instead, it mutates the location holding the package to hold the package's contents. The Vault system [3] also has linear existential types. Formally, opening a Vault existential package introduces a new binding. In practice, the Vault type-checker infers where to put **open** statements and how to rewrite terms using the bindings that these statements introduce.

Smith and Volpano [13, 14] describe an integration of *universal* types into C. Their technical development is somewhat similar to ours, but they leave the treatment of structures to future work. It is precisely structures that motivate existential types and our treatment of them.

The well-studied problem of polymorphic references in ML [5, 19, 17] also results from quantified types, aliasing, and mutation, so it is natural to suppose the work presented here is simply the logical dual of the same problem. We have not found the correspondence between the two issues particularly illuminating, but we nonetheless point out similarities that may suggest a duality.

In this work's notation, if NULL can have any pointer type, the polymorphic-reference problem is that a naive type system might permit the following:

$$(1) \quad \textbf{let } x : \forall \alpha.(\alpha*) = \texttt{NULL in}$$
$$(2) \quad \textbf{let } zero : \text{int} = 0 \textbf{ in}$$
$$(3) \quad \textbf{let } pzero : \text{int}* = \&zero \textbf{ in}$$
$$(4) \quad x := \&pzero \;;$$
$$(5) \quad *x := 0 \;;$$
$$(6) \quad *pzero := zero$$

The problem is giving x type $\forall \alpha.(\alpha*)$ (as opposed to $(\forall \alpha.\alpha)*$ or a monomorphic type), which allows us to treat the same location as though it had types int** and int*. The example assigns to x at an *instantiated* type (line 4) and *then* instantiates x at a different type (line 5). In contrast, our unsoundness example with existential types assigns to a value at an *unopened* type only *after* creating an alias at the opened type.

The "value restriction" is a very clever way to prevent types like $\forall \alpha.(\alpha*)$ by exploiting that expressions of such types cannot be values in ML. It effectively prevents certain types for a mutable locations' *contents*. In contrast, our "no witness changes" solution prevents certain types for a mutation's *location*.

With the exception of linear type systems, we know of no treatment of universal types that actually permits the types of values at mutable locations to change, as our "no aliases at the opened type" solution does. It is unclear what an invariant along these lines would look like for polymorphic references.

6   Acknowledgments

I am grateful for relevant discussions with Rob DeLine, Manuel Fähndrich, Greg Morrisett, David Walker, Kevin Watkins, Yanling Wang, and Steve Zdancewic.

References

1. Kim B. Bruce, Luca Cardelli, and Benjamin C. Pierce. Comparing object encodings. *Information and Computation*, 155:108–133, 1999.
2. *Cyclone User's Manual*, 2001. http://www.cs.cornell.edu/projects/cyclone.
3. Robert DeLine and Manuel Fähndrich. Enforcing high-level protocols in low-level software. In *ACM Conference on Programming Language Design and Implementation*, pages 59–69, Snowbird, UT, June 2001.
4. Dan Grossman. Existential types for imperative languages: Technical results. Technical Report 2001-1854, Cornell University Computer Science, October 2001.
5. Robert Harper. A simplified account of polymorphic references. *Information Processing Letters*, 51(4):201–206, August 1994.
6. Trevor Jim, Greg Morrisett, Dan Grossman, Michael Hicks, James Cheney, and Yanling Wang. Cyclone: A safe dialect of C. In *2002 USENIX Annual Technical Conference*, Monterey, CA, June 2002. To appear.
7. Konstantin Läufer. Type classes with existential types. *Journal of Functional Programming*, 6(3):485–517, May 1996.
8. B. Liskov et al. *CLU Reference Manual*. Springer-Verlag, 1984.
9. Robin Milner, Mads Tofte, Robert Harper, and David MacQueen. *The Definition of Standard ML (Revised)*. MIT Press, 1997.
10. Yasuhiko Minamide, Greg Morrisett, and Robert Harper. Typed closure conversion. In *23rd ACM Symposium on Principles of Programming Languages*, pages 271–283, St. Petersburg, FL, January 1996.
11. J.C. Mitchell and G.D. Plotkin. Abstract types have existential type. *ACM Transactions on Programming Languages and Systems*, 10(3):470–502, 1988. Preliminary version in 12th ACM Symposium on Principles of Programming Languages, 1985.
12. Greg Morrisett, David Walker, Karl Crary, and Neal Glew. From System F to typed assembly language. *ACM Transactions on Programming Languages and Systems*, 21(3):528–569, May 1999.
13. Geoffrey Smith and Dennis Volpano. Towards an ML-style polymorphic type system for C. In *6th European Symposium on Programming*, volume 1058 of *Lecture Notes in Computer Science*, pages 341–355, Linköping, Sweden, April 1996. Springer-Verlag.
14. Geoffrey Smith and Dennis Volpano. A sound polymorphic type system for a dialect of C. *Science of Computer Programming*, 32(2–3):49–72, 1998.
15. *The Glasgow Haskell Compiler User's Guide, Version 5.02*, 2001. http://www.haskell.org/ghc/docs/latest/set/book-users-guide.html.
16. *The Hugs 98 User Manual*, 2001. http://www.cse.ogi.edu/PacSoft/projects/Hugs/pages/hugsman/index.html.
17. Mads Tofte. Type inference for polymorphic references. *Information and Computation*, 89:1–34, November 1990.
18. David Walker and Greg Morrisett. Alias types for recursive data structures. In *Workshop on Types in Compilation*, volume 2071 of *Lecture Notes in Computer Science*, pages 177–206, Montreal, Canada, September 2000. Springer-Verlag.
19. Andrew K. Wright and Matthias Felleisen. A syntactic approach to type soundness. *Information and Computation*, 115(1):38–94, 1994.
20. Hongwei Xi. Imperative programming with dependent types. In *15th IEEE Symposium on Logic in Computer Science*, pages 375–387, Santa Barbara, CA, June 2000.

Another Type System for In-Place Update

David Aspinall[1] and Martin Hofmann[2]

[1] LFCS Edinburgh, Mayfield Rd, Edinburgh EH9 3JZ, UK
da@dcs.ed.ac.uk,
WWW: www.dcs.ed.ac.uk/home/da
[2] Institut für Informatik, Oettingenstraße 67, 80538 München, Germany
mhofmann@informatik.uni-muenchen.de,
WWW: www.tcs.informatik.uni-muenchen.de/~mhofmann

Abstract. Linear typing schemes guarantee single-threadedness and so
the soundness of in-place update with respect to a functional semantics.
But linear schemes are restrictive in practice, and more restrictive than
necessary to guarantee soundness of in-place update. This has prompted
research into static analysis and more sophisticated typing disciplines, to
determine when in-place update may be safely used, or to combine linear
and non-linear schemes. Here we contribute to this line of research by
defining a new typing scheme which better approximates the semantic
property of soundness of in-place update for a functional semantics. Our
typing scheme includes two kinds of products ($\otimes$ and $\times$), which allows
data structures with or without sharing to be defined. We begin from the
observation that some data is used only in a "read-only" context after
which it may be safely re-used before being destroyed. Formalizing the in-
place update interpretation and giving a machine model semantics allows
us to refine this observation. We define three *usage aspects* apparent from
the semantics, which are used to annotate function argument types. The
aspects are (1) used destructively, (2) used read-only but shared with
result, and (3) used read-only and not shared.

1 Introduction

The distinctive advantage of pure functional programming is that program functions may be viewed as ordinary mathematical functions. Powerful proof principles such as equational reasoning with program terms and mathematical induction are sound, without needing to use stores or other auxiliary entities, as is
invariably required when reasoning about imperative programs.

Consider the functional implementation of linked list reversal, as shown in
Fig. 1 (for the moment, ignore the first argument to cons). This definition of
reversal is readily verified by induction and equational reasoning over the set of
finite lists. On the other hand, implementing reversal imperatively using pointers
is (arguably) more cumbersome and error prone and, more seriously, would be
harder to verify using complicated reasoning principles for imperative programs.

The advantage of an imperative implementation, of course, is that it modi-
fies its argument in-place whereas in a traditional functional implementation the

D. Le Métayer (Ed.): ESOP 2002, LNCS 2305, pp. 36–52, 2002.
© Springer-Verlag Berlin Heidelberg 2002

result must be created from scratch and garbage collection is necessary in order salvage heap space. We are interested in the possibility of having the best of both worlds by using a semantics-preserving translation of functional programs into imperative ones which use in-place update and need no garbage collection. In previous work by the second author, a first-order functional language called

```
def list reverse_aux (list l, list acc) =
    match l with
         nil -> acc
       | cons(d,h,t) -> reverse_aux(t,cons(d,h,acc))

def list reverse (list l) = reverse_aux(l, nil)

def list append(list l, list m) =
    match l with
         nil -> m
       | cons(d,h,t) -> cons(d,h,append(t,m))
```

Fig. 1. LFPL examples

LFPL was defined, together with such a translation. LFPL relies on some user intervention to manage memory but without compromising the functional semantics in any way. This works by augmenting (non-nil) constructors of inductive datatypes such as cons with an additional argument of an abstract "diamond" resource type $\diamond$ whose elements can be thought of as heap-space areas, loosely corresponding to Tofte-Talpin's notion of *regions* [TT97].

To construct an element of an inductive type, we must supply a value of the $\diamond$ abstract type. The only way of obtaining values of type $\diamond$ is by deconstructing elements of recursive types in a pattern match. The first argument to each use of cons in Fig. 1 is this value of type $\diamond$; the cons on the right hand side of the match is "justified" by the preceding cons-pattern. The correspondence need not always be as local; in particular, values of type $\diamond$ may be passed as arguments to and returned by functions, as well as appearing in components of data structures.

We can give a compositional translation of LFPL into C by mapping $\diamond$ to the type void * (a universal pointer type), and implementing cons as

```
list_t cons(void *d, entry_t hd, list_t tl){
    d->head=hd; d->tail=tl; return d;
}
```

Here, list_t is the type of pointers to a C struct with appropriately typed entries head, tail, and we have elided (compulsory) typecasts to reduce clutter. As expected, nil is implemented as a function returning a null pointer. When receiving a non-null argument of type list_t we can save its entries as local variables and subsequently use the pointer itself as an argument to cons(). This implements pattern matching. For details of the translation, see [Hof00].

The main result of [Hof00] was that the semantics of the C translation agrees with the functional semantics of the soure program *provided* the latter admitted a linear typing for inductive types and ◇ types, i.e., bound variables of inductive type are used at most once. In particular, this linearity guarantees that the memory space pointed to by a ◇-value is not needed anywhere else. This prevents function definitions like:

```
def list twice (list l) =
  match l with
    nil -> nil
  | cons(d,h,t) -> cons(d,0,cons(d,0,twice(l)))
```

The functional semantics of `twice` maps a list l to a list twice as long as l with zero entries; on the other hand, the LFPL translation to C of the above code computes a circular list. As one would expect, the translation of append in Fig. 1 appends one linked list to another in place; again, the translation of a non-linear phrase like `append(l,l)` results in a circular list, disagreeing with the functional semantics. As an aside: we can implmenent `twice` in LFPL with the typing `list[int*<>]` -> `list[int]`, where the argument list provides the right amount of extra space. In recent unpublished work with Steffen Jost and Dilsun Kırlı, we have shown that the position of ◇ types and their arguments can be automatically inferred, using integer linear programming.

Linear typing together with the resource type ◇ seems restrictive at first sight. In particular, without dynamic creation of memory in the translation, no function can be written that increases the size of its input. Yet surprisingly, a great many standard examples from functional programming fit very naturally into the LFPL typing discipline, among them, insertion sort, quick sort, tree sort, breadth-first traversal of a tree and Huffman's algorithm. Moreover, in [Hof00] it was shown that every non size-increasing function on lists over booleans in the complexity class ETIME can be represented.

In spite of this positive outlook, the linear typing discipline, as any other typing scheme, rejects many semantically valid programs. In our context a program is semantically valid if its translation to imperative code computes its functional semantics. We cannot hope to catch all semantically valid programs by a typing discipline, of course, but we can try to refine the type system to reduce the "slack", i.e., the discrepancy between the semantically valid programs and those which pass the typing discipline.

In this paper we address one particular source for slack, namely the implicit assumption that every access to a variable is potentially destructive, i.e., changes the memory region pointed to or affected by this variable. This is overly conservative: multiple uses of a variable need not compromise semantic validity, as long as only the last in a series of multiple uses is destructive (and moreover the results of the earlier accesses do not interfere with the ultimate destructive access). A safe static approximation of this idea in the context of LFPL is the goal of this paper. We present a type system which is more general than linear typing in that it permits multiple uses of variables in certain cases, yet is sound in the sense that for well-typed LFPL programs the imperative translation computes the functional semantics.

1.1   Usage Aspects for Variables

Some examples will help to motivate our type system. A first example is the function `sumlist` : *list[int]* -> *int* which computes the sum of the elements in an integer list.

```
def int sumlist(list[int] l) =
    match l with
        nil -> 0
      | cons(d,h,t) -> h + sumlist(t)
```

With the destructive pattern matching scheme of LFPL, we must consider that l is destroyed after evaluating `sumlist(l)`, although the list would actually remain intact under any reasonable implementation. We can avoid losing the list by returning it along with the result, rebuilding it as we compute the sum of the elements. But this leads to a cumbersome programming style, and one has to remember that `sumlist'` : *list[int]* -> *int* * *list[int]* returns its argument unmodified. A better solution is to say that from the definition above, we see that the list is not destroyed (because the $\diamond$-value d is not used), so we would like to assign `sumlist` a type which expresses that it does not destroy its argument.

Not only should the `sumlist` function inspect its argument list without modifying it, but the result it returns no longer refers to the list. This means that an expression like

```
cons(d,sumlist(l),reverse(l))
```

where d is of type $\diamond$, should also be soundly implemented, if we assume that evaluation occurs from left to right. In other words, we can freely use the value of `sumlist(l)` even after l is destroyed.

This is not the case for functions which inspect data structures without modifying them, but return a result which contains some part of the argument. An example is the function `nth_tail` which returns the nth tail of a list:

```
def list nth_tail(int n, list l) =
    if n<=0 then l else match l with
                nil -> nil
              | cons(d,h,t) -> nth_tail(n-1, t)
```

Unlike `sumlist`, the result of `nth_tail` may be *shared* (aliased) with the argument. This means an expression like

```
cons(d,nth_tail(2,l),nil)
```

will be sound, but

```
cons(d,nth_tail(2,l),cons(d',reverse(l),nil))
```

will *not* be soundly implemented by the in-place update version, so the second expression should not be allowed in the language. (If l=[1,2,3], the expression should evaluate to the list [[3],[3,2,1]] but the in-place version would yield [[1],[3,2,1]]). Simpler example functions in the same category as `nth_tail` include projection functions and the identity function.

As a final example, consider again the append function in Fig. 1. The imperative implementation physically appends the second list to the first one and returns the so modified first argument. Thus, the first list l has been *destroyed* so we should treat that in the same way as arguments to reverse. But the second list m is *shared* with the result, and so should be treated in the same way as arguments to nth_tail. This suggests that we should consider the way a function operates on each of its arguments.

These observations lead us to distinguish three *usage aspects* of variables, which are the central innovation in our type system. The usage aspects are:

- Aspect 1: modifying use, e.g., l in reverse(l)
- Aspect 2: non-modifying use, but shared with result, e.g., m in append(l,m)
- Aspect 3: non-modifying use, not shared with result, e.g., l in sumlist(l).

The numbers are in increasing order of "safety" or "permissiveness" in the type system. Variables may only be accessed once with aspect 1. Variables can be used many times with aspect 2, but this prevents an aspect 1 usage later if intermediate results are retained. Finally, variables can be freely used with aspect 3, the pure "read-only" usage. Perhaps surprisingly, these exact distinctions appear to be novel, but they are closely connected to several other analyses appearing in related work [Wad90,Ode92,Kob99] — see Section 5 for precise comparisons.

Our type system decorates function arguments with usage aspects, and then tracks the way that variables are used. For example, we have the following types:

```
 reverse : list[t]^1 -> list[t]
sumlist : list[t]^3 -> int
nth_tail : list[t]^2 * int^3 -> list[t]
  append : list[t]^1 * list[t]^2 -> list[t]
```

Heap-free types such as *int* will always have the read-only aspect 3. Functions which have a heap-free result (like sumlist) may have aspect 3 for their non heap-free arguments, provided they are not modified when computing the result.

1.2 Sharing in Data Structures

The strict linear type system in LFPL prevents sharing in data structures, which can lead to bad space behaviour in some programs. The append function shows how we might be able to allow some limited sharing within data structures but still use an in-place update implementation, provided we take care over when modification is allowed. For example, we would like to allow the expression

let x=append(u,w) **and** y=append(v,w) **in** e

provided that we don't modify both x and y in e; after either has been modified we should not refer to the other. Similarly, we would like to allow a tree which has sharing amongst subtrees, in the simplest case a node constructed like this:

let u=node(d,a,t,t) **in** e

(where d:<> and a is a label). This data structure should be safe so long as we do not modify both branches of u. The kinds of data structure we are considering here have a DAG-like layout in memory.

The "not modifying both parts" flavour of these examples leads us to include two kinds of products in our language. Consider binary trees. In a linear setting we have two kinds of trees, one corresponding to trees laid out in full in memory ($\otimes$-trees), the other corresponding more to an object-oriented representation ($\times$-trees) under which a tree can be sent messages asking it to return the outermost constructor or to evolve into one of its subtrees. In ordinary functional programming these two are extensionally equivalent; in the presence of linearity constraints they differ considerably. The $\otimes$-trees allow simultaneous access to all their components thus encompassing e.g., computing the list of leaf labellings, whereas access to the $\times$-trees is restricted to essentially search operations. Conversely, $\otimes$-trees are more difficult to construct; we must ensure that their overall size is polynomially bounded which precludes in particular the definition of a function which constructs the full binary tree of *depth n*. On the other hand, the typing rules would allow construction of a full binary $\times$-tree, which is represented as a rather small DAG. The novelty here is that we can reflect in the type system the kind of choices that a programmer would normally make in selecting the best data representation for a purpose.

The product already in LFPL as studied to date is the tensor product (denoted by $\otimes$, resp. * in code), accessed using a pattern matching construct:

```
match p with x*y -> e
```

This allows both x and y to be accessed simultaneously in e. (Typing rules are shown in the next section). Given a $\otimes$-product of two lists, we can access (maybe modify) both components; to be sound, the two lists must have no sharing.

The cartesian product (denoted $\times$, resp. X in code) which corresponds to the & connective of linear logic has a different behaviour. We may access one component or the other, but not both; this means that the two components may have sharing. With our usage aspects, we can be more permissive than allowing just access to one component of the product. We can safely allow access to both components, so long as at most one component is modified, and if it is, the other one is not referenced thereafter. The pairing rule for cartesian products has a special side condition which allows this. Cartesian products are accessed via projection functions:

```
fst : (t X u)^2 -> t
snd : (t X u)^2 -> u
```

The usage aspect 2 here indicates that the result shares with the argument, which is the other part of enforcing the desired behaviour.

To allow data structures with sharing, we can give constructors arguments of cartesian product types. Ideally, we would allow the user to choose exactly where cartesian products are used and where $\otimes$-products are used, to allow the user to define datatypes appropriate for their application. For the purpose of exposition in this paper, however, we will treat both lists and tree types as primitives, and consider just the $\otimes$-product style data structures as used in LFPL.

O'Hearn and Pym's "bunched implications" [OP99] are also based on $\otimes$ and $\times$ coexisting. In our case, $\times$ is not a true categorical product since the $\times$-pairing operation $\langle -, - \rangle$ is partial; it was shown in [Hof99] that implementing $\langle e_1, e_2 \rangle$ as a closure ($\lambda t.$if t then e_1 else e_2) recovers the categorical product, but it requires heap space, violating heap size boundedness.

2   Syntax and Typing

Syntax. The grammar for the types and terms of our improved LFPL is given in Fig. 2. For brevity, we use N also for the type of booleans (as in C). Types not containing diamonds $\diamond$, lists $\mathsf{L}(-)$ or trees $\mathsf{T}(-)$ are called *heap-free*, e.g. N and $\mathsf{N} \otimes \mathsf{N}$ are heap-free. We use x and variants to range over (a set of) variables and f to range over function symbols.

$$
\begin{aligned}
A ::=&\ \mathsf{N} \quad | \quad \diamond \quad | \quad \mathsf{L}(A) \quad | \quad \mathsf{T}(A) \quad | \quad A_1 \otimes A_2 \quad | \quad A_1 \times A_2 \\
e ::=&\ c \quad | \quad f(x_1, \ldots, x_n) \quad | \quad x \quad | \quad \mathsf{let}\ x = e_x\ \mathsf{in}\ e \quad | \quad \mathsf{if}\ x\ \mathsf{then}\ x_1\ \mathsf{else}\ x_2 \\
&\ | \quad e_1 \otimes e_2 \quad | \quad \mathsf{match}\ x\ \mathsf{with}\ (x_1 \otimes x_2) {\Rightarrow} e \quad | \quad (e_1, e_2) \quad | \quad \mathsf{fst}(e) \quad | \quad \mathsf{snd}(e) \\
&\ | \quad \mathsf{nil} \quad | \quad \mathsf{cons}(x_d, x_h, x_t) \quad | \quad \mathsf{match}\ x\ \mathsf{with}\ \mathsf{nil} {\Rightarrow} e_n | \mathsf{cons}(x_d, x_h, x_t) {\Rightarrow} e_c \\
&\ | \quad \mathsf{leaf}(x_d, x_a) \quad | \quad \mathsf{node}(x_d, x_a, x_l, x_r) \\
&\ | \quad \mathsf{match}\ x\ \mathsf{with}\ \mathsf{leaf}(x_d, x_a) {\Rightarrow} e_l | \mathsf{node}(x_d, x_a, x_l, x_r) {\Rightarrow} e_n
\end{aligned}
$$

Fig. 2. LFPL grammar

To simplify the presentation, we restrict the syntax so that most term formers can only be applied to variables. In practice, we can define the more general forms such as $f(e_1, \ldots, e_n)$ easily as syntactic sugar for nested let-expressions. Also, compared with [Hof00] we will use a different translation scheme, where every non-nullary constructor of inductive type takes exactly one $\diamond$-argument, rather than a $\diamond$-argument for every ordinary argument of inductive type. This is closer to the Java compilation described in [AH01].

A program consists of a series of (possibly mutually recursive) function definitions of the form $f(x_1, \ldots, x_n) = e_f$. These definitions must be well-typed. To help ensure this, a program is given together with a signature Σ, which is a finite function from *function symbols* to first-order function types with usage aspects, i.e. of the form $A_1^{i_1}, \ldots, A_n^{i_n} \to A$. In the typing rules we will assume a fixed program with signature Σ.

We keep track of *usage aspects* for variables as introduced above. We write $x \overset{i}{:} A$ to mean that $x{:}A$ will be used with aspect $i \in \{1, 2, 3\}$ in the subject of the typing judgement. A *typing context* Γ is a finite function from identifiers to types A with usage aspects. If $x \overset{i}{:} A \in \Gamma$ we write $\Gamma(x) = A$ and $\Gamma[x] = i$.

We use familiar notation for extending contexts. If $x \notin \mathrm{dom}(\Gamma)$ then we write $\Gamma, x \overset{i}{:} A$ for the extension of Γ with $x \overset{i}{:} A$. More generally, if $\mathrm{dom}(\Gamma) \cap \mathrm{dom}(\Delta) = \emptyset$

then we write Γ, Δ for the disjoint union of Γ and Δ. If such notation appears in the premise or conclusion of a rule below it is implicitly understood that these disjointness conditions are met. We write $e[x/y]$ for the term obtained from e by replacing all occurrences of the free variable y in e by x. We consider terms modulo renaming of bound variables.

In a couple of the typing rules we need some additional notation for manipulating usage aspects on variables. The "committed to i" context Δ^i is the same as Δ, but each declaration $x \overset{2}{:} A$ of an aspect 2 (aliased) variable is replaced with $x \overset{i}{:} A$. If we have two contexts Δ_1, Δ_2 which only differ on usage aspects, so $\mathrm{dom}(\Delta_1) = \mathrm{dom}(\Delta_2)$ and $\Delta_1(x) = \Delta_2(x)$ for all x, then we define the merged context $\Gamma = \Delta_1 \wedge \Delta_2$ by $\mathrm{dom}(\Gamma) = \mathrm{dom}(\Delta_1)$, $\Gamma(x) = \Delta_1(x)$, $\Gamma[x] = \min(\Delta_1(x), \Delta_2(x))$. The merged context takes the "worst" usage aspect of each variable.

Signatures. We treat constructors as function symbols declared in the signature. We also include primitive arithmetic and comparison operations in the signature. Specifically, we can assume Σ contains a number of declarations:

$$
\begin{aligned}
&+, -, <, > : \mathsf{N}^3, \mathsf{N}^3 \to \mathsf{N} \\
&\mathsf{nil}_A \qquad : \mathsf{L}(A) \\
&\mathsf{cons}_A \qquad : \Diamond^1, A^2, \mathsf{L}(A)^2 \to \mathsf{L}(A) \\
&\mathsf{leaf}_A \qquad : \Diamond^1, A^2 \to \mathsf{T}(A) \\
&\mathsf{node}_A \qquad : \Diamond^1, A^2, \mathsf{T}(A)^2, \mathsf{T}(A)^2 \to \mathsf{T}(A) \\
&\mathsf{fst}_{A \times B} \quad : (A \times B)^2 \to A \\
&\mathsf{snd}_{A \times B} \quad : (A \times B)^2 \to B
\end{aligned}
$$

for suitable types A as used in the program. The comma between argument types is treated as a $\otimes$-product, which means that these typings, and the corresponding elimination rules below, describe lists and trees with simultaneous access to subcomponents. Hence they must be implemented without sharing unless the access is guaranteed to be read-only. (For trees $\mathsf{ST}(A)$ with unrestricted sharing between components we could use the typing:

$$\mathsf{sharednode}_A : \Diamond^1, (A \times \mathsf{ST}(A) \times \mathsf{ST}(A))^2 \to \mathsf{ST}(A).$$

In this typing, there can be sharing amongst the label and subtrees, but still no sharing with the $\Diamond$ argument, of course, since the region pointed to by the $\Diamond$-argument is overwritten to store the constructed cell.)

Typing rules. Now we explain the typing rules, shown in Fig. 2, which define a judgement of the form $\Gamma \vdash e : A$. Most rules are straightforward. We use an affine linear system, so include WEAK. In VAR, variables are given the default aspect 2, to indicate sharing. If the result is a value of heap-free type, then with RAISE we can promote variables of aspect 2 to aspect 3 to reflect that they do not share with the result. The rule DROP goes the other way and allows us to assume that a variable is used in a more destructive fashion than it actually is.

$$\frac{}{\vdash c : \mathsf{N}} \ (\text{CONST}) \qquad \frac{}{x \overset{2}{:} A \vdash x : A} \ (\text{VAR}) \qquad \frac{\Gamma \vdash e : A}{\Gamma, \Delta \vdash e : A} \ (\text{WEAK})$$

$$\frac{\Gamma \vdash e : A \qquad A \text{ heap-free}}{\Gamma^3 \vdash e : A} \ (\text{RAISE}) \qquad \frac{\Gamma, x \overset{i}{:} A \vdash e : B \qquad j \leq i}{\Gamma, x \overset{j}{:} A \vdash e : B} \ (\text{DROP})$$

$$\frac{f : A^{i_1}, \ldots, A^{i_n} \to B \text{ in } \Sigma}{x_1 \overset{i_1}{:} A_1, \ldots, x_n \overset{i_n}{:} A_n \vdash f(x_1, \ldots, x_n) : B} \ (\text{FUN})$$

$$\frac{\Gamma \vdash e_1 : C \qquad \Gamma \vdash e_2 : C}{\Gamma, x \overset{3}{:} \mathsf{N} \vdash \text{if } x \text{ then } e_1 \text{ else } e_2 : C} \ (\text{IF})$$

$$\frac{\Gamma, \Delta_1 \vdash e_1 : A \quad \Delta_2, \Theta, x \overset{i}{:} A \vdash e_2 : B \quad \begin{array}{l} \text{Either } \forall z.\Delta_1[z] = 3, \\ \text{or } i = 3, \forall z.\Delta_1[z] \geq 2, \Delta_2[z] \geq 2 \end{array}}{\Gamma^i, \Theta, \Delta_1^i \wedge \Delta_2 \vdash \text{let } x = e_1 \text{ in } e_2 : B} \ (\text{LET})$$

$$\frac{}{x_1 \overset{2}{:} A_1, x_2 \overset{2}{:} A_2 \vdash x_1 \otimes x_2 : A_1 \otimes A_2} \ (\otimes\text{-PAIR})$$

$$\frac{\Gamma, \Delta_1 \vdash e_1 : A_1 \qquad \Theta, \Delta_2 \vdash e_2 : A_2 \qquad \text{condition } \star}{\Gamma, \Theta; \Delta_1 \wedge \Delta_2 \vdash (e_1, e_2) : A_1 \times A_2} \ (\times\text{-PAIR})$$

$$\frac{\Gamma, x_1 \overset{i_1}{:} A_1, x_2 \overset{i_2}{:} A_2 \vdash e : B \qquad i = \min(i_1, i_2)}{\Gamma, x \overset{i}{:} A_1 \otimes A_2 \vdash \text{match } x \text{ with } (x_1 \otimes x_2) \Rightarrow e : B} \ (\text{PAIR-ELIM})$$

$$\frac{\begin{array}{l} \Gamma \vdash e_{\mathsf{nil}} : B \\ \Gamma, x_d \overset{i_d}{:} \Diamond, x_h \overset{i_h}{:} A, x_t \overset{i_t}{:} \mathsf{L}(A) \vdash e_{\mathsf{cons}} : B \qquad i = \min(i_d, i_h, i_t) \end{array}}{\Gamma, x \overset{i}{:} \mathsf{L}(A) \vdash \text{match } x \text{ with } \mathsf{nil} \Rightarrow e_{\mathsf{nil}} | \mathsf{cons}(x_d, x_h, x_t) \Rightarrow e_{\mathsf{cons}} : B} \ (\text{LIST-ELIM})$$

$$\frac{\begin{array}{l} \Gamma, x_d \overset{i_d}{:} \Diamond, x_a \overset{i_a}{:} A \vdash e_{\mathsf{leaf}} : B \\ \Gamma, x_d \overset{i_d}{:} \Diamond, x_a \overset{i_a}{:} A, x_l \overset{i_l}{:} \mathsf{T}(A), x_r \overset{i_r}{:} \mathsf{T}(A) \vdash e_{\mathsf{node}} : B \quad i = \min(i_a, i_d, i_l, i_r) \end{array}}{\Gamma, x \overset{i}{:} \mathsf{T}(A) \vdash \text{match } x \text{ with } \mathsf{leaf}(x_d, x_a) \Rightarrow e_{\mathsf{leaf}} | \mathsf{node}(x_d, x_a, x_l, x_r) \Rightarrow e_{\mathsf{node}} : B} \ (\text{TREE-ELIM})$$

Fig. 3. Typing rules

The LET rule is somewhat intricate. The context is split into three pieces: variables specific to the definition e_1, in Γ; variables specific to the body e_2, in Θ; and common variables, in Δ_1 and Δ_2, which may be used with different aspects in e_1 and e_2. First, we type-check the definition to find its type A. Then we type-check the body using some usage aspect i for the bound variable x. The way the bound variable x is used in the body is used to commit any aliased variables belonging to e_1. For example, if x is used destructively in e_2, then all aliased variables in Γ and Δ_1 are used destructively in the overall expression; this accounts for the use of Γ^i and Δ^i in the conclusion. The aspects in Δ_1 and Δ_2 are merged in the overall expression, taking into account the way that x is used in e_2. The side condition prevents any common variable z being modified in e_1 or e_2 before it is referenced in e_2. More exactly, $\Delta_1[z] = 1$ is not allowed (the value of the variable would be destroyed in the binding); $\Delta_1[z] = 3$ is always allowed (the value of the variable has no heap overlap with the binding value), and $\Delta_1[z] = 2$ is allowed provided neither $i = 1$ nor $\Delta_2[z] = 1$ (the value of the common variable may have aliasing with e_2, provided it is not partly or completely destroyed in e_2: the modification may happen before the reference). As an instance of LET, we get a derived rule of contraction for aspect 3 variables.

The only constructor rules we need are for the two kinds of pairs. The rule for constructing a $\times$-pair ensures that all variables which are shared between the components have aspect at least 2. The "condition $\star$" in rule $\times$-PAIR is:

- $\Delta_1[z] \geq 2$ and $\Delta_2[z] \geq 2$ for all $z \in \mathrm{dom}(\Delta_1) = \mathrm{dom}(\Delta_2)$.

which ensures that no part of memory shared between the components is destroyed when the pair is constructed. (A more liberal condition which considers evaluation order is possible, but we omit it here.)

In the destructor rules we type-check the branches in possibly extended contexts, and then pass the worst-case usage aspect as the usage for the term being destructed. For example, if we destroy one half of a pair in PAIR-ELIM, so x_1 has usage aspect 1, then the whole pair is considered destroyed in the conclusion.

3   Imperative Operational Semantics

To establish the correctness of our typing rules, we need to formalize the intended in-place update interpretation of the language. In [Hof00], a translation to 'C' and a semantics for the target sublanguage for 'C' was used. Here we instead use an abstract machine model; this allows us to more easily consider alternative translations to other languages, such as the Java translation given in [AH01], or a typed assembly language interpretation, as given in [AC02]. The interpretation we consider here is closest to the Java translation from [AH01].

Let Loc be a set of *locations* which model memory addresses on a heap. We use l to range over elements of Loc. Next we define two sets of values, *stack values* SVal, ranged over by v, and *heap values* HVal, ranged over by h, thus:

$$v ::= n \quad | \quad l \quad | \quad \mathrm{NULL} \quad | \quad (v, v)$$
$$h ::= v \quad | \quad \{\mathsf{f_1} = v_1 \ldots \mathsf{f_n} = v_n\}$$

A stack value is either an integer n, a location l, a null value NULL, or a pair of stack values (v, v). A heap value is either a stack value or an n-ary record consisting of named fields with stack values. A stack S:Var $\rightharpoonup$ SVal is a partial mapping from variables to stack values, and a heap σ:Loc $\rightharpoonup$ HVal is a partial mapping from locations to heap values. Evaluation of an expression e takes place with a given stack and heap, and yields a stack value and a possibly updated heap. Thus we have a relation of the form $S, \sigma \vdash e \leadsto v, \sigma'$ expressing that the evaluation of e under stack S and heap σ terminates and results in stack value v. As a side effect the heap is modified to σ'.

The only interesting cases in the operational semantics are the ones for the heap datatypes, which make use of $\Diamond$-values as heap locations. For example, the following rules for cons:

$$\frac{S, \sigma \vdash e_d \leadsto l_d, \sigma' \qquad S, \sigma' \vdash e_h \leadsto v_h, \sigma'' \qquad S, \sigma'' \vdash e_t \leadsto v_t, \sigma'''}{S, \sigma \vdash \mathsf{cons}(e_d, e_h, e_t) \leadsto l_d, \sigma'''[l_d \mapsto \{\mathsf{hd}=v_h, \mathsf{tl}=v_t\}]}$$

$$\frac{S, \sigma \vdash e \leadsto l, \sigma' \qquad \sigma'(l) = \{\mathsf{hd}=v_h, \mathsf{tl}=v_t\}}{S[x_d \mapsto l, x_h \mapsto v_h, x_t \mapsto v_t], \sigma' \vdash e_{\mathsf{cons}} \leadsto v, \sigma''}{S, \sigma \vdash \mathsf{match}\ e\ \mathsf{with}\ \mathsf{nil} \Rightarrow e_{\mathsf{nil}} | \mathsf{cons}(x_d, x_h, x_t) \Rightarrow e_{\mathsf{cons}} \leadsto v, \sigma''}$$

In the constructor rule, the first argument e_d of cons is a term of $\Diamond$ type, which we evaluate to a heap location l_d. We then evaluate the head and the tail of the list in turn, propagating any changes to the heap. Finally, the result is the location l_d where we make the cons cell by updating the heap, using a record with hd and tl fields. The match rule performs the opposite operation, breaking apart a cons-cell.

This operational semantics describes the essence of our in-place update interpretation of the functional language, without considering more complex translations or optimizations that might be present in a real compiler.

4   Correctness

In this section we will prove that for a typable program, the imperative operational semantics is sound with respect to a functional (set-theoretic) semantics.

Set-theoretic interpretation. We define the set-theoretic interpretation of types $[\![A]\!]$, by setting $[\![\mathsf{N}]\!] = \mathbf{Z}$, $[\![\Diamond]\!] = \{0\}$, $[\![\mathsf{L}(A)]\!] =$ finite lists over $[\![A]\!]$, $[\![\mathsf{T}(A)]\!] =$ binary $[\![A]\!]$-labelled trees, and $[\![A \otimes B]\!] = [\![A \times B]\!] = [\![A]\!] \times [\![B]\!]$. To each program $(\Sigma, (e_f)_{f \in \mathrm{dom}(\Sigma)})$ we can now associate a mapping ρ such that $\rho(f)$ is a *partial* function from $[\![A_1]\!] \times \ldots [\![A_n]\!]$ to $[\![B]\!]$ for each $f : A_1^{i_1}, \ldots, A_n^{i_n} \to B$. This meaning is given in the standard fashion as the least fixpoint of an appropriate compositionally defined operator, as follows. A *valuation* of a context Γ is a function η such that $\eta(x) \in [\![\Gamma(x)]\!]$ for each $x \in \mathrm{dom}(\Gamma)$; a valuation of a signature Σ is a function ρ such that $\rho(f) \in [\![\Sigma(f)]\!]$ whenever $f \in \mathrm{dom}(\Sigma)$. To each expression e such that $\Gamma \vdash_\Sigma e : A$ we assign an element $[\![e]\!]_{\eta, \rho} \in [\![A]\!] \cup \{\bot\}$ in the obvious way: function symbols and variables are interpreted according to the valuations;

basic functions and expression formers are interpreted by the eponymous set-theoretic operations, ignoring the $\Diamond$-type arguments in the case of constructor functions. The formal definition of $[\![-]\!]_{\eta,\rho}$ is by induction on terms. A *program* $(\Sigma, (e_f)_{f \in \text{dom}(\Sigma)})$ is then the least valuation ρ such that

$$\rho(f)(v_1, \ldots, v_n) = [\![e_f]\!]_{\rho,\eta}$$

where $\eta(x_i) = v_i$, for any $f \in \text{dom}(\Sigma)$.

Notice that this set-theoretic semantics does not say anything about space usage and treats $\Diamond$ as a single-point type; its only purpose is to pin down the functional denotations of programs so that we can formally state a correctness result for the in-place update operational interpretation.

Heap regions. Given a stack value v, a type A and a heap σ we define the associated *region* $R_A(v, \sigma)$ as the least set of locations satisfying

- $R_N(n, \sigma) = \emptyset$,
- $R_\Diamond(l, \sigma) = \{l\}$,
- $R_{A \times B}((v_1, v_2), \sigma) = R_{A \otimes B}((v_1, v_2), \sigma) = R_A(v_1, \sigma) \cup R_B(v_2, \sigma)$,
- $R_{L(A)}(\text{NULL}, \sigma) = \emptyset$,
- $R_{L(A)}(l, \sigma) = \{l\} \cup R_A(h, \sigma) \cup R_{L(A)}(t, \sigma)$ when $\sigma(l) = \{\text{hd} = h, \text{tl} = t\}$ (otherwise $\emptyset$),
- $R_{T(A)}(l, \sigma) = \{l\} \cup R_A(v, \sigma)$, when $\sigma(l) = \{\text{label} = v\}$,
- $R_{T(A)}(l, \sigma) = \{l\} \cup R_A(v, \sigma) \cup R_{T(A)}(t_l, \sigma) \cup R_{T(A)}(t_r, \sigma)$, when $\sigma(l) = \{\text{label} = v, \text{left} = t_l, \text{right} = t_r\}$ (otherwise $\emptyset$).

It should be clear that $R_A(v, \sigma)$ is the part of the (domain of) σ that is relevant for v. Accordingly, if $\sigma(l) = \sigma'(l)$ for all $l \in R_A(v, \sigma)$ then $R_A(v, \sigma) = R_A(v, \sigma')$. If A is a heap-free type, then $R_A(v, \sigma) = \emptyset$.

Meaningful stack values in a heap. Next, we need to single out the meaningful stack values and relate them to the corresponding semantic values. A stack value is *meaningful* for a particular type and heap if it has a sensible interpretation in the heap for that type. For instance, if $\sigma(a) = \{\text{hd} = 1, \text{tl} = \text{NULL}\}$ then a would be a meaningful stack value of type $L(N)$ with respect to σ and it would correspond to the semantic list $[1]$. Again, w.r.t. that same heap (a, a) would be a meaningful stack value of type $L(A) \times L(A)$ corresponding to the semantic pair $([1], [1]) \in [\![L(A) \times L(A)]\!]$. That same value (a, a) will also be a meaningful stack value of type $L(A) \otimes L(A)$ in case it will be used in a read only fashion. This occurs for example in the term $f(x \otimes x)$ when $f : (A \otimes A)^3 \to B$. This means that "meaningfulness" is parametrised by the aspect with which the value is going to be used. No distinction is made, however, between aspects 2 and 3 in this case.

Given a stack value v, a type A, a heap σ, a denotation $a \in [\![A]\!]$ and an aspect $i \in \{1, 2, 3\}$, we define a five-place relation $v \Vdash^\sigma_{A,i} a$ which expresses that v is a meaningful stack value of type A with respect to heap σ corresponding to semantic value a in aspect i. It is defined inductively as follows:

- $n \Vdash^\sigma_{N,i} n'$, if $n = n'$.

- $l \Vdash^\sigma_{\diamond,i} 0$.
- $(v_1, v_2) \Vdash^\sigma_{A_1 \times A_2, i} (a_1, a_2)$ if $v_k \Vdash^\sigma_{A_k, i} a_k$ for $k = 1, 2$.
- $(v_1, v_2) \Vdash^\sigma_{A_1 \otimes A_2, i} (a_1, a_2)$ if $v_k \Vdash^\sigma_{A_k, i} a_k$ for $k = 1, 2$. Additionally, $R_{A_1}(v_1, \sigma) \cap R_{A_2}(v_2, \sigma) = \emptyset$ in case $i = 1$.
- NULL $\Vdash^\sigma_{L(A), i}$ nil.
- $l \Vdash^\sigma_{L(A), i}$ cons(h, t), if $\sigma(l) = \{$hd$=v_h,$ tl $= v_t\}$, $l \Vdash^\sigma_{\diamond, i} 0$ and $v_h \Vdash^\sigma_{A, i} h$ and $v_t \Vdash^\sigma_{L(A), i} t$. Additionally, $R_\diamond(l, \sigma)$, $R_A(v_h, \sigma)$, $R_{L(A)}(v_t, \sigma)$ are pairwise disjoint in case $i = 1$.
- $l \Vdash^\sigma_{T(A), i}$ leaf(a) if $\sigma(l) = \{$label$=v_a\}$ and $l \Vdash^\sigma_{\diamond, i} 0$ and $v_a \Vdash^\sigma_A a$. Additionally, $R_\diamond(l, \sigma) \cap R_A(v_a) = \emptyset$ in case $i = 1$.
- $l \Vdash^\sigma_{T(A), i}$ node(a, l, r) if $\sigma(l) = \{$label$=v_a,$ left$=v_l,$ right$=v_r\}$ and $l \Vdash^\sigma_{\diamond, i} 0$ and $v_a \Vdash^\sigma_{A, i} a$ and $v_l \Vdash^\sigma_{A, i} l$ and $v_r \Vdash^\sigma_{A, i} r$. Additionally $R_\diamond(l, \sigma)$, $R_A(v_a, \sigma)$, $R_{T(A)}(v_l, \sigma)$, $R_{T(A)}(v_r, \sigma)$ are pairwise disjoint in case $i = 1$.

Notice that $\Vdash^\sigma_{A, 2}$ and $\Vdash^\sigma_{A, 3}$ are identical, whereas $\Vdash^\sigma_{A, 1}$ prevents any "internal sharing" within $\otimes$-product types in the heap representation. We extend this relation to stacks and valuations for a context, by defining $S \Vdash^\sigma_\Gamma \eta$ thus:

- $S(x) \Vdash^\sigma_{\Gamma(x), \Gamma[x]} \eta(x)$ for each $x \in$ dom(Γ)
- $x \neq y$ and $R_{\Gamma, x}(S, \sigma) \cap R_{\Gamma, y}(S, \sigma) \neq \emptyset$ implies $\Gamma[x] \geq 2, \Gamma[y] \geq 2$.

where as a shorthand, $R_{\Gamma, x}(S, \sigma) =_{\text{def}} R_{\Gamma(x)}(S(x), \sigma)$. So $S \Vdash^\sigma_\Gamma \eta$ holds if stack S and heap σ are meaningful for the valuation η at appropriate types and aspects, and moreover, the region for each aspect 1 variable does not overlap with the region for any other variable. (Informally: the aspect 1 variables are safe to update.) Below we use the shorthand $R_\Gamma(S, \sigma) =_{\text{def}} \bigcup_{x \in \text{dom}(\Gamma)} R_{\Gamma, x}(S, \sigma)$.

Correctness theorem. With this definition of meaningfulness in place, we can prove that the evaluation of a term under a meaningful stack and heap gives a meaningful result corresponding to the set-theoretic semantics. As usual, we prove a stronger statement to get an inductive argument through.

Theorem 1. *Assume the following data and conditions:*

1. *a program P over some signature Σ with meaning ρ,*
2. *a well-typed term $\Gamma \vdash e : C$ over Σ for some Γ, e, C,*
3. *a heap σ, a stack S and a valuation η, such that $S \Vdash^\sigma_\Gamma \eta$*

Then $S, \sigma \vdash e \rightsquigarrow v, \sigma'$ for some (uniquely determined) v, σ' if and only if $[\![e]\!]_{\eta, \rho}$ is defined. Moreover, in this case the following hold:

1. $R_C(v, \sigma') \subseteq R_\Gamma(S, \sigma)$,
2. *if $l \notin R_\Gamma(S, \sigma)$ then $\sigma(l) = \sigma'(l)$,*
3. *if $l \in R_{\Gamma, x}(S, \sigma)$ and $\Gamma[x] \geq 2$ then $\sigma(l) = \sigma'(l)$,*
4. $v \Vdash^{\sigma'}_{C, 2} [\![e]\!]_{\eta, \rho}$,
5. $S \Vdash^\sigma_{\Gamma 1} \eta$ *implies $v \Vdash^{\sigma'}_{C, 1} [\![e]\!]_{\eta, \rho}$ and $R_C(v, \sigma') \cap R_{\Gamma, x}(S, \sigma) = \emptyset$ when $\Gamma[x] = 3$.*

This theorem expresses both the meaningfulness of the representation of semantic values on the machine, and the correctness of the operational semantics
with respect to the set-theoretic semantics. The five consequences capture the
expected behaviour of the imperative operational semantics and the variable aspects. In brief: (1) no new memory is consumed; (2) heap locations outside those
reachable from input variables are unchanged in the result heap; (3) in-place updates are only allowed for locations in the regions of aspect 1 variables; (4) the
operational semantics agrees with the set-theoretic result for aspects 2 and 3; (5)
if the heap additionally has no variable-variable overlaps or "internal" sharing
for aspect 2 variables, then the meaningfulness relation also holds in aspect 1 (in
particular, there is no internal sharing within the result value v), and moreover,
there is no overlap between the result region and the region of any aspect 3
variable. This means it is safe to use the result in an updating context.

Specialising this perhaps daunting theorem to the particular case of a unary
function on lists yields the following representative corollary:

Corollary 1. *Let P be a program having a function symbol $f : L(N)^i \to L(N)$.*

*If σ is a store and l is a location such that l points in σ to a linked list with
integer entries $w = [x_1, \ldots, x_n]$ in σ then $\rho(f)(w)$ is defined iff $[x \mapsto l], \sigma \vdash
f(x) \rightsquigarrow v, \sigma'$ for some v, σ' and in this case v points in σ' to a linked list with
integer entries $\rho(f)(w)$.*

Additionally, one can draw conclusions about the heap region of the result list
depending on the value of i.

In further work (partly underway) we are examining the two kinds of product
in more detail, and considering array types with and without sharing between
entries. We are also looking at dynamically allocated store via built-in functions
new :$\to \diamond$ and dispose : $\diamond^3 \to$ N. These built-ins can be implemented by interfacing to an external memory manager, for example, using `malloc` and `free`
system calls augmented with a free list. This allows more functions to be defined
but breaks the heap-bounded nature of the system, in general.

5 Conclusions and Related Work

We defined an improved version of the resource-aware linear programming language LFPL, which includes *usage aspect* annotation on types. We also added
datatypes based on cartesian products, to allow sharing in data structures on
the heap. Using an operational semantics to formalize the in-place update interpretation, we proved that evaluation in the language is both type-sound for a
memory model and correct for a set-theoretic functional semantics.

The philosophy behind LFPL is that of providing a *static guarantee* that
efficient in-place implementations are used, while allowing as many programs as
possible. The guarantee is enforced by the type system. This is in contrast to
various other proposed systems which perform static analysis during compilation, or mix linear and non-linear typing schemes, to achieve compilations which
are often efficient in practice, but which provide no absolute guarantee. In its
pure form, LFPL does not include any instructions for allocating heap space,

so all computation is done in-place, using constant heap space. This guarantee is provided for any program which can be written in the language. Apart from differences in philosophy, our usage aspects and their semantic motivation from the memory model are somewhat novel compared with previous work. Related ideas and annotations do already appear in the literature, although not always with semantic soundness results. We believe that our system is simpler than much of the existing work, and in particular, the use of the resource type $\Diamond$ is crucial: it is the appearance of $\Diamond^1$ in the typing of constructors like cons that expresses that constructors are given an in-place update interpretation. Without the resource type $\Diamond$ there would be no aspect 1 component.

Here is a necessarily brief comparison with some of the previous work. The closest strand of work begins with Wadler's introduction of the idea of a sequential let [Wad90]. If we assume that e_1 is evaluated before e_2 in the expression

let $x=e_1$ in $e_2[x]$

then we can allow sharing of a variable z between e_1 and e_2, as long as z is not modified in e_1 and some other side-conditions which prevent examples like

let $x=y$ in append(x, y).

Our rule for let follows similar ideas. Odersky [Ode92] built on Wadler's idea of the sequential let. He has an *observer* annotation, which corresponds to our aspect 2 annotations: not modified, but still occurs in the result. He too has side conditions for the let rule which ensure soundness, but there is no proof of this (Odersky's main result is a type reconstruction algorithm). Kobayashi [Kob99] introduces *quasi-linear* types. This typing scheme also allows sharing in let expressions. It has a δ-*usage* which corresponds roughly to our aspect 3 usage. Kobayashi's motivation was to statically detect points where deallocation occurs; this requires stack-managed extra heap, augmenting region analysis [TT97]. Kobayashi also allows non-linear use of variables (we might similarly add an extra aspect to LFPL to allow non-linear variables, if we accepted the use of a garbage collector). Kobayashi proves a traditional type soundness (subject reduction) property, which shows an internal consistency of his system, whereas we have characterised and proved equivalence with an independently meaningful semantic property. It might well be possible to prove similar results to ours for Kobayashi's system, but we believe that by considering the semantical property at the outset, we have introduced a rather more natural syntactic system, with simpler types and typing rules.

There is much other related work on formal systems for reasoning or type-checking in the presence of aliasing, including for example work by Reynolds, O'Hearn and others [Rey78,OTPT95,Rey00,IO01]; work on the imperative λ-calculus [YR97]; uniqueness types [BS96], usage types for optimised compilation of lazy functional programs [PJW00] and program analyses for destructive array updates [DP93,WC98] as automated in PVS [Sha99]. There is also related work in the area of compiler construction and typed assembly languages, where researchers have investigated static analysis techniques for determining when optimisations such as in-place update or compile-time garbage collection are admissible; recent examples include shape analysis [WSR00], alias types [SWM00], and static capabilities [CWM99], which are an alternative and more permissive form of region-based memory management. One of our future goals is to relate our work back to research on compiler optimizations and typed low-level languages, in the hope that we can *guarantee* that certain optimizations will always be possible in LFPL, by virtue of its type system. This is in contrast to the behaviour of many present optimizing compilers, where it is often difficult for the programmer to be sure if a certain desirable optimization will performed by the compiler or not. Work in this directions has begun in [AC02], where a typed assembly language is developed which has high-level types designed to support compilation from LFPL, to obviate the need for garbage collection.

We see the work reported here as a step along the way towards a powerful high-level language equipped with notions of resource control. There are more steps to take. We want to consider richer type systems closer to those used in present functional programming languages, in particular, including polymorphic and higher-order types. For the latter, recent work by the second author [Hof02] shows that a large class of functions on lists definable in a system with higher-order functions can be computed in bounded space. Another step is to consider inference mechanisms for adding resource annotations, including the ◇ arguments (we mentioned some progress on this in Section 1) and usage aspects, as well as the possibility of automatically choosing between ⊗-types and ×-types. Other work-in-progress was mentioned at the end of the previous section. We are supporting some of the theoretical work with the ongoing development of an experimental prototype compiler for LFPL; see the first author's web page for more details.

Acknowledgements. The authors are grateful to Michal Konečný and Robert Atkey for discussion and comments on this work.

References

[AC02]   David Aspinall and Adriana Compagnoni. Heap bounded assembly language. Technical report, Division of Informatics, University of Edinburgh, 2002.

[AH01]   David Aspinall and Martin Hofmann. Heap bounded functional programming in Java. Implementation experiments, 2001.

[BS96]   E. Barendsen and S. Smetsers. Uniqueness typing for functional languages with graph rewriting semantics. *Mathematical Structures in Computer Science*, 6:579–612, 1996.

[CWM99] Karl Crary, David Walker, and Greg Morrisett. Typed memory management in a calculus of capabilities. In *Proceedings ACM Principles of Programming Languages*, pages 262–275, 1999.

[DP93]   M. Draghicescu and S. Purushothaman. A uniform treatment of order of evaluation and aggregate update. *Theoretical Computer Science*, 118(2):231–262, September 1993.

[Hof99]   Martin Hofmann. Linear types and non size-increasing polynomial time computation. In *Logic in Computer Science (LICS)*, pages 464–476. IEEE, Computer Society Press, 1999.

[Hof00]   Martin Hofmann. A type system for bounded space and functional in-place update. *Nordic Journal of Computing*, 7(4):258–289, 2000. An extended abstract has appeared in *Programming Languages and Systems*, G. Smolka, ed., Springer LNCS, 2000.

[Hof02]   Martin Hofmann. The strength of non size-increasing computation. In *Proceedings ACM Principles of Programming Languages*, 2002.

[IO01]   Samin Ishtiaq and Peter W. O'Hearn. BI as an assertion language for mutable data structures. In *Conference Record of POPL 2001: The 28th ACM SIGPLAN-SIGACT Symposium on Principles of Programming Languages*, pages 14–26, New York, 2001. ACM.

[Kob99]   Naoki Kobayashi. Quasi-linear types. In *Proceedings ACM Principles of Programming Languages*, pages 29–42, 1999.

[Ode92]   Martin Odersky. Observers for linear types. In B. Krieg-Brückner, editor, *ESOP '92: 4th European Symposium on Programming, Rennes, France, Proceedings*, pages 390–407. Springer-Verlag, February 1992. Lecture Notes in Computer Science 582.

[OP99]   Peter W. O'Hearn and David J. Pym. The logic of bunched implications. *Bulletin of Symbolic Logic*, 5(2):215–243, 1999.

[OTPT95]   P. W. O'Hearn, M. Takeyama, A. J. Power, and R. D. Tennent. Syntactic control of interference revisited. In *MFPS XI, Conference on Mathematical Foundations of Program Semantics*, volume 1 of *Electronic Notes in Theoretical Computer Science*. Elsevier, 1995.

[PJW00]   Simon Peyton-Jones and Keith Wansbrough. Simple usage polymorphism. In *Proc. 3rd ACM SIGPLAN Workshop on Types in Compilation, Montreal*, September 2000.

[Rey78]   J. C. Reynolds. Syntactic control of interference. In *Proc. Fifth ACM Symp. on Princ. of Prog. Lang. (POPL)*, 1978.

[Rey00]   John C. Reynolds. Intuitionistic reasoning about shared mutable data structure. In Jim Davies, Bill Roscoe, and Jim Woodcock, editors, *Millennial Perspectives in Computer Science*, pages 303–321, Houndsmill, Hampshire, 2000. Palgrave.

[Sha99]   Natarajan Shankar. Efficiently executing PVS. Technical report, Computer Science Laboratory, SRI International, 1999.

[SWM00]   Frederick Smith, David Walker, and Greg Morrisett. Alias types. In G. Smolka, editor, *Programming Languages and Systems*, volume 1782, pages 366–381. Springer LNCS, 2000.

[TT97]   M. Tofte and J.-P. Talpin. Region-based memory management. *Information and Computation*, 132(2):109–176, 1997.

[Wad90]   Philip Wadler. Linear types can change the world. In M. Broy and C. B. Jones, editors, *IFIP TC 2 Working Conference on Programming Concepts and Methods*, pages 561–581, Sea of Gallilee, Israel, 1990. North-Holland.

[WC98]   Mitchell Wand and William D. Clinger. Set constraints for destructive array update optimization. In *Proc. IEEE Conf. on Computer Languages '98*, pages 184–193, 1998.

[WSR00]   Reinhard Wilhelm, Mooly Sagiv, and Thomas Reps. Shape analysis. In *Proceedings Compiler Construction, CC 2000*, 2000.

[YR97]   H. Yang and U. Reddy. Imperative lambda calculus revisited, 1997.

Soft Concurrent Constraint Programming[*]

Stefano Bistarelli[1], Ugo Montanari[2], and Francesca Rossi[3]

[1] Istituto per le Applicazioni Telematiche, C.N.R. Pisa,
Area della Ricerca, Via G. Moruzzi 1, I-56124 Pisa, Italy
Email: Stefano.Bistarelli@iat.cnr.it
[2] Dipartimento di Informatica, Università di Pisa,
Corso Italia 40, I-56125 Pisa, Italy
Email: ugo@di.unipi.it
[3] Dipartimento di Matematica Pura ed Applicata, Università di Padova
Via Belzoni 7, 35131 Padova, Italy
Email: frossi@math.unipd.it

Abstract. Soft constraints extend classical constraints to represent multiple consistency levels, and thus provide a way to express preferences, fuzziness, and uncertainty. While there are many soft constraint solving algorithms, even distributed ones, by now there seems to be no concurrent programming framework where soft constraints can be handled. In this paper we show how the classical concurrent constraint (cc) programming framework can work with soft constraints, and we also propose an extension of cc languages which can use soft constraints to prune and direct the search for a solution. We believe that this new programming paradigm, called soft cc (scc), can be very useful in many web-related scenarios. In fact, the language level allows web agents to express their interaction and negotiation protocols, and also to post their requests in terms of preferences, and the underlying soft constraint solver can find an agreement among the agents even if their requests are incompatible.

1 Introduction

The concurrent constraint (cc) language [16] is a very interesting computational framework able to merge together constraint solving and concurrency. The main idea is to choose a *constraint system* and use constraints to model communication and synchronization among concurrent agents.

Until now, constraints in cc were *crisp* in the sense that only a yes/no answer could be defined. Recently the classical idea of *crisp* constraint has been shown to be too weak to represent real problems and a big effort has been done toward the use of soft constraints [13, 11, 15, 12, 18, 5, 6, 3].

Many real-life situations are, in fact, easily described via constraints able to state the necessary requirements of the problems. However, usually such requirements are not hard, and could be more faithfully represented as preferences, which should preferably be satisfied but not necessarily. In real life, we are often challenged with over-constrained problems, which do not have any solution, and this also leads to the use of preferences or in general of soft constraints rather than classical constraints.

---

[*] Research supported in part by the the MURST Projects TOSCA and NAPOLI.

D. Le Métayer (Ed.): ESOP 2002, LNCS 2305, pp. 53–67, 2002.

Generally speaking, a soft constraint is just a classical constraint plus a way to associate, either to the entire constraint or to each assignment of its variables, a certain element, which is usually interpreted as a level of preference or importance. Such levels are usually ordered, and the order reflects the idea that some levels are better than others. Moreover, one has also to say, via suitable combination operators, how to obtain the level of preference of a global solution from the preferences in the constraints.

Many formalisms have been developed to describe one or more classes of soft constraints. For instance consider the Fuzzy CSPs [11, 15], where the crisp constraints are extended with a level of preference represented by a real number between 0 and 1, or the probabilistic CSPs [12], where the probability to be in the real problem is assigned to each constraint. Some other examples are the Partial CSPs [13] or the valued CSPs [18] where a preference is assigned to each constraint, in order to also solve overconstrained problems.

We think that many network-related problem could be represented and solved by using soft constraints. Moreover, the possibility to use a concurrent language on top of a soft constraint system, could lead to the birth of new protocols with an embedded constraint satisfaction and optimization framework.

In particular, the constraints could be related to a quantity to be minimized but they could also satisfy policy requirements given for performance or administrative reasons. This leads to change the idea of QoS in routing and to speak of *constraint-based* routing [1, 10, 14, 8]. Constraints are in fact able to represent in a declarative fashion the needs and the requirements of agents interacting over the web.

The features of soft constraints could also be useful in representing routing problems where an imprecise state information is given [9]. Moreover, since QoS is only a specific application of a more general notion of Service Level Agreement (SLA), many applications could be enhanced by using such a framework. As an example consider E-commerce: here we are always looking for establishing an agreement between a merchant, a client and possibly a bank. Also, all auction-based transactions need an agreement protocol. Moreover, also security protocol analysis have shown to be enhanced by using security levels instead of a simple notion of secure/insecure level [2]. All these considerations advocate for the need of a soft constraint framework where optimal answers are extracted.

In the paper, we use one of the frameworks able to deal with soft constraints [4, 5]. The framework is based on a semiring structure that is equipped with the operations needed to combine the constraints present in the problem and to choose the best solutions. According to the choice of the semiring, this framework is able to model all the specific soft constraint notions mentioned above. We compare the semiring-based framework with constraint systems *"a la Saraswat"* and then we show how use it inside the cc framework. The next step is the extension of the syntax and operational semantics of the language to deal with the semiring levels. Here, the main novelty with respect to cc is that tell and ask agents are equipped with a preference (or consistency) threshold which is used to prune the search.

2   Background

2.1   Concurrent Constraint Programming

The concurrent constraint (cc) programming paradigm [16] concerns the behaviour of a set of concurrent agents with a shared store, which is a conjunction of constraints. Each computation step possibly adds new constraints to the store. Thus information is monotonically added to the store until all agents have evolved. The final store is a refinement of the initial one and it is the result of the computation. The concurrent agents do not communicate with each other, but only with the shared store, by either checking if it entails a given constraint (*ask* operation) or adding a new constraint to it (*tell* operation).

Constraint Systems. A constraint is a relation among a specified set of variables. That is, a constraint gives some information on the set of possible values which these variables may assume. Such information is usually not complete since a constraint may be satisfied by several assignments of values of the variables (in contrast to the situation that we have when we consider a valuation, which tells us the only possible assignment for a variable). Therefore it is natural to describe constraint systems as systems of *partial* information [16].

The basic ingredients of a constraint system defined following the information systems idea are a set D of *primitive constraints* or *tokens*, each expressing some partial information, and an entailment relation $\vdash$ defined on $\wp(D) \times D$ (or its extension defined on $\wp(D) \times \wp(D))$[1] satisfying: 1. $u \vdash P$ for all $P \in u$ (reflexivity) and 2. if $u \vdash v$, and $v \vdash z$, then $u \vdash z$ (transitivity). We also define $u \approx v$ if $u \vdash v$ and $v \vdash u$.

As an example of entailment relation consider D as the set of equations over the integers; then $\vdash$ includes the pair $\langle \{x = 3, x = y\}, y = 3 \rangle$, which means that the constraint $y = 3$ is entailed by the constraints $x = 3$ and $x = y$. Given $X \in \wp(D)$, let $\overline{X}$ be the set X closed under entailment. Then, a constraint in an information system $\langle \wp(D), \vdash \rangle$ is simply an element of $\overline{\wp(D)}$ (that is, a set of tokens).

As it is well known, $\langle \overline{\wp(D)}, \subseteq \rangle$ is a complete algebraic lattice, the compactness of $\vdash$ gives us algebraicity of $\overline{\wp(D)}$, with least element $true = \{P \mid \emptyset \vdash P\}$, greatest element D (which we will mnemonically denote $false$), glbs (denoted by $\sqcap$) given by the closure of the intersection and lubs (denoted by $\sqcup$) given by the closure of the union. The lub of chains is, however, just the union of the members in the chain. We use a, b, c, d and e to stand for elements of $\overline{\wp(D)}$; $c \geq d$ means $c \vdash d$.

The hiding operator: Cylindric Algebras. In order to treat the hiding operator of the language, a general notion of existential quantifier is introduced which is formalized in terms of cylindric algebras. This leads to the concept of *cylindric constraint system* over an infinite set of variables V such that for each variable $x \in V$, $\exists_x : \wp(D) \to \wp(D)$ is an operation satisfying: 1. $u \vdash \exists_x u$; 2. $u \vdash v$ implies $(\exists_x u) \vdash (\exists_x v)$; 3. $\exists_x (u \sqcup \exists_x v) \approx (\exists_x u) \sqcup (\exists_x v)$; 4. $\exists_x \exists_y u \approx \exists_y \exists_x u$.

Procedure calls. In order to model parameter passing, *diagonal elements* are added to the primitive constraints. We assume that, for x, y ranging in V, $\overline{\wp(D)}$ contains a constraint d_{xy} which satisfies the following axioms: 1. $d_{xx} = true$, 2. if $z \neq x, y$ then

---

[1] The extension is s.t. $u \vdash v$ iff $u \vdash P$ for every $P \in v$.

$d_{xy} = \exists_z (d_{xz} \sqcup d_{zy})$, 3. if $x \neq y$ then $d_{xy} \sqcup \exists_x (c \sqcup d_{xy}) \vdash c$. Note that the in the previous definition we assume the cardinality of the domain for x, y and z greater than 1. Note also that, if $\vdash$ models the equality theory, then the elements d_{xy} can be thought of as the formulas $x = y$.

The language. The syntax of a cc program is show in Table 1: P is the class of programs, F is the class of sequences of procedure declarations (or clauses), A is the class of agents, c ranges over constraints, and x is a tuple of variables. Each procedure is defined (at most) once, thus nondeterminism is expressed via the $+$ combinator only. We also assume that, in $p(x) :: A, vars(A) \subseteq x$, where $vars(A)$ is the set of all variables occurring free in agent A. In a program $P = F.A$, A is the initial agent, to be executed in the context of the set of declarations F. This corresponds to the language considered in [16], which allows only guarded nondeterminism.   In order to better understand the extension of

Table 1: cc syntax

$P ::= F.A$	$A ::= success \mid fail \mid tell(c) \rightarrow A \mid E \mid A\|A \mid \exists_x A \mid p(x)$
$F ::= p(x) :: A \mid F.F$	$E ::= ask(c) \rightarrow A \mid E + E$

the language that we will introduce later, let us remind here (at least) the meaning of the tell and ask agents. The other constructs are easily understandable.

- agent "$ask(c) \rightarrow A$" checks whether constraint c is entailed by the current store and then, if so, behaves like agent A. If c is inconsistent with the current store, it fails, and otherwise it suspends, until c is either entailed by the current store or is inconsistent with it;
- agent "$tell(c) \rightarrow A$" adds constraint c to the current store and then, if the resulting store is consistent, behaves like A, otherwise it fails.

A formal treatment of the cc semantics can be found in [16, 7].

2.2   Soft Constraints

Several formalization of the concept of *soft constraints* are currently available. In the following, we refer to the one based on c-semirings [5, 3], which can be shown to generalize and express many of the others.

A soft constraint may be seen as a constraint where each instantiations of its variables has an associated value from a partially ordered set which can be interpreted as a set of preference values. Combining constraints will then have to take into account such additional values, and thus the formalism has also to provide suitable operations for combination ($\times$) and comparison ($+$) of tuples of values and constraints. This is why this formalization is based on the concept of c-semiring, which is just a set plus two operations.

C-semirings. A semiring is a tuple $\langle A, +, \times, \mathbf{0}, \mathbf{1} \rangle$ such that: 1. A is a set and $\mathbf{0}, \mathbf{1} \in A$; 2. $+$ is commutative, associative and $\mathbf{0}$ is its unit element; 3. $\times$ is associative, distributes over $+$, $\mathbf{1}$ is its unit element and $\mathbf{0}$ is its absorbing element.

A *c-semiring* is a semiring $\langle A, +, \times, \mathbf{0}, \mathbf{1} \rangle$ such that $+$ is idempotent, $\mathbf{1}$ is its absorbing element and $\times$ is commutative. Let us consider the relation $\leq_S$ over A such that $a \leq_S b$ iff $a + b = b$. Then it is possible to prove that (see [5]): 1. $\leq_S$ is a partial order; 2. $+$ and $\times$ are monotone on $\leq_S$; 3. $\mathbf{0}$ is its minimum and $\mathbf{1}$ its maximum; 4. $\langle A, \leq_S \rangle$ is a complete lattice and, for all $a, b \in A$, $a + b = lub(a, b)$.

Moreover, if $\times$ is idempotent, then: $+$ distribute over $\times$; $\langle A, \leq_S \rangle$ is a complete distributive lattice and $\times$ its glb. Informally, the relation $\leq_S$ gives us a way to compare semiring values and constraints. In fact, when we have $a \leq_S b$, we will say that b is *better than* a. In the following, when the semiring will be clear from the context, $a \leq_S b$ will be often indicated by $a \leq b$.

Problems. Given a semiring $S = \langle A, +, \times, \mathbf{0}, \mathbf{1} \rangle$, a finite set D (the domain of the variables) and an ordered set of variables V, a *constraint* is a pair $\langle def, con \rangle$ where $con \subseteq V$ and $def : D^{|con|} \rightarrow A$. Therefore, a constraint specifies a set of variables (the ones in con), and assigns to each tuple of values of these variables an element of the semiring. Consider two constraints $c_1 = \langle def_1, con \rangle$ and $c_2 = \langle def_2, con \rangle$, with $|con| = k$. Then $c_1 \sqsubseteq_S c_2$ if for all k-tuples t, $def_1(t) \leq_S def_2(t)$. The relation $\sqsubseteq_S$ is a partial order.

A *soft constraint problem* is a pair $\langle C, con \rangle$ where $con \subseteq V$ and C is a set of constraints: con is the set of variables of interest for the constraint set C, which however may concern also variables not in con. Note that a classical CSP is a SCSP where the chosen c-semiring is: $S_{CSP} = \langle \{false, true\}, \vee, \wedge, false, true \rangle$. Fuzzy CSPs [17] can instead be modeled in the SCSP framework by choosing the c-semiring $S_{FCSP} = \langle [0, 1], max, min, 0, 1 \rangle$. Many other "soft" CSPs (Probabilistic, weighted, ...) can be modeled by using a suitable semiring structure ($S_{prob} = \langle [0, 1], max, \times, 0, 1 \rangle$, $S_{weight} = \langle \mathcal{R}, min, +, 0, +\infty \rangle$, ...).

Figure 1 shows the graph representation of a fuzzy CSP. Variables and constraints are represented respectively by nodes and by undirected (unary for c_1 and c_3 and binary for c_2) arcs, and semiring values are written to the right of the corresponding tuples. The variables of interest (that is the set con) are represented with a double circle. Here we assume that the domain D of the variables contains only elements a and b.

Fig. 1: A fuzzy CSP

Combining and projecting soft constraints. Given two constraints $c_1 = \langle def_1, con_1 \rangle$ and $c_2 = \langle def_2, con_2 \rangle$, their *combination* $c_1 \otimes c_2$ is the constraint $\langle def, con \rangle$ defined by $con = con_1 \cup con_2$ and $def(t) = def_1(t \downarrow_{con_1}^{con}) \times def_2(t \downarrow_{con_2}^{con})$, where $t \downarrow_Y^X$ denotes the tuple of values over the variables in Y, obtained by projecting tuple t from X to Y. In words, combining two constraints means building a new constraint involving all the variables of the original ones, and which associates to each tuple of domain values for such variables a semiring element which is obtained by multiplying the elements associated by the original constraints to the appropriate subtuples.

Given a constraint $c = \langle def, con \rangle$ and a subset I of V, the *projection* of c over I, written $c \Downarrow_I$ is the constraint $\langle def', con' \rangle$ where $con' = con \cap I$ and $def'(t') = \sum_{t/t \downarrow^{con}_{I \cap con} = t'} def(t)$. Informally, projecting means eliminating some variables. This is done by associating to each tuple over the remaining variables a semiring element which is the sum of the elements associated by the original constraint to all the extensions of this tuple over the eliminated variables. In short, combination is performed via the multiplicative operation of the semiring, and projection via the additive one.

Solutions. The *solution* of an SCSP problem $P = \langle C, con \rangle$ is the constraint $Sol(P) = (\bigotimes C) \Downarrow_{con}$. That is, we combine all constraints, and then project over the variables in con. In this way we get the constraint over con which is "induced" by the entire SCSP.

For example, the solution of the fuzzy CSP of Figure 1 associates a semiring element to every domain value of variable x. Such an element is obtained by first combining all the constraints together. For instance, for the tuple $\langle a, a \rangle$ (that is, $x = y = a$), we have to compute the minimum between 0.9 (which is the value assigned to $x = a$ in constraint c_1), 0.8 (which is the value assigned to $\langle x = a, y = a \rangle$ in c_2) and 0.9 (which is the value for $y = a$ in c_3). Hence, the resulting value for this tuple is 0.8. We can do the same work for tuple $\langle a, b \rangle \rightarrow 0.2$, $\langle b, a \rangle \rightarrow 0$ and $\langle b, b \rangle \rightarrow 0$. The obtained tuples are then projected over variable x, obtaining the solution $\langle a \rangle \rightarrow 0.8$ and $\langle b \rangle \rightarrow 0$.

Sometimes it may be useful to find only a semiring value representing the least upper bound among the values yielded by the solutions. This is called the *best level of consistency* of an SCSP problem P and it is defined by $blevel(P) = Sol(P) \Downarrow_\emptyset$ (for instance, the fuzzy CSP of Figure 1 has best level of consistency 0.8). We also say that: P is α-consistent if $blevel(P) = \alpha$; P is consistent iff there exists $\alpha > 0$ such that P is α-consistent; P is inconsistent if it is not consistent.

3   Concurrent Constraint Programming over Soft Constraints

Given a semiring $S = \langle A, +, \times, \mathbf{0}, \mathbf{1} \rangle$ and an ordered set of variables V over a finite domain D, we will now show how soft constraints with a suitable pair of operators form a semiring, and then, we evidentiate the properties needed to map soft constraints over constraint systems *"a la Saraswat"*.

We start by giving the definition of the carrier set of the semiring.

Definition 1 (functional constraints). *We define* $\mathcal{C} = (V \rightarrow D) \rightarrow A$ *as the set of all possible constraints that can be built starting from* $S = \langle A, +, \times, \mathbf{0}, \mathbf{1} \rangle$, D *and* V.

A generic function describing the assignment of domain elements to variables will be denoted in the following by $\eta : V \rightarrow D$. Thus a constraint is a function which, given an assignment η of the variables, returns a value of the semiring.

Note that in this *functional* formulation, each constraint is a function and not a pair representing the variable involved and its definition. Such a function involves all the variables in V, but it depends on the assignment of only a finite subset of them. We call this subset the *support* of the constraint. For computational reasons we require each support to be finite.

Definition 2 (constraint support). *Consider a constraint* $c \in \mathcal{C}$. *We define his support as* $supp(c) = \{v \in V \mid \exists \eta, d_1, d_2.c\eta[v := d_1] \neq c\eta[v := d_2]\}$, *where*

$$\eta[v := d]v' = \begin{cases} d & \text{if } v = v', \\ \eta v' & \text{otherwise.} \end{cases}$$

Note that $c\eta[v := d_1]$ means $c\eta'$ where η' is η modified with the association $v := d_1$ (that is the operator $[\,]$ has precedence over application).

Definition 3 (functional mapping). *Given any soft constraint* $\langle def, \{v_1, \ldots, v_n\}\rangle \in C$, *we can define its corresponding function* $c \in \mathcal{C}$ *as* $c\eta[v_1 := d_1] \ldots [v_n := d_n] = def(d_1, \ldots, d_n)$. *Clearly* $supp(c) \subseteq \{v_1, \ldots, v_n\}$.

Definition 4 (Combination and Sum). *Given the set* $\mathcal{C}$, *we can define the combination and sum functions* $\otimes, \oplus : \mathcal{C} \times \mathcal{C} \to \mathcal{C}$ *as follows:*

$$(c_1 \otimes c_2)\eta = c_1\eta \times_S c_2\eta \qquad and \qquad (c_1 \oplus c_2)\eta = c_1\eta +_S c_2\eta.$$

Notice that function $\otimes$ has the same meaning of the already defined $\otimes$ operator (see Section 2.2) while function $\oplus$ models a sort of disjunction.

By using the $\oplus_S$ operator we can easily extend the partial order $\leq_S$ over $\mathcal{C}$ by defining $c_1 \sqsubseteq c_2 \iff c_1 \oplus_S c_2 = c_2$.

We can also define a unary operator that will be useful to represent the unit elements of the two operations $\oplus$ and $\otimes$. To do that, we need the definition of constant functions over a given set of variables.

Definition 5 (constant function). *We define function* $\bar{a}$ *as the function that returns the semiring value* a *for all assignments* η, *that is,* $\bar{a}\eta = a$. *We will usually write* $\bar{a}$ *simply as* a.

It is easy to verify that each constant has an empty support. An example of constants that will be useful later are $\bar{0}$ and $\bar{1}$ that represent respectively the constraint associating **0** and **1** to all the assignment of domain values.

Theorem 1 (Higher order semiring). *The structure* $S_C = \langle \mathcal{C}, \oplus, \otimes, \mathbf{0}, \mathbf{1}\rangle$ *where*
- $\mathcal{C} : (V \to D) \to A$ *is the set of all the possible constraints that can be built starting from S, D and V as defined in Definition 1,*
- $\otimes$ *and* $\oplus$ *are the functions defined in Definition 4, and*
- **0** *and* **1** *are constant functions defined following Definition 5,*

is a c-semiring.

The next step is to look for a notion of token and of entailment relation. We define as tokens the functional constraints in $\mathcal{C}$ and we introduce a relation $\vdash$ that is an entailment relation when the multiplicative operator of the semiring is idempotent.

Definition 6 ($\vdash$ relation). *Consider the high order semiring carrier set* $\mathcal{C}$ *and the partial order* $\sqsubseteq$. *We define the relation* $\vdash \subseteq \wp(\mathcal{C}) \times \mathcal{C}$ *s.t. for each* $C \in \wp(\mathcal{C})$ *and* $c \in \mathcal{C}$, *we have* $C \vdash c \iff \bigotimes C \sqsubseteq c$.

The next theorem shows that when the multiplicative operator of the semiring is idempotent, the $\vdash$ relation satisfies all the properties needed by an entailment.

Theorem 2 ($\vdash$ with idempotent $\times$ is an entailment relation). *Consider the higher order semiring carrier set $\mathcal{C}$ and the partial order $\sqsubseteq$. Consider also the relation $\vdash$ of Definition 6. Then, if the multiplicative operation of the semiring is idempotent, $\vdash$ is an entailment relation.*

Note that in this setting the notion of token (constraint) and of set of tokens (set of constraints) closed under entailment is used indifferently. In fact, given a set of constraint functions C_1, its closure w.r.t. the entailment is a set $\bar{C}_1$ that contains all the constraints greater than $\bigotimes C_1$. This set is univocally representable by the constraint function $\bigotimes C_1$.

The definition of the entailment operator $\vdash$ on top of the higher order semiring $S_C = \langle \mathcal{C}, \oplus, \otimes, \mathbf{0}, \mathbf{1} \rangle$ and of the $\sqsubseteq$ relation leads to the notion of *soft constraint system*. It is also important to notice that in [16] is claimed the constraint system to be a *complete algebraic* lattice. Here we do not ask for this algebraicity since the algebraicity of the structure $\mathcal{C}$ strictly depends on the properties of the semiring.

Non-idempotent $\times$. If the constraint system is defined on top of a non-idempotent multiplicative operator, we cannot obtain a $\vdash$ relation satisfying all the properties of an entailment. Nevertheless, we can give a *denotational* semantics to the constraint store, as described in Section 4, using the operations of the higher order semiring.

To treat the hiding operator of the language, a general notion of existential quantifier has to be introduced by using notions similar to those used in cylindric algebras. Note however that cylindric algebras are first of all boolean algebras. This could be possible in our framework only when the $\times$ operator is idempotent.

Definition 7 (hiding). *Consider a set of variables V with domain D and the corresponding soft constraint system $\mathcal{C}$. We define for each $x \in V$ the hiding function $(\exists_x c)\eta = \sum_{d_i \in D} c\eta[x := d_i]$.*

Notice that x does not belong to the support of $\exists_x c$.

To model parameter passing we need instead to define what diagonal elements are.

Definition 8 (diagonal elements). *Consider an ordered set of variables V and the corresponding soft constraint system $\mathcal{C}$. Let us define for each $x, y \in V$ a constraint $d_{xy} \in \mathcal{C}$ s.t., $d_{xy}\eta[x := a, y := b] = \mathbf{1}$ if $a = b$ and $d_{xy}\eta[x := a, y := b] = \mathbf{0}$ if $a \neq b$. Notice that $supp(d_{xy}) = \{x, y\}$.*

Using cc on top of a Soft Constraint System. The major problem in using a soft constraint system in a cc language is the interpretation of the *consistency* notion necessary to deal with the ask and tell operations.

Usually SCSPs with best level of consistency equal to $\mathbf{0}$ are interpreted as inconsistent, and those with level greater than $\mathbf{0}$ as consistent, but we can be more general. In fact, we can define a suitable function α that, given the best level of the actual store, will map such a level over the classical notion of consistency/inconsistency. More precisely, given a semiring $S = \langle A, +, \times, \mathbf{0}, \mathbf{1} \rangle$, we can define a function $\alpha : A \rightarrow \{false, true\}$.

Function α has to be at least monotone, but functions with a richer set of properties could be used.[2]

Whenever we need to check the consistency of the store, we will first compute the best level and then we will map such a value by using function α over *true* or *false*.

It is important to notice that changing the α function (that is, by mapping in a different way the set of values A over the boolean elements *true* and *false*), the same cc agent yields different results: by using a high cut level, the cc agent will either finish with a failure or succeed with a high final best level of consistency of the store. On the other side, by using a low level, more programs will end in a success state.

4   Soft Concurrent Constraint Programming

The next step in our work is now to extend the syntax of the language in order to directly handle the cut level. This means that the syntax and semantics of the tell and ask agents have to be enriched with a threshold to specify when ask/tell agents have to fail, succeed or suspend.

Given a soft constraint system $\langle S, D, V \rangle$ and the corresponding structure $\mathcal{C}$, the syntax of agents in soft concurrent constraint *scc* programming is given in Table 2.   The

Table 2: scc syntax

$P :: = F.A$	$A :: = stop \mid tell(c) \rightarrow^a A \mid E \mid A\|A \mid \exists X.A \mid p(X)$
$F :: = p(X) :: A \mid F.F$	$E :: = ask(c) \rightarrow^a A \mid E + E$

main difference w.r.t. original *cc* syntax is the presence of a semiring element a to be checked whenever an *ask* or *tell* operation is performed. More precisely, the semiring level a will be used as a cut level to prune computations that are not good enough.

We present here a structural operational semantics for scc programs, in the SOS style, which consists of defining the semantic of the programming language by specifying a set of *configurations* Γ, which define the states during execution, a relation $\rightarrow \subseteq \Gamma \times \Gamma$ which describes the *transition* relation between the configurations, and a set T of *terminal* configurations.

The set of configurations represent the evolutions of the agents and the modifications in the constraint store.

Definition 9 (configurations). *The set of configurations for a soft cc system is the set* $\Gamma = \{\langle A, \sigma \rangle\} \cup \{\langle success, \sigma \rangle\}$ *where* $\sigma \in \mathcal{C}$. *The set of terminal configurations is the set* $T = \{\langle success, \sigma \rangle\}$ *and the transition rule for the scc language are defined in Table 3.*

Here is a brief description of the most complex rules:

---

[2] In a different environment some of the authors use a similar function to map elements from a semiring to another, by using abstract interpretation techniques.

Table 3: Transition rules for scc

$$\langle stop, \sigma \rangle \longrightarrow \langle success, \sigma \rangle \tag{Stop}$$

$$\frac{(\sigma \otimes c) \Downarrow_{\emptyset} \not\prec a}{\langle tell(c) \rightarrow^a A, \sigma \rangle \longrightarrow \langle A, \sigma \otimes c \rangle} \tag{Valued-tell}$$

$$\frac{\sigma \vdash c, \sigma \Downarrow_{\emptyset} \not\prec a}{\langle ask(c) \rightarrow^a A, \sigma \rangle \longrightarrow \langle A, \sigma \rangle} \tag{Valued-ask}$$

$$\frac{\langle A_1, \sigma \rangle \longrightarrow \langle A'_1, \sigma' \rangle}{\langle A_1 \| A_2, \sigma \rangle \longrightarrow \langle A'_1 \| A_2, \sigma' \rangle} \quad \frac{\langle A_1, \sigma \rangle \longrightarrow \langle success, \sigma' \rangle}{\langle A_1 \| A_2, \sigma \rangle \longrightarrow \langle A_2, \sigma' \rangle} \tag{Parallelism}$$
$$\langle A_2 \| A_1, \sigma \rangle \longrightarrow \langle A_2 \| A'_1, \sigma' \rangle \qquad \langle A_2 \| A_1, \sigma \rangle \longrightarrow \langle A_2, \sigma' \rangle$$

$$\frac{\langle E_1, \sigma \rangle \longrightarrow \langle A_1, \sigma' \rangle}{\langle E_1 + E_2, \sigma \rangle \longrightarrow \langle A_1, \sigma' \rangle} \tag{Nondeterminism}$$
$$\langle E_2 + E_1, \sigma \rangle \longrightarrow \langle A_1, \sigma' \rangle$$

$$\frac{\langle A[y/x], \sigma \rangle \longrightarrow \langle A', \sigma' \rangle}{\langle \exists_x A, \sigma \rangle \longrightarrow \langle A', \sigma' \rangle} \text{ with } y \text{ fresh} \tag{Hidden variables}$$

$$\langle p(y), \sigma \rangle \longrightarrow \langle A[y/x], \sigma \rangle \text{ when } p(x) :: A \tag{Procedure call}$$

Valued-tell The valued-tell rule checks for the α-consistency of the SCSP defined by the store $\sigma \cup c$. The rule can be applied only if the store $\sigma \cup c$ is b-consistent with $b \not\preceq a$. In this case the agent evolves to the new agent A over the store $\sigma \otimes c$.

Valued-ask The semantics of the valued-ask is extended in a way similar to what we have done for the valued-tell action. This means that, to apply the rule, we need to check if the store σ entails the constraint c and also if the store is "consistent enough" w.r.t. the threshold a set by the programmer.

Nondeterminism and parallelism The composition operators $+$ and $\|$ are not modified w.r.t. the classical ones: a parallel agent will succeed if all the agents succeeds; a nondeterministic rule chooses any agent whose guard succeeds.

Hidden variables The semantics of the existential quantifier is similar to that described in [16] by using the notion of *freshness* of the new variable added to the store.

Observables. Given the transition system as defined in the previous section, we now define what we want to observe of the program behaviours described by the transitions. To do this we define for each agent A the set of constraints

$$\mathcal{S}_A = \{\sigma \Downarrow_{var(A)} | \langle A, \mathbf{1} \rangle \rightarrow^* \langle success, \sigma \rangle\}$$

that collects the results of the successful computations that the agent can perform. The computed store σ is projected over the variables of the agent A to discard any *fresh* variable introduced in the store by the $\exists$ operator. In this paper we only consider a semantics that collects success states. We plan to extend the operational semantics to collect also failing and suspending computations.

The observable S_A could be refined by considering, instead of the set of successful computations starting from $\langle A, 1 \rangle$, only a subset of them. One could be interested in considering for example only the *best* computations: in this case, all the computations leading to a store worse than one already collected are disregarded. With a pessimistic view, the representative subset could instead collect all the worst computations (that is, all the computations better than others are disregarded). Finally, also a set containing both the best and the worst computations could be considered. These options are reminiscent of Hoare, Smith and Egli-Milner powerdomains respectively.

Let us also notice that different cut levels in the ask and tell operations could lead to a different final sets S_A. In fact, it can be proved that if the thresholds of the ask and tell operations of the program are not worse than a given α, we can be sure to find in the final store only solutions not worse than α. This observation can be useful when we are looking just for the best stores reachable from an initial given agent. In fact, we can move the cut up and down (in a way similar to a binary search) and perform a branch and bound exploration of the search tree in order to find the final success sets.

5 A Simple Example

In the following we will show the behaviour of some of the rules of our transition system. We consider in this example a soft constraint system over the fuzzy semiring. Consider the constraint

$$c(x,y) = \frac{1}{1+|x-y|} \qquad \text{and} \qquad c'(x) = \begin{cases} 1 & \text{if } x \leq 10, \\ 0 & \text{otherwise.} \end{cases}$$

Let's now evaluate the agent $\langle tell(c) \rightarrow^{0.4} ask(c') \rightarrow^{0.8} stop, 1 \rangle$ in the empty starting store 1.

By applying the *Valued-tell* rule we need to check $(1 \otimes c) \Downarrow_0 \not< 0.4$. Since $1 \otimes c = c$ and $c \Downarrow_0 = 1$, the agent can perform the step, and it reaches the state $\langle ask(c') \rightarrow^{0.8} stop, c \rangle$. Now we need to check (by following the rule of *Valued-ask*) if $c \vdash c'$ and $c \Downarrow_0 \not< 0.8$. While the second relation easily holds, the first one does not hold (in fact, for $x = 11$ and $y = 10$ we have $c'(x) = 0$ and $c(x,y) = 0.5$). If instead we consider the constraint $c''(x,y) = \frac{1}{1+2\times|x-y|}$ in place of c', then the condition $c \vdash c''$ easily holds and the agent $ask(c'') \rightarrow^{0.8} stop$ can perform its last step, reaching the *stop* and *success* states: $\langle stop, c \otimes c'' \rangle \rightarrow \langle success, c \otimes c'' \rangle$.

6 A Possible Application

We consider in this section a network problem, involving a set of processes running on distinct locations and sharing some variables, over which they need to synchronize.

Each process is connected to a set of variables, shared with other processes, and it can perform several moves. Each of such moves involves performing an action over some or all the variables connected to the process. An action over a variable consists of giving a certain value to that variable. A special value "idle" models the fact that a process does not perfom any action over a variable. Each process has also the possibility of not moving at all: in this case, all its variables are given the idle value.

The desired behavior of a network of such processes is that, at each move of the entire network: 1) processes sharing a variable perform the same action over it; 2) as few processes as possible remain idle.

To describe a network of processes with these features, we use an SCSP where each variable models a shared variable, and each constraint models a process and connects the variables corresponding to the shared variables of that process. The domain of each variable in this SCSP is the set of all possible actions, including the idle one. Each way of satisfying a constraint is therefore a tuple of actions that a process can perform on the corresponding shared variables.

In this scenario, softness can be introduced both in the domains and in the constraints. In particular, since we prefer to have as many moving processes as possible, we can associate a penalty to both the idle element in the domains, and to tuples containing the idle action in the constraints. As for the other domain elements and constraint tuples, we can assign them suitable preference values to model how much we like that action or that process move.

For example, we can use the semiring $S = \langle [-\infty, 0], max, +, -\infty, 0 \rangle$, where 0 is the best preference level (or, said dually, the weakest penalty), $-\infty$ is the worst level, and preferences (or penalties) are combined by summing them. According to this semiring, we can assign value $-\infty$ to the idle action or move, and suitable other preference levels to the other values and moves. Figure 2 gives the details of a part of a network and it

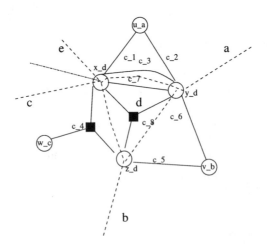

Fig. 2: The SCSP describing part of a process network.

shows eight processes (that is, $c_1, \ldots, c_8$) sharing a total of six variables. In this example, we assume that processes c_1, c_2 and c_3 are located on site a, processes c_5 and c_6 are located on site b, and c_4 is located on site c. Processes c_7 and c_8 are located on site d.

Site e connects this part of the network to the rest. Therefore, for example, variables x_d, y_d and z_d are shared between processes located in distinct locations.

As desired, finding the best solution for the SCSP representing the current state of the process network means finding a move for all the processes such that they perform the same action on the shared variables and there is a minimum number of idle processes. However, since the problem is inherently distributed, it does not make sense, and it might not even be possible, to centralize all the information and give it to a single soft constraint solver.

On the contrary, it may be more reasonable to use several soft constraint solvers, one for each network location, which will take care of handling only the constraints present in that location. Then, the interaction between processes in different locations, and the necessary agreement to solve the entire problem, will be modelled via the scc framework, where each agent will represent the behaviour of the processes in one location.

More precisely, each scc agent (and underlying soft constraint solver) will be in charge of receiving the necessary information from the other agents (via suitable asks) and using it to achieve the synchronization of the processes in its location. For this protocol to work, that is, for obtaining a global optimal solution without a centralization of the work, the SCSP describing the network of processes has to have a tree-like shape, where each node of the tree contains all the processes in a location, and the agents have to communicate from the bottom of the tree to its root. In fact, the proposed protocol uses a sort of Dynamic Programming technique to distribute the computation between the locations. In this case the use of a tree shape allows us to work, at each step of the algorithm, only locally to one of the locations. In fact, a non tree shape would lead to the construction of non-local constraints and thus require computations which involve more than one location at a time. In our example, the tree structure we will use is the one shown in Figure 3(a), which also shows the direction of the child-parent relation links (via arrows). Figure 3(b) describes instead the partition of the SCSP over the four involved locations. The gray connections represent the synchronization to be assured between distinct locations. Notice that, w.r.t. Figure 2, we have duplicated the variables representing variables shared between distinct locations, because of our desire to first perform a local work and then to communicate the results to the other locations.

The scc agents (one for each location plus the parallel composition of all of them) are therefore defined as follows:

$$A_a : \exists_{u_a}(tell(c_1(x_a, u_a) \wedge c_2(u_a, y_a) \wedge c_3(x_a, y_a)) \rightarrow tell(end_a = true) \rightarrow stop)$$
$$A_b : \exists_{v_b}(tell(c_5(y_b, v_b) \wedge c_6(z_b, v_b)) \rightarrow tell(end_b = true) \rightarrow stop)$$
$$A_c : \exists_{w_c}(tell(c_4(x_c, w_c, z_c)) \rightarrow tell(end_c = true) \rightarrow stop)$$
$$A_d : ask(end_a = true \wedge end_b = true \wedge end_c = true \wedge end_d = true) \rightarrow$$
$$tell(c_7(x_d, y_d) \wedge c_8(x_d, y_d, z_d) \wedge x_a = x_d = x_c \wedge y_a = y_d = y_b \wedge z_b = z_d = z_c)$$
$$\rightarrow tell(end_d = true) \rightarrow stop$$
$$A : A_a \mid A_b \mid A_c \mid A_d$$

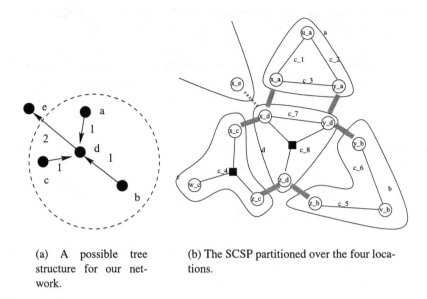

(a) A possible tree structure for our network.

(b) The SCSP partitioned over the four locations.

Fig. 3: The ordered process network.

Agents A_a, A_b, A_c and A_d represent the processes running respectively in the location a, b, c and d. Note that, at each ask or tell, the underlying soft constraint solver will only check (for consistency or entailment) a part of the current set of constraints: those local to one location. Due to the tree structure chosen for this example, where agents A_a, A_b, and A_c correspond to leaf locations, only agent A_d shows all the actions of a generic process: first it needs to collect the results computed separately by the other agents (via the ask); then it performs its own constraint solving (via a tell), and finally it can set its end flag, that will be used by a parent agent (in this case the agent corresponding to location e, which we have not modelled here).

7   Conclusions and Future Work

We have shown that cc languages can deal with soft constraints. Moreover, we have extended their syntax to use soft constraints also to direct and prune the search process at the language level. We believe that such a new programming paradigm could be very useful for web and internet programming.

In fact, in several network-related areas, constraints are already being used [2, 1, 10, 14, 8]. The soft constraint framework has the advantage over the classical one of selecting a "best" solution also in overconstrained or underconstrained systems. Moreover, the need to express preferences and to search for optimal solutions shows that soft constraints can improve the modelling of web interaction scenarios.

Acknowledgements. We are indebted to Paolo Baldan for invaluable suggestions.

References

[1] Awduche, D., Malcolm, J., Agogbua, J., O'Dell, M., McManus, J.: Rfc2702: Requirements for traffic engineering over mpls. Technical report, Network Working Group (1999)

[2] Bella, G., Bistarelli, S.: Sof constraints for security protocol analysis: Confidentiality. In Ramakrishnan, I., ed.: Proc. of PADL 2001, 3rd international symposium on Practical Aspects of Declarative Languages. Volume 1990 of LNCS., Springer-Verlag (2001) 108–122

[3] Bistarelli, S.: Soft Constraint Solving and programming: a general framework. PhD thesis, Dipartimento di Informatica, Università di Pisa, Italy (2001) TD-2/01.

[4] Bistarelli, S., Montanari, U., Rossi, F.: Constraint Solving over Semirings. In: Proc. IJ-CAI95, San Francisco, CA, USA, Morgan Kaufman (1995)

[5] Bistarelli, S., Montanari, U., Rossi, F.: Semiring-based Constraint Solving and Optimization. Journal of the ACM **44** (1997) 201–236

[6] Bistarelli, S., Montanari, U., Rossi, F.: Semiring-based Constraint Logic Programming: Syntax and Semantics. ACM Transactions on Programming Languages and System (TOPLAS) (2001) To Appear.

[7] Boer, F.D., Palamidessi, C.: A fully abstract model for concurrent constraint programming. In Abramsky, S., Maibaum, T., eds.: Proc. TAPSOFT/CAAP. Volume 493., Springer-Verlag (1991)

[8] Calisti, M., Faltings, B.: Distributed constrained agents for allocating service demands in multi-provider networks,. Journal of the Italian Operational Research Society **XXIX** (2000) Special Issue on Constraint-Based Problem Solving.

[9] Chen, S., Nahrstedt, K.: Distributed qos routing with imprecise state information. In: Proc. International Conference on Computer, Communications and Networks (ICCCN'98). (1998)

[10] Clark, D.: Rfc1102: Policy routing in internet protocols. Technical report, Network Working Group (1989)

[11] Dubois, D., Fargier, H., Prade, H.: The calculus of fuzzy restrictions as a basis for flexible constraint satisfaction. In: Proc. IEEE International Conference on Fuzzy Systems, IEEE (1993) 1131–1136

[12] Fargier, H., Lang, J.: Uncertainty in constraint satisfaction problems: a probabilistic approach. In: Proc. European Conference on Symbolic and Qualitative Approaches to Reasoning and Uncertainty (ECSQARU). Volume 747 of LNCS., Springer-Verlag (1993) 97–104

[13] Freuder, E., Wallace, R.: Partial constraint satisfaction. AI Journal **58** (1992)

[14] Jain, R., Sun, W.: QoS/Policy/Constraint-based routing. In: Carrier IP Telephony 2000 Comprehensive Report. International Engineering Consortium (2000) ISBN: 0-933217-75-7.

[15] Ruttkay, Z.: Fuzzy constraint satisfaction. In: Proc. 3rd IEEE International Conference on Fuzzy Systems. (1994) 1263–1268

[16] Saraswat, V.: Concurrent Constraint Programming. MIT Press (1993)

[17] Schiex, T.: Possibilistic constraint satisfaction problems, or "how to handle soft constraints?". In: Proc. 8th Conf. of Uncertainty in AI. (1992) 269–275

[18] Schiex, T., Fargier, H., Verfaille, G.: Valued Constraint Satisfaction Problems: Hard and Easy Problems. In: Proc. IJCAI95, San Francisco, CA, USA, Morgan Kaufmann (1995) 631–637

Programming Languages for Compressing Graphics

Morgan McGuire, Shriram Krishnamurthi, and John F. Hughes

Computer Science Department
Brown University
Providence, RI, USA
Contact: sk@cs.brown.edu

Abstract. Images are programs. They are usually simple instructions to a very specialized interpreter that renders them on screen. Image formats therefore correspond to different programming languages, each with distinctive properties of program size and accuracy. Image-processing languages render large images from small pieces of code. We present Evolver, a language and toolkit that perform the reverse transformation.

The toolkit accepts images in conventional graphics formats like JPEG and uses genetic algorithms to grow a program in the Evolver language that generates a similar image. Because the program it produces is often significantly smaller than the input image, Evolver can be used as a compression tool.

The language balances the tradeoff between having many features, which improves compression, and fewer features, which improves searching. In addition, by being programmatic descriptions, the rendered images scale much better to multiple resolutions than fixed-size images. We have implemented this system and present examples of its use.

1 Introduction

The growing volume of data on the Web has resulted in enormous demands on network bandwidth. Improvements in network access, such as the increasing availability of high-speed connections outside commercial venues, have simply resulted in correspondingly larger data and the greater use of bandwidth-hungry formats. Web designers have come to rely on such availability, producing denser sites, and users in turn have higher expectations. As a result, the principal cost for many sites is simply that of leasing sufficient bandwidth. This cost dwarfs that of providing and maintaining content. Since visual formats are central to many Web interfaces, their compression is of key importance in making existing bandwidth more effective. Keeping visual formats small will have obvious benefits to Web designers, site administrators and users.

The common approach to compressing data is to use a standard lossless compression algorithm, such as the many variants of Lempel-Ziv [19], which reduce redundancy using a dictionary. Some formats like JPEG [18] are tuned specifically for graphics by accepting imperfect (lossy) compression and reverse

D. Le Métayer (Ed.): ESOP 2002, LNCS 2305, pp. 68–82, 2002.

engineering the human visual system to determine where compression artifacts will have the least perceptual impact. There are unfortunately limitations with these approaches that preclude many improvements:

- They still result in fairly large files. The benefits of compression are limited by the artifacts introduced when the nature of the image does not match the compression technique. For instance, JPEG was designed for images whose frequency decomposition to is similar to photographs. It is less effective on images with many high-frequency components, e.g., diagrams with sharp distinctions between differently colored regions or images containing text. GIF was designed for images just like these, but produces dithered and poorly colored results for natural images like photographs. Neither performs well when both kinds of data are contained in a single image.
- The resulting images are at a fixed resolution. Proper display on devices of varying resolution will only grow in importance as new devices such as PDAs are deployed as browsers.
- Because the output format is fixed, the server administrator cannot trade space for time. In particular, running the compression utility, which is a one-shot activity that benefits all users, for a longer time will not result in a smaller or better image.

Designers address some of these problems by replacing static entities with programs that generate them (e.g., Flash, SVG objects). Even a basic image is, in the abstract, a program. For example, a GIF file contains a series of run-length encoded rasters. The run-length blocks can be considered instructions for a very primitive machine which produces its output in the form of an image.

Formats make the idea of transmitting a program as a form of compression more explicit. Formats such as Flash, Shockwave and SVG [3] use a richer underlying language that keeps objects distinct and resolution-independent, allowing implementors to describe vector-based graphics. Flash and Shockwave also add time-varying instructions and loops to enable animation. The virtual machines for these programs are Web browser plug-ins. Using Java to generate animations is an extreme example of this same principle, namely *programmatic compression*:

a program is often much smaller than the output it generates.[1]

A program is also much more capable of scaling by resolution (recall Knuth's METAFONT [11] for generating fonts from typeface descriptions).

The Flash approach reflects a valuable principle, but has many practical shortcomings. It requires the manual construction of programs from constituent arcs, lines, shades, and so forth. Many complex entities, such as texture-mapped regions, are difficult or impossible to specify using so-called vector graphics primitives. Professional Web designers thus prefer to use tools such as Adobe Photoshop to generate high-quality images with effects like drop shadow, texture, and compositing of scanned/digital photographs. An artist can create such an

---

[1] For a non-visual example, consider programs that generate the digits in the decimal expansion of π.

image in Photoshop and import it into a tool like Flash as a JPEG, but this immediately loses the benefits of a programmatic description, such as effective scaling and extreme compression. The result is a comparably large and pixellated image embedded in an otherwise small and resolution-independent vector description. Ideally, designers should generate images with their favorite general purpose tools like Photoshop; *the compression technique must integrate into their existing design flow.*

The rest of this paper is organized as follows. Section 2 outlines the principles underlying Evolver, our language for graphical image compression. Section 3 provides the details of Evolver's language and tools. Section 4 describes some of our results. Section 5 discusses related work. Finally, section 6 offers concluding remarks and discusses directions for future work.

2   Generating Image Descriptions

The display software for a GIF must decode the format's run-length encoding, thereby effectively acting as an interpreter. Similarly, JPEG images depend on the encoding of small blocks of an image; the display software must again decode the data for display. As a more extreme example, various "fractal compression" algorithms rely on more complex encodings; iterated function systems [1, 4] and partitioned iterated function systems [10] rely on the idea that small parts of an image may resemble translated, rotated, scaled-down copies of other larger portions; a simple version of the key idea is that some savings can be found by representing the smaller portion via this transformation rather than directly.[2] Each of these compression algorithms can be seen as exploiting some known characteristic of images: the tendency to be scan-line coherent, the tendency to have large blocks with small variation, or the tendency to have little pieces that look like scaled versions of larger pieces. The result of each of these insights is a particular program (a decoder) that takes a certain amount of data (the "GIF" or "JPEG" or "PIFS" image) and converts it to an image (a rectangular array of colors).

Note that certain types of image are well-suited to each of these approaches: scanned-text compresses pretty well with GIF, in part because of the long "white" runs between the lines. Photos of natural phenomena seem to be well-suited to iterated-function-system compression. And JPEG works well on interior photos, where things like walls present relatively large, relatively constant areas. These techniques tend to produce large files or introduce artifacts when applied to the wrong kind of images.

One might therefore imagine an image format that stored an image either as a GIF or a JPEG or a PIFS, by trying each one and selecting the one with the best compression results; the particular type used could be indicated with a few bits in a header. But from this, a more general approach suggests itself: why not consider *all* possible programs, not just the handful that have been written down

---

[2] Discovering the correct transformations is the hard part of the compression process.

as JPEG or GIF decompressors, that can generate an image and simply record the one that best generates *this* image? (Note that in this case, the decoder and the data it operates on are all considered part of "the program"; indeed, the decoder-and-data model of generating images is only one of many possibilities.)

While the idea of searching "all possible programs" seems ludicrous at first blush (there are an infinite number of them, for example), searching a rich collection of programs turns out to be feasible with some insight into the design of the language in which the programs are written and the goal of the program.

Evolver

We present Evolver, a collection of tools for visual image compression. Because artists are skilled at the use of image manipulation software, not programming, Evolver presents a simple interface: the designer provides an image (the *source image*) built with their favorite tools. Evolver reduces this image to an Evolver language program (the *description*) which, by rendering a reasonable approximation of the image and being small, exploits the power of programmatic compression.

Evolver has two parts. The first program is an encoder, which consumes the source image and produces its description. It does this by searching the space of all legal descriptions to find ones that generate an image that is visually similar to the source image. The second, a decoder, is a fast interpreter for the Evolver language, which renders the description as an image for the client. The decoder is currently implemented in Java [7], and is hence easy to deploy in Web contexts.[3]

Evolver confronts two hard problems. First, it is difficult to search the space of all programs, because the space is large, and small changes to the source of a program can lead to large changes in its output. Second, it's difficult to create an objective measure of visual similarity. Evolver therefore employs randomized search algorithms. Our current implementation uses *genetic algorithms*, following Karl Sims's ideas from a decade ago [17]; that is, *Evolver breeds a program that generates the desired image*. We could use other algorithms such as simulated annealing instead.

Because it uses an optimizer to search, the effectiveness of Evolver depends on the choice of an appropriate fitness function. We could obtain a perfect image match by subtracting the current approximation from the original and requiring that the difference be zero; this would, however, take unreasonably long to converge. This also fails to exploit the feature that several different descriptions can render identical-looking images within the tolerance of the human visual system. We instead use more flexible metrics that account for desirable visual properties, such as matching texture and shape, rather than individual pixel values. For example, it is acceptable to compress one white noise image into another

---

[3] The Java bytecode for the decoder is substantially larger than the descriptions it decompresses into images; we assume that for practical deployment the Java decoder would be downloaded once and used many times, so its size does not pose a problem.

where no individual pixel matches, so long as we preserve the statistical properties of the noise. We are not aware of a pre-existing compression technique that uses the property that two noise signals with the same statistics are visually indistinguishable.

Evolver rewards longer runs by producing higher quality matches. Some of these programs grow in size to improve the approximation. Over time, however, Evolver may also find smaller programs that generate the same image. Therefore, Evolver presents the designer a range of images corresponding to the original; the designer can pick the smallest or best, or even choose several for use in different contexts.[4] The image's description (an Evolver program) then becomes the object distributed to clients.

3   The Evolver Language

Evolver's success relies crucially on the choice of language. Not all choices of languages automatically accomplish compression. For instance, consider the trivial, single-instruction language whose one instruction consumes the coordinates and color of a point and shades it accordingly. Slavishly translating each pixel in the source image into an instruction in this language would accomplish little, and might well expand the size of the description. In contrast, because many images contain considerable redundancy, adding abstraction mechanisms to the language can lead to programs that account for this redundancy, thus removing it in the image's description. Run-length encoding is a simple example of this: a "repeat n times" mechanism in the trivial language above would allow it to implement run-length encoding.

The benefit of a larger language is obvious: the more powerful its instructions, the greater the likelihood that a concise description exists in the language. Another benefit of a larger language is that it allows us to encode something of our knowledge of the structure of images. The `Collage` primitive of Evolver, described later in this section, is a good example of this kind of domain-specific construct.

The benefits that ensue from large languages mask a significant shortcoming. The larger the language, and the greater its parameterizations, the harder the genetic algorithm needs to work to find even valid programs,[5] much less ones that render a useful approximation to the source image. *This is the central tension in the design of Evolver's language.* To understand the explosion of search

---

[4] The smallest and best criteria can be combined into a single criterion by accumulating the per-pixel color value differences between Evolver's result image and the source image and counting the number of bits needed to encode those deltas against each description. This is overly strict because different pixel values do not necessarily produce visually different images. In practice, there is no established algorithm for reliably measuring the perceptual error in an image approximation and we are left with appealing to a human observer to obtain the best results.

[5] Sims finessed this issue by creating a language/breeding system in which every possible mutation was a valid program. We follow a similar approach, and discuss this issue further in section 5.

complexity that results from adding language features, consider variable binding, a feature that is useful in programming languages used by humans but is particularly difficult for a search program to use effectively. The search program must both bind a variable and use that binding for it to contribute compression. Evolving both of those code fragments simultaneously in a way that increases match quality may be a low probability occurrence. In contrast, highly nested and self-similar programs are easy for the search program to generate but look nothing like the programs a human would write. Furthermore, Evolver optimizes globally over an image, and may perform filter steps that affect different portions of an image differently, in clever ways a human is unlikely to engineer.

The Evolver language is a simple, functional language, based on that used by Sims. It provides a rich set of primitives that render various shapes on screen. We describe these primitives in groups, with some brief rationale given for each. All primitives operate on (and produce) *matrices*, which correspond to pixel samples in an image; thus a matrix is a 3D array of values arranged into a rectangular array of color *vectors*, where a vector is a triple of *scalars*, and a scalar is a number between -1.0 and 1.0. In some cases, it's natural to do something to the *first* entry of each triple; the array of all these "first entries" will be called the "first channel" of the matrix. Because at display time, each triple is interpreted as the red, green, and blue components of a pixel, we'll sometimes speak of the "red channel" as well.[6]

The interpretation of an Evolver program depends on the *dimensions* of the final image; all matrices in the program are of these same dimensions, which enables resolution independence. Some of the primitives in the Evolver language use stock images as constants, which do not mesh well with resolution independence. To address this, a high-resolution stock image is appropriately filtered to the matrix size and then sampled at the given size. This means an Evolver program is really parameterized by the output image dimensions; the primitives are designed to have the characteristic that a low-resolution result of a program looks like a scaled-down version of a high-resolution result of the same program.

We allow values to be coerced between scalar, vector, and matrix types. Vector values can be derived from a matrix by operations like "compute the average color the image." This has the advantage that it is reasonably scale-independent: whether the images we're working with are 10x10 or 300x300, the average of all pixels is roughly the same. Scalars can be obtained from vectors by chosing a single channel or the average. A scalar is coerced to a vector by repeating it three times; a vector is coerced to a matrix by repeating it the necessary number of times.

The full Evolver language grammar in BNF notation is given by:

```
ELValue := ELMatrix | ELScalar | ELVector
ELOperator := Add | Sub | Blur | Noise | ...
ELCall := ELOperator x ELExpression*
```

---

[6] The mapping from the interval $[-1.0, 1.0]$ to colors is due to Sims: negative values are clamped to no intensity; numbers between 0 and 1 map to the full range of intensities.

```
ELExpression := ELCall | ELScalar | ELVector
ELMatrix := ELVector*
ELVector := ELScalar x ELScalar x ELScalar
```

where an ELScalar is a real number between -1 and 1.

3.1   Fitness Function

Our fitness function, which may be simplistic by the standards of the computer vision community, attempts to match properties of images that are known to affect the human visual system. The properties we use are:

 - edges,
 - per-pixel intensity,
 - pixel color,
 - average color over large regions (image segments),
 - average color over small regions.

We compute these properties of the input and current image, and sum the differences along each of these metrics. We choose the sum to avoid preferring generations that succeed in a few metrics but greatly fail in the others.

Edges are a crude measure of frequency data, so an area in an image that has high frequency will appear densely populated with edges. High-frequency areas (such as images of leaves and grass) will match poorly with low-frequency images such as gradients and constants, and well with other high-frequency areas such as noise and stock images. We tried to employ the magnitude of the gradient of the image, which is a better measure of local frequency content, but found that it gave poor matches compared with the edge detector.

3.2   Language Primitives

The language grammar reveals that the core of Evolver lies in its set of primitives. The details are not essential to the larger point and are too large to print here. Instead, we provide detailed information on the Web:

http://www.cs.brown.edu/people/morgan/evolver/

Here, we describe the categories of primitives with some commentary on the graphical motivation for each type of primitive.

Variation Sources To produce compact representations of nearly-constant areas of an image (which are often good targets for compression), it helps to have some functions that produce slowly-varying signals, which can then be arithmetically mapped to generate periodic signals (via sin or cos), or can be used directly to represent slowly-varying regions of the input images. Similarly, band-limited noise has been known to be very valuable in texture generation [5]; we therefore include primitives that generate this directly. In all cases, we use Perlin's noise

Fig. 1. A few of Evolver's image primitives.

function, but with a constant "seed" so that the results are reproducible. Finally, purely statistical information about an image can help to generate patterns that may be likely to resemble those appearing in other images "like" this one; we therefore have primitives that are images such as those shown in figure 1. (Note that none of these images was actually in the test data set.)

Mathematical Transformations Following Sims, we allow basic arithmetic operations on matrices, and element-wise transformations such as mathematical (sine, cosine) and logical (and, or) operations. Some specialized operations include ExpandRange, which expands the dynamic range of a matrix's contents from (0, 1) to (-1, 1). This has the effect of enhancing the contrast in an image, while reducing the average brightness.

Color Some primitives reinterpret or convert channels between RGB and HSV.

Geometric Pattern Generation Tools A few primitives help with the representation of images that have some geometric regularity to them, by providing various natural transformations. These include symmetric mirrors, splits and zooms.

Combinations Naturally, some of the most important primitives are those that combine images in interesting ways; ordinary arithmetic operations have been discussed above, but the following operations are richer, and preliminary evidence suggests that Rotate, HueShift, and Interpolate are powerful enough to be selected often by Evolver.
Rotate(matrix, matrix): Rotates the first image by the average value of the red channel of the second argument (averaged over whole image); tiles missing areas.
Interpolate(matrix, matrix, matrix): Linearly interpolates the first and third arguments using the second as the blending value.
Distort(matrix, matrix): Displaces the pixels of the first argument by the values of the second (as if refracting through glass).
EnvironmentMap(matrix, matrix): Interprets the first argument as a height map and uses the second as a color environment map (as if reflecting the second image).

HueShift(matrix, matrix): Shift the overall hue of the first argument by average red value of the second argument.
Collage(matrix*): Colors different segments with different textures.

The last of these deserves special comment: because it is hard for Evolver to determine how to partition the image, we start the search with a "Collage" primitive. This depends on a first step: we take the target image and compute a "segmentation" of it, breaking it into regions of similar hue. The segmentation algorithm is relatively naive, and tends to produce regions which may not represent terribly precise segmentations, but which are extremely amenable to run-length encoding, and hence can be compactly represented. This segmentation is provided as "data" to the evolver program (and its size is taken into account when we measure compression!); the primitive collage(m1, m2, ...) creates an image where pixels from segment 1 are taken from the matrix m1, those from segment 2 are taken from matrix m2, and so on.

3.3   Linguistic Observations

Many of the primitives were chosen because they worked well in Sims's original work; others were included because they have proven useful in image processing. Evolver's language, as with most other programming languages, grows through an evolutionary process. The language we currently have reflects a very capable set of primitives that renders a diverse stable of images.

Our primitive set is not minimal by any means: several primitives can be built from simple combinations of other primitives. They were included as a way of injecting domain knowledge into the search process to make it converge faster. For example, a translation operation can be generated as an application of the form distort(matrix m, matrix c) where c is a constant matrix, and indeed, Evolver often uses this idiom; thus including Translate as a new primitive is natural.

In general, we inject domain knowledge at three points:

- The selection of primitives, as explained above.
- The mutation strategy: one of our mutations involves adjusting a scalar by a small amount, for example. Large adjustments caused too-drastic changes in the results; tiny adjustments made it hard to ever "get where we needed to be." Hence we chose a modest average adjustment to scalars. Similarly, in the mutations that wrap an expression in a larger one or trim away part of an expression, we recognized the need to balance the frequencies of these operations so that the size of expressions did not tend to grow without bound.
- The fitness function: by adjusting the fitness function to be sensitive to approximate edge-placement, we made substantial improvements over an earlier L^2-distance function. The better that one can match the fitness function to the human visual system, the better the results will be.

4   Experimental Results

Our test data set was a series of outdoor photographs by Philip Greenspun available on photo.net. We loaded each image into the encoder and allowed it to run for a fixed period of time. In each case, the encoder segmented the image and ran for 10 minutes on each segment, then combined the segments using the collage operator and ran for an additional 10 minutes on the combined expression. The parameters used to tune the genetic algorithm will be available on our website.

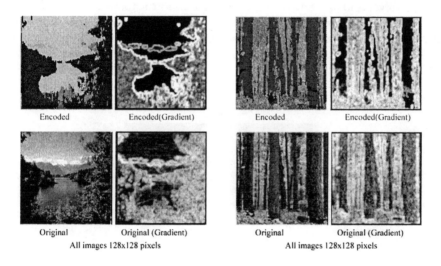

Encoded   Encoded(Gradient)   Encoded   Encoded(Gradient)

Original   Original (Gradient)   Original   Original (Gradient)

All images 128x128 pixels   All images 128x128 pixels

Fig. 2. Some uses of Evolver.

The figure on the left shows a poor result from Evolver. The source image is in the lower left corner. This is an image of a lake surrounded by trees, with mountains in the distance. In the lower right is an image showing the magnitude of the gradient of the source image. This is not used by the encoder but is useful for evaluating the quality of the results and understanding the matcher. Light values in the gradient correspond to areas of high frequency, like leaves, and dark values correspond to low frequencies like sky.

The upper left image shows the image after compression by Evolver and the upper right shows the gradient of this image. While the encoding contains visible artifacts and is thus inferior to the compression available through a GIF or JPEG, it demonstrates that the evolutionary approach is clearly feasible. Evolver correctly matches the hue and intensity in the image, creating bright green areas where the trees were illuminated and dark green areas where the trees were in shadow. The sky and lake are a uniform grey, averaging the color of the lake and mountains. The clouds are pink. Looking at the gradient, we see that the encoder matched high frequency textures to the tree areas and low frequencies to the lake and sky. The mountains are absent entirely. This is because the segmentation failed to distinguish between the sky and mountains, so Evolver created a single texture for both of them.

The figure on the right shows a much better result. The source image is a close-up view of some maple trees. After 40 minutes, Evolver successfully matched both the frequency, color and texture of the source image. The encoded image has minimal artifacts, and thus indicates that Evolver can successfully function as a compression algorithm.

As a multiresolution experiment, we compressed an 128x128 original image using Evolver and as a 64x64 JPEG. The goal was to store the image using very few bits without losing all detail. We then decompressed and displayed the image at 768x768. Evolver's procedural representation preserves high frequency detail. The small JPEG image is blocky when viewed at 12x the encoding size. Below are zoomed in views of a few pixels from each to show the difference.

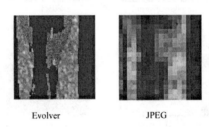

Evolver   JPEG

Virtual environments often suffer from low texture resolution. When the viewer is very close to a surface, textures appear either blurry or blocky. It has long been known that procedural textures are a solution to this problem. Traditionally, procedural textures could only be used for textures like wood grain and checkerboards that were easy for humans to synthesize algorithms for. Evolver is important for this problem because it is a method for taking an arbitrary image texture and making a procedural texture from it.

Note that Evolver will add texture at higher frequencies than appear in the original image. This is only mathematically possible because it may add the wrong information; it is not sampling the original scene at a higher frequency but trying to simulate what the results of that process would be. Because Evolver uses natural images as part of its input data set, it is predisposed to creating detail that has the same statistical properties as that found in real images. If Evolver matches a stock leaf texture to a forest, it is likely that zooming in will show individual leaves and not blocks. Of course, it is also possible that from a distance carpet and leaves look the same and on zooming in the viewer will discover that Evolver carpeted the forest instead. The user can control this process by picking an appropriate set of primitive images.

5 Other Related Work

There is a long history of procedural graphics languages. Papert's LOGO language [15], Henderson's Picture Language [9], Knuth's TEXand Metafont [11] are some early and familiar examples. Programmable shading languages like Renderman [8, 16] continue to play an important role in graphics.

Perlin, and Worley independently worked on many procedural texturing algorithms which are summarized in their book [5]. This work all assumes a human writes the code manually, which is prohibitively difficult for complicated textures such as actual photographs.

Barnsley [1] introduced the idea of iterated function systems ("fractals") for compression. These are much richer graphics languages than JPEG or GIF but less general than Evolver, which does not rely on self-similarity for compression.

Massalin's *superoptimizer* [12] tries all sequences of assembly language instructions to find the smallest one equivalent to a given input function. That is, the superoptimizer conducts a comprehensive search of the state space of programs. It therefore clearly represents an extreme instance of optimization. While the superoptimizer finds a globally optimal solution, it is clearly infeasible in the large space that Evolver searches.

Nicholas et al. [13] have studied the problem of *typed* genetic programming to improve the convergence speed of genetic programs. These works are not immediately applicable to ours, because they consider much weaker languages whose type domains we cannot adopt. We believe it is important to use a typed language in Evolver, and intend to do this as future work.

Beretta, et al. [2] describe a technique for compressing images using genetic algorithms. Nordin, et al. [14] describes a similar program for images and sound. Both of these systems use primitive languages (at the machine instruction level) and operate on 8x8 or 16x16 blocks. We build on their results by using genetic algorithms for compression and the observation that dividing the image into separate regions speeds convergence. Evolver differs in that it uses an image segmentation based on objects, not arbitrary blocks, and features a rich image processing language. Our approach avoids the blocky artifacts from these systems and allows Evolver to capture details in a multi-resolution fashion. It also gives Evolver the potential for much higher compression ratios, since 8x8 blocks can achieve at most a factor of 64:1 compression.

Our work is directly inspired by Karl Sims [17], who used genetic algorithms to evolve images on a connection machine with a high level language. In his experiments, the fitness function was the user's aesthetic preference, and the human and computer interacted to form visually pleasing abstract images. We use a language and genetic algorithm similar to Sims but apply it to image compression to synthesize programs that create actual photographs.

6 Conclusions and Future Work

We have presented the Evolver framework, a collection of tools for compressing graphical images. At its heart, Evolver consists of a simple, functional graphics description language, and its corresponding interpreter, which resides on client computers. Given an image to compress, Evolver breeds a description that generates an image that the designer considers acceptably close to the source image. This program is generated once on the server, and used many times on numerous clients.

Because the image is rendered by a program, Evolver offers many benefits not found in traditional formats and compressors. Image descriptions are resolution-independent, so the same description can render both a thumbnail image and the actual one, with graceful degradation. The genetic algorithms reward patience: by running longer, they can produce better approximations to the original image, or find smaller programs that generate acceptable approximations. The resulting image description can be extremely small, and can be replaced with smaller descriptions as they become available. Different genetic algorithms are better-suited to different kinds of images, so as Evolver encounters new families of images, it simply needs new mating techniques; since the output is still a rendering program in the same language, the client does not need to make changes. Even if the language does grow, an enriched interpreter would still handle any older images.

So far, we have only discussed the use of Evolver to compress static images. We are also conducting experiments on compressing animations. On the one hand, animations appear to offer a considerable challenge. It can be fairly time-consuming to generate a description of even a single static image; how much longer would it take to generate a small program that generates a *sequence* of images? Indeed, this problem seems practically intractable.

There are, in fact, several feasible ways of approaching animations. One obvious approach is to treat each frame individually, apply Evolver to each frame in turn, and add a single instruction to its language to encapsulate a sequence of frames. We can improve the convergence by exploiting temporal locality by using the description for one frame as the initial description for the next.

In the ideal case, Evolver will incorporate a second language, dedicated to animations. This second language would capture attributes such as a consistent darkening of all pixels in a region (perhaps indicating nightfall). This again exploits the programmatic principle that a large difference in bit-wise information may be captured by a small set of instructions. Various MPEG encoding standards use "difference" data of this sort, which we hope to exploit for designing the animation language.

More importantly, we see Evolver pointing to numerous research opportunities for the programming languages community. First, the genetic algorithms in Evolver need a type system to guide the generation of programs; currently, Evolver uses fairly ad hoc techniques to prevent the generation of invalid programs. Second, there are likely to be several static analyses that, with small extensions to the intermediate language, will encourage "suitable" programs (at the expense of some diversity), yielding quicker convergence. Third, Evolver may be able to benefit from some of the features of existing graphical languages, such as FRAN [6]; we were forced to use Java because Haskell currently lacks the rich graphics library and widespread applet support necessary to deploy Evolver, but the language's design in no way precludes, and indeed encourages, implementation in a functional language. Finally, Evolver points to a new criterion for the design of some domain-specific languages: to be suitable for creation of programs by other programs, especially through a simple but highly iterative process such as evolution.

Ultimately, our goal is not to develop radical new compression schemes—we defer to others for whom that is a primary research interest. Instead, we believe that Evolver's true value lies in the philosophy that it embodies:

- Many problems in science and engineering are solved by changing representations. Programming languages are pervasive, and can therefore serve as a useful alternate representation in many domains. Converting a domain's data into code makes it possible to leverage the techniques and tools of programming languages—such as semantics-preserving program transformations and interpreters, respectively—to tackle difficult problems.
- Leveraging steerable, probabilistic search techniques, such as genetic algorithms, permits the selective injection of domain knowledge into optimization problems.
- The burgeoning availability of cycles creates possibilities for whole new styles of programs. These may employ, and can even exploit, non-standard notions of "correctness". In Evolver, for instance, the validity of an approximation is determined entirely by the judgment of the designer's visual sensory system.

We believe that this is an important design pattern that can be used to effectively open a radical new approach to hard problems in several domains.

Acknowledgments

This work has been supported in part by the NSF Science and Technology Center for Computer Graphics and Scientific Visualization, Adobe Systems, Alias/Wavefront, Department of Energy, IBM, Intel, Microsoft, Sun Microsystems, and TACO, and NSF Grant ESI 0010064. Nature photographs courtesy of and copyright to Philip Greenspun (http://photo.net/philg/). Fish and sunrise images courtesy of and copyright to Morgan McGuire. We thank Nick Beaudrot for his help writing the toolkit.

References

1. M. F. Barnsley and A. E. Jacquin. Application of recurrent iterated function systems to images. In *Proceedings SPIE Visual Communications and Image Processing '88*, volume 1001, pages 122–131, 1988.
2. M. Beretta and A. Tettamanzi. An evolutionary approach to fuzzy image compression. In *Proceedings of the Italian Workshop on Fuzzy Logic (WILF 95)*, pages 49–57, Naples, Italy, 1996. World Scientific.
3. World Wide Web Consortium. Scalable vector graphics (SVG) 1.0 specification, 2001. http://www.w3.org/TR/SVG/.

4. S. Demko, L. Hodges, and B. Naylor. Construction of fractal objects with iterated function systems. In B. A. Barsky, editor, *Computer Graphics (Proceedings of ACM SIGGRAPH 85)*, volume 19 (3), pages 271–278, San Francisco, California, July 1985.

5. D. Ebert, K. Musgrave, D. Peachey, K. Perlin, and S. Worley. *Texturing and Modeling: A Procedural Approach, second edition.* AP Professional, 1998.

6. Conal Elliott and Paul Hudak. Functional reactive animation. In *Proceedings of the ACM SIGPLAN International Conference on Functional Programming (ICFP '97)*, volume 32(8), pages 263–273, 1997.

7. James Gosling, Bill Joy, and Guy Lewis Steele, Jr. *The Java Language Specification.* Addison-Wesley, 1996.

8. Pat Hanrahan and Jim Lawson. A language for shading and lighting calculations. In *Computer Graphics (Proceedings of ACM SIGGRAPH 90)*, volume 24 (4), pages 289–298, Dallas, Texas, August 1990. ISBN 0-201-50933-4.

9. Peter Henderson. Functional geometry. In *Symposium on Lisp and Functional Programming*, pages 179 – 187, New York, 1982. ACM Press.

10. Hau-Lai Ho and Wai-Kuen Cham. Attractor image coding using lapped partitioned iterated function systems. In *Proceedings ICASSP-97 (IEEE International Conference on Acoustics, Speech and Signal Processing)*, volume 4, pages 2917–2920, Munich, Germany, 1997.

11. D. Knuth. *TEX and METAFONT : new directions in typesetting.* Digital Press and the American Mathematical Society, 1979.

12. H. Massalin. Superoptimizer: A look at the smallest program. In *Proceedings of the 2nd International Conference on Architectural Support for Programming Languages and Operating System (ASPLOS)*, volume 22, pages 122–127, New York, NY, 1987. ACM Press.

13. Nicholas F. McPhee and Riccardo Poli. A schema theory analysis of the evolution of size in genetic programming with linear representations. In *Genetic Programming, Proceedings of EuroGP 2001*, LNCS, Milan, 2001. Springer-Verlag.

14. Peter Nordin and Wolfgang Banzhaf. Programmatic compression of images and sound. In John R. Koza, David E. Goldberg, David B. Fogel, and Rick L. Riolo, editors, *Genetic Programming 1996: Proceedings of the First Annual Conference*, pages 345–350, Stanford University, CA, USA, 28–31 July 1996. MIT Press.

15. S. A. Papert. Teaching children thinking. Technical Report A. I. MEMO 247 and Logo Memo 2, AI Laboratory, Massachusetts Institute of Technology, Cambridge, Massachusetts, 1971.

16. Pixar. The renderman interface, version 3.1, 1989. http://www.pixar.com/renderman/developers_corner/rispec/.

17. K. Sims. Interactive evolution of equations for procedural models. In *Proceedings of IMAGINA conference, Monte Carlo, January 29-31, 1992*, 1992.

18. Gregory K. Wallace. The JPEG still picture compression standard. *Communications of the ACM*, 34(4):30–44, 1991.

19. Jacob Ziv and Abraham Lempel. A universal algorithm for sequential data compression. *IEEE Transactions on Information Theory*, IT-23(3):337–343, 1977.

An Accumulative Parallel Skeleton for All

Zhenjiang HU[1,3], Hideya IWASAKI[2], and Masato TAKEICHI[1]

[1] The University of Tokyo
{hu,takeichi}@ipl.t.u-tokyo.ac.jp
[2] The University of Electro-Communications
iwasaki@cs.uec.ac.jp
[3] PRESTO 21, Japan Science and Technology Corporation

Abstract. Parallel skeletons intend to encourage programmers to build a parallel program from ready-made components for which efficient implementations are known to exist, making the parallelization process simpler. However, it is neither easy to develop *efficient* parallel programs using skeletons nor to use skeletons to manipulate *irregular* data, and moreover there lacks a *systematic* way to optimize skeletal parallel programs. To remedy this situation, we propose a *novel* parallel skeleton, called accumulate, which not only efficiently describes data dependency in computation but also exhibits nice algebraic properties for manipulation. We show that this skeleton significantly eases skeletal parallel programming in practice, efficiently manipulating both regular and irregular data, and systematically optimizing skeletal parallel programs.

1   Introduction

With the increasing popularity of parallel programming environments such as PC cluster, more and more people, including those who have little knowledge of parallel architecture and parallel programming, are hoping to write parallel programs. This situation eagerly calls for models and methodologies which can assist programming parallel computers effectively and correctly.

The *data parallel* model [HS86] turns out to be one of the most successful ones for programming massively parallel computers. To support parallel programming, this model basically consists of two parts:

- *a parallel data structure* to model a uniform collection of data which can be organized in a way that each element can be manipulated in parallel; and
- *a fixed set of parallel skeletons* on the parallel data structure to abstract parallel structures of interest, which can be used as building blocks to write parallel programs. Typically, these skeletons include element-wise arithmetic and logic operations, reductions, prescans, and data broadcasting.

This model not only provides programmers an easily understandable view of a *single execution stream* of a parallel program, but also makes the parallelizing process easier because of explicit parallelism of the skeletons.

Despite these promising features, the application of current data parallel programming suffers from several problems which prevent it from being practically

D. Le Métayer (Ed.): ESOP 2002, LNCS 2305, pp. 83–97, 2002.

used. Firstly, because parallel programming relies on a set of parallel primitive skeletons for specifying parallelism, programmers often find it hard to choose proper ones or to integrate them well in order to develop *efficient* parallel programs. Secondly, the skeletal parallel programs are difficult to be optimized. The major difficulty lies in the construction of rules meeting the *skeleton-closed* requirement for transformation among skeletons [Bir87,SG99]. Thirdly, skeletons are assumed to manipulate regular data structure. Unfortunately, for *irregular* data like nested lists where the sizes of inner lists are remarkably different, the parallel semantics of skeletons would lead to load imbalance which may nullify the effect of parallelism in skeletons. For more detailed discussion of these problems, see Section 3.

To remedy this situation, we propose in this paper a *new* parallel skeleton, which can significantly eases skeletal parallel programming, efficiently manipulating both regular and irregular data, and systematically optimizing skeletal parallel programs. Our contributions, which make skeletal programming more practical, can be summarized as follows.

- We define a *novel* parallel skeleton (Section 4), called accumulate, which can not only efficiently describe data dependency in a computation through an *accumulating* parameter, but also exhibits nice algebraic properties for manipulation. It can be considered as a higher order list homomorphism, which abstracts a computation requiring more than one pass and provides a better recursive interface for parallel programming.

- We give a single but general rule (Theorem 4 in Section 5), based on which we construct a framework for systematically optimizing skeletal parallel programs. Inspired by the success of the shortcut deforestation [GLJ93] for optimizing sequential programs in compilers, we give a specific shortcut law for fusing compositional style of skeletal parallel programs, but paying much more attention to guaranteeing skeleton-closed parallelism. Our approach using a single rule is in sharp contrast to the existing ones [SG99,KC99] based on a huge set of transformation rules developed in a rather ad-hoc way.

- We propose a flattening rule (Theorem 5 in Section 6), enabling accumulate to deal with both regular and irregular nested data structures efficiently. Compared to the work by Blelloch [Ble89,Ble92] where the so-called *segmented scan* is proposed to deal with irregular data, our rule is more general and powerful, and can be used to systematically handle a wider class of skeletal parallel programs.

The organization of this paper is as follows. After briefly reviewing the notational conventions and some basic concepts in the BMF parallel model in Section 2, we illustrate with a concrete example the problems in skeletal parallel programming in Section 3. To resolve these problems, we begin by proposing a new general parallel skeleton called accumulate, and show how one can easily program with this new skeleton in Section 4. Then in Section 5, we develop a general rule for optimization of skeletal parallel programs. Finally, we give a powerful theorem showing that accumulate can be used to efficiently manipulate irregular data in Section 6. Related work and discussions are given in Section 7.

2   BMF and Parallel Computation

We will address our method on the BMF data parallel programming model [Bir87,Ski90], though the method itself is not limited to the BMF model. We choose BMF because it can provide us a concise way to describe both programs and transformation of programs. Those who are familiar with the functional language Haskell [JH99] should have no problem in understanding the programs in this paper. From the notational viewpoint, the main difference is that we use more symbols or special parentheses to shorten the expressions so that manipulation of expressions can be performed in a more concise way.

Functions. *Function application* is denoted by a space and the argument which may be written without brackets. Thus $f\,a$ means $f\,(a)$. Functions are curried, and application associates to the left. Thus $f\,a\,b$ means $(f\,a)\,b$. Function application binds stronger than any other operator, so $f\,a \oplus b$ means $(f\,a) \oplus b$, not $f\,(a \oplus b)$. *Function composition* is denoted by a centralized circle $\circ$. By definition, we have $(f \circ g)\,a = f\,(g\,a)$. Function composition is an associative operator, and the identity function is denoted by id. Infix binary operators will often be denoted by $\oplus$, $\otimes$ and can be *sectioned*; an infix binary operator like $\oplus$ can be turned into unary or binary functions by $a \oplus b = (a \oplus)\,b = (\oplus b)\,a = (\oplus)\,a\,b$.

Parallel Data Structure: Join Lists. *Join lists* (or *append lists*) are finite sequences of values of the same type. A list is either the empty, a singleton, or the concatenation of two other lists. We write $[\,]$ for the empty list, $[a]$ for the singleton list with element a (and $[\cdot]$ for the function taking a to $[a]$), and $x \mathbin{+\!\!+} y$ for the concatenation (join) of two lists x and y. Concatenation is associative, and $[\,]$ is its unit. For example, $[1] \mathbin{+\!\!+} [2] \mathbin{+\!\!+} [3]$ denotes a list with three elements, often abbreviated to $[1, 2, 3]$. We also write $a : x$ for $[a] \mathbin{+\!\!+} x$. If a list is constructed on by the constructor of $[\,]$ and $:$, we call it *cons list*.

Parallel Skeletons: map, reduce, scan, zip. It has been shown [Ski90] that BMF [Bir87] is a nice architecture-independent parallel computation model, consisting of a small fixed set of specific higher order functions which can be regarded as parallel skeletons suitable for parallel implementation. Four important higher order functions are *map, reduce, scan* and *zip*.

Map is the skeleton which applies a function to every element in a list. It is written as an infix $*$. Informally, we have

$$k * [x_1, x_2, \ldots, x_n] = [k\,x_1, k\,x_2, \ldots, k\,x_n].$$

Reduce is the skeleton which collapses a list into a single value by repeated application of some associative binary operator. It is written as an infix $/$. Informally, for an associative binary operator $\oplus$, we have

$$\oplus/\,[x_1, x_2, \ldots, x_n] = x_1 \oplus x_2 \oplus \cdots \oplus x_n.$$

Scan is the skeleton that accumulates all intermediate results for computation of reduce. Informally, for an associative binary operator $\oplus$ and an initial value e, we have

$$\oplus \#_e [x_1, x_2, \ldots, x_n] = [e, e \oplus x_1, e \oplus x_1 \oplus x_2, \ldots, e \oplus x_1 \oplus x_2 \oplus \cdots \oplus x_n].$$

Note that this definition is a little different from that in [Bir87]; the e there is assumed to be the unit of $\oplus$. In fact efficient implementation of the scan skeleton does not need this restriction.

Zip is the skeleton that merges two lists into a single one by paring the corresponding elements. The resulting list has the same length as that of shorter one. Informally, we have

$$[x_1, x_2, \ldots, x_n] \Upsilon [y_1, y_2, \ldots, y_n] = [(x_1, y_1), (x_2, y_2), \ldots, (x_n, y_n)].$$

It has been shown that these four operators have nice massively parallel implementations on many architectures [Ski90,Ble89]. If k and $\oplus$ need $O(1)$ parallel time, then $k*$ can be implemented using $O(1)$ parallel time, and both $\oplus/$ and $\oplus\#_e$ can be implemented using $O(\log N)$ parallel time, where N denotes the size of the list. For example, $\oplus$ can be computed in parallel on a tree-like structure with the combining operator $\oplus$ applied in the nodes, while $k*$ is computed in parallel with k applied to each of the leaves. The study on efficient parallel implementation of $\oplus\#_e$ can be found in [Ble89], though the implementation may be difficult to understand.

3   Limitations of the Existing Skeletal Parallel Programming

In this section, we are using a simple but practical example, the *lines-of-sight problem* (*los* for short), to explain in detail the limitations (problems) of the existing approach to parallel programming using skeletons, clarifying the motivation and the goal of this work.

Given a terrain map in the form of a grid of altitudes, an observation point, and a set of rays, the lines-of-sight problem is to find which points are visible along these rays originating at the observation point (as in Figure 1). A point on a ray is visible if and only if no other point between it and the observation point has a greater vertical angle. More precisely, $los : Point \to [[Point]] \to [[Bool]]$ accepts as input an observation point p_0 and a list of rays where each ray is a list of points, and returns a list of lists where corresponding element is a boolean value showing whether the point is visible or not.

This problem is of practical interest, and a simpler version (considering only a single line) was informally studied in [Ble89] where an efficient parallel program was given without explanation how it was obtained. Now the question is how to make use of the four BMF skeletons in Section 2 to develop an efficient parallel program for this problem.

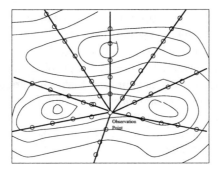

Fig. 1. Altitude Map

3.1 Programming Efficient Skeletal Programs

Developing *efficient* programs with skeletons is hard because it requires both a proper choice of skeletons and an efficient combination of them. Using skeletons, one often tries to solve a problem by composition of several passes so that each pass can be described in terms of a parallel skeleton. Considering the subproblem *los*1 which just checks whether the points in a *single* ray *ps* are visible or not from the observation point p_0, one may solve the problem by the following three passes.

1. Compute the vertical angles for each point.
2. For each point, compute the maximum angle among all the points between this point and the observation point, which can again be solved by two passes:
   (a) gathering all angles of the points between this point and the observation point;
   (b) computing the maximum of the angles.
3. For each point, compare its angle with the maximum angle obtained in step 2.

Therefore one could come up with the following program:

$$
\begin{aligned}
los1 \; p_0 \; ps \; = \; \textbf{let} \quad & \\
as \; & = \; (angle \; p_0) * ps && \text{— Pass 1} \\
ass \; & = \; (\mathbin{+\!\!\!+}) \#_{[\,]} \, ([\cdot] * as) && \text{— Pass 2 (a)} \\
mas \; & = \; maximum * ass && \text{— Pass 2 (b)} \\
vs \; & = \; (\lambda \, (x, y) \rightarrow x > y) * (as \; \Upsilon \; mas) && \text{— Pass 3} \\
\textbf{in} \quad & \\
vs \quad &
\end{aligned}
$$

However, this multi-pass program has the problem of introducing many intermediate data structures (such as *as*, *ass*, and *mas*) passed between skeletons. This may result in a terribly inefficient programs (the above definition *los*1 is such an example) with high computation and communication cost especially in a distributed system [KC99]; these intermediate data structures have to be distributed to processors and each result must be gathered to the master processor.

As a matter of fact, even for a simpler subproblem like Pass 2 (a), solving it in terms of skeleton is actually not an easy task. One approach for coping with this problem is to derive a *homomorphism* [Col95,Gor96,HTC98], resulting in skeletal parallel programs in the form of $(\oplus /) \circ (f*)$. Though homomorphisms may deal well with programming using *map* and *reduce* skeletons, they cannot directly support programming with the skeleton of *scan* [Ble89] which uses an accumulating parameter.

3.2   Skeleton Composition

As argued, most inefficiency specific to skeletal parallel programs originates from many intermediate data structures passed from one skeleton to another. Therefore, it is essential to fuse compositions of skeletons to eliminate unnecessary intermediate data structures, to save both computation and communication cost.

The major difficulty for this fusion lies in the construction of rules meeting the *skeleton-closed* requirement that the result of fusion of skeletons should give a skeleton again [Bir87,SG99]. Recall the program for Pass 2 (a):

$$ass \ = \ + \!\!\!+ \, /\!\!/_{[]}([\cdot] * as).$$

It cannot be fused into a program using a single skeleton of *map*, *reduce*, or *scan*. One may hope to fuse it into a form something like $(\lambda \, e \, \lambda \, a \ \rightarrow \ e \ +\!\!\!+ \, [a]) /\!\!/_{[]}$, but this is incorrect because the underlined binary operator is not associative. The key problem for optimization turns out to be how to systematically fuse skeletal parallel programs.

3.3   Nested Parallelism

Consider the program of Pass 2 (b) in the definition of *los1*:

$$mas \ = \ maximum * ass.$$

Let $ass = [as_1, as_2, \ldots, as_n]$. This expression is quite inefficient when the lengths of $as_1, as_2, \ldots, as_n$ are quite different. To see this more clearly, consider an extreme case of

$$maximum * [[1], [2], [1, 2, 3, 4, \ldots, 100]],$$

and assume that we have three processors. If we naively use one processor to compute *maximum* on each element list, computation time will be dominated by the processor which computes *maximum* $[1, 2, \ldots, 100]$, and the load imbalance cancels the effect of parallelism in the *map* skeleton.

Generally, the nested parallelism problem can be formalized as: "under what condition of f, the function $f*$ can be implemented efficiently no matter how different the sizes of the element lists are?" Blelloch [Ble89,Ble92] gave a *case study*, showing that if f is $\oplus \#_e$, then $f*$ is called *segmented scan* and can be implemented efficiently. But how to systematically cope with skeletal parallel programs remains unclear.

A concrete but more involved example is the lines-of-sight problem, which can be solved by

$$los\ p_0\ pss\ =\ (los1\ p_0) * pss$$

where pss may be an imbalanced (irregular) data, and $los1\ p_0$ is a rather complicated function.

4   An Accumulative Parallel Skeleton

From this section, we propose a new general parallel skeleton to resolve the problems raised in Section 3, showing how one can easily program with this new skeleton, how skeletal parallel programs can be systematically optimized, and how nested parallelism can be effectively dealt with.

4.1   The Skeleton accumulate

We believe that the skeleton itself should be able to describe data dependency naturally. Map and zip describe parallel computation without data dependency, reduce describes parallel computation with an *upward* (bottom-up) data dependency, and scan describes parallel computation with an *upward* and a simple *downward* (top-down) data accumulation. Compared with these skeletons, our new accumulative skeleton can describe both upward and downward data dependency in a more general way.

Definition 1 (accumulate). Let g, p, q be functions, and $\oplus$ and $\otimes$ be associative operators. The skeleton accumulate is defined by

$$\begin{aligned} \text{accumulate}\ [\,]\ e\quad &= g\ e \\ \text{accumulate}\ (a:x)\ e &= p(a,e)\ \oplus\ \text{accumulate}\ x\ (e \otimes q\ a). \end{aligned}$$

We write $[\![g, (p, \oplus), (q, \otimes)]\!]$ for the function accumulate.   □

It is worth noting that this skeleton, looking a bit complicated, is the simplest form combining two basic recursive forms of *foldl* and *foldr* [Gib96]; $(p, \oplus)$ corresponds to *foldr*, $(q, \otimes)$ corresponds to *foldl*, and g is to connect these two parts.

As a quick example of this skeleton, $los1$ in Section 3 can be defined as

$$\begin{aligned} los1\ p_0 = [\![&\lambda m \to [\,], \\ &(\lambda(p, maxAngle) \to \textbf{if}\ a > maxAngle\ \textbf{then}\ [\textsf{T}]\ \textbf{else}\ [\textsf{F}], +\!\!+\,), \\ &(id, max)]\!]. \end{aligned}$$

More examples can be found in Section 4.4.

4.2   Parallelizability of accumulate

To see that accumulate is indeed a parallel skeleton, we will show that it can be implemented efficiently in parallel. As a matter of fact, the recursive definition for accumulate belongs to the class of parallelizable recursions defined in [HTC98]. The following theorem gives the resulting parallel version for accumulate.

Theorem 1 (Parallelization). The function accumulate defined in Definition 1 can be parallelized to the following divide-and-conquer program.

$$
\begin{aligned}
\text{accumulate } [] \; e &= g \; e \\
\text{accumulate } x \; e &= \mathit{fst} \; (\text{accumulate}' \; x \; e) \\
\text{accumulate}' \; [a] \; e &= (p \; (a, e) \oplus g \; (e \otimes q \; a), p \; (a, e), q \; a) \\
\text{accumulate}' \; (x \mathbin{+\!\!+} y) \; e &= \textbf{let} \; (r_1, s_1, t_1) = \text{accumulate}' \; x \; e \\
&\qquad\qquad (r_2, s_2, t_2) = \text{accumulate}' \; y \; (e \otimes t_1) \\
&\qquad \textbf{in} \; (s_1 \oplus r_2, \; s_1 \oplus s_2, \; t_1 \otimes t_2)
\end{aligned}
$$

Proof. Apply the parallelization theorem in [HTC98] followed by the tupling calculation [HITT97].   □

It is worth noting that accumulate′ can be implemented in parallel on a multiple processor system supporting bidirectional tree-like communication, using the time of $O(\log N)$ where N denotes the length of the input list, provided that $\oplus, \otimes, p, q$ and g can be computed in a constant time. Two passes are employed; an upward pass in the computation can be used to compute the third component of accumulate′ x e before a downward pass is used to compute the first two values of the triple.

4.3   An Abstraction of Multi-pass Computation

Let us see why it is necessary to have this special skeleton accumulate rather than implementing it using existing skeletons, although it can be described in terms of the existing skeletons according to the diffusion theorem [HTI99].

Theorem 2 (Diffusion). The skeleton accumulate can be diffused into the following composition of skeletal functions.

$$
\begin{aligned}
\text{accumulate } x \; e = \; &\textbf{let} \; y \mathbin{+\!\!+} [e'] = \otimes \#_e (q * x)) \\
&\qquad z = x \Upsilon y \\
&\textbf{in} \; (\oplus / \, (p * z)) \oplus (g \; e')
\end{aligned}
$$
□

The resulting skeletal program after diffusion cannot be efficiently implemented just according to the parallel semantics of each skeleton. To see this, consider the simplest composition of two skeleton of $\oplus/(p * z)$ when computed on a distributed parallel machine. It would be performed by the following two passes.

1. Compute $p * z$ by distributing data z among processors, performing $p*$ in a parallel way, and collecting data from processors to form data w.

2. Compute $\oplus/w$ by <u>distributing data w among processors</u>, performing $\oplus/$ in a parallel way, and <u>collecting data from processors</u> to form the result.

The underlined two parts are obviously not necessary, but this multiple-pass computation would not be avoidable unless $(\oplus/) \circ (p*)$ can be fused into a single existing skeleton[1]. To resolve this problem, one must introduce a new skeleton to capture (abstract) this kind of multiple-pass program. Our skeleton accumulate is exactly designed for this abstraction, while it can be efficiently implemented without actual intermediate data distribution and collection.

4.4   Parallel Programming with accumulate

The skeleton accumulate uses an accumulating parameter which can be used to describe complicated dependency of computation in a natural way. In contrast, the existing skeletal parallel programming requires that all dependency must be explicitly specified by using intermediate data.

We have shown in Section 4.1 that computation function $los1$ can be easily described by accumulate. In fact, the new skeleton is so powerful and general that it can be used to describe the skeletons without sacrificing the performance in order, as summarized in the following theorem.

Theorem 3 (Skeletons in accumulate).

$$f * x = [\![\lambda\_ \to [\,], (\lambda(a, \_) \to [f\ a], +\!\!+\,), (\_, \_)]\!]\ x\ \_$$
$$\oplus/\ x = [\![\lambda\_ \to \iota_\oplus, (\lambda(a, \_) \to a, \oplus), (\_, \_)]\!]\ x\ \_$$
$$\oplus\#_e = [\![[\cdot], (\lambda(a, e) \to [e], +\!\!+\,), (id, \oplus)]\!]$$ □

Note that in the above theorem, $\_$ is used to represent a "don't care" value with consistent type.

Powerful and general, accumulate can be used to solve many problems in a rather straightforward way, that is *not* more difficult than solving the problems in sequential setting [HIT01]. Consider a simple example computing a polynomial value, a case study in [SG99] and an exercise in [Ble90]:

$$poly\ [a_1, a_2, \ldots, a_N]\ x\ =\ a_1 \times x + a_1 \times x^2 + \cdots + a_N \times x^N.$$

It can be easily defined by the following recursive definition with an accumulating parameter storing x^i.

$$poly\ as\ x = poly'\ as\ x$$
$$\textbf{where } poly'\ [\,]\ e = 0$$
$$poly'\ (a : as)\ e = a \times e + poly\ as\ (e \times x)$$

That is,

$$poly = [\![\lambda e \to 0, (\lambda(a, e) \to a \times e, +), (id, \times)]\!].$$

It follows from the Parallelization Theorem that we have obtained an $O(\log N)$ parallel time program for evaluating a polynomial.

---

[1] Note that we cannot fuse it into $\otimes/$ where $a \otimes r = p\ a \oplus r$, because $\otimes$ may not be associative.

5 Optimizing Skeletal Parallel Programs

To fuse several skeletons into one for eliminating unnecessary intermediate data structures passed between skeletons, one would try to develop rules for performing algebraic transformations on skeletal parallel program like [SG99]. For instance, here is a possible algebraic transformation which eliminates an intermediate list:

$$f * (g * x) = (f \circ g) * x.$$

Unfortunately, one would need a huge set of rules to account for all possible combinations of skeletal functions. In this paper, we borrow the idea of shortcut deforestation [GLJ93] for optimization of sequential programs, and reduce the entire set to a *single* rule, by standardizing the way in which *join* lists are consumed by accumulate and standardizing the way in which they are produced.

5.1 The Fusion Rule

First, we explain the shortcut deforestation theorem, known as foldr-build rule [GLJ93].

Lemma 1 (foldr-build Rule). If we have $gen : \forall \beta. (A \to \beta \to \beta) \to \beta \to \beta$ for some fixed A, then

$$\mathsf{foldr}\ (\oplus)\ e\ (\mathsf{build}\ gen) = gen\ (\oplus)\ e,$$

where foldr and build are defined by

$$
\begin{aligned}
\mathsf{foldr}\ (\oplus)\ e\ [] \quad &= e \\
\mathsf{foldr}\ (\oplus)\ e\ (a : x) &= a \oplus \mathsf{foldr}\ (\oplus)\ e\ x \\
\mathsf{build}\ gen \quad\quad\ &= gen\ (:)\ [].
\end{aligned}
$$
□

Noticing that accumulate can be described in terms of foldr as

$$\mathsf{accumulate}\ =\ \mathsf{foldr}\ (\lambda a \lambda r\ \to (\lambda e \to p(a,e) \oplus r(e \otimes q\ a)))\ g,$$

we obtain a rule for fusion of accumulate from Lemma 1:

$$[\![g, (p, \oplus), (q, \otimes)]\!]\ (\mathsf{build}\ gen) = gen\ (\lambda a \lambda r\ \to (\lambda e \to p(a,e) \oplus r(e \otimes q\ a)))\ g.$$

However, this rule has a practical problem for being used to fuse skeletal parallel programs. The reason is that skeletal functions produce *join* lists rather than cons lists, due to the requirement of associativity in their definitions. For example, for the definition of $f*$:

$$f * x = [\![\lambda_- \to [], (\lambda(a, \_) \to [f\ a], +\!\!+), (\_, \_)]\!]\ x\ \_$$

it would be more natural to consider $f*$ as a production of a join list using the constructors of $[]$, $[\cdot]$, and $+\!\!+$. To resolve this problem, we standardize the production of join lists by defining a new function buildJ as

$$\mathsf{buildJ}\ gen = gen\ (+\!\!+)\ [\cdot]\ [],$$

and accordingly standardize the list consumption by transforming $[\![g, (p, \oplus), (q, \otimes)]\!]$ based on the parallelization theorem to

$$
\begin{aligned}
[\![g, (p, \oplus), (q, \otimes)]\!]\ x &= \textit{fst} \circ \textsf{accumulate}' \\
\textsf{accumulate}'\ [] &= \lambda e \to (g\ e, \_, \_) \\
\textsf{accumulate}'\ [a] &= \lambda e \to (p\ (a, e) \oplus g\ (e \otimes q\ a), p\ (a, e), q\ a) \\
\textsf{accumulate}'\ (x +\!\!+ y) &= \textsf{accumulate}'\ x \odot_{\oplus, \otimes} \textsf{accumulate}'\ y
\end{aligned}
$$

where $\odot_{\oplus, \otimes}$ is defined by

$$
\begin{aligned}
(u \odot_{\oplus, \otimes} v)\ e = \textbf{let}\ &(r_1, s_1, t_1) = u\ e \\
&(r_2, s_2, t_2) = v\ (e \otimes t_1) \\
\textbf{in}\ &(s_1 \oplus r_2,\ s_1 \oplus s_2,\ t_1 \otimes t_2).
\end{aligned}
$$

Therefore, we obtain the following general and practical fusion theorem for accumulate.

Theorem 4 (Fusion (Join Lists)). If for some fixed A we have $gen : \forall \beta. (\beta \to \beta \to \beta) \to (A \to \beta) \to \beta \to \beta$ then

$$
\begin{aligned}
&[\![g, (p, \oplus), (q, \otimes)]\!]\ (\textsf{buildJ}\ gen)\ e \\
&= \textit{fst}\ (gen\ (\odot_{\oplus, \otimes})\ (\lambda a \to (\lambda e \to (p\ (a, e) \oplus g\ (e \otimes q\ a), p\ (a, e), q\ a))) \\
&\qquad\ (\lambda e \to (g\ e, \_, \_))\ e)
\end{aligned}
$$
$\square$

For the skeletons in the form of $[\![\lambda\_ \to e, (\lambda(a, \_) \to p'\ a, \oplus), (\_, \_)]\!]$, like *map* and *reduce*, which do not need a accumulating parameter, we can specialize Theorem 4 to the following corollary for fusion with these skeletons.

Corollary 1. If for some fixed A we have $gen : \forall \beta. (A \to \beta \to \beta) \to (A \to \beta) \to \beta \to \beta$ and then

$$
\begin{aligned}
&[\![\lambda\_ \to d, (\lambda(a, \_) \to p'a, \oplus), (\_, \_)]\!]\ (\textsf{buildJ}\ gen)\ \_ \\
&= gen\ (\oplus)\ (\lambda a \to p'\ a \oplus d)\ d
\end{aligned}
$$
$\square$

5.2 Warm Fusion

To apply Theorem 4 for fusion, we must standardize those skeletal parallel programs to be fused in terms of accumulate for consuming join lists and of buildJ for producing join lists. We may deal with this by the following two methods:

- *Standardizing library functions by hand.* We can standardize frequently used functions by hand. For example, the followings define *map* and *scan* in the required form.

$$
\begin{aligned}
f * x &= \textsf{buildJ}\ (\lambda c \lambda s \lambda n \to [\![\lambda\_ \to n, (\lambda(a, \_) \to s\ (f\ a), c), (\_, \_)]\!]\ x\ \_) \\
\oplus \#_e x &= \textsf{buildJ}\ (\lambda c \lambda s \lambda n \to [\![s, (\lambda(a, e) \to s\ e, c), (id, \oplus)]\!]\ x\ e)
\end{aligned}
$$

Following this idea, one may redefine their library functions such as *maximum* in this form, as done in sequential programming like [GLJ93] which rewrites most prelude functions of Haskell in the form of foldr-build form. This approach is rather practical [GLJ93], but needs preprocessing.

– *Standardizing* accumulate *automatically.* For a user-defined function in terms of accumulate, we may build a type inference system to automatically abstract the data constructors of join lists appearing in the program to derive its buildJ form. Many studies have been devoted to this approach on the context of sequential programming [LS95,Chi99], which may be adapted to our use.

Consider the function *alleven* defined by *alleven* $x = \wedge\,/\,(even * x)$, which judges whether all the elements of a list are even. We can perform fusion systematically (automatically) as follows. Note that this program cannot be fused in the existing framework.

$$\wedge\,/\,(even * x)$$
$$= \quad \{\text{ def. of } reduce \text{ and } map \,\}$$
$$[\![\lambda_- \rightarrow \mathsf{T}, (\lambda(a,\_) \rightarrow a, \wedge), (\_,\_)]\!]$$
$$\quad (\mathsf{buildJ}\ (\lambda c \lambda s \lambda n \rightarrow [\![\lambda_- \rightarrow n, (\lambda(a,\_) \rightarrow s\ (even\ a), c), (\_,\_)]\!]\ x\ \_)) \ _-$$
$$= \quad \{\text{ Corollary 1 }\}$$
$$[\![\lambda_- \rightarrow \mathsf{T}, (\lambda(a,\_) \rightarrow even\ a \wedge \mathsf{T}, \wedge), (\_,\_)]\!]\ x\ _-$$
$$= \quad \{\text{ simplification }\}$$
$$[\![\lambda_- \rightarrow \mathsf{T}, (\lambda(a,\_) \rightarrow even\ a, \wedge), (\_,\_)]\!]\ x\ _-$$

Theorem 4 can be applied to a wider class of skeletal parallel programs, including the useful program patterns such as (1) $(f_1*) \circ (f_2*) \circ \cdots \circ (f_n*)$, (2) $(\oplus\,/) \circ (f*)$, (3) $(\oplus\,/) \circ (\otimes \#_e)$, (4) $(f*) \circ (\oplus \#_e) \circ (g*)$, (5) $(\oplus_1 \#_{e_1}) \circ (\oplus_2 \#_{e_2})$. Recall the lines-of-sight problem in Section 3 where we obtain the following compositional program for Pass 2 (b) after expansion of *ass* and *as*:

$$mas = (maximum/) * ((+\!\!\!+\,) \#_{[]}\,([\cdot] * (angle * ps))).$$

We can fuse it into a single one [HIT01].

6   Dealing with Nested Skeletons

Our new skeleton accumulate can deal with nested data structures very well, especially *irregular* ones whose elements may have quite different sizes. To be concrete, given a list of lists, we are considering efficient implementation of a computation which maps some function f in terms of accumulate to every sublist.

In order to process a given nested (maybe irregular) list[2] efficiently, we first use *flatten* : $[[a]] \rightarrow [(Bool, a)]$ to transform the nested list into a flat list of pairs [Ble92]. Each element in this flat list is a pair of *flag*, a boolean value, and an element of inner list of the original nested list. If the element is the first of an inner list, *flag* is T, otherwise *flag* is F. For example, a nested list

$$[[x_1, x_2, x_3], [x_4, x_5], [x_6], [x_7, x_8]]$$

is flattened into the list

$$[(\mathsf{T}, x_1), (\mathsf{F}, x_2), (\mathsf{F}, x_3), (\mathsf{T}, x_4), (\mathsf{F}, x_5), (\mathsf{T}, x_6), (\mathsf{T}, x_7), (\mathsf{F}, x_8)].$$

---

[2] For simplicity, we assume that each element list is nonempty. Actually, it not difficult to introduce an additional tag to deal with empty list.

Using the flattened representation, each processor can be assigned almost the same number of data elements, and therefore, reasonable load balancing between processors can be achieved. For the above example, if there are four processors, they are assigned to $[(\mathsf{T}, x_1), (\mathsf{F}, x_2)]$, $[(\mathsf{F}, x_3), (\mathsf{T}, x_4)]$, $[(\mathsf{F}, x_5), (\mathsf{T}, x_6)]$, and $[(\mathsf{T}, x_7), (\mathsf{F}, x_8)]$, respectively. Note that elements of the same inner list may be divided and assigned to more than one processor.

Our theorem concerning nested lists states that mapping the function accumulate to every sublist can be turned into a form applying another accumulate to the flattened representation of the given nested list.

Theorem 5 (Flattening). If xs is a nested list which is not empty and does not include empty list, then

$$(\lambda\, x\ \rightarrow\ [\![g, (p, \oplus), (q, \otimes)]\!]\, x\ e_0)\ *\ xs$$
$$=\ v\ \text{where}\ (\_, v, \_)\ =\ [\![g', (p', \oplus'), (q', \otimes')]\!]\ (\text{flatten}\ xs)\ (\mathsf{T}, e_0)$$

    where

$$
\begin{aligned}
g'\,(z, a) &= (\mathsf{T}, [\,], a) \\
p'\,((\mathsf{T}, x), (z, a)) &= (\mathsf{T}, [p\,(x, e_0)], a) \\
p'\,((\mathsf{F}, x), (z, a)) &= (\mathsf{F}, [p\,(x, a)], a) \\
q'\,(\mathsf{T}, x) &= (\mathsf{T}, e_0 \otimes q\,x) \\
q'\,(\mathsf{F}, x) &= (\mathsf{F}, q\,x) \\
(z, vs \mathbin{+\!\!+} [v], a) \oplus' (\mathsf{T}, ws, b) &= (z, vs \mathbin{+\!\!+} [v \oplus g\,b] \mathbin{+\!\!+} ws, a) \\
(z, vs \mathbin{+\!\!+} [v], a) \oplus' (\mathsf{F}, [w] \mathbin{+\!\!+} ws, b) &= (z, vs \mathbin{+\!\!+} [v \oplus w] \mathbin{+\!\!+} ws, a) \\
(z, a) \otimes' (\mathsf{T}, b) &= (\mathsf{T}, b) \\
(z, a) \otimes' (\mathsf{F}, b) &= (z, a \otimes b)
\end{aligned}
$$

      □

Due to space limination, we cannot give a proof of the theorem. The key point of this theorem is that the transformed program is just a simple application of accumulate to the flattened list. It follows from the implementation of accumulate that we obtain an efficient implementation for the map of accumulate.

7   Related Work and Discussions

Our design of accumulate for parallel programming is related to the Third Homomorphism Theorem [Gib96], which says that if a problem can be solved in terms of both *foldl* (top down) and *foldr* (bottom up), then it can be solved in terms of a list homomorphism which can be implemented in parallel in a divide-and-conquer way. However, it remains open how to construct such list homomorphism from two solutions in terms of *foldl* and *foldr*. Rather than finding a way for this construction, we provide accumulate for parallel programming, and it can be regarded as an *integration* of both *foldl* and *foldr*.

Optimizing skeletal parallel programs is a challenge, and there have been several studies. A set of optimization rules, together with performance estimation, have been proposed in [SG99], which are used to guide fusion of several skeletons into one. This, however, would need a huge set of rules to account for all possible combinations of skeletal functions. In contrast, we reduce this set to a *single* rule (Fusion Theorem), by standardizing both the way in which *join* lists are consumed by accumulate and the way in which they are produced. This idea is related to the shortcut deforestation [GLJ93,LS95,Chi99] which has proved to be practically useful for optimization of sequential programs. Another approach is to refine the library functions to reveal their internal structure for optimization in a compiler [KC99]. We deal with this problem in programming instead of compiler reconstruction.

As for nested parallelism or the form $f*$, our work is related to that by Blelloch [Ble89,Ble92] who showed that if f is $\oplus \#_e$, than we know that $(\oplus \#_e)*$ can be implemented efficiently. Here we treat more complicated f including *scan* as its special case, showing that $(\lambda x.[\![g, (p, \oplus), (q, \otimes)]\!] \ x \ e_0)*$ can be efficiently implemented.

This work is a continuation of our effort to apply the so-called program calculation technique to the development of efficient parallel programs [HTC98]. As a matter of fact, our new skeleton accumulate comes out of the recursive pattern which is parallelizable in [HTC98,HTI99]. Based on these results, this paper made a significant progress towards practical use of skeletons for parallel programming, showing how to program with accumulate, how to systematically optimize skeletal programs, and how to deal with irregular data.

Although we have implemented a small prototype system basically for testing the idea in this paper, we believe that it should be more important to see how efficient the idea in a real parallelizing compiler. In addition, we have not taken account of those skeletons for data communication.

Acknowledgments

We thank the anonymous referees for their suggestions and comments.

References

[Bir87]   R. Bird. An introduction to the theory of lists. In M. Broy, editor, *Logic of Programming and Calculi of Discrete Design*, pages 5–42. Springer-Verlag, 1987.

[Ble89]   Guy E. Blelloch. Scans as primitive operations. *IEEE Trans. on Computers*, 38(11):1526–1538, November 1989.

[Ble90]   G. E. Blelloch. Prefix sums and their applications. Technical Report CMU-CS-90-190, Carnegie-Mellon Univ., 1990.

[Ble92]   G.E. Blelloch. NESL: a nested data parallel language. Technical Report CMU-CS-92-103, School of Computer Science, Carnegie-Mellon University, January 1992.

[Chi99]   O. Chitil. Type inference builds short cut to deforestation. In *Proceedings of 1999 ACM SIGPLAN International Conference on Functional Programming*, pages 249–260. ACM Press, 1999.

[Col95]   M. Cole. Parallel programming with list homomorphisms. *Parallel Processing Letters*, 5(2), 1995.

[Gib96]   J. Gibbons. The third homomorphism theorem. *Journal of Functional Programming*, 6(4):657–665, 1996.

[GLJ93]   A. Gill, J. Launchbury, and S. Peyton Jones. A short cut to deforestation. In *Proc. Conference on Functional Programming Languages and Computer Architecture*, pages 223–232, Copenhagen, June 1993.

[Gor96]   S. Gorlatch. Systematic efficient parallelization of scan and other list homomorphisms. In *Annual European Conference on Parallel Processing, LNCS 1124*, pages 401–408, LIP, ENS Lyon, France, August 1996. Springer-Verlag.

[HIT01]   Z. Hu, H. Iwasaki, and M. Takeichi. An accumulative parallel skeleton for all. Technical Report METR 01–05, University of Tokyo, September 2001. Available from `http://www.ipl.t.u-tokyo.ac.jp/ ~hu/pub/metr01-05.ps.gz`.

[HITT97]   Z. Hu, H. Iwasaki, M. Takeichi, and A. Takano. Tupling calculation eliminates multiple data traversals. In *ACM SIGPLAN International Conference on Functional Programming*, pages 164–175, Amsterdam, The Netherlands, June 1997. ACM Press.

[HS86]   W.D. Hills and Jr. G. L. Steele. Data parallel algorithms. *Communications of the ACM*, 29(12):1170–1183, 1986.

[HTC98]   Z. Hu, M. Takeichi, and W.N. Chin. Parallelization in calculational forms. In *25th ACM Symposium on Principles of Programming Languages*, pages 316–328, San Diego, California, USA, January 1998.

[HTI99]   Z. Hu, M. Takeichi, and H. Iwasaki. Diffusion: Calculating efficient parallel programs. In *1999 ACM SIGPLAN Workshop on Partial Evaluation and Semantics-Based Program Manipulation*, pages 85–94, San Antonio, Texas, January 1999. BRICS Notes Series NS-99-1.

[JH99]   S. Peyton Jones and J. Hughes, editors. *Haskell 98: A Non-strict, Purely Functional Language*. Available online: `http://www.haskell.org`, February 1999.

[KC99]   G. Keller and M. M. T. Chakravarty. On the distributed implementation of aggregate data structures by program transformation. In J. Rolim et al., editor, *4th International Workshop on High-Level Parallel Programming Models and Supportive Environments* (LNCS 1586), pages 108–122, Berlin, Germany, 1999. Springer-Verlag.

[LS95]   J. Launchbury and T. Sheard. Warm fusion: Deriving build-catas from recursive definitions. In *Proc. Conference on Functional Programming Languages and Computer Architecture*, pages 314–323, La Jolla, California, June 1995.

[SG99]   Christian Lengauer Sergei Gorlatch, Christoph Wedler. Optimization rules for programming with collective operations. In Mikhail Atallah, editor, *IPPS/SPDP'99. 13th Int. Parallel Processing Symp. & 10th Symp. on Parallel and Distributed Processing*, pages 492–499, 1999.

[Ski90]   D.B. Skillicorn. Architecture-independent parallel computation. *IEEE Computer*, 23(12):38–51, December 1990.

Higher-Order Intensional Type Analysis

Stephanie Weirich

Department of Computer Science, Cornell University
Ithaca, NY 14850, USA
sweirich@cs.cornell.edu

Abstract. Intensional type analysis provides the ability to analyze abstracted types at run time. In this paper, we extend that ability to higher-order and kind-polymorphic type constructors. The resulting language is elegant and expressive. We show through examples how it extends the repertoire of polytypic definitions and the domain of valid types for those definitions.

1 Polytypic Programming

Some functions are naturally defined by examining the type structure of their arguments. For example, a *polytypic* pretty printer can format any data structure by decomposing it into basic parts, guided by its argument's type. Without such analysis, one must write a separate pretty printer for every data type and constantly update each one as the data types evolve. Polytypic programming, on the other hand, simplifies the maintenance of software by allowing functions to automatically adapt to changes in the representation of data. Other classic examples of polytypic operations include debuggers, comparison functions and mapping functions. The theory behind describing such operations has been developed in a variety of frameworks [1, 2, 4, 8, 12, 14, 17, 18, 27, 28, 30, 31].

Nevertheless, no single existing framework encompasses all polytypic definitions. These systems are limited by what polytypic operations they may express and by what types they may examine. These deficiencies are unfortunate because advanced languages depend crucially on these features. Only some frameworks for polytypism may express operations over parameterized data structures, such as maps and folds [14, 17, 18, 27]. Yet parametric polymorphism is essential to modern typed programming languages. It is intrinsic to functional programming languages, such as ML [21] and Haskell [24], and also extremely important to imperative languages such as Ada [16] and Java [3, 11]. Furthermore, only some frameworks for polytypism may examine types with binding structure, such as polymorphic or existential types [2, 4, 30]. However, these types are becoming increasingly more important. Current implementations of the Haskell language [19, 29] include a form of existential type and first class polymorphism. Existential types are particularly useful for implementing dynamically extensible systems that may be augmented at run time with new operations and new types of data [13]. Also, the extension of polytypic programming to an object-oriented language will require the ability to examine types with binding structure.

D. Le Métayer (Ed.): ESOP 2002, LNCS 2305, pp. 98–114, 2002.

What is necessary to accommodate all types and all operations? First, because a quantified type hides type information, the semantics of the language must provide that information at run time to examine polymorphic and existential types. Second, the class of polytypic operations including mapping functions, reductions, zipping functions and folds must be defined in terms of *higher-order type constructors* instead of types. Such type constructors are "functions" such as *list* or *tree*, that are parameterized by other types.[1]

There is no reason why one system should not be able to define polytypic operations over both type constructors and quantified types. In fact, the two abilities are complementary if we represent quantified types with type constructors, using higher-order abstract syntax [25, 30]. For example, we may represent the type $\forall \alpha. \alpha \rightarrow \alpha$ as the constant $\forall_\star$ applied to the type function $(\lambda \alpha{:}\star. \alpha \rightarrow \alpha)$.

In this paper, we address the previous limitations of polytypic programming and demonstrate how well these abilities fit together by extending Harper and Morrisett's seminal type-passing framework of *intensional type analysis* [12] to higher-order polytypism. In their language λ_i^{ML}, polytypic operations are defined by run-time examination of the structure of first-order types with the special term *typerec*. In λ_i^{ML}, an analyzable type is either *int*, *string*, a product type composed of two other types, or a function type composed of two other types. As these simple type constructors form an inductive datatype, *typerec* defines a fold (or catamorphism) over its type argument. For example, the result of analyzing types such as $\tau_1 \times \tau_2$ is defined in terms of analyses of τ_1 and τ_2. With the inclusion of type constructors that take a higher-order argument (such as $\forall_\star$ with argument of kind $\star \rightarrow \star$) the type structure of the language is no longer inductive. Previously, Trifonov *et al.* [30] avoided this issue by using the kind-polymorphic type constructor $\forall$ of kind $\forall \chi.(\chi \rightarrow \star) \rightarrow \star$ instead of $\forall_\star$ to represent kind-polymorphic types. As the argument of $\forall$ does not have a negative occurrence of the kind $\star$, the type structure remains inductive.

Hinze [14] has observed that we may define polytypic operations over type constructors by viewing a polytypic definition as an *interpretation* of the entire type constructor language, instead of a fold over the portion of kind type. However, his framework is based on compile-time definitions of polytypic functions (as opposed to run-time type analysis) and so cannot instantiate these functions with polymorphic or existential types. Here, we use this idea to extend Harper and Morrisett's *typerec* to a run-time interpreter for the type language, and extend it to higher-order type constructors and quantified types.

In the rest of this section, we review λ_i^{ML} and Hinze's framework for polytypic programming. In Section 2 we extend *typerec* to constructors of function kind. Because a polytypic definition is a model of the type language, it inhabits a unary *logical relation* indexed by the kind of the argument type constructor. A simple generalization in Section 3 extends this *typerec* to inhabit multi-place logical relations. Furthermore, in Section 4 we generalize *typerec* to constructors

---

[1] Just as terms are described by types, type constructors are described by kinds κ. The kind $\star$ contains all types. Higher-order constructors (functions from kind κ_1 to kind κ_2) have kind $\kappa_1 \rightarrow \kappa_2$.

of polymorphic kind. This extension admits the analysis of the $\forall$ constructor and encompasses as a special case the previous approach of Trifonov *et al.* [30]. Also, incorporating kind polymorphism enables further code sharing; without it, polytypic definitions must be duplicated for each kind of type argument. Finally, in Sections 5 and 6 we compare our approach with other systems and conclude with ideas for future extension.

1.1 Intensional Type Analysis

Harper and Morrisett's language λ_i^{ML} [12] introduced intensional type analysis with the *typerec* term. For example, *typetostring* (of type $\forall \alpha\colon \star . string$) uses *typerec* to produce a string representation of any type.[2]

$$typetostring = \Lambda\alpha\colon \star.\ typerec[\lambda\beta\colon \star.\ string]\ \alpha$$
$$int \quad \Rightarrow \texttt{"int"}$$
$$string \Rightarrow \texttt{"string"}$$
$$\to \quad \Rightarrow \Lambda\beta\colon \star.\lambda x\colon string\,.\Lambda\gamma\colon \star.\lambda y\colon string\,.\texttt{"("}\ \texttt{++}\ x\ \texttt{++}\ \texttt{" -> "}\ \texttt{++}\ y\ \texttt{++}\ \texttt{")"}$$
$$\times \quad \Rightarrow \Lambda\beta\colon \star.\lambda x\colon string\,.\Lambda\gamma\colon \star.\lambda y\colon string\,.\texttt{"("}\ \texttt{++}\ x\ \texttt{++}\ \texttt{" * "}\ \texttt{++}\ y\ \texttt{++}\ \texttt{")"}$$

The annotation $[\lambda\beta\colon \star.\ string]$ on *typerec* above is used for type-checking. If α, the argument to *typerec*, is instantiated with the type *int* or *string*, this term immediately returns the appropriate string. If α is a product or function type (in the $\times$ and $\to$ branches), *typerec* inductively calls itself to provide the strings of the subcomponents of the type. In these branches, the type variables β and γ are bound to the subcomponent types, and the term variables x and y are bound to the inductively computed strings. The rules below show the operation of *typerec* over various arguments, providing the inductively computed results to the product and function branches.

$$typerec[c]\ int\ \bar{e} \mapsto e_{int}$$
$$typerec[c]\ string\ \bar{e} \mapsto e_{string}$$
$$typerec[c]\ (c_1 \times c_2)\ \bar{e} \mapsto e_\times\ [c_1]\ (typerec[c]\ c_1\ \bar{e})\ [c_2]\ (typerec[c]\ c_2\ \bar{e})$$
$$typerec[c]\ (c_1 \to c_2)\ \bar{e} \mapsto e_\to\ [c_1]\ (typerec[c]\ c_1\ \bar{e})\ [c_2]\ (typerec[c]\ c_2\ \bar{e})$$

The symbol $\bar{e}$ abbreviates the branches of the *typerec* ($int \Rightarrow e_{int}, string \Rightarrow e_{string}, \to \Rightarrow e_\to, \times \Rightarrow e_\times$). In this paper we will be deliberately vague about what type constructors comprise these branches and add new branches as necessary.

What is the return type of a *typerec* term? The typing judgment below reflects that this term is an induction over the structure of the analyzed type, c'. The annotation c applied to the argument type c' forms the return type of the *typerec* expression. For example, in *typetostring* above, the result type is $(\lambda\beta\colon \star.\ string)\alpha$ or *string*. In each branch, c' is specialized. For example, the *int* branch is of type $c\ int$, while the product branch takes two arguments of type $c\ \alpha$ and $c\ \beta$ to an expression of type $c(\alpha \times \beta)$. The context Γ contains assumptions about the types and kinds of the free type and term variables found inside c, c' and $\bar{e}$.

$$\frac{\Gamma \vdash c'\colon \star \quad \Gamma \vdash c\colon \star \to \star \quad \Gamma \vdash e_{int}\colon c\ int \quad \Gamma \vdash e_{string}\colon c\ string \\ \Gamma \vdash e_\to\ \colon \forall \alpha\colon \star.c\ \alpha \to \forall\beta\colon \star.c\ \beta \to c(\alpha \to \beta) \\ \Gamma \vdash e_\times\ \colon \forall \alpha\colon \star.c\ \alpha \to \forall\beta\colon \star.c\ \beta \to c(\alpha \times \beta)}{\Gamma \vdash typerec[c]\ c'\ \bar{e}\colon c\ c'}$$

---

[2] We use $\texttt{++}$ as an infix function for string concatenation.

$$size\langle\alpha\rangle\eta = \eta(\alpha)$$
$$size\langle\lambda\alpha{:}\kappa.c\rangle\eta = \Lambda\alpha{:}\kappa.\lambda x{:}Size\langle\kappa\rangle\alpha.(size\langle c\rangle\eta\{\alpha\mapsto x\})$$
$$size\langle c_1 c_2\rangle\eta = (size\langle c_1\rangle\eta)\;[c_2]\;(size\langle c_2\rangle\eta)$$
$$size\langle int\rangle\eta = \lambda x{:}\,int\,.0$$
$$size\langle string\rangle\eta = \lambda x{:}\,string\,.0$$
$$size\langle\times\rangle\eta = \Lambda\alpha{:}\star.\lambda x{:}(\alpha\to int).\Lambda\beta{:}\star.\lambda y{:}(\beta\to int).\lambda v:\alpha\times\beta.x(\pi_1 v)+y(\pi_2 v)$$
$$size\langle+\rangle\eta = \Lambda\alpha{:}\star.\lambda x{:}(\alpha\to int).\Lambda\beta{:}\star.\lambda y{:}(\beta\to int).$$
$$\lambda v:\alpha+\beta.\;case\;v(inj_1\,w\Rightarrow xw\mid inj_2\,w\Rightarrow yw)$$

Fig. 1. *size*

However, *typerec* may not express all polytypic definitions. For example, we cannot use it to define a term of type $\forall\alpha{:}\star\to\star.\forall\beta{:}\star.\alpha\;\beta\to int$, that counts the number of values of type β in a data structure of type $\alpha\;\beta$. Call this operation *fsize*. For example, if $c_1 = \lambda\alpha{:}\star.\alpha\times int$ and $c_2 = \lambda\alpha{:}\star.\alpha\times\alpha$, then *fsize*$[c_1]$ and *fsize*$[c_2]$ are constant functions returning 1 and 2 respectively. If α is instantiated with *list*, *fsize*$[list]$ is the standard length function.

As α is of higher-kind, we must apply it to some type in order to analyze it. We might try to define *fsize* as

$$fsize = \Lambda\alpha{:}\star\to\star.\Lambda\beta{:}\star.\;typerec[\lambda\gamma.\gamma\to int](\alpha\;\beta)\dots$$

However, this approach is not correct. At run time, β will be instantiated before *typerec* analyzes $(\alpha\;\beta)$. The value returned by *typerec* will depend on what β is replaced with. If β is instantiated by *int*, then $c_1\beta$ and $c_2\beta$ will be the same type, and analysis cannot produce different results. Therefore, to define *fsize* we must analyze α independently of β.

1.2 Higher-Order Polytypism

How should we extend *typerec* to higher-order type constructors? What should the return type of such an analysis be? Hinze [14] observed that a polytypic definition should be an *interpretation* of the type language with elements of the term language. This interpretation must sound — *i.e.* when two types are equal, their interpretations are equal — so that we can reason about the behavior of a polytypic definition. A sound interpretation of higher-order types is to interpret type functions as term functions and type application as term application. Then β-equality between types $(i.e.(\lambda\alpha{:}\kappa.c_1)c_2 = c_2\{c_1/\alpha\})$ will be preserved by β-equality in the term language. The constants of the type language $(int, string, \to, \times)$ may be mapped to any term (of an appropriate type) providing the flexibility to define a number of different polytypic operations.

For example, the definition of the polytypic operation *size* is in Figure 1. This operation is defined by induction over a type constructors c. It is also parameterized by a finite map η (an environment) mapping type variables to terms. We use $\emptyset$ as the empty map, extend a map with a new mapping from the type variable α to the term e with the notation $\eta\{\alpha\mapsto e\}$, and retrieve the mapping for a type variable with $\eta(\alpha)$. All variables in the argument of *size* should be in the domain of η. The first three lines of the definition in this figure are common to polytypic definitions. The definition for variables is determined by retrieving the mapping of the variable from environment. The environment is extended in the definition of *size* for type functions ($\lambda\alpha{:}\kappa.c$). As a type function is of higher kind, it is defined to be a polymorphic function from the *size* of the type argument, to the *size* of the body of the type constructor, with the environment updated to provide a mapping for the type variable occurring in the body. The type of x is determined by the kind of α and is explained in the following. Because a type function maps to a polymorphic term function, a type application produces a term application.

The last four cases determine the behavior of *size*. Intuitively, *size* produces an iterator over a data structure that adds the "sizes" of all of its parts. We would like to use this operation in the definition of *fsize* as follows. Because *list* is a type constructor, the specialization $size\langle list \rangle$ maps a function to compute the "size" of values of some type β, to a function to compute the "size" of the entire list of type $list\ \beta$. If we supply the constant function $\lambda x{:}\beta.1$ for the list elements, we produce the desired length function for lists. Therefore, we may define *fsize* specialized by any closed type constructor c as $\Lambda\beta{:}{\star}.size\langle c \rangle[\beta](\lambda x{:}\beta.1)$.[3] For base types, such as *int* or *string*, *size* produces the constant function $\lambda x.0$, because they should not be included in computing the size. The type constructors $+$ and $\times$ are both parameterized by the two subcomponents of the $+$ or $\times$ types (α and β) and functions to compute their sizes (x and y).

For example, we can use many of the above definitions to compute $size\langle \lambda\alpha.\alpha \times string \rangle$. The slightly simplified result, when all of the definitions have been applied, is below. It is a function that when given an argument to compute the size of terms of type α, should accept a pair and apply this argument to the first component of the pair. (As the second component of the pair is of type *string*, its *size* is 0).

$$size\langle \lambda\alpha.\alpha \times string \rangle = \Lambda\alpha{:}\star.\lambda w{:}(\alpha \rightarrow int).\lambda v{:}(\alpha \times string).w(\pi_1 v) + 0$$

Because type functions are mapped to term functions, the *type* of the polytypic definition (such as *size*) will be determined by the *kind* of the type constructor analyzed. In each instance, the definition of $size\langle c \rangle$ will be of type $Size\langle \kappa \rangle c$ where κ is the kind of c and $Size\langle \kappa \rangle c$ is defined by induction on the structure of κ. If the constructor c is of kind $\star$, then $Size\langle \star \rangle c$, is a function type from c to *int*. Otherwise, if c is of higher kind then *size* is parameterized by a corresponding *size* argument for the type argument to c.

$$Size\langle \star \rangle c = c \rightarrow int$$
$$Size\langle \kappa_1 \rightarrow \kappa_2 \rangle c = \forall\alpha{:}\kappa_1.Size\langle \kappa_1 \rangle\alpha \rightarrow Size\langle \kappa_2 \rangle(c\alpha)$$

Why does the definition of *size* make sense? Though *size* is determined by the syntax of a type, a type is actually an equivalence class of syntactic expressions. To be well-defined, a polytypic function must return equivalent terms for

---

[3] Unlike λ_i^{ML} where types are analyzed at run time, in this framework polytypic functions are created and specialized to their type arguments at compile-time, so we may not make $fsize\langle c \rangle$ polymorphic over c.

all equivalent types, no matter how the types are expressed. For example, $size$ instantiated with $(\lambda\alpha{:}\star.\alpha \times string)\,int$ must be equal to $size\,\langle int \times string \rangle$ because these two types are equal by β-equality. Because the term functions provide the necessary equational properties, the definition of $size$ is sound. Therefore, though the interpretations of the type operators $(int, \rightarrow, \times)$ may change for each polytypic operation, the interpretations of functions $(\lambda\alpha{:}\kappa.c)$, variables α, and applications $(c_1 c_2)$ remain constant in every polytypic definition. As a result, the types of polytypic operations can be expressed using the following notation.

Definition 1. *A polykinded type, written $c\langle\kappa\rangle c'$, where c is a type constructor of kind $\star \rightarrow \star$, and c' a type constructor of kind κ, is defined by induction on the structure of the kind κ by:*

$$c\langle\star\rangle c' = cc' \qquad c\langle\kappa_1 \rightarrow \kappa_2\rangle c' = \forall\alpha{:}\kappa_1.c\langle\kappa_1\rangle\alpha \rightarrow c\langle\kappa_2\rangle(c'\alpha)$$

For example, we express $Size\langle\kappa\rangle c$ in this notation as $(\lambda\alpha{:}\star.\alpha \rightarrow int)\langle\kappa\rangle c$.

2   The Semantics of Higher-Order *typerec*

Hinze's framework specifies how to define a polytypic function at compile time by translating closed types into terms. However, in some cases, such as in the presence of polymorphic recursion, first-class polymorphism, or separate compilation it is not possible to specialize all type abstractions at compile time. Therefore, we extend a language supporting run-time type analysis to polytypic definitions over higher-order type constructors. We do so by changing the behavior of λ_i^{ML}'s *typerec* to be an *interpreter* of the type language at run time.

There is a close correspondence between the polykinded types and the typing judgment for *typerec*. Each of the branches of *typerec* may be written as a polykinded type. For example, the branch $e_\times$ is of type $c\langle\star \rightarrow \star \rightarrow \star\rangle\times = \forall\alpha{:}\star.c\alpha \rightarrow \forall\beta{:}\star.c\beta \rightarrow c(\alpha \times \beta)$. Carrying the analogy further suggests that we may extend *typerec* to all type constructors by relaxing the restriction that the argument to *typerec* be of kind $\star$, and by using a polykinded type to describe the result of *typerec*. We use $\oplus$ to notate arbitrary type constructor constants (such as $int, \rightarrow, \times$, called operators) and assume each $\oplus$ is of kind $\kappa_\oplus$.

$$\frac{\Gamma \vdash c' : \kappa \qquad \Gamma \vdash c : \star \rightarrow \star \qquad \Gamma \vdash e_\oplus : c\langle\kappa_\oplus\rangle\,\oplus \qquad (\forall e_\oplus \in \bar{e})}{\Gamma \vdash typerec[c]\,c'\bar{e} : \boxed{c\langle\kappa\rangle c'}}$$

Unfortunately, this judgment is not complete. As in the definition of $size\langle c\rangle\eta$, the operational semantics for higher-order *typerec* must involve some sort of environment η and the typing judgment must describe that environment.

In the following, we introduce higher-order *typerec* and describe how to typecheck a *typerec* term. We conclude this section with a number of examples demonstrating *typerec* extended to type constructors with binding constructs. To make these examples concrete, we change the semantics of the *typerec* term of λ_i^{ML}. The syntax of this language appears in Figure 2; we refer the reader to other sources [12, 23] for the semantics not involved with *typerec*. Type constructors

---

$(kinds)$ $\kappa ::= \star \mid \kappa_1 \to \kappa_2$ $(op's)$ $\oplus ::= int \mid \to \mid \times \mid + \mid \ldots$
$(con's)$ $c ::= \alpha \mid \lambda\alpha{:}\kappa.c \mid c_1 c_2 \mid \oplus$ $(types)$ $\sigma ::= T(c) \mid int \mid \sigma \to \sigma \mid \forall\alpha{:}\kappa.\sigma \mid \ldots$
$(exp's)$ $e ::= i \mid x \mid \lambda x{:}\sigma.e \mid e_1 e_2 \mid fix\ x{:}\sigma.e \mid \Lambda\alpha{:}\kappa.e \mid e[c] \mid typerec[c][\Gamma,\eta,\rho]\ c\ \ \bar{e} \mid \ldots$

Fig. 2. Syntax

---

and types are separate syntactic classes in this language, with an injection $T(c)$ between the type constructors of kind $\star$ and the types. Consequently, we must slightly modify the definition of the base case of a polykinded type so that it produces a type instead of a type constructor: $c\langle\star\rangle c' = T(cc')$.

We define the operational semantics for higher-order *typerec* by structural induction on its type constructor argument.

$typerec[c][\Gamma',\eta,\rho]\ \alpha\ \ \bar{e} \mapsto \eta(\alpha)$
$typerec[c][\Gamma',\eta,\rho]\ (c_1 c_2)\ \ \bar{e} \mapsto (typerec[c][\Gamma',\eta,\rho]\ c_1\ \ \bar{e})[\rho(c_2)](typerec[c][\Gamma',\eta,\rho]\ c_2\ \ \bar{e})$
$typerec[c][\Gamma',\eta,\rho]\ (\lambda\alpha{:}\kappa.c)\ \ \bar{e} \mapsto$
$\quad \Lambda\beta{:}\kappa.\lambda x{:}c\langle\kappa\rangle\beta.\ typerec[c][\Gamma'\{\alpha \mapsto \kappa\},\eta\{\alpha \mapsto x\},\rho\{\alpha \mapsto \beta\}]\ c\ \ \bar{e}$
$typerec[c][\Gamma',\eta,\rho]\ \oplus\ \bar{e} \mapsto e_\oplus$

The environment component η of *typerec* interprets the free type variables in its argument. For type checking (see below) the context Γ' lists the kinds of these variables. When analysis reaches a variable, *typerec* uses η to provide the appropriate value. For the analysis of type application $c_1 c_2$, *typerec* applies the analyzed constructor function c_1 to the analyzed argument c_2. In this rule, we must be careful that the free type variables in c_2 do not escape their scope, so we replace all of the free type variables occurring in c_2. For this substitution, we add an additional environment ρ mapping type variables to types. We substitute of all free variables of c_2 in the domain of ρ with $\rho(c_2)$. When the argument to *typerec* is a type constructor abstraction, the context and the term and type environments are extended. For operators, *typerec* returns the appropriate branch.

A reassuring property of this *typerec* is that it derives the original operational rules. For example, λ_i^{ML}'s *typerec* has the following evaluation for product types:

$$typerec[c]\ (c_1 \times c_2)\ \ \bar{e} \mapsto e_\times[c_1]\ (typerec[c]\ c_1\ \ \bar{e})\ [c_2]\ (typerec[c]\ c_2\ \ \bar{e})$$

With higher-order type analysis, because $c_1 \times c_2$ is the operator $\times$ applied to c_1 and c_2, the rule for type-constructor application generates the same behavior.

To typecheck a *typerec* term the context Γ' below describes the kinds of the variables in the domain of η and ρ. To check that Γ',η and ρ are well-formed, we formulate a new judgment $\Gamma; c \vdash \Gamma' \mid \eta \mid \rho$. This judgment is derived from two inference rules. The first rule states that the empty context and the empty environments are always valid.

$$\frac{}{\Gamma; c \vdash \emptyset \mid \emptyset \mid \emptyset} \qquad \frac{\Gamma; c \vdash \Gamma' \mid \eta \mid \rho \quad \Gamma \vdash c' : \kappa \quad \Gamma \vdash e : c\langle\kappa\rangle c' \quad \alpha \notin Dom(\Gamma,\Gamma')}{\Gamma; c \vdash \Gamma'\{\alpha \mapsto \kappa\} \mid \eta\{\alpha \mapsto e\} \mid \rho\{\alpha \mapsto c'\}}$$

In the second rule, if we add a new type variable α of kind κ to Γ', its mapping in ρ must be to a type constructor c' also of kind κ, and its mapping in η must be to a term with type indexed by κ. Note that as we add to Γ' only type variables that are not in Γ, the domains of Γ and Γ' must be disjoint. With this judgment, we can state the formation rule for *typerec*.

$$\frac{\Gamma \vdash c : \star \to \star \quad \Gamma; c \vdash \Gamma' \mid \eta \mid \rho \quad \Gamma, \Gamma' \vdash c' : \kappa' \quad \Gamma \vdash e_\oplus : c\langle \kappa_\oplus \rangle \oplus \quad (\forall e_\oplus \in \bar{e})}{\Gamma \vdash typerec[c][\Gamma', \eta, \rho] \, c' \, \bar{e} : c\langle \kappa' \rangle (\rho(c'))}$$

This rule and the rules for the dynamic semantics are appropriate because they satisfy type preservation. Looking at the four operational rules for *typerec*, we can see that no matter which one applies, if the original term was well-typed then the resulting term also has the same type. Furthermore, a closed, well-typed *typerec* term is never stuck; for any type constructor argument, one of the four operational rules must apply. These two properties may be used to syntactically prove type safety for this language [32].

We may implement *size* with higher-order *typerec* below (when Γ', η and ρ are empty, we elide them):

$$
\begin{aligned}
size &= \Lambda\alpha{:}\star \to \star.\, typerec[\lambda\beta{:}\star.\beta \to int] \; \alpha \\
int &\Rightarrow \lambda y{:}\, int\, .0 \\
string &\Rightarrow \lambda y{:}\, string\, .0 \\
\times &\Rightarrow \Lambda\beta{:}\star.\lambda x{:}\beta \to int\,.\Lambda\gamma{:}\star.\lambda y{:}\gamma \to int\,.\lambda v{:}\beta \times \gamma.\; x(\pi_1 v) + y(\pi_2 v) \\
+ &\Rightarrow \Lambda\beta{:}\star.\lambda x{:}\beta \to int\,.\Lambda\gamma{:}\star.\lambda y{:}\gamma \to int\,. \\
&\quad\; \lambda v{:}\beta + \gamma.\; case \; v \; (inj_1 \, z \Rightarrow x(z) \mid inj_2 \, z \Rightarrow y(z))
\end{aligned}
$$

This example demonstrates a few deficiencies of the calculus presented so far. First, what about recursive types? We cannot compute *size* for lists and trees without them. What about polymorphic or existential types? Must we limit *size* to constructors of kind $\star \to \star$, even though *typerec* can operate over constructors of any kind? We address these limitations in the rest of the paper.

2.1 Recursive Types

We have two choices to add recursive types to our system. Both versions are created with the type constructor $\mu_\star$ (of kind $(\star \to \star) \to \star$). In the first case, an *equi-recursive* type is definitionally equivalent to its unrolling, *i.e.* $\mu_\star c = c(\mu_\star c)$. Therefore, we must make analysis of $(\mu_\star c)$ equal to that of $(c(\mu_\star c))$. We do so with an evaluation rule for *typerec* that takes the fixed point of its argument as the interpretation of a recursive type[4]

$$typerec[c][\Gamma, \eta, \rho] \, \mu_\star \, \bar{e} \; \mapsto \; \Lambda\alpha{:}\star \to \star.\lambda x{:}(c\langle \star \to \star \rangle \alpha).\, fix \; f{:}(c\langle \star \rangle \mu_\star \alpha).\; (x[\mu_\star \alpha] f)$$

The alternative is to include *iso-recursive* types: those that require explicit term coercions. In other words, there is no equational rule for $\mu_\star$, but the calculus includes two terms that witness the isomorphism.

$$roll_{\mu_\star c} : c(\mu_\star c) \to \mu_\star c \qquad unroll : \mu_\star c \to c(\mu_\star c)$$

---

[4] In a call-by-value calculus this rule is ill-typed because we are taking the fixed point of an expression that is not necessarily of function type. To support this rule in such a calculus we would require that c return a function type for any argument.

With iso-recursive types, we have the most flexibility in the definition of poly-typic functions. Without an equivalence rule governing $\mu_\star$, we are free to interpret it in any manner, as long as its branch in *typerec* has the correct type determined by the kind of $\mu_\star$. For a given c, this type is

$$c\langle(\star \rightarrow \star) \rightarrow \star\rangle\mu_\star = \forall\alpha{:}\star \rightarrow \star.[\forall\beta{:}\star.T(c\beta) \rightarrow T(c(\alpha\beta))] \rightarrow T(c(\mu_\star\alpha))$$

In most polytypic terms, the *typerec* branch for iso-recursive $\mu_\star$ will match the evaluation rule for equi-recursive $\mu_\star$.[5] For example, the $\mu_\star$ branch for *size* is below. The difference between it and the rule for equi-recursive types is an η-expansion around $x[\mu_\star\alpha]f$ that allows the explicit *unroll* coercion.

$$\mu_\star \Rightarrow \Lambda\alpha{:}\star \rightarrow \star.\lambda x{:}(\forall\beta{:}\star.T(\beta \rightarrow int) \rightarrow T(\alpha\beta \rightarrow int)).$$
$$\textit{fix } f{:}T(\mu_\star\alpha \rightarrow int).\lambda y{:}T(\mu_\star\alpha).\ x\ [\mu_\star\alpha]\ f\ (\textit{unroll } y)$$

In this branch, α is the body of the recursive type, and x is the result of *typerec* over that body. The definition of *size* for a recursive type should be a recursive function that accepts an argument y of recursive type, unrolls it to type $T(\alpha(\mu_\star\alpha))$, and calls x to produce *size* for this object. The call to x needs an argument that computes the size of $\mu_\star\alpha$. This argument is the result we are computing in the first place. Therefore, we use *fix* to name this result f and supply it to x.

2.2   F2 Polymorphism

The type constructor constants $\forall_\star$ and $\exists_\star$ (of kind $(\star \rightarrow \star) \rightarrow \star$) use higher-order abstract syntax [25] to describe polymorphic and existential[6] types of F2 [10, 26, 22]. These types are a subset of the polymorphic and existential types of λ_i^{ML}— they may only abstract constructors of kind $\star$ instead of any kind. The relationship between these type constructors and the corresponding types are:

$$T(\forall_\star c) = \forall\alpha{:}\star.T(c\alpha) \qquad T(\exists_\star c) = \exists\alpha{:}\star.T(c\alpha)$$

We can extend *size* with a branch for $\exists_\star$. For this branch, we must provide a function to calculate the size of the hidden type. We use the constant function zero, as that is result of *size* for types.

$$\exists_\star \Rightarrow \Lambda\alpha{:}\star \rightarrow \star.\lambda r{:}(\forall\beta{:}\star.T(\beta \rightarrow int) \rightarrow T(\alpha\beta \rightarrow int)).$$
$$\lambda x{:}T(\exists\alpha).\ \textit{let}\langle\beta, y\rangle = \textit{unpack } x \textit{ in } r\ [\beta]\ (\lambda x{:}\beta.0)\ y$$

With *size* we were fortunate that we could compute the value of *size* for the hidden type of an existential without analyzing it, as it was a constant function. However, for many polytypic functions, the function we pass to operate on the hidden type may itself be polytypic. Often it is the polytypic function

---

[5] In Section 3 we discuss a example that does not.

[6] We create an object of existential type $(\exists\alpha{:}\kappa.\sigma)$ with the term *pack*$\langle c, e\rangle$ *as* $\exists\alpha{:}\kappa.\sigma$ (where e has type $\sigma\{c/\alpha\}$) and destruct the existentially typed e_1 with the term *let*$\langle\beta, x\rangle = $ *unpack* e_1 *in* e_2 which binds β and x to the hidden type and term of e_1 within e_2.

$$\boxed{\Gamma \vdash e : \sigma}$$

$$\frac{\begin{array}{c} \Gamma; c \vdash \Gamma' \mid \eta \mid \rho_1 \mid \ldots \mid \rho_n \\ \Gamma, \Gamma' \vdash c' : \kappa \qquad \Gamma \vdash c : \star^n \to \star \\ \Gamma \vdash e_\oplus : c\langle \kappa_\oplus \rangle^n \oplus \ldots \oplus \qquad (\forall e_\oplus \in \bar{e}) \end{array}}{\Gamma \vdash typerec^n[c][\Gamma', \eta, \rho_1 \ldots \rho_n]\ c'\ \bar{e} : c\langle \kappa \rangle^n \rho_1(c') \ldots \rho_n(c')}$$

$$\boxed{e \mapsto e'}$$

$$typerec^n[c][\Gamma', \eta, \rho_1, \ldots, \rho_n]\ \oplus\ \bar{e} \mapsto \eta_\oplus$$

$$typerec^n[c][\Gamma', \eta, \rho_1, \ldots, \rho_n]\ \alpha\ \bar{e} \mapsto \eta(\alpha)$$

$$typerec^n[c][\Gamma', \eta, \rho_1, \ldots, \rho_n]\ (c_1 c_2)\ \bar{e} \mapsto (typerec^n[c][\Gamma', \eta, \rho_1, \ldots, \rho_n]\ c_1\ \bar{e})$$
$$[\rho_1(c_2)] \ldots [\rho_n(c_2)]\ (typerec^n[c][\Gamma', \eta, \rho_1, \ldots, \rho_n]\ c_2\ \bar{e})$$

$$typerec^n[c][\Gamma', \eta, \rho_1, \ldots, \rho_n]\ (\lambda \alpha{:}\kappa.c')\ \bar{e} \mapsto \Lambda \beta_1{:}\kappa. \ldots \Lambda \beta_n{:}\kappa.\lambda x{:}c\langle \kappa \rangle^n \beta_1 \ldots \beta_n.$$
$$(typerec^n[c][\Gamma'\{\alpha \mapsto \kappa\}, \eta\{\alpha \mapsto x\}, \rho_1\{\alpha \mapsto \beta_1\}, \ldots, \rho_n\{\alpha \mapsto \beta_n\}]\ c'\ \bar{e})$$

Fig. 3. Semantics for multi-place *typerec*

itself, called recursively. This fact is not surprising considering the impredicative nature of $\forall_\star$ and $\exists_\star$ types: since the quantifiers range over *all* types we need an appropriate definition at all types.

For example, consider the simple function *copy* that creates an identical version of its argument. At base types, it is an identity function, at higher types, it breaks apart its argument and calls itself recursively.

$$fix\ copy : (\forall \alpha : \star. T(\alpha \to \alpha)).$$
$$\Lambda \alpha : \star.\ typerec[\lambda \alpha{:} \star .\alpha \to \alpha]\ \alpha$$
$$int \Rightarrow \lambda i{:} int\ .i$$
$$\to\ \Rightarrow \Lambda \alpha{:} \star.\lambda r_\alpha{:}T(\alpha \to \alpha).\Lambda \beta{:} \star.\lambda r_\beta{:}T(\beta \to \beta).\lambda f{:}T(\alpha \to \beta).r_\beta \circ f \circ r_\alpha$$
$$\times\ \Rightarrow \Lambda \alpha{:} \star.\lambda r_\alpha{:}T(\alpha \to \alpha).\Lambda \beta{:} \star.\lambda r_\beta{:}T(\beta \to \beta).\lambda x{:}T(\alpha \times \beta).\langle r_\alpha(\pi_1 x), r_\beta(\pi_2 x) \rangle$$
$$\mu_\star \Rightarrow \Lambda \alpha{:} \star \to \star.\lambda r{:} \forall \beta{:} \star .T(\beta \to \beta) \to T(\alpha \beta \to \alpha \beta).$$
$$fix\ f{:}T(\mu_\star \alpha \to \mu_\star \alpha).\lambda x{:}T(\mu_\star \alpha).\ roll\ (r\ [\mu_\star \alpha]\ f\ (unroll\ x))$$
$$\forall_\star \Rightarrow \Lambda \alpha{:} \star \to \star.\lambda r{:} \forall \beta{:} \star .T(\beta \to \beta) \to T(\alpha \beta \to \alpha \beta).$$
$$\lambda x{:}T(\forall_\star \alpha).\Lambda \beta{:} \star .r\ (copy\ [\beta])\ (x[\beta])$$
$$\exists_\star \Rightarrow \Lambda \alpha{:} \star \to \star.\lambda r{:} \forall \beta{:} \star .T(\beta \to \beta) \to T(\alpha \beta \to \alpha \beta).\lambda x{:}T(\exists_\star \alpha).$$
$$let\langle \beta, y \rangle = unpack\ x\ in\ pack\langle \beta, r\ (copy\ [\beta])\ y \rangle\ as\ \exists \beta{:} \star .\alpha \beta$$

3   Multi-place Polykinded Types

Unfortunately, with the calculus we have just developed we cannot implement several important examples of polytypic programming. For example, consider generic map. Given a function f, this map copies a data-structure parameterized by the type α, replacing every component x of type α, with fx. For example, if map is specialized to lists, then its type is $\forall \alpha : \star .\forall \beta : \star .(\alpha \to \beta) \to (list\ a) \to (list\ \beta)$. However, while the operation of generic map is guided by the structure of the type constructor *list*, this type is not a polykinded type of the form $c\langle \star \to \star \rangle list$. By an analogy with logical relations, Hinze observed that by extending the definition of polykinded types in the following way, we may define generic map.

Definition 2. *A* multi-place polykinded type, *written* $c\langle\kappa\rangle^n c_1 \ldots c_n$, *where c is of kind* $\star_1 \to \ldots \to \star_n \to \star$ *and c_i is of kind* κ *for* $1 \leq i \leq n$, *is defined by induction on κ as:*

$$c\langle\star\rangle^n c_1 \ldots c_n = T(c\ c_1 \ldots c_n)$$
$$c\langle\kappa_1 \to \kappa_2\rangle^n c_1 \ldots c_n = \forall\beta_1{:}\kappa_1.\ldots.\forall\beta_n{:}\kappa_1.c\langle\kappa_1\rangle^n\beta_1\ldots\beta_n \to c\langle\kappa_2\rangle^n(c_1\beta_1)\ldots(c_n\beta_n)$$

Now the type of generic map may be expressed as $\forall\alpha{:}\star \to \star.(\to)\langle\star \to \star\rangle^2\alpha\ \alpha$. If map is instantiated with the type constructor *list*, we get the expected type:

$$(\to)\langle\star \to \star\rangle^2 list\ list = \forall\alpha{:}\star.\forall\beta{:}\star.(\alpha \to \beta) \to (list\ \alpha \to list\ \beta).$$

Generalizing the definition of polykinded types forces us to also generalize *typerec* to *typerec*^{n} and expand ρ to a set of type environments $\rho_1 \ldots \rho_n$ (see Figure 3). On type abstraction, n type variables are abstracted and $\rho_1 \ldots \rho_n$ are extended with these variables. We use these environments to provide substitutions for the n type arguments in a type application. With *typerec*^{2} we may implement map, essentially a two-place version of *copy*.

Surprisingly, we can write useful functions when n is zero, such as a version of *typetostring* below.[7] In this code, *gensym* creates a unique string for each variable name, and *let* $x = e_1$ *in* e_2 is the usual abbreviation for $(\lambda x{:}\sigma.e_2)e_1$.

```
typetostring :  ∀α : ⋆. string .
typetostring =  Λα:⋆. typerec⁰[string] α
  int ⇒  "int"
  →  ⇒  λx:string.λy:string. "(" x ++  " -> " ++ y ++  ")"
  ×  ⇒  λx:string.λy:string. "(" x ++  " * " ++ y ++  ")"
  μ⋆ ⇒  λr:string →string. let x = gensym () in "mu"++ x ++ "." ++ (r x)
  ∀⋆ ⇒  λr:string →string. let x = gensym () in "all"++ x ++ "." ++ (r x)
  ∃⋆ ⇒  λr:string →string. let x = gensym () in "ex"++ x ++ "." ++ (r x)
```

Note that this example does not follow the pattern of iso-recursive types, which would be $\mu_\star \Rightarrow \lambda r{:}string \to string.fix\ f{:}string.rf$. In that case, the string representation of a recursive type would be infinitely long, witnessing the fact that a recursive type is an infinitely large type.

4   Kind Polymorphism

Why is there a distinction between types σ, and type constructors c, necessitating the irritating conversion $T()$? The reason is that we cannot analyze all types. In particular, we cannot analyze polymorphic types where the kind of the bound variable is not $\star$. We may analyze only those types created with the constructor $\forall_\star$. Trifonov *et al.*[30] (hereafter TSS) use the term *fully-reflexive* to refer to a

---

[7] For comparison, we could have also extended the *typerec*^{1} version of *typetostring* (in Section 1.1). In the new branches, r would be of type $\forall\alpha{:}\star.string \to string$ instead of $string \to string$ as above, so a dummy type argument must be supplied when r is used.

$$\kappa ::= \ldots \mid \chi \mid \forall\chi.\kappa \qquad \oplus ::= \ldots \mid \forall \mid \exists \mid \forall^+ \qquad c ::= \ldots \mid \Lambda\chi.c \mid c[\kappa] \mid c\langle\kappa\rangle^n c_1 \ldots c_n$$
$$\sigma ::= \ldots \mid \forall^+\chi.\sigma \qquad e ::= \ldots \mid \Lambda^+\chi.e \mid e[\kappa]^+$$

Fig. 4. Additions for kind polymorphism

calculus where analysis operations are applicable to all types, and argue that this property is important for a type analyzing language.

A naive idea to make this language *fully-reflexive* would be to limit polymorphism to that of F2, *i.e.*, allow types only of the form $\forall\alpha: \star .\sigma$. However, then we cannot express the type of the $e_{\forall_\star}$ branch as it quantifies over a constructor of kind $\star \to \star$. We could then extend the language to allow types that quantify over constructors of kind $\star \to \star$, and add a constructor $(\forall_{\star\to\star})$ of kind $((\star \to \star) \to \star) \to \star$, but then the $e_{\forall_{\star\to\star}}$ branch would quantify over variables of kind $(\star \to \star) \to \star$. In general, we have a vicious cycle: for each type that we add to the calculus, we need a more complicated type to describe its branch in *typerec*. We could break this cycle by adding an infinite number of type constructors $\forall_\kappa$, thereby allowing construction of all polymorphic types. However, then *typerec* would require an infinite number of branches to cover all such types.

TSS avoid having an infinite number of branches for polymorphic types by introducing *kind polymorphism*. By holding the kind of the bound variable abstract, they may write one branch for all such types. Furthermore, they require kind polymorphism to analyze polymorphic types. As their type analysis is based on structural induction, they cannot handle $\forall_\star$ with a negative occurrence of $\star$ in the kind of its argument. With kind polymorphism, the $\forall$ constructor has kind $\forall\chi.(\chi \to \star) \to \star$, without such a negative occurrence.

Our version of *typerec*, as it is not based on induction, can already analyze $\forall_\star$. So their second motivation for kind polymorphism does not apply. However, in this system with kind-indexed types, we do have a separate and additional reason for adding kind polymorphism – our higher-order *typerec* term is naturally kind polymorphic and we would like to express that fact in the type system.

Like TSS, we include two forms of kind polymorphism: First, we extend the type constructor language to F2 by adding kind variables (χ), polymorphic kinds $(\forall\chi.\kappa)$, and type constructors supporting kind abstraction $(\Lambda\chi.c)$ and application $(c[\kappa])$. This polymorphism allows us to express the kind of the $\forall$ and $\exists$ constructors. Second, we also allow terms to abstract $(\forall^+\chi.e)$ and apply $(e[\kappa]^+)$ kinds, so that the $\forall$ branch of *typerec* may be polymorphic over the domain kind. We use the constructor $\forall^+$ to describe the type of kind-polymorphic terms. This constructor is also represented with higher-order abstract syntax: it is of kind $(\forall\chi.\star) \to \star$, where its argument describes how the type depends on the abstract kind χ.

To extend type analysis to polymorphic kinds we must extend the definition of $c\langle\kappa\rangle\alpha$ for the new kind forms χ and $\forall\chi.\kappa$. Therefore, we add polykinded types to the type constructor language and the following axioms to judge equality of type constructors, including a new axiom for polymorphic kinds:

$$\Gamma \vdash c\langle\star\rangle^n c_1 \ldots c_n = c c_1 \ldots c_n : \star$$
$$\Gamma \vdash c\langle\kappa_1 \to \kappa_2\rangle^n c_1 \ldots c_n =$$
$$\forall[\kappa_1](\lambda\alpha_1{:}\kappa_1.\ldots\forall[\kappa_1](\lambda\alpha_n{:}k_1.\,(c\langle\kappa_1\rangle^n\alpha_1\ldots\alpha_n) \to c\langle\kappa_2\rangle^n(c_1\alpha_1)\ldots(c_n\alpha_n))\ldots) : \star$$
$$\Gamma \vdash c\langle\forall\chi.\kappa\rangle^n c_1 \ldots c_n = \forall^+(\Lambda\chi.c\langle\kappa\rangle^n(c_1[\chi])\ldots(c_n[\chi])) : \star$$

Furthermore, we must extend the operational semantics of *typerec* to cover arguments that are kind abstractions or kind applications. By the above definition, *typerec* must produce a kind polymorphic term when reaching a kind polymorphic constructor. Therefore, an argument to *typerec* of a polymorphic kind pushes the *typerec* through the kind abstraction. Likewise, when we reach a kind application during analysis, we propagate the analysis through.

$$typerec^n[c][\Gamma,\eta,\overline{\rho}]\,(\Lambda\chi.c)\;\overline{e} \mapsto \Lambda^+\chi.\,typerec^n[c][\Gamma,\eta,\overline{\rho}]\,(c[\chi])\;\overline{e}$$
$$typerec^n[c][\Gamma,\eta,\overline{\rho}]\,(c[\kappa])\;\overline{e} \mapsto (typerec^n[c][\Gamma,\eta,\overline{\rho}]\,c\;\overline{e})[\kappa]^+$$

With kind polymorphism, we express the type of *size* more precisely as $\forall^+\chi.\forall\alpha{:}\chi.\,T((\lambda\beta:\star.\beta \to int)\langle\chi\rangle\alpha)$. We can also extend *size* to general existential types. Before, as $\exists_\star$ hides type constructors of kind $\star$, we used the constant zero function as the *size* of the hidden type. Here, because the hidden type constructor may be of any kind, we must use a recursive call to define *size*.

$$\exists \Rightarrow \Lambda^+\chi.\Lambda\alpha{:}\chi \to \star.\lambda r : \forall\beta{:}\chi.\,T(c\langle\chi\rangle\beta) \to T(\alpha\beta \to int).$$
$$\lambda x{:}T(\exists[\chi]\alpha).\,let\,\langle\beta,y\rangle = unpack\,x\,in\;r\;[\beta]\;(size[\chi][\beta])\;y$$

4.1 Example: typetostring

Unfortunately, even though we may analyze the entire type language, we cannot extend *typetostring* to create strings of all constructors. As kind polymorphism is parametric, we cannot differentiate constructors with polymorphic kinds. However, by giving *typetostring* a kind-polymorphic type we can produce many string representations.

$$typetostring : \forall^+\chi.\forall\alpha{:}\chi.\,T(string\langle\chi\rangle^0)$$

How do we use *typetostring* to produce strings of higher-order type constructors? When χ is not $\star$, the result of *typetostring* is not a *string*. However, we may analyze $string\langle\chi\rangle^0$ to produce a string when χ is a function kind. Using a technique similar to *type-directed partial evaluation* [5] we may *reify* a term of type $string\langle\chi\rangle^0$ into a string. To do so, we require *app* and *lam* to create string abstractions and applications.

$lam : (string \to string) \to string$ $app : string \to (string \to string)$
$lam = \lambda x{:}string \to string\,.\,let\,b = gensym()\,in$ $app = \lambda x{:}string\,.\lambda y{:}string\,.$
   "(lambda" $++b\,++"."++(x b)\,++")"$ "(" $++x\,++"\;"\,++y\,++")"$

Below, let $c = \lambda\alpha{:}\star.(\alpha \to string) \times (string \to \alpha)$

$ReifyReflect = typerec[c]\;\alpha$
$string \Rightarrow \langle\lambda y{:}string\,.y, \lambda y{:}string\,.y\rangle$
$\quad\to\quad \Rightarrow \Lambda\alpha_1{:}\star.\lambda r_1{:}c\alpha_1.\Lambda\alpha_2{:}\star.\lambda r_2{:}c\alpha_2.$
$\qquad\qquad let\langle reify_1, reflect_1\rangle = r_1; \langle reify_2, reflect_2\rangle = r_2\,in$
$\qquad\qquad \langle\lambda y{:}\alpha_1 \to \alpha_2.lam(reify_2 \circ y \circ reflect_1), \lambda y{:}string\,.reflect_2 \circ app\;y\;\circ reify_1\rangle$

The result of *reify*, the first component of *ReifyReflect* above, composed with *typetostring* is a string representation of the long $\beta\eta$-normal form of the type constructor. What if that constructor has a polymorphic kind? We cannot extend *ReifyReflect* to analyze $string\langle\forall\chi.\kappa\rangle^0$, because parametric kind polymorphism prevents us from writing the functions $klam : (\forall^+\chi.\ string) \rightarrow string$ and $kapp : string \rightarrow \forall\chi^+.\ string$.

We also need *ReifyReflect* to create string representations of polymorphic types. In the previous version of *typetostring*, for the constructor $\forall_\star$, the inductive argument r was of type $string \rightarrow string$. With kind polymorphism, the type of this argument $(T(string\langle\chi\rangle^0))$ is dependent on χ the kind abstracted by $\forall$. In order to call r, we need to manufacture a value of this type — we need to *reflect* a string into the appropriate argument for the inductive call in *typetostring*:

$$\forall \;\Rightarrow\; \Lambda^+\chi.\;\; \Lambda\alpha{:}\chi \rightarrow \star.\;\; \lambda r{:}T(string\langle\chi\rangle^0) \;\rightarrow\; string\,.$$
$$\quad let\; \langle reify, reflect\rangle = ReifyReflect[string\langle\chi\rangle^0]$$
$$\qquad v = gensym\,()\; in\;\; \texttt{"all"} \;+\!\!+\; v \;+\!\!+\;\; \texttt{"."} \;+\!\!+\; (r\;(reflect\;v))$$

Again, because *ReifyReflect* is limited to kinds of the form $\star$ or $\kappa_1 \rightarrow \kappa_2$, we can only accept the types of F_ω [10] (*i.e.*, types such as $\forall[\star \rightarrow \star](\lambda\alpha{:}\star \rightarrow \star.c)$ but not $\forall[\forall\chi.\kappa](\lambda\alpha{:}\forall\chi.\kappa.c)$). And just as we cannot extend *ReifyReflect* to kind-polymorphic constructors, we cannot extend *typetostring* to kind-polymorphic types (those formed by $\forall^+$). While this calculus is fully-reflexive, we cannot completely discriminate all of the type constructors of this language.

4.2   Analysis of Polymorphic Types

In Section 2, we were reassured when the operation of higher-order *typerec* over product types mirrored that of λ_i^{ML}. How does analysis of polymorphic and existential types differ when *typerec* is viewed as a structural induction (as in TSS) and as an interpretation of the type language?

In the first case (which we distinguish by *typerec*^{i}) we have the following operational rule for polymorphic types; when c' is analyzed, its argument β is also examined with the same analysis.

$$typerec^i[c]\ (\forall[\kappa]c')\ \bar{e} \;\mapsto\; e_\forall\ [\kappa]^+[c']\ (\Lambda\beta{:}\kappa.\ typerec^i[c]\ (c'\beta)\ \bar{e})$$

With higher-order *typerec*, we may derive the following rule for polymorphic types. Here, the result of analysis of the argument to c' may be supplied in x.

$$typerec[c][\Gamma', \eta, \rho]\ (\forall[\kappa]c')\ \bar{e} \mapsto^*$$
$$e_\forall\ [\kappa]^+[c']\ (\Lambda\beta{:}\kappa.\lambda x{:}T(c\langle\kappa\rangle\beta).\ typerec[c][\Gamma'\{\alpha \mapsto \kappa\}, \eta\{\alpha \mapsto x\}, \rho\{\alpha \mapsto \beta\}]\ (c'\alpha)\ \bar{e})$$

However, many examples of polytypic functions defined by higher-order *typerec* (such as *copy*) create a fixed point of the Λ-abstracted *typerec* term, and it is this fixed point applied to β that eventually replaces x. Therefore, as above, the argument to c' is examined with the same analysis. The difference between the two versions is similar to the difference between iso- and equi-recursive types. Because we have more expressiveness in the analysis of type constructors with higher-order *typerec*, we have more flexibility in the analysis of quantified types. TSS's calculus may implement *copy* (though they must restrict the kind of its argument to $\star$) but not *typetostring*.

5   Related Work

In lifting type analysis to higher-order constructors, this work is related to induction over datatypes with embedded function spaces and, more specifically, to those datatypes representing higher-order abstract syntax. Meijer and Hutton [20] describe how to extend catamorphisms to datatypes with embedded functions by simultaneously computing an inverse. Fegaras and Sheard [9] simplify this process, noting that when the analyzed function is *parametric*, an inverse is not required. TSS employ their technique for the type level analysis of recursive types in the language λ_i^Q [30], using the kind language to enforce that the argument to $\mu_\star$ is parametric. Likewise, in a language for expressing induction over higher-order abstract syntax, Despeyroux *et al.* [6, 7], use a modal type to indicate parametric functions. In this paper, because only terms analyze types, all analyzed type functions are parametric and so we do not require such additional typing machinery.

6   Conclusions and Future Work

The goal of this work is to extend polytypic programming to encompass the features of expressive and advanced type systems. Here, we provide an operational semantics for type constructor polytypism by extending *typerec* to cover higher-order types. By casting these operations in a type-passing framework, we extend polytypic definitions over type constructors (such as *size* and *map*) to situations where type abstraction cannot be specialized away at compile time. With type passing, we also extend the domain of polytypic definitions to include first-class polymorphic and existential types. With the addition of kind polymorphism and polykinded types, we allow the types of polytypic operations to be explicitly and accurately described. Finally, by extending *typerec* to constructors of polymorphic kind we allow the analysis of constructors such as ∀ and ∃ in a flexible manner and provide insight to the calculus of TSS.

We hope to extend this work in the future with type-level type analysis. The languages λ_i^{ML} and λ_i^Q include *Typerec* that analyzes types to produce other types. This operator is often important in describing the types of polytypic definitions. Hinze *et al.* [15] provide a number of examples of higher-order polytypic term definitions that require higher-order polytypic type definitions. However, adding an operator to analyze higher-order constructors will require machinery at the kind level like TSS's λ_i^Q [30] or Despeyroux *et al.* [6, 7].

This work suggests other areas of future research. First, because this framework depends on a type-passing semantics, it is important to investigate and develop compiler optimizations that would eliminate unneeded run-time analysis. Furthermore, while intensional type analysis has traditionally been used in the context of type-based compilation, we would like to incorporate this system in an expressive user language. Finally, because this language supports the analysis of types with binding structure, it may be applicable to adding polytypic programming to object-oriented languages.

Acknowledgments. Thanks to Dan Grossman, Michael Hicks, Greg Morrisett, Steve Zdancewic and the anonymous reviewers for helpful suggestions.

References

1. Martín Abadi, Luca Cardelli, Benjamin Pierce, and Gordon Plotkin. Dynamic typing in a statically-typed language. *ACM Transactions on Programming Languages and Systems*, 13(2):237–268, April 1991.
2. Martín Abadi, Luca Cardelli, Benjamin Pierce, and Didier Rémy. Dynamic typing in polymorphic languages. *Journal of Functional Programming*, 5(1):111–130, January 1995.
3. Gilad Bracha, Martin Odersky, David Stoutamire, and Philip Wadler. Making the future safe for the past: Adding genericity to the Java programming language. In Craig Chambers, editor, *Object Oriented Programming: Systems, Languages, and Applications (OOPSLA)*, pages 183–200, Vancouver, BC, 1998.
4. Karl Crary and Stephanie Weirich. Flexible type analysis. In *Proceedings of the Fourth ACM SIGPLAN International Conference on Functional Programming*, pages 233–248, Paris, September 1999.
5. O. Danvy. Type-directed partial evaluation. In *POPL'96: The 23rd ACM SIGPLAN-SIGACT Symposium on Principles of Programming Languages, St. Petersburg, Florida, January 1996*, pages 242–257, 1996.
6. Joëlle Despeyroux and Pierre Leleu. Recursion over objects of functional type. *Mathematical Structures in Computer Science*, 11:555–572, 2001.
7. Joëlle Despeyroux, Frank Pfenning, and Carsten Schürmann. Primitive recursion for higher-order abstract syntax. In *Third International Conference on Typed Lambda Calculi and Applications*, volume 1210 of *Lecture Notes in Computer Science*, pages 147–163, Nancy, France, April 1997. Springer-Verlag.
8. Catherine Dubois, François Rouaix, and Pierre Weis. Extensional polymorphism. In *Twenty-Second ACM Symposium on Principles of Programming Languages*, pages 118–129, San Francisco, January 1995.
9. L. Fegaras and T. Sheard. Revisiting catamorphisms over datatypes with embedded functions. In *Twenty-Third ACM Symposium on Principles of Programming Languages*, St. Petersburg Beach, Florida, January 1996.
10. Jean-Yves Girard. *Interprétation fonctionelle et élimination des coupures de l'arithmétique d'ordre supérieur*. PhD thesis, Université Paris VII, 1972.
11. James Gosling, Bill Joy, and Guy Steele. *The Java Language Specification*. Addison-Wesley, 1996.
12. Robert Harper and Greg Morrisett. Compiling polymorphism using intensional type analysis. In *Twenty-Second ACM Symposium on Principles of Programming Languages*, pages 130–141, San Francisco, January 1995.
13. Michael Hicks, Stephanie Weirich, and Karl Crary. Safe and flexible dynamic linking of native code. In R. Harper, editor, *Types in Compilation: Third International Workshop, TIC 2000; Montreal, Canada, September 21, 2000; Revised Selected Papers*, volume 2071 of *Lecture Notes in Computer Science*, pages 147–176. Springer, 2001.
14. Ralf Hinze. Polytypic values possess polykinded types. In Roland Backhouse and J.N. Oliveira, editors, *Proceedings of the Fifth International Conference on Mathematics of Program Construction (MPC 2000)*, Ponte de Lima, Portugal, July 2000.

114   Stephanie Weirich

15. Ralf Hinze, Johan Jeuring, and Andres L oh. Type-indexed data types. Available at http://www.cs.uu.nl/~johanj/publications/publications.html, 2001.
16. International Organisation for Standardisation and International Electrotechnical Commission. *Ada Reference Manual: Language and Standard Libraries*, 6.0 edition, December 1994. International Standard ISO/IEC 8652:1995.
17. Patrick Jansson and Johan Jeuring. PolyP - a polytypic programming language extension. In *Twenty-Fourth ACM Symposium on Principles of Programming Languages*, pages 470–482, Paris, France, 1997.
18. C.B. Jay, G. Bellè, and E. Moggi. Functorial ML. *Journal of Functional Programming*, 8(6):573–619, November 1998.
19. Mark P Jones and Alastair Reid. *The Hugs 98 User Manual*. Yale Haskell Group and Oregon Graduate Institute of Science and Technology. Available at http://cvs.haskell.org/Hugs/pages/hugsman/index.html.
20. Erik Meijer and Graham Hutton. Bananas in space: Extending fold and unfold to exponential types. In *Conf. Record 7th ACM SIGPLAN/SIGARCH and IFIP WG 2.8 Int. Conf. on Functional Programming Languages and Computer Architecture, FPCA'95, La Jolla, San Diego, CA, USA, 25-28 June 1995*, pages 324–333. ACM Press, New York, 1995.
21. Robin Milner, Mads Tofte, Robert Harper, and David MacQueen. *The Definition of Standard ML (Revised)*. The MIT Press, Cambridge, Massachusetts, 1997.
22. John C. Mitchell and Gordon D. Plotkin. Abstract types have existential type. *ACM Transactions on Programming Languages and Systems*, 10(3):470–502, July 1988.
23. Greg Morrisett. *Compiling with Types*. PhD thesis, Carnegie Mellon University, School of Computer Science, Pittsburgh, Pennsylvania, December 1995.
24. Simon L. Peyton Jones and J. Hughes (editors). Report on the programming language Haskell 98, a non-strict purely functional language. Technical Report YALEU/DCS/RR-1106, Yale University, Department of Computer Science, February 1999. Available from http://www.haskell.org/definition/.
25. Frank Pfenning and Conal Elliott. Higher-order abstract syntax. In *ACM SIGPLAN Conference on Programming Language Design and Implementation*, pages 199–208, Atlanta, GA, USA, June 1988.
26. John C. Reynolds. Types, abstraction and parametric polymorphism. In *Information Processing '83*, pages 513–523. North-Holland, 1983. Proceedings of the IFIP 9th World Computer Congress.
27. Fritz Ruehr. Structural polymorphism. In Roland Backhouse and Tim Sheard, editors, *Informal Proceedings Workshop on Generic Programming, WGP'98, Marstrand, Sweden, 18 June 1998.*, 1998.
28. T. Sheard. Type parametric programming. Technical Report CSE 93-018, Oregon Graduate Institute, 1993.
29. The GHC Team. *The Glasgow Haskell Compiler User's Guide*, version 5.02 edition. Available at http://www.haskell.org/ghc/.
30. Valery Trifonov, Bratin Saha, and Zhong Shao. Fully reflexive intensional type analysis. In *Fifth ACM SIGPLAN International Conference on Functional Programming*, pages 82–93, Montreal, September 2000.
31. Philip Wadler and Stephen Blott. How to make ad-hoc polymorphism less ad-hoc. In *Sixteenth ACM Symposium on Principles of Programming Languages*, pages 60–76. ACM, 1989.
32. Stephanie Weirich. *Programming With Types*. PhD thesis, Cornell University, 2002. Forthcoming.

Branching Types*

Joe B. Wells[1] and Christian Haack[1]

Heriot-Watt University
http://www.cee.hw.ac.uk/ultra/

Abstract. Although systems with intersection types have many unique capabilities, there has never been a fully satisfactory explicitly typed system with intersection types. We introduce λ^B with *branching types* and types which are quantified over *type selectors* to provide an explicitly typed system with the same expressiveness as a system with intersection types. Typing derivations in λ^B effectively squash together what would be separate parallel derivations in earlier systems with intersection types.

1 Introduction

1.1 Background and Motivation

Intersection Types. Intersection types were independently invented near the end of the 1970s by Coppo and Dezani [3] and Pottinger [15]. Intersection types provide type polymorphism by listing type instances, differing from the more widely used ∀-quantified types [8, 16], which provide type polymorphism by giving a type scheme that can be instantiated into various type instances. The original motivation was for analyzing and/or synthesizing λ-models as well as in analyzing normalization properties, but over the last twenty years the scope of research on intersection types has broadened.

Intersection types have many unique advantages over ∀-quantified types. They can characterize the behavior of λ-terms more precisely, and can be used to express exactly the results of many program analyses [13, 1, 25, 26]. Type polymorphism with intersection types is also more flexible. For example, Urzyczyn [20] proved the λ-term

$$(\lambda x.z(x(\lambda fu.fu))(x(\lambda vg.gv)))(\lambda y.yyy)$$

to be untypable in the system F_ω, considered to be the most powerful type system with ∀-quantifiers measured by the set of pure λ-terms it can type. In contrast, this λ-term is typable with intersection types satisfying the *rank-3* restriction [12]. Better results for automated type inference (ATI) have also been obtained for intersection types. ATI for type systems with ∀-quantifiers that are more powerful than the very-restricted Hindley/Milner system is a murky area,

---

* This work was partly supported by NSF grants CCR 9113196, 9417382, 9988529, and EIA 9806745, EPSRC grants GR/L 36963 and GR/R 41545/01, and Sun Microsystems equipment grant EDUD-7826-990410-US.

D. Le Métayer (Ed.): ESOP 2002, LNCS 2305, pp. 115–132, 2002.

and it has been proven for many such type systems that ATI algorithms can not
be both complete and terminating [11, 23, 24, 20]. In contrast, ATI algorithms
have been proven complete and terminating for the rank-k restriction for every
finite k for several systems with intersection types [12, 10].

We use intersection types in typed intermediate languages (TILs) used in
compilers. Using a TIL increases reliability of compilation and can support useful type-directed program transformations. We use intersection types because
they support both more accurate analyses (as mentioned above) and interesting
type/flow-directed transformations [5, 19, 7, 6] that would be very difficult using
∀-quantified types. When using a TIL, it is important to regularly check that
the intermediate program representation is in fact well typed. Provided this is
done, the correctness of any analyses encoded in the types is maintained across
transformations. Thus, it is important for a TIL to be *explicitly* typed, i.e., to
have type information attached to internal nodes of the program representation.
This is necessary both for efficiency and because program transformations can
yield results outside the domain of ATI algorithms. Unfortunately, intersection
types raise troublesome issues for having an explicitly typed representation. This
is the main motivation for this paper.

The Trouble with the Intersection-Introduction Rule. The important
feature of a system with intersection types is this rule:

$$\frac{E \vdash M : \sigma; \quad E \vdash M : \tau}{E \vdash M : \sigma \wedge \tau} \ (\wedge\text{-intro})$$

The proof terms are the same for both premises and the conclusion! No syntax is
introduced. A system with this rule does not fit into the proofs-as-terms (PAT,
a.k.a. propositions-as-types and Curry/Howard) correspondence, because it has
proof terms that do not encode deductions. Unfortunately, this is inadequate
for many needs, and there is an immediate dilemma in how to make a type-
annotated variant of the system. The usual strategy fails immediately, e.g.:

$$\frac{E \vdash (\lambda x{:}\sigma.\, x) : (\sigma \to \sigma); \quad E \vdash (\lambda x{:}\tau.\, x) : (\tau \to \tau)}{E \vdash (\lambda x{:}\boxed{???}.\, x) : (\sigma \to \sigma) \wedge (\tau \to \tau)}$$

Where $\boxed{???}$ appears, what should be written? This trouble is related to the fact
that the $\wedge$ type constructor is not a truth-functional propositional connective.

Earlier Approaches. In the language Forsythe [17], Reynolds annotates the
binding of $(\lambda x.M)$ with a list of types, e.g., $(\lambda x{:}\sigma_1| \cdots |\sigma_n.\, M)$. If the abstraction
body M is typable with a fixed type τ for each type σ_i for x, then the abstraction
gets the type $(\sigma_1 \to \tau) \wedge \cdots \wedge (\sigma_n \to \tau)$. However, this approach can not handle
dependencies between types of nested variable bindings, e.g., this approach can
not give $K = (\lambda x.\lambda y.x)$ the type $\tau_K = (\sigma \to (\sigma \to \sigma)) \wedge (\tau \to (\tau \to \tau))$.

Pierce [14] improves on Reynolds's approach by using a **for** construct which
gives a type variable a finite set of types to range over, e.g., K can be annotated

as (**for** $\alpha \in \{\sigma, \tau\}.\lambda x{:}\alpha.\,\lambda y{:}\alpha.\,x$) with the type τ_K. However, this approach can not represent some typings, e.g., it can not give the term $M_f = \lambda x.\lambda y.\lambda z.(xy, xz)$ the type $(((\alpha \to \delta) \wedge (\beta \to \epsilon)) \to \alpha \to \beta \to (\delta \times \epsilon)) \wedge ((\gamma \to \gamma) \to \gamma \to \gamma \to (\gamma \times \gamma))$. Pierce's approach could be extended to handle more complex dependencies if simultaneous type variable bindings were added, e.g., M_f could be annotated as:

$$\textbf{for } \{[\theta \mapsto \alpha, \kappa \mapsto \beta, \eta \mapsto \delta, \nu \mapsto \epsilon], [\theta \mapsto \gamma, \kappa \mapsto \gamma, \eta \mapsto \gamma, \nu \mapsto \gamma]\}.$$
$$\lambda x : (\theta \to \eta) \wedge (\kappa \to \nu).\,\lambda y : \theta.\,\lambda z : \kappa.\,(xy, xz)$$

Even this extension of Pierce's approach would still not meet our needs. First, this approach needs intersection types to be associative, commutative, and idempotent (ACI). Recent research suggests that non-ACI intersection types are needed to faithfully encode flow analyses [1]. Second, this approach arranges the type information inconveniently because it must be found from enclosing type variable bindings by a tree-walking process. This is bad for flow-based transformations, which reference arbitrary subterms from distant locations. Third, reasoning about typed terms in this approach is not compositional. It is not possible to look at an arbitrary subterm independently and determine its type.

The approach of λ^{CIL} [25, 26] is essentially to write the typing derivations as terms, e.g., K can be "annotated" as $\bigwedge((\lambda x{:}\sigma.\,\lambda y{:}\sigma.\,x), (\lambda x{:}\tau.\,\lambda y{:}\tau.\,x))$ in order to have the type τ_K. Here $\bigwedge(M, N)$ is a *virtual* tuple where the type erasure of M and N must be the same. In λ^{CIL}, subterms of an untyped term can have many disjoint representatives in a corresponding typed term. This makes it tedious and time-consuming to implement common program transformations, because *parallel contexts* must be used whenever subterms are transformed.

Venneri succeeded in completely removing the ($\wedge$-intro) rule from a type system with intersection types, but this was for combinatory logic rather than the λ-calculus [21, 4], and the approach seems unlikely to be transferable to the λ-calculus.

1.2   Contributions of This Paper

Our Approach: Branching Types. In this paper, we define and prove the basic properties of λ^{B}, a system with *branching types* which represent the effect of simultaneous derivations in the old style. Consider this untyped λ-term:

$$M_a = \lambda a.\lambda b.\lambda c.\ c\,(\lambda d.\ d\,a\,b)$$

In an intersection type system, M_a can have type $(\tau \wedge \sigma)$, where τ and σ are:

$$\tau = (i \to b) \to i \to \tau^c \to b$$
$$\tau^c = (\tau^d \to b) \to b$$
$$\tau^d = (i \to b) \to i \to b$$

$$\sigma = r \to ((r \to r) \wedge (b \to b)) \to (\sigma^c \to b) \to b$$
$$\sigma^c = ((\sigma_1^d \to b) \wedge (\sigma_2^d \to b))$$
$$\sigma_1^d = r \to (r \to r) \to b$$
$$\sigma_2^d = r \to (b \to b) \to b$$

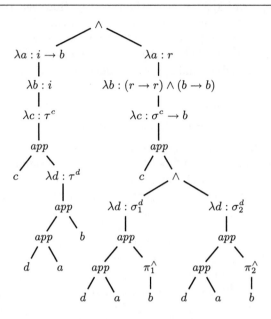

Fig. 1. A syntax tree in a λ^{CIL}-style system

$\Lambda(\mathsf{join}\{f = *, g = *\})$
|
$\lambda a : \{f = i \rightarrow b, g = r\}$
|
$\lambda b : \{f = i, g = \sigma^{bg}\}$
|
$\lambda c : \{f = \tau^c, g = \sigma^{cg} \rightarrow b\}$
|
app

c $\Lambda\{f = *, g = \mathsf{join}\{h = *, l = *\}\}$
|
$\lambda d : \{f = \tau^d, g = \{h = \sigma_1^d, l = \sigma_2^d\}\}$
|
app

app $[\{f = *, g = \{h = (j, *), l = (k, *)\}\}]$
/ \\ |
d a b

Fig. 2. A syntax tree in our system λ^{B}

In λ^B, correspondingly the term M_a can be annotated to have the type ρ where:

$$\rho = \forall(\text{join}\{f = *, g = *\}). \{f = \tau, g = \sigma^g\}, \text{ where } \tau \text{ is as above}$$
$$\sigma^g = r \rightarrow \sigma^{bg} \rightarrow (\sigma^{cg} \rightarrow b) \rightarrow b$$
$$\sigma^{bg} = \forall(\text{join}\{j = *, k = *\}). \{j = r \rightarrow r, k = b \rightarrow b\}$$
$$\sigma^{cg} = \forall(\text{join}\{h = *, l = *\}). \{h = \sigma_1^d \rightarrow b, l = \sigma_2^d \rightarrow b\}$$

Figure 1 shows the syntax tree of the corresponding explicitly typed term in a λ^{CIL}-style system and figure 2 shows the corresponding syntax tree in λ^B.

The λ^{CIL} tree can be seen to have 2 uses of ($\wedge$-intro), one at the root, and one inside the right child of the root. In the λ^B tree, the left branch of the λ^{CIL} tree is effectively named f, the right branch g, and the left and right subbranches of the inner ($\wedge$-intro) rule are named $g.h$ and $g.l$. Every type τ has a kind κ which indicates its branching shape. For example, the result type of the sole leaf occurrence of b has the kind $\{f = *, g = \{h = *, l = *\}\}$. This corresponds to the fact that in the λ^{CIL} derivation the leaf b is duplicated 3 times and occurs in the branches f, $g.h$, and $g.l$.

Each intersection type $\rho_1 \wedge \rho_2$ in this particular λ^{CIL} derivation has a corresponding type of the shape $\forall(\text{join}\{f_1 = *, f_2 = *\}).\{f_1 = \rho'_1, f_2 = \rho'_2\}$ in the λ^B derivation. A type of the shape $\forall P.\rho'$ has a *type selector parameter* P which is a pattern indicating what possible *type selector arguments* are valid to supply. Each parameter P has 2 kinds, its *inner kind* $\lfloor P \rfloor$ and its *outer kind* $\lceil P \rceil$. The kind of a type $\forall P.\rho'$ is $\lfloor P \rfloor$ and the kind of ρ' must be $\lceil P \rceil$.

One of the most important features of λ^B is its equivalences among types. The first two type equivalence rules are:

$$\forall *.\tau \;\simeq\; \tau \qquad\qquad \forall\{f_i = P_i\}^{i \in I}.\{f_i = \tau_i\}^{i \in I} \;\simeq\; \{f_i = \forall P_i.\tau_i\}^{i \in I}$$

To illustrate their use, we explain why the application of b to its type selector argument is well-typed in the example given above. The type of b at its binding site is written as $\{f = i, g = \sigma^{bg}\}$ and has kind $\{f = *, g = *\}$. Because the leaf occurrence of b must have kind $\{f = *, g = \{h = *, l = *\}\}$, the type at that location is expanded by the typing rules to be $\{f = i, g = \{h = \sigma^{bg}, l = \sigma^{bg}\}\}$. Then, using the additional names

$$P_{jk} = \text{join}\{j = *, k = *\}$$
$$\sigma_2^{bg} = \{j = r \rightarrow r, k = b \rightarrow b\}$$

so that $\sigma^{bg} = \forall P_{jk}.\sigma_2^{bg}$, the equivalences are applied to the type as follows to lift the occurrences of $\forall P$ to outermost position:

$$\{f = i, g = \{h = \sigma^{bg}, l = \sigma^{bg}\}\}$$
$$\simeq \{f = (\forall * .i), g = \forall\{h = P_{jk}, l = P_{jk}\}.\{h = \sigma_2^{bg}, l = \sigma_2^{bg}\}\}$$
$$\simeq \forall\{f = *, g = \{h = P_{jk}, l = P_{jk}\}\}.\{f = i, g = \{h = \sigma_2^{bg}, l = \sigma_2^{bg}\}\}$$

The final type is the type actually used in figure 2. The type selector parameter of the final type effectively says, "in the f branch, no type selector argument can be supplied and in the $g.h$ and $g.l$ branches, a choice between

j and k can be supplied". This is in fact what the type selector argument $\{f = *, g = \{h = (j, *), l = (k, *)\}\}$ does; it supplies no choice in the f branch, a choice of j in the $g.h$ branch, and a choice of k in the $g.l$ branch. The $*$ in $(j, *)$ means that after the choice of j is supplied, no further choices are supplied. The use of type selector parameters and arguments in terms takes the place of the $\wedge$-introduction and $\wedge$-elimination rules of a system with intersection types.

The example just preceding of the type of b illustrated 2 of the 3 type equivalence rules. The third rule, which is particularly important because it allows using the usual typing rules for λ-calculus abstraction and application, is this:

$$\{f_i = \sigma_i\}^{i \in I} \rightarrow \{f_i = \tau_i\}^{i \in I} \simeq \{f_i = \sigma_i \rightarrow \tau_i\}^{i \in I}$$

We now give an example of where this rule was used in the earlier typing example. The binding type of c is a branching type, but the type of the leaf occurrence of c needs to be a function type in order to be applied to its argument. Fortunately, the type equivalence gives the following, providing exactly the type needed:

$$\{f = (\tau^d \rightarrow b) \rightarrow b, g = \sigma^{cg} \rightarrow b\} \simeq \{f = \tau^d \rightarrow b, g = \sigma^{cg}\} \rightarrow \{f = b, g = b\}$$

Another important feature of λ^B is its reduction rules which manipulate and simplify the type annotations as needed. As an example, consider the λ^B term $M = (\Lambda P_1.\Lambda P_2.\lambda x^\tau.x)[A]$, where:

$$P_1 = \{f = \mathsf{join}\{j = *, k = *\}, g = *\}, \quad P_2 = \{f = *, g = \mathsf{join}\{h = *, l = *\}\}$$
$$\tau = \{f = \{j = \alpha_1, k = \alpha_2\}, g = \{h = \beta_1, l = \beta_2\}\}, \quad A = \{f = *, g = (h, *)\}$$

The term M first reduces to $\Lambda P_1.(\Lambda P_2.\lambda x^\tau.x)[A]$, by a (β_Λ)-step where P_1 and A pass through each other without interacting. By another (β_Λ)-step, it reduces to $\Lambda P_1.\Lambda P_2'.(\lambda x^\sigma.x)[A']$, where:

$$P_2' = \{f = *, g = *\}, \sigma = \{f = \{j = \alpha_1, k = \alpha_2\}, g = \beta_1\}, \text{ and } A' = \{f = *, g = *\}$$

Finally, it reduces to $\Lambda P_1.\lambda x^\sigma.x$, removing the trivial P_2' and A' by a $(*_\Lambda)$-step and a $(*_\Lambda)$-step.

Recent Related Work. Ronchi Della Rocca and Roversi have a system called Intersection Logic (IL) [18] which is similar to λ^B, but has nothing corresponding to our explicitly typed terms. IL has a meta-level operation corresponding to our equivalence for function types. IL has nothing corresponding to our other type equivalences, because IL does not group parallel occurrences of its equivalent of type selector parameters and arguments, but instead works with equivalence classes of derivations modulo permutations of what we call *individual* type selector parameters and arguments. We expect that the use of these equivalence classes will cause great difficulty with the proofs. Much of the proof burden for the IL system (corresponding to a large portion of this paper) is inside the 1-line proof of their lemma 4 in the calculation of $S(\Pi, \Pi')$ where S is not constructively specified. A proof-term-labelled version of IL is presented, but the proof terms are pure λ-terms and thus the proof terms do not represent entire derivations.

Capitani, Loreti, and Venneri have designed a similar system called HL (Hyperformulae Logic) [2]. HL is quite similar to IL, although it seems overall to have a less complicated presentation. HL has nothing corresponding to our equivalences on types. The set of properties proved for HL in [2] is not exactly the same as the set of properties proved for IL in [18], e.g., there is no attempt to directly prove any result related to reduction of HL proofs as there is for IL, although this could be obtained indirectly via their proofs of equivalence with traditional systems with intersection types. HL is reported in [18] to have a typed version of an untyped calculus like that in [9], but in fact there is no significant connection between [2] and [9] and there is no explicitly typed calculus associated with HL.

For both IL and HL, there are proofs of equivalence with earlier systems with intersection types. These proofs show that the proof-term-annotated versions of IL and HL can type the same sets of pure untyped λ-terms as a traditional system with intersection types. We expect that this could also be done for our system λ^B, but we have not yet bothered to complete such a proof because it is a theoretical point which does not directly affect our ability to use λ^B as a basis for representing analysis information in implementations.

Summary of Contributions (i.e., the Conclusion). In this paper, we present λ^B, the first typed calculus with the power of intersection types which is Church-style, i.e., typed terms do not have multiple disjoint subterms corresponding to single subterms in the corresponding untyped term. We prove for λ^B subject reduction, and soundness and completeness of typed reduction w.r.t. β-reduction on the corresponding untyped λ-terms. The main benefit of λ^B will be to make it easier to use technology (both theories and software) already developed for the λ-calculus on typed terms in a type system having the power and flexibility of intersection types. Due to the experimental performance measurements reported in [7], we do not expect a substantial size benefit in practice from λ^B over λ^{CIL}. In the area of logic, λ^B terms may be useful as typed realizers of the so-called *strong conjunction*, but we are not currently planning on investigating this ourselves.

2   Some Notational Conventions

We use expressions of the form $\{f_i = E_i\}^I$, where I is a finite index set, the f_i's are drawn from a fixed set of labels and the E_i are expressions that may depend on i. Such an expression stands for the set $\{(f_i, E_i) \mid i \in I\}$.

Let an expression E be called *partially defined* whenever E is built using partial functions. Such an expression E defines an object iff all of its subexpressions are also defined; this will depend on the valuation for E's free variables. Given a binary relation $\mathcal{R}$ and partially defined expressions E_1 and E_2, let $(E_1 \; \mathcal{R}^\perp \; E_2)$ hold iff either both E_1 and E_2 are undefined or E_1 denotes an object x_1 and E_2 an object x_2 such that $(x_1 \; \mathcal{R} \; x_2)$.

3   Types and Kinds

3.1   Kinds

Let Label be a countably infinite set of labels. Let f and g range over Label. The set Kind of *kinds* is defined by the following pseudo-grammar:

$$\kappa \in \text{Kind} ::= * \mid \{f_i = \kappa_i\}^I$$

We define a partial order on kinds, inductively by the following rules:

$$\frac{}{* \leq \kappa} \qquad\qquad \frac{(\kappa_i \leq \kappa_i') \text{ for all } i \text{ in } I}{\{f_i = \kappa_i\}^I \leq \{f_i = \kappa_i'\}^I}$$

Lemma 1. *The relation $\leq$ is a partial order on the set of kinds.* $\qquad\square$

3.2   Types

The sets Parameter of *type selector parameters* and IndParameter of *individual type selector parameters* are defined by the following pseudo-grammar:

$$P \in \text{Parameter} ::= \bar{P} \mid \{f_i = P_i\}^I$$
$$\bar{P} \in \text{IndParameter} ::= * \mid \text{join}\{f_i = \bar{P}_i\}^I$$

Given a parameter P, let P's *inner kind* $\lfloor P \rfloor$ and *outer kind* $\lceil P \rceil$ be defined as follows:

$$\lfloor * \rfloor = *, \quad \lfloor \text{join}\{f_i = \bar{P}_i\}^I \rfloor = *, \qquad\qquad \lfloor \{f_i = P_i\}^I \rfloor = \{f_i = \lfloor P_i \rfloor\}^I$$
$$\lceil * \rceil = *, \quad \lceil \text{join}\{f_i = \bar{P}_i\}^I \rceil = \{f_i = \lceil \bar{P}_i \rceil\}^I, \quad \lceil \{f_i = P_i\}^I \rceil = \{f_i = \lceil P_i \rceil\}^I$$

Let TypeVar be a countably infinite set of type variables. Let α and β range over TypeVar. Let the set of types Type be given by the following pseudo-grammar:

$$\sigma, \tau \in \text{Type} ::= \alpha \mid \sigma \to \tau \mid \{f_i = \tau_i\}^I \mid \forall P.\tau$$

The relation assigning kinds to types is given by these rules:

$$\frac{}{\alpha : *} \qquad \frac{\sigma : \kappa; \quad \tau : \kappa}{\sigma \to \tau : \kappa} \qquad \frac{\tau_i : \kappa_i \text{ for every } i \text{ in } I}{\{f_i = \tau_i\}^I : \{f_i = \kappa_i\}^I} \qquad \frac{\tau : \lceil P \rceil}{\forall P.\tau : \lfloor P \rfloor}$$

Note that every type has at most one kind. A type τ is called *well-formed* if there is a kind κ such that $(\tau : \kappa)$. A well-formed type is called *individual* if its kind is $*$. A well-formed type is called *branching* if its kind is not $*$. Individual types correspond to single types in the world of intersection types, whereas branching types correspond to collections of types where each type in the collection would occur in a separate derivation.

3.3   Type Equivalences

In order to be able to treat certain types as having essentially the same meaning, we define an equivalence relation on the set of types as follows. A binary relation $\mathcal{R} \subseteq \mathsf{Type} \times \mathsf{Type}$ is called *compatible* if it satisfies the following rules:

$$(\sigma \mathrel{\mathcal{R}} \sigma') \Rightarrow ((\sigma \to \tau) \mathrel{\mathcal{R}} (\sigma' \to \tau))$$
$$(\tau \mathrel{\mathcal{R}} \tau') \Rightarrow ((\sigma \to \tau) \mathrel{\mathcal{R}} (\sigma \to \tau'))$$
$$((\tau_j \mathrel{\mathcal{R}} \tau'_j) \wedge (j \notin I)) \Rightarrow (\{f_i = \tau_i\}^I \cup \{f_j = \tau_j\} \mathrel{\mathcal{R}} \{f_i = \tau_i\}^I \cup \{f_j = \tau'_j\})$$
$$(\tau \mathrel{\mathcal{R}} \sigma) \Rightarrow ((\forall P.\tau) \mathrel{\mathcal{R}} (\forall P.\sigma))$$

Let $\succ$ be the least compatible relation that contains all instances of the rules (1) through (3), below. Let $\succeq$ denote the reflexive and transitive closure of $\succ$, and $\simeq$ the least compatible equivalence relation that contains all instances of (1) through (3).

$$\forall *.\tau \mathrel{\mathcal{R}} \tau \tag{1}$$
$$\forall \{f_i = P_i\}^I.\{f_i = \tau_i\}^I \mathrel{\mathcal{R}} \{f_i = \forall P_i.\tau_i\}^I \tag{2}$$
$$\{f_i = \sigma_i\}^I \to \{f_i = \tau_i\}^I \mathrel{\mathcal{R}} \{f_i = \sigma_i \to \tau_i\}^I \tag{3}$$

Lemma 2. *If $(\tau \simeq \sigma)$ and $(\tau : \kappa)$ then $(\sigma : \kappa)$.* $\square$

Lemma 3 (Confluence).

1. *If $\tau_1 \succ \tau_2$ and $\tau_1 \succ \tau_3$, then there is a type τ_4 such that $\tau_2 \succ \tau_4$ and $\tau_3 \succ \tau_4$.*
2. *If $\tau_1 \succeq \tau_2$ and $\tau_1 \succeq \tau_3$, then there is a type τ_4 such that $\tau_2 \succeq \tau_4$ and $\tau_3 \succeq \tau_4$.*

$\square$

Proof Sketch. An inspection of the reduction rules shows the following: Whenever a redex τ contains another redex σ, then σ still occurs in the contractum of τ. Moreover, σ doesn't get duplicated in the contraction step. For this reason, statement (1) holds. Statement (2) follows from (1) by a standard argument. $\square$

Lemma 4 (Termination). *There is no infinite sequence $(\tau_n)_{n \in \mathbb{N}}$ such that $\tau_n \succ \tau_{n+1}$ for all n in $\mathbb{N}$.* $\square$

Proof. Define a weight function $\|\cdot\|$ on types by

$$\|\tau\| = \left(\begin{array}{c} \text{(no. of occurrences of labels in } \tau) \\ + \text{ (no. of occurrences of } * \text{ in } \tau) \end{array} \right)$$

An inspection of the reduction rules shows that $\tau \succ \sigma$ implies $\|\tau\| > \|\sigma\|$. Therefore, every reduction sequence is finite. $\square$

3.4   Normal Types

A type τ is called *normal* if there is no type σ such that $\tau \succ \sigma$. We abbreviate the statement that τ is normal by $\mathsf{normal}(\tau)$. For any type τ, let $\mathsf{nf}(\tau)$ be the unique normal type σ such that $\tau \succeq \sigma$, which is proven to exist by Lemma 5 below.

Lemma 5.
For every type τ there is a unique normal type σ such that $\tau \succeq \sigma$.   □

Lemma 6. $(\tau \simeq \sigma)$ *if and only if* $(\mathsf{nf}(\tau) = \mathsf{nf}(\sigma))$.   □

An important property of normal types is that their top-level structure reflects the top-level structure of their kinds. In particular, if a type is normal and individual, then it is not of the form $\{f_i = \tau_i\}^I$. This is made precise in the following lemma:

Lemma 7. *If* $(\tau : \{f_i = \kappa_i\}^I)$ *and* τ *is normal, then there is a family* $(\tau_i)_{i \in I}$ *of normal types such that* $(\tau = \{f_i = \tau_i\}^I)$ *and* $(\tau_i : \kappa_i)$ *for all i in I.*   □

4   Expansion and Selection for Types

4.1   Expansion

For the typing rules, we need to define some auxiliary operations on types. First, we define a partial function expand from Type $\times$ Parameter to Type. Applying expand to the pair (τ, P) adjusts the type τ of branching shape $\lfloor P \rfloor$ to the new branching shape $\lceil P \rceil$ (of which $\lfloor P \rfloor$ is an initial segment) by duplicating subterms of τ. The duplication is caused by the second of the defining equations below. The expansion operation is used in the typing rule that corresponds to the intersection introduction rule, in order to adjust the types of free variables to a new branching shape. The additional branches in the new branching shape $\lceil P \rceil$ correspond to different type derivations for the same term in an intersection type system.

$$
\begin{aligned}
\mathsf{expand}(\tau, *) &= \tau, & &\text{if } \mathsf{normal}(\tau) \\
\mathsf{expand}(\tau, \mathsf{join}\{f_i = \bar{P}_i\}^I) &= \{f_i = \mathsf{expand}(\tau, \bar{P}_i)\}^I, & &\text{if } \mathsf{normal}(\tau) \\
\mathsf{expand}(\{f_i = \tau_i\}^I, \{f_i = P_i\}^I) &= \{f_i = \mathsf{expand}(\tau_i, P_i)\}^I, & &\text{if } \mathsf{normal}(\{f_i = \tau_i\}^I) \\
\mathsf{expand}(\tau, P) &= \mathsf{expand}(\mathsf{nf}(\tau), P), & &\text{if } \neg\mathsf{normal}(\tau)
\end{aligned}
$$

Lemma 8.

1. *If* $(\lfloor P \rfloor \leq \kappa)$ *and* $(\tau : \kappa)$, *then* $\mathsf{expand}(\tau, P)$ *is defined.*
2. $(\tau : \lfloor P \rfloor)$ *if and only if* $\mathsf{expand}(\tau, P) : \lceil P \rceil$.   □

Lemma 9.
If $(\sigma \to \tau : \kappa)$, *then* $(\mathsf{expand}(\sigma \to \tau, P) \simeq^\perp \mathsf{expand}(\sigma, P) \to \mathsf{expand}(\tau, P))$.   □

4.2   Type Selector Arguments and Selection

The sets Argument of *type selector arguments* and IndArgument of *individual type selector arguments* are defined by the following pseudo-grammar:

$$A \in \mathsf{Argument} ::= \bar{A} \mid \{f_i = A_i\}^I$$
$$\bar{A} \in \mathsf{IndArgument} ::= * \mid f, \bar{A}$$

We define two relations that assign kinds to arguments:

$$\frac{}{* : *} \qquad \frac{\bar{A} : *}{f, \bar{A} : *} \qquad \frac{A_i : \kappa_i \quad \text{for all } i \text{ in } I}{\{f_i = A_i\}^I : \{f_i = \kappa_i\}^I}$$

$$\frac{}{* \lhd \kappa} \qquad \frac{\bar{A} \lhd \kappa_j}{f_j, \bar{A} \lhd \{f_i = \kappa_i\}^I} \text{ if } j \in I \qquad \frac{A_i \lhd \kappa_i \quad \text{for all } i \text{ in } I}{\{f_i = A_i\}^I \lhd \{f_i = \kappa_i\}^I}$$

Note that for every argument A there is exactly one kind κ such that $(A : \kappa)$. On the other hand, there are many kinds κ such that $(A \lhd \kappa)$.

Lemma 10. *If $(A \lhd \kappa)$ and $(\kappa \le \kappa')$, then $(A \lhd \kappa')$.*   □

We define two partial functions select^i and select^b. Both go from $\mathsf{Type} \times \mathsf{Argument}$ to Type. The two functions are similar. The main difference is that select^i performs selections on individual (joined) types, whereas select^b performs selections on branching types. We define the functions in two steps, first for the case where the function's first argument is a normal type:

$$\mathsf{select}^i(\tau, *) = \tau, \quad \text{if } \tau \text{ is individual}$$
$$\mathsf{select}^i(\forall (\mathsf{join}\{f_i = \bar{P}_i\}^I).\{f_i = \tau_i\}^I, (f_j, \bar{A})) = \mathsf{select}^i(\forall \bar{P}_j.\tau_j, \bar{A}), \quad \text{if } (j \in I)$$
$$\mathsf{select}^i(\{f_i = \tau_i\}^I, \{f_i = A_i\}^I) = \{f_i = \mathsf{select}^i(\tau_i, A_i)\}^I$$

$$\mathsf{select}^b(\tau, *) = \tau$$
$$\mathsf{select}^b(\{f_i = \tau_i\}^I, (f_j, \bar{A})) = \mathsf{select}^b(\tau_j, \bar{A}), \quad \text{if } (j \in I)$$
$$\mathsf{select}^b(\{f_i = \tau_i\}^I, \{f_i = A_i\}^I) = \{f_i = \mathsf{select}^b(\tau_i, A_i)\}^I$$

Now, for the case where the function's first argument is a type that isn't normal:

$$\mathsf{select}^i(\tau, A) = \mathsf{select}^i(\mathsf{nf}(\tau), A)$$
$$\mathsf{select}^b(\tau, A) = \mathsf{select}^b(\mathsf{nf}(\tau), A)$$

Lemma 11.

1. *If $(\tau : \kappa)$ and $\mathsf{select}^i(\tau, A)$ is defined, then $(A : \kappa)$.*
2. *If $(\tau : \kappa)$ and $(\mathsf{select}^i(\tau, A) = \tau')$, then $(\tau' : \kappa)$.*
3. *If $(\tau : \kappa)$ and $\mathsf{select}^b(\tau, A)$ is defined, then $(A \lhd \kappa)$.*

□

Lemma 12. *If $(f \in \{\mathsf{select}^i, \mathsf{select}^b\})$ and $(\sigma \to \tau : \kappa)$, then $(f(\sigma \to \tau, A) \simeq^\perp f(\sigma, A) \to f(\tau, A))$.*   □

5   Terms and Typing Rules

Let TermVar be a countably infinite set of λ-term variables. Let x range over TermVar. Let the set Term of explicitly typed λ-terms be given by the following pseudo-grammar:

$$M, N \in \text{Term} ::= \Lambda P.M \mid M[A] \mid \lambda x^\tau.M \mid M \ N \mid x^\tau$$

The λx binds the variable x in the usual way.[1] We identify terms that are equal up to renaming of bound variables.

A *type environment* is defined to be a finite function from TermVar to Type. We use the metavariable E to range over type environments. We extend the definitions of expansion, kind assignment and type equality to type environments:

$$\text{expand}(E, P)(x) \;=\; \text{expand}(E(x), P)$$

$$E : \kappa \overset{\text{def}}{\Longleftrightarrow} E(x) : \kappa \text{ for all } x \text{ in } \text{dom}(E)$$

$$E \simeq E' \overset{\text{def}}{\Longleftrightarrow} \begin{cases} \text{dom}(E) = \text{dom}(E') \text{ and} \\ (E(x) \simeq E'(x)) \text{ for all } x \text{ in } \text{dom}(E) \end{cases}$$

Typing judgement are of the form:

$$E \vdash M : \tau \text{ at } \kappa$$

The valid typing judgement are those that can be proven using the typing rules in Figure 3.

(ax) $\dfrac{}{E \vdash x^{E(x)} : E(x) \text{ at } \kappa}$ if $(E : \kappa)$

($\rightarrow_i$) $\dfrac{E[x \mapsto \sigma] \vdash M : \tau \text{ at } \kappa}{E \vdash \lambda x^\sigma.M : \sigma \rightarrow \tau \text{ at } \kappa}$

($\rightarrow_e$) $\dfrac{E \vdash M : \sigma \rightarrow \tau \text{ at } \kappa; \quad E \vdash N : \sigma \text{ at } \kappa}{E \vdash M \ N : \tau \text{ at } \kappa}$

($\forall_i$) $\dfrac{\text{expand}(E, P) \vdash M : \tau \text{ at } \lceil P \rceil}{E \vdash \Lambda P.M : \forall P.\tau \text{ at } \lfloor P \rfloor}$

($\forall_e$) $\dfrac{E \vdash M : \tau \text{ at } \kappa}{E \vdash M[A] : \tau' \text{ at } \kappa}$ if $(\text{select}^i(\tau, A) = \tau')$

($\simeq$) $\dfrac{E \vdash M : \tau \text{ at } \kappa}{E \vdash M : \tau' \text{ at } \kappa}$ if $(\tau \simeq \tau')$

Fig. 3. Typing Rules

---

[1] In this language, ΛP does *not* bind any variables!

Lemma 13.

1. *If $(E \vdash M : \tau$ at $\kappa)$, then $(\tau : \kappa)$.*
2. *If $(E \vdash M : \tau$ at $\kappa)$, then $(E : \kappa)$.*
3. *If $(E \vdash M : \tau$ at $\kappa)$ and $E \simeq E'$, then $(E' \vdash M : \tau$ at $\kappa)$.* □

6 Expansion, Selection and Substitution for Terms

In this section, we define auxiliary operations that are needed for the statements of the term reduction rules.

6.1 Expansion

In order to define substitution and β-reduction, we need to extend the expand operation to terms. This is necessary because the branching shape of type annotations changes when a term is substituted into a new context. First, expand is extended to parameters, arguments and kinds, by the following equations where X ranges over Parameter $\cup$ Argument $\cup$ Kind:

$$\text{expand}(X, *) = X$$
$$\text{expand}(X, \text{join}\{f_i = \bar{P}_i\}^I) = \{f_i = \text{expand}(X, \bar{P}_i)\}^I$$
$$\text{expand}(\{f_i = X_i\}^I, \{f_i = P_i\}^I) = \{f_i = \text{expand}(X_i, P_i)\}^I$$

Now, the expand operation is inductively extended to terms:

$$\text{expand}(\Lambda P'.M, P) = \Lambda(\text{expand}(P', P)). \, \text{expand}(M, P)$$
$$\text{expand}(M[A], P) = (\text{expand}(M, P))[\text{expand}(A, P)]$$
$$\text{expand}(\lambda x^\tau.M, P) = \lambda x^{\text{expand}(\tau, P)}. \, \text{expand}(M, P)$$
$$\text{expand}(M \, N, P) = (\text{expand}(M, P)) \, (\text{expand}(N, P))$$
$$\text{expand}(x^\tau, P) = x^{\text{expand}(\tau, P)}$$

Lemma 14. *If $(E \vdash M : \tau$ at $\kappa)$ and $(\lfloor P \rfloor \leq \kappa)$,
then $(\text{expand}(E, P) \vdash \text{expand}(M, P) : \text{expand}(\tau, P)$ at $\text{expand}(\kappa, P))$.* □

Corollary 1. *If $(E \vdash M : \tau$ at $\lfloor P \rfloor)$,
then $(\text{expand}(E, P) \vdash \text{expand}(M, P) : \text{expand}(\tau, P)$ at $\lceil P \rceil)$.* □

6.2 Substitution

A *substitution* is a finite function from TermVar to Term. We extend the operation expand to substitutions as follows:

$$\text{expand}(s, P)(x) = \text{expand}(s(x), P)$$

We now define the *application of a substitution s to a term M*. The definition is by induction on the structure of the term:

$$s(\Lambda P.M) = \Lambda P. \text{ expand}(s, P)(M)$$
$$s(M[A]) = (s(M))[A]$$
$$s(\lambda x^\tau.M) = \lambda x^\tau.\ s(M), \quad \text{if } x \text{ does not occur freely in ran}(s) \text{ and } x \notin \text{dom}(s)$$
$$s(M\ N) = s(M)\ s(N)$$
$$s(x^\tau) = s(x), \quad \text{if } x \in \text{dom}(s)$$
$$s(x^\tau) = x^\tau, \quad \text{if } x \notin \text{dom}(s)$$

We write $M[x := N]$ for the term that results from applying the singleton substitution $\{(x, N)\}$ to M.

We define typing judgement for substitutions as follows:

$$(E' \vdash s : E \text{ at } \kappa) \overset{\text{def}}{\Longleftrightarrow} (E' \vdash s(x^{E(x)}) : E(x) \text{ at } \kappa) \text{ for all } x \text{ in dom}(E)$$

Lemma 15. *If $(E' \vdash s : E \text{ at } \lfloor P \rfloor)$,*
then $(\text{expand}(E', P) \vdash \text{expand}(s, P) : \text{expand}(E, P) \text{ at } \lceil P \rceil)$. $\qquad\square$

Lemma 16. *If $(E \vdash M : \tau \text{ at } \kappa)$ and $(E' \vdash s : E \text{ at } \kappa)$,*
then $(E' \vdash s(M) : \tau \text{ at } \kappa)$. $\qquad\square$

6.3 Selection

The preceding treatment of substitution prepares for the definition of β-reduction of terms of the form $((\lambda x^\tau.M)N)$. We also need to define reduction of terms of the form $(\Lambda P.M)[A]$. To this end, we extend the select^b to parameters, arguments and kinds, by the following equations where X ranges over Parameter $\cup$ Argument $\cup$ Kind:

$$\text{select}^b(X, *) = X$$
$$\text{select}^b(\{f_i = X_i\}^I, (f_j, \bar{A})) = \text{select}^b(X_j, \bar{A}), \quad \text{if } j \in I$$
$$\text{select}^b(\{f_i = X_i\}^I, \{f_i = A_i\}^I) = \{f_i = \text{select}^b(X_i, A_i)\}^I$$

Lemma 17. *$(A \lhd \kappa)$ if and only if $\text{select}^b(\kappa, A)$ is defined.* $\qquad\square$

The select^b operation is extended to terms by induction on the structure of the term:

$$\text{select}^b(\Lambda P'.M, A) = \Lambda(\text{select}^b(P', A)).\ \text{select}^b(M, A)$$
$$\text{select}^b(M[A'], A) = (\text{select}^b(M, A))[\text{select}^b(A', A)]$$
$$\text{select}^b(\lambda x^\tau.M, A) = \lambda x^{\text{select}^b(\tau, A)}.\ \text{select}^b(M, A)$$
$$\text{select}^b(M\ N, A) = (\text{select}^b(M, A))\ (\text{select}^b(N, A))$$
$$\text{select}^b(x^\tau, A) = x^{\text{select}^b(\tau, A)}$$

The select^b operation is extended to type environments as follows:

$$\text{select}^b(E, A)(x) = \text{select}^b(E(x), A)$$

Lemma 18. *If $(E \vdash M : \tau$ at $\kappa)$ and $(A \lhd \kappa)$,*
then $(\mathsf{select}^b(E, A) \vdash \mathsf{select}^b(M, A) : \mathsf{select}^b(\tau, A)$ at $\mathsf{select}^b(\kappa, A))$.   □

7 Reduction Rules for Terms

We define a partial function match from Parameter $\times$ Argument to Parameter $\times$ Argument $\times$ Argument.[2] This function is needed for the reduction rule (β_Λ) for type selection.

$$\overline{\mathsf{match}(*, \bar{A}) = (*, *, \bar{A})} \qquad \overline{\mathsf{match}(\bar{P}, *) = (\bar{P}, *, \lceil \bar{P} \rceil)}$$

$$\frac{\mathsf{match}(\bar{P}_j, \bar{A}) = (\bar{P}', \bar{A}^s, A^a)}{\mathsf{match}(\mathsf{join}\{f_i = \bar{P}_i\}^I, (f_j, \bar{A})) = (\bar{P}', (f_j, \bar{A}^s), A^a)} \text{ if } j \in I$$

$$\frac{\mathsf{match}(P_i, A_i) = (P_i', A_i^s, A_i^a) \quad \text{for all } i \text{ in } I}{\mathsf{match}(\{f_i = P_i\}^I, \{f_i = A_i\}^I) = (\{f_i = P_i'\}^I, \{f_i = A_i^s\}^I, \{f_i = A_i^a\}^I)}$$

A parameter or argument is called *trivial* if it is also a kind.

Lemma 19.

1. *If P is a trivial parameter and $(\forall P.\tau : \kappa)$, then $(\forall P.\tau \simeq \tau)$.*
2. *If A is a trivial argument and $(\mathsf{select}^i(\tau, A) = \tau')$, then $(\tau' \simeq \tau)$.*   □

The reduction relation for terms is defined as the least compatible relation of terms that contains the following axioms:

$$
\begin{array}{lll}
(\beta_\lambda) & ((\lambda x^\tau.M)N) \to (M[x := N]) \\
(\beta_\Lambda) & (\Lambda P.M)[A] \to \Lambda P'.((\mathsf{select}^b(M, A^s))[A^a]), \\
& \quad \text{if } \mathsf{match}(P, A) = (P', A^s, A^a) \text{ and neither } P \text{ nor } A \text{ is trivial} \\
(*_\Lambda) & (\Lambda P.M) \to M, \quad \text{if } P \text{ is trivial} \\
(*_A) & (M[A]) \to M, \quad \text{if } A \text{ is trivial}
\end{array}
$$

Theorem 1 (Subject Reduction). *If $(M \to N)$ and $(E \vdash M : \tau$ at $\kappa)$, then $(E \vdash N : \tau$ at $\kappa)$.*   □

Proof. For (β_λ), one uses Lemma 16. For $(*_A)$ and $(*_\Lambda)$, one uses Lemma 19. For (β_Λ) one uses Lemma 18 and some other technical Lemmas, which we have omitted because of space constraints.   □

---

[2] In the second rule, note that $\lceil P \rceil \in$ Argument for all parameters P.

8   Correspondence of Typed and Untyped Reduction

The set UntypedTerm of *untyped terms* is defined by the following pseudo-grammar:

$$M, N \in \mathsf{UntypedTerm} ::= x \mid \lambda x.M \mid M\,N$$

Substitution for untyped terms is defined as usual, and so is β-reduction:

$$(\beta) \qquad (\lambda x.M)N \to M[x := N]$$

Let $\to^*$ denote the reflexive and transitive closure of $\to$. We define a map $|\cdot|$ from Term to UntypedTerm that erases type-annotations:

$$|\Lambda P.M| = |M| \qquad |\lambda x^\tau.M| = \lambda x.|M| \qquad |x^\tau| = x$$
$$|M[A]| = |M| \qquad |MN| = |M|\,|N|$$

Lemma 20.

1. If $\mathsf{expand}(M, P)$ *is defined, then* $(|\mathsf{expand}(M, P)| = |M|)$.
2. If $M[x := N]$ *is defined, then* $|M[x := N]| = |M|[x := |N|]$.
3. If $\mathsf{select}^b(M, A)$ *is defined, then* $(|\mathsf{select}^b(M, A)| = |M|)$. $\qquad\square$

Theorem 2 (Soundness of Reduction).
If $M, N \in$ Term *and* $M \to N$, *then* $|M| \to^* |N|$. $\qquad\square$

Lemma 21.

1. *Any sequence of* (β_Λ), $(*_\Lambda)$ *and* $(*_A)$ *reductions is terminating.*
2. *If* M *reduces to* N *by a* (β_Λ), $(*_\Lambda)$ *or* $(*_A)$ *reduction, then* $|M| = |N|$.
3. *If* $\mathsf{select}^i(\forall P.\tau, A)$ *is defined, then so is* $\mathsf{match}(P, A)$.
4. *A well-typed term that is free of* (β_Λ), $(*_\Lambda)$ *or* $(*_A)$ *redices is of the form*

$$\Lambda P_1 \ldots \Lambda P_n.M[A_1] \ldots [A_m]$$

where $n, m \geq 0$, *the* P_i's *and* A_i's *are not trivial, and* M *is either a variable, a* λ-*abstraction or an application.* $\qquad\square$

Theorem 3 (Completeness of Reduction).
If M *is well-typed and* $|M| \to |N|$, *then* $(M \to^* N)$. $\qquad\square$

Proof Sketch. The proof uses the previous lemma. To simulate a β-reduction step of the type erasure of M, one first applies (β_Λ), $(*_\Lambda)$ and $(*_A)$-reductions until no more such reductions are possible. Because it is well-typed, the resulting term allows a β_λ-reduction that simulates the β-reduction of the type erasure. $\qquad\square$

References

[1] T. Amtoft, F. Turbak. Faithful translations between polyvariant flows and polymorphic types. In *Programming Languages & Systems, 9th European Symp. Programming*, vol. 1782 of *LNCS*, pp. 26–40. Springer-Verlag, 2000.

[2] B. Capitani, M. Loreti, B. Venneri. Hyperformulae, parallel deductions and intersection types. *Electronic Notes in Theoretical Computer Science*, 50, 2001. Proceedings of ICALP 2001 workshop: Bohm's Theorem: Applications to Computer Science Theory (BOTH 2001), Crete, Greece, 2001-07-13.

[3] M. Coppo, M. Dezani-Ciancaglini. An extension of the basic functionality theory for the λ-calculus. *Notre Dame J. Formal Logic*, 21(4):685–693, 1980.

[4] M. Dezani-Ciancaglini, S. Ghilezan, B. Venneri. The "relevance" of intersection and union types. *Notre Dame J. Formal Logic*, 38(2):246–269, Spring 1997.

[5] A. Dimock, R. Muller, F. Turbak, J. B. Wells. Strongly typed flow-directed representation transformations. In *Proc. 1997 Int'l Conf. Functional Programming*, pp. 11–24. ACM Press, 1997.

[6] A. Dimock, I. Westmacott, R. Muller, F. Turbak, J. B. Wells. Functioning without closure: Type-safe customized function representations for Standard ML. In *Proc. 2001 Int'l Conf. Functional Programming*, pp. 14–25. ACM Press, 2001.

[7] A. Dimock, I. Westmacott, R. Muller, F. Turbak, J. B. Wells, J. Considine. Program representation size in an intermediate language with intersection and union types. In *Proceedings of the Third Workshop on Types in Compilation (TIC 2000)*, vol. 2071 of *LNCS*, pp. 27–52. Springer-Verlag, 2001.

[8] J.-Y. Girard. *Interprétation Fonctionnelle et Elimination des Coupures de l'Arithmétique d'Ordre Supérieur*. Thèse d'Etat, Université de Paris VII, 1972.

[9] A. J. Kfoury. A linearization of the lambda-calculus. *J. Logic Comput.*, 10(3), 2000. Special issue on Type Theory and Term Rewriting. Kamareddine and Klop (editors).

[10] A. J. Kfoury, H. G. Mairson, F. A. Turbak, J. B. Wells. Relating typability and expressibility in finite-rank intersection type systems. In *Proc. 1999 Int'l Conf. Functional Programming*, pp. 90–101. ACM Press, 1999.

[11] A. J. Kfoury, J. B. Wells. A direct algorithm for type inference in the rank-2 fragment of the second-order λ-calculus. In *Proc. 1994 ACM Conf. LISP Funct. Program.*, pp. 196–207, 1994.

[12] A. J. Kfoury, J. B. Wells. Principality and decidable type inference for finite-rank intersection types. In *Conf. Rec. POPL '99: 26th ACM Symp. Princ. of Prog. Langs.*, pp. 161–174, 1999.

[13] J. Palsberg, C. Pavlopoulou. From polyvariant flow information to intersection and union types. *J. Funct. Programming*, 11(3):263–317, May 2001.

[14] B. C. Pierce. Programming with intersection types, union types, and polymorphism. Technical Report CMU-CS-91-106, Carnegie Mellon University, Feb. 1991.

[15] G. Pottinger. A type assignment for the strongly normalizable λ-terms. In J. R. Hindley, J. P. Seldin, eds., *To H. B. Curry: Essays on Combinatory Logic, Lambda Calculus, and Formalism*, pp. 561–577. Academic Press, 1980.

[16] J. C. Reynolds. Towards a theory of type structure. In *Colloque sur la Programmation*, vol. 19 of *LNCS*, pp. 408–425, Paris, France, 1974. Springer-Verlag.

[17] J. C. Reynolds. Design of the programming language Forsythe. In P. O'Hearn, R. D. Tennent, eds., *Algol-like Languages*. Birkhauser, 1996.

[18] S. Ronchi Della Rocca, L. Roversi. Intersection logic. In *Computer Science Logic, CSL '01*. Springer-Verlag, 2001.

[19] F. Turbak, A. Dimock, R. Muller, J. B. Wells. Compiling with polymorphic and polyvariant flow types. In *Proc. First Int'l Workshop on Types in Compilation*, June 1997.

[20] P. Urzyczyn. Type reconstruction in $\mathbf{F}_\omega$. *Math. Structures Comput. Sci.*, 7(4):329–358, 1997.

[21] B. Venneri. Intersection types as logical formulae. *J. Logic Comput.*, 4(2):109–124, Apr. 1994.

[22] J. B. Wells. Typability and type checking in the second-order λ-calculus are equivalent and undecidable. In *Proc. 9th Ann. IEEE Symp. Logic in Comp. Sci.*, pp. 176–185, 1994. Superseded by [24].

[23] J. B. Wells. Typability is undecidable for F+eta. Tech. Rep. 96-022, Comp. Sci. Dept., Boston Univ., Mar. 1996.

[24] J. B. Wells. Typability and type checking in System F are equivalent and undecidable. *Ann. Pure Appl. Logic*, 98(1–3):111–156, 1999. Supersedes [22].

[25] J. B. Wells, A. Dimock, R. Muller, F. Turbak. A typed intermediate language for flow-directed compilation. In *Proc. 7th Int'l Joint Conf. Theory & Practice of Software Development*, pp. 757–771, 1997. Superseded by [26].

[26] J. B. Wells, A. Dimock, R. Muller, F. Turbak. A calculus with polymorphic and polyvariant flow types. *J. Funct. Programming*, 200X. To appear. Supersedes [25].

Exceptions, Continuations and Macro-expressiveness

James Laird

COGS, University of Sussex, UK
e-mail: jiml@cogs.susx.ac.uk

Abstract. This paper studies the the problem of expressing exceptions using first-class continuations in a functional-imperative language. The main result is that exceptions *cannot* be macro-expressed using first-class continuations and references (contrary to "folklore"). This is shown using two kinds of counterexample. The first consists of two terms which are equivalent with respect to contexts containing continuations and references, but which can be distinguished using exceptions. It is shown, however, that there are no such terms which do not contain `callcc`. However, there is a Π_1 sentence of first-order logic which is satisfied when interpreted in the domain of programs containing continuations and references but not satisfied in the domain of programs with exceptions and references. This is used to show that even when `callcc` is omitted from the source language, exceptions still cannot be expressed using continuations and references.

1 Introduction

All practical functional programming languages have operators for manipulating the flow of control, typically either first-class *continuations* or *exceptions*. There are clear differences between these features; the former are *statically* scoped, whilst the latter are handled *dynamically*. But how significant are these distinctions? (After all, many instances of control can be written using either continuations or exceptions.) This can be seen as a question of *relative expressive power*: can exceptions be expressed in terms of continuations and vice-versa [3]? The difficulty lies in formalising this problem; there is a consensus that translations between languages should be the basis for comparing their expressive power but different notions of what constitutes a satisfactory translation have been proposed in different contexts [11, 7, 1]. Having settled on one of them, a second problem is that translations compare whole languages rather than specific features, as Felleisen notes [1]:

> ... claims [about expressiveness] only tend to be true in specific language universes for specific conservative language restrictions: they often have no validity in other contexts!

For example, Lillibridge [6] has shown that adding ML-style exceptions to the simply-typed λ-calculus allows recursion to be encoded whilst adding `callcc`

D. Le Métayer (Ed.): ESOP 2002, LNCS 2305, pp. 133–146, 2002.

does not, and so by this measure exceptions are more powerful than continuations. However, "realistic" languages include some form of recursion directly and so this notion of expressiveness based on computational strength is too coarse to distinguish exceptions from `callcc` in general.

A more fine-grained approach is obtained if the translations between languages are restricted to those which preserve common structure — the terms themselves and their contextual equivalences — intact. Riecke and Thielecke [12] have shown that in the context of a simple functional language, exceptions cannot be expressed as a macro in terms of continuations and vice-versa, by giving terms of the simply-typed λ-calculus which are contextually equivalent when continuations are added to the language but inequivalent if exceptions are added, and terms which are equivalent in the presence of exceptions but not continuations. This does not resolve the issue, however, for languages like ML or Scheme which combine exceptions or continuations with assignable *references*. Thielecke [14] has shown that in the presence of state it is still the case that exception-handling cannot be used to macro-express `callcc`. He also observes that "...it is known (and one could call it "folklore") that in the presence of storable procedures, exceptions can be implemented by storing a current handler continuation." (An example of such an implementation is given in [10].) The inference drawn from this fact in [14] is that in the presence of higher-order references, continuations are strictly more expressive than exceptions, although, as we shall see, the implementation *fails* to conform to the criteria given in [1] and adopted in [12, 14] for a translation to be used to compare expressiveness.

1.1 Contribution of This Paper

The main formal results contained in this paper are two counterexamples to the assertion that exceptions can be expressed in terms of continuations and references. (An appendix gives (Standard ML of New Jersey) code corresponding to these examples.) Section 2 describes a language with exceptions, continuations and references, and gives some background on the theory of expressivenes of programming languages. The first counterexample (Section 3) is of the kind used in [12, 14]; two terms which are observationally equivalent in a language with continuations and references but which can be distinguished when exceptions are added. In fact, these two terms are actually equated by various "theories of control" such as the λC [2] and $\lambda \mu$-calculi [9], and hence these theories *are not sound* in the presence of exceptions.

However, the terms used in the first counterexample contain `callcc`, so it does not exclude the possibility that exceptions (in the absence of continuations) can be reduced to continuations and references. In fact, it is shown in Section 4 that no counterexample of the same form can exclude this possibility — because the implementation of exceptions using `callcc` and references preserves equivalences between terms which don't contain `callcc`.

Hence to show that the λ-calculus with exceptions and references cannot be reduced to the λ-calculus with continuations and references (Section 5), it proves necessary to develop the theory of expressiveness by describing a new and more general kind of counterexample to relative expressiveness — a Π_1 formula of the associated logic of programs which is satisfied in the domain of programs containing continuations and references, but not satisfied when programs can contain exceptions.

2   Exceptions, Continuations and References

Following [1], a programming language $\mathcal{L}$ will be formally considered to be a tuple $\langle \mathrm{Tm}_\mathcal{L}, \mathrm{Prog}_\mathcal{L} \subseteq_\mathcal{L}, \mathrm{Eval}_\mathcal{L} \rangle$ consisting of the terms of $\mathcal{L}$ (phrases generated from a signature Σ_L — a set of constructors with arities), the well-formed programs of $\mathcal{L}$ and the terminating programs of $\mathcal{L}$ respectively ($M \in \mathrm{Eval}_L$ will be written $M \Downarrow_\mathcal{L}$). $\mathcal{L}'$ is a conservative extension of $\mathcal{L}$ ($\mathcal{L} \subseteq \mathcal{L}'$) if $\mathrm{Tm}_\mathcal{L} \subseteq \mathrm{Tm}_{\mathcal{L}'}$, $\mathrm{Prog}_\mathcal{L} = \mathrm{Prog}_{\mathcal{L}'} \cap \mathrm{Tm}_\mathcal{L}$ and $\mathrm{Eval}_\mathcal{L} = \mathrm{Eval}_{\mathcal{L}'} \cap \mathrm{Prog}_\mathcal{L}$.

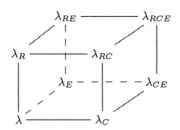

Fig. 1. A hierarchy of functional languages with side-effects

The languages considered here will all be contained within λ_{RCE}, a λ-calculus extended with exceptions, continuations and references. The various fragments of λ_{RCE} — λ-calculus with just references, with just exceptions, with just continuations, with exceptions and references, and with continuations and references — will be referred to as λ_R, λ_E, λ_C, λ_{RE} and λ_{RC} respectively (Figure 1). Terms of λ_{RCE} are formed according to the following grammar:

$M ::= x \mid * \mid \lambda x.M \mid M\,M \mid$
       abort $M \mid$ callcc $M \mid$
       new_exn $\mid$ raise $M \mid$ handle $M\,M \mid$
       new $\mid M := M \mid {!}M$.

We shall consider a typed form of λ_{RCE}, although the results described here apply (in a modified form) in an untyped setting as well. Types are generated from a basis — including a type unit containing the single value $*$, an empty type $\mathbf{0}$, and a type exn of exceptions — by $\Rightarrow$ and a type constructors for references:

$T ::= \text{unit} \mid \mathbf{0} \mid \text{exn} \mid T \Rightarrow T \mid T\,\text{ref}$

Terms are derived in contexts of typed variables; the typing judgements for exceptions, references and continuations are as follows:

$$\frac{}{\vdash \mathtt{new}_T{:}T \text{ ref}} \quad \frac{\Gamma \vdash M{:}T \text{ ref} \quad \Gamma \vdash N{:}T}{\Gamma \vdash M{:}=N{:}\mathtt{unit}} \quad \frac{\Gamma \vdash M{:}T \text{ ref}}{\Gamma \vdash !M{:}T}$$

$$\frac{}{\vdash \mathtt{new\_exn}{:}\mathtt{exn}} \quad \frac{\Gamma \vdash M{:}\mathtt{exn}}{\Gamma \vdash \mathtt{raise}\, M{:}S} \quad \frac{\Gamma \vdash M{:}\mathtt{exn} \quad \Gamma \vdash N{:}\mathtt{unit}}{\Gamma \vdash \mathtt{handle}\, M\, N{:}\mathtt{unit}}$$

$$\frac{\Gamma \vdash M{:}\mathbf{0}}{\Gamma \vdash \mathtt{abort}\, M{:}T} \quad \frac{\Gamma \vdash M{:}(T{\Rightarrow}S){\Rightarrow}T}{\Gamma \vdash \mathtt{callcc}\, M{:}T}$$

Reference and exception variables have been given the local declarations **new** and **new_exn** (although the counterexample of Section 3 also shows that global exceptions cannot be expressed by continuations and references). *Evaluation contexts* are used to pick out the next redex, and to represent continuations.

Definition 1. *Evaluation contexts are given by the following grammar:*
$$E[\cdot] ::= [\cdot] \mid E[\cdot]\, M \mid V\, E[\cdot] \mid$$
$$\quad\quad \mathtt{callcc}\, E[\cdot] \mid$$
$$\quad\quad E[\cdot] := M \mid V := E[\cdot] \mid !E[\cdot] \mid$$
$$\quad\quad \mathtt{raise}\, E[\cdot] \mid \mathtt{handle}\, E[\cdot]\, M \mid \mathtt{handle}\, h\, E[\cdot]$$
where M ranges over general terms, and V over values (variables, exception and reference names, and lambda abstractions).

Our exceptions are essentially a simplified version of Gunther, Rémy and Riecke's "simple exceptions" [3]. A modified notion of evaluation context is used to determine which handler will trap an exception; for each exception name h, $E_h[\cdot]$ ranges over the evaluation contexts which do not have a **handle** h in their spine.
$$E[\cdot] ::= [\cdot] \mid E_h[\cdot]\, M \mid V\, E_h[\cdot] \mid$$
$$\quad\quad \mathtt{callcc}\, E_h[\cdot] \mid$$
$$\quad\quad E_h[\cdot] := M \mid V := E_h[\cdot] \mid !E_h[\cdot] \mid$$
$$\quad\quad \mathtt{raise}\, E_h[\cdot] \mid \mathtt{handle}\, E_h[\cdot]\, M \mid \mathtt{handle}\, k\, E_h[\cdot]\ (k \neq h)$$
(Call-by-value) evaluation of programs is given by small-step reduction in an environment $\mathcal{E}$ consisting of a set of exception names, a set of reference names or locations $\mathcal{E}[L]$ and a state $\mathcal{E}[S]$, which is a partial map from L to values of λ_{RCE}.

Definition 2. *Operational semantics of λ_{RCE} is given by the reflexive transitive closure of the following relation between terms* of type $\mathbf{0}$ *in an environment $\mathcal{E}$ (containing a set of locations $\mathcal{E}[L]$, store $\mathcal{E}[S]$ and set of exception names $\mathcal{E}[Ex]$):*

$$E[\lambda x.M\, V], \mathcal{E} \longrightarrow E[M[V/x]], \mathcal{E}$$
$$E[\mathtt{new}], \mathcal{E}[L] \longrightarrow E[x], \mathcal{E}[L \cup \{x\}] : x \notin \mathcal{E}[L]$$
$$E[x := V], \mathcal{E}[S] \longrightarrow E[*], \mathcal{E}[S[x \mapsto V]] : x \in \mathcal{E}[L]$$
$$E[!x], \mathcal{E}[S] \longrightarrow E[S(x)], \mathcal{E}\ : S(x){\downarrow}$$
$$E[\mathtt{new\_exn}], \mathcal{E}[Ex] \longrightarrow E[h], \mathcal{E}[Ex \cup \{h\}] : h \notin \mathcal{E}[Ex]$$
$$E[\mathtt{handle}\, h *], \mathcal{E} \longrightarrow E[*], \mathcal{E} : h \in \mathcal{E}[Ex]$$
$$E[\mathtt{handle}\, h\, E_h[\mathtt{raise}\, h]], \mathcal{E} \longrightarrow E[*], \mathcal{E}h \in \mathcal{E}[Ex]$$
$$E[\mathtt{callcc}\, V], \mathcal{E} \longrightarrow E[V\, \lambda x.\mathtt{abort}\, E[x]], \mathcal{E}$$
$$E[\mathtt{abort}\, M], \mathcal{E} \longrightarrow M, \mathcal{E}$$

For a program (closed term) M : unit, let κ : unit $\Rightarrow$ **0** be a variable not occurring free in M, then $M \Downarrow$ if $\kappa M, \{\} \twoheadrightarrow \kappa *, \mathcal{E}$.

The standard notions of contextual approximation and equivalence will be used:
$M \lesssim_X N$ if for all closing λ_X-contexts, $C[M] \Downarrow$ implies $C[N] \Downarrow$.
$M \simeq_X N$ if $M \lesssim_X N$ and $N \lesssim_X M$.

Notation: $M; N$ will be used for $(\lambda x.N) M$ ($x \notin FV(N)$, let $x = N$ in M for $(\lambda x.M) N$, new_exn $h.M$ for $(\lambda x.M)$ new_exn and new $x := V.M$ for $(\lambda x.x :=$ $V; M)$ new. At each type T there is a divergent term $\perp^T : T = \text{new}_{\text{unit} \Rightarrow T} \, y.y :=$ $(\lambda x.!y \, x).!y *$.

2.1   Macro-expressiveness: Some Simple Examples

The common basis of the various comparisons [11, 7, 1] of expressiveness is the notion of a *reduction* or translation between programming languages.

Definition 3. *A reduction from $\mathcal{L}_1$ to $\mathcal{L}_2$ is a (recursively definable) mapping $\phi : \text{Tm}_{\mathcal{L}_1} \to \text{Tm}_{\mathcal{L}_2}$ such that:*

- *if $M \in \text{Prog}_{\mathcal{L}_1}$ then $\phi(M) \in \text{Prog}_{\mathcal{L}_2}$,*
- *$\phi(M) \Downarrow_{\mathcal{L}_2}$ if and only if $M \Downarrow_{\mathcal{L}_1}$.*

ϕ is compositional if it extends to a map on contexts such that $\phi(C[M]) = \phi(C)[\phi(M)]$.

However, existence of such a reduction (whether compositional or not) merely amounts to the possibility of writing an interpreter for $\mathcal{L}_1$ in $\mathcal{L}_2$. As a test of expressiveness it is unlikely to be sufficient to distinguish between Turing-complete languages. A finer notion of relative expressiveness can be obtained by introducing additional criteria for determining a suitable notion of translation, such as the requirement that a reduction from $\mathcal{L}_1$ to $\mathcal{L}_2$ should preserve their common structure in the following sense.

Definition 4. *Let ϕ be a reduction from $\mathcal{L}_1$ to $\mathcal{L}_2$, and $\mathcal{L} \subseteq \mathcal{L}_1, \mathcal{L}_2$. Then ϕ preserves $\mathcal{L}$-contexts if for all contexts $C[\cdot]$ of $\mathcal{L}$, $\phi(C[M]) = C[\phi(M)]$. If $\mathcal{L} = \mathcal{L}_1 \cap \mathcal{L}_2$ we shall just say that ϕ preserves contexts.*

The strength of this condition is clearly directly related to the content of $\mathcal{L}$; when the two languages are disjoint it has no force whereas when $\mathcal{L}_2 \subseteq \mathcal{L}_1$ it is equivalent to the notion of *eliminability* [1]; constructors $F_1, \dots, F_n$ in a language $\mathcal{L}$ are *eliminable* if there is a translation ϕ from $\mathcal{L}$ to $\mathcal{L} - \{F_1, \dots F_n\}$ such that for every $G \notin \{F_1, \dots, F_n\}$, $\phi(G(M_1 \dots M_n)) = G(\phi(M_1) \dots \phi(M_n))$ — i.e. ϕ preserves $\mathcal{L}$ contexts.

$F_1, \dots F_n$ are *macro-eliminable* if in addition each F_i is expressible as a "syntactic abstraction"; a context $A_i[\cdot] \dots [\cdot]$ of $\mathcal{L} - \{F_1, \dots, F_n\}$ such that $\phi(F_i(M_1 \dots M_n))$ $= A_i[(\phi(M_1)] \dots [(\phi(M_n)]$ — i.e. ϕ is compositional. We shall use syntactic abstractions for defining compositional translations.

As an example we shall first show that the forms of raise and handle used here have the full expressive power of Gunther, Rémy and Riecke's simple exceptions [3] by giving syntactic abstractions for the latter. Simple exceptions differ from our "even simpler" exceptions in that they can carry values; there is a type-constructor _ exn and at each type T there is an operation $raise_T$, typable as follows:

$$\frac{\Gamma \vdash M : T \text{ exn} \quad \Gamma \vdash N : T}{\Gamma \vdash raise_T\ M\ N : S}$$

In the presence of state, exceptions carrying values of type T can be expressed by storing the latter in a reference of type T ref and raising and handling an associated value of type exn.

The second difference between simple exceptions and those in λ_{RCE} is that the handle operation for the former applies a handler function when it catches an exception: the simple-exception handler handle L with M in N has the typing rule:

$$\frac{\Gamma \vdash L : S \text{ exn} \quad \Gamma \vdash M : S \Rightarrow T \quad \Gamma \vdash N : T}{\Gamma \vdash \text{handle } L \text{ with } M \text{ in } N : T.}$$

The operational semantics for simple exceptions is given by an appropriate notion of evaluation context (see [3]), and the evaluation rules:

$$E[\text{handle } h \text{ with } V \text{ in } U], \mathcal{E} \longrightarrow E[U], \mathcal{E}$$
$$E[\text{handle } h \text{ with } V \text{ in } E_h[raise_T\ h\ U]], \mathcal{E} \longrightarrow E[V\ U], \mathcal{E}.$$

We can simulate simple exception handling by raising an additional exception which escapes from the handler function if the main body of the program evaluates without raising an exception.

Proposition 1. *Simple exceptions are macro-eliminable in $\mathcal{L}$.*

Proof. The following syntactic abstractions for simple exceptions simulate the reduction rules appropriately, and generate an equivalent notion of evaluation context:

$\phi(T \text{ exn}) = (\phi(T) \text{ ref} \Rightarrow (\text{exn} \Rightarrow \text{unit})) \Rightarrow \text{unit},$
$\phi(\text{new\_exn}_T) = \text{new\_exn } x.\text{new}_T\ y.\lambda g.((g\ y)\ x),$
$\phi(raise_T M\ N) = \phi(M)\ (\lambda xy.y := \phi(N); \text{raise } x),$
$\phi(\text{handle } L \text{ with } M \text{ in } N) = \text{let } \phi(L) = l, \phi(M) = m, k = \text{new\_exn}, z = \text{new}_T \text{ in }$
$(\text{handle } k\ (l\ \lambda xy.\text{handle } y\ (z := \phi(N); \text{raise } k); z := m\ !x)); !z$

3   Interference between Control Effects

Another sense in which a translation may preserve program structure is as follows.

Definition 5. *If $\mathcal{L} \subseteq \mathcal{L}_1, \mathcal{L}_2$, then $\phi : \mathcal{L}_1 \to \mathcal{L}_2$ preserves $\mathcal{L}$-terms in context if it extends to $\mathcal{L}_1$-contexts and for all contexts $C[\cdot]$ of $\mathcal{L}_1$ and all terms M of $\mathcal{L}$, $\phi(C[M]) = \phi(C)[M]$.*

Lemma 1. *If ϕ is compositional and preserves $\mathcal{L}$-contexts then ϕ preserves $\mathcal{L}$-terms in context.*

Proof. For any $\mathcal{L}$ term M, $\phi(M) = M$ (as M is a 0-ary $\mathcal{L}$-context) and hence $\phi(C[M]) = \phi(C)[\phi(M)] = \phi(C)[M]$.

A translation which preserves terms in context will also preserve observational equivalences — this is the basis for a useful test given in [1]; a necessary condition for a compositional and context-preserving reduction to exist.

Proposition 2. *If there is a reduction $\phi : \mathcal{L}_2 \to \mathcal{L}_1$ which preserves $\mathcal{L}$-terms in context then for all M_1, M_2 in $\mathcal{L}$, $M \lesssim_{\mathcal{L}_1} N$ implies $M \lesssim_{\mathcal{L}_2} N$.*

Proof. For any $\mathcal{L}_2$ context $C[\cdot]$, $C[M] \Downarrow$ implies $\phi(C[M]) = \phi(C)[M] \Downarrow$ implies $\phi(C)[N] = \phi(C[N]) \Downarrow$ implies $C[N] \Downarrow$.

Our first example showing that exceptions cannot be expressed using continuations and references is of this form; we shall show that exceptions can be used to break a simple and natural equivalence which holds in λ_{RC}. Moreover, an equivalence which is at the basis of several "equational theories of control", such as Felleisen's $\lambda\mathcal{C}$-calculus [2], and Parigot's $\lambda\mu$-calculus [9] (which has been proposed as a "a metalanguage for functional computation with control" by Ong and Stewart [8]).

Proposition 3. *For any $E[\cdot] : S$, $M : T$ in λ_{RC}:*
$$E[\text{callcc}\, M] \simeq_{RC} \text{callcc}\, \lambda k^{S \Rightarrow T}.E[M\, \lambda y.k\, E[y]]$$

This equivalence is a typed version of the rule C_{lift} which is a key axiom of Sabry and Felleisen's equational theory of the λ-calculus with callcc [13], where it is shown to be sound using a cps translation. To prove that it holds in λ_{RC}, we use an approximation relation. Let $\sim$ be the least *congruence* on terms of λ_{RC} such that for all evaluation contexts $E[\cdot] : S$ and $M : T$, $E[\text{callcc}\, M] \sim$ $\text{callcc}\, \lambda k^{S \Rightarrow T}.E[M\, \lambda y.k\, E[y]]$,
and for all $E[\cdot]$ such that if x is not free in $E[\cdot]$ or M, $E[M] \sim \lambda x.E[x]\, M$.
We extend $\sim$ straightforwardly to a relationship on environments: $\mathcal{E} \sim \mathcal{E}'$ if $\mathcal{E}[L] = \mathcal{E}'[L]$ and for all $x \in \mathcal{E}[L]$, $\mathcal{E}[S](x) \sim \mathcal{E}'[S](x)$.

Lemma 2. *If $M, \mathcal{E} \sim M', \mathcal{E}'$ and $M', \mathcal{E}' \longrightarrow M'', \mathcal{E}''$ then $\exists \widehat{M}, \widehat{\mathcal{E}}$ such that $M, \mathcal{E} \twoheadrightarrow \widehat{M}, \widehat{\mathcal{E}}$ and $\widehat{M}, \widehat{\mathcal{E}} \sim M'', \mathcal{E}''$.*

Corollary 1. *If $M \sim M'$, then $M \Downarrow$ if and only if $M' \Downarrow$.*

To prove Proposition 3, it suffices to observe that for any $C[\cdot]$, $C[E[\text{callcc}\, M]] \sim$ $C[\text{callcc}\, \lambda k^{S \Rightarrow T}.E[M\, \lambda y.k\, E[y]]]$ and so by Lemma 2, $C[E[\text{callcc}\, M]] \Downarrow$ if and only if $C[\text{callcc}\, \lambda k^{S \Rightarrow T}.E[M\, \lambda y.k\, E[y]]] \Downarrow$.

However, because exceptions and continuations both manipulate the flow of control they can "interfere" with each other, breaking this equivalence, *even between terms which do not contain exceptions*. For instance, suppose f is a variable of type ($\text{unit} \Rightarrow \text{unit}$) $\Rightarrow \text{unit} \Rightarrow$ ($\text{unit} \Rightarrow \text{unit}$). Then we have ($\text{callcc}\, f$) $* \simeq_{RC} \text{callcc}\, \lambda k.(f\, \lambda y.k\, (y\, *))\, *$, as this is an instance of the equivalence proved in Proposition 3, with $E[\cdot] = [\cdot]\, *$.

Proposition 4. $\lambda f.((\text{callcc } f) *) \not\approx_{RCE} \lambda f.\text{callcc } \lambda k.((f \lambda y.k (y *)) *).$

Proof. Let $N \equiv \lambda g x.(\text{handle } h (g \lambda v.\text{raise } h); \text{raise } e.$
Then $(\text{callcc } N) *$ raises exception h but $\text{callcc } \lambda k.(N \lambda y.k (y *)) *$ raises exception e, and so if:
$C_1[\cdot] \equiv \text{new\_exn } h, e.\text{handle } h (\lambda f.[\cdot] N),$
$C_2[\cdot] \equiv \text{new\_exn } h, e.\text{handle } e (\lambda f.[\cdot] N),$
then $C_1[E[\text{callcc } f]] \Downarrow$ and $C_1[\text{callcc } \lambda k.E[f \lambda y.k E[y]]] \Downarrow,$
but $C_2[\text{callcc } \lambda k.E[f \lambda y.k E[y]]] \Downarrow$ and $C_2[E[\text{callcc } f]] \Downarrow.$

Corollary 2. *Exceptions are not macro-eliminable in λ_{RCE}.*

The fact that exceptions cannot be expressed in control calculi based on first-class continuations such as λC or $\lambda \mu$ has already been shown in [12]. But the result given here is stronger — these calculi are not even sound for reasoning about exception-free programs if there is the possibility that they might interact with exceptions. This is an important point of difference between control calculi and the (call-by-value) λ-calculus, which is notable for its robustness in the presence of side-effects.

4   Implementing Exceptions with Continuations

We have established that exceptions, continuations and references cannot be satisfactorily reduced to continuations and references, but this leaves open the problem of whether exceptions and references can be reduced to exceptions and continuations. In other words, is there a translation from λ_{RE} into λ_{RC} which preserves only the terms or contexts of λ_R? The existence of even a limited reduction of this kind would lend some plausibility to the claim that continuations (with references) are more expressive than exceptions, because it is known not to be possible to reduce continuations and references to exceptions and references [14].

Moreover, it is possible to give alternative operational semantics of exceptions combined with continuations. For example, New Jersey SML includes an additional type constructor — control_cont— for "primitive continuations" which ignore enclosing exception handlers, and control operators — capture and escape — corresponding to callcc and throw, for manipulating them. For programs without exceptions, substituting capture and escape for callcc and throw yields an equivalent program, but this is not true in the presence of exceptions, and in fact the counterexample of Section 3 is not valid for primitive continuations.

However, exceptions *cannot* break any equivalence between λ_R terms which is not broken by continuations and references, because there is an implementation of exceptions using continuations and references which preserves terms of λ_R in context. This implementation is essentially as described in [10]. Exception names are represented as references of type $(\text{unit} \Rightarrow 0) \Rightarrow (\text{unit} \Rightarrow 0) \Rightarrow 0$ — they are not used to store anything, but can be tested for equality — define:

If $M = N$ then L else $L' \equiv (M := \lambda xy.y *); (N := \lambda xy.x *); (!M \, \lambda z.L \, \lambda z.L')$.
The current continuation of each handler is stored in a stack, which is represented as "handler function" inside a reference variable exh. Raising an exception simply applies the value of exh to the exception name, which then replaces the current continuation with the relevant handler continuation, and resets exh. Non-compositionality of the implementation stems from the global nature of exh; access to this variable must be shared by all parts of a term, but it must be initialized at the start of each program.

Thus the implementation can be represented as a translation ψ on *terms* of λ_{RE} defined by the following syntactic abstractions:

$\psi(\text{new\_exn}) = \text{new}$,
$\psi(\text{handle } M \, N) = \text{let } old = !exh$
$\qquad\qquad\quad \text{in callcc } \lambda k.exh := \lambda y.\text{If } \psi(M) = y \text{ then } (exh := old; (k \, \psi(N)))$
$\qquad\qquad\qquad\qquad\qquad\qquad\qquad\qquad\qquad\qquad\quad \text{else } (old \, y))$,
$\psi(\text{raise } M)) = !exh \, \psi(M)$.

This yields a translation ϕ on *programs*: $\phi(M) = \text{new } exh := \lambda x.\bot.\psi(M)$ such that if $\phi(C)[\cdot] =_{df} \text{new } exh := \lambda x.\bot.\psi(C)[\cdot]$ then ϕ preserves λ_R terms-in-context.

Proposition 5. *For any program M of λ_{RE}, $M \Downarrow$ if and only if $\phi(M) \Downarrow$.*

Proof. Define ψ as a map on evaluation contexts as follows:
$\psi([\cdot]) = [\cdot], \psi(E[V [\cdot]]) = \psi(E)[\psi(V) [\cdot]], \ldots,$
$\psi(E[\text{raise} [\cdot]]) = \psi(E)[(!exh [\cdot]], \psi(E[\text{handle } h [\cdot]]) = \psi(E)[[\cdot]; !exh \, h]$.
This map is used to define an operation $\ulcorner E[\cdot] \urcorner$ which extracts the current contents of exh, represented as a list of pairs $(h, E[\cdot])$ of names and handler contexts:
$\ulcorner [\cdot] \urcorner = [], \ulcorner E[V [\cdot]] \urcorner = \ulcorner E[\cdot] \urcorner, \ldots, \ulcorner E[\text{handle } h [\cdot]] \urcorner = \ulcorner E[\cdot] \urcorner :: (h, \psi(E[\cdot]))$.
An inductive proof of soundness can then be based on the following facts:
$E[\psi(E'[M])], \mathcal{E}[exh \mapsto l] \twoheadrightarrow E[\psi(E')[\psi(M)], \mathcal{E}[exh \mapsto l :: \ulcorner E'[\cdot] \urcorner]$,
and if $E[M], \mathcal{E} \longrightarrow E[M'], \mathcal{E}'$ then:
$\psi(E)[\psi(M)], \mathcal{E}[exh \mapsto l] \twoheadrightarrow \psi(E)[\psi(M')], \mathcal{E}'[exh \mapsto l]$.

Corollary 3. *Equivalence of λ_R terms with respect to λ_{RCE} contexts is conservative over equivalence of λ_R terms with respect to λ_{RC} contexts.*

Thus the implementation cannot be soundly extended to one which preserves λ_{RC} terms in context; the proof of Proposition 4 provides a counterexample — $\phi(C_2)[(\text{callcc } f) *]$ converges.

5   Expressiveness and First-Order Formulas

Does Corollary 3 entail that exceptions can be expressed using continuations and references if we don't have continuations in our source language? We might reasonably take the fact that the implementation of exceptions preserves λ_R equivalences to be *the* sufficient condition for it to be a satisfactory reduction of λ_{RE} to λ_{RC}. However, we shall show that no translation from λ_{RE} to λ_{RC} can exist which adheres to our original criteria — compositionality and preservation of contexts — as such a translation will preserve the truth of all Π_1 statements which do not mention exceptions, whereas there is a such a statement which is true in λ_{RC} but not in λ_{RE}.

Definition 6. *For a programming language $\mathcal{L}$, let the* object language of $\mathcal{L}$, $\mathrm{obj}(\mathcal{L})$, *be the language of first-order logic with two unary predicates* Prog *and* Eval *and terms generated from* $\Sigma_{\mathcal{L}}$, *together with a distinct set of logical variables* x, y, z, ...
Let $\mathcal{M}(\mathcal{L})$ be the $\mathrm{obj}(\mathcal{L})$-structure with the domain $\mathrm{Tm}_{\mathcal{L}}$ in which each term of $\mathrm{obj}(\mathcal{L})$ is interpreted as the corresponding term of $\mathcal{L}$, and $\mathcal{M}(\mathcal{L}) \models$ Prog(t) if and only if $t \in \mathrm{Prog}_{\mathcal{L}}$ and $\mathcal{M}(\mathcal{L}) \models$ Eval(t) if and only if $t \in \mathrm{Eval}_{\mathcal{L}}$.

Proposition 6. *If there is a compositional and context-preserving translation $\phi : \mathcal{L}_1 \to \mathcal{L}_2$ then for all Π_1 sentences of $\mathrm{obj}(\mathcal{L}_1 \cap \mathcal{L}_2))$, if $\mathcal{M}(\mathcal{L}_2) \models \theta$ then $\mathcal{M}(\mathcal{L}_1) \models \theta$.*

Proof. If $\mathcal{M}(\mathcal{L}_1) \not\models \forall y_1 \ldots y_n.\theta(y_1, \ldots, y_n)$ then there exist terms $M_1, \ldots M_n$ in $\mathcal{L}_1$ such that $\mathcal{M}(\mathcal{L}_1) \models \neg\theta(M_1, \ldots, M_n)$. It is then straightforward to show by structural induction that $\mathcal{M}(\mathcal{L}_2) \models \neg\theta(\phi(M_1), \ldots, \phi(M_n))$, and hence $\mathcal{M}(\mathcal{L}_2) \not\models \forall y_1 \ldots y_n.\theta$ as required.

So to show that there is no compositional and context-preserving reduction from $\mathcal{L}_1$ to $\mathcal{L}_2$, it is sufficient to find a Π_1 sentence θ of $\mathrm{obj}(\mathcal{L}_1 \cap \mathcal{L}_2)$ such that $\mathcal{M}(\mathcal{L}_2) \models \theta$ and $\mathcal{M}(\mathcal{L}_1) \not\models \theta$. In a λ-calculus-based language this *includes* all counterexamples in the form of a contextual equivalence of $\mathcal{L}_2$ which is broken in $\mathcal{L}_1$ since contextual equivalence of values U, V can be expressed in $\mathrm{obj}(\mathcal{L})$ by the Π_1 sentence $\forall x.\mathrm{Eval}(x\, U) \iff \mathrm{Eval}(x\, V)$. But we gain access to new counterexamples which are not of this form; we shall give a context $C[\cdot]$ and a value U of λ_R such that for $\theta \equiv \forall x, y.\mathrm{Prog}(C[x]) \wedge \mathrm{Eval}(y\, C[x]) \implies \mathrm{Eval}(y\, U)$ we have $\mathcal{M}(\lambda_{RC}) \models \theta$ and $\mathcal{M}(\lambda_{RE}) \not\models \theta$.

Let $T = (\mathrm{unit} \Rightarrow 0) \Rightarrow 0$, $U = \lambda g : T.g$, and $C[\cdot] \equiv V \lambda f : T.([\cdot] : 0)$, where $V \equiv \lambda F.\lambda g.\lambda x.\mathrm{new}\, z := \lambda a.((z := \lambda y.x\, *); g\, a).F\, \lambda w.!z\, w$. So θ represents the assertion that for any $M : 0$ containing only $f : (\mathrm{unit} \Rightarrow 0) \Rightarrow 0$ free, $V \lambda f.M \lesssim \lambda g.g$.

Proposition 7. $\mathcal{M}(\lambda_{RE}) \not\models \theta$.

Proof. Let $M \equiv \mathrm{new\_exn}\, h.(\mathrm{handle}\, h\, (f\, \lambda x.\mathrm{raise}\, h); \bot); f\, \lambda w.\bot$ and $D[\cdot] \equiv \mathrm{new\_exn}\, k.\mathrm{handle}\, k\, ((([\cdot]\, \lambda x.\mathrm{handle}\, k\, (x\, *); \bot)\, \lambda y.\mathrm{raise}\, k); \bot)$. Then $D[V \lambda f.M] \Downarrow$ but $D[\lambda g.g] \Uparrow$.

The proof that $\mathcal{M}(\lambda_{RC}) \models \theta$ can be outlined via a series of lemmas about $\lesssim_{RC}$ and $\simeq_{RC}$. First we show that terms of type 0 containing only $f : T \Rightarrow 0$ free can be reduced to a "head-normal form".
Write $\mathrm{new}\, \bar{y} := \bar{v}.M$ for $\mathrm{new}\, y_1.\mathrm{new}\, y_2 \ldots \mathrm{new}\, y_n.y_1 := v_1; y_2 := v_2; \ldots; y_n := v_n.M$.

Lemma 3. *If $M : \mathbf{0}$ is a λ_{RC} term containing only $f : T \Rightarrow \mathbf{0}$ free, then there are some λ_{RC}-values $U : T, \overline{v}$ such that $M \lesssim_{RC} \mathbf{new}\,\overline{y} := \overline{v}.f\,U$.*

Proof. The following facts (proved using approximation relations) are used to inductively *reduce* terms of type $M : \mathbf{0}$ to head-normal form:
$E[\mathbf{abort}\,M] : \mathbf{0} \simeq_{RC} M$
$E[\mathbf{callcc}\,M] : \mathbf{0} \simeq_{RC} E[M\,\lambda x.\mathbf{abort}\,E[x]]$
$E[\mathbf{new}\,z.M] \simeq_{RC} \mathbf{new}\,z.E[M]$
$\mathbf{new}\,\overline{y} := \overline{v}.E[!y_i] \simeq_{RC} \mathbf{new}\,\overline{y} := \overline{v}.E[v_i]$
$\mathbf{new}\,\overline{y} := \overline{v}.E[y_i := U] \simeq_{RC}$
$\mathbf{new}\,y_1 := v_1 \ldots y_{i-1} := v_{i-1}.y_{i+1} := v_{i+1} \ldots y_n := v_n.y_i := U.E[*]$.
If this reduction process *does not* terminate, then M is equivalent to $\bot_{\mathbf{0}}$.

The following lemma is proved using approximation relations.

Lemma 4. i *If a is not free in W then:*
   $\mathbf{new}\,z := \lambda a.((z := W); M).\mathbf{new}\,\overline{y} := \overline{v}.!z\,U$
   $\simeq_{RC} \mathbf{new}\,z := W.\mathbf{new}\,\overline{y} := \overline{v}.M[U/a]$.
ii *For any term $M(f)$ and value V which do not contain z free:*
   $\mathbf{new}\,z := V.M[\lambda y.!z\,y/f] \simeq_{RC} M[V/f]$.

The final lemma is a refinement of Lemma 3.

Lemma 5. *For any term $M \equiv \mathbf{new}\,\overline{y} := \overline{v}.\lambda w.N : \mathbf{unit} \Rightarrow \mathbf{0}$, containing only $x : \mathbf{unit} \Rightarrow \mathbf{0}$ free, $M \lesssim_{RC} x$.*

Proposition 8. *For any λ_{RC}-term $M(f) : \mathbf{0}$ which contains only $f : (\mathbf{unit} \Rightarrow \mathbf{0}) \Rightarrow \mathbf{0}$ free, $V\,\lambda f.M \lesssim_{RC} \lambda g.g$.*

Proof. By Lemma 3, there exist $U, \overline{v}$ such that $M \lesssim_{RC} \mathbf{new}\,\overline{y} := \overline{v}.f\,U$ and hence $V\,\lambda f.M$
$\lesssim_{RC} \lambda gx.\mathbf{new}\,z := \lambda a.(z := \lambda b.x\,*); g\,a.(\mathbf{new}\,\overline{y} := \overline{v}.f\,U)[\lambda w.!z\,w/f]$
$\simeq_{RC} \lambda gx.\mathbf{new}\,z := \lambda a.(z := \lambda b.x\,*); g\,a.(\mathbf{new}\,\overline{y} := \overline{v}.!z\,U)[\lambda w.!z\,w/f]$
$\lesssim_{RC} \lambda gx.\mathbf{new}\,z := \lambda b.x\,*.\mathbf{new}\,\overline{y} := \overline{v}.g\,U[\lambda w.!z\,w/f]$ (By Lemma 4.i)
$\simeq_{RC} \lambda gx.\mathbf{new}\,\overline{y} := \overline{v}.g\,U[\lambda b.x\,*/f]$ (By Lemma 4.ii)
$\simeq_{RC} \lambda gx.g\,(\mathbf{new}\,\overline{y} := \overline{v}.U)[\lambda b.x\,*/f]$
$\lesssim_{RC} \lambda gx.g\,x$ (By Lemma 5) $\simeq_{RC} \lambda g.g$.

Corollary 4. *There is no compositional and context-preserving reduction from λ_{RE} to λ_{RC}.*

6   Conclusions

What relevance do these results have to the design, implementation and application of programming languages? Whilst expressiveness can mean the facility to write concise, flexible and efficient programs, the kind of expressive power which is embodied in our counterexamples does not appear to be particularly useful. Indeed, quite the reverse — combining continuations and exceptions gives the "power" to write programs with unpredictable behaviour, and this should be balanced against the usefulness of these effects when permitting such combinations. A better way to combine the simplicity of exceptions with the power of continuations could be to provide dynamically bound control constructs which still allow complex, continuation-style behaviour, such as *prompts* [3].

The difficulty of predicting on an ad hoc basis how control effects will interact suggests that more formal ways of reasoning about them would be useful. One possibility is equational reasoning using "control calculi" such as $\lambda\mathcal{C}$ [2] or $\lambda\mu$ [8]. The counterexample in Section 3 shows the limitations of these calculi, however, in that their equational theories are not consistent with the presence of exceptions.

There are many other ways to model or reason about control, but one which deserves mention is *game semantics*. The results described here arose from a semantic study of exceptions and continuations in a fully abstract games model [4, 5]. Thus one of the conclusions they support is a methodological one; game semantics — with its focus on definability and full abstraction — can be a useful tool for investigating relative expressiveness. Moreover game-based reasoning can be readily converted into syntactic examples (using definability results) which can be understood in isolation from the semantics.

Acknowledgments

I would like to thank Guy McCusker and the referees for their comments.

References

1. Matthias Felleisen. On the expressive power of programming languages. In *Science of Computer Programming*, volume 17, pages 35–75, 1991.
2. Matthias Felleisen, Daniel P. Friedman, Eugene E. Kohlbecker, and Bruce Duba. A syntactic theory of sequential control. *Theoretical Computer Science*, 52:205 – 207, 1987.
3. C. Gunter, D. Rémy, and J. Riecke. A generalization of exceptions and control in ML like languages. In *Proceedings of the ACM Conference on Functional Programming and Computer Architecture*, pages 12–23, 1995.
4. J. Laird. Full abstraction for functional languages with control. In *Proceedings of the Twelfth International Symposium on Logic In Computer Science, LICS '97*. IEEE Computer Society Press, 1997.
5. J. Laird. A fully abstract game semantics of local exceptions. In *Proceedings of the Sixteenth International Symposium on Logic In Computer Science, LICS '01*. IEEE Computer Society Press, 2001.
6. M. Lillibridge. Unchecked exceptions can be strictly more powerful than Call/CC. *Higher-Order and Symbolic Computation*, 12(1):75–104, 1999.
7. J. Mitchell. On abstraction and the expressive power of programming languages. In *Proc. Theor. Aspects of Computer Software*, pages 290–310, 1991.
8. C.-H. L. Ong and C. Stewart. A Curry-Howard foundation for functional computation with control. In *Proceedings of ACM SIGPLAN-SIGACT syposium on Principles of Programming Languages, Paris, January 1997*. ACM press, 1997.

9. M. Parigot. $\lambda\mu$ calculus: an algorithmic interpretation of classical natural deduction. In *Proc. International Conference on Logic Programming and Automated Reasoning*, pages 190–201. Springer, 1992.
10. J. Reynolds. *Theories of Programming Languages*. Cambridge University Press, 1998.
11. Jon G. Riecke. *The Logic and Expressibility of Simply-Typed Call-by-Value and Lazy Languages*. PhD thesis, Massachusetts Institute of Technology, 1991. Available as technical report MIT/LCS/TR-523 (MIT Laboratory for Computer Science).
12. J. Riecke and H. Thielecke. Typed exceptions and continuations cannot macro-express each other. In J. Wiedermann, P. van Emde Boas and M. Nielsen, editor, *Proceedings of ICALP '99*, volume 1644 of *LNCS*, pages 635 –644. Springer, 1999.
13. A. Sabry and M. Felleisen. Reasoning about programs in continuation-passing style. *LISP and Symbolic Computation*, 6(3/4):289–360, 1993.
14. H. Thielecke. On exceptions versus continuations in the presence of state. In *Proceedings of ESOP 2000*, volume 1782 of *LNCS*. Springer, 2000.

Appendix

```
(* SML_NJ code corresponding to sections 3 - 5.*)
(* Counterexample from section 3: *)
open SMLofNJ.Cont;
exception E;exception F
fun M y x = ((y (fn z => raise E)) handle E =>();raise F);
(* (callcc (fn k => (M (fn x => throw k x)))) ();
   raises exception E whereas
   callcc (fn k =>  ((M (fn x => throw k (x ())))  ()));
   raises exception F *)


(* Implementation of exceptions  described in section 4:*)
fun diverge x = diverge x;
val exhandler = ref (fn x:unit ref => (diverge ()):unit);
val new_exn M = = M (ref ());
fun handle_xn h x = let val old = !exhandler in
                    (callcc (fn k =>
                    ((exhandler := (fn y =>
                    (if (y = h)
                        then ((exhandler:= old);(throw k ()))
                        else  (old y))));
                    ((fn v => ((exhandler:= old);v)) (x ()))))))
 end;
(*It's necessary to ``thunk'' the second argument to handle_xn.*)
fun raise_xn h  = diverge (!exhandler h);


(*Counterexample from section 5: *)
datatype Empty = empty of Empty;
```

```
fun V g (f: (unit -> Empty) -> Empty) (x:unit -> Empty) =
let val z = (ref diverge) in
  ((z:= (fn u => ((z:= (fn y => x ()));(f u))));
  ((diverge (g (fn w => (!z w)))))):Empty
 end;
fun N f = let exception H in
          (diverge (f (fn w=>raise H)) handle H=>();f diverge)
end;
fun arg1 x = diverge (diverge (x ()) handle F => ());
fun arg2 z = raise F;
(*diverge (((V N) arg1) arg2) handle F=>(); converges, *)
(*diverge (((fn g => g) arg1) arg2) handle F =>(); diverges.*)
```

A Theory of Second-Order Trees

Neal Glew

aglew@acm.org

Abstract. This paper describes a theory of second-order trees, that is, finite and infinite trees where nodes of the tree can bind variables that appear further down in the tree. Such trees can be used to provide a natural and intuitive interpretation for type systems with equirecursive types and binding constructs like universal and existential quantifiers. The paper defines the set of *binding trees*, and a subset of these called *regular binding trees*. These are similar to the usual notion of regular trees, but generalised to take into account the binding structure. Then the paper shows how to interpret a second-order type system with recursive quantifiers as binding trees, and gives a sound and complete axiomatisation of when two types map to the same tree. Finally the paper gives a finite representation for trees called *tree automata*, and gives a construction for deciding when two automata map to the same tree. To tie everything together, the paper defines a mapping from types to automata, thus giving a decision procedure for when two types map to the same tree.

1   Introduction

In the theory of type systems there are two approaches to recursive types, the *isorecursive* and *equirecursive* approach. In the *isorecursive approach*, the types rec $\alpha.\tau$ and $\tau\{\alpha := $ rec $\alpha.\tau\}$[1] are considered different but isomorphic types. The expression language includes type coercions[2] $\mathsf{roll}(e)$ and $\mathsf{unroll}(e)$ for converting a value of one type to the other. The isorecursive approach is easier to construct decision procedures for, and is easier to prove sound; but it requires programs to contain type coercions. In the *equirecursive approach*, the types rec $\alpha.\tau$ and $\tau\{\alpha := $ rec $\alpha.\tau\}$ are considered equal, and there are no expression-level constructs for dealing with recursive types. The presence of this equality makes it more difficult to develop decision procedures for equality and subtyping, and more difficult to prove the type system sound. However, there are no type coercions in programs, and more types are equivalent. For example, rec $\alpha.\tau$ and rec $\alpha.(\tau\{\alpha := \tau\})$ are equal in the equirecursive types approach but are not intercoercible in the isorecursive approach.

A more fundamental problem with the equirecursive approach is that previous work on formalising it has gaps (see below). This paper fills these gaps by providing solid foundations for second-order type systems with equirecursive types.

---

[1] The notation $x\{y := z\}$ denotes the capture avoiding substitution of z for y in x.

[2] A type coercion changes the type of an expression but has no runtime effect.

D. Le Métayer (Ed.): ESOP 2002, LNCS 2305, pp. 147–161, 2002.

Amadio and Cardelli [AC93] were the first to investigate the equirecursive approach. They proposed the *tree interpretation* of recursive types, which is based on the idea that if the equality between rec $\alpha.\tau$ and $\tau\{\alpha := \text{rec } \alpha.\tau\}$ is applied repeatedly then recursive types expand into infinite trees that have no recursive quantifiers. Then, types are equal exactly when their fully-expanded trees are the same. Furthermore, subtyping can first be defined on trees and then lifted to types. Amadio and Cardelli defined a suitable tree model for a first-order type system, and a definition of subtyping between trees. Then they gave a set of type equality and subtyping rules, and proved them sound and complete with respect to the tree interpretation. Finally they gave an algorithm for deciding type equality and subtyping. Their algorithm is exponential time in the worst case, which is much worse than the linear time algorithm in the isorecursive approach.

Kozen et al. [KPS95] reduced this exponential time complexity to polynomial time. First they defined term automata,[3] which, like types, are a finite representation for trees. Briefly, a term automaton is finite state machine. Each state represents a collection of nodes in a tree, the initial state is the root of the tree, and the transition function gives the children for each node and the labels on the edges to these children. Kozen et al. gave an intersection-like construction on term automata that can be used to decide equality and subtyping in quadratic time. In both Amadio and Cardelli and Kozen et al.'s work, only first-order systems were considered, and their results do not generalise in a straightforward manner to second-order types.

Colazzo and Ghelli [CG99] investigated a second-order type system with equirecursive quantifiers. They gave a coinductively defined set of type rules (type rules are normally defined inductively), and described and proved correct an algorithm for deciding subtyping. They did not show the relation between their rules and Amadio and Cardelli's rules. Nor did they analyse the complexity of their algorithm, although they conjectured it was exponential. Their algorithm is essentially a search algorithm with the curious feature that it cuts off search when it sees the same subtyping judgement for the third, not second, time. They were able to show that this criterion is necessary and sufficient, but never gave an intuitive explanation.

This paper extends the tree interpretation and idea of tree automata from first-order to second-order trees. The first contribution is a notion of second-order finite and infinite trees suitable as a semantic model for types. The second contribution is a proof that the usual equality rules for equirecursive types are sound and complete for this model. The third contribution is notion of tree automata suitable for second-order trees. The fourth contribution is a polynomial time decision procedure for type equality. This paper deals only with equality and subtyping is left to future work. Since equality is not something specific to types, I will call them terms in the sequel. The rest of the paper presents each contribution in turn. Full details including proofs are available in a companion technical report [Gle02].

---

[3] This paper will call Kozen et al.'s term automata, tree automata.

2   Preliminaries

The theory is meant to be general and to abstract over everything else in the term system. Therefore, I will assume the term language consists of variables, recursive quantifiers, and terms build from node labels $nl \in NL$. Each node label will take a number of arguments, which will be identified using labels $\ell \in L$, and for each argument may bind a certain number of variables. The function $spec \in NL \rightarrow L \xrightarrow{\text{fin}} \mathbb{N}$ defines which arguments a node label takes and how many variables it binds for each. For example, the system $\mathcal{F}_{\leq \mu}$ of Colazzo and Ghelli has $NL = \{\top, \rightarrow, \forall\}$, $L = \{\text{arg}, \text{bnd}, \text{bdy}, \text{res}\}$, and $spec = \{(\rightarrow, \text{arg}, 0), (\rightarrow, \text{res}, 0), (\forall, \text{bnd}, 0), (\forall, \text{bdy}, 1)\}$. In this system, $\forall$ is a quantifier for bounded polymorphic types and binds one variable in its body (label bdy), so its specification is 1; the bound (label bnd) does not bind a variable, so its specification is 0. The rest of the paper will not refer to $spec$, instead it will use functions $\text{LABELS}(nl) = \text{dom}(spec(nl))$ and $\text{BIND}(nl, \ell) = spec(nl)(\ell)$.

Notations and Conventions $A \rightharpoonup B$ is the set of all partial functions from A to B; $A \xrightarrow{\text{fin}} B$ is the set of partial functions from A to B with finite domain. If e_1 and e_2 are possibly undefined expressions then $e_1 = e_2$ means that either both are defined and equal or both are undefined. A^* is the set of finite sequences of elements from A; ϵ is the empty sequence; prefix, concatenation, and append are written using juxtaposition; if $x, y \in A^*$ then $x \leq y$ means that x is a prefix of y. $|\cdot|$ is used both as the size of a set and the length of a sequence. $A + B$ is the disjoint union of A and B; tags in this font will be used for injections, which tags correspond to which arms should be clear. If f is a function then $f\{x \mapsto y\}$ is the same function except that it maps x to y. If R is an equivalence relation then $[R]$ is the set of its equivalence classes and $[x]_R$ is the equivalence class of x under R.

3   Binding Trees

Binding trees are just finite or infinite trees whose nodes are labeled by node labels or by variables in a De Bruijn representation [Bru72] and whose edges are labeled by L. A node labeled nl has edges labeled by $\text{LABELS}(nl)$ and variables are leafs. This can be formalised as follows.

Definition 1 *The set of binding trees is defined as:*

$$Tree = \{t : L^* \rightharpoonup NL + \mathbb{N} \mid$$
$$\epsilon \in \text{dom}(t) \wedge (p\ell \in \text{dom}(t) \Leftrightarrow \exists nl : t(p) = \text{nl}(nl) \wedge \ell \in \text{LABELS}(nl))\}$$

Distance between two trees is defined as $d(t_1, t_2) = 2^{-\min\{n \mid t_1(p) \neq t_2(p) \wedge n = |p|\}}$ *where* $2^{-\min \emptyset} = 0$.

For example, the term $\forall \alpha.\text{rec } \beta.(\alpha \rightarrow \forall \gamma.\beta)$ maps to the tree $\{(\epsilon, \text{nl}(\forall)), (\text{bdy}, \text{nl}(\rightarrow)), (\text{bdyarg}, \text{var}(0)), (\text{bdyres}, \text{nl}(\forall)), (\text{bdyresbdy}, \text{nl}(\rightarrow)), \ldots\}$ (tree t1 in

Figure 1). De Bruijn indices are used to get a unique representation for the binding structure. The term above maps to the above tree rather than to an α-equivalence class of trees, as it would if explicit variables were used in trees.

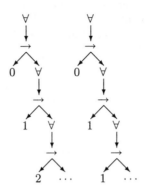

Fig. 1. Example trees t1, on left, and t2, on right.

Recursive quantifiers will be interpreted as fixed points of maps on *Tree*, so it is important that such fixed points exist. In fact, (*Tree*, d) is a complete ultrametric space, which means that contractive maps on it have unique fixed points (c.f. [Kap77]). A map f is *contractive* on a metric space (X, d) if there exists a $c \in [0, 1)$ such that $d(f(x_1), f(x_2)) \leq cd(x_1, x_2)$ for all x_1 and x_2 in X—that is, f maps all pairs a certain fraction closer together.

The following two tree constructors will be needed latter. The first builds a tree whose root is the free variable n, and the second builds a tree with root nl and the given trees as the children of the root.

Definition 2 *Tree* VAR(n) *is* $\{(\epsilon, \text{var}(n))\}$ *and tree* NL($nl, \ell = t_\ell)_{\ell \in \text{LABELS}(nl)}$ *is* $\{(\epsilon, \text{nl}(nl))\} \cup \{(\ell p, t_\ell(p)) \mid \ell \in \text{LABELS}(nl) \land p \in \text{dom}(t_\ell)\}$ *if* $t_\ell \in$ *Tree*.

3.1   Regular Trees

Not all trees are expressible using terms or automata, so it is important to define a subset of trees that are. In the theory of first-order trees, these are called regular trees, and are defined as those with a finite number of subtrees. This definition is inadequate for binding trees, as tree t1 in Figure 1 (which should be regular) has a subtree of the form VAR(n) for each $n \in \mathbb{N}$. The problem is that the De Bruijn indices represent conceptually the same variable as possibility different tree nodes. The definition of regular trees needs to take into account the binding structure and De Bruijn representation. Before giving the definition, two preliminary concepts are needed.

Definition 3 *The number of variables bound along path p in tree t is:*

$$\text{BIND}(t, \epsilon) = 0$$
$$\text{BIND}(t, p\ell) = \text{BIND}(t, p) + \text{BIND}(nl, \ell) \text{ where } t(p) = \mathsf{nl}(nl)$$

The number of variables bound from path p_1 to p_2 where $p_1 \leq p_2$ in tree t is $\text{BIND}(t, p_1 \to p_2) = \text{BIND}(t, p_2) - \text{BIND}(t, p_1)$.

The key to regular trees is that variable nodes that conceptually refer to the same variable (e.g., the same free variable or are bound by the same node) should be considered equal. The next definition makes precise what a variable node in a tree refers to.

Definition 4 *The variable identified by path p of tree t where $t(p) = \mathsf{var}(n)$ is:*

$$\text{VAROF}(t, p) = \begin{cases} \mathsf{free}(n - \text{BIND}(t, p)) & \text{BIND}(t, p) \leq n \\ \mathsf{bound}(p_1, \ell, i) & p_1\ell \leq p \wedge i = n - \text{BIND}(t, p_1\ell \to p) \wedge \\ & \text{BIND}(t, p_1\ell \to p) \leq n < \text{BIND}(t, p_1 \to p) \end{cases}$$

For example, $\text{VAROF}(\mathsf{t1}, \mathsf{bdyarg}) = \mathsf{bound}(\epsilon, \mathsf{bdy}, 0)$ and if t' is the subtree along the bdy edge then $\text{VAROF}(t', \mathsf{resbdyarg}) = \mathsf{free}(0)$.

Using this, when two subtrees of a tree might be equal is defined coinductively as follows.

Definition 5 *A relation R is an equivalence of t's subtrees exactly when R is an equivalence relation on $\text{dom}(t)$ and $p_1 \, R \, p_2$ implies either*

- $t(p_1) = \mathsf{nl}(nl)$, $t(p_2) = \mathsf{nl}(nl)$, and $p_1\ell \, R \, p_2\ell$ for all $\ell \in \text{LABELS}(nl)$,
- $\text{VAROF}(t, p_1) = \mathsf{free}(n)$ and $\text{VAROF}(t, p_2) = \mathsf{free}(n)$, or
- $\text{VAROF}(t, p_1) = \mathsf{bound}(p_1', \ell, n)$, $\text{VAROF}(t, p_2) = \mathsf{bound}(p_2', \ell, n)$, and $p_1' \, R \, p_2'$.

However, more is needed. Consider this tree $\mathsf{t2}$ in Figure 1. There exists an equivalence of this trees subtrees that relates all the $\forall$ nodes and has a finite number of equivalence classes. However, no term or term automata generates this tree. The problem is that the variable on path $\mathsf{bdyresbdyarg}$ binds not to the nearest $\forall$ but to the previous one, and terms never have this kind of binding structure. Therefore I define nonoverlapping equivalences to rule out these kinds of binding structures.

Definition 6 *An equivalence R of t's subtrees is nonoverlapping exactly when $\text{VAROF}(t, p_3) = \mathsf{bound}(p_1, \ell, n)$ and $p_1 < p_2 < p_3$ implies $(p_1, p_2) \notin R$.*

A tree t is regular if there exists a nonoverlapping equivalence of t's subtrees with a finite number of equivalence classes. RegTree is the set of regular trees.

While the definition of regular binding trees is not nearly as elegant as that for regular trees without binding, it nevertheless does define exactly the set of trees that are expressible by terms or automata, as will be proven later.

It turns out that trees have a greatest nonoverlapping equivalence of their subtrees; later sections will use this to define a canonical term for each tree and to prove completeness of the equality rules.

Definition 7 *For $t \in Tree$, EQST(t) is the union of the nonoverlapping equivalences of t's subtrees.*

Theorem 8 *If $t \in Tree$ then EQST(t) is a nonoverlapping equivalence of t's subtrees. Hence, $t \in RegTree$ if and only if EQST(t) has finite number of equivalence classes.*

Proof sketch: The proof shows that EQST(t)'s transitive closure is a nonoverlapping equivalence of t's subtrees. Then it is a subset and thus equal to EQST(t), so the latter is a nonoverlapping equivalence of t's subtrees. Since EQST(t) is a union of equivalence relations, its transitive closure is an equivalence relation. Since the other conditions for equivalence of subtrees are monotonic in the relation, it is easy to show that EQST(t)'s transitive closure is an equivalence of t's subtrees. The tricky part is to show that it is nonoverlapping. Space does not permit showing the details, these are in the companion technical report [Gle02].
□

One final operator on trees is needed latter. It is the *shifting* operation common to De Bruijn representations, and returns an identical tree except that the tree's free variables are incremented by a constant.

Definition 9 *The shift of a tree t by n is:*

$$\text{SHIFT}(t, n) = \lambda p. \begin{cases} \text{var}(n + i) & t(p) = \text{var}(i) \wedge i \geq \text{BIND}(t, p) \\ t(p) & otherwise \end{cases}$$

4   Terms

The second-order term language with recursive quantifiers is:

$$\tau ::= \alpha \mid nl(\ell = \overrightarrow{\alpha_\ell} . \tau_\ell)_{\ell \in \text{LABELS}(nl)} \mid \text{rec } \alpha.\tau$$

where α ranges over term variables and $\overrightarrow{\alpha}$ is a sequence of term variables. Terms are considered equal up to alpha conversion, where for $nl(\ell = \overrightarrow{\alpha_\ell} . \tau_\ell)$, $\overrightarrow{\alpha_\ell}$ binds in τ_ℓ, and for rec $\alpha.\tau$, α binds in τ.

Not all phrases matching the above grammar are considered terms, but only those that satisfy two further constraints. In terms of the from $nl(\ell = \overrightarrow{\alpha_\ell} . \tau_\ell)$ it must be that $\mid \overrightarrow{\alpha_\ell} \mid = \text{BIND}(nl, \ell)$. In terms of the form rec $\alpha.\tau$ it must be that $\tau \downarrow \alpha$, where the latter means that τ is syntactically contractive in α and is defined as:

$$\begin{aligned} \beta \downarrow \alpha & \Leftrightarrow \alpha \neq \beta \\ nl(\ell = \overrightarrow{\alpha_\ell} . \tau_\ell) \downarrow \alpha & \\ \text{rec } \beta.\tau \downarrow \alpha & \Leftrightarrow \alpha = \beta \vee \tau \downarrow \alpha \end{aligned}$$

Intuitively, $\tau \downarrow \alpha$ if mapping α to τ is not equivalent to the identity mapping, for which any term is a fixed point. Instead mapping α to τ produces a term whose outer most constructor is independent of α, and can have only one fixed point.

4.1   Terms to Trees

The interpretation of terms as trees depends upon the interpretation of its free variables. An environment η is a mapping from term variables to *Tree*. Terms under a binder are interpreted in a shifted environment.

Definition 10

$$\text{SHIFT}(\eta, \alpha_0 \cdots \alpha_{n-1}) = \lambda\beta. \begin{cases} \text{VAR}(i) & \beta = \alpha_i \\ \text{SHIFT}(\eta(\beta), n) & \beta \notin \{\alpha_0, \ldots, \alpha_{n-1}\} \end{cases}$$

With these preliminaries, the interpretation of a term as a tree is straightforward.

Definition 11

$$\begin{aligned} [\![\alpha]\!]_\eta &= \eta(\alpha) \\ [\![nl(\ell =\overrightarrow{\alpha_\ell} .\tau_\ell)]\!]_\eta &= \text{NL}(nl, \ell = [\![\tau_\ell]\!]_{\text{SHIFT}(\eta, \overrightarrow{\alpha_\ell})}) \\ [\![\text{rec } \alpha.\tau]\!]_\eta &= \text{fix}([\![\alpha.\tau]\!]_\eta) \\ [\![\alpha.\tau]\!]_\eta &= \lambda t.[\![\tau]\!]_{\eta\{\alpha \mapsto t\}} \end{aligned}$$

where $\text{fix}(\cdot)$ *maps a contractive function to its unique fixed point*

It is easy to show that a term's interpretation is a uniquely defined tree, and the proof also shows that syntactically contractive term and variable pairs define contractive maps.

Theorem 12 *If η maps term variables to Tree then $[\![\tau]\!]_\eta \in$ Tree. If $\tau \downarrow \alpha$ then $[\![\alpha.\tau]\!]_\eta$ is contractive.*

The interpretation of terms as trees produces a regular tree. Also, all regular trees are also expressible as terms; this is proven in the section on completeness.

Theorem 13 *If η maps term variables to RegTree then $[\![\tau]\!]_\eta \in$ RegTree.*

4.2   Term-Equality Rules

The term-equality rules derive judgements of the form $\vdash \tau_1 = \tau_2$ intended to mean that terms τ_1 and τ_2 are equal. The rules are essentially those of Amadio and Cardelli:

$$(\text{eqsym}) \frac{\vdash \tau_2 = \tau_1}{\vdash \tau_1 = \tau_2} \qquad (\text{eqtrans}) \frac{\vdash \tau_1 = \tau_2 \quad \vdash \tau_2 = \tau_3}{\vdash \tau_1 = \tau_3} \qquad (\text{eqvar}) \frac{}{\vdash \alpha = \alpha}$$

$$(\text{eqnl}) \frac{\vdash \tau_\ell = \sigma_\ell}{\vdash nl(\ell =\overrightarrow{\alpha_\ell} .\tau_\ell) = nl(\ell =\overrightarrow{\alpha_\ell} .\sigma_\ell)} \qquad (\text{eqrec}) \frac{\vdash \tau = \sigma}{\vdash \text{rec } \alpha.\tau = \text{rec } \alpha.\sigma}$$

$$(\text{eqroll}) \frac{}{\vdash \text{rec } \alpha.\tau = \tau\{\alpha := \text{rec } \alpha.\tau\}}$$

$$(\text{equnq}) \frac{\vdash \tau_1 = \sigma\{\alpha := \tau_1\} \quad \vdash \tau_2 = \sigma\{\alpha := \tau_2\}}{\vdash \tau_1 = \tau_2} \quad (\sigma \downarrow \alpha)$$

The first two rules express that equality is symmetric and transitive. The next three rules express that equality is closed under all the term constructors and that equality is reflexive. Together these five rules make equality a congruence relation. The last two rules are the interesting ones. Rule (eqroll) expresses that rec $\alpha.\tau$ is the fixed point of the mapping of α to τ, and is the rule from the introduction that defines the equirecursive approach. Rule (equnq) expresses the fact that contractive mappings have unique fixed points. The hypotheses expresses that τ_1 and τ_2 are a fixed points of the mapping α to σ; the side condition expresses that the mapping is contractive; and the conclusion expresses that the two fixed points are equal.

It is straightforward to prove the rules sound, that is, that provably equal terms map to the same tree.

Theorem 14 (Soundness) *If* $\vdash \tau_1 = \tau_2$ *then* $[\![\tau_1]\!]_\eta = [\![\tau_2]\!]_\eta$ *for all environments* η.

4.3   Completeness

It is more difficult to show the converse, that terms that map to the same tree are provably equal. Amadio and Cardelli showed completeness by defining something called *systems of equations*. Unfortunately, it seems very difficult to define systems of equations for second-order terms. So I use a different approach to showing completeness, which also works in the first-order setting. The idea is to define a canonical term for every regular tree and show that a term is provably equal to the canonical term for its tree. Completeness then follows by transitivity.

I will define canonical terms for trees with respect to particular kinds of environments called distinguishing environments. These are environments of the form $\eta(\alpha) = \mathrm{VAR}(g(\alpha))$ for some g that is a bijection from term variables to $\mathbb{N}$.

Definition 15 *If* $t \in RegTree$, η *is distinguishing, and* R *is a nonoverlapping equality of* t's *subtrees with a finite number of equivalence classes, then* T, S, $\mathrm{TERMOF}_\eta(t, R)$, *and* $\mathrm{TERMOF}_\eta(t)$ *are defined as follows:*

- *If* f *maps* $[R]$ *to term variables,* f *maps the pair* $([p]_R, \ell)$ *to a sequence of term variables of length* $\mathrm{BIND}(nl, \ell)$ *when* $t(p) = nl(nl)$ *and* $\ell \in \mathrm{LABELS}(nl)$, S *is a subset of* $[R]$, *and* $p \in \mathrm{dom}(t)$ *then:*

$$\mathsf{T}^{t,\eta,R,f}_{S,p} = \begin{cases} f([p]_R) & [p]_R \in S \\ \mathrm{rec}\ f([p]_R).\mathsf{S}^{t,\eta,R,f}_{S\cup\{[p]_R\},p} & [p]_R \notin S \end{cases}$$

$$\mathsf{S}^{t,\eta,R,f}_{S,p} = \begin{cases} \beta & \mathrm{VAROF}(t,p) = \mathrm{free}(n)\ \wedge \\ & \eta(\beta) = \mathrm{VAR}(n) \\ f([p']_R, \ell)_n & \mathrm{VAROF}(t,p) = \mathrm{bound}(p', \ell, n) \\ nl(\ell = f([p]_R, \ell).\mathsf{T}^{t,\eta,R,f}_{S,p\ell}) & t(p) = nl(nl) \end{cases}$$

- $\mathrm{TERMOF}_\eta(t, R) = \mathsf{T}^{t,\eta,R,f}_{\emptyset,\epsilon}$ *for some appropriate* f *that maps to fresh variables*

$-$ TERMOF$_\eta(t)$ = TERMOF$_\eta(t,$ EQST$(t))$

These terms do map to the tree they are based on, and this shows that every regular tree is expressible using a term.

Theorem 16 *If $t \in \text{RegTree}$ and η is distinguishing then $[\![\text{TERMOF}_\eta(t)]\!]_\eta = t$.*

The key technical result used to show completeness is that every term is provably equal to the canonical term for its tree.

Lemma 17 *If η is distinguishing then $\vdash \text{TERMOF}_\eta([\![\tau]\!]_\eta) = \tau$.*

Proof sketch: The proof is ultimately by induction on the structure of τ. If τ has the form $nl(\ell = \overrightarrow{\alpha_\ell} . \tau_\ell)$ then TERMOF$_\eta([\![\tau]\!]_\eta)$ has the form rec $\alpha.nl(\ell = \overrightarrow{\alpha_\ell} . \sigma_\ell)$. If the induction hypothesis is $\vdash \sigma_\ell\{\alpha := \text{TERMOF}_\eta([\![\tau]\!]_\eta)\} = \tau_\ell$ (1), then the result follows by rules (eqnl), (eqroll), and (eqtrans). If τ has the form rec $\alpha.\sigma$ then the key is to have the induction hypothesis $\vdash \text{TERMOF}_\eta([\![\tau]\!]_\eta) = \sigma\{\alpha := \text{TERMOF}_\eta([\![\tau]\!]_\eta)\}$ (2). Then by (eqroll), $\vdash \tau = \sigma\{\alpha := \tau\}$ and the result follows by rule (equnq). The key then, is to get the induction hypothesis to satisfy properties (1) and (2). The proof first defines for each subterm σ of τ a pair of terms (σ_1, σ_2) satisfying properties (1) and (2). Next it shows that the trees for these two terms and a corresponding subtree of $[\![\tau]\!]_\eta$ are all the same. Finally it shows by induction on σ that $\vdash \sigma_1 = \sigma_2$. Details are in the companion technical report [Gle02]. □

Completeness follows easily from this last lemma.

Theorem 18 (Completeness) *If η is distinguishing and $[\![\tau_1]\!]_\eta = [\![\tau_2]\!]_\eta$ then $\vdash \tau_1 = \tau_2$.*

Proof: By Lemma 17, $\vdash \text{TERMOF}_\eta([\![\tau_1]\!]_\eta) = \tau_1$ and $\vdash \text{TERMOF}_\eta([\![\tau_2]\!]_\eta) = \tau_2$. Since $[\![\tau_1]\!]_\eta = [\![\tau_2]\!]_\eta$, TERMOF$_\eta([\![\tau_1]\!]_\eta)$ = TERMOF$_\eta([\![\tau_2]\!]_\eta)$. The result follows by (eqsym) and (eqtrans). □

5   Binding Tree Automata

The final step of my programme is to give a decision algorithm for term equality. The algorithm is in terms of a finite representation for trees, similar to the term automata of Kozen et al. The basic idea is that an automaton is given as input a path and gives as output the node at the end of that path. Automata are state machines, that is, each label in the path causes the automaton to transition from one state to another, starting with an initial state, and the state obtained at the end of the path determines the output. Rather than output the node in the form a tree does, that is, as an element of $NL + \mathbb{N}$, the automaton outputs either a node label, a free variable index, or a bound variable. A bound variable is specified as a state, label, and index; the idea being that the variable is bound by the most recent occurrence of the binder generated by the state, along the edge given by the label.

A few preliminaries are needed for the definition. If $\delta \in Q \times L \rightharpoonup Q$ for some Q then δ^* is its extension to L^*, specifically $\delta^*(q, \epsilon) = q$ and $\delta^*(q, p\ell) = \delta(\delta^*(q, p), \ell)$. If $\delta^*(q_1, p) = q_2$ then p is a path from q_1 to q_2; if in addition $\delta^*(q_1, p') \neq q$ for all $p' \leq p$ then p is a q-less path from q_1 to q_2.

Definition 19 *A binding tree automaton is a quadruple* (Q, i, δ, sl) *satisfying:*

- Q *is a finite set called the states of the automaton.*
- $i \in Q$ *is the initial state.*
- $\delta \in Q \times L \rightharpoonup Q$ *is the transition function.*
- $sl \in Q \rightarrow NL + \mathbb{N} + Q \times L \times \mathbb{N}$ *is the labeling or output function.*
- $(q, \ell) \in \mathrm{dom}(\delta) \Leftrightarrow sl(q) = \mathsf{nl}(nl) \wedge \ell \in \mathrm{LABELS}(nl)$.
- $sl(q) = \mathsf{fvar}(q', \ell, n)$ *implies that:*
    - $sl(q') = \mathsf{nl}(nl)$,
    - $\ell \in \mathrm{LABELS}(nl)$,
    - $0 \leq n < \mathrm{BIND}(nl, \ell)$, *and*
    - *if p is a path from i to q then there are paths p_1 and p_2 such that $p = p_1 \ell p_2$, p_1 is a path from i to q', and p_2 is q'-less (from $\delta(q', \ell)$ to q).*

5.1 Automata to Trees

This section explains how an automaton generates a tree. Letting t represent this tree then intuitively: if $sl(\delta^*(i, p)) = \mathsf{nl}(nl)$ then $t(p) = \mathsf{nl}(p)$; if $sl(\delta^*(i, p)) = \mathsf{bvar}(n)$ then $\mathrm{VAROF}(t, p) = \mathsf{free}(n)$; finally, if $sl(\delta^*(i, p)) = \mathsf{fvar}(q', \ell, n)$ then $\mathrm{VAROF}(t, p) = \mathsf{bound}(p', \ell, n)$ where p' is the longest path from i to q' that is a prefix of p.

The formal definition extends the state space to include enough information to compute the De Bruijn indices for free and bound variables. An extended state is a triple consisting of a state of the automaton, the number of variables bound along the path so far (needed to determine free variables), and a function $f \in Q \rightarrow \mathbb{N}$, which gives the number of variables bound since the last occurrence of each state (need to determine bound variables). The transition function is lifted to extended states in such a way as to track the binding information, and the labeling function is lifted to extended states to use the binding information to generate nodes for trees. Then the tree of an automaton at a path is just the lifted labeling function of the lifted transition function on the path.

Definition 20 *The tree associated with an automaton is defined as follows:*

$$
\begin{aligned}
\mathrm{SHIFT}(f, q := n) &= \lambda q'. \begin{cases} 0 & q' = q \\ f(q') + n & q' \neq q \end{cases} \\
\hat{\delta}((q, n, f), \ell) &= (\delta(q, \ell), n + i, \mathrm{SHIFT}(f, q := i)) \\
&\quad \textit{where } sl(q) = \mathsf{nl}(nl) \wedge i = \mathrm{BIND}(nl, \ell) \\
\hat{sl}(q, n, f) &= \begin{cases} \mathsf{nl}(nl) & sl(q) = \mathsf{nl}(nl) \\ \mathsf{var}(n + i) & sl(q) = \mathsf{bvar}(i) \\ \mathsf{var}(f(q') + i) & sl(q) = \mathsf{fvar}(q', \ell, i) \end{cases} \\
\mathrm{TREE}((Q, i, \delta, sl), qnf) &= \lambda p. \hat{sl}(\hat{\delta}^*(qnf, p)) \\
\hat{\imath} &= (i, 0, \lambda q.0) \\
\mathrm{TREE}(Q, i, \delta, sl) &= \mathrm{TREE}((Q, i, \delta, sl), \hat{\imath})
\end{aligned}
$$

It is not hard to see that automata generate trees, in fact, they generate regular trees.

Theorem 21 *If ta is an automaton then* TREE$(ta) \in RegTree$.

Proof sketch: Let $R = \{(p_1, p_2) \mid \delta^*(i, p_1) = \delta^*(i, P)\}$ where $ta = (Q, i, \delta, sl)$. Then R is a nonoverlapping equivalence of TREE(ta)'s subtrees. It is clearly an equivalence relation. The other conditions for being an equivalence essentially follow from the fact that TREE$(ta)(p)$ is determined by $\delta^*(i, p)$'s label. It is nonoverlapping because of the last condition in the definition of tree automata.
□

The converse is also true—regular trees are expressible as tree automata.

Theorem 22 *If t is a regular tree then there exists an automaton ta such that* TREE$(ta) = t$.

Proof: The proof uses the equivalence classes of EQST(t) as the states Q. The initial state i is $[\epsilon]$. If $t(p) = $ nl(nl) then $sl([p]) = $ nl(nl); if VAROF$(t, p) = $ free(n) then $sl([p]) = $ bvar(n); if VAROF$(t, p) = $ bound(p', ℓ, n) then $sl([p]) = $ fvar$([p'], \ell, n)$. The transition function δ is $\lambda([p], \ell).[p\ell]$. The conditions for equivalence of subtrees ensure that sl and δ are consistently defined. It is easy to check that this defines an automaton, the last part of the last condition follows from EQST(t) being nonoverlapping. An easy induction shows that $\hat{\delta}^*(\hat{i}, p) = ([p], \text{BIND}(t, p), f)$ where f is such that if p' is such that $p = p'\ell p''$ and p' is the largest strict prefix of p in $[p']$ then $f([p']) = \text{BIND}(t, p'\ell \to p)$. Then it is easy to show that $\hat{sl}([p], \text{BIND}(t, p), f) = t(p)$.
□

5.2 Equality Algorithm

Two trees are different if they differ at some path, but more specifically if they differ at some minimal path. This minimal path will be in the domain of both trees. Therefore to determine if two automata generate the different trees, it suffices to search for paths in their common domain that have different outputs. If the outputs along some path are the same up to but not including the last state then the number of variables bound up to the last state is the same. Thus, two free variable states will differ exactly when their indices differ, free variable states will differ from bound variable states, and bound variable states will differ if the most recent occurrence of the binding state occurred at different prefixes of the path. Thus determining if the outputs are different requires only keeping track of the states and the correspondence between binding states. As in Kozen et al., this can be expressed as a deterministic finite state automaton. The states of this equality automaton are triples, one state from each automata, and the correspondence between binding states. The transition function updates the states according to the input automata's transition functions and updates the correspondence. The accepting states are those where the output of the two states differs according to the binding state correspondence. The two trees differ if the language of the equality automaton is nonempty. The correspondence between binding states can be expressed as *partial bijections*, introduced next.

Definition 23 *The partial bijections between A and B are $A \leftrightharpoons B = \{R \in \mathcal{P}(A \times B) \mid (a_1, b_1) \in R \wedge (a_2, b_2) \in R \Rightarrow (a_1 = a_2 \Leftrightarrow b_1 = b_2)\}$. Bijection update of R by a maps to b is $R\{a \leftrightharpoons b\} = \{(a', b') \in R \mid a' \neq a \wedge b' \neq b\} \cup \{(a, b)\}$.*

Definition 24 *The equality deterministic finite state automaton (over alphabet L) of two automata $ta_1 = (Q_1, i_1, \delta_1, sl_1)$ and $ta_2 = (Q_2, i_2, \delta_2, sl_2)$ is:*

$$\begin{aligned}
&\text{CORRESPOND}(sl_1, sl_2, q_1, q_2, R) = \\
&\quad \vee(sl_1(q_1) = \mathsf{nl}(nl) \wedge sl_2(q_2) = \mathsf{nl}(nl)) \\
&\quad \vee(sl_1(q_1) = \mathsf{bvar}(n) \wedge sl_2(q_2) = \mathsf{bvar}(n)) \\
&\quad \vee(sl_1(q_1) = \mathsf{fvar}(q_1', \ell, n) \wedge sl_2(q_2) = \mathsf{fvar}(q_2', \ell, n) \wedge q_1' \; R \; q_2') \\
&\text{EQUAL}(ta_1, ta_2) = \\
&\quad (Q_1 \times Q_2 \times (Q_1 \leftrightharpoons Q_2), \\
&\quad (i_1, i_2, \emptyset), \\
&\quad \lambda(q_1, q_2, R, \ell).(\delta_1(q_1, \ell), \delta_2(q_2, \ell), R\{q_1 \leftrightharpoons q_2\}), \\
&\quad \{(q_1, q_2, R) \mid \neg\text{CORRESPOND}(sl_1, sl_2, q_1, q_2, R)\})
\end{aligned}$$

The next theorem proves the correctness of this construction.

Theorem 25 $\text{TREE}(ta_1) = \text{TREE}(ta_2) \Leftrightarrow L(\text{EQUAL}(ta_1, ta_2)) = \emptyset$

Proof sketch: The main part of the proof shows that if $\text{TREE}(ta_1)(p') = \text{TREE}(ta_2)(p')$ for $p' < p$ then: $\text{TREE}(ta_1)(p) = \text{TREE}(ta_2)(p)$ if and only if $p \in L(\text{EQUAL}(ta_1, ta_2))$; from which the result easily follows. This property holds because of the correspondence between an automaton's tree and its state labels, and because $q_1 \; R \; q_2$, where $\delta^*(i, p) = (\_, \_, R)$, if and only if the most recent occurrence of q_1 and q_2 are at the same prefix of p. $\quad\square$

The previous theorem gives an algorithm for deciding the equality of the trees of two automata. Since emptiness of a deterministic finite state automaton's language is linear time, and the equality automaton is exponential in the size of the tree automata, it is an exponential algorithm. However, an optimisation yields a polynomial time algorithm. This optimisation is based on the following lemma.

Lemma 26 *If $ta_1 = (Q_1, i_1, \delta_1, sl_1)$ and $ta_2 = (Q_2, i_2, \delta_2, sl_2)$ are automata, $p_2 \neq \epsilon$, $p_3 \neq \epsilon$, $\delta_1^*(i_1, p_1) = \delta_1^*(i_1, p_1 p_2) = \delta_1^*(i_1, p_1 p_2 p_3) = q_1$, $\delta_2^*(i_2, p_1) = \delta_2^*(i_2, p_1 p_2) = \delta_2^*(i_2, p_1 p_2 p_3) = q_2$, and $p \notin L(\text{EQUAL}(ta_1, ta_2))$ for $p \not\geq p_1 p_2 p_3$ then $L(\text{EQUAL}(ta_1, ta_2)) = \emptyset$.*

This lemma says that the search for a word in $L(\text{EQUAL}(ta_1, ta_2))$ does not need to search the entire space $Q_1 \times Q_2 \times (Q_1 \leftrightharpoons Q_2)$, but only needs to search until it sees the same $Q_1 \times Q_2$ pair three times. It is insufficient to stop after seeing the same pair twice, as in Colazzo and Ghelli's algorithm. For example, consider the following two automata:[4]

---

[4] The notation for automata depicts states as circles with $x = y$ inside; x is the state's identifier, and y is the states label, either a node label, a natural number for a free variable, or a $\mathsf{b}n$ for a variable bound by state n. An arrow not from another circle points to the initial state. The transition function is depicted with arrows between the circles labeled by L.

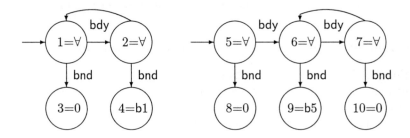

The path bdybdybdy produces the pair $(2, 6)$ for the second time, and while bdybnd is not accepted by the equality automaton, bdybdybdybnd is accepted. The problem is that states 4 and 9 are part of repetitive structures and the path bdybnd checks that the first repetition of 4 matches the first repetition of 9, but not that the other repetitions match. The path bdybdybdybnd checks whether the second repetitions match. Only when both the first and second repetitions match will all repetitions necessarily match.

With an appropriate choice of representation and implemented carefully, the above algorithm is quadratic in the sizes of the input automata.

6 Putting It Together

The previous section gave an algorithm for deciding equality of two automata, so an algorithm to convert terms into automata gives an algorithm for deciding term equality. This section gives that algorithm and its correctness.

First an algorithm to convert terms into automata. The states of this automaton are the parts of the term not involved with recursive quantifiers.

Definition 27 *The set* PROPER(τ) *is the subterms of τ that are not recursive quantifiers or variables bound by recursive quantifiers of τ. Every subterm of τ can be mapped to* PROPER(τ) *as follows: if $\sigma \in$ PROPER(τ) then PROPER$(\tau, \sigma) = \sigma$;* PROPER$(\tau, \mathsf{rec}\ \alpha.\sigma) = $ PROPER(τ, σ); *if α is a subterm of τ bound by the subterm* $\mathsf{rec}\ \alpha.\sigma$ *then* PROPER$(\tau, \alpha) = $ PROPER$(\tau, \mathsf{rec}\ \alpha.\sigma)$.

PROPER(τ, σ) is uniquely defined for all subterms σ of τ, because recursive quantifiers are required to be syntactically contractive.

Armed with these constructs, the automaton of a term is easily defined.

Definition 28 *If η is distinguishing then*

$$\text{AUTOMATONOF}_\eta(\tau) = (\text{PROPER}(\tau), \text{PROPER}(\tau, \tau), \delta, sl)$$

where δ and sl are as follows. If $\sigma = nl(\ell =\vec{\alpha_\ell} .\sigma_\ell)$ then $\delta(\sigma, \ell) = $ PROPER(τ, σ_ℓ) and $sl(\sigma) = \mathsf{nl}(nl)$. If σ is variable subterm of τ that is free in τ then $sl(\sigma) = \mathsf{bvar}(n)$ where $\eta(\sigma) = \text{VAR}(n)$. If σ is a variable subterm of τ that is bound by the nth binder of edge ℓ of σ' subterm of τ then $sl(\sigma) = \mathsf{fvar}(\sigma', \ell, n)$.

The automaton of a term is defined so that its tree is the same as the term's tree.

Theorem 29 *If η is distinguishing then* $\text{TREE}(\text{AUTOMATONOF}_\eta(\tau)) = [\![\tau]\!]_\eta$.

Finally, all the previous results can be combined into a decision procedure for equality of terms. Since the algorithm for equality of automata is quadratic and the conversion from terms to automata produces a linear output in linear time, the decision procedure below is quadratic.

Theorem 30 *If η is distinguishing then:*

$$\vdash \tau_1 = \tau_2 \quad \Leftrightarrow \quad L(\text{EQUAL}(\text{AUTOMATONOF}_\eta(\tau_1), \text{AUTOMATONOF}_\eta(\tau_2)) = \emptyset$$

Proof:

$$\vdash \tau_1 = \tau_2$$
$$\Leftrightarrow \quad \langle \text{Theorem 14 and Theorem 18} \rangle$$
$$[\![\tau_1]\!]_\eta = [\![\tau_2]\!]_\eta$$
$$\Leftrightarrow \quad \langle \text{Theorem 29} \rangle$$
$$\text{TREE}(\text{AUTOMATONOF}_\eta(\tau_1)) = \text{TREE}(\text{AUTOMATONOF}_\eta(\tau_2))$$
$$\Leftrightarrow \quad \langle \text{Theorem 25} \rangle$$
$$L(\text{EQUAL}(\text{AUTOMATONOF}_\eta(\tau_1), \text{AUTOMATONOF}_\eta(\tau_2))) = \emptyset$$

$\square$

7   Summary and Future Work

This paper has shown how to give a natural interpretation to a second-order term system with recursive quantifiers. In particular it extends the well known tree interpretation, introduced by Amadio and Cardelli, to second-order constructs by defining a theory of trees with binding. It gives an appropriate generalisation of regularity to binding trees, and shows that regular trees characterise both those generated by terms and by automata. It shows the usual set of equality rules are sound and complete in the second-order case. It generalises Kozen et al.'s term automata to the second-order case, providing a polynomial time decision procedure for equality of terms. The result is a natural and intuitive theory of second-order type systems with equirecursive types.

The obvious next step is to add subtyping to the theory. The main idea is to define subtyping on trees coinductively. Then it should be possible to show that a certain set of rules is sound and complete with respect to this definition. Interestingly, the rules I believe are sound and complete are a nonconservative extension of rules for $\mathcal{F}_\le$ with the Kernel-Fun rule for bounded quantification (c.f. [Pie94] and [CG99]). Finally, it should be possible to extend the construction for equality of automata's trees to subtyping in a way that combines my ideas for second-order constructs with Kozen et al.'s ideas for subtyping and a simple idea for dealing with bounded variables. The result should be a polynomial time algorithm for deciding subtyping in a system with Kernel-Fun recursively-bounded quantifiers and equirecursive types.

Another extension of the ideas is to higher-order kinds. Languages like ML and Haskell allow the definition of type constructors, which could be thought of as type variables with second-order kinds. Thus at a minimum, it would be good to include this in the theory if not a larger system with a fuller set of kinds. Full $\mathcal{F}_\omega$ (c.f. [Gir71] and [Gir72]) with equirecursive types is likely to be undecidable since it contains the simply-typed lambda calculus with recursive functions at the type level, for which equality is at least as hard as the halting problem. But, it might be possible to restrict $\mathcal{F}_\omega$ with equirecursive types to a decidable system, perhaps by allowing only syntactically-contractive recursive types.

References

[AC93]   Roberto Amadio and Luca Cardelli. Subtyping recursive types. *ACM Transactions on Progamming Languages and Systems*, 15(4):575–631, September 1993.

[Bru72]   N. De Bruijn. Lambda-calculus notation with nameless dummies, a tool for automatic formula manipulation. *Indag. Mat.*, 34:381–392, 1972.

[CG99]   Dario Colazzo and Giorgio Ghelli. Subtyping recursive types in kernel fun. In *1999 Symposium on Logic in Computer Science*, pages 137–146, Trento, Italy, July 1999.

[Gir71]   Jean-Yves Girard. Une extension de l'interprétation de Gödel à l'analyse, et son application à l'élimination de coupures dans l'analyse et la théorie des types. In J. E. Fenstad, editor, *Proceedings of the Second Scandinavian Logic Symposium*, pages 63–92. North-Holland Publishing Co., 1971.

[Gir72]   Jean-Yves Girard. *Interprétation fonctionelle et élimination des coupures de l'arithmétique d'ordre supérieur*. PhD thesis, Université Paris VII, 1972.

[Gle02]   Neal Glew. A theory of second-order trees. Technical Report TR2001-1859, Department of Computer Science, Cornell University, 4130 Upson Hall, Ithaca, NY 14853-7501, USA, January 2002.

[Kap77]   Irving Kaplansky. *Set Theory and Metric Spaces*. Chelsea Pub Co, 2nd edition, June 1977.

[KPS95]   Dexter Kozen, Jens Palsberg, and Michael Schwartzbach. Efficient recursive subtyping. *Mathematical Structures in Computer Science*, 5(1):113–125, March 1995.

[Pie94]   Benjamin Pierce. Bounded quantification is undecidable. *Information and Computation*, 112:131–165, 1994.

Tool Support for Improving Test Coverage

Susan Horwitz

University of Wisconsin and GrammaTech, Inc.
`horwitz@cs.wisc.edu`

Abstract. Testing is a critical part of the software-engineering process. Coverage tools provide information about which components are exercised by a test suite, but they do not assist programmers with the important problem of how to increase coverage. We propose a tool to address that problem: Using the program's control and flow dependences, the tool helps programmers determine where to focus their efforts, and how to force a chosen component to be exercised.

1 Introduction

A common approach to testing software is the use of coverage criteria [5]; for example, using the all-statements criterion, a program is 100% covered if after running the program on all test inputs, every statement has been executed at least once. Tools such as Rational's PureCoverage [14], Bullseye Testing Technology's C-Cover [4], and Software Research, Inc's TCAT [15] help the programmer by measuring coverage: the tools instrument the program so that when it runs, a record is kept of which components executed. The tools can then report untested components to the programmer. However, these tools provide no help with the important problem of how to increase coverage.

Given a set of program components that have not yet been executed, the programmer must decide which component(s) to focus on next. The programmer would like to know, for each component:

- How easy will it be to find an input that causes the component to execute.
- How much benefit will there be in causing that component to execute; i.e., how many of the other currently untested components are also likely to be executed using the same, or similar inputs.

Furthermore, once the programmer has selected a component on which to concentrate, help is needed to determine how to force the execution of that component.

Example: Consider the program shown in Figure 1, which reads information about one employee, reads a print option, and then prints information either about the employee's average hours worked per day, or the current week's pay. (Apologies for the poor structure of the code – the use of the goto permits certain features of the proposed approach to be illustrated.) Comments on the right label the predicates, and line numbers are given on the left. Assume that the code has been tested on one input file, and that the untested statements are

D. Le Métayer (Ed.): ESOP 2002, LNCS 2305, pp. 162–177, 2002.

```
(1)   read(jobCode, hourlyRate, hours);
(2)   read(printOption);
(3)   if (printOption == AV_HOURS) {                          /* pred 1 */
(4)      print("av. hours per day = ", hours/5.0);
(5)   }
(6)   else if (printOption == WEEKS_PAY) {                    /* pred 2 */
(7)              if (jobCode == SALARIED) {                   /* pred 3 */
(8)                 pay = 40*hourlyRate;
(9)              }
(10)           else { if (hours > 40) {                       /* pred 4 */
(11)                     basePay = 40*hourlyRate;
(12)                     overtime = (hours-40)*1.5*hourlyRate;
(13)                     pay = basePay+overtime;
(14)                  }
(15)              else {
(16)                     pay = hours*hourlyRate;
(17)                     goto L;
(18)                  }
(19)              }
(20)           if (hours > 60) {                              /* pred 5 */
(21)              pay += BONUS;
(22)           }
(23)        L: print("weekly pay = ", pay);
(24)      }
(25)   else print("unknown print option: ", printOption);
(26)   print("all done!");
```

Fig. 1. An example program. This code has been tested on one input file, and the untested code is shown using bold font.

those shown using bold font. In this example, there are two blocks of untested code: The first (lines (6) - (24)) is the block that executes when predicate 1 evaluates to *false* and predicate 2 evaluates to *true* (i.e., when the input print option is WEEKS_PAY). The second (line (25)) is the single-line block that executes when both predicates 1 and 2 evaluate to *false* (i.e., when the input print option is neither AV_HOURS nor WEEKS_PAY). Within the first untested block, different code will execute depending on the values of predicates 3, 4, and 5. □

As mentioned above, the programmer would like help in choosing a key component of the program such that

- It will not be too difficult to figure out what input values will cause that component to execute.
- Many of the untested components in the program are likely to be executed using the same, or similar input values.

In this example, the same (small) amount of effort is required to force either of the outer two untested blocks to execute: in both cases, predicate 1 must evaluate to *false*; in the first case, predicate 2 must then evaluate to *true*, and in the second case, it must evaluate to *false*. However, the payoff in the first case is much greater: all but one of the untested components are in the block that is reached when predicate 1 is *false* and predicate 2 is *true*; only a single untested component is reached when both predicates are *false*. Given these observations, it is clear that it would be very useful to have a tool that:

- Guides the programmer to choose to concentrate on producing an input file that will cause predicate 2 to execute and to evaluate to *true*, and
- Assists the programmer in producing that file by indicating:
  - That in order to reach predicate 2, it is necessary first to reach predicate 1, and to have it evaluate to *false*, and
  - That the value of the variable `printOption` used in predicates 1 and 2 comes from the read statement at line (2) in the program.

A tool that has access to the program's control and flow dependences (defined in Section 2) can provide help with both of these problems, as described in sections 3, 4, and 5.

In the remainder of the paper, as in the example above, we assume that the criterion of interest is the all-statements criterion. However, it should be clear that the ideas presented apply equally well to other criteria, such as the all-branches criterion, that involve individual components (nodes or edges of the program's control-flow graph). Also, while our example program is written in C, the ideas presented here can be applied to any program for which control and flow dependences can be computed. Language features that make those computations difficult include interprocedural control flow (e.g., throw-catch or exceptions) parallelism (e.g., Java threads), and the use of standard libraries. Those issues are currently being addressed by a number of researchers, including [13], [10,6, 11] and [12].

2   Background

2.1   Control Dependences

Intuitively, control dependences capture the fact that the number of times some program component will execute, or whether it will execute at all, may depend on the value of some predicate. For example, the statements in the *true* branch of an `if-then-else` statement will execute only if the condition evaluates to *true* (so those statements are said to be *true-control-dependent* on the `if` predicate), while the statements in the *false* branch will execute only if the condition evaluates to *false* (so those statements are said to be *false-control-dependent* on the `if` predicate).

Control dependences are defined in terms of the program's control-flow graph (CFG) [7]. For the purposes of defining control dependences, the `enter` node of a CFG is considered to be a predicate (that always evaluates to *true*) whose *true* control child in the CFG is the first statement in the program, and whose *false* control child in the CFG is a special `exit` node that follows the last statement in the program.

Definition 1. *A node n in a program's CFG is **v-control-dependent** on a node m iff n postdominates m's v CFG successor, but does not postdominate m (by definition, every node postdominates itself).*

Example: Figures 2 and 3 show the control-flow and control-dependence graphs for the program in Figure 1. Note that predicate 5 is *true*-control-dependent on both predicate 3 and predicate 4, because it postdominates both of their *true* successors in the CFG, but does not postdominate either of their *false* successors. Statement (23), L: `print("weekly pay = ...")` is not control dependent on predicates 3, 4, or 5, because it postdominates both CFG successors of each of those predicates (i.e., it executes whether they evaluate to *true* or to *false*). □

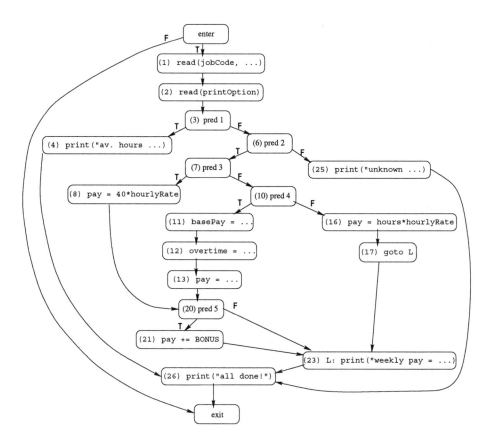

Fig. 2. The Control Flow Graph (CFG) for the example program.

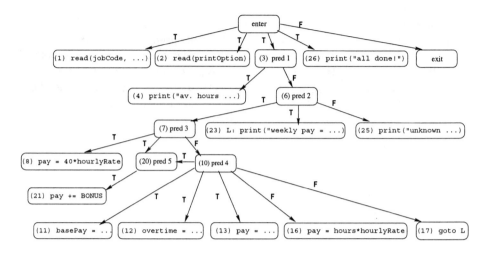

Fig. 3. The Control Dependence Graph for the example program.

2.2   Flow Dependences

Flow dependences are essentially *def-use* chains [1], representing the flow of values in the program.

Definition 2. *Node n is **flow dependent** on node m iff m defines a variable x, n uses x, and there is an x-definition-free path in the CFG from m to n.*

Example (refer to Figure 2): Statement (21), `pay += BONUS`, uses the variable `pay`. That variable is defined at three places in the program: statements (8), (13), and (16). There are `pay`-definition-free paths in the control-flow graph from (8) to (21), and from (13) to (21); therefore, statement (21) is flow dependent on statements (8) and (13). There is *no* path in the control-flow graph from (16) to (21); therefore, statement (21) is not flow dependent on statement (16). □

3   Choosing the Next Component on Which to Focus

As discussed in the Introduction, when a programmer is trying to increase coverage, an important issue is which component to focus on next. In this section, we discuss using control dependences to address this issue. In particular, we describe how to compute three metrics that can be used to help answer the following two questions for each predicate in the program:

1. How easy will it be to find an input that causes the predicate to be executed?
2. How much benefit will there be in causing that predicate to be executed; i.e., how many of the currently untested components in the program will also be executed using the same, or similar inputs?

After defining the metrics, we first discuss the time required to compute them, then how they, together with additional information provided by the tool, can be used by the programmer to choose the next component on which to focus.

3.1   A Metric for the Ease of Forcing Execution of Component C

There may be many paths in a program's control-flow graph to a given component C (where a component is a statement or a predicate). C will execute if any one of those paths is followed. Following a particular path requires that the predicates along the path evaluate to the appropriate values. However, sometimes a predicate is actually irrelevant: if component C post-dominates a predicate in the control-flow graph, then C will execute regardless of the predicate's value.

Example: In the control-flow graph in Figure 2, all paths to statement (26), `print("all done!")`, include predicate 1; however, statement (26) will execute whether predicate 1 evaluates to *true* or to *false*, since it postdominates predicate 1 in the control-flow graph. Similarly, all paths to statement (23), `L: print("weekly pay = ", pay)` include predicates 1, 2, 3, and 4; however, since statement (23) post-dominates predicates 3 and 4, the values of those two predicates are not actually relevant to the execution of statement (23). □

An estimate of the effort needed to force an untested component C to execute can be computed by finding the path from a tested component to C that contains the fewest "relevant" predicates; i.e., we can define an *Ease-of-Execution* metric whose value is the number of relevant predicates on that path. The idea is that the programmer can reuse the part of the input that caused the component at the start of the path to execute, but then must figure out what the rest of the input must be to force execution to follow the path to C. Of course, this provides only a rough estimate of the actual effort needed to force C to execute, since in practice the predicates in a program are not independent, and it may be easier for the programmer to force a predicate to evaluate to one value than to another value. Nevertheless, we believe that this metric (when used with the other metrics defined in the next section) will be useful in helping the programmer to choose the next component on which to focus. In this context, absolute precision is not required, there just needs to be a reasonable correlation between the actual effort required and the values of the metrics for most components.

Example (refer to Figure 2): Consider statement (25), `print("unknown print option: ", printOption)`, in the example program. The Ease-of-Execution metric for this statement is 2, since it requires that both predicates 1 and 2 evaluate to *false*. The metric for statement (11), `basePay = 40*rate`, is 4, since it executes only when predicates 1 – 4 evaluate to *false*, *true*, *false*, *true*, respectively. Now consider predicate 5: `if (hours>60)`, at line (20). Note that there are two paths in the program's control-flow graph from the already-executed predicate 1 to this predicate: both start by following the *false* edge out of predicate 1, and the *true* edge out of predicate 2. One path then takes the *true* edge out of predicate 3, while the other takes the *false* edge out of predicate 3 and the *true* edge out of predicate 4. Thus, the first path includes 3 relevant predicates, while the second path includes 4 relevant predicates. Since the value of the metric is determined by the path with the fewest relevant predicates, the metric for predicate 5 is 3. ☐

This Ease-of-Execution metric can be computed efficiently for each component C using the program's control-dependence graph by finding the path in that graph from a tested predicate (or from the **enter** node) to C that includes the fewest predicates. In the control-dependence graph, each such path corresponds to one or more paths in the control-flow graph – the predicates on the control-dependence-graph path are the "relevant" predicates on the corresponding control-flow-graph paths (the possibility of irrelevant predicates is what can cause a single control-dependence-graph path to correspond to more than one control-flow-graph path).

Example: In the control-dependence graph in Figure 3 the path from predicate 1 to statement (25) includes two predicates (predicate 1 itself, and predicate 2); thus, as discussed above, the metric for that statement is 2. Similarly, the path to statement (11) contains four predicates, and there are two paths to predicate 5, one containing three predicates and the other containing four. The table in Figure 4 gives the Ease-of-Execution metric for each untested component in the example program. ☐

Untested Component	Ease Metric	Untested Component	Ease Metric	Untested Component	Ease Metric
line (6)	1	line (12)	4	line (21)	4
line (7)	2	line (13)	4	line (23)	2
line (8)	3	line (16)	4	line (25)	2
line (10)	3	line (17)	4		
line (11)	4	line (20)	3		

Fig. 4. The Ease-of-Execution metric for each untested component C in the example program: the number of predicates on the shortest path from a tested predicate (in this example, always predicate 1) to C in the program's control-dependence graph.

3.2   Two Metrics for the Benefit of Forcing Predicate P to Execute

Finding an input that forces a particular predicate P to execute and to evaluate to a specific value v can help improve test coverage in two ways:

1. There will be a set S of previously untested components that are guaranteed to execute whenever P evaluates to v, but that might not execute if P does not evaluate to v. Thus, forcing P to evaluate to v is guaranteed to increase coverage by at least the size of set S.
2. There will be another set T of previously untested components whose Ease-of-Execution metrics will decrease; thus, forcing P to execute and to evaluate to v will have "made progress" toward forcing the execution of each member of set T.

For instance, in our example program:

1. When predicate 2 evaluates to *true*, lines (7) and (23) are guaranteed to execute.
2. Predicate 2 evaluating to *true* lowers the Ease-of-Execution metric of statements (8), (10), (11), (12), (13), (16), (17), (20), and (21) by at least 2, possibly more, depending on the values of predicates 3, 4, and 5. Predicate 2 evaluating to *true* lowers the Ease-of-Execution metric of statement (25) by 1.

These observations suggest two useful metrics to report to the programmer for each predicate P, and each possible value v of P:

Must-Execute-Set Metric: The number of untested components that *must* execute if P executes and evaluates to v, and might not execute otherwise (the value of this metric is 2 for the pair (predicate 2, *true*) in the example program).

Improved-Ease-Set Metric: The total amount by which the ease metrics of untested components are guaranteed to be lowered if P executes and evaluates to v (the value of this metric is 19 for the pair (predicate 2, *true*) in the example program).

The two metrics can be computed efficiently using the control-dependence graph. Recall that component C is v-control-dependent on predicate P iff C postdominates P's v-successor (in the control-flow graph) but does not postdominate P. This means that if P evaluates to v, then C is guaranteed to execute, while if P evaluates to some other value, C may not execute. Thus, it seems that the Must-Execute-Set Metric for predicate P and value v could simply be the number of untested components that are v-control-dependent on P. However, there is a subtlety involving backedges in the control-flow graph. Such edges can cause a component C that dominates predicate P in the control-flow graph to be control dependent on P. For example, as illustrated in Figure 5, all of the statements in the body of a do-while loop dominate the loop predicate, and are also control dependent on it. If component C dominates predicate P, then whenever P executes, C will have already executed; i.e., C will be tested regardless of the value to which P executes, and therefore it would be wrong to include C when computing (P,v)'s Must-Execute-Set Metric (since that set is supposed to include only components that might *not* execute if P does not evaluate to v). Fortunately, this is an easy problem to solve: it simply requires that all backedges be removed from the control-flow graph before computing control dependences. (In the example of Figure 5, this would have the effect of removing all outgoing control-dependence edges from the while predicate.) Given control dependences computed using a control-flow graph with no backedges, the Must-Execute-Set Metric for each predicate P and value v is the number of untested components that are v-control-dependent on P.

The Improved-Ease-Set Metric can be computed for each predicate P and value v by determining, for each untested component C reachable in the control-dependence graph from P, how many predicates are on the shortest path from

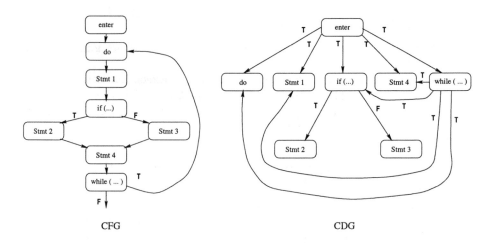

CFG   CDG

Fig. 5. Control-flow and control-dependence graphs for a `do-while` loop.

P to C (counting P itself when considering paths that start with a control-dependence edge labeled with a value other than v, and not counting P when considering paths that start with one of P's outgoing v edges). If the number of predicates is less than C's current Ease-of-Execution metric, then the difference in values is added to (P,v)'s Improved-Ease-Set Metric.

Note that we are proposing to supply the two "benefit" metrics only for predicates (rather than for all program components). It is true that forcing a statement S to execute also guarantees the execution of the other statements in the same weak region [2]. For example, forcing the statement on line (11) of our example program to execute guarantees that the statements on lines (12) and (13) will also execute. However, since only predicates have control-dependence successors, there is no obvious analog to the Improved-Ease-Set Metric for statements. Furthermore, in order to force a statement S to execute, the programmer must consider how to force the predicates that control S's execution to execute, and to evaluate to the appropriate values. Therefore, it seems reasonable for the programmer, and thus the tool, to concentrate on predicates.

Example: For each of the five predicates P in the example program, and for each value v to which P could evaluate, the table in Figure 6 lists the untested components that are guaranteed to execute if P evaluates to v (those that are v-control-dependent on P), those whose ease metrics are guaranteed to decrease if P evaluates to v (with the amount of decrease in parentheses), and the values of the two "benefit" metrics. □

3.3   Complexity

Ease-of-Execution Metric: The computation of the Ease-of-Execution metric for all untested components in the program can be performed using a single breadth-first search in the control-dependence graph. The queue is initialized to include

Predicate	Value	Must Execute	Has Lowered Ease Metric	Metric 1	Metric 2
pred 1	*true*	- none -	- none -	0	0
	false	6	7(-1), 8(-1), 10(-1), 11(-1), 12(-1), 13(-1), 16(-1), 17(-1), 23(-1), 25(-1)	1	10
pred 2	*true*	6, 7, 23	8(-2), 10(-2), 11(-2), 12(-2), 13(-2), 16(-2), 17(-2), 20(-2)	3	16
	false	6, 25	- none -	2	0
pred 3	*true*	7, 8, 20	21(-3)	3	3
	false	7, 10	11(-3), 12(-3), 13(-3), 16(-3), 17(-3), 20(-2), 21(-2)	2	19
pred 4	*true*	10, 11, 12, 13, 20	21(-3)	5	3
	false	10, 16, 17	- none -	3	0
pred 5	*true*	20, 21	- none -	2	0
	false	20	- none -	1	0

Fig. 6. For each predicate in the example program, and for each possible value, the untested components that must execute, those whose ease metrics are guaranteed to be lowered (and by how much), and the values of the Must-Execute-Set Metric (Metric 1) and the Improved-Ease-Set Metric (Metric 2).

all nodes that are control-dependence successors of some tested predicate, with metric = 1. Each time a node n is removed from the queue, each of its successors is considered. If a successor has not yet been visited, then its value is set to n's value + 1, and it is enqueued. The time required is linear in the size of the control-dependence graph.

Must-Execute-Set Metric: As stated in Section 3.2, the value of this metric for predicate P and value v is the number of untested components that are v-control-dependent on P. This number can be computed in time proportional to the number of components that are v-control-dependent on P simply by checking each one to see whether it has been tested.

Improved-Ease-Set Metric: The Improved-Ease-Set Metric for predicate P and value v can be computed by using breadth-first search to find the shortest path in the control-dependence graph from P to each untested component C, starting by putting all of P's v-successors on the queue. If the path to C is shorter than the current value of C's Ease-of-Execution Metric, then the difference in values is added to the running total for (P,v)'s Improved-Ease-Set Metric. In the worst case, this computation is linear in the size of the control-dependence graph.

Interprocedural Analysis To handle complete programs, control-dependence graphs are built for each procedure, and are connected by adding an edge from each node `call Proc` to `Proc`'s `enter` node. The techniques described above for computing the Ease-of-Execution and Improved-Ease-Set metrics work with a trivial extension in the interprocedural case: When during the breadth-first search a node `call Proc` is enqueued, if `Proc`'s `enter` node has not yet been visited, all of its successors should also be enqueued. In the case of the Ease-of-

Execution metric, those nodes should also be given the same metric value as the call node. In the case of the Improved-Ease-Set metric, the length of the current path (counting the new interprocedural edges, as well as the edges out of the enter node as having length zero) should be compared to the nodes' recorded Ease-of-Execution metric value, updating (P,v)'s Improved-Ease-Set metric if appropriate.

When computing the interprocedural Must-Execute-Set metric for predicate P and value v, the call nodes that are v-control-dependent on P must be handled specially: for each such node, call Proc, the number of untested components that are *true*-control-dependent on Proc's enter node must be included in the value of the metric. However, they should not be added multiple times when there are multiples calls to Proc that are v-control-dependent on P. A straightforward way to implement the computation of (P,v)'s Must-Execute-Set metric is to do a breadth-first search from P, initializing the queue to include all of P's v-control successors. The search continues only from call nodes (following their outgoing interprocedural edges) and from enter nodes (following their outgoing *true* edges). The final value of the metric is the number of untested components encountered during the search. The time required to compute the metric for (P,v) is proportional to the number of nodes that are v-control-dependent on P, plus the number of nodes that are *true*-control-dependent on the enter node for some procedure Proc called from a node that is v-control-dependent on P.

4   Using the Metrics

Our proposed testing tool will use the three metrics computed for each untested (predicate, value) pair to determine an ordering on those pairs, which will be reported to the programmer. One window will be used to display the program itself, and another window will be used to display the sorted list of pairs (with the values of the three metrics).

Experiments will be needed to determine the best way to compute the ordering (and, while a good default will be used, the programmer will also be given the opportunity to define alternative ways of combining the metric values to produce a sorted list). One reasonable possibility is to sort the pairs using the Ease-of-Execution metric as the primary key (sorting from low to high), the Must-Execute-Set metric as the secondary key (sorting from high to low), and the Improved-Ease-Set metric as the third key (sorting from high to low). The intuition is that predicates with low Ease-of-Execution metrics represent "low-hanging fruit"; i.e., it will be relatively easy for the programmer to figure out how to force those predicates to execute. By providing the two "benefit" metrics as well, the programmer can avoid wasting time focusing on those "easy" predicates that are unprofitable because their execution is not likely to cause very many untested components to execute.

Example: The information that would be provided to the programmer using this approach is shown in Figure 7. □

Predicate	Value	Ease-of-Execution Metric	Must-Execute-Set Metric	Improved-Ease-Set Metric
1: if (printOption == AV_HOURS)	false	0	1	10
2: if (printOption == WEEKS_PAY)	true	1	3	16
	false	1	2	0
3: if (jobCode == SALARIED)	true	2	3	3
	false	2	2	19
4: if (hours > 40)	true	3	5	3
	false	3	3	0
5: if (hours > 60)	true	3	2	0
	false	3	1	0

Fig. 7. The untested (predicate, value) pairs for the example program, sorted using the Ease-of-Execution metric as the primary key (sorted from low to high), the Must-Execute-Set metric as the secondary key (sorted from high to low), and the Improved-Ease-Set metric as the third key (sorted from high to low). The values of the three metrics are also shown.

The tool will also provide a way for the programmer to see the components that have contributed to the values of the three metrics: When the programmer chooses one of the predicate-value pairs (P, v) – by clicking on that line in the table – the tool will change the display of the program as follows:

– The text of the program is scrolled if necessary, so that the selected predicate is visible on the screen.
– The "relevant" predicates for P are displayed using red font. (If those predicates are not visible on the screen, a separate window is used to display the names of the files and procedures that contain relevant predicates.) Clicking on a relevant predicate causes the display of the value to which it must execute in order to follow the path to P.
– The components that are (interprocedurally) v-control-dependent on P are displayed using green font (again, a separate window is used to indicate where to find those components that are not on-screen).
– The components whose Ease-of-Execution metrics would decrease if P evaluates to v are displayed using blue font.

5   Help with Forcing the Execution of Predicate P

Once the programmer has selected a predicate-value pair (P, v) on which to focus, the next task is to consider what input values will cause P to execute and to evaluate to v. Our tool, which has access to the program's control and flow dependences can help in several ways.

5.1   The Reduced CFG

First, the tool can use the same information that was used to compute P's Ease-of-Execution metric to compute a reduced control-flow graph. Recall that the Ease-of-Execution metric was based on finding the shortest path in the control-dependence graph from an already-executed component C to P. Initially, the reduced control-flow graph includes only the paths that start from the beginning of the program, go through C, then reach P via a path in the CFG that corresponds to the control-dependence-graph path from C to P. The control and flow dependences induced by this reduced CFG are then computed and used to find all of the statements that involve computations that might affect which path is actually followed at runtime (i.e., the statements in the backward inter-procedural slice from P [9]).[1] Irrelevant statements (those not in the slice) are removed, further reducing the size of the reduced CFG. The input statements in the reduced CFG are highlighted, using different colors for the ones that are relevant, and the ones that are irrelevant (an input statement is irrelevant if some input must be provided at that point, but the actual value can be arbitrary). Finally, the tool allows the user to "walk back" along the flow dependence edges in the reduced control-flow graph, to help illustrate the flow of values.

Example: Suppose that the programmer has decided to concentrate on forcing predicate 5 to evaluate to *true* (this is an unlikely choice, but is good for illustrative purposes). The Ease-of-Execution metric for predicate 5 was based on a control-dependence-graph path starting at (already executed) predicate 1. There is only one path in the CFG from the beginning of the program to predicate 1: nodes (1), (2), and (3). The control-dependence path from predicate 1 to predicate 5 goes via predicates 2 and 3. There is only one CFG path that corresponds to this control-dependence-graph path; that CFG path includes nodes (3), (6), (7), (8), and (20). Thus, the initial reduced CFG would contain just seven nodes: (1), (2), (3), (6), (7), (8), and (20). Since the statement at node (8), pay = 40 * hourlyRate, has no direct or transitive effect on any of the predicates, that node would also be eliminated. The code that corresponds to the final reduced control-flow graph is shown in Figure 8. Each predicate is annotated with the value to which it must evaluate in order to reach predicate 5; boxes are used to indicate the relevant inputs, and underlining is used to indicate the (single) irrelevant input. If the programmer asks to see the source of the value of variable hours used in predicate 5, the tool would display the input of that variable at line (1). Similarly, the programmer could ask to see the sources of the values of the variables used at the other relevant predicates. In this example, the information provided by the tool would quickly lead the programmer to understand that using SALARIED as the first input (for variable jobCode), an arbitrary value as the second input (for variable hourlyRate), a value greater than 60 for the third input (for variable hours), and WEEKS_PAY for

---

[1] We assume that input statements are chained together by control dependences as described in [3] so that every input statement in the reduced CFG is in the slice from P.

the final input (for variable `printOption`) would cause predicate 5 to evaluate to *true*. □

```
(1)   read(jobCode, hourlyRate, hours);
(2)   read(printOption);
(3)   if (printOption == AV_HOURS) {          /* pred 1: must be FALSE */

(5)   }
(6)   else if (printOption == WEEKS_PAY) {    /* pred 2: must be TRUE */
(7)              if (jobCode == SALARIED) {    /* pred 3: must be TRUE */

(9)             }

(20)            if (hours > 60) {              /* pred 5 */
```

Fig. 8. The reduced version of the example program that is relevant to forcing predicate 5 to evaluate to *true*. The relevant inputs are indicated using boxes and the one irrelevant input is underlined.

5.2   Forbidden Predicate-Value Pairs

As discussed in Section 3.1, there may be multiple paths in the control-flow graph (and in the control-dependence graph) to a given predicate P. One example, caused by the use of a goto, was given in Section 3.1. However, non-structured code is not the only cause; for example, a predicate in a procedure that is called from multiple call sites will be reachable via multiple paths. While it is reasonable to start by considering the control-dependence path with the fewest predicates, the programmer may prefer to consider other paths as well. For example, the path used to compute the Ease-of-Execution metric for (P, v) might include a predicate-value pair (pred, val) such that the programmer cannot easily figure out how to force pred to evaluate to val. In this case, the programmer may wish to see a different reduced CFG that does not involve this problem pair. To permit this, our tool will allow the programmer to specify a set of prohibited predicate-value pairs; the tool will first find the best path in the control-dependence graph to P that does not include any prohibited pairs, and will then produce the corresponding reduced CFG. Computing the new path can be implemented easily and efficiently by using breadth-first search in the control-dependence graph from which edges that correspond to the forbidden pairs have been removed.

Example: Assume that the programmer has chosen to force predicate 5 to evaluate to *true*, but specifies that (predicate 3, true) is forbidden. The re-computation of the control-dependence-graph path would produce: (predicate 1, false)(predicate 2, true)(predicate 3, false)(predicate 4, true), because that is the shortest path in the control-dependence graph from predicate 1 to predicate 5 that does not include the forbidden predicate-value pair. The code that corresponds to the (final) reduced CFG that would be produced in this case is shown in Figure 9. □

```
(1)    read(jobCode, hourlyRate, hours);
(2)    read(printOption);
(3)    if (printOption == AV_HOURS) {          /* pred 1: must be FALSE */

(5)    }
(6)    else if (printOption == WEEKS_PAY) {    /* pred 2: must be TRUE */
(7)              if (jobCode == SALARIED) {    /* pred 3: must be FALSE */

(9)              }
(10)             else { if (hours > 40) {      /* pred 4: must be TRUE */
(14)                    }
(19)             }
(20)             if (hours > 60) {             /* pred 5 */
```

Fig. 9. The reduced version of the example program that is relevant to forcing predicate 5 to evaluate to *true*, given that the pair (predicate 3, true) is forbidden. The relevant inputs are indicated using boxes and the one irrelevant input is underlined.

6   Summary, Current Status, and Future Work

Testing is one of the most difficult aspects of software engineering. In practice, testers use tools that tell them what percentage of their code is covered by a given test suite, and their goal is to reach some level of coverage (typically something like 85%). While existing tools track code coverage, they do not provide help with the vital problem of how to increase coverage. We have proposed the design of a tool that does address this problem. The tool uses information about the program's control dependences to help the programmer to select (predicate, value) pairs such that it will not be too difficult to find an input that causes the selected predicate to evaluate to the chosen value, and such that forcing that evaluation will make good progress toward increasing code coverage. The tool then uses both control and flow dependences to help the programmer choose an input that will cause the selected predicate to execute, and to evaluate to the chosen value.

We have implemented an initial prototype of the tool using GrammaTech's CodeSurfer system [8]. CodeSurfer is an ideal platform on which to build since it provides many of the facilities needed to support our proposed tool:

- CodeSurfer processes C programs, computing their control and flow dependences.
- It provides an API that gives access to the program's CFG, control-dependence, and flow-dependence edges.
- It can import the program-coverage data gathered by PureCoverage [14], mapping per-line coverage information to per-CFG-node information.
- It provides high-level operations such as program slicing and chopping.

Future work includes completing the implementation of the tool and evaluating how well it works in practice, as well as investigating other uses for control and flow dependences in the context of testing. For example:

- How well does the Ease-of-Execution metric predict the actual effort required to force a given predicate to evaluate to a given value?
- How effective is the use of the reduced CFG in helping the programmer to write a test input that forces the chosen predicate to execute and to evaluate to the chosen value?
- Can control and flow dependences help with the problem of how to reuse existing test inputs when writing new ones?
- Can control and flow dependences help with the problem of automatic test-input generation?

Acknowledgements

This work was supported in part by the National Science Foundation under grants CCR-9970707, CCR-9987435 and DMI-0060607.

References

1. A. Aho, R. Sethi, and J. Ullman. Addison-Wesley, Reading, MA, 1986.
2. T. Ball. What's in a region - or - computing control dependence regions in linear time for reducible control-flow. *ACM Trans. on Programming Languages and Systems*, 2(1-4):1–16, 1993.
3. S. Bates and S. Horwitz. Incremental program testing using program dependence graphs. In *Proc. ACM Symp. on Principles of Programming Languages (POPL)*, pages 384–396, January 1993.
4. Bullseye Testing Technology C-Cover. http://www.bullseye.com.
5. M. Davis and E. Weyuker. A formal notion of program-based test data adequacy. *Inform. and Contr.*, 56(1-2):52–71, Jan-Feb 1983.
6. M. Dwyer et al. Slicing multi-threaded Java programs: A case study. Technical Report 99-7, Kansas State University Computing and Information Sciences, 1999.
7. J. Ferrante, K. Ottenstein, and J. Warren. The program dependence graph and its use in optimization. *ACM Trans. on Programming Languages and Systems*, 9(3):319–349, July 1987.
8. GrammaTech, Inc. Codesurfer user guide and reference manual, 2000.
9. S. Horwitz, T. Reps, and D. Binkley. Interprocedural slicing using dependence graphs. *ACM Trans. on Programming Languages and Systems*, 12(1):26–60, January 1990.
10. J. Krinke. Static slicing of threaded programs. In *Proc. ACM SIGPLAN/SIGSOFT Workshop on Program Analysis for Tools and Software Eng.*, June 1998.
11. M. Nanda and S. Ramesh. Slicing concurrent programs. In *Proc. Int. Symp. on Software Testing and Analysis*, August 2000.
12. A. Rountev and B. Ryder. Points-to and side-effect analyses for programs built with precompiled libraries. In *Int. Conf. on Compiler Construction*, April 2001.
13. S. Sinha, M. Harrold, and G. Rothermel. System-dependence-graph-based slicing of programs with arbitrary interprocedural control flow. In *Int. Conf. on Software Eng.*, pages 432–441, May 1999.
14. Rational Software. http://www.rational.com/products/pqc/index.jsp.
15. Software Research, Inc. http://www.soft.com/products/web/tcat.java.html.

Data Space Oriented Tiling

Mahmut Kandemir

Department of Computer Science and Engineering
The Pennsylvania State University
University Park, PA 16802, USA
kandemir@cse.psu.edu

Abstract. An optimizing compiler can play an important role in enhancing data locality in array-intensive applications with regular data access patterns. This paper presents a compiler-based data space oriented tiling approach (DST). In this strategy, the data space (i.e., the array index space) is logically divided into chunks (called data tiles) and each data tile is processed in turn. In processing a data tile, our approach traverses the entire iteration space of all nests in the code and executes all iterations (potentially coming from different nests) that access the data tile being processed. In doing so, it also takes data dependences into account. Since a data space is common across all nests that access it, DST can potentially achieve better results than traditional tiling by exploiting inter-nest data locality. This paper also shows how data space oriented tiling can be used for improving the performance of software-managed scratch pad memories.

1 Introduction

Iteration space tiling (also called loop blocking) [9, 1] is a loop-oriented optimization aiming at improving data locality. The idea behind tiling is to divide a given iteration space into chunks such that the data elements accessed by a given chunk fit in the available cache memory capacity. Previously-published work iteration space tiling reports significant improvements in cache miss rates and program execution times. Compilers use iteration space tiling mainly to create the blocked version of a given nested loop automatically. Note that, in general, it is difficult to guarantee that the array elements accessed by a given iteration space tile will fit in the cache. This problem occurs because tile shapes and tiling style are decided based on loop behavior rather than the data elements accessed. In particular, most of the current approaches to tiling do not consider the shape of the data regions (from different arrays) touched by an iteration space tile.

In this paper, we discuss and evaluate data space oriented tiling (DST), a variant of classical iteration space oriented tiling, to achieve better data locality than classical tiling. Instead of tiling iteration space first, and then considering data space requirements of the resulting tiles (data regions) in data space, DST takes a data space oriented approach. Specifically, it first logically divides data space into tiles (called data space tiles or data tiles for short), and then processes

---

D. Le Métayer (Ed.): ESOP 2002, LNCS 2305, pp. 178–193, 2002.

each data tile in sequence. Processing a data tile involves determining the set of loop iterations that access the elements in that data tile and executing these iterations taking into account data dependences. Since it starts its analysis from data space, DST has two main advantages over iteration space tiling:

- Since data space of a given array is shared across all nests that access the corresponding array, DST has a more global view of the program-wide access pattern (than iteration space tiling). This is especially true if one can come up with strategies to summarize access patterns of multiple nests on a given array.
- Working on data space allows compiler to take layout constraints into account better. For instance, in selecting a data tile shape, in addition to other parameters, the compiler can also consider memory layout of the array in question.

This paper describes a data space oriented tiling approach and presents a strategy for determining data tile shapes and sizes automatically. It also shows how DST can be used in conjunction with a scratch pad memory (SPM).

The remainder of this paper is organized as follows. Section 2 revises classical iteration space tiling and discusses how it improves data locality. Section 3 presents description of data space oriented tiling, focusing in particular on issues such as selection of data tile shapes, traversing iteration space, and handling data dependences. Section 4 discusses an application of DST to optimizing the effectiveness of scratch pad memories, which are compiler-managed on-chip SRAMs. Section 5 concludes the paper with a summary of our major contributions.

2 Review of Iteration Space Tiling

An important technique used to improve cache performance (data locality) by making better use of cache lines is iteration space tiling (also called loop blocking) [1, 2, 9]. In tiling, data structures that are too big to fit in the cache are (logically) broken up into smaller pieces that will fit in the cache. In other words, instead of operating on entire columns or rows of a given array, tiling enables operations on multi-dimensional sections of arrays at one time. The objective here is to keep the active sections of the arrays in faster levels of memory hierarchy (e.g., data caches) as long as possible so that when a data item (array element) is reused, it can be accessed from the faster memory instead of the slower memory.

For an illustration of tiling, consider the matrix-multiply code given in Figure 1(a). Let us assume that the layouts of all the arrays are row-major. It is easy to see that, from the cache locality perspective, this loop nest may not exhibit a very good performance (depending on the actual array sizes and cache capacity). The reason is that, although array U_2 has temporal reuse in the innermost loop (the k loop) and successive iterations of this loop access consecutive elements from array U_0 (i.e., array U_0 has spatial reuse in the innermost loop), the successive accesses to array U_1 touch different rows of this array. Obviously, this is not a good style of access for a row-major array. Using state-of-the-art optimizing compiler technology (e.g., [5]), we can derive the code shown in Figure 1(b), given the code in Figure 1(a). In this optimized code, the array U_0 has temporal reuse in the innermost loop (the j loop now) and the arrays U_1 and U_2 have spatial reuses, meaning that the successive iterations of the innermost loop touch consecutive elements from both the arrays.

However, unless the faster memory in question is large enough to hold the entire $N \times N$ array U_1, many elements of this array will probably be replaced from the cache before they are reused in successive iterations of the outermost i loop. Instead of operating on individual array elements, tiling achieves reuse of array sections by performing the calculations (in our case matrix multiplication) on array sections (in our case sub-matrices). Figure 1(c) shows the tiled version of Figure 1(b). This tiled version is from [1]. In the tiled code, the loops kk and jj are called the tile loops, whereas the loops i, k, and j are called the element loops. It is important to choose the tile size (blocking factor) B such that all the $B^2 + 2NB$ array items accessed by the element loops i, k, j should fit in the faster memory (e.g., cache). In other words, the tiled version of the matrix-multiply code operates on $N \times B$ sub-matrices of arrays U_0 and U_2, and a $B \times B$ sub-matrix of array U_1 at one time. Assuming that the matrices in this example are in main memory to begin with, ensuring that $B^2 + 2NB$ array elements can be kept in cache might be sufficient to obtain high levels of performance. In practice, however, depending on the cache size, cache associativity, and absolute array addresses in memory, cache conflicts can occur. Consequently, the tile size B is set to a much smaller value than necessary [1].

```
for(i = 1; i ≤ N; i + +)
  for(j = 1; j ≤ N; j + +)
    for(k = 1; k ≤ N; k + +)
      U₂[i][j]+ = U₀[i][k] * U₁[k][j];
```

(a)

```
for(i = 1; i ≤ N; i + +)
  for(k = 1; k ≤ N; k + +)
    for(j = 1; j ≤ N; j + +)
      U₂[i][j]+ = U₀[i][k] * U₁[k][j];
```

(b)

```
for(kk = 1; kk ≤ N; kk = kk + B)
  for(jj = 1; jj ≤ N; jj = jj + B)
    for(i = 1; i ≤ N; i + +)
      for(k = kk; k ≤ min(N, kk + B − 1); k + +)
        for(j = jj; j ≤ min(N, jj + B − 1); j + +)
          U₂[i][j]+ = U₀[i][k] * U₁[k][j];
```

(c)

Fig. 1. (a) Matrix-multiply nest. (b) Locality-optimized version. (c) Tiled version.

3   Description of Data Space Oriented Tiling

The traditional iteration space tiling tiles the iteration space taking into account data dependences in the code. In such a tiling strategy, it is not guaranteed that the array elements accessed by a given iteration space tile form a region (which we can refer to as data tile) that exhibits locality. Also, since each nest is tiled independently from other nests in the code, it may not be possible to exploit potential data reuse between different nests due to common array regions accessed.

In contrast, data space oriented tiling (DST) takes a different approach. Instead of focussing on iteration space, it first considers data space (e.g., an array). Specifically, it divides a given array into logical partitions (data tiles) and processes each data tile in turn. In processing a data tile, it traverses the entire iteration space of all nests in the code and executes all iterations (potentially coming from different nests) that access the current data tile being processed. In doing so, it takes data dependences into account. Note that since a data space is common across all nests that access it, DST can potentially achieve better results than traditional tiling by exploiting inter-nest locality. Note also that, as opposed to tradition tiling, this data oriented tiling approach can also handle imperfectly-nested loops easily as it is not restricted by the way the loops in the nests are structured.

In [4], Kodukula et al. present a data oriented tiling strategy called data shackling, which is similar to our approach in spirit. However, there are significant differences between these two optimization strategies. First, the way that a data tile shape is determined in [4] is experimental. Since they mainly focus on linear algebra codes, they decided that using square (or rectilinear) tiles would work well most of the time; that is, such tiles lead to legal (semantics-preserving) access patterns. In comparison, we first summarize the access patterns of multiple nests on data space using data relation vectors, and then select a suitable tile shape so as to minimize the communication volume. Second, their optimization strategy considers only a single imperfectly-nested loop at a time, while we attempt to optimize all the nests in the code simultaneously. Therefore, our approach is expected to exploit inter-nest data reuse better. Third, we also present an automated strategy to handle data dependences. Instead, their work is more oriented towards determining legality for a given data tile (using a polyhedral tool). Finally, the application domains of these two techniques are also different. The approach discussed in [4] is specifically designed for optimizing cache locality. As will be explained later in the paper, we instead mainly focus on improving memory energy consumption of a scratch pad memory based architecture. Therefore, in our case, optimizing inter-nest reuse is more important.

To illustrate the difference between iteration space oriented tiling and data space oriented tiling, we consider the scenario in Figure 2 where an array is manipulated using three separate nests and there are no intra-nest or inter-nest data dependences in the code. As shown on the upper-left portion of the figure, the array is divided into two sections (regions): a and b. The iteration spaces of the nests are divided into four regions. Each region is identified using letters a or b to indicate the data region it accesses. Figure 2 also shows three possible execution orders. In the execution order (I), the traditional tiling approach is shown, assuming that the sections in the iteration space are processed from left-to-right and top-to-bottom. We clearly see that there are frequent transitions between a-blocks and b-blocks, which is not good from the data locality perspective. The execution order (II) illustrates a data oriented approach which restricts its optimization scope to a single nest at a time (as in [4]). That is, it handles nests one-by-one, and in processing a nest it clusters iterations that access a given data region. Consequently, it does not incur transitions between a-blocks and b-blocks in executing a given nest, a big advantage over the scheme in (I). However, in going from one nest to another, it incurs transitions between a-blocks and b-blocks. Finally, the execution order (III) represents our approach. In this strategy, we process data regions one-by-one, and in processing a region, we execute all iterations from all nests that access the said region. Therefore, our approach first executes iterations (considering all nests) that access a-block, and then executes all iterations that access b-blocks. Consequently, there is only one transition between a-blocks and b-blocks. However, there are many issues that need to be addressed. First, in some cases, inherent data dependences in the program may not allow interleaving loop iterations from different nests. Second, in general, a given code may contain multiple arrays that need to be taken into account. Third, shape of the data regions might also have a significant impact on the success of the strategy (in particular, when we have data dependences). Data space oriented tiling is performed in two steps: (i) selecting an array (called the seed array) and determining a suitable tile shape for that array, and (ii) iterating through data tiles and for each tile executing all iterations (from all nests in the code) that manipulate array elements in the data tile. In the remainder of this paper, we address these issues in detail.

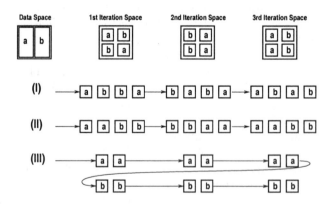

Fig. 2. Comparison of iteration space oriented tiling and data space oriented tiling.

The loop iterators surrounding any statement can be represented as an $n \times 1$ column vector: $\boldsymbol{i} = [i_1, i_2, \cdots, i_n]^T$, where n is the number of enclosing loop iterators. The loop bounds of the iterators can be described by a system of inequalities which define the polyhedron $\mathcal{A}\boldsymbol{i} \leq \boldsymbol{b}$ where $\mathcal{A}$ is an $l \times n$ integer matrix and b is an l vector. The integer values taken by i define the iteration space of the iterators.

The data storage of an array U_0 can also be viewed as a (rectilinear) poly-hedron. The index domain of array U_0 can be described using index vectors: $a = \left[a_1, a_2, \cdots, a_{dim(U_0)}\right]^T$, where $dim(U_0)$ refers to the dimensionality of U_0. The index vectors have a certain range which describe the size of the array, or data space: $\mu_{LB} \leq a \leq \mu_{UB}$, where the $dim(U_0) \times 1$ vectors μ_{LB} and μ_{UB} correspond to lower and upper bounds of the array, respectively. In this paper, we assume that $\mu_{LB} = [1, 1, \cdots, 1, 1]$; that is, the lowest index value in each subscript position is 1.

The subscript function for a reference to array U_0 represents a mapping from iteration space to data space. An iteration vector i is said to access (or reference) an array element indexed by a if there exists a subscript function (or array reference) $R_{U_0}(.)$ such that $R_{U_0}(i) = a$. In our context, an array reference can be written as an affine mapping that has the form $Li + o$, where L is a $dim(U_0) \times n$ matrix and o is a $dim(U_0) \times 1$ vector. For example, an array reference such as $U_0[i-1][i+j+2]$ in a two-level nested loop (where i is the outer loop and j is the inner loop) can be represented as

$$R_{U_0}(i) = Li + o = \begin{bmatrix} 1 & 0 \\ 1 & 1 \end{bmatrix} \begin{bmatrix} i \\ j \end{bmatrix} + \begin{bmatrix} -1 \\ 2 \end{bmatrix},$$

where $i = \begin{bmatrix} i & j \end{bmatrix}^T$. When there is no confusion, we write $R_{U_0} \in N_k$ to indicate that the reference $R_{U_0}(.)$ appears in nest N_k.

3.1   Array Selection and Tile Shapes

The first step in DST is selecting a suitable array (called the seed array) from among the arrays declared in the code and determining a suitable data tile shape for this array. Once the shape of the tile has been determined, its sizes in different dimensions can be found by scaling up its shape.

Let us assume for now that we have already selected a seed array, U_0. A data tile corresponds to set of array elements in a data space (array). To define a suitable data tile for a given seed array, we need to consider the access pattern of each nest on the said array. For a given seed array U_0 and a nest N_i, the seed element of U_0 with respect to nest N_i, denoted s_{U_0,N_i}, is the lexicographically smallest element of the array accessed by N_i. Based on this definition, the global seed element g_{U_0} for array U_0 is the smallest array element accessed by all nests in the code. In cases where there is not such a global seed, we select an element which is accessed by most of the nests.

Using this global seed element, we determine a seed iteration for each nest as follows. The seed iteration of nest N_i with respect to array U_0 is an iteration i_{sU_0,N_i} that among the elements accessed by this iteration, g_{U_0} is the smallest one in lexicographic sense. If there are multiple seed iterations (for a given nest), we select the lexicographically smallest one. Then, we define the footprint of nest N_i with respect to array U_0 (denoted $\mathcal{F}_{U_0,N_i}$) as the set of elements accessed by i_{sU_0,N_i}. More precisely, $\mathcal{F}_{U_0,N_i} = \{f \mid f = R_{U_0}(i_{sU_0,N_i}) \text{ for all } R_{U_0} \in N_i\}$.

Let us define a set of vectors $(\mathcal{V}_{U_0,N_i})$, called data relation vectors, on the data space of U_0 using the elements in the footprint $\mathcal{F}_{U_0,N_i}$. Specifically, let $\mathcal{F}_{U_0,N_i} =$

$\{f_1, f_2, \cdots, f_k\}$, where the elements in this set are ordered lexicographically, f_1 being the lexicographically smallest one. Each $v_j \in \mathcal{V}$ represents a vector between f_i and f_k, where $k > i$. In other words, by doing so, we define a set of lexicographically positive vectors between all data point pairs in $\mathcal{F}_{U_0,N_i}$. We can write $\mathcal{V}_{U_0,N_i}$ as a matrix $[v_1; v_2; \cdots; v_L]$. This matrix is termed as the local data relation matrix.

The global data relation matrix of array U_0 (denoted $\mathcal{G}_{U_0}$) is the combination of local data relation matrices coming from individual nests; that is, $\mathcal{G}_{U_0} = [\mathcal{V}_{U_0,N_1}; \mathcal{V}_{U_0,N_2}; \cdots \mathcal{V}_{U_0,N_P}]$, where P is the number of nests in the code. If desired, the (column) vectors in $\mathcal{G}_{U_0}$ can be re-ordered according to their frequency of occurrence. Our approach uses $\mathcal{G}_{U_0}$ to define tile shapes on data space. Specifically, we first find the vectors in $\mathcal{G}_{U_0}$ and cover the entire data space (of the array in question) using these vectors. The positions of these vectors on the data space is used in selecting a data tile shape. Our objective in selecting a data tile shape is to ensure that, when executing a group of iterations that access the elements in a given data tile, the number of non-tile elements accessed should be minimized as much as possible. Obviously, the shape of the data tile plays a major role in determining the number of the non-tile elements accessed.

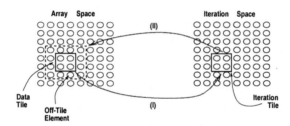

Fig. 3. Going from data tile to iteration tile and off-tile (non-tile) elements.

We next define communication volume as the number of non-tile elements accessed during the execution of iterations that manipulate the elements in the tile. It should be noted that, for a given data tile, the execution of each nest might incur a non-zero communication volume. We then try to minimize the global (over all nests) communication volume. It should also be noted that a non-tile element access occurs due to a relation vector that crosses a tile boundary (i.e., one of its end-points are inside the tile whereas the other end-point lies outside the tile). As an example, consider the iteration space and data space shown in Figure 3. Considering the data tile on the left side of the figure, our approach determines an iteration tile (on the iteration space). This activity is marked (I) in the figure. The iterations in the iteration tile are the ones that access the array elements in the data tile. We will make a more accurate definition of iteration tile later in the paper. Next, the entire set of array elements accessed by this iteration tile is determined. This step corresponds to (II) in the figure. These array elements are delimited using a dashed box in the figure. The array elements that are within the dashed box but outside the data tile are called off-tile (or non-tile) elements. The objective of our tile selection strategy is to minimize the number of off-tile elements.

A given data tile can be defined using a set of hyperplanes. Specifically, data tiles in an M-dimensional space can be defined by M families of parallel hyperplanes (or planes), each of which is an $(M - 1)$-dimensional hyperplane. Data tiles so defined are parallelepipeds (except for those near the boundary of the data space) and each tile is an M-dimensional subset of the data space. Thus, the shape of the tiles is defined by the families of planes and the size of the tiles is defined by the distance of separation between adjacent pairs of parallel planes in each of the M families. We can represent a given tile to array U_0 using M vectors, where the ith vector p_i $(1 \leq i \leq M)$ corresponds to the ith boundary of the tile. These vectors can collectively be written as a matrix $P_{U_0} = [p_1; p_2; \cdots; p_M]$. Alternatively, a given data tile can be defined using another matrix, H_{U_0}, each row of which is perpendicular to a given tile boundary. It can be shown that $H_{U_0} = P_{U_0}^{-1}$. Consequently, to define a data tile, we can either specify the columns of P_{U_0} or the rows of H_{U_0}.

We then try to select a tile shape such that the number of data relation vectors intersected by tile boundaries will be minimum. As mentioned earlier, each such vector (also referred to as the communication vector) represents two elements, one of which is within the tile whereas the other is outside the tile. Note that such vectors are the most important ones to concentrate on as the vectors with both the ends are outside can be converted to either the communication vectors or the vectors which are contained completely in the tile by making the tile large enough. It should also be noted that using H_{U_0} and $\mathcal{G}_{U_0}$, we can represent the communication requirements in a concise manner. Specifically, since data tiles are separated by tile boundaries (defined by H_{U_0}), a communication vector must cross the tile boundary between the tiles. A non-zero entry in $\mathcal{G}'_{U_0} = H_{U_0}\mathcal{G}_{U_0}$, say the entry in (i, j), implies that communication is incurred due to the jth communication vector poking the ith tile boundary. The amount of communication across a tile boundary, defined by the ith row of H_{U_0}, is a function of the sum of the entries in the ith row of $\mathcal{G}'_{U_0}$.

Based on this, we can formulate the problem of finding tiling planes as that of finding a transformation H_{U_0} such that the communication volume (due to communication vectors) will be minimum. Note that the communication volume is proportional to:

$$\sum_{i=1}^{M} \sum_{j=1}^{S} \sum_{k=1}^{M} h_{i,k} v_{k,j}.$$

As an example, let us consider the code fragment given below, which consists of two separate nests. Figure 4(a) shows the local data relation vectors for each nest as well as the global data relation vector (only the first 3×3 portion of the array is shown for clarity). Figure 4(b) shows how the global data relation vectors can be used to cover the entire data space. This picture is then used to select a suitable tile shape. It should be noted that the global data relation matrix in this example is:

$$\mathcal{G}_{U_0} = \begin{bmatrix} 0 & 1 \\ 1 & 1 \end{bmatrix}.$$

$$for(i = 1; i \leq N - 1; i + +)$$
$$for(j = 1; j \leq N - 1; j + +)$$
$$\{U_0[i][j], U_0[i+1][j+1]\};$$
$$for(i = 1; i \leq N; i + +)$$
$$for(j = 1; j \leq N - 1; j + +)$$
$$\{U_0[i][j], U_0[i][j+1]\};$$

Assuming a data tile capacity (size) of six elements, Figure 4(c) shows three alternative data tile shapes with their communication vectors. It should be noted that each tile in this figure has a different communication volume. For example, the data tile in (I) has a communication volume of 12, corresponding to six in-coming edges and six out-going edges. The tile in (II), on the other hand, has a communication volume of 14. Finally, the tile (III) has a communication volume of 10. Consequently, for the best results, tile (III) should be selected. In fact, it is easy to see that, in this example, if the dimension sizes of the rectangular data tile (as in (I) and (II)) are n (vertical) and m (horizontal), then the communication volume is $4n + 2(m - 1)$. For the tile in (III), on the other hand, the corresponding figure is $2(m+n)$. As an example, if $n = m = 50$, the communication volume of the tile in (III) is 32% less than the one in (I).

To show how our approach derives the tile shown in (III) for the example code fragment above, let us define H_{U_0} as:

$$H_{U_0} = \begin{bmatrix} h_{11} & h_{12} \\ h_{21} & h_{22} \end{bmatrix}.$$

Consequently,

$$\mathcal{G}'_{U_0} = H_{U_0}\mathcal{G}_{U_0} = \begin{bmatrix} h_{11} & h_{12} \\ h_{21} & h_{22} \end{bmatrix} \begin{bmatrix} 0 & 1 \\ 1 & 1 \end{bmatrix} = \begin{bmatrix} h_{11} + h_{12} & h_{12} \\ h_{21} + h_{22} & h_{22} \end{bmatrix}.$$

To minimize the communication volume, the sum of (the absolute values of) the entries in this last matrix should be minimum. This is because, as we have discussed above, each non-zero entry in $\mathcal{G}'_{U_0}$ represents a communication along one surface of the tile. In mathematical terms, we need to select h_{11}, h_{12}, h_{21}, and h_{22} such that $|h_{11} + h_{12}| + |h_{12}| + |h_{21} + h_{22}| + |h_{22}|$ should be minimized. A possible set of values for minimizing this is $h_{11} = 1$, $h_{12} = 0$, $h_{21} = -1$, and $h_{22} = 1$, respectively, which gives us:

$$H_{U_0} = \begin{bmatrix} 1 & 0 \\ -1 & 1 \end{bmatrix},$$

which, in turn, means

$$P_{U_0} = H_{U_0}^{-1} = \begin{bmatrix} 1 & 0 \\ 1 & 1 \end{bmatrix}.$$

Recall that each column of the P_{U_0} matrix represents a boundary of data tile. So, the P_{U_0} matrix above represents the data tile (III) illustrated in Figure 4(c). We next explain how a data tile is actually scaled up.

After selecting a data tile shape, it is scaled up in each dimension. In scaling up a data tile, we consider the iterations that follow the seed iteration in execution order. The left part of Figure 4(d) shows the global data relation vectors defined by the seed iteration and three other iterations that follows it. We

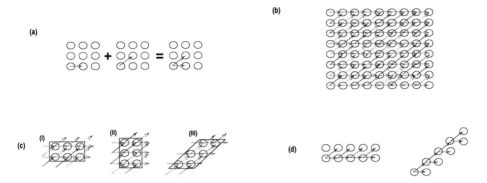

Fig. 4. (a) Local and global data relation vectors. (b) Data space covered by global data relation vectors. (c) Three different data tile shapes with their communication vectors. (d) Scaling up tile size based on array layout. (e) Tiling the entire data space.

can include as many iterations as possible as long as the maximum (allowable) capacity of a data tile is not exceeded. As will be discussed later in the paper, the maximum capacity of a data tile depends on the application at hand and the memory architecture under consideration. The iterations that (follow the seed iteration and) are included in determining the size of a tile constitute an iteration tile. It should be noted, however, that we do not necessarily include the iterations that immediately follow the seed. Instead, we can take into account array layout and determine a suitable iteration tile such that the spatial locality is exploited as much as possible. For example, as we can see on the left portion of Figure 4(d), for this example, progressing the relation vectors (that is, stretching the data tile) along the horizontal axis makes sense since the array layout is row-major. If, however, the array layout was column-major, it would be more beneficial to stretch the tile along the vertical exis as illustrated one the right side of Figure 4(d). Our current implementation takes the maximum capacity of the tile and the array layout into account, and determines the iterations in the iteration tile. Note that, for a given data tile, each nest may have a different iteration tile.

As will be explained in detail in the next section, once a suitable data tile (shape/size) has been selected, our approach considers data tiles one-by-one, and for each data tile, executes iterations that access the array elements in the tile. It should be noted, however, iterations that manipulate elements in a given tile may also access elements from different arrays. Assuming that we have tiles for these arrays as well, these accesses may also incur communication (i.e., accesses to non-tile elements). Consequently, just considering the seed array and its communication volume may not be sufficient in obtaining an overall satisfactory performance (that is, minimizing the communication volume due to all arrays and all nets). It should also be noted that the selection of the seed array is very important as it determines the execution order of loop iterations, how the iterations from different nests are interleaved, and tile shapes for other arrays. Our current approach to the problem of selecting the most suitable seed array is as follows. Since the number of arrays in a given code is small, we consider each array in turn as the seed array and compute the size of the overall communication set. Then, we select the array which leads to overall minimum communication when used as the seed.

3.2   Traversing Iteration Space

In this subsection, we assume that there exists no data dependences in the code. Once a seed array has been determined and a data tile shape/size has been selected, our approach divides the array into tiles. The tiles are exact copies of each other except maybe at the boundaires of the array space. It then re-structures the code so that the (re-structured) code, when executing, reads each data tile, executes loop iterations (possibly from different nests) that accesses its elements, and moves to the next tile. Since, as explained in the previous section, we are careful in selecting the most suitable tile shape, in executing iterations for a given tile, the number of off-tile (non-tile) elements will be minimum.

However, we need to be precise in defining the iterations that manipulate the elements in a given tile. This is because even iterations that are far apart from each other can occasionally access the same element in a given tile. For this purpose, we use the concept of the iteration tile given above. Let us focus on a specific data tile of T elements:

$$DT_{U_0} = \{a_1, a_2, \cdots, a_{T-1}, a_T\},$$

assuming that $g_{U_0} = a_1$ and H_{U_0} is the corrsponding tile matrix. Let

$$IT_{U_0,N_i} = \{i_1, i_2, \cdots, a_{T-1}, a_T\}$$

be the corresponding iteration tile for nest N_i, where $i_{sU_0,N_i} = i_1$.

When DT_{U_0} is processed, the corresponding IT_{U_0} is determined. This IT, in turn, determines the data tiles for the other arrays in the code. This is depicted in Figure 5, assuming that there are three arrays in the code and a single nest: U_0 (the seed array), U_1, and U_2. We first determine the data tile for U_0 (the seed array). Then, using this data tile, we find the corresponding iteration tile. After that, using this iteration tile, we determine data tiles for arrays U_1 and U_2. Once this iteration tile is executed, our approach processes the next tile from U_0 and so on. If there exist multiple nests in the code being optimized, when we process the data tile, we execute all iterations from the corresponding iteration tiles of all nests. Let us number the tiles in a given data space (array) from 1 to Y. Let us also denote $DT_{U_0}(j)$ the jth data tile (from array U_0) and $IT_{U_0,N_i}(j)$ the corresponding iteration tile from nest N_i. We process data tiles and execute corresponding iteration tiles in the following order (in Y steps):

$$DT_{U_0}(1) : IT_{U_0,N_1}(1), IT_{U_0,N_2}(1), \cdots, IT_{U_0,N_P}(1)$$
$$DT_{U_0}(2) : IT_{U_0,N_1}(2), IT_{U_0,N_2}(2), \cdots, IT_{U_0,N_P}(2)$$
$$\vdots \quad \vdots \qquad \vdots \qquad \vdots$$
$$DT_{U_0}(Y) : IT_{U_0,N_1}(Y), IT_{U_0,N_2}(Y), \cdots, IT_{U_0,N_P}(Y)$$

In other words, the iterations from different nests are interleaved. This is possible as we assumed that no data dependence exists in the code. When there are data dependences, however, the execution order of loop iterations is somewhat restricted as discussed in the next section.

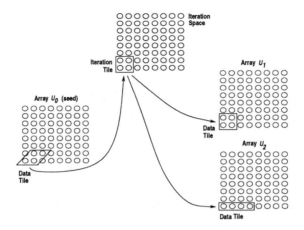

Fig. 5. Determining data tiles of non-seed arrays using the iteration tile defined by the data tile of the seed array.

3.3   Handling Data Dependences

As mentioned earlier, ideally, we would like to execute loop iterations as follows. We consider data tiles from the array one-by-one, and for each data tile, we execute all loop iterations (and only those iterations) that access array elements in the tile. However, if the communication volume of data tile is not zero, this ideal execution pattern would not happen. This is because, in executing some iterations, we might need to access elements from other tiles as well. Obviously, if we are able to select a good data tile (using the strategy explained earlier), the number of such non-tile accesses will be minimized. Note that, even in a loop without data dependences, we can experience non-tile accesses. However, when data dependences exist in the code, we can expect that such off-tile accesses will be more as the iterations that access the elements in the current tile might involve in data dependence relationships with other iterations.

For the sake of presentation, let us assume that there are two nests in the code (N_1 and N_2) and a single array (U_0). Assume that $DT_{U_0}(1)$ is a data tile for array U_0 and let $IT_{U_0,N_1}(1)$ and $IT_{U_0,N_2}(1)$ be the corresponding iteration tiles for nests N_1 and N_2. Assume further that $IT'_{U_0,N_1}(1)$ is the set of iterations (in N_1) other than those in $IT_{U_0,N_1}(1)$. Note that $IT_{U_0,N_1}(1)$ and $IT'_{U_0,N_1}(1)$ are disjoint and their union gives the iteration space of nest N_1. We can define a similar $IT'_{U_0,N_2}(1)$ set for nest N_2. Consider now the iteration sets $IT_{U_0,N_1}(1)$, $IT'_{U_0,N_1}(1)$, $IT_{U_0,N_2}(1)$, and $IT'_{U_0,N_2}(1)$ shown in Figure 6(a). If there are no data dependences in the code, when processing $DT_{U_0}(1)$, we can execute $IT_{U_0,N_1}(1)$ followed by $IT_{U_0,N_2}(1)$. Note that this corresponds to the ideal case as these two iteration sets, namely, $IT_{U_0,N_1}(1)$ and $IT_{U_0,N_2}(1)$, access the same data tile, so executing them one after another (without an intervening iteration from $IT'_{U_0,N_1}(1)$ or $IT'_{U_0,N_2}(1)$) represents the best possible scenario. Note also that even if there are data dependences between iterations in $IT_{U_0,N_1}(1)$ (and/or between iterations in $IT_{U_0,N_2}(1)$) but not across iterations of different sets, we can still execute $IT_{U_0,N_1}(1)$ followed by $IT_{U_0,N_2}(1)$, provided that we execute iterations in $IT_{U_0,N_1}(1)$ (and also in $IT_{U_0,N_2}(1)$) in their original execution order. This execution order is also valid if there are dependences from $IT_{U_0,N_1}(1)$ (resp. $IT_{U_0,N_2}(1)$) to $IT'_{U_0,N_1}(1)$ (resp. $IT'_{U_0,N_2}(1)$) only. These cases are superimposed in Figure 6(b). Once all the iterations in $IT_{U_0,N_1}(1)$ and $IT_{U_0,N_2}(1)$ have been executed, we can proceed with $DT_{U_0}(2)$. The dashed arrow in Figure 6(b) represents the execution order of these sets.

Suppose now that there exists a dependence from an iteration $i' \in IT'_{U_0,N_1}(1)$ to an iteration $i \in IT_{U_0,N_1}(1)$ as shown in Figure 6(c). Assume further that there exists a dependence from an iteration $i' \in IT'_{U_0,N_2}(1)$ to an iteration $i \in IT_{U_0,N_2}(1)$. In this case, it is not possible to execute $IT_{U_0,N_1}(1)$ followed by $IT_{U_0,N_2}(1)$ as doing so would modify the original semantics of the code (i.e., violate data dependences). To handle this case, our approach breaks $IT'_{U_0,N_1}(1)$ into two groups, $IT'_{U_0,N_1}(1a)$ and $IT'_{U_0,N_1}(1b)$, such that there is a dependence from $IT'_{U_0,N_1}(1a)$ to $IT_{U_0,N_1}(1)$, but not from $IT'_{U_0,N_1}(1b)$ to $IT_{U_0,N_1}(1)$. This situation is depicted in Figure 6(d). Note that in the degenerate case one of $IT'_{U_0,N_1}(1a)$ and $IT'_{U_0,N_1}(1b)$ can be empty. Similarly, we also divide $IT'_{U_0,N_2}(1)$ into two groups: $IT'_{U_0,N_1}(1a)$ and $IT'_{U_0,N_1}(1b)$. Then, a suitable order of execution (during processing $DT_{U_0}(1)$) is $IT'_{U_0,N_1}(1a)$, $IT'_{U_0,N_2}(1a)$, $IT_{U_0,N_1}(1)$, $IT_{U_0,N_2}(1)$, which is also illustrated in Figure 6(d). It should be noticed that, in this scenario, although we need to execute sets $IT'_{U_0,N_1}(1a)$, $IT'_{U_0,N_2}(1a)$ before $IT_{U_0,N_1}(1)$, $IT_{U_0,N_2}(1)$, we are still able to execute $IT_{U_0,N_1}(1)$ and $IT_{U_0,N_2}(1)$ one after another, which is good from the locality viewpoint.

Let us now consider the scenario in Figure 6(e) that indicates data dependences from $IT_{U_0,N_1}(1)$ and $IT'_{U_0,N_1}(1)$ to $IT_{U_0,N_2}(1)$ and $IT'_{U_0,N_2}(1)$. To handle this case, we break $IT'_{U_0,N_1}(1)$ into two subsets, $IT'_{U_0,N_1}(1a)$ and $IT'_{U_0,N_1}(1b)$, such that there are no dependences from the set $IT'_{U_0,N_1}(1b)$ to the set $IT'_{U_0,N_2}(1)$. Then, the preferred execution order is shown Figure 6(f).

4   Application of Data Space Oriented Tiling

There are several applications of data space oriented tiling. One of these is improving cache locality in array-dominated applications. Since DST captures data accesses in a global (procedure-wide) manner, it has better potential for improving cache locality compared to conventional iteration space oriented tiling. In this section, however, we focus on a similar yet different application area: using data space oriented tiling for exploiting an on-chip scratch pad memory (SPM).

Scratch pad memories (SPMs) are alternatives to conventional cache memories in embedded computing world [7, 8]. These small on-chip memories, like

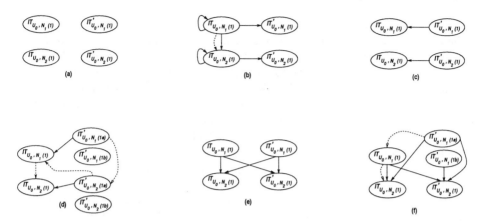

Fig. 6. Different iteration sets and dependences between them. Note that a solid arrow denotes a data dependence, whereas a dashed arrow denotes a legal execution order.

caches, provide fast and low-power access to data and instructions; but, they differ from conventional data caches in that their contents are managed by software instead of hardware. Since the software is in full control of what the contents of the SPM will be at a given time, it is easy to predict memory access times in an SPM-based system, a desired property for real-time embedded systems. Since there is a large difference between access latencies and energy consumptions of these memories, it is important to satisfy as many data requests as possible from SPM. Our compiler-based approach to SPM management determines the contents of the SPM (at every program point) and schedules all data movements between the SPM and off-chip data memory at compile-time. The actual data movements (between SPM and off-chip data memory), however, take place at run-time. In other words, we divide the task of exploiting the software-controlled SPM between compiler and run-time (hardware). It should also be mentioned that in order to benefit from an SPM, the energy (and performance) gains obtained through optimized locality should not be offset by the runtime overheads (e.g., explicit data copies between SPM and off-chip memory). That is, a data item (array element) should be moved to the SPM only if it is likely that it will be accessed from the SPM large number of times (that is, if it exhibits high data reuse).

Our approach works as follows. It first optimizes the code using DST as explained above. It then reads data tiles from off-chip data memory to SPM and executes all iterations that manipulate the data in the SPM. When these iterations are finished, a new set of data tiles are brought into SPM and the corresponding loop iterations are executed, and so on. It should be noted that if, during its stay in the SPM, the data tile has been modified (through a write command) it should be written back to the off-chip memory when it needs to be replaced by another data tile. Figure 7 gives a sketch of the SPM optimization algorithm based on data space oriented tiling. To keep the presentation clear, we assume that all arrays are of the same size and dimensionality, and all arrays are accessed in each nest. After determining the seed array and the most suitable tile shape from the viewpoint of communication volume, the first loop in this figure iterates over data tiles. In each iteration, we read the corresponding data tiles from the off-chip memory to the SPM. Then, the second loop nest determines the corresponding iteration tiles from all nests and also computes the set of iterations ($\mathcal{I}'$) that should be executed before these iterations (due to data dependences). The compiler then generates code to execute these iterations and updates the iteration sets by eliminating the already executed iterations from further consideration. It should be noted that this is a highly-simplified presentation. In general, the iterations in $\mathcal{I}'$ and $IT_{U_0,N_j}(i)$ might be dependent on each other. In executing the iterations in a given set, we stick to the original execution order (not to violate any dependences). After that, it checks whether the data tiles have been updated while they are in the SPM. If so, they need to be written back to the main memory. This concludes an iteration of the outermost for-loop in Figure 7.

INPUT: a set of nests N_j, $1 \leq j \leq P$ accessing K arrays
$\quad$ $\mathcal{I}_j$: the iteration set of the jth nest

ALGORITHM:
determine the seed array U_0 and data tile shape;
for each data tile i, $1 \leq i \leq Y$
$\quad$ generate code to read $DT_{U_0}(i), DT_{U_1}(i), \cdots, DT_{U_K}(i)$
$\quad\quad$ from main memory;
$\quad$ $\mathcal{I}_{res} = \emptyset$;
$\quad$ for each nest N_j, $1 \leq j \leq P$
$\quad\quad$ $\mathcal{I}_{rem} = \bigcup \mathcal{I}_k$, $1 \leq k \leq j$
$\quad\quad$ determine $IT_{U_0,N_j}(i)$ and $IT'_{U_0,N_j}(i)$;
$\quad\quad$ determine $\mathcal{I}' \subset \mathcal{I}_{rem}$ such that:
$\quad\quad\quad$ (i) there is a dependence from $\mathcal{I}'$ to $IT_{U_0,N_j}(i)$
$\quad\quad\quad$ (ii) there is no dependence from $(\mathcal{I}_{rem} - \mathcal{I}')$
$\quad\quad\quad\quad$ to $IT_{U_0,N_j}(i)$
$\quad\quad$ $\mathcal{I}_{res} = \mathcal{I}_{res} \bigcup \mathcal{I}'$;
$\quad$ endfor;
$\quad$ for each nest N_j, $1 \leq j \leq P$
$\quad\quad$ generate code to execute iterations in $\mathcal{I}'$
$\quad\quad\quad$ (if they have not been executed so far);
$\quad\quad$ generate code to execute iterations in $IT_{U_0,N_j}(i)$
$\quad\quad\quad$ (if they have not been executed so far);
$\quad$ endfor;
$\quad$ update $\mathcal{I}_k$, $1 \leq k \leq j$
$\quad$ for each U_l, $1 \leq l \leq K$
$\quad\quad$ if $DT_{U_l}(i)$ is modified, then write it back
$\quad\quad\quad$ to main memory;
$\quad$ endfor;
endfor;

Fig. 7. An SPM optimization algorithm based on DST.

5 Conclusions

This paper presents a compiler-based strategy for optimizing data accesses in regular array-dominated applications. Our approach, called data space oriented tiling, is a variant of classical iteration space tiling. It improves over the latter by working with better data tile shapes and by exploiting inter-nest data reuse. This paper also shows how data space oriented tiling can be used to improve the effectiveness of a scratch pad memory.

References

1. S. Coleman and K. McKinley. Tile size selection using cache organization and data layout. In Proc. *the ACM SIGPLAN Conference on Programming Language Design and Implementation*, June 1995.
2. F. Irigoin and R. Triolet. Super-node partitioning. In Proc. *the 15th Annual ACM Symposium on Principles of Programming Languages*, pages 319–329, January 1988.
3. M. Kandemir, J. Ramanujam, M. Irwin, N. Vijaykrishnan, I. Kadayif, and A. Parikh. Dynamic management of scratch-pad memory space. In Proc. *the 38th Design Automation Conference,* Las Vegas, NV, June 2001.
4. I. Kodukula, N. Ahmed, and K. Pingali. Data-centric multi-level blocking. In Proc. *the SIGPLAN Conference on Programming Language Design and Implementation*, June 1997.
5. W. Li. *Compiling for NUMA Parallel Machines.* Ph.D. Dissertation, Computer Science Department, Cornell University, Ithaca, NY, 1993.
6. M. O'Boyle and P. Knijnenburg. Non-singular data transformations: Definition, validity, applications. In Proc. *the 6th Workshop on Compilers for Parallel Computers*, pages 287–297, 1996.
7. P. R. Panda, N. D. Dutt, and A. Nicolau. Efficient utilization of scratch-pad-memory in embedded processor applications. In Proc. *the European Design and Test Conference (ED&TC'97),* Paris, March 1997.
8. L. Wang, W. Tembe, and S. Pande. Optimizing on-chip memory usage through loop restructuring for embedded processors. In Proc. *the 9th International Conference on Compiler Construction,* March 30–31 2000, pp. 141–156, Berlin, Germany.
9. M. Wolfe. *High Performance Compilers for Parallel Computing*, Addison-Wesley Publishing Company, 1996.
10. J. Xue and C.-H. Huang. Reuse-driven tiling for data locality. In *Languages and Compilers for Parallel Computing*, Z. Li et al., Eds., Lecture Notes in Computer Science, Volume 1366, Springer-Verlag, 1998.

Propagation of Roundoff Errors in Finite Precision Computations: A Semantics Approach[1]

Matthieu Martel

CEA – Recherche Technologique
LIST-DTSI-SLA
CEA F91191 Gif-Sur-Yvette Cedex, France
e-mail: ttmmartel@cea.fr

Abstract. We introduce a concrete semantics for floating-point operations which describes the propagation of roundoff errors throughout a computation. This semantics is used to assert the correctness of an abstract interpretation which can be straightforwardly derived from it.
In our model, every elementary operation introduces a new first order error term, which is later combined with other error terms, yielding higher order error terms. The semantics is parameterized by the maximal order of error to be examined and verifies whether higher order errors actually are negligible. We consider also coarser semantics computing the contribution, to the final error, of the errors due to some intermediate computations.
Keywords: Numerical Precision, Abstract Interpretation, Floating-point Arithmetic, IEEE Standard 754.

1 Introduction

Often, the results of numerical programs are accepted with suspicion because of the approximate numbers used during the computations. In addition, it is often hard for a programmer to understand how precise a result is, or to understand the nature of the imprecision [6, 13]. In this article, we present the theoretical basis of an abstract interpreter which estimates the accuracy of a numerical result and which detects the elementary operations that introduce the most imprecision. The implementation of this tool is described in [9]. Compared with other approaches, we do not attempt to compute a better estimation of what a particular execution of a numerical program would return if the computer were using real number. Instead, we statically point out the places in the code which possibly introduce significant errors for a large set of executions.

From our knowledge, the propagation of roundoff errors and the introduction of new errors at each stage of a computation is a phenomenon which has almost never been studied in a semantics framework. Some dynamic stochastic methods have been proposed but they cannot guarantee the correctness of the estimation

---

[1] This work was supported by the RTD project IST-1999-20527 "DAEDALUS" of the European FP5 programme.

D. Le Métayer (Ed.): ESOP 2002, LNCS 2305, pp. 194–208, 2002.
© Springer-Verlag Berlin Heidelberg 2002

in all cases [1, 2, 11, 16, 17]. Recently, Eric Goubault has proposed a static analysis based on abstract interpretation [3] which can compute the contribution of each first order error, due to the inaccuracy of one floating-point operation, to the final error associated with a result [7]. This new approach differs from the existing ones in that it not only attempts to estimate the accuracy of a result, but also provides indications on the source of the imprecision. It also differs from much other work in that it models the propagation of errors on initial data (sensitivity analysis) as well as the propagation of roundoff errors due to the intermediate floating-point computations (this can dominate the global error in some cases).

We develop a general concrete semantics $\mathcal{S}^{\mathcal{L}^*}$ for floating-point operations which explains the propagation of roundoff errors during a computation. Elementary operations introduce new first order error terms which, once combined, yield higher order error terms. $\mathcal{S}^{\mathcal{L}^*}$ models the roundoff error propagation in finite precision computations for error terms of any order and is based on IEEE Standard 754 for floating-point numbers [12]. By modelling the propagation of errors in the general case, $\mathcal{S}^{\mathcal{L}^*}$ contributes to the general understanding of this problem and provide a theoretical basis for many static analyses. In particular, $\mathcal{S}^{\mathcal{L}^*}$ can be straightforwardly adapted to define abstract interpretations generalizing the one of [7].

Next we propose some approximations of $\mathcal{S}^{\mathcal{L}^*}$. We show that for any integer n, $\mathcal{S}^{\mathcal{L}^*}$ can be approximated by another semantics $\mathcal{S}^{\mathcal{L}^n}$ which only computes the contribution to the global error of the error terms of order at most n, as well as the residual error, i.e. the global error due to the error terms of order higher than n. Approximations are proven correct by means of Galois connections. For example, $\mathcal{S}^{\mathcal{L}^1}$ computes the contribution to the global error of the first order errors. In addition, in contrast to [7], $\mathcal{S}^{\mathcal{L}^1}$ does verifie that the contribution to the global error of the error terms of order greater than one is negligible. Finally, we introduce coarser semantics which compute the contribution, to the global error in the result of a computation, of the errors introduced by some pieces of code in the program. These semantics provide less information than the most general ones but use non-standard values of smaller size. In practice, this allows the user to first detect which functions of a program introduce most errors and, next, to examine in more detail which part of an imprecise function increases the error [9]. We introduce a partial order relation $\dot{\subseteq}$ on the set of the partitions of the program points and we show that, for two partitions $\mathcal{J}_1 \dot{\subseteq} \mathcal{J}_2$, the semantics based on $\mathcal{J}_1$ approximates the semantics based on $\mathcal{J}_2$.

Section 2 gives an overview of the techniques developed in this article and Section 3 briefly describes some aspects of IEEE Standard 754. In Section 4 and Section 5, we introduce the semantics detailing the contribution, to the global error, of the error terms of any order and of order at most n, respectively. In Section 6, we introduce a coarser semantics which computes the contribution of the error introduced in pieces of code partitioning the program. We show that the semantics based on certain partitions are comparable. Section 7 concludes.

2 Overview

In this section, we illustrate how the propagation of roundoff errors is treated in our model using as an example a simple computation involving two values $a_{\mathbb{F}} = 621.3$ and $b_{\mathbb{F}} = 1.287$. For the sake of simplicity, we assume that $a_{\mathbb{F}}$ and $b_{\mathbb{F}}$ belong to a simplified set of floating-point numbers composed of a mantissa of four digits written in base 10. We assume that initial errors are attached to $a_{\mathbb{F}}$ and $b_{\mathbb{F}}$, and we write $a = 621.3 + 0.05\varepsilon_1$ and $b = 1.287 + 0.0005\varepsilon_2$ to indicate that the value of the initial error on $a_{\mathbb{F}}$ (resp. $b_{\mathbb{F}}$) is 0.05 (resp. 0.0005). ε_1 and ε_2 are formal variables related to static program points. a and b are called *floating-point numbers with errors*. Let us focus on the product $a_{\mathbb{F}} \times b_{\mathbb{F}}$ whose exact result is $a_{\mathbb{F}} \times b_{\mathbb{F}} = 799.6131$. This computation carried out with floating-point numbers with errors yields $a \times b = 799.6131 + 0.06435\varepsilon_1 + 0.31065\varepsilon_2 + 0.000025\varepsilon_1 \times \varepsilon_2$ The difference between $\alpha_{\mathbb{F}} \times b_{\mathbb{F}}$ and 621.35×1.2875 is 0.375025 and this error stems from the fact that the initial error on a (resp. b) was multiplied by b (resp. a) and that a second order error corresponding to the multiplication of both errors was introduced. So, at the end of the computation, the contribution to the global error of the initial error on a (resp. b) is 0.06435 (resp. 0.31065) and corresponds to the coefficient attached to the formal variable ε_1 (resp. ε_2). The contribution of the second order error due to the initial errors on both a and b is given by the term $0.000025\varepsilon_1 \times \varepsilon_2$ which we will write as $0.000025\varepsilon_{12}$ in the following. Finally, the number 799.6131 has too many digits to be representable in our floating-point number system. Since IEEE Standard 754 ensures that elementary operations are correctly rounded, we may claim that the floating-point number computed by our machine is 799.6 and that a new error term $0.0131\varepsilon_{\times}$ is introduced by the multiplication. To sum up, we have

$$a \times b = 799.6 + 0.06435\varepsilon_1 + 0.31065\varepsilon_2 + 0.000025\varepsilon_{12} + 0.0131\varepsilon_{\times}$$

At first sight, one could believe that the precision of the computation mainly depends on the initial error on a since it is 100 times larger than the one on b. However the above result indicates that the final error is mainly due to the initial error on b. Hence, to improve the precision of the final result, one should first try to increase the precision on b (whenever possible). Note that, as illustrated by the above example and in contrast to most of existing methods [14, 16], we do not attempt to compute a better approximation of the real number that the program would output if the computer were using real numbers. Since we are interested in detecting the errors possibly introduced by floating-point numbers, we always work with the floating-point numbers used by the machine and we compute the errors attached to them.

3 Preliminary Definitions

3.1 IEEE Standard 754

IEEE Standard 754 was introduced in 1985 to harmonize the representation of floating-point numbers as well as the behavior of the elementary floating-point operations [6, 12]. This standard is now implemented in almost all modern processors and, consequently, it provides a precise semantics, used as a basis in this article, for the basic operations occurring in high-level programming languages. First of all, a *floating-point number* x in base β is defined by

$$x = s \cdot (d_0.d_1 \ldots d_{p-1}) \cdot \beta^e = s \cdot m \cdot \beta^{e-p+1}$$

where $s \in \{-1, 1\}$ is the sign, $m = d_0 d_1 \ldots d_{p-1}$ is the *mantissa* with digits $0 \leq d_i < \beta$, $0 \leq i \leq p-1$, p is the *precision* and e is the exponent, $e_{min} \leq e \leq e_{max}$. A floating-point number x is *normalized* whenever $d_0 \neq 0$. Normalization avoids multiple representations of the same number. IEEE Standard 754 specifies a few values for p, e_{min} and e_{max}. Simple precision numbers are defined by $\beta = 2$, $p = 23$, $e_{min} = -126$ and $e_{max} = +127$; Double precision numbers are defined by $\beta = 2$, $p = 52$, $e_{min} = -1022$ and $e_{max} = +1023$. $\beta = 2$ is the only allowed basis but slight variants also are defined by IEEE Standard 854 which, for instances, allows $\beta = 2$ or $\beta = 10$. IEEE Standard 754, also introduces *denormalized numbers* which are floating-point numbers with $d_0 = d_1 = \ldots = d_k = 0$, $k < p-1$ and $e = e_{min}$. Denormalized numbers make underflow gradual [6]. Finally, the following special values also are defined:

- NaN (Not a Number) resulting from an illegal operation,
- the values $\pm\infty$ corresponding to overflows,
- the values $+0$ and -0 (signed zeros[2]).

We do not consider the extended simple and extended double formats, also defined by IEEE Standard 754, whose implementations are machine-dependent. In the rest of this paper, the notation $\mathbb{F}$ indifferently refers to the set of simple or double precision numbers, since our assumptions conform to both types. $\mathbb{R}$ denotes the set of real numbers.

IEEE 754 Standard defines four rounding modes for elementary operations between floating-point numbers. These modes are towards $-\infty$, towards $+\infty$, towards zero and to the nearest. We write them $\circ_{-\infty}$, $\circ_{+\infty}$, $\circ_0$ and $\circ_\sim$ respectively. Let $\mathbb{R}$ denote the set of real numbers and let $\uparrow_\circ : \mathbb{R} \to \mathbb{F}$ be the function which returns the roundoff of a real number following the rounding mode $\circ \in \{\circ_{-\infty}, \circ_{+\infty}, \circ_0, \circ_\sim\}$. IEEE standard 754 specifies the behavior of the elementary operations $\diamond \in \{+, -, \times, \div\}$ between floating-point numbers by

$$f_1 \diamond_{\mathbb{F},\circ} f_2 = \uparrow_\circ (f_1 \diamond_{\mathbb{R}} f_2) \qquad (1)$$

IEEE Standard 754 also specifies how the square root function must be rounded in a similar way to Equation (1) but does not specify, for theoretical reasons [15], the roundoff of transcendental functions like sin, log, etc.

In this article, we also use the function $\downarrow_\circ : \mathbb{R} \to \mathbb{R}$ which returns the error ω due to using $\uparrow_\circ (r)$ instead of f. We have $\downarrow_\circ (r) = r - \uparrow_\circ (r)$.

Let us remark that the elementary operations are total functions on $\mathbb{F}$, i.e. that the result of operations involving special values are specified. For instance,

---

[2] Remark that 0 is neither a normalized nor denormalized number.

$1 \div +\infty = 0$, $+\infty \times 0 = \text{NaN}$, etc. [6, 10]. However, for the sake of simplicity, we do not consider these special values, assuming that any operation has correct operands and does not return an overflow or a NaN.

3.2 Standard Semantics

To study the propagation of errors along a sequence of computations, we consider arithmetic expressions annotated by static labels ℓ, ℓ_1, ℓ_2, etc. and generated by the grammar of Equation (2).

$$a^\ell ::= r^\ell \mid a_0^{\ell_0} +^\ell a_1^{\ell_1} \mid a_0^{\ell_0} -^\ell a_1^{\ell_1} \mid a_0^{\ell_0} \times^\ell a_1^{\ell_1} \mid a_0^{\ell_0} \div^\ell a_1^{\ell_1} \mid F^\ell(a_0^{\ell_0}) \qquad (2)$$

r denotes a value in the domain of floating-point numbers with errors and F denotes a transcendental function $\sqrt{\ }$, sin, etc. For any term generated by the above grammar, a unique label is attached to each sub-expression. These labels, which correspond to the nodes of the syntactic tree, are used to identify the errors introduced during a computation by an initial datum or a given operator. For instance, in the expression $r_0^{\ell_0} +^\ell r_1^{\ell_1}$ the initial errors corresponding to r_0 and r_1 are attached to the formal variables ε_{ℓ_0} and ε_{ℓ_1} and the new error introduced by the addition during the computation is attached to ε_ℓ.

In the remainder of this article, the set of all the labels occurring in a program is denoted $\mathcal{L}$. We use the small step operational semantics defined by the reduction rules below, where $\Diamond \in \{+, -, \times, \div\}$. These rules correspond to a left to right evaluation strategy of the expressions.

$$\frac{a_0^{\ell_0} \rightarrow a_2^{\ell_2}}{a_0^{\ell_0} \Diamond^\ell a_1^{\ell_1} \rightarrow a_2^{\ell_2} \Diamond^\ell a_1^{\ell_1}} \qquad \frac{a_1^{\ell_1} \rightarrow a_2^{\ell_2}}{r_0^{\ell_0} \Diamond^\ell a_1^{\ell_1} \rightarrow r_0^{\ell_0} \Diamond^\ell a_2^{\ell_2}}$$

$$\frac{r = r_0 \Diamond^\ell r_1}{r_0^{\ell_0} \Diamond^\ell r_1^{\ell_1} \rightarrow r^\ell} \qquad \frac{a_0^{\ell_0} \rightarrow a_1^{\ell_1}}{F^\ell(a_0^{\ell_0}) \rightarrow F^\ell(a_1^{\ell_1})} \qquad \frac{r = F^\ell(r_0)}{F^\ell(r_0^{\ell_0}) \rightarrow r^\ell}$$

In the following, we introduce various domains for the values r and we specify various implementations of the operators $\Diamond$. We only deal with arithmetic expressions because the semantics of the rest of the language (which is detailed in [8]) presents little interest. The only particularity concerns loops and conditionals, when the result of a comparison between floating-point numbers differs from the same comparison in $\mathbb{R}$. In this case, the semantics in $\mathbb{F}$ and $\mathbb{R}$ lead to the execution of different pieces of code. Our semantics mimics what the computer does and follows the execution path resulting from the evaluation of the test in $\mathbb{F}$. However, the errors cannot be computed any longer.

Labels are only attached to the arithmetic expressions because no roundoff error is introduced elsewhere. A label ℓ is related to the syntactic occurrence of an operator. If an arithmetic operation $\Diamond^\ell$ is executed many times then the coefficient attached to ε_ℓ denotes the sum of the roundoff errors introduced by each instance of $\Diamond$. For instance if the assignment $x = r_1^{\ell_1} \Diamond^\ell r_2^{\ell_2}$ is carried out inside a loop then, in the floating-point number with error denoting the value of x after n iterations, the coefficient attached to ε_ℓ is the sum of the roundoff errors introduced by $\Diamond^\ell$ during the n first iterations.

4 Floating-Point Numbers with Errors

In this section, we define the general semantics $\mathcal{S}^{\mathcal{L}^*}$ of floating-point numbers with errors. $\mathcal{S}^{\mathcal{L}^*}$ computes the errors of any order made during a computation. Intuitively, a number r^ℓ occurring at point ℓ and corresponding to an initial datum r is represented by the floating-point number with errors $r^{\ell \mathcal{L}^*} = (f\varepsilon + \omega^\ell \varepsilon_\ell) \in \mathbb{R}^{\mathcal{L}^*}$ where $f = \uparrow_\circ r$ is the floating-point number approximating r and $\omega^\ell = \downarrow_\circ r$. The functions $\uparrow_\circ$ and $\downarrow_\circ$ are defined in Section 3.1. f and ω^ℓ are written as coefficients of a formal series and ε and ε_ℓ are formal variables related to the value f known by the computer and the error between r and f.

A number r occurring at point ℓ_0 and corresponding to the result of the evaluation of an expression $a_0^{\ell_0}$ is represented by the series

$$r^{\ell_0 \mathcal{L}^*} = f\varepsilon + \sum_{u \in \overline{\mathcal{L}^+}} \omega^u \varepsilon_u \tag{3}$$

where $\mathcal{L}$ is a set containing all the labels occurring in $a_0^{\ell_0}$ and $\overline{\mathcal{L}^+}$ is a subset of the words on the alphabet $\mathcal{L}$. $\overline{\mathcal{L}^+}$ is formally defined further in this Section. In Equation (3), f is the floating-point number approximating r and is always attached to the formal variable ε. Let ℓ be a word made of one character. In the formal series $\sum_{u \in \overline{\mathcal{L}^+}} \omega^u \varepsilon_u$, $\omega^\ell \varepsilon_\ell$ denotes the contribution to the global error of the first order error introduced by the computation of the operation labelled ℓ during the evaluation of $a_0^{\ell_0}$. $\omega^\ell \in \mathbb{R}$ is the scalar value of this error term and ε_ℓ is a formal variable. For a given word $u = \ell_1 \ell_2 \ldots \ell_n$ such that $n \geq 2$, ε_u denotes the contribution to the global error of the nth order error due to the combination of the errors made at points $\ell_1 \ldots \ell_n$. For instance, let us consider the multiplication at point ℓ_3 of two initial data $r_1^{\ell_1} = (f_1 \varepsilon + \omega_1^{\ell_1} \varepsilon_{\ell_1})$ and $r_2^{\ell_2} = (f_2 \varepsilon + \omega_2^{\ell_2} \varepsilon_{\ell_2})$.

$$r_1^{\ell_1} \times^{\ell_3} r_2^{\ell_2} = \uparrow_\circ (f_1 f_2)\varepsilon + f_2 \omega_1^{\ell_1} \varepsilon_{\ell_1} + f_1 \omega_2^{\ell_2} \varepsilon_{\ell_2} + \omega_1^{\ell_1} \omega_2^{\ell_2} \varepsilon_{\ell_1 \ell_2} + \downarrow_\circ (f_1 f_2)\varepsilon_{\ell_3} \tag{4}$$

As shown in Equation (4), the floating-point number computed by this multiplication is $\uparrow_\circ (f_1 f_2)$. The initial first order errors $\omega_1^{\ell_1} \varepsilon_{\ell_1}$ and $\omega_2^{\ell_2} \varepsilon_{\ell_2}$ are multiplied by f_2 and f_1 respectively. In addition, the multiplication introduces a new first order error $\downarrow_\circ (f_1 f_2)\varepsilon_{\ell_3}$, due to the approximation made by using the floating-point number $\uparrow_\circ (f_1 f_2)$ instead of the real number $f_1 f_2$. Finally, this operation also introduces an error whose weight is $\omega_1^{\ell_1} \omega_2^{\ell_2}$ and which is a second order error. We attach this coefficient to the formal variable $\varepsilon_{\ell_1 \ell_2}$ denoting the contribution to the global error of the second order error in ℓ_1 and ℓ_2.

From a formal point of view, let $\mathcal{L}^*$ denote the set of words of finite length on the alphabet $\mathcal{L}$. ϵ denotes the empty word, $|u|$ denotes the size of the word u and $u.v$ denotes the concatenation of the words u and v. We introduce the equivalence relation $\sim$ which identifies the words made of the same letters. $\sim$ makes concatenation commutative.

Definition 1 $\sim \subseteq \mathcal{L}^* \times \mathcal{L}^*$ *is the greatest equivalence relation R such that $u\ R\ v$ implies $u = \ell.u'$, $v = v'.\ell.v''$ and $u'\ R\ v'.v''$.*

Let $\overline{\mathcal{L}^*}$ be the quotient set $\mathcal{L}^*/\sim$. An equivalence class in $\overline{\mathcal{L}^*}$ is denoted by the smallest element u of the class w.r.t. the lexicographical order. $\overline{\mathcal{L}^+}$ denotes the set $\overline{\mathcal{L}^*} \setminus \{\epsilon\}$. For any word $u \in \overline{\mathcal{L}^+}$, the formal variable ε_u is related to a nth order error whenever $n = |u|$. $\varepsilon_\epsilon = \varepsilon$ is related to the floating-point number f known by the computer instead of the real value. In this article, the symbols f and ω^ϵ are used indifferently to denote the coefficient of the variable ε_ϵ.

Let $\mathcal{F}(\mathcal{D}, \overline{\mathcal{L}^*}) = \{\sum_{u \in \overline{\mathcal{L}^*}} \omega^u \varepsilon_u\ :\ \forall u,\ \omega^u \in \mathcal{D}\}$ be the domain of the formal series (ordered componentwise) whose formal variables are annotated by elements of $\overline{\mathcal{L}^*}$ and which coefficients ω^u belong to $\mathcal{D}$. The semantics $\mathcal{S}^{\mathcal{L}^*}$ uses the domain $\mathbb{R}^{\mathcal{L}^*} = \mathcal{F}(\mathbb{R}, \overline{\mathcal{L}^*})$ for floating-point numbers with errors. The elementary operations on $\mathbb{R}^{\mathcal{L}^*}$ are defined in Figure 1. $\mathcal{W}$ denotes a set of words on an alphabet containing $\mathcal{L}$ and $\mathcal{W}^+$ denotes $\mathcal{W} \setminus \{\epsilon\}$. For now, $\mathcal{W} = \overline{\mathcal{L}^*}$ but some alternatives are treated later in this article.

$$r_1 +^{\ell_i} r_2 \stackrel{\text{def}}{=} \uparrow_\circ (f_1 + f_2)\varepsilon + \sum_{u \in \mathcal{W}^+} (\omega_1^u + \omega_2^u)\varepsilon_u + \downarrow_\circ (f_1 + f_2)\varepsilon_{\ell_i} \tag{5}$$

$$r_1 -^{\ell_i} r_2 \stackrel{\text{def}}{=} \uparrow_\circ (f_1 - f_2)\varepsilon + \sum_{u \in \mathcal{W}^+} (\omega_1^u - \omega_2^u)\varepsilon_u + \downarrow_\circ (f_1 - f_2)\varepsilon_{\ell_i} \tag{6}$$

$$r_1 \times^{\ell_i} r_2 \stackrel{\text{def}}{=} \uparrow_\circ (f_1 f_2)\varepsilon + \sum_{\substack{u \in \mathcal{W} \\ v \in \mathcal{W} \\ |u.v| > 0}} \omega_1^u \omega_2^v \varepsilon_{u.v} + \downarrow_\circ (f_1 f_2)\varepsilon_{\ell_i} \tag{7}$$

$$(r_1)^{-1^{\ell_i}} \stackrel{\text{def}}{=} \uparrow_\circ (f_1^{-1})\varepsilon + \frac{1}{f_1} \sum_{n \geq 1} (-1)^n \left(\sum_{u \in \mathcal{W}^+} \frac{\omega^u}{f_1} \varepsilon_u \right)^n + \downarrow_\circ (f_1^{-1})\varepsilon_{\ell_i} \tag{8}$$

$$r_1 \div^{\ell_i} r_2 \stackrel{\text{def}}{=} r_1 \times^{\ell_i} (r_2)^{-1^{\ell_i}} \tag{9}$$

Fig. 1. Elementary operations for the semantics $\mathcal{S}^{\mathcal{L}^*}$.

In Figure 1, the formal series $\sum_{u \in \overline{\mathcal{L}^*}} \omega^u \varepsilon_u$ related to the result of an operation $\Diamond^{\ell_i}$ contains the combination of the errors on the operands as well as a new error term $\downarrow_\circ (f_1 \Diamond_\mathbb{R} f_2)\varepsilon_{\ell_i}$ corresponding to the error introduced by the operation $\Diamond_\mathbb{F}$ occurring at point ℓ_i. The rules for addition and subtraction are natural. The elementary errors are added or subtracted componentwise in the formal series and the new error due to point ℓ_i corresponds to the roundoff of the result. Multiplication requires more care because it introduces higher-order errors due to the multiplication of the elementary errors. Higher-order errors appear when multiplying error terms. For instance, for $\ell_1, \ell_2 \in \mathcal{L}$, and for first order errors $\omega_1^{\ell_1} \varepsilon_{\ell_1}$ and $\omega_2^{\ell_2} \varepsilon_{\ell_2}$, the operation $\omega_1^{\ell_1} \varepsilon_{\ell_1} \times \omega_2^{\ell_2} \varepsilon_{\ell_2}$ introduces a second-order error term written $(\omega_1^{\ell_1} \times \omega_2^{\ell_2})\varepsilon_{\ell_1 \ell_2}$. The formal series resulting from the computation of $r_1^{-1^{\ell_i}}$ is obtained by means of a power series development. Note that, since a power series is only defined as long as it is convergent, the above technique cannot be used for any value of r_1. In the case of the inverse function, the convergence disc of the series $\sum_{n \geq 0}(-1)^n x^n = (1+x)^{-1}$ has radius $\rho = 1$. So, in Equation (8), we require $-1 < \sum_{u \in W^+} \frac{\omega^u}{f_1} < 1$. This constraint means that Equation (8) is correct as long as the absolute value of the sum of the elementary errors is less than the related floating-point number.

For an expression $a_0^{\ell_0}$ such that $\mathrm{Lab}(a_0^{\ell_0}) \subseteq \mathcal{L}$, the semantics $\mathcal{S}^{\mathcal{L}^*}$ is defined by the domain $\mathbb{R}^{\mathcal{L}^*}$ for values and by the reduction rules $\to^{\mathcal{L}}$ obtained by substituting the operators on $\mathbb{R}^{\mathcal{L}^*}$ to the operators $\Diamond$ in the reduction rules of Section 3.

Concerning the correctness of the operations defined by equations (5) to (9), it is a trivial matter to verify that both sides of these equations denote the same quantity, i.e. for any operator $\Diamond$ and any numbers $r_1 = \sum_{u \in W} \omega_1^u \varepsilon_u$, $r_2 = \sum_{u \in W} \omega_2^u \varepsilon_u$ and $r = r_1 \Diamond^{\ell_i} r_2 = \sum_{u \in W} \omega^u \varepsilon_u$, we have

$$\sum_{u \in W} \omega^u = \left(\sum_{u \in W} \omega_1^u\right) \Diamond \left(\sum_{u \in W} \omega_2^u\right) \tag{10}$$

However, this is too weak a correctness criterion since it does not examine whether a given error term is correctly propagated during a computation. For example, Equation (11) incorrectly models the propagation of errors since it inverts the errors attached to ε_{ℓ_1} and ε_{ℓ_2}.

$$(f_1 \varepsilon + \omega^{\ell_1} \varepsilon_{\ell_1}) +^{\ell_i} (f_2 \varepsilon + \omega^{\ell_2} \varepsilon_{\ell_2}) \stackrel{\mathrm{bad!}}{=} \uparrow_\circ (f_1 + f_2)\varepsilon + \omega^{\ell_1} \varepsilon_{\ell_2} + \omega^{\ell_2} \varepsilon_{\ell_1} + \downarrow_\circ (f_1 + f_2)\varepsilon_{\ell_i} \tag{11}$$

Defining addition by a generalization of Equation (11) leads to an undesirable formula satisfying the correctness criterion of Equation (10). We aim at showing that no such confusion was made in our definitions of the elementary operations, mainly for multiplication and division. So we compare the variations of the terms occurring in both sides of the equations (5) to (9) as a finite number of the coefficients ω_1^u and ω_2^u are slightly modified. The variations of r_1 and r_2 are given by $\frac{\partial^n}{\partial \omega_{k_1}^{u_1} \ldots \omega_{k_n}^{u_n}}$ for a finite subset $\omega_{k_1}^{u_1}, \ldots \omega_{k_n}^{u_n}$ of the coefficients, with $k_i = 1$ or 2, $u_i \in \mathcal{W}^+$, $1 \leq i \leq n$. We first introduce Lemma 2 which deals with first order partial derivatives.

Lemma 2 *Let $\Diamond \in \{+, -, \times, \div\}$ be a usual operator on formal series and let $\Diamond^{\ell_i} \in \{+^{\ell_i}, -^{\ell_i}, \times^{\ell_i}, \div^{\ell_i}\}$ be the operators defined in Equations (5) to (9). For any $r_1 = \sum_{u \in W} \omega_1^u \varepsilon_u$, $r_2 = \sum_{u \in W} \omega_2^u \varepsilon_u$ and for any $u_0 \in \mathcal{W}^+ \setminus \{\ell_i\}$ we have*

$$\frac{\partial(r_1 \Diamond r_2)}{\partial \omega_1^{u_0}} = \frac{\partial(r_1 \Diamond^{\ell_i} r_2)}{\partial \omega_1^{u_0}} \quad and \quad \frac{\partial(r_1 \Diamond r_2)}{\partial \omega_2^{u_0}} = \frac{\partial(r_1 \Diamond^{\ell_i} r_2)}{\partial \omega_2^{u_0}} \tag{12}$$

Lemma 2 ensures that the variation of a single error term in the input series is correctly managed in our model. Proofs are detailed in [8]. Proposition 3 below generalizes Lemma 2 to the variation of a finite number of coefficients.

Proposition 3 *Let $\Diamond \in \{+, -, \times, \div\}$ denote an usual operator on formal series and let $\Diamond^{\ell_i} \in \{+^{\ell_i}, -^{\ell_i}, \times^{\ell_i}, \div^{\ell_i}\}$ denote the operators defined in Equations (5) to (9). For any $r_1 = \sum_{u \in \mathcal{W}} \omega_1^u \varepsilon_u$, $r_2 = \sum_{u \in \mathcal{W}} \omega_2^u \varepsilon_u$ and for any $\omega_{k_1}^{u_1}, \ldots \omega_{k_n}^{u_n}$, $k_i = 1$ or 2, $u_i \in \mathcal{W}^+ \setminus \{\ell_i\}$, $1 \le i \le n$, we have:*

$$\frac{\partial^n (r_1 \Diamond r_2)}{\partial \omega_{k_1}^{u_1} \ldots \omega_{k_n}^{u_n}} = \frac{\partial^n (r_1 \Diamond^{\ell_i} r_2)}{\partial \omega_{k_1}^{u_1} \ldots \omega_{k_n}^{u_n}} \tag{13}$$

As a conclusion, let us remark that the incorrect definition of addition given in Equation (11) satisfies neither Lemma 2, nor Proposition 3.

For transcendental functions, given a number $r^{\mathcal{L}^n} = \sum_{u \in \overline{\mathcal{L}^n}} \omega^u \varepsilon_u$ and a function F, we aim at determining how a given error term ω^u related to $r^{\mathcal{L}^n}$ is modified in $F(r^{\mathcal{L}^n})$. This is done by means of power series developments, as for the inverse function of Equation (8). However, let us remark that the functions $\uparrow_\circ (F(x))$ and $\downarrow_\circ (F(x))$ must be used carefully, since IEEE Standard 754 only specifies how to roundoff the elementary operations $+$, $-$, $\times$ and $\div$ and the square root function. For another function $F \in \{\sin, \exp, \ldots\}$ machine-dependent criteria must be considered to determine $\uparrow_\circ (F(x))$ [8].

5   Restriction to Errors of the nth Order

The semantics $\mathcal{S}^{\mathcal{L}^*}$, introduced in Section 4, computes the errors of any order made during a computation. This is a general model for error propagation but it is commonly admitted that, in practice, errors of order greater than one or (rarely) two are negligible [5]. However, even if, from a practical point of view, we are only interested in detailing the contribution of the first n order errors to the global error, for $n = 1$ or $n = 2$, a safe semantics must check that higher order errors actually are negligible.

We introduce a family $(\mathcal{S}^{\mathcal{L}^n})_{n \in \mathbb{N}}$ of semantics such that the semantics $\mathcal{S}^{\mathcal{L}^n}$ details the contribution to the global error of the errors of order at most n. In addition, $\mathcal{S}^{\mathcal{L}^n}$ collapses into the coefficient of a single formal variable of the series the whole contribution of the errors of order higher than n. A value r is represented by

$$r = f\varepsilon + \sum_{u \in \overline{\mathcal{L}^+}, \, |u| \le n} \omega^u \varepsilon_u + \omega^\varsigma \varepsilon_\varsigma \tag{14}$$

The term $\omega^\varsigma \varepsilon_\varsigma$ of the series aggregates the elementary errors of order higher than n. Starting with $n = 1$, one can examine the contribution of the first order errors to the global error in a computation. If the ω^ς coefficient is negligible in the result, then the semantics $\mathcal{S}^{\mathcal{L}^1}$ provides enough information to understand the nature of the error. Otherwise, $\mathcal{S}^{\mathcal{L}^1}$ states that there is a higher order error which is not negligible but does not indicate which operation mainly makes this error grow. This information can be obtained by the semantics $\mathcal{S}^{\mathcal{L}^n}$ for an adequate value of n.

Let $\mathcal{L}^n$ be the set of words of length at most n on the alphabet $\mathcal{L}$ and let $\overline{\mathcal{L}^n} = (\mathcal{L}^n/\sim) \cup \{\varsigma\}$. $\varsigma \notin \mathcal{L}^*$ is a special word representing all the words of size greater than n. We define the new concatenation operator

$$u \cdot_n v = \begin{cases} u.v \text{ if } |u.v| \leq n \text{ and } u, v \neq \varsigma \\ \varsigma \text{ otherwise} \end{cases} \quad (15)$$

For the sake of simplicity, we write $u.v$ instead of $u \cdot_n v$ whenever it is clear that u and v belong to $\overline{\mathcal{L}^n}$. The domain of floating-point numbers with errors of order at most n is $\mathbb{R}^{\mathcal{L}^n} = \mathcal{F}(\mathbb{R}, \overline{\mathcal{L}^n})$. The elementary operations on $\mathbb{R}^{\mathcal{L}^n}$ are defined by the equations (5) to (9) of Section 4 in which $\mathcal{W} = \overline{\mathcal{L}^n}$.

Let $\mathcal{S}^{\mathcal{L}^n}$ denote the semantics defined by the domain $\mathbb{R}^{\mathcal{L}^n}$ for values and by the reduction rules of Section 2. The semantics $\mathcal{S}^{\mathcal{L}^n}$ indicates the contribution to the global error of the elementary errors of order at most n.

The correctness of the semantics $(\mathcal{S}^{\mathcal{L}^n})_{n \in \mathbb{N}}$ stems from the fact that, for any n, $\mathcal{S}^{\mathcal{L}^n}$ is a conservative approximation of $\mathcal{S}^{\mathcal{L}^*}$. Furthermore, for any $1 \leq m \leq n$, $\mathcal{S}^{\mathcal{L}^m}$ is a conservative approximation of $\mathcal{S}^{\mathcal{L}^n}$. So, the semantics of order m can always be considered as being a safe approximation of the semantics of order n, for any $n > m$. To prove the previous claims we introduce the following Galois connections [3,4] in which $m \leq n$.

$$\langle \wp(\mathcal{F}(\mathbb{R}, \overline{\mathcal{L}^n})), \subseteq \rangle \; \overset{\gamma^{m,n}}{\underset{\alpha^{n,m}}{\leftrightarrows}} \; \langle \mathcal{F}(\mathbb{R}, \overline{\mathcal{L}^m}), \sqsubseteq \rangle \quad (16)$$

$\wp(X)$ denotes the power set of X and $\sqsubseteq$ denotes the componentwise ordering on formal series. $\alpha^{n,m}$ and $\gamma^{m,n}$ are defined by

$$\alpha^{n,m} \left(\bigcup_{i \in I} \sum_{u \in \overline{\mathcal{L}^n}} \omega_i^u \varepsilon_u \right) \overset{\text{def}}{=} \sum_{u \in \overline{\mathcal{L}^m} \backslash \{\varsigma\}} \left(\bigvee_{i \in I} \omega_i^u \right) \varepsilon_u + \bigvee_{i \in I} \left(\sum_{u \in (\overline{\mathcal{L}^n} \backslash \overline{\mathcal{L}^m}) \cup \{\varsigma\}} \omega^u \right) \varepsilon_\varsigma$$

$$\gamma^{m,n} \left(\sum_{u \in \overline{\mathcal{L}^m}} \nu^u \varepsilon_u \right) \overset{\text{def}}{=} \left\{ \sum_{u \in \overline{\mathcal{L}^n}} \omega^u \varepsilon_u \; : \; \begin{array}{l} \omega^u \leq \nu^u \text{ if } u \in \overline{\mathcal{L}^m} \backslash \{\varsigma\} \\ \sum_{u \in (\overline{\mathcal{L}^n} \backslash \overline{\mathcal{L}^m}) \cup \{\varsigma\}} \omega^u \leq \nu^\varsigma \end{array} \right\}$$

The abstraction of the coefficients attached to ε_u, for any $u \in \overline{\mathcal{L}^m} \backslash \{\varsigma\}$, is natural. $\alpha^{n,m}$ also adds the coefficients of the terms of order higher than m and appends the result to ε_ς. Next the supremum is taken between the terms $\nu_i^\varsigma \varepsilon_\varsigma$, $i \in I$. $\gamma^{m,n}$ maps a series $\sum_{u \in \overline{\mathcal{L}^m}} \nu^u \varepsilon_u \in \mathcal{F}(\mathbb{R}, \overline{\mathcal{L}^m})$ to the set of series of the form $\sum_{u \in \overline{\mathcal{L}^n}} \omega^u \varepsilon_u \in \mathcal{F}(\mathbb{R}, \overline{\mathcal{L}^n})$ whose coefficients ω^u are less than ν^u for any $u \in \overline{\mathcal{L}^m} \backslash \{\varsigma\}$ and such that ν^ς is greater than the sum of the remaining terms. The correctness of the elementary operations in $\mathcal{F}(\mathbb{R}, \overline{\mathcal{L}^m})$, w.r.t. the correctness of the same operations in $\mathcal{F}(\mathbb{R}, \overline{\mathcal{L}^n})$ stems from Lemma 4.

Lemma 4 *Let ℓ_i be a program point, let $R^{\mathcal{L}^n}, S^{\mathcal{L}^n} \in \wp(\mathcal{F}(\mathbb{R}, \overline{\mathcal{L}^n}))$ be sets of floating-point numbers with errors and let $r^{\mathcal{L}^m} = \alpha^{n,m}(R^{\mathcal{L}^n})$, $s^{\mathcal{L}^m} = \alpha^{n,m}(S^{\mathcal{L}^n})$, $1 \leq m \leq n$. For any operator $\diamond \in \{+, -, \times, \div\}$ we have*

$$R^{\mathcal{L}^n} \diamond^{\ell_i} S^{\mathcal{L}^n} \subseteq \gamma^{m,n}(r^{\mathcal{L}^m} \diamond^{\ell_i} s^{\mathcal{L}^m})$$

Proofs are given in [8]. To extend Lemma 4 to sequences of reduction steps, we introduce the mapping $\mathcal{R}$ defined by Equation (17). $\mathrm{Lab}(a_0^{\ell_0})$ is the set of labels occurring in $a_0^{\ell_0}$.

$$\mathcal{R}(a_0^{\ell_0}) \;:\; \begin{vmatrix} \mathrm{Lab}(a_0^{\ell_0}) \to \mathcal{F}(\mathbb{R}, \overline{\mathcal{L}^n}) \\ \ell \quad \mapsto \begin{cases} r \text{ if } a^\ell = r^\ell \\ \perp \text{ otherwise} \end{cases} \end{vmatrix} \tag{17}$$

$\mathcal{R}(a_0^{\ell_0})(\ell)$ returns a value if the sub-expression a^ℓ in $a_0^{\ell_0}$ is a value and $\perp$ otherwise.

Proposition 5 *Let $a_0^{\ell_0 \mathcal{L}^m}$ and $a_0^{\ell_0 \mathcal{L}^n}$ be syntactically equivalent expressions such that for any $\ell \in \mathcal{L}$, $\mathcal{R}(a_0^{\ell_0 \mathcal{L}^n})(\ell) \in \gamma^{m,n}(\mathcal{R}(a_0^{\ell_0 \mathcal{L}^m})(\ell))$. If $a_0^{\ell_0 \mathcal{L}^m} \to a_1^{\ell_1 \mathcal{L}^m}$ then $a_0^{\ell_0 \mathcal{L}^n} \to a_1^{\ell_1 \mathcal{L}^n}$ such that $a_1^{\ell_1 \mathcal{L}^m}$ and $a_1^{\ell_1 \mathcal{L}^n}$ are syntactically equivalent expressions and for all $\ell \in \mathcal{L}$, $\mathcal{R}(a_1^{\ell_1 \mathcal{L}^n})(\ell) \in \gamma^{m,n}(\mathcal{R}(a_1^{\ell_1 \mathcal{L}^m})(\ell))$.*

Given an arithmetic expression $a_0^{\ell_0}$, Proposition 5 shows how to link $\mathcal{S}^{\mathcal{L}^n}(a_0^{\ell_0})$ to $\mathcal{S}^{\mathcal{L}^{n+1}}(a_0^{\ell_0})$ for any integer $n \geq 0$. The semantics $\mathcal{S}^{\mathcal{L}^n}$ is based on the domain $\mathbb{R}^{\mathcal{L}^n} = \mathcal{F}(\mathbb{R}, \overline{\mathcal{L}^n})$. The semantics $\mathcal{S}^{\mathcal{L}^*}$ can be viewed as a simple instance of this model, since the operations on $\mathbb{R}^{\mathcal{L}^*}$, as defined in Section 4, correspond to the ones of equations (5) to (9) with $\mathcal{W} = \mathcal{L}^*$. Conversely, the semantics $\mathcal{S}^{\mathcal{L}^0}$ uses floating-point numbers with errors of the form $\omega^\epsilon \varepsilon_\epsilon + \omega^\varsigma \varepsilon_\varsigma$ and computes the global error done during a computation. In short, there is a chain of Galois connections between the semantics of any order:

$$\mathcal{S}^{\mathcal{L}^*}(a_0^{\ell_0}) \;\leftrightarrows\; \ldots \; \mathcal{S}^{\mathcal{L}^n}(a_0^{\ell_0}) \;\leftrightarrows\; \mathcal{S}^{\mathcal{L}^{n-1}}(a_0^{\ell_0}) \;\ldots\; \leftrightarrows\; \mathcal{S}^{\mathcal{L}^0}(a_0^{\ell_0})$$

$\mathcal{S}^{\mathcal{L}^*}(a_0^{\ell_0})$ is the most informative result since it indicates the contribution of the elementary errors of any order. $\mathcal{S}^{\mathcal{L}^0}(a_0^{\ell_0})$ is the least informative result which only indicates the global error made during the computation.

6   Coarse Grain Errors

In this section, we introduce a new semantics that generalizes the ones of Section 4 and Section 5. Intuitively, we no longer consider elementary errors corresponding to the errors due to individual operations and we instead compute errors due to pieces of code partitioning the program. For instance, one may be interested in the contribution to the global error of the whole error due to an intermediate formula or due to a given line in the program code.

In practice, these new semantics are important to reduce the memory size used to store the values. From a theoretical point of view, it is necessary to prove that they are correct with respect to the general semantics $\mathcal{S}^{\mathcal{L}^*}$ of Section 4.

We show that the different partitions of the program points can be partially ordered in such a way that we can compare the semantics based on comparable partitions. Let $\mathcal{J} = \{J_1, J_2, \ldots, J_p\} \in \mathcal{P}(\mathcal{L})$ be a partition of the program points. We consider now the words on the alphabet $\mathcal{J}$. $\mathcal{J}^n$ denotes the words of maximal length n and $\overline{\mathcal{J}^n} = (\mathcal{J}^n / \sim) \cup \{\varsigma\}$. The concatenation operator $\cdot_n$ related to $\overline{\mathcal{J}^n}$ is defined in Equation (15).

For a maximal order of error $n \in \mathbb{N}$, we consider the family of domains $(\mathcal{F}(\mathbb{R}, \overline{\mathcal{J}^n}))_{\mathcal{J} \in \mathcal{P}(\mathcal{L})}$, equivalently denoted $(\mathbb{R}^{\mathcal{J}^n})_{\mathcal{J} \in \mathcal{P}(\mathcal{L})}$. Basically, a unique label identifies all the operations of the same partition. A value $r^{\mathcal{J}^n} \in \mathbb{R}^{\mathcal{J}^n}$ is written

$$r^{\mathcal{J}^n} = f\varepsilon + \sum_{\substack{u \in \overline{\mathcal{J}^{n+}} \\ u = J_1 \dots J_k \ \forall i, \ 1 \leq i \leq k, \ \ell_i \in J_i}} \left(\sum_{v = \ell_1 \dots \ell_k \in \overline{\mathcal{L}^n}} \omega^v \right) \varepsilon_u = f\varepsilon + \sum_{u \in \overline{\mathcal{J}^{n+}}} \omega^u \varepsilon_u$$

If $|u| = 1$, the word $u = J$ is related to the first order error due to the operations whose label belongs to J. The elementary operations on $\mathbb{R}^{\mathcal{J}^n}$ are defined by the equations (5) to (9) of Section 4 in which $\mathcal{W} = \overline{\mathcal{J}^n}$.

Remark that this semantics generalizes the semantics of Section 5 which is based on a particular partition $\mathcal{J} = \{\{\ell\} \ : \ \ell \in \mathcal{L}\}$. Another interesting partition consists of using singletons for the initial data and collapsing all the other program points. This enables us to determine the contribution, to the global error, of initial errors on the program inputs (sensitivity analysis).

In the rest of this section, we compare the semantics based on different partitions of the labels. Intuitively, a partition $\mathcal{J}_1$ is coarser than a partition $\mathcal{J}_2$ if $\mathcal{J}_1$ collapses some of the elements of $\mathcal{J}_2$. For a maximal order of error n and using this ordering, the partition $\mathcal{J} = \{\{\ell\} \ : \ \ell \in \mathcal{L}\}$ corresponds to $\mathcal{S}^{\mathcal{L}^n}$ and is the finest partition. We show that any semantics based on a partition $\mathcal{J}_2$, coarser than a partition $\mathcal{J}_1$, is an approximation of the semantics based on $\mathcal{J}_1$. Consequently, any semantics based on a partition of the program points is an approximation of the general semantics $\mathcal{S}^{\mathcal{L}^n}$ and $\mathcal{S}^{\mathcal{L}^*}$ defined in Section 4 and 5. The partial ordering on the set of partitions is defined below.

Definition 6 *Let $\mathcal{J}_1$ and $\mathcal{J}_2$ be two partitions of the set $\mathcal{L}$. $\mathcal{J}_1$ is a coarser partition of $\mathcal{L}$ than $\mathcal{J}_2$ and we write $\mathcal{J}_1 \dot{\subseteq} \mathcal{J}_2$ iff $\forall J_2 \in \mathcal{J}_2, \ \exists J_1 \in \mathcal{J}_1 \ : \ J_2 \subseteq J_1$.*

If $\mathcal{J}_1 \dot{\subseteq} \mathcal{J}_2$ then some components of the partition $\mathcal{J}_2$ are collapsed in $\mathcal{J}_1$. $\dot{\subseteq}$ is used in the following to order the partitions of the set $\mathcal{L}$ of labels. The *translation function* $\tau_{\mathcal{J}_2^n, \mathcal{J}_1^n}$ maps words on the alphabet $\overline{\mathcal{J}_2^n}$ to words on $\overline{\mathcal{J}_1^n}$ as follows.

$$\tau_{\mathcal{J}_2^n, \mathcal{J}_1^n}(J_2.u) = J_1.\tau_{\mathcal{J}_2^n, \mathcal{J}_1^n}(u) \text{ where } J_1 \in \mathcal{J}_1, \ J_2 \subseteq J_1$$

The correctness of any semantics based on a partition $\mathcal{J}_1$ of $\mathcal{L}$ stems from the fact that, for any $\mathcal{J}_2 \in \mathcal{P}(\mathcal{L})$ such that $\mathcal{J}_1 \dot{\subseteq} \mathcal{J}_2$, there is a Galois connection

$$\langle \wp(\mathcal{F}(\mathbb{R}, \overline{\mathcal{J}_2^n})), \subseteq \rangle \ \underset{\alpha^{\mathcal{J}_2^n, \mathcal{J}_1^n}}{\overset{\gamma^{\mathcal{J}_1^n, \mathcal{J}_2^n}}{\leftrightarrows}} \ \langle \mathcal{F}(\mathbb{R}, \overline{\mathcal{J}_1^n}), \sqsubseteq \rangle$$

defined by

$$\alpha^{\mathcal{J}_2^n, \mathcal{J}_1^n} \left(\bigcup_{i \in I} \sum_{u \in \overline{\mathcal{J}_2^n}} \omega_i^u \varepsilon_u \right) \overset{\text{def}}{=} \sum_{u \in \overline{\mathcal{J}_2^n}} \left(\bigvee_{i \in I} \omega_i^u \right) \varepsilon_{\tau_{\mathcal{J}_2^n, \mathcal{J}_1^n}(u)}$$

$$\gamma^{\mathcal{J}_1^n,\mathcal{J}_2^n}\left(\sum_{v\in\overline{\mathcal{J}_1^n}}\nu^u\varepsilon_v\right)\overset{\text{def}}{=}\left\{\sum_{u\in\overline{\mathcal{J}_2^n}}\omega^u\varepsilon_u\ :\ \sum_{\tau_{\mathcal{J}_2^n,\mathcal{J}_1^n}(u)=v}\omega^u\le\nu^v\right\}$$

Let J be an element of the coarser partition $\mathcal{J}_1$. For any first order error term $\omega^u\varepsilon_u$ attached to a floating-point number with errors $r^{\overline{\mathcal{J}_2^n}}=\sum_{u\in\overline{\mathcal{J}_2^n}}\omega^u\varepsilon_u$, the abstraction $\alpha^{\mathcal{J}_2^n,\mathcal{J}_1^n}(\{r^{\overline{\mathcal{J}_2^n}}\})$ defines the coefficient ν_J attached to ε_J as being the sum of the coefficients $\omega_{J'}$ such that $J'\in\mathcal{J}_2$ and $J'\subseteq J$. The abstraction of sets of numbers is next defined in the usual way, by taking the supremum of the coefficients for each component. The function $\gamma^{\mathcal{J}_1^n,\mathcal{J}_2^n}$ returns the set of floating-point numbers with errors for which $\sum_{\tau_{\mathcal{J}_2^n,\mathcal{J}_1^n}(u)=v}\omega^u\le\nu^v$. Lemma 7 assesses the correctness of the operations defined by Equations (5) to (9) for the domains introduced in this section.

Lemma 7 *Let ℓ_i be a program point, let $\mathcal{J}_1$ and $\mathcal{J}_2$ be partitions of $\mathcal{L}$ such that $\mathcal{J}_1\dot\subseteq\mathcal{J}_2$ and let $R^{\mathcal{J}_2^n},S^{\mathcal{J}_2^n}\in\wp(\mathcal{F}(\mathbb{R},\overline{\mathcal{J}_2^n}))$. If $r^{\mathcal{J}_1^n}=\alpha^{\mathcal{J}_2^n,\mathcal{J}_1^n}(R^{\mathcal{J}_2^n})$, $s^{\mathcal{J}_1^n}=\alpha^{\mathcal{J}_2^n,\mathcal{J}_1^n}(S^{\mathcal{J}_2^n})$ then for any operator $\Diamond\in\{+,-,\times,\div\}$ we have*

$$R^{\mathcal{J}_2^n}\Diamond^{\ell_i}S^{\mathcal{J}_2^n}\in\gamma^{\mathcal{J}_1^n,\mathcal{J}_2^n}(r^{\mathcal{J}_1^n}\Diamond^{\ell_i}s^{\mathcal{J}_1^n})$$

The proof is given in [8]. The semantics defined by the domain $\mathbb{R}^{\mathcal{J}^n}$ for values and by the reduction rules of Section 3 is denoted $\mathcal{S}^{\mathcal{J}^n}$. Proposition 8 establishes the link between the semantics $\mathcal{S}^{\mathcal{J}_1^n}$ and $\mathcal{S}^{\mathcal{J}_2^n}$ for comparable partitions $\mathcal{J}_1\dot\subseteq\mathcal{J}_2$ of the set $\mathcal{L}$ of labels.

Proposition 8 *Let $\mathcal{J}_1$ and $\mathcal{J}_2$ be partitions of $\mathcal{L}$ such that $\mathcal{J}_1\dot\subseteq\mathcal{J}_2$ and let $a_0^{\ell_0\mathcal{J}_1^n}$ and $a_0^{\ell_0\mathcal{J}_2^n}$ be syntactically equivalent expressions such that for all $\ell\in\mathcal{L}$, $\mathcal{R}(a_0^{\ell_0\mathcal{J}_2^n})(\ell)\in\gamma^{\mathcal{J}_1^n,\mathcal{J}_2^n}(\mathcal{R}(a_0^{\ell_0\mathcal{J}_1^n})(\ell))$. If $a_0^{\ell_0\mathcal{J}_1^n}\rightarrow a_1^{\ell_1\mathcal{J}_1^n}$ then $a_0^{\ell_0\mathcal{J}_2^n}\rightarrow a_1^{\ell_1\mathcal{J}_2^n}$ such that $a_1^{\ell_1\mathcal{J}_1^n}$ and $a_1^{\ell_1\mathcal{J}_2^n}$ are syntactically equivalent expressions and for all $\ell\in\mathcal{L}$, $\mathcal{R}(a_1^{\ell_1\mathcal{J}_2^n})(\ell)\in\gamma^{\mathcal{J}_1^n,\mathcal{J}_2^n}(\mathcal{R}(a_1^{\ell_1\mathcal{J}_2^n})(\ell))$.*

As a consequence, for a given order of error n and for a given chain C of partitions, there is a chain of Galois connections between the semantics based on the partitions of C. Let us assume that

$$C=\mathcal{J}_0=\{\mathcal{L}\}\dot\subseteq\ \ldots\ \dot\subseteq\ \ldots\ \dot\subseteq\mathcal{J}_k\dot\subseteq\ \ldots\ \dot\subseteq\{\{\ell\}\ :\ell\in\mathcal{L}\}$$

By combining Proposition 5 and Proposition 8, we can also link the semantics $\mathcal{S}^{\mathcal{J}_k^n}$ and $\mathcal{S}^{\mathcal{J}_k^{n+1}}$ for any $\mathcal{J}_k\in C$ and any $n\in\mathbb{N}$. This is summed up in Figure 2. For any integer n and partition $\mathcal{J}_k$, $\mathcal{S}^{\mathcal{J}_k^n}$ describes a particular semantics; $\mathcal{S}^{\mathcal{L}^*}$ is the most informative semantics and, conversely, the semantics $\mathcal{S}^{\mathcal{L}^0}$ that computes one global error term is the least informative semantics; for all $k>0$ $\mathcal{S}^{\mathcal{J}_k^0}=\mathcal{S}^{\mathcal{L}^0}$ (for $n=0$, any partition yields the same semantics); $\mathcal{S}^{\mathcal{J}_0^2}$ computes the global first order and second order errors made during a computation; finally, for any $\mathcal{J}_k$, $\mathcal{S}^{\mathcal{J}_k^1}$ computes the contribution to the global error of the first order errors made in the different pieces of code identified by $\mathcal{J}_k$.

Let us remark that the values in $\mathbb{R}^{\mathcal{J}_1^n}$ contain less terms than the ones in $\mathbb{R}^{\mathcal{J}_2^n}$ if $\mathcal{J}_1\dot\subseteq\mathcal{J}_2$. Hence, using coarser partitions leads to significantly fewer computations.

$$\mathcal{S}^{\mathcal{J}_0^*}(a_0^{\ell_0}) \leftrightarrows \ldots \overset{\gamma^{n,n+1}}{\underset{\alpha^{n+1,n}}{\leftrightarrows}} \mathcal{S}^{\mathcal{J}_0^n}(a_0^{\ell_0}) \overset{\gamma^{n-1,n}}{\underset{\alpha^{n,n-1}}{\leftrightarrows}} \ldots \leftrightarrows \mathcal{S}^{\mathcal{J}_0^0}(a_0^{\ell_0})$$

$$\updownarrow \qquad \updownarrow \qquad \alpha^{\mathcal{J}_1^n,\mathcal{J}_0^n}\updownarrow\downarrow\gamma^{\mathcal{J}_0^n,\mathcal{J}_1^n} \qquad \updownarrow \qquad \updownarrow$$

$$\mathcal{S}^{\mathcal{J}_1^*}(a_0^{\ell_0}) \leftrightarrows \ldots \qquad \leftrightarrows \qquad \mathcal{S}^{\mathcal{J}_1^n}(a_0^{\ell_0}) \qquad \leftrightarrows \quad \ldots \leftrightarrows \mathcal{S}^{\mathcal{J}_1^0}(a_0^{\ell_0})$$

$$\updownarrow \qquad \updownarrow \qquad \updownarrow \qquad \updownarrow \qquad \updownarrow$$

$$\ldots \quad \leftrightarrows \ldots \quad \leftrightarrows \qquad \ldots \qquad \leftrightarrows \quad \ldots \leftrightarrows \quad \ldots$$

$$\updownarrow \qquad \updownarrow \qquad \updownarrow \qquad \updownarrow \qquad \updownarrow$$

$$\mathcal{S}^{\mathcal{L}^*}(a_0^{\ell_0}) \leftrightarrows \ldots \quad \leftrightarrows \qquad \mathcal{S}^{\mathcal{L}^n}(a_0^{\ell_0}) \qquad \leftrightarrows \quad \ldots \leftrightarrows \mathcal{S}^{\mathcal{L}^0}(a_0^{\ell_0})$$

Fig. 2. Links between the semantics $\mathcal{S}^{\mathcal{J}_k^n}$ for a given order of error n and for a chain of partitions $\mathcal{J}_0 \dot{\subseteq} \mathcal{J}_1 \dot{\subseteq} \ldots \dot{\subseteq} \mathcal{J}_k \dot{\subseteq} \ldots \dot{\subseteq} \{\{\ell\} : \ell \in \mathcal{L}\}$.

7   Conclusion

The semantics introduced in this article models the propagation of roundoff errors and the introduction of new errors at each stage of a computation. We use a unified framework, mainly based on the equations of Figure 1, to compute the contribution, to the global error, of the errors due to pieces of code partitioning the program and up to a maximal order of error. Lemma 2 and Proposition 3 are essential to ensure the correctness of the operators of Figure 1. They also represent a stronger correctness criterion for the operators introduced in [7]. Another important point is that $\mathcal{S}^{\mathcal{L}^n}$ not only details the propagation of the errors of order $\leq n$ but also verifies that higher order error terms actually are negligible.

A tool has been developed which implements an abstract interpretation based on the semantics introduced in this article. The real coefficients of the error series are abstracted by intervals of multi-precision floating-point numbers. This tool is described in [9]. Current work concerns the precision of the abstract interpretation in loops and is proceeding in two directions. First, because narrowings do not yield information to improve the precision of the error terms, we really need finely-tuned widening operators for our domain. This should enable us to restrict the number of cases where a loop is stable but is declared unstable by the abstract interpreter because of the approximations made during the analysis. The second way to improve the precision in loops consists of using a relational analysis. A first solution was proposed in [7] that can be used when the errors made at the iterations n and $n + 1$ are related by a linear transformation. We are also working on the non-linear cases, using mathematical tools developed for the study of dynamical systems.

Acknowledgements

I would like to thank Eric Goubault, Sylvie Putot and Nicky Williams for their suggestions on earlier drafts of this paper.

References

1. F. Chaitin-Chatelin and V. Fraysse. *Lectures on Finite Precision Computations.* SIAM, 1996.
2. F. Chaitin-Chatelin and E. Traviesas. Precise, a toolbox for assessing the quality of numerical methods and software. In *IMACS World Congress on Scientific Computation, Modelling and Applied Mathematics*, 2000.
3. P. Cousot and R. Cousot. Abstract interpretation: A unified lattice model for static analysis of programs by construction of approximations of fixed points. *Principles of Programming Languages 4*, pages 238–252, 1977.
4. P. Cousot and R. Cousot. Abstract interpretation frameworks. *Journal of Logic and Symbolic Computation*, 2(4):511–547, 1992.
5. M. Daumas and J. M. Muller, editors. *Qualité des Calculs sur Ordinateur.* Masson, 1997.
6. D. Goldberg. What every computer scientist should know about floating-point arithmetic. *ACM Computing Surveys*, 23(1), 1991.
7. E. Goubault. Static analyses of the precision of floating-point operations. In *Static Analysis Symposium, SAS'01*, number 2126 in LNCS. Springer-Verlag, 2001.
8. E. Goubault, M. Martel, and S. Putot. Concrete and abstract semantics of fp operations. Technical Report DRT/LIST/DTSI/SLA/LSL/01-058, CEA, 2001.
9. E. Goubault, M. Martel, and S. Putot. Asserting the precision of floating-point computations: a simple abstract interpreter. In *ESOP'02*, 2002.
10. J. R. Hauser. Handling floating-point exceptions in numeric programs. *ACM Transactions on Programming Languages and Systems*, 18(2), 1996.
11. W. Kahan. The improbability of probabilistic error analyses for numerical computations. Technical report, Berkeley University, 1991.
12. W. Kahan. Lecture notes on the status of IEEE standard 754 for binary floating-point arithmetic. Technical report, Berkeley University, 1996.
13. D. Knuth. *The Art of Computer Programming - Seminumerical Algorithms.* Addison Wesley, 1973.
14. P. Langlois and F. Nativel. Improving automatic reduction of round-off errors. In *IMACS World Congress on Scientific Computation, Modelling and Applied Mathematics*, volume 2, 1997.
15. V. Lefevre, J.M. Muller, and A. Tisserand. Toward correctly rounded transcendentals. *IEEE Transactions on Computers*, 47(11), 1998.
16. M. Pichat and J. Vignes. The numerical study of unstable fixed points in a chaotic dynamical system. In *IMACS World Congress on Scientific Computation, Modelling and Applied Mathematics,*, volume 2, 1997.
17. J. Vignes. A survey of the CESTAC method. In *Proceedings of Real Numbers and Computer Conference*, 1996.

Asserting the Precision of Floating-Point Computations: A Simple Abstract Interpreter[*]

Eric Goubault, Matthieu Martel, and Sylvie Putot

CEA - Recherche Technologique, LIST-DTSI-SLA
CEA F91191 Gif-Sur-Yvette Cedex, France
e-mail : [goubault,mmartel,sputot]@cea.fr

1 Introduction

The manipulation of real numbers by computers is approximated by floating-point arithmetic, which uses a finite representation of numbers. This implies that a (small in general) rounding error may be committed at each operation. Although this approximation is accurate enough for most applications, there are some cases where results become irrelevant because of the precision lost at some stages of the computation, even when the underlying numerical scheme is stable. In this paper, we present a tool for studying the propagation of rounding errors in floating-point computations, that carries out some ideas proposed in [3], [7]. Its aim is to detect automatically a possible catastrophic loss of precision, and its source. The tool is intended to cope with real industrial problems, and we believe it is specially appropriate for critical instrumentation software. On these numerically quite simple programs, we believe our tool will bring some very helpful information, and allow us to find possible programming errors such as potentially dangerous double/float conversions, or blatant instabilities or losses of accuracy. The techniques used being those of static analysis, the tool will not compete on numerically intensive codes with a numerician's study of stability. Neither is it designed for helping to find better numerical schemes. But, it is automatic and in comparison with a study of sensitivity to data, brings about the contribution of rounding errors occuring at every intermediary step of the computation. Moreover, static analyzes are sure (but may be pessimistic) and consider a set of possible executions and not just one, which is the essential requirement a verification tool for critical software must meet.

2 Main Features

Basically, the error $r - f$ between the results f and r of the same computation done with floating-point and real numbers is decomposed into a sum of error terms corresponding to the elementary operations done to obtain f. An elementary operation introduces a new rounding error which is then added, multiplied

---

[*] This work was supported by the RTD project IST-1999-20527 "DAEDALUS" of the European FP5 programme.

D. Le Métayer (Ed.): ESOP 2002, LNCS 2305, pp. 209–212, 2002.
© Springer-Verlag Berlin Heidelberg 2002

etc. by the next operations on the approximated partial result. For example, let x and y be initial data and let us assume that errors are attached to these numbers (we assume that we only have three digits of precision). The notation $x^{\ell_1} = 1.01\varepsilon + 0.005\varepsilon_{\ell_1}$ indicates that the floating-point value of x is 1.01 and that an error of magnitude 0.005 was introduced on this value at point ℓ_1. If $y^{\ell_2} = 10.1\varepsilon + 0.05\varepsilon_{\ell_2}$ then $x +^{\ell_3} y = 11.1\varepsilon + 0.005\varepsilon_{\ell_1} + 0.05\varepsilon_{\ell_2} + 0.01\varepsilon_{\ell_3}$ and $x \times^{\ell_3} y = 10.2\varepsilon + 0.0505\varepsilon_{\ell_1} + 0.0505\varepsilon_{\ell_2} + 0.001\varepsilon_{\ell_3} + 0.00025\varepsilon_{\varsigma}$. In $x +^{\ell_3} y$, the errors terms on x and y are added and this operation, done at point ℓ_3, introduces a new error term $0.001\varepsilon_{\ell_3}$ due to the truncation of the result. $x \times^{\ell_3} y$ also introduces an higher order error term $0.00025\varepsilon_{\varsigma}$ due to the factor $0.005\varepsilon_{\ell_1} \times 0.05\varepsilon_{\ell_2}$.

More generally, a floating-point number f with errors is denoted by an *error series* $f\varepsilon + \sum_{\ell \in \mathcal{L}} \omega^{\ell}\varepsilon_{\ell}$ where $\mathcal{L}$ is a set of syntactic program points and $\omega^{\ell}\varepsilon_{\ell}$ is the contribution to the global error of the error introduced at the point $\ell \in \mathcal{L}$ and propagated in the following computations. The tool described in this article implements an abstract interpretation [1] based on this model, where the value f and the coefficients ω^{ℓ} are abstracted by intervals.

As shown in Figure 1, the main window of the analyzer displays the code of the program being analyzed, the list of identifiers occurring in the abstract environment at the end of the analysis and a graph representation of the abstract value related to the selected identifier in the list. Scrollbars on the sides of the graph window are used to do various kinds of zooms.

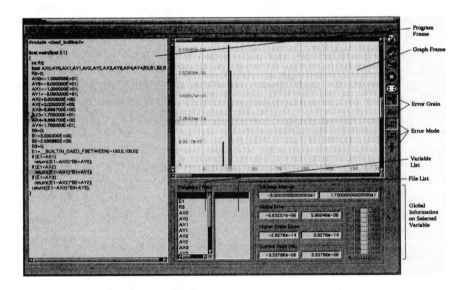

Fig. 1. Main window of the analyzer.

The graph represents the error series of a variable *id* and thus shows the contribution of the operations to the global error on *id*. The operations are identified with their program point which is displayed on the X-axis.

In Figure 1, the bars indicate the maximum of the absolute values of the interval bounds. This enables to assert the correctness of the code, when the errors have a small magnitude. This kind of graph is well suited to identify some numerical errors, but other kinds of errors, like cancellations [2], are more easily detected by graphs showing relative errors. Different types of graphs can be drawn by clicking the adequate button in the right-hand side toolbar. The graph and program code frames are connected in the graphical user interface in such a way that clicking on a column of the graph makes the code frame emphasizes the related program block and conversely. This enables the user to easily identify which piece of code mainly contributes to the error on the selected variable. Another interesting feature is that different grains of program points (like code lines or functions) can be selected by clicking the adequate button. Hence, for the analysis of a program made of many functions, the user may first identify which functions introduce the most important errors and next refine the result.

In the example of Figure 1, a typical program of an instrumentation sofware is being analyzed. It is basically an interpolation function with thresholds. One can see from the graph at the right-hand side of the code that the only sources of imprecision for the final result of the main function are: the floating-point approximation of the constant 2.999982 at line 20 (click on the first bar to outline the corresponding line in the C code), which is negligible, the 2nd `return` line 26 (second bar in the graph), and the 3rd `return` line 28 (third and last bar in the error graph), the last two ones being the more important. In fact, using `_BUILTIN_DAED_FBETWEEN` (an assertion of the analyzer), we imposed that E1 takes its value at the entry of the function between -100 and 100. So the analyzer derives that the function does not go through the first `return`. Then it derives that the function can go through the 4th and last `return`, but the multiplication is by zero and the constant is exact in the expression returned, so that there is no imprecision due to that case. The user can deduce from this that if he wants to improve the result, he can improve the accuracy of the computation of the 2nd and 3rd `return`. One simple way is to improve the accuracy of the two subtractions in these two expressions (using `double E1` in particular), whereas the improvement of the precision of the constant 2.999982 is not the better way. Notice that the analyzer also finds that the higher-order errors are always negligible. It will also be demonstrated that simple looping programs, such as linear filters can be proved stable or unstable accordingly by the analyzer, so the method does also work for loops (to a certain amount of precision).

3   Implementation

We are at a point where we have a first prototype of a static analyzer for full ANSI C programs, which abstracts floating-point variables by series of intervals. For the time being, if it can parse all ANSI C, it does not interpret aliases, arrays and struct information on the code. Nevertheless, it is already interprocedural, using simple static partitioning techniques [6].

The analyzer is based on a simple abstract interpreter [4] developed at CEA. The interval representing the floating-point value is implemented using classical floating-point numbers, and higher precision is used for the errors (necessary because numerical computations are done on these errors, and they must be done more accurately than usual floating-point). We use a library for multiprecision arithmetic, MPFR [5], based on GNU MP, but which provides the exact features of IEEE754, in particular the rounding modes. The interface is based on Trolltech's QT and communicates with the analyzer through data files.

The computational cost of the analysis is really reasonable. To give an idea, on small toy examples, typically a loop including a few operations, the analysis takes less than 0.1 second. On a more complex example of about 500 lines, with no loop, it takes only 45 seconds.

4 Conclusion and Future Work

The current implementation of our prototype already gives some interesting results on simple programs, which we propose to show during the demo. Concerning the threats detected by the analyzer, various reasons like cancellations or instabilites in loops may contribute to the loss of precision and some phenomena are easier to detect with a particular graph representation of the errors. In interaction with users, we are working on the best way to represent the many results collected by the analysis as well as on the methodology needed to their treatment. We also work on improving the precision of the analysis in loops. Because narrowings do not improve the analysis for the error terms, the approximation made by widenings must be fairly precise. We also plan to use relational lattices as discussed in [3].

References

1. P. Cousot and R. Cousot. Abstract interpretation: A unified lattice model for static analysis of programs by construction of approximations of fixed points. *Principles of Programming Languages 4*, pages 238–252, 1977.
2. D. Goldberg. What every computer scientist should know about floating-point arithmetic. *ACM Computing Surveys*, 23(1), 1991.
3. E. Goubault. Static analyses of the precision of floating-point operations. In *SAS'01*, LNCS. Springer-Verlag, 2001.
4. E. Goubault, D. Guilbaud, A. Pacalet, B. Starynkévitch, and F. Védrine. A simple abstract interpreter for threat detection and test case generation. In *Proceedings of WAPATV'01 (ICSE'01)*, May 2001.
5. G. Hanrot, V. Lefevre, F. Rouillier, and P. Zimmermann. The MPFR library. Institut de Recherche en Informatique et Automatique, 2001.
6. N. D. Jones and S. S. Muchnick. A flexible approach to interprocedural flow analysis and programs with recursive data structures. In *Proceedings of the 9th ACM Symposium on Principles of Programming Languages*, 1982.
7. M. Martel. Propagation of rounding errors in finite precision computations: a semantics approach. ESOP, 2002.

A Modular, Extensible Proof Method for Small-Step Flow Analyses

Mitchell Wand and Galen B. Williamson

College of Computer Science
Northeastern University
Boston, MA 02115, USA
{wand,gwilliam}@ccs.neu.edu

Abstract. We introduce a new proof technique for showing the correctness of 0CFA-like analyses with respect to small-step semantics. We illustrate the technique by proving the correctness of 0CFA for the pure λ-calculus under arbitrary β-reduction. This result was claimed by Palsberg in 1995; unfortunately, his proof was flawed. We provide a correct proof of this result, using a simpler and more general proof method. We illustrate the extensibility of the new method by showing the correctness of an analysis for the Abadi-Cardelli object calculus under small-step semantics.

1 Introduction

Sestoft [10, 11] has shown the correctness of 0CFA [12] with respect to call-by-value and call-by-name evaluation, using an evaluation semantics for the former and the Krivine machine for the latter. Palsberg [9] attempted to show that 0CFA was correct with respect to small-step semantics under arbitrary β-reduction; unfortunately, his proof was flawed. Our attempts to extend Palsberg's proof to more complex languages led us to discover flaws in the proof of one of the main theorems upon which his correctness result depends.

In this paper, we fix Palsberg's proof, working out some key details omitted from his paper and introducing a new proof technique that we believe will be easier to extend to more complex languages. Our proof is based on the observation that reduction carries most of the local structure of the source expression into the result expression, modifying only a few key terms. We illustrate the extensibility of our proof technique by showing the correctness of an analysis for the Abadi-Cardelli object calculus [1].

We begin in Sect. 2 by presenting the syntax and semantics of the language we will analyze, the λ-calculus, along with a few syntactic annotations and their properties. In Sect. 3, we present our control flow analysis, following Palsberg's constraint-generation system. In Sect. 4, we present our reformulation of Palsberg's proof of correctness, along with a description of precisely where his proof goes wrong. In Sect. 5, we apply our proof technique to an analysis of the Abadi-Cardelli object calculus.

D. Le Métayer (Ed.): ESOP 2002, LNCS 2305, pp. 213–227, 2002.

2   The Language

The syntax of our language is shown in Fig. 1. It is the standard untyped lambda calculus consisting of variable, abstraction, and application expressions. However, our analysis will require that expressions carry labels, so we define the set of expression labels Lab, and we use l to range over this set. We define two restrictions of Lab: Lab^b to the set of binding labels, and Lab^λ to the set of abstraction labels. We use β to range over Lab^b. Binding labels appear only on variable expressions, and on the bound variables in lambda expressions. (We have adapted the use of binding labels from [4].) In Fig. 2, we define lab, the obvious map from expressions to their labels.

$$
\begin{array}{ll}
l \in Lab & \text{Labels} \\
Lab^\lambda \subseteq Lab & \text{Abstraction Labels} \\
\beta \in Lab^b \subseteq Lab & \text{Binding Labels} \\
x \in Var & \text{Variables} \\
e ::= x^\beta \mid (e_1\ e_2)^l \mid \lambda^l x^\beta.e_0 & \text{Expressions}
\end{array}
$$

Fig. 1. Syntax

$$
\begin{aligned}
\mathsf{lab}(x^\beta) &= \beta \\
\mathsf{lab}(\lambda^l x^\beta.e_0) &= l \\
\mathsf{lab}((e_1\ e_2)^l) &= l
\end{aligned}
$$

Fig. 2. The map lab from expressions to their labels

In Fig. 3 we show the definitions of change of variable, $e\{y/x\}$, and substitution, $e[e'/x]$, to make explicit these two operations' effects (or lack thereof) on expression labels. The lemma which follows indicates precisely the limits of this effect.

$$
\begin{aligned}
x^\beta\{y/x\} &= y^\beta & x^\beta[e/x] &= e \\
z^\beta\{y/x\} &= z^\beta & y^\beta[e/x] &= y^\beta \\
(e_1\ e_2)^l\{y/x\} &= (e_1\{y/x\}\ e_2\{y/x\})^l & (e_1\ e_2)^l[e/x] &= (e_1[e/x]\ e_2[e/x])^l \\
(\lambda^l x^\beta.e_0)\{y/x\} &= (\lambda^l x^\beta.e_0) & (\lambda^l x^\beta.e_0)[e/x] &= (\lambda^l x^\beta.e_0) \\
(\lambda^l z^\beta.e_0)\{y/x\} &= \lambda^l z^\beta.(e_0\{y/x\}) & (\lambda^l y^\beta.e_0)[e/x] &= (\lambda^l z^\beta.e_0\{z/y\}[e/x]) \\
& (z \neq y) & & (z\ \text{fresh})
\end{aligned}
$$

Fig. 3. Change of variables and substitution

Lemma 2.1. $\mathsf{lab}(e_0[e/x]) = \mathsf{lab}(e_0)$, *unless* $e_0 = x^\beta$, *for some* $\beta \in Lab^b$.

Proof. By inspection of the definition of substitution, observing that variable renaming preserves labels.

Our semantics is unrestricted β-reduction, and we define the redex and reduction contexts in Fig. 4.

$$((\lambda^{l_0} x^\beta.e_0)\ e)^l \rightarrow e_0[e/x]$$
$$E ::= [\,]\ |\ \lambda^l x^\beta.E\ |\ (E\ e)^l\ |\ (e\ E)^l$$

Fig. 4. Semantics: the redex and reduction contexts

We introduce a syntactic notion of *well-labelledness* for expressions, along with *binding environments*. Intuitively, an expression is well-labelled when all of the labels on variable expressions match the binding labels appearing on the lambda expressions that bind them. To formulate well-labelledness, define a binding environment to be a finite map from variables to the labels of their respective binders:

$$\Gamma : Var \rightarrow Lab^{\mathrm{b}}\ .$$

Consider the expression $\lambda^l x^\beta.e_0$. A binding environment Γ would be "correct" for the expression e_0 only if $\Gamma(x) = \beta$. We formalize this notion of a binding environment being correct for an expression into *labelling judgements* of the form $\Gamma \vdash e$ wl, which says simply that the expression e is well-labelled under the binding environment Γ. Well-labelledness for expressions is captured precisely by the set of rules for deriving labelling judgements shown in Fig. 5. For convenience, we say that an expression e is well-labelled, written $\vdash e$ wl, iff there exists a labelling environment Γ such that $\Gamma \vdash e$ wl.

$$\frac{\Gamma(x) = \beta \quad \beta = \beta'}{\Gamma \vdash x^{\beta'}\ \mathsf{wl}} \quad \textbf{[var-wl]}$$

$$\frac{\Gamma \vdash e_1\ \mathsf{wl} \quad \Gamma \vdash e_2\ \mathsf{wl}}{\Gamma \vdash (e_1\ e_2)^l\ \mathsf{wl}} \quad \textbf{[app-wl]}$$

$$\frac{\Gamma[x \mapsto \beta] \vdash e_0\ \mathsf{wl}}{\Gamma \vdash \lambda^l x^\beta.e_0\ \mathsf{wl}} \quad \textbf{[abs-wl]}$$

Fig. 5. The rules for deriving labelling judgements

Finally, we define a subterm relation $\in_E$, shown in Fig. 6.

$$
\begin{aligned}
e_0 \in_E e \quad \text{iff} \quad & (e = e_0) \\
& \lor\ (e = (\lambda^l x^\beta.e_1) \land e_0 \in_E e_1) \\
& \lor\ (e = (e_1\ e_2)^{l'} \land (e_0 \in_E e_1 \lor e_0 \in_E e_2))
\end{aligned}
$$

Fig. 6. The subterm relation $\in_E$

The following lemma expresses some properties of well-labelledness that should be familiar from typing. (See [7], pp. 244-5.)

Lemma 2.2. *Let e be an expression and let Γ be a binding environment.*

1. *If $\Gamma \vdash e$ wl and $e' \in_E e$, then there exists a Γ' extending Γ such that $\Gamma' \vdash e'$ wl.*
2. *If $x \notin \mathsf{fv}(e)$, then for all $\beta \in Lab^b$, $\Gamma \vdash e$ wl iff $\Gamma[x \mapsto \beta] \vdash e$ wl.*
3. *If $\Gamma[x \mapsto \beta] \vdash e$ wl and $y \notin \mathsf{dom}(\Gamma)$, then $\Gamma[y \mapsto \beta] \vdash e\{y/x\}$ wl.*
4. *If $\Gamma[x \mapsto \beta] \vdash e$ wl and $\Gamma \vdash e_0$ wl, then $\Gamma \vdash e[e_0/x]$ wl.*

Proof. Each property is proved by a straightforward induction, the first by induction on the definition of $e' \in_E e$, and the remaining three by induction on the size of e.

Finally, we show that well-labelledness is preserved under reduction.

Lemma 2.3. *If $\Gamma \vdash e$ wl and $e \to e'$, then $\Gamma \vdash e'$ wl.*

Proof. Since $e \to e'$, choose the reduction context E and redex r such that $r \to s$, $e = E[r]$, and $e' = E[s]$. We proceed by induction on the structure of E.

In the base case, we have $E = [\ ]$. Then $e = r$, $e' = s$, $\Gamma \vdash r$ wl, and we must show $\Gamma \vdash s$ wl. Since r is a redex, $r = ((\lambda^{lo} x^\beta.e_0)\ e_1)^l$, so $s = e_0[e_1/x]$. Since $\Gamma \vdash r$ wl, we have $\Gamma \vdash \lambda^{lo} x^\beta.e_0$ wl and $\Gamma \vdash e_1$ wl by [**app-wl**]. Thus, $\Gamma[x \mapsto \beta] \vdash e_0$ wl by [**abs-wl**]. Then by Lemma 2.2, part 4, we have $\Gamma \vdash e_0[e_1/x]$ wl and thus $\Gamma \vdash s$ wl.

In the induction step, consider first $E = \lambda^{lo} x^\beta.E_0$. In this case, $e = E[r] = \lambda^{lo} x^\beta.E_0[r]$, and we have

$$\Gamma \vdash \lambda^{lo} x^\beta.E_0[r]\ \mathsf{wl} \Rightarrow \Gamma[x \mapsto \beta] \vdash E_0[r]\ \mathsf{wl} \quad (\text{by } [\mathbf{abs\text{-}wl}])$$
$$\Rightarrow \Gamma[x \mapsto \beta] \vdash E_0[s]\ \mathsf{wl} \quad\quad (\text{by IH})$$
$$\Rightarrow \Gamma \vdash \lambda^{lo} x^\beta.E_0[s]\ \mathsf{wl} \quad (\text{by } [\mathbf{abs\text{-}wl}])$$

Consider next $E = (E_1\ e_2)^l$. Then $e = E[r] = (E_1[r]\ e_2)^l$, and we have

$$\Gamma \vdash (E_1[r]\ e_2)^l\ \mathsf{wl} \Rightarrow \Gamma \vdash E_1[r]\ \mathsf{wl} \wedge \Gamma \vdash e_2\ \mathsf{wl} \quad (\text{by } [\mathbf{app\text{-}wl}])$$
$$\Rightarrow \Gamma \vdash E_1[s]\ \mathsf{wl} \quad\quad\quad\quad (\text{by IH})$$
$$\Rightarrow \Gamma \vdash (E_1[s]\ e_2)^l\ \mathsf{wl} \quad (\text{by } [\mathbf{app\text{-}wl}])$$

In the final case, $E = (e_1\ E_2)^l$, and the proof is similar to the previous case.

3   The Analysis

We derive our analysis from the constraint-based analysis of [9]. The analysis of an expression is specified by a constraint system (see Defn. 4.1) that is generated from the program text [2]. A solution to these constraints will give an approximation to the possible results of evaluating each program point.

The constraint system consists of a collection of conditional inclusions between sets. In general, there will be one set for each program point and for each bound variable. Palsberg uses two sets of metavariables $[\![\lambda^l]\!]$ and $[\![\nu^l]\!]$ as names for these sets; Nielson and Nielson [8] formulate these as abstract caches $\widehat{C}$ and $\widehat{\rho}$. Other researchers, e.g. [3, 6], convert terms to A-normal form or the like, and use variables as program points. We introduce labels for each program point and for each bound variable (following [4]). Because denoted and expressed values in our language coincide, we need only a single cache Φ.

The labelling behavior of our semantics follows Palsberg's: when one term reduces to another, the label on the source term will disappear, and the result term will keep its previous label. This means that a given label may appear in many different places as its term is copied. Our notion of well-labelledness ensures that the label on a variable instance matches the label on its binder.

We express flow information using a single map. This abstract cache maps labels to *abstract values*, which are sets of abstraction labels.

$$\Phi \in \widehat{Cache} = Lab \to \widehat{Val}$$
$$\widehat{Val} = \mathcal{P}(Lab^\lambda)$$

An abstract value is a set of abstraction labels because abstractions are the only values in our language. If our language had scalars, they would also be abstracted into the set $\widehat{Val}$.

The analysis of an expression e is the following set of constraints [9]:

$$[\![e]\!] = \bigcup_{\substack{\lambda^{lo} x^\beta . e_0 \in_E e \\ (e_1 \ e_2)^l \in_E e}} R((e_1 \ e_2)^l, \lambda^{lo} x^\beta . e_0) \quad \cup \quad \bigcup_{\lambda^{lo} x^\beta . e_0 \in_E e} \{ \ \{l_0\} \subseteq \Phi(l_0) \ \} \ ,$$

where the set $R((e_1 \ e_2)^l, (\lambda^{lo} x^\beta . e_0))$ consists of the following two constraints:

$$\{l_0\} \subseteq \Phi(\mathsf{lab}(e_1)) \Rightarrow \Phi(\mathsf{lab}(e_2)) \subseteq \Phi(\beta)$$
$$\{l_0\} \subseteq \Phi(\mathsf{lab}(e_1)) \Rightarrow \Phi(\mathsf{lab}(e_0)) \subseteq \Phi(l) \ .$$

The first comprehension ensures that every abstraction term in the expression is matched against every application term in the expression. Palsberg gives a nice description of the two constraints in R:

- *The first constraint.* If the operator of [the application] evaluates to an abstraction with label l_0, then the bound variable of that abstraction may be substituted with everything to which the operand of [the application] can evaluate.
- *The second constraint.* If the operator of [the application] evaluates to an abstraction with label l_0, then everything to which the body of the abstraction evaluates is also a possible result of evaluating the whole application. [9, p. 280]

The second comprehension consists of a single constraint $\{l_0\} \subseteq \Phi(l_0)$ for every abstraction label appearing in the source expression. These constraints ensure that each abstraction is predicted as a possible value for itself.

4   Correctness

Our proof of correctness for the analysis is based on an entailment relation between constraint systems, $A \vdash A'$. This entailment expresses the property that all of the constraints in A' can be derived from those in A by the formal system in Def. 4.2 below. We have formulated the proof in this way so as to most closely follow the results in [9].

We begin by formalizing our constraint language.

Definition 4.1. *Let V and U be sets. A* constraint system A *over V and U is a finite set of Horn clauses, defined by the following grammar:*

$$
\begin{array}{ll}
s \in V & \textit{Set Variables} \\
c \in U & \textit{Constants} \\
I ::= \{c\} \subseteq s \mid s \subseteq s & \textit{Atomic Formulas} \\
H ::= I \mid I \Rightarrow H & \textit{Horn Clauses} \\
A \in \mathrm{fin}(H) & \textit{Constraint Systems}
\end{array}
$$

A solution *of a constraint system of V and U is a map $\Phi : V \to \mathcal{P}(U)$ such that $\Phi \models A$, where $\Phi \models A$ is defined by:*

$$
\begin{array}{ll}
\Phi \models A & \textit{iff } \forall\, H \in A, \Phi \models H \\
\Phi \models \{c\} \subseteq s & \textit{iff } \{c\} \subseteq \Phi(s) \\
\Phi \models s_1 \subseteq s_2 & \textit{iff } \Phi(s_1) \subseteq \Phi(s_2) \\
\Phi \models I \Rightarrow H & \textit{iff } \Phi \models I \Rightarrow \Phi \models H
\end{array}
$$

For our constraint systems, V will be *Lab* and U will be *Lab*$^{\lambda}$.

Definition 4.2. *If A is a constraint system, and H is a Horn clause, then the judgement $A \vdash H$ ("A entails H") holds if it is derivable using the following five rules:*

$$
\frac{}{A \vdash H} \quad \textit{if } H \in A \qquad\qquad\qquad \textit{(Discharge)}
$$

$$
\frac{}{A \vdash P \subseteq P} \qquad\qquad\qquad\qquad\qquad \textit{(Reflexivity)}
$$

$$
\frac{A \vdash P \subseteq P' \qquad A \vdash P' \subseteq P''}{A \vdash P \subseteq P''} \qquad\qquad \textit{(Transitivity)}
$$

$$
\frac{A \vdash X \qquad A \vdash X \Rightarrow Y}{A \vdash Y} \qquad\qquad \textit{(Modus Ponens)}
$$

$$
\frac{A \vdash P' \subseteq P'' \qquad A \vdash P \subseteq P'' \Rightarrow Q' \subseteq Q'' \qquad A \vdash Q \subseteq Q'}{A \vdash P \subseteq P' \Rightarrow Q \subseteq Q''} \qquad \textit{(Weakening)}
$$

If A, A' are constraint systems, then $A \vdash A'$ if and only if for every $H \in A'$, we have $A \vdash H$.

Definition 4.2 is verbatim from [9], except that we overload the "turnstyle" operator, $\vdash$, so that the right hand side can be either a single constraint or a constraint system (set of clauses) with the conjunction of these clauses implied, as it already is for $\models$.

We have formulated our proof in terms of constraint systems and deductions so as to most closely follow the results in [9]. Our results could easily be reformulated in terms of preservation of solutions (for all Φ, if $\Phi \models A$ then $\Phi \models A'$). Such a formulation would also expose the analogy with the Subject Reduction Theorem.

Lemma 4.3. $\vdash$ *is reflexive, transitive, and solution-preserving. If $A \supseteq A'$, then $A \vdash A'$.*

Proof. Trivial, relying on the definition of $\Phi \models A$ above. See Lem. 4.2 in [9].

Since our analysis is a comprehension over applications and abstractions that occur in the expression to be analyzed, it will be useful to have a characterization of the applications and abstractions that occur in the result expression, in terms of the applications and abstractions that occur in the source expression. The following relation captures the possible differences between terms in the result of a reduction and the terms in the source expression that gave rise to them.

Definition 4.4. *If r is a β-redex and s is an expression such that $r \to s$, E is a reduction context, and e, e' are expressions such that $e \in_E E[r]$ and $e' \in_E E[s]$, then define $\$(e, e')$ iff either*

1. *$\mathsf{lab}(e) = \mathsf{lab}(e')$, or*
2. *$e = r$ and $e' = s$, or else*
3. *$r = ((\lambda^{l_0}x^\beta.e_0)\ e_1)^l$, $s = e_0[e_1/x]$, $e = x^\beta$ and $e' = e_1$.*

The following lemma shows that every abstraction or application in the result expression arises from an abstraction or application in the original term with the same label and with immediate subterms that either have the same label as the subterms in the original, or else whose subterms differ in the very specific ways delineated by Definition 4.4.

Lemma 4.5. *Assume r is a redex and s an expression such that $r \to s$, and E is a reduction context such that $\vdash E[r]$ wl. Then*

1. *If $(e'_1\ e'_2)^l \in_E E[s]$, then there exists a $(e_1\ e_2)^l \in_E E[r]$ such that $\$(e_1, e'_1)$ and $\$(e_2, e'_2)$.*
2. *If $\lambda^l x^\beta.e'_1 \in_E E[s]$, then there exists a $\lambda^l x^\beta.e_1 \in_E E[r]$ such that $\$(e_1, e'_1)$.*

Proof. Since r is a redex, it must be of the form $((\lambda^{l_0}y^\beta.e_0)\ e)^l$ and thus $s = e_0[e/y]$. We must show that for each $(e'_1\ e'_2)^{l'} \in_E E[s]$, there exists an application $(e_1\ e_2)^{l'} \in_E E[r]$, and for each $\lambda^{l_0}x^{\beta'}.e'_3 \in_E E[s]$, there exists an abstraction $\lambda^{l_0}x^{\beta'}.e_3 \in_E E[r]$, such that for $i = 1\ldots 3$, $\$(e_i, e'_i)$.

Consider every abstraction or application node in $E[s]$. Each such node in e and in the interiors of E and e_0 looks like the node labelled l_1 in Fig. 7. These

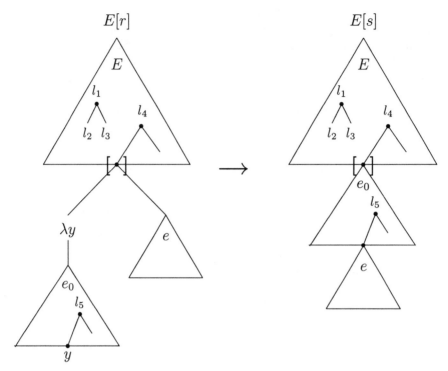

Fig. 7. The tree representations of $E[r]$ and $E[s]$

nodes were unaffected by the reduction, and their children are covered by case
(1) of Defn. 4.4.

The remaining nodes in $E[s]$ are like those labelled l_4 and l_5. Since there is
a unique hole in E, there is exactly one node like that labelled l_4, which has the
hole in E as a child. This node is covered by case (2) of Defn. 4.4, since it has s
as a child after the reduction, and it had r as a child before the reduction.

This leaves nodes in $E[s]$ like that labelled l_5 in the figure. These nodes are
covered by case (3) of Defn. 4.4, since they have a copy of e as a child after
the reduction, as a result of substituting for an occurrence of y in the redex.
However, Defn. 4.4 requires that the labels on these occurrences of y must all
have been β, the label on the bound variable in the redex. This requirement
is satisfied easily using the well-labelledness of $E[r]$. Since $\vdash E[r]$ wl, choose a
labelling environment Γ such that $\Gamma \vdash E[r]$ wl. Thus, since $r \in_E E[r]$, by part
(1) of Lem. 2.2, there exists a Γ' extending Γ such that $\Gamma' \vdash r$ wl. Then by
[**app-wl**] and [**abs-wl**], we have $\Gamma'[y \mapsto \beta] \vdash e_0$ wl. Thus, since any instance of
y substituted for in the reduction must have been a free occurrence of y in e_0,
by inspection of the rules for labelling judgements, we can see that the label on
each such occurrence must have been $\Gamma'[y \mapsto \beta](y) = \beta$.

A more formal, but considerably more lengthy, proof could be constructed
based on the concept of case analysis of tree addresses in the style of Brainerd
[5].

The next lemma states that terms in the result of a reduction have smaller flow information than the terms in the source expression to which they are related by $.

Lemma 4.6. *If r is a redex and s an expression such that $r \to s$, E is a reduction context such that $\vdash E[r]$ wl, and e and e' are expressions such that $e \in_E E[r]$, $e' \in_E E[s]$, and $\$(e, e')$, then $\llbracket E[r] \rrbracket \vdash \Phi(\mathsf{lab}(e')) \subseteq \Phi(\mathsf{lab}(e))$.*

Proof. We note that since r is a redex and $r \to s$, we have $r = ((\lambda^{l_0} x^\beta.e_0)\ e_1)^l$ and $s = e_0[e_1/x]$. We have

$$\llbracket E[r] \rrbracket \vdash \llbracket r \rrbracket = \llbracket ((\lambda^{l_0} x^\beta.e_0)\ e_1)^l \rrbracket\ ,$$

and thus,

$$\llbracket r \rrbracket \vdash \{\ \{l_0\} \subseteq \Phi(l_0)\ ,$$
$$\{l_0\} \subseteq \Phi(l_0) \Rightarrow \Phi(\mathsf{lab}(e_1)) \subseteq \Phi(\beta)\ ,$$
$$\{l_0\} \subseteq \Phi(l_0) \Rightarrow \Phi(\mathsf{lab}(e_0)) \subseteq \Phi(l)\ \}\ .$$

Therefore, by two applications of Modus Ponens, we have

$$\llbracket r \rrbracket \vdash \Phi(\mathsf{lab}(e_1)) \subseteq \Phi(\beta)\ , \tag{1}$$

and

$$\llbracket r \rrbracket \vdash \Phi(\mathsf{lab}(e_0)) \subseteq \Phi(l)\ . \tag{2}$$

We proceed by cases on the definition of $\$(e, e')$:

1. Trivial.
2. Since $e = r$ and $e' = s$, we have $\mathsf{lab}(e) = \mathsf{lab}(r) = l$ and $\mathsf{lab}(e') = \mathsf{lab}(s) = \mathsf{lab}(e_0[e_1/x])$. By Lem. 2.1, unless $e_0 = x$, $\mathsf{lab}(e_0[e_1/x]) = \mathsf{lab}(e_0)$, and the result follows trivially. Consider instead $e_0 = x$. Since $\vdash E[r]$ wl, choose a labelling environment Γ such that $\Gamma \vdash E[r]$ wl. Then by Lem. 2.2, there exists a Γ' extending Γ such that $\Gamma' \vdash r$ wl, and thus, we have $\Gamma'[x \mapsto \beta] \vdash e_0$ wl by [**app-wl**] and [**abs-wl**]. Now, since $\Gamma'[x \mapsto \beta] \vdash e_0$ wl, $\Gamma'[x \mapsto \beta](x) = \beta$, and $e_0 = x$, we must have $\mathsf{lab}(e_0) = \beta$ by [**var-wl**]. We also have $e_0[e_1/x] = x^\beta[e_1/x] = e_1$, and thus, $\mathsf{lab}(s) = \mathsf{lab}(e_1)$. By (1) and (2) then, we have $\llbracket r \rrbracket \vdash \Phi(\mathsf{lab}(e_1)) \subseteq \Phi(\beta) \subseteq \Phi(l)$, and thus, since $e = r$ and $e' = s$, we have $\llbracket E[r] \rrbracket \vdash \Phi(\mathsf{lab}(e')) \subseteq \Phi(\mathsf{lab}(e))$, by Transitivity of both $\vdash$ and $\subseteq$.
3. Since $e = x^\beta$ and $e' = e_1$, $\mathsf{lab}(e) = \beta$ and $\mathsf{lab}(e') = \mathsf{lab}(e_1)$, by (1) and Transitivity of $\vdash$, we have $\llbracket E[r] \rrbracket \vdash \Phi(\mathsf{lab}(e')) \subseteq \Phi(\mathsf{lab}(e))$.

Now we turn to the main theorem, which shows that constraints are preserved under reduction. That is, the constraints of the result term are entailed by the constraints of the source term. The correctness of the analysis is a consequence of this entailment: the flow information of the result term is predicted by (contained in) the flow information of the source term.

We replace the inductive structure of Palsberg's proof of the equivalent theorem ([9, Thm. 4.10]) by a flat structure that matches the flat, non-inductive structure of the definition of the analysis.

Theorem 4.7. *If $e_X \to e_Y$, and there exists a Γ_X such that $\Gamma_X \vdash e_X$ wl, then $[\![e_X]\!] \vdash [\![e_Y]\!]$ and $[\![e_X]\!] \vdash \Phi(\mathrm{lab}(e_Y)) \subseteq \Phi(\mathrm{lab}(e_X))$.*

Proof. Since $e_X \to e_Y$, choose a reduction context E, redex r, and corresponding reductum s such that $e_X = E[r] \to E[s] = e_Y$. Since r is a redex, it must be of the form $((\lambda^{l_0} y^\beta.e_0)\ e)^l$ and thus $s = e_0[e/y]$. We need to show $[\![E[r]]\!] \vdash [\![E[s]]\!]$, where

$$[\![E[s]]\!] = \bigcup_{\substack{\lambda^{l'_0} x^{\beta'}.e'_3 \in_\mathsf{E} E[s] \\ (e'_1\ e'_2)^{l'} \in_\mathsf{E} E[s]}} R((e'_1\ e'_2)^{l'}, \lambda^{l'_0} x^{\beta'}.e'_3) \cup \bigcup_{\lambda^{l'_0} x^{\beta'}.e'_3 \in_\mathsf{E} E[s]} \{\ \{l'_0\} \subseteq \Phi(l'_0)\ \}\ .$$

Let $(e'_1\ e'_2)^{l'} \in_\mathsf{E} E[s]$ and $\lambda^{l'_0} x^{\beta'}.e'_3 \in_\mathsf{E} E[s]$. Since $e_X = E[r]$ is well-labelled, by Lem. 4.5, there exists an application $(e_1\ e_2)^{l'} \in_\mathsf{E} E[r]$, and there exists an abstraction $\lambda^{l'_0} x^{\beta'}.e_3 \in_\mathsf{E} E[r]$, such that $\mathbb{S}(e_i, e'_i)$ for $i = 1\dots3$. By Lem. 4.6 then, we have $[\![E[r]]\!] \vdash \Phi(\mathrm{lab}(e'_i)) \subseteq \Phi(\mathrm{lab}(e_i))$ for $i = 1\dots3$.

Now, by the definition of $[\![E[r]]\!]$, since $(e_1\ e_2)^{l'} \in_\mathsf{E} E[r]$ and $\lambda^{l'_0} x^{\beta'}.e_3 \in_\mathsf{E} E[r]$, we have

$$[\![E[r]]\!] \vdash R((e_1\ e_2)^{l'}, \lambda^{l'_0} x^{\beta'}.e_3)\ .$$

Thus we have

$$[\![E[r]]\!] \vdash \{l'_0\} \subseteq \Phi(\mathrm{lab}(e_1)) \Rightarrow \Phi(\mathrm{lab}(e_2)) \subseteq \Phi(\beta)$$

and

$$[\![E[r]]\!] \vdash \{l'_0\} \subseteq \Phi(\mathrm{lab}(e_1)) \Rightarrow \Phi(\mathrm{lab}(e_3)) \subseteq \Phi(l')\ .$$

Now, since we have $[\![E[r]]\!] \vdash \Phi(\mathrm{lab}(e'_i)) \subseteq \Phi(\mathrm{lab}(e_i))$ for each e'_i and its corresponding e_i, we have

$$[\![E[r]]\!] \vdash \Phi(\mathrm{lab}(e'_1)) \subseteq \Phi(\mathrm{lab}(e_1))$$
$$[\![E[r]]\!] \vdash \{l'_0\} \subseteq \Phi(\mathrm{lab}(e_1)) \Rightarrow \Phi(\mathrm{lab}(e_2)) \subseteq \Phi(\beta)$$
$$\underline{[\![E[r]]\!] \vdash \Phi(\mathrm{lab}(e'_2)) \subseteq \Phi(\mathrm{lab}(e_2))}$$
$$[\![E[r]]\!] \vdash \{l'_0\} \subseteq \Phi(\mathrm{lab}(e'_1)) \Rightarrow \Phi(\mathrm{lab}(e'_2)) \subseteq \Phi(\beta')$$

and

$$[\![E[r]]\!] \vdash \Phi(\mathrm{lab}(e'_1)) \subseteq \Phi(\mathrm{lab}(e_1))$$
$$[\![E[r]]\!] \vdash \{l'_0\} \subseteq \Phi(\mathrm{lab}(e_1)) \Rightarrow \Phi(\mathrm{lab}(e_3)) \subseteq \Phi(l')$$
$$\underline{[\![E[r]]\!] \vdash \Phi(\mathrm{lab}(e'_3)) \subseteq \Phi(\mathrm{lab}(e_3))}$$
$$[\![E[r]]\!] \vdash \{l'_0\} \subseteq \Phi(\mathrm{lab}(e'_1)) \Rightarrow \Phi(\mathrm{lab}(e'_3)) \subseteq \Phi(l')$$

by Weakening in both cases. But these two constraints are exactly the constraints in $R((e'_1\ e'_2)^{l'}, \lambda^{l'_0} x^{\beta'}.e'_3)$, and so we have shown

$$[\![E[r]]\!] \vdash \bigcup_{\substack{\lambda^{l'_0} x^{\beta'}.e'_3 \in_\mathsf{E} E[s] \\ (e'_1\ e'_2)^{l'} \in_\mathsf{E} E[s]}} R((e'_1\ e'_2)^{l'}, \lambda^{l'_0} x^{\beta'}.e'_3)\ .$$

Now, since $\lambda^{l'_0} x^{\beta'}.e_0 \in_E E[r]$, we have $[\![E[r]]\!] \vdash \{ \{l'_0\} \subseteq \Phi(l'_0) \}$, and so we have

$$[\![E[r]]\!] \vdash \bigcup_{\lambda^{l'_0} x^{\beta'}.e'_3 \in_E E[s]} \{ \{l'_0\} \subseteq \Phi(l'_0) \} \ .$$

Thus we have $[\![E[r]]\!] \vdash [\![E[s]]\!]$, which is $[\![e_X]\!] \vdash [\![e_Y]\!]$.

Finally, we show $[\![e_X]\!] \vdash \Phi(\mathsf{lab}(e_Y)) \subseteq \Phi(\mathsf{lab}(e_X))$. Since $e_X = E[r]$ and $e_Y = E[s]$, obviously we have $e_X \in_E E[r]$ and $e_Y \in_E E[s]$. Now, if $E = [\ ]$, then $E[r] = r$ and $E[s] = s$, and we have $\$(E[r], E[s])$. If instead $E \neq [\ ]$, then $\mathsf{lab}(E[r]) = \mathsf{lab}(E[s])$, and again we have $\$(E[r], E[s])$. Thus, since $r \rightarrow s$, and $\vdash E[r]$ wl, by Lem. 4.6, we have $[\![e_X]\!] \vdash \Phi(\mathsf{lab}(E[r])) \subseteq \Phi(\mathsf{lab}(E[s]))$.

The following corollary states that if an expression converges to a value, then the label on the value is among those predicted by the analysis of the expression.

Corollary 4.8. *If $\vdash e$ wl and e converges to a value v, then $[\![e]\!] \vdash \{\mathsf{lab}(v)\} \subseteq \Phi(\mathsf{lab}(e))$.*

Note that much information is lost by this corollary: while it shows that the label of a result value is predicted, it does not tell us anything about the internal structure of this value, which may be arbitrarily complex, but is guaranteed to obey the constraints of $[\![e]\!]$.

We can now characterize the difficulty in Palsberg's theorem [9, Thm. 4.10] corresponding to our Thm. 4.7. Palsberg's proof proceeds by induction on the structure of e_X. While considering the case in which $e_X = (e_1 \ e_2)^l$ and $e_1 \rightarrow e'_1$ (that is, the reduction occurs in the operator subterm), he invokes the induction hypothesis to get $[\![e_1]\!] \vdash [\![e'_1]\!]$. He then shows that for every $\lambda^{l_0} x.e'$ in $(e'_1 \ e_2)^l$, $[\![(e_1 \ e_2)^l]\!] \vdash R((e'_1 \ e_2)^l, \lambda^{l_0} x.e')$. However, he needs to show $[\![(e'_1 \ e_2)^l]\!] \vdash R((e''_1 \ e''_2)^l, \lambda^{l_0} x.e')$ for *every* $(e''_1 \ e''_2)^l$ in $(e'_1 \ e_2)^l$.

Any repair of this error would require an induction hypothesis that accounted for the context in which the reduction appeared. This approach is complicated by the mismatch between any inductive approach and the non-inductive formulation of the analysis used by Palsberg. We made several increasingly baroque attempts to repair the proof, and were eventually led to abandon a formal inductive structure in favor of the "flat" characterization of Lem. 4.5.

5 The Abadi-Cardelli Object Calculus

We presume the reader is familiar with the Abadi-Cardelli Object Calculus [1]. Our syntax is shown in Fig. 8. We have adopted a slightly non-standard syntax to facilitate the presentation. Subterms are labelled with superscripts; bound variables of comprehensions are presented as subscripts, e.g. $\langle \ldots \rangle^l_i$. We elide the range of the bound variable i, relying on the fact that this calculus neither adds nor removes methods from an object. For any program, the set of method names is finite.

$$
\begin{array}{ll}
m & \text{Method Names} \\
x & \text{Identifiers} \\
\mu ::= m =^l (b)e & \text{Methods} \\
b ::= x^\beta & \text{Variables} \\
e ::= b \mid \langle \mu_i \rangle_i^l \mid (e.m)^l \mid (e \Leftarrow (\mu))^l & \text{Expressions}
\end{array}
$$

Fig. 8. Syntax of the Object Calculus

The reduction rules of the object calculus are shown in Fig. 9. Reductions may be carried out in arbitrary contexts, and well-labelledness works in the usual manner.

$$
(\langle m_i =^{l_i} (x_i^{\beta_i})e_i \rangle_i^{l_1}.m_j)^{l_2}
$$
$$
\rightarrow e_j[\langle m_i =^{l_i} (x_i^{\beta_i})e_i \rangle_i^{l_1}/x_j] \qquad \text{(Red Sel)}
$$

$$
(\langle m_i =^{l_i} (x_i^{\beta_i})e_i \rangle_i^{l_1} \Leftarrow (m_j =^{l_2} (x^\beta)e))^{l_3}
$$
$$
\rightarrow \langle m_j =^{l_2} (x^\beta)e, \ m_i =^{l_i} (x_i^{\beta_i})e_i \mid_{i, \ i \neq j} \rangle^{l_3} \quad \text{(Red Upd)}
$$

Fig. 9. Reduction Rules of the Object Calculus

We think of objects as sets of abstractions, indexed by method name. As with the lambda-calculus, we label each object by the expression in which it was created, either by an object expression or by an update expression. Methods are similarly identified by labels.

For this analysis, the cache will have two arguments: a label and a method name, and will return a set of method labels. The intention is that $\Phi(l, m)$ will contain all the labels of methods that might be the m-method of an object labelled l.

We define $\Phi(l) \sqsubseteq \Phi(l')$ as the conjunction of the formulas $\Phi(l, m) \subseteq \Phi(l', m)$ for all method names m.

For dealing with the analysis, ordinary comprehensions are cumbersome. We introduce reverse comprehensions:

$$
(\mathsf{ForEach} \ x \in X \ \triangleright \ f(x))
$$

in place of the more usual $\{f(x) \mid x \in X\}$ or $\bigcup_{x \in X} f(x)$, depending on whether $f(x)$ is a formula or a set of formulas.

We may now define the analysis $[\![e]\!]$ of a term e as the set of Horn clauses defined by:

$$\llbracket e \rrbracket = (\mathsf{ForEach}\ \langle m_i =^{l_i} (x_i^{\beta_i})e_i\rangle_i^l \in_{\mathsf{E}} e \rhd \{l_i\} \subseteq \Phi(l, m_i))$$
$$\cup\,(\mathsf{ForEach}\ (e_1.m)^l \in_{\mathsf{E}} e, m =^{l'} (x^\beta)e_2 \in_{\mathsf{E}} e$$
$$\rhd \{l'\} \subseteq \Phi(\mathsf{lab}(e_1), m) \Rightarrow \Phi(\mathsf{lab}(e_1)) \sqsubseteq \Phi(\beta),$$
$$\{l'\} \subseteq \Phi(\mathsf{lab}(e_1), m) \Rightarrow \Phi(\mathsf{lab}(e_2)) \sqsubseteq \Phi(l))$$
$$\cup\,(\mathsf{ForEach}\ (e_1 \Leftarrow (m =^{l_1} (x^\beta)e_1'))^l \in_{\mathsf{E}} e$$
$$\rhd (\forall n \neq m)(\Phi(\mathsf{lab}(e_1), n) \subseteq \Phi(l, n)),$$
$$\{l_1\} \subseteq \Phi(l, m))$$

As in Sect. 3, each comprehension in the analysis has an intuitive relation to the semantics:

- Every m-method that appears in an object is a possible m-method of that object.
- If an m-method of an object is selected, then the object is among the possible values of the method's bound variable, and the value of the method's body is among the possible values of the selection expression.
- If an object is created by updating the m-method of some object, then every n-method of the old object is a possible n-method of the new object (for $n \neq m$), and the new method is a possible m-method of the new object.

We now proceed as in Sect. 4.

Definition 5.1. *If r is a redex and s is an expression such that $r \to s$, E is a reduction context, and e, e' are expressions such that $e \in_{\mathsf{E}} E[r]$ and $e' \in_{\mathsf{E}} E[s]$, then define $\$(e, e')$ iff either*

1. $\mathsf{lab}(e) = \mathsf{lab}(e')$,
2. $e = r$ and $e' = s$, or else
3. $r = (\langle m_i =^{l_i} (x_i^{\beta_i})e_i\rangle_i^{l_1}.m_j)^{l_2}$ and $s = e_j[\langle m_i =^{l_i} (x_i^{\beta_i})e_i\rangle_i^{l_1}/x_j]$ and $e = x_j^{\beta_j}$ and $e' = \langle m_i =^{l_i} (x_i^{\beta_i})e_i\rangle_i^{l_1}$.

Lemma 5.2. *Assume r is a redex and s an expression such that $r \to s$, E is a reduction context, and $\vdash E[r]$ wl. Then*

1. *If $(m =^l (x^\beta)e_1') \in_{\mathsf{E}} E[s]$, then there exists a $(m =^l (x^\beta)e_1) \in_{\mathsf{E}} E[r]$ such that $\$(e_1, e_1')$.*
2. *If $(e_1'.m)^l \in_{\mathsf{E}} E[s]$, then there exists a $(e_1.m)^l \in_{\mathsf{E}} E[r]$ such that $\$(e_1, e_1')$.*
3. *If $(e_1' \Leftarrow (m =^{l_2} (x^\beta)e_2'))^{l_1} \in_{\mathsf{E}} E[s]$, then there exists a $(e_1 \Leftarrow (m =^{l_2} (x^\beta)e_2))^{l_1} \in_{\mathsf{E}} E[r]$ such that $\$(e_1, e_1')$ and $\$(e_2, e_2')$.*
4. *If $\langle m_i =^{l_i'} (b_i)e_i'\rangle_i^l \in_{\mathsf{E}} E[s]$ then either*
   (a) There exists $\langle m_i =^{l_i'} (b_i)e_i\rangle_i^l \in_{\mathsf{E}} E[r]$ such that $\$(e_i, e_i')$ for all i, or
   (b) $r \to s$ is an instance of (Red Upd) and $s = \langle m_i =^{l_i'} (b_i)e_i'\rangle_i^l$ and there exists $(\langle m_i =^{l_i} (x_i^{\beta_i})e_i\rangle_i^l \Leftarrow (m_j =^{l_2} (x^\beta)e))^l \in_{\mathsf{E}} E[r]$ such that for all i,

$$l_i' = l_i,\ b_i = x_i^{\beta_i},\ e_i' = e_i \quad \text{for } i \neq j$$
$$l_i' = l_2,\ b_i = x^\beta,\ e_i' = e \quad \text{for } i = j$$

Proof. By an analysis like the one for Lem. 4.5. The only additional case is that of an object constructed by (Red Upd). But in this case we know exactly what the redex must have looked like, and it is described in the last case of the lemma.

Lemma 5.3. *If r is a redex and s an expression such that $r \to s$, E is a reduction context, $\vdash E[r]$ wl, and e and e' are expressions such that $e \in_E E[r]$, $e' \in_E E[s]$, and $\$(e, e')$, then $[\![E[r]]\!] \vdash \Phi(\mathsf{lab}(e')) \sqsubseteq \Phi(\mathsf{lab}(e))$.*

Proof. By cases on the definition of $\$(e, e')$, as in the proof of Lem. 4.6.

Theorem 5.4. *If $e_X \to e_Y$, and $\vdash e_X$ wl, then $[\![e_X]\!] \vdash [\![e_Y]\!]$ and $[\![e_X]\!] \vdash \Phi(\mathsf{lab}(e_Y)) \sqsubseteq \Phi(\mathsf{lab}(e_X))$.*

Proof. From the constraints in $[\![E[r]]\!]$, we need to deduce each of the constraints in $[\![E[s]]\!]$, given by

$$
\begin{aligned}
[\![E[s]]\!] = &(\mathsf{ForEach}\ \langle m_i =^{l'_i} (x_i^{\beta_i}) e_i \rangle_i^l \in_E E[s] \ \triangleright\ \{l'_i\} \subseteq \Phi(l, m_i)) \\
&\cup (\mathsf{ForEach}\ (e_1.m)^l \in_E E[s], m =^{l'} (x^\beta) e_2 \in_E E[s] \\
&\quad \triangleright\ \{l'\} \subseteq \Phi(\mathsf{lab}(e_1), m) \Rightarrow \Phi(\mathsf{lab}(e_1)) \sqsubseteq \Phi(\beta), \\
&\qquad \{l'\} \subseteq \Phi(\mathsf{lab}(e_1), m) \Rightarrow \Phi(\mathsf{lab}(e_2)) \sqsubseteq \Phi(l)) \\
&\cup (\mathsf{ForEach}\ (e_1 \Leftarrow (m =^{l_1} (x^\beta) e'_1))^l \in_E E[s] \\
&\quad \triangleright\ (\forall n \neq m)(\Phi(\mathsf{lab}(e_1), n) \subseteq \Phi(l, n)), \\
&\qquad \{l_1\} \subseteq \Phi(l, m))
\end{aligned}
$$

First consider the case $(\mathsf{ForEach}\ \langle m_i =^{l'_i} (x_i^{\beta_i}) e_i \rangle_i^l \in_E E[s] \ \triangleright\ \{l'_i\} \subseteq \Phi(l, m_i))$. By Lem. 5.2, if $\langle m_i =^{l'_i} (b_i) e'_i \rangle_i^l \in_E E[s]$ then either

1. There exists $\langle m_i =^{l'_i} (b_i) e_i \rangle_i^l \in_E E[r]$ such that $\$(e_i, e'_i)$ for all i, or
2. $r \to s$ is an instance of (Red Upd) and $s = \langle m_i =^{l'_i} (b_i) e'_i \rangle_i^l$ and there exists $r = (\langle m_i =^{l_i} (x_i^{\beta_i}) e_i \rangle_i^{l_1} \Leftarrow (m_j =^{l_2} (x^\beta) e))^l \in_E E[r]$ such that for all i,

$$
\begin{aligned}
l'_i = l_i, \ b_i = x_i^{\beta_i}, \ e'_i = e_i \quad &\text{for } i \neq j \\
l'_i = l_2, \ b_i = x^\beta, \ e'_i = e \quad &\text{for } i = j
\end{aligned}
$$

In the first case, each of the formulas $\{l'_i\} \subseteq \Phi(l, m_i)$ is already in $[\![E[r]]\!]$. In the second case, since $E[r]$ contains the update term r, $[\![E[r]]\!]$ contains the formulas

$$
\begin{aligned}
\Phi(l_1, m_i) \subseteq \Phi(l, m_i) \quad &i \neq j \\
\{l_2\} \subseteq \Phi(l, m_j)
\end{aligned}
$$

which describe the possible methods in abstract object l. Since r contains an object term, $[\![E[r]]\!]$ also contains the formulas $\{l_i\} \subseteq \Phi(l_1, m_i)$ for each i.

We can now consider each of the formulas $\{l'_i\} \subseteq \Phi(l, m_i)$. For $i \neq j$, $[\![E[r]]\!] \vdash \{l_i\} \subseteq \Phi(l_1, m_i) \subseteq \Phi(l, m_i)$, and $l'_i = l_i$, so $[\![E[r]]\!] \vdash \{l'_i\} \subseteq \Phi(l, m_i)$, as desired. For $i = j$, $[\![E[r]]\!] \vdash \{l_2\} \subseteq \Phi(l, m_j)$, but $l'_i = l_2$ and $m_i = m_j$, so $[\![E[r]]\!] \vdash \{l'_i\} \subseteq \Phi(l, m_j)$ as desired.

For the remaining cases, we rely on Lem. 4.6, as in Thm. 4.7. The second half follows analogously to the second half of Thm. 4.7.

6   Conclusion and Further Work

We have introduced a novel proof technique for the correctness of constraint-based flow analyses, and used it to provide a complete proof for the central theorem of [9]. By matching the structure of the proof to the flat structure of the analysis, we have not only clarified the overall flow of the proof, but we have also exposed the crucial effects of reduction on the subterms of the expression under analysis. Furthermore, by structuring the case analysis of the proof around reduction contexts and redices instead of around the reductions of whole expressions, we have simplified the necessary steps of the proof. Finally, we have demonstrated our technique's extensibility by applying it to an analysis for a larger language.

We intend to investigate how well our proof technique will scale up to analyses of larger, more realistic languages. In particular, we would like to know how well it handles analyses that do not take the whole program into account. A related investigation is to consider coinductive analyses like [8], in which not all expressions are analyzed.

References

[1] M. Abadi and L. Cardelli. A theory of primitive objects: Untyped and first-order systems. *Information and Computation*, 125(2):78–102, Mar. 1996.

[2] A. Aiken and N. Heintze. Constraint-based program analysis. In *POPL'95 Tutorial*, January 1995.

[3] P. D. Blasio, K. Fisher, and C. Talcott. Analysis for concurrent objects. In H. Bowman and J. Derrick, editors, *Proc. 2nd IFIP Workshop on Formal Methods for Open Object-Based Distributed Systems (FMOODS)*, pages 73–88, Canterbury, UK, July 1997. Chapman and Hall, London.

[4] C. Bodei, P. Degano, F. Nielson, and H. R. Nielson. Control flow analysis for the π-calculus. In *Proceedings of CONCUR'98*, pages 611–638, Berlin, Heidelberg, and New York, 1998. Springer-Verlag.

[5] W. S. Brainerd. Tree generating regular systems. *Information and Control*, 14(2):217–231, 1969.

[6] C. Flanagan and M. Felleisen. Set-based analysis for full scheme and its use in soft-typing. Technical Report COMP TR95-253, Department of Computer Science, Rice University, Oct. 1995.

[7] J. C. Mitchell. *Foundations for Programming Languages*. MIT Press, Cambridge, MA, 1996.

[8] F. Nielson and H. R. Nielson. Infinitary control flow analysis: a collecting semantics for closure analysis. In *Proceedings 24th Annual ACM Symposium on Principles of Programming Languages*, pages 332–345. ACM, Jan. 1997.

[9] J. Palsberg. Closure analysis in constraint form. *ACM Transactions on Programming Languages and Systems*, 17(1):47–62, January 1995.

[10] P. Sestoft. Replacing function parameters by global variables. Master's thesis, DIKU, University of Copenhagen, Copenhagen, 1989.

[11] P. Sestoft. *Analysis and efficient implementation of functional programs*. PhD thesis, DIKU, University of Copenhagen, Copenhagen, 1991.

[12] O. Shivers. *Control-Flow Analysis of Higher-Order Languages*. PhD thesis, Carnegie-Mellon University, May 1991.

A Prototype Dependency Calculus

Peter Thiemann

Universität Freiburg
thiemann@informatik.uni-freiburg.de

Abstract. Dependency has been identified as the main ingredient underlying many program analyses, in particular flow analysis, secrecy and integrity analysis, and binding-time analysis. Driven by that insight, Abadi, Banerjee, Heintze, and Riecke [1] have defined a dependency core calculus (DCC). DCC serves as a common target language for defining the above analyses by translation *to* DCC.

The present work considers the opposite direction. We define a Prototype Dependency Calculus (PDC) and define flow analysis, secrecy analysis, and region analysis by translation *from* PDC.

1 Introduction

Dependency plays a major role in program analysis. There are two broad kinds of dependency, value dependency and control dependency. A value dependency from v to v' states that value v' is constructed from v, so that there is a direct influence of v on v'. A typical value dependency arises from the use of a primitive operation, $v' = p(v)$, or from just passing the value as a parameter. A control dependency from v to v' describes an indirect influence where v controls the construction of v'. A typical example of a control dependency is "$v' = $ if v then ...". Although v does not contribute to v', it still controls the computation of v'.

Many program analysis questions are derived from dependency information. A flow analysis answers questions like: which program points may have contributed to the construction of a value? Hence, a flow analysis is only interested in value dependencies. A region analysis answers similar questions, but instead of yielding answers in terms of program points, the analysis computes regions, which we regard as abstractions of sets of program points. Other analyses, like secrecy and binding-time analyses, also need to consider control dependencies. Here, the typical question is: if a particular value changes, which other values may also change?

The dependency core calculus DCC [1] is an attempt to unify a number of calculi that rely on dependency information. DCC builds on Moggi's computational metalanguage [10]. It formalizes the notion of dependency using a set of monads T_ℓ, indexed by the elements of a lattice. The idea is that each element ℓ of the lattice stands for a certain level of dependency and that computations up to that level must occur in monad T_ℓ (an ℓ-computation). In particular, the bind-operator of DCC guarantees that the outcome of an ℓ-computation can be constructed only from the results of ℓ'-computations, where $\ell' \sqsubseteq \ell$ in the lattice.

D. Le Métayer (Ed.): ESOP 2002, LNCS 2305, pp. 228–242, 2002.

DCC has a denotational semantics and there are translations *from* various calculi — a two-level lambda calculus (binding-time analysis), SLam (secrecy analysis), a flow-type system (flow analysis) — into DCC. Each translation instantiates L to a suitable lattice — {*static, dynamic*}, {*low-security, high-security*}, powerset of the set of program points — and uses a variant of the monadic translation.

This beautiful approach has a number of drawbacks:

- There is no direct link from DCC to the region calculus [20]. The DCC authors [4] have made a separate effort to build a DCC-style denotational model for it.

  However, the region calculus is an important program analysis which relies on dependecy information to reason about memory allocation and memory reuse.
- DCC does not have a notion of polymorphism and it does not seem easy to extend it in this way. In particular, while a fixed number of regions can be tackled with a fixed lattice of dependency levels (viz. the flow-type system), an extension to region polymorphism does not seem to be possible.

  An extension to polymorphism is possible in the denotational model of the region calculus due to Banerjee et al [4]. But, as the authors point out in the conclusion, it is not clear how to unify this model with their work on DCC.

The present work approaches the problems from the other side. Instead of giving a target calculus that can be used as a common meta-language, we start from a prototypical calculus that collects all sensible dependency information. Instantiating this calculus to a particular analysis means to chop away part of the information that it provides. The appeal of this approach is that

- it can provide a common framework for a range of analyses: analyses can be factored through PDC and exploit PDC's minimal typing property for implementing the analyses;
- it scales easily to polymorphism;
- it can be mapped to all the problems that have been translated to DCC;
- it can be mapped to region calculus;
- a non-interference result for the PDC would give rise to corresponding properties for all analyses that are images of PDC;
- it uncovers an interesting connection between region calculus, dependency analysis, and flow analysis.

The main novelty of PDC is the modeling of dependency information as a graphical effect. That is, the effect of evaluating an expression e is a relation that approximates the data and control flow during the evaluation. The mappings from PDC to other calculi are abstraction mappings that cut away excess information.

There are also drawbacks in this approach. In particular, the evaluation strategy (call-by-value) is built into the calculus and some proofs need to be redone when changing the strategy. DCC avoids this by being based on the computational metalanguage. However, for a call-by-value language, the DCC authors recommend a modified vDCC calculus that has a slightly different model for non-interference. It is hard to argue for the completeness of PDC. It might be that we missed an important kind of dependency in the construction. We cannot be certain until we encounter an analysis, which is not an image of PDC.

Related Work The present work draws heavily on the large body of work on type-based program analysis. We cannot aim for completeness here, for a good overview see the recent survey paper by Palsberg in the PASTE'01 workshop. Particularly influencing are the works on region calculus [20], on effect systems [13, 14, 17], on flow analysis [19], on secrecy and security analysis [8, 16, 21, 22], on binding-time analysis [3, 5, 6, 9, 12].

The only unifying efforts that we are aware of are the works of Abadi, Banerjee, Heintze, and Riecke [1, 4] that we discussed above.

Abadi et al [2] have defined a labeled lambda calculus which enables tracking of dependencies. From the labels present in a normalized expression they compute a pattern that matches lambda expressions with the same normal form. A cache maps these patterns to their respective normal forms. While their labeled expressions only represent the final results, our graphical approach can provide information about intermediate results, too.

Contributions We introduce the PDC and give its static and dynamic semantics. Next, we prove standard properties about its type system, culminating in a minimal typing result. We prove the soundness of the static semantics with respect to an instrumented big-step operational semantics. We define type preserving translations from PDC to the region calculus, to a particular flow analysis, and to SLam (a calculus of secrecy)[1]. Our translations shed some light on the relation between flow analysis and region analysis: a flow analysis is concerned with program points while a region analysis is concerned with portions of memory. In our setting, a region is an abstraction for a set of program points (which shares a common pool of memory to store its results).

2   The Calculus PDC

In this section, we fix the syntax of PDC, define its static semantics, and give an instrumented dynamic (big-step operational) semantics. Finally, we prove type preservation with respect to the static semantics.

2.1   Syntax

An expression, *Expr*, is a variable, a recursive function, a function application, a let-expression, a base-type constant, a primitive operation, or a conditional.

Similar to labeled expressions in flow analysis, all expressions carry a source label, $s \in Source$. Contrary to labels in flow analysis, these source labels need

---

[1] This is found in an extended version of the paper.

$$Expr \ni e \quad ::= x^s \mid \mathbf{rec}^s \ f(x) \ e \mid e@^s e \mid \mathbf{let}^s \ x = e \ \mathbf{in} \ e \mid$$
$$\qquad\qquad c^s \mid \mathbf{op}^s(e) \mid \mathbf{if}^s \ e \ e \ e$$
$$\quad s \quad \in Source$$
$$AType \ni \phi \quad ::= (\tau, s)$$
$$Type \ni \tau \quad ::= \alpha \mid \mathbf{B} \mid \phi \xrightarrow{\ \epsilon\ } \phi$$
$$\quad \epsilon \quad \in Effect = \mathbf{P}(Source \times Source \times Indicator)$$
$$\quad \iota \quad \in Indicator = \{V, W, C\} \qquad where \qquad V \sqsubset W \ and \ W \sqsubset C$$
$$TE \ \in \ Variable \xrightarrow{\ fin\ } AType$$

Fig. 1. Syntax of PDC

not be unique. In fact, they should be looked upon as variables that may be substituted later on.

We shall not define explicitly the underlying expressions of an applied lambda calculus. Rather, we define them intuitively through an erasure mapping $|\cdot|$, where $|e|$ is an expression with the same structure as e, but all source annotations removed.

An annotated type, ϕ, is a pair (τ, s) where τ is a type and s is a source annotation. A type can be a type variable, a base type, or a function type. The function arrow is decorated with a source annotation and an effect ϵ. An effect is a labeled graph where the edges are *atomic* dependencies.

An atomic dependency is either a value dependency (s, s', V) (written as $(s, s')_V$), a control dependency (s, s', C) (written as $(s, s')_C$), or a weak control dependency (s, s', W) (written as $(s, s')_W$). A control dependency is weak, if it does not lead to the construction or examination of a value. If we do not care about the kind of dependency, we write (s, s'). Dependency indicators are totally ordered by $V \sqsubset W$ and $W \sqsubset C$. An effect always stands for the least reflexive and transitive relation generated by its atomic dependencies, as formalized by the judgement $(s, s, \iota) \in \epsilon$:

$$(e\text{-}atom)\frac{(s, s', \iota) \in \epsilon}{(s, s', \iota) \in \epsilon} \qquad (e\text{-}refl) \ (s, s, \iota) \in \epsilon$$

$$(e\text{-}trans)\frac{(s_1, s_2, \iota_1) \in \epsilon \quad (s_2, s_3, \iota_2) \in \epsilon}{(s_1, s_3, \iota_1 \sqcup \iota_2) \in \epsilon}$$

That is, if there is a single control dependency on the path from s to s', then there is a control dependency $(s, s')_C$. If all atomic steps on the path from s to s' are value dependencies, then there is a value dependency $(s, s')_V$.

For comparison with the simply-typed lambda calculus, we define:

$$BType \ni \zeta \quad ::= \alpha \mid \mathbf{B} \mid \zeta \to \zeta$$
$$BTE \ \in \ Variable \xrightarrow{\ fin\ } BType$$

$$(var)\frac{TE(x) = (\tau, s'')}{TE, s \vdash x^{s'} : (\tau, s') \, ! \, \{(s, s')_W, (s'', s')_V\}}$$

$$(rec)\frac{TE[f \mapsto (\phi' \xrightarrow{\epsilon} \phi, s'), x \mapsto \phi'], s' \vdash e : \phi \, ! \, \epsilon}{TE, s \vdash \mathbf{rec}^{s'} \, f(x) \, e : (\phi' \xrightarrow{\epsilon} \phi, s') \, ! \, \{(s, s')_C\}}$$

$$(app)\frac{TE, s \vdash e_1 : (\phi' \xrightarrow{\epsilon} \phi, s'') \, ! \, \epsilon_1 \qquad TE, s \vdash e_2 : \phi' \, ! \, \epsilon_2}{TE, s \vdash e_1 @^{s'} e_2 : \phi \, ! \, \epsilon_1 \cup \epsilon_2 \cup \epsilon \cup \{(s, s'')_C\}} \qquad \phi = (\tau, s')$$

$$(let)\frac{TE, s \vdash e_1 : \phi_1 \, ! \, \epsilon_1 \qquad TE[x : \phi_1], s \vdash e_2 : \phi_2 \, ! \, \epsilon_2}{TE, s \vdash \mathbf{let}^{s'} \, x = e_1 \text{ in } e_2 : \phi_2 \, ! \, \epsilon_1 \cup \epsilon_2} \qquad \phi_2 = (\tau, s')$$

$$(const)\frac{}{TE, s \vdash c^{s'} : (B, s') \, ! \, \{(s, s')_C\}}$$

$$(op)\frac{TE, s \vdash e : (B, s'') \, ! \, \epsilon}{TE, s \vdash \mathbf{op}^{s'}(e) : (B, s') \, ! \, \epsilon \cup \{(s'', s')_C\}}$$

$$(if)\frac{TE, s \vdash e_1 : (B, s'') \, ! \, \epsilon_1 \qquad TE, s'' \vdash e_2 : \phi \, ! \, \epsilon_2 \qquad TE, s'' \vdash e_3 : \phi \, ! \, \epsilon_3}{TE, s \vdash \mathbf{if}^{s'} \, e_1 \, e_2 \, e_3 : \phi \, ! \, \epsilon_1 \cup \epsilon_2 \cup \epsilon_3} \qquad \phi = (\tau, s')$$

Fig. 2. Static Semantics of PDC

The set $BType$ is exactly the set of types for a simply-typed lambda calculus. BTE ranges over type environments for this calculus, wheras TE ranges over annotated type environments for PDC.

We extend the erasure function to types. Type erasure $|\cdot| : AType \rightarrow BType$ maps an annotated type to a bare type ($BType$) by $|(\alpha, s)| = \alpha$, $|(\mathbf{B}, s)| = \mathbf{B}$, and $|(\phi' \xrightarrow{\epsilon} \phi'', s')| = |\phi'| \rightarrow |\phi''|$. Technically, we should be using two different sets of type variables, one ranging over $Type$ and the other ranging over $BType$, but context will ensure that no ambiguities arise.

Despite the presence of type variables in the type language, there is no polymorphism. The sole purpose of the type variables is to provide a principal typing property to the type system.

2.2 Static Semantics

The static semantics defines the typing judgement $TE, s \vdash e : \phi \, ! \, \epsilon$ in Fig. 2 in the style of a type and effect system. The type environment TE binds variables to annotated types. The source label s on the left side of the turnstile denotes the source label of the program location that causes e to evaluate, in the sense of a control dependency. For example, the condition expression in a conditional causes one of the "then" or "else" expressions to evaluate. Hence (viz. rule (if)), its source label drives the evaluation of the branches. The annotated type $\phi = (\tau, s)$

consists of the real type τ and the source label of the last expression that either created the value of e or passed it on. As mentioned before, the effect ϵ is just a labeled relation, which stands for its least reflexive, transitive closure. It expresses the relation between the values in the environment, the sources labels in e, and the value computed by e.

The rule (*var*) gives rise to one weak control dependency and one value dependency. The value dependency arises due to "copying" the value from the environment (with source s'') to the result area of the expression (with source s'). The control dependency arises from the source s to the left of the turnstile. No parts of the value are examined or constructed, so it is only a weak control dependency.

The rule (*rec*) produces just one control dependency: the allocation of the closure is caused by s. But it also provides the explanation for the pair s'', ϵ on the function arrow. When applying the function, s'' will be the cause for applying the function, *i.e.*, the source of the application context. The effect ϵ is the dependency relation that the function promises to construct. Otherwise, the rule is just the usual rule for a recursive function.

In the function application rule (*app*), the source s is the cause for evaluating e_1, e_2, and also the body of the closure that is computed by e_1. The latter control dependency is created by the atomic dependency $(s, s'')_C$. There is an additional control dependency from the creation of the closure s''' and the result of the whole expression s'. As usual, the application of a function causes the release of its latent effect (the dependency relation ϵ). The relations resulting from the subexpressions are unioned together (and closed under reflexivity and transitivity).

The let expression has no surprises (*let*). However, it is important to see that the evaluation of e_1 can be independent of the evaluation of e_2 if the variable x does not appear in e_1.

The allocation of a constant (*const*) is caused by the context s, so there is a control dependency.

A primitive operation, shown in rule (*op*), is quite similar. The result of the operation is not part of the argument, but still it depends on the input value. Hence, it gives rise to a control dependency and collects the dependency relation from the subexpression.

A conditional expression (*if*) evaluates the condition in the outer context s. The result lives at source s'' and *it* causes the evaluation of either e_1 or e_2.

2.3   Subtyping

The most important bit to understand about this section is that the static semantics is not meant to be prescriptive, in the sense that it limits the applicability of a function. On the contrary, the idea is that every simply-typed program can be completed to a PDC expression (by adding source annotations), which is type correct. In order to obtain this descriptive property, we introduce a notion of subtyping which only works at the level of annotations. This is a typical step in program analysis [6].

First, we define the notion of an effect subset, $\epsilon_1 \sqsubseteq \epsilon_2 \, ! \, \epsilon$. It means that in the presence of ϵ, ϵ_1 is a subeffect of ϵ_2.

$$\emptyset \sqsubseteq \epsilon_2 \, ! \, \emptyset \qquad \qquad \frac{\epsilon_1' \sqsubseteq \epsilon_2 \, ! \, \epsilon' \qquad \epsilon_1'' \sqsubseteq \epsilon_2 \, ! \, \epsilon''}{(\epsilon_1' \cup \epsilon_2') \sqsubseteq \epsilon_2 \, ! \, (\epsilon' \cup \epsilon'')}$$

$$\frac{(s, s', \iota) \in \epsilon_2}{\{(s, s', \iota)\} \sqsubseteq \epsilon_2 \, ! \, \emptyset} \qquad \qquad \frac{(s, s', \iota) \notin \epsilon_2}{\{(s, s', \iota)\} \sqsubseteq \epsilon_2 \, ! \, \{(s, s', \iota)\}}$$

The subtyping judgement is $\vdash \phi \leq \phi \, ! \, \epsilon$ with the usual typing rule for subsumption, which includes subeffecting, too:

$$(sub)\frac{TE, s \vdash e : \phi \, ! \, \epsilon \qquad \vdash \phi \leq \phi' \, ! \, \epsilon' \qquad \epsilon \cup \epsilon' \subseteq \epsilon''}{TE, s \vdash e : \phi' \, ! \, \epsilon''}$$

Subtyping is more complicated than usual because it adds to the dependency effect. Subtyping only introduces value dependencies because it only "connects" different source annotations.

$$(sub\text{-}base)\frac{}{\vdash (\mathbf{B}, s) \leq (\mathbf{B}, s') \, ! \, \{(s, s')_V\}}$$

$$(sub\text{-}fun)\frac{\vdash \phi_2 \leq \phi_1 \, ! \, \epsilon \qquad \vdash \phi_1' \leq \phi_2' \, ! \, \epsilon' \qquad \epsilon_1 \sqsubseteq \epsilon_2 \, ! \, \epsilon''}{\vdash (\phi_1 \xrightarrow{\epsilon_1} \phi_1', s_1) \leq (\phi_2 \xrightarrow{\epsilon_2} \phi_2', s_2) \, ! \, \epsilon \cup \epsilon' \cup \epsilon'' \cup \{(s_1, s_2)_V\}}$$

The best reading of a subtyping judgement $\vdash \phi \leq \phi' \, ! \, \epsilon$ is in terms of the subsumption rule, $i.e.$, as a conversion of a value of type ϕ to the expected type ϕ'. The effect ϵ of the subtyping judgement registers the dependencies established by the conversion. In this reading, the rule ($sub\text{-}base$) is obvious. The rule ($sub\text{-}fun$) has the usual contravariant behavior in the argument part and covariant behavior in the result part and in all other components.

2.4   Basic Properties

The static semantics of PDC is closely tied to the simply-typed lambda calculus. Each expression of the simply-typed lambda calculus can be completed to a typable PDC expression and, vice versa, the erasure of a PDC expression yields a simply-typed lambda expression.

Lemma 1 (Erasure). If $TE, s \vdash e : \phi \, ! \, \epsilon$ then $|TE| \vdash_{st} |e| : |\phi|$ in the system of simple types.

Lemma 2 (Type Extension). If $|\phi| = |\phi'|$, then there exists a smallest ϵ so that $\vdash \phi \leq \phi' \, ! \, \epsilon$.

Proof. Case **B**: In this case, $\phi = (\mathbf{B}, s)$ and $\phi' = (\mathbf{B}, s')$. Clearly, $\vdash (\mathbf{B}, s) \leq (\mathbf{B}, s') \, ! \, \{(s, s')_V\}$, by definition of $\leq$.

Case $\rightarrow$: In this case, $\phi = (\phi_{1a} \xrightarrow{\epsilon_f} \phi_{1r}, s)$ and $\phi' = (\phi'_{1a} \xrightarrow{\epsilon'_f} \phi'_{1r}, s')$. Furthermore, $|\phi_{1a}| = |\phi'_{1a}|$ as well as $|\phi_{1r}| = |\phi'_{1r}|$. By induction, there exist ϵ_a and ϵ_r so that $\vdash \phi'_{1a} \leq \phi_{1a} ! \epsilon_a$ and $\vdash \phi_{1r} \leq \phi'_{1r} ! \epsilon_r$. Furthermore, define ϵ' by $\epsilon_f \sqsubseteq \epsilon'_f ! \epsilon'$. Setting $\epsilon = \epsilon_a \cup \epsilon_r \cup \epsilon' \cup \{(s, s')_V\}$, we obtain that $\vdash \phi \leq \phi' ! \epsilon$, as claimed.

Lemma 3 (Completion). *If $BTE \vdash_{st} e_0 : \zeta$ then for all s and TE where $|TE| = BTE$ there exist e, ϕ, and ϵ such that $|e| = e_0$, $|\phi| = \zeta$, and $TE, s \vdash e : \phi ! \epsilon$.*

Furthermore, for each ϕ' and ϵ' so that $TE, s \vdash e : \phi' ! \epsilon'$ and $|\phi'| = \zeta$ it holds that $\vdash \phi \leq \phi' ! \epsilon''$ and $\epsilon \cup \epsilon'' \subseteq \epsilon'$.

Lemma 4 (Minimal Type). *Suppose that $BTE \vdash_{st} e_0 : \zeta$ is a principal typing for e in the system of simple types. Then there exist TE, s, e, ϕ, and ϵ with $|TE| = BTE$, $|e| = e_0$, $|\phi| = \zeta$ and $TE, s \vdash e : \phi ! \epsilon$, so that, for all TE', ϕ', e', and ϵ' with $|TE'| = BTE$, $|e'| = e_0$, $|\phi'| = \zeta$ and $TE', s \vdash e' : \phi' ! \epsilon'$, it holds that $\vdash \phi \leq \phi' ! \epsilon''$ and $\epsilon \subseteq \epsilon'$ and $\epsilon'' \subseteq \epsilon'$.*

Finally, a technical result that shows that the value of an expression depends on its control dependency. For this result, we need an assumption about the types in the environment, which is captured by the following definition:

An annotated type is *well-formed* if the judgement ϕ wft is derivable using the rules

$$(\alpha, s) \text{ wft} \qquad (\mathbf{B}, s) \text{ wft} \qquad \frac{\phi' \text{ wft} \quad \phi \text{ wft} \quad (s', s) \in \epsilon \quad \phi = (\tau, s)}{(\phi' \xrightarrow{\epsilon} \phi, s') \text{ wft}}$$

If $TE = \{x_1 : \phi_1, \ldots, x_n : \phi_n\}$ then TE wft holds if ϕ_i wft, for all $1 \leq i \leq n$.

Lemma 5 (Output Types). *Suppose that $TE, s \vdash e : (\tau, s') ! \epsilon$ where TE wft. Then $(s, s') \in \epsilon$.*

2.5 Dynamic Semantics

The dynamic semantics of PDC is defined using a big-step operational semantics. The judgement $VE, s \vdash e \Downarrow r$ states that with variable bindings VE and current "cause for the evaluation" s, the expression e evaluates to a return value r, where r is either a value paired with a dependency graph or an error ERR. Values, v, are either base-type constants or closures. Each value is tagged with a source annotation, s, that describes where the value has been created or passed through. The dependency graph tracks the actual dependencies that have occured during computation. Here is the formal definition of return values:

$$v ::= c \mid (VE, \lambda x . e)$$
$$w ::= v^s$$
$$r ::= w, \epsilon \mid ERR$$

$$(ev\text{-}var)\frac{VE(x) = v^{s''}}{VE, s \vdash x^{s'} \Downarrow v^{s'}, \{(s,s')_W, (s'',s')_V\}}$$

$$(ev\text{-}rec)\frac{}{VE, s \vdash \mathbf{rec}^{s'} \ f(x) \ e \Downarrow (VE \downarrow fv(\mathbf{rec}^{s'} \ f(x) \ e), \mathbf{rec} \ f(x) \ e)^{s'}, \{(s,s')_C\}}$$

$$(ev\text{-}app)\frac{\begin{array}{c} VE, s \vdash e_1 \Downarrow (VE', \mathbf{rec} \ f(x) \ e)^{s''}, \epsilon_1 \\ VE, s \vdash e_2 \Downarrow w_2, \epsilon_2 \\ VE'[f \mapsto (VE', \mathbf{rec} \ f(x) \ e)^{s''}, x \mapsto w_2], s'' \vdash e \Downarrow v^{s'''}, \epsilon \end{array}}{VE, s \vdash e_1 @^{s'} e_2 \Downarrow v^{s'}, \epsilon_1 \cup \epsilon_2 \cup \epsilon \cup \{(s,s'')_C\}}$$

$$(ev\text{-}let)\frac{VE, s \vdash e_1 \Downarrow w_1, \epsilon_1 \qquad VE[x \mapsto w_1], s \vdash e_2 \Downarrow v^{s'''}, \epsilon_2}{VE, s \vdash \mathbf{let}^{s'} \ x = e_1 \ \mathbf{in} \ e_2 \Downarrow v^{s'}, \epsilon_1 \cup \epsilon_2}$$

$$(ev\text{-}const)\frac{}{VE, s \vdash c^{s'} \Downarrow c^{s'}, \{(s,s')_C\}}$$

$$(ev\text{-}op)\frac{VE, s \vdash e \Downarrow c^{s''}, \epsilon}{VE, s \vdash \mathbf{op}^{s'}(e) \Downarrow (\mathbf{op}(c))^{s'}, \epsilon \cup \{(s'',s')_C\}}$$

$$(ev\text{-}if\text{-}true)\frac{VE, s \vdash e_1 \Downarrow c^{s''}, \epsilon_1 \quad c \neq \mathbf{false} \qquad VE, s'' \vdash e_2 \Downarrow v^{s'''}, \epsilon_2}{VE, s \vdash \mathbf{if}^{s'} \ e_1 \ e_2 \ e_3 \Downarrow v^{s'}, \epsilon_1 \cup \epsilon_2}$$

$$(ev\text{-}if\text{-}false)\frac{VE, s \vdash e_1 \Downarrow \mathbf{false}^{s''}, \epsilon_1 \qquad VE, s'' \vdash e_3 \Downarrow v^{s'''}, \epsilon_3}{VE, s \vdash \mathbf{if}^{s'} \ e_1 \ e_2 \ e_3 \Downarrow v^{s'}, \epsilon_1 \cup \epsilon_3}$$

Fig. 3. Dynamic Semantics

Figure 3 defines the inference rules for the judgement $VE, s \vdash e \Downarrow r$. Figure 4 shows an excerpt of the error transitions, namely those for the rule (*ev-app*). There are two more for (*ev-let*), two for (*ev-op*), and three for (*ev-if-true*) as well as for (*ev-if-false*). They are constructed in the usual way, so that evaluation propagates errors strictly.

2.6   Type Preservation

To establish a connection between the static semantics and the dynamic semantics, we define a typing relation for values $\vdash_v w : \phi$ and value environments as follows:

$$\vdash_v c^s : (\mathbf{B}, s)$$

$$\frac{\vdash_v VE : TE \qquad TE[f : (\phi' \xrightarrow{\epsilon} \phi, s), x : \phi'], s \vdash e : \phi \ ! \ \epsilon}{\vdash_v (VE, \mathbf{rec} \ f(x) \ e)^s : (\phi' \xrightarrow{\epsilon} \phi, s)}$$

$$\frac{\vdash_v w_i : \phi_i}{\vdash_v \{x_i : w_i\} : \{x_i : \phi_i\}}$$

$$(ev\text{-}app\text{-}err1)\frac{VE, s \vdash e_1 \Downarrow c^{s''}, \epsilon_1}{VE, s \vdash e_1 @^{s'} e_2 \Downarrow ERR}$$

$$(ev\text{-}app\text{-}err2)\frac{VE, s \vdash e_1 \Downarrow ERR}{VE, s \vdash e_1 @^{s'} e_2 \Downarrow ERR}$$

$$(ev\text{-}app\text{-}err3)\frac{VE, s \vdash e_1 \Downarrow (VE', s'', \mathbf{rec}\ f(x)\ e)^{s'''}, \epsilon_1 \qquad VE, s \vdash e_2 \Downarrow ERR}{VE, s \vdash e_1 @^{s'} e_2 \Downarrow ERR}$$

$$(ev\text{-}app\text{-}err4)\frac{\begin{array}{c}VE, s \vdash e_1 \Downarrow (VE', s'', \mathbf{rec}\ f(x)\ e)^{s'''}, \epsilon_1 \\ VE, s \vdash e_2 \Downarrow w_2, \epsilon_2 \\ VE'[x \mapsto w_2], s'' \vdash e \Downarrow ERR\end{array}}{VE, s \vdash e_1 @^{s'} e_2 \Downarrow ERR}$$

Fig. 4. Error Transitions (Excerpt)

This enables us to prove the following by induction on the derivation of the evaluation judgement.

Lemma 6 (Type Preservation). *If* $TE, s \vdash e : \phi\ !\ \epsilon$ *and* $VE, s \vdash e \Downarrow w, \epsilon'$ *and* $\vdash_v VE : TE$ *then* $\vdash_v w : \phi$ *and* $\epsilon' \subseteq \epsilon$.

3   Translations

In this section, we demonstrate that the region calculus and a calculus for flow analysis are both images of PDC.

3.1   Region Calculus

We consider a simply-typed variant of the region calculus without region polymorphism and without the letregion construct. Polymorphism is out of the scope of the present work.

Figure 5 summarizes syntax and static semantics of the region calculus, where we take *Region* as a set of region variables. To simplify the translation, we have made subeffecting into a separate rule, rather than including it in the rule for functions (as in [20]).

Suppose now that we are given a derivation for the PDC judgement $TE, s \vdash e : \phi\ !\ \epsilon$. From this we construct a derivation for a corresponding judgement in the region calculus in two steps. In the first step, we extract an equivalence relation on source annotations from the PDC derivation. The equivalence classes of this relation serve as our region variables. In the second step, we translate a PDC expressions to an expression of the region calculus and map the type derivation accordingly. The main step here is the mapping from source annotations to their equivalence classes.

$$\rho \in Region$$
$$e_r ::= x \mid \textbf{rec } f(x)\, e_r \textbf{ at } \rho \mid e_r @ e_r \mid \textbf{let } x = e_r \textbf{ in } e_r \mid$$
$$c \textbf{ at } \rho \mid op(e_r) \textbf{ at } \rho \mid \textbf{if } e_r\, e_r\, e_r$$

$$\phi ::= (\theta, \rho)$$
$$\theta ::= \alpha \mid \mathbf{B} \mid \phi \xrightarrow{\ \varepsilon\ } \phi$$
$$\varepsilon \subseteq Region$$

$$(r\text{-}var)\frac{RTE(x) = \phi}{RTE \vdash_r x : \phi \,!\, \emptyset}$$

$$(r\text{-}rec)\frac{RTE[f \mapsto (\phi' \xrightarrow{\ \varepsilon\ } \phi, \rho'), x \mapsto \phi'] \vdash_r e : \phi \,!\, \varepsilon}{RTE \vdash_r \textbf{rec } f(x)\, e \textbf{ at } \rho' : (\phi' \xrightarrow{\ \varepsilon\ } \phi, \rho') \,!\, \{\rho\}}$$

$$(r\text{-}app)\frac{RTE \vdash_r e_1 : (\phi' \xrightarrow{\ \varepsilon\ } \phi, \rho) \,!\, \varepsilon_1 \qquad RTE \vdash_r e_2 : \phi' \,!\, \varepsilon_2}{RTE \vdash_r e_1 @ e_2 : \phi \,!\, \varepsilon_1 \cup \varepsilon_2 \cup \varepsilon \cup \{\rho\}}$$

$$(r\text{-}let)\frac{RTE \vdash_r e_1 : \phi_1 \,!\, \varepsilon_1 \qquad RTE[x : \phi_1] \vdash_r e_2 : \phi_2 \,!\, \varepsilon_2}{RTE \vdash_r \textbf{let } x = e_1 \textbf{ in } e_2 : \phi_2 \,!\, \varepsilon_1 \cup \varepsilon_2}$$

$$(r\text{-}const)\frac{}{RTE \vdash_r c \textbf{ at } \rho' : (B, \rho') \,!\, \{\rho'\}}$$

$$(r\text{-}op)\frac{RTE \vdash_r e : (B, \rho'') \,!\, \varepsilon}{RTE \vdash_r op(e) \textbf{ at } \rho' : (B, \rho') \,!\, \varepsilon \cup \{\rho'', \rho'\}}$$

$$(r\text{-}if)\frac{RTE \vdash_r e_1 : (B, \rho'') \,!\, \varepsilon_1 \qquad RTE \vdash_r e_2 : \phi \,!\, \varepsilon_2 \qquad RTE \vdash_r e_3 : \phi \,!\, \varepsilon_3}{RTE \vdash_r \textbf{if } e_1\, e_2\, e_3 : \phi \,!\, \varepsilon_1 \cup \varepsilon_2 \cup \varepsilon_3}$$

$$(r\text{-}subeff)\frac{RTE \vdash_r e : \phi \,!\, \varepsilon \quad \varepsilon \subseteq \varepsilon'}{RTE \vdash_r e : \phi \,!\, \varepsilon'}$$

Fig. 5. Syntax and Static Semantics of the Region Calculus

For the first step, the computation of the equivalence relation, the function α extracts a set of pairs from effects, annotated types, and type environments. The most important part is that *control dependencies are ignored by* α.

$$
\begin{aligned}
\alpha(\emptyset) &= \emptyset \\
\alpha(\epsilon \cup \epsilon') &= \alpha(\epsilon) \cup \alpha(\epsilon') \\
\alpha((s, s')_V) &= \{(s, s')\} \\
\alpha((s, s')_W) &= \emptyset \\
\alpha((s, s')_C) &= \emptyset \\[4pt]
\alpha(\mathbf{B}, s) &= \emptyset \\
\alpha(\phi' \xrightarrow{\ \epsilon\ } \phi, s) &= \alpha(\phi') \cup \alpha(\phi) \cup \alpha(\epsilon) \\[4pt]
\alpha([x_1 : \phi_1, \ldots]) &= \alpha(\phi_1) \cup \ldots
\end{aligned}
$$

The *extract* of a type derivation is the union of the results of applying α to each occurrence of a type environment, an annotated type, and an effect in every step of the derivation (we sidestep the formal definition, which should be obvious). Then, we define the relation $\equiv \subseteq Source \times Source$ as the smallest equivalence relation containing the extract. We denote the equivalence classes of $\equiv$ by $[s]_\equiv$ or just $[s]$.

In the second step, we translate the parts of an RC type derivation using the function $\beta_\equiv$. For expressions it is defined as follows.

$$
\begin{aligned}
\beta_\equiv(x^s) &= x \\
\beta_\equiv(\mathtt{rec}^s\ f(x)\,e) &= \mathtt{rec}\ f(x)\,\beta_\equiv(e)\ \mathtt{at}\ [s]_\equiv \\
\beta_\equiv(e_1 @^s e_2) &= \beta_\equiv(e_1) @ \beta_\equiv(e_2) \\
\beta_\equiv(\mathtt{let}^s\ x = e_1\ \mathtt{in}\ e_2) &= \mathtt{let}\ x = \beta_\equiv(e_1)\ \mathtt{in}\ \beta_\equiv(e_2) \\
\beta_\equiv(c^s) &= c\ \mathtt{at}\ [s]_\equiv \\
\beta_\equiv(\mathtt{op}^s(e)) &= \mathtt{op}(e)\ \mathtt{at}\ [s]_\equiv \\
\beta_\equiv(\mathtt{if}^s\ e_1\ e_2\ e_3) &= \mathtt{if}\ \beta_\equiv(e_1)\ \beta_\equiv(e_2)\ \beta_\equiv(e_3)
\end{aligned}
$$

For types and effects, it is defined by

$$
\begin{aligned}
\beta_\equiv(\mathbf{B}, s) &= (\mathbf{B}, [s]_\equiv) \\
\beta_\equiv(\phi' \xrightarrow{\ \epsilon\ } \phi, s) &= (\beta_\equiv(\phi') \xrightarrow{\ \beta_\equiv(\epsilon)\ } \beta_\equiv(\phi), [s]_\equiv)
\end{aligned}
$$

$$
\begin{aligned}
\beta_\equiv(\emptyset) &= \emptyset \\
\beta_\equiv(\epsilon \cup \epsilon') &= \beta_\equiv(\epsilon) \cup \beta_\equiv(\epsilon') \\
\beta_\equiv((s, s')_V) &= \emptyset \\
\beta_\equiv((s, s')_W) &= \emptyset \\
\beta_\equiv((s, s')_C) &= \{[s']_\equiv\}
\end{aligned}
$$

With these definition, we can show the following correspondence.

Lemma 7. *Let $TE, s \vdash e : \phi\,!\,\epsilon$ and $\equiv$ be defined as described above. Then $\beta_\equiv(TE) \vdash_r \beta_\equiv(e) : \beta_\equiv(\phi)\,!\,\beta_\equiv(\epsilon)$.*

Proof. By induction on the derivation of $TE, s \vdash e : \phi\,!\,\epsilon$. Note that uses of the subsumption rule can be mapped to the subeffecting rule (*r-subeff*) because subtyping only gives rise to value dependencies, which are equated by $\equiv$.

3.2   Flow Calculus

We consider a simply-typed flow calculus comparable to 0CFA [7, 15, 18, 19]. Figure 5 summarizes syntax and static semantics of the flow calculus. In this calculus, each subexpression is labeled by a location ℓ. The calculus uses subtyping in the usual way. The type judgement $FTE \vdash_f e_f : (\theta, L)$ means that the value of e_f is constructed and passed through (at most) the locations mentioned in L.

The mapping to PDC is straightforward for the flow calculus. Firstly, it ignores all control dependencies. Next, it maps source annotations to locations

$$\ell \in Location$$
$$e_f ::= x^\ell \mid \mathbf{rec}^\ell \ f(x) \, e_f \mid e_f @^\ell e_f \mid \mathbf{let}^\ell \ x = e_f \ \mathbf{in} \ e_f \mid$$
$$c^\ell \mid \mathbf{op}^\ell(e_f) \mid \mathbf{if}^\ell \ e_f \ e_f \ e_f$$

$$L \subseteq Location$$
$$\phi ::= (\theta, L)$$
$$\theta ::= \alpha \mid \mathbf{B} \mid \phi \to \phi$$

$$(f\text{-}var)\frac{FTE(x) = (\theta, L)}{FTE \vdash_f x^\ell : (\theta, \{\ell\} \cup L)}$$

$$(f\text{-}rec)\frac{FTE[f \mapsto (\phi' \to \phi, L'), x \mapsto \phi'] \vdash_f e : \phi}{FTE \vdash_f \mathbf{rec}^\ell \ f(x) \, e : (\phi' \to \phi, \{\ell\})}$$

$$(f\text{-}app)\frac{FTE \vdash_f e_1 : (\phi' \to \phi, L) \qquad FTE \vdash_f e_2 : \phi' \qquad \ell \in L'}{FTE \vdash_f e_1 @^\ell e_2 : \phi} \phi = (\theta, L')$$

$$(f\text{-}let)\frac{FTE \vdash_f e_1 : \phi_1 \qquad FTE[x : \phi_1] \vdash_f e_2 : \phi_2}{FTE \vdash_f \mathbf{let}^\ell \ x = e_1 \ \mathbf{in} \ e_2 : \phi_2}$$

$$(f\text{-}const)\frac{}{FTE \vdash_f c^\ell : (B, \{\ell\})}$$

$$(f\text{-}op)\frac{FTE \vdash_f e : (B, L)}{FTE \vdash_f \mathbf{op}^\ell(e) : (B, \{\ell\})}$$

$$(f\text{-}if)\frac{FTE \vdash_f e_1 : (B, L) \qquad FTE \vdash_f e_2 : \phi \qquad FTE \vdash_f e_3 : \phi \qquad \ell \in L'}{FTE \vdash_f \mathbf{if}^\ell \ e_1 \ e_2 \ e_3 : \phi} \phi = (\theta, L')$$

$$(f\text{-}sub)\frac{FTE \vdash_f e : \phi \qquad \vdash_f \phi \le \phi'}{FTE \vdash_f e : \phi'}$$

$$\frac{L \subseteq L'}{\vdash_f (\mathbf{B}, L) \le (\mathbf{B}, L')} \qquad \frac{\vdash_f \phi_1' \le \phi_1 \qquad \vdash_f \phi_2 \le \phi_2' \qquad L \subseteq L'}{\vdash_f (\phi_1 \to \phi_2, L) \le (\phi_1' \to \phi_2', L')}$$

Fig. 6. Syntax and Static Semantics of the Flow Calculus

(without lack of generality, we assume the identify mapping because there is always a PDC derivation where all source annotations are distinct). Then, to compute the set L for a type, we take its source annotation and close it under the current dependency graph.

Hence, define

$$
\begin{aligned}
F(s, \epsilon) &= \{s' \mid (s', s)_V \in \epsilon\} \\
F((\mathbf{B}, s), \epsilon) &= (\mathbf{B}, F(s, \epsilon)) \\
F((\phi \xrightarrow{\epsilon'} \phi', s), \epsilon) &= (F(\phi, \epsilon) \to F(\phi', \epsilon \cup \epsilon'), F(s, \epsilon)) \\
F([x_1 : \phi_1, \ldots], \epsilon) &= [x_1 : F(\phi_1, \epsilon), \ldots]
\end{aligned}
$$

and then we can prove that

Lemma 8. If $TE, s \vdash e : \phi \, ! \, \epsilon$ then $F(TE, \emptyset) \vdash_f e : F(\phi, \epsilon)$.

4 Conclusion

We have defined a prototype dependency calculus, PDC, which subsumes important dependency-based program analyses. It is the first calculus that subsumes both the region calculus and other calculi like flow analysis and the SLam calculus for secrecy analysis. Other analyses, in particular binding-time analyses, would also be easy to derive.

We are presenting a number of typed translations into the above calculi. Taken together with the soundness proofs of these calculi, these results give some confidence in the construction of PDC, but ultimately we aim at proving a noninterference result directly for PDC.

On the positive side, the extension to a polymorphic base language and to polymorphic properties seems straightforward. However, it must be expected that such an extension loses the principal typing property enjoyed by PDC.

Another interesting extension would be to cover further effect-based analyses, like side-effects or communication.

References

1. M. Abadi, A. Banerjee, N. Heintze, and J. G. Riecke. A core calculus of dependency. In A. Aiken, editor, *Proc. 26th Annual ACM Symposium on Principles of Programming Languages*, pages 147–160, San Antonio, Texas, USA, Jan. 1999. ACM Press.
2. M. Abadi, B. Lampson, and J.-J. Lévy. Analysis and caching of dependencies. In R. K. Dybvig, editor, *Proc. International Conference on Functional Programming 1996*, pages 83–91, Philadelphia, PA, May 1996. ACM Press, New York.
3. K. Asai. Binding-time analysis for both static and dynamic expressions. In *Static Analysis*, pages 117–133, 1999.
4. A. Banerjee, N. Heintze, and J. G. Riecke. Region analysis and the polymorphic lambda calculus. In *Proc. of the 14th Annual IEEE Symposium on Logic in Computer Science*, pages 88–97, Trento, Italy, July 1999. IEEE Computer Society Press.
5. L. Birkedal and M. Welinder. Binding-time analysis for Standard-ML. In P. Sestoft and H. Søndergaard, editors, *Proc. ACM SIGPLAN Workshop on Partial Evaluation and Semantics-Based Program Manipulation PEPM '94*, pages 61–71, Orlando, Fla., June 1994. University of Melbourne, Australia. Technical Report 94/9, Department of Computer Science.
6. D. Dussart, F. Henglein, and C. Mossin. Polymorphic recursion and subtype qualifications: Polymorphic binding-time analysis in polynomial time. In Mycroft [11], pages 118–136.
7. N. Heintze. Control-flow analysis and type systems. In Mycroft [11], pages 189–206.
8. N. Heintze and J. G. Riecke. The SLam calculus: Programming with security and integrity. In L. Cardelli, editor, *Proc. 25th Annual ACM Symposium on Principles of Programming Languages*, pages 365–377, San Diego, CA, USA, Jan. 1998. ACM Press.
9. F. Henglein and C. Mossin. Polymorphic binding-time analysis. In D. Sannella, editor, *Proceedings of European Symposium on Programming*, volume 788 of *Lecture Notes in Computer Science*, pages 287–301. Springer-Verlag, Apr. 1994.

10. E. Moggi. Notions of computations and monads. *Information and Computation*, 93:55–92, 1991.
11. A. Mycroft, editor. *Proc. International Static Analysis Symposium, SAS'95*, number 983 in Lecture Notes in Computer Science, Glasgow, Scotland, Sept. 1995. Springer-Verlag.
12. F. Nielson and H. R. Nielson. Automatic binding-time analysis for a typed lambda calculus. *Science of Computer Programming*, 10:139–176, 1988.
13. F. Nielson, H. R. Nielson, and C. Hankin. *Principles of Program Analysis*. Springer Verlag, 1999.
14. H. R. Nielson, F. Nielson, and T. Amtoft. Polymorphic subtyping for effect analysis: The static semantics. In M. Dam, editor, *Proceedings of the Fifth LOMAPS Workshop*, number 1192 in Lecture Notes in Computer Science. Springer-Verlag, 1997.
15. J. Palsberg and P. O'Keefe. A type system equivalent to flow analysis. In *Proc. 22nd Annual ACM Symposium on Principles of Programming Languages*, pages 367–378, San Francisco, CA, Jan. 1995. ACM Press.
16. P. Ørbæk and J. Palsberg. Trust in the λ-calculus. *Journal of Functional Programming*, 7(6):557–591, Nov. 1997.
17. J.-P. Talpin and P. Jouvelot. The type and effect discipline. *Information and Computation*, 111(2):245–296, 1994.
18. Y. M. Tang and P. Jouvelot. Control-flow effects for closure analysis. In *Proceedings of the 2nd Workshop on Static Analysis*, number 81-82 in Bigre Journal, pages 313–321, Bordeaux, France, Oct. 1992.
19. Y. M. Tang and P. Jouvelot. Effect systems with subtyping. In W. Scherlis, editor, *Proc. ACM SIGPLAN Symposium on Partial Evaluation and Semantics-Based Program Manipulation PEPM '95*, pages 45–53, La Jolla, CA, June 1995. ACM Press.
20. M. Tofte and J.-P. Talpin. Region-based memory management. *Information and Computation*, 132(2):109–176, 1997.
21. D. Volpano and G. Smith. A type-based approach to program security. In M. Bidoit and M. Dauchet, editors, *TAPSOFT'97: Theory and Practice of Software Development*, number 1214 in Lecture Notes in Computer Science, pages 607–621, Lille, France, Apr. 1997. Springer-Verlag.
22. D. Volpano, G. Smith, and C. Irvine. A sound type system for secure flow analysis. *Journal of Computer Security*, 4(3):1–21, 1996.

Automatic Complexity Analysis

Flemming Nielson[1], Hanne Riis Nielson[1], and Helmut Seidl[2]

[1] Informatics and Mathematical Modelling, The Technical University of Denmark,
DK-2800 Kongens Lyngby, Denmark
{nielson,riis}@imm.dtu.dk
[2] Fachbereich IV – Informatik, Universität Trier, D-54286 Trier, Germany
seidl@uni-trier.de

Abstract. We consider the problem of automating the derivation of tight asymptotic complexity bounds for solving Horn clauses. Clearly, the solving time crucially depends on the "sparseness" of the computed relations. Therefore, our asymptotic runtime analysis is accompanied by an asymptotic sparsity calculus together with an asymptotic sparsity analysis. The technical problem here is that least fixpoint iteration *fails* on asymptotic complexity expressions: the intuitive reason is that $O(1) + O(1) = O(1)$ but $O(1) + \cdots + O(1)$ may return any value.

Keywords: Program analysis, Horn clauses, automatic complexity analysis, sparseness.

1 Introduction

A program analyzer workbench should aid the analysis designer in the construction of efficient program analyses. In particular, the workbench has to provide a specification language in which the program properties to be analyzed can be conveniently formalized. Typically, the program analyzer generated from such a specification consists of a frontend for compiling the input program together with the specification into a constraint system which then is solved.

Here, we consider an approach where (some fragment of) predicate logic serves as a specification language for the analysis. Thus, we use predicates to represent program properties and Horn clause-like implications to formalize their inter-dependencies. The notion of predicates denoting relations is stronger than using just classical bit vectors or set constraints as provided by the BANE system [1] and makes the construction of control-flow analyses very easy (see [11, 12] for recent examples). There are three further reasons for the interest in an analyzer workbench based on this approach:

– The task of the frontend is reduced to the extraction of certain input relations from the program which then together with the clause specifying the analysis is supplied to the solver algorithm. Thus, it is possible to rapidly add new frontends for further languages to be analyzed.

D. Le Métayer (Ed.): ESOP 2002, LNCS 2305, pp. 243–261, 2002.

- The task of computing the result is reduced to computing the desired model of a formula. As minor syntactical variations of formulas can have major impacts on the efficiency of solving, the task of tuning of the analysis boils down to tuning of formulas. Transformations along these lines were reported in [12] and are currently studied in the context of [13]. And finally,
- The generated program analyzers have *predictable* performance. This is the topic of the present paper.

Clearly, any good algorithm should be *predictable* – although only few are sufficiently well understood. Here, by predictability we mean two things. First, the algorithm should return the expected answers – this has classically been called *correctness*. But second, the algorithm also should return the answer in a reliable amount of time – meaning that the algorithm either always should be fast or, should allow an easy to understand classification of inputs into those which are rapidly doable and others which potentially take longer.

Our goal in this paper is to obtain safe estimations for the asymptotic complexities of the generated analyzers. For ease of presentation we explain our approach for a very simple fragment of predicate logic only, namely, for *Horn clauses*. For these, McAllester has presented a complexity meta-theorem [11] which reduces the complexity estimation for clause solving to counting of "prefix firings". These numbers, however, as well as practical clause solving times crucially depend on the "sparseness" of involved relations. Therefore, we develop an asymptotic sparsity calculus which formalizes this notion and allows to automate the necessary calculations. We use this calculus both to derive an automatic complexity estimator and also to design a sparsity analysis which infers asymptotic sparsity information for predicates for which no sparsity information has been provided by the user. This is particularly important for auxiliary predicates that are not part of the original formulation of the analysis but have been introduced during clause tuning (see, e.g., [12, 13] for an example).

The technical problem here stems from the observation that classical least fixpoint iteration fails on asymptotic expressions: $O(1) + O(1) = O(1)$ but $O(1) + \cdots + O(1)$ may return any value. We overcome this difficulty by relying on an interesting theorem about uniform finite bounds on the number of iterations needed for "nice" functions to reach their *greatest* fixpoints – even in presence of decreasing chains of unbounded lengths.

The paper is organized as follows. We introduce basic notions about Horn clauses in section 2. In section 3 we report on McAllester's complexity meta-theorem. In sections 4 and 5 we present the technical ideas onto which our analysis is based. In section 6 we explain the asymptotic sparsity analysis. In section 7 we sketch our implementation and present results for various benchmark clauses.

2   Horn Clauses

In this section, we recall the classical notion of Horn clauses (without function symbols) as our constraint formalism. A Horn clause is a conjunction of implications of the form:

$$g_1, \ldots, g_m \Rightarrow r(X_1, \ldots, X_k)$$

where $g_1, \ldots, g_m$ is a (possibly empty) list of assumptions and $r(X_1, \ldots, X_k)$ is the conclusion. W.l.o.g. we assume that the argument tuples of predicates in goals or conclusions are always given by *mutually distinct* variables. Thus, the goals g_i occurring as assumptions either are queries $s(Y_1, \ldots, Y_n)$ to predicates or equality constraints between variables or variables and constants:

$$g \quad ::= \quad s(Y_1, \ldots, Y_k) \quad | \quad X = Y \quad | \quad X = a$$

for variables $X, Y, Y_1, \ldots, Y_k$ and atoms a.

Horn clauses are interpreted over a universe $\mathcal{U}$ of atomic values (or atoms). For simplicity (and by confusing syntax and semantics here), we assume that all atoms occurring in the clause are contained in $\mathcal{U}$. Then given interpretations ρ and σ for predicate symbols and (a superset of) occurring variables, respectively, we define the satisfaction relation $(\rho, \sigma) \models t$ (t a goal or clause) as follows.

$$
\begin{array}{lll}
(\rho, \sigma) \models r(X_1, \ldots, X_k) & \text{iff} & (\sigma X_1, \ldots, \sigma X_k) \in \rho\, r \\
(\rho, \sigma) \models X = Y & \text{iff} & \sigma X = \sigma Y \\
(\rho, \sigma) \models X = a & \text{iff} & \sigma X = a \\
(\rho, \sigma) \models g_1, \ldots, g_m \Rightarrow r(X_1, \ldots, X_k) & \text{iff} & (\sigma X_1, \ldots, \sigma X_k) \in \rho\, r \\
& & \text{whenever } \forall i : (\rho, \sigma) \models g_i \\
(\rho, \sigma) \models c_1 \wedge \ldots \wedge c_n & \text{iff} & \forall j : (\rho, \sigma) \models c_j
\end{array}
$$

In particular, we call an interpretation ρ of the predicate symbols in $\mathcal{R}$ a *solution* of c provided $(\rho, \sigma) \models c$ for all variable assignments σ of the free variables in c.

The set of all interpretations of predicate symbols in $\mathcal{R}$ over $\mathcal{U}$ forms a complete lattice (w.r.t. componentwise set inclusion on relations). It is well-known that the set of all solutions of a clause is a Moore family within this lattice. We conclude that for every clause c and interpretation ρ_0 there is a least solution ρ of c with $\rho_0 \sqsubseteq \rho$. An algorithm which, given c and ρ_0, computes ρ is called a *Horn clause solver*. In the practical application, e.g., of a program analyzer workbench, the initial interpretation ρ_0 assigns to input predicates relations which have been extracted from the program to be analyzed. Depending on the input predicates, the clause c (representing the analysis) defines certain output predicates which return the desired information about the program to be analyzed.

3   Concrete Calculation of Runtimes

In [11], McAllester proposes an efficient Horn clause solver. In particular, he determines the complexity of his algorithm by means of the number of *prefix firings* of the clause. Let ρ be an interpretation of the predicate symbols. Let $p \equiv g_1, \ldots, g_m$ denote a sequence of goals and $A = Vars(p)$ the set of variables occurring in p. Then the set $\mathcal{T}_\rho[p]$ of *firings* of p (relative to ρ) is the set of all variable assignments for which all goals g_i succeed. Thus, this set is given by:

$$\mathcal{T}_\rho[p] = \{\sigma : A \to \mathcal{U} \mid \forall i : (\sigma, \rho) \models g_i\}$$

In particular, if p is empty, then $Vars(p) = \emptyset$, and $\mathcal{T}_\rho[p]$ only consists of a single element, namely, the empty assignment (which we denote by $\emptyset$ as well). The set $\mathcal{F}_\rho[c]$ of *prefix firings* of a clause c is given by the set of all firings of prefixes of sequences of assumptions occurring in c.

Let us now without loss of generality assume that each implication $p \Rightarrow r(args)$ is *bottom-up bound*, i.e., each variable occurring in $args$ also occurs in the list p of assumptions[1]. McAllester's result then can be stated as follows:

Theorem 1 (McAllester). *Let c be a Horn clause of size $\mathcal{O}(1)$ and ρ_0 an initial interpretation of the predicate symbols occurring in c. Then the least solution ρ of c with $\rho_0 \sqsubseteq \rho$ can be computed in time $\mathcal{O}(|\rho| + |\mathcal{F}_\rho[c]|)$, i.e., asymptotically equals the cardinality of ρ plus the number of prefix firings relative to ρ.*   □

Thus, computing the complexity of Horn clause solving reduces to asymptotically counting the number of prefix firings. In simple applications, this can be done manually by looking at the clause and exploiting background knowledge about the occurring relations. In more complicated applications, however, this task quickly becomes tedious — making a mechanization of the asymptotic counting desirable. This is what we are going to do now.

We observe that computing sets of firings can be reduced to the application of a small set of operations on relations and sets of variable assignments: For sets of variables $A \subseteq V$, we define an *extension* operator $\mathrm{ext}_{A,V}$ which maps subsets $\mathcal{E} \subseteq A \rightarrow \mathcal{U}$ to subsets of $V \rightarrow \mathcal{U}$ by "padding" the variable assignments in all possible ways, i.e.:

$$\mathrm{ext}_{A,V}\, \mathcal{E} \;=\; \{\sigma : V \rightarrow \mathcal{U} \mid (\sigma|_A) \in \mathcal{E}\}$$

In particular for $A = \emptyset$ and $\mathcal{E} = \{\emptyset\}$, $\mathrm{ext}_{A,V}\, \mathcal{E} = V \rightarrow \mathcal{U}$.

For sets of variable assignments $\mathcal{E}_1 \subseteq A \rightarrow \mathcal{U}$ and $\mathcal{E}_2 \subseteq B \rightarrow \mathcal{U}$, we define an extended *intersection* operation $\cap_{A,B}$ by extending the variable assignments in both sets $\mathcal{E}_i$ to the union $V = A \cup B$ first and computing the intersection then:

$$\mathcal{E}_1 \cap_{A,B} \mathcal{E}_2 \;=\; (\mathrm{ext}_{A,V}\, \mathcal{E}_1) \cap (\mathrm{ext}_{B,V}\, \mathcal{E}_2)$$

For simplicity, we omit these extra indices at "$\cap$" if no confusion can arise. Using this generalized intersection operation, we can compute the set of firings of a list p of assumptions inductively by:

$$\mathcal{T}_\rho[] = \{\emptyset\} \qquad\qquad \mathcal{T}_\rho[p, g] = \mathcal{T}_\rho[p] \cap \mathcal{T}_\rho[g]$$

— given that we are provided with the sets of firings for individual goals. Accordingly, the number $\mathcal{C}_\rho[t]$ of prefix firings associated to a list of goals or conjunction of implications t inductively can be computed by:

$$\mathcal{C}_\rho[] = 1 \qquad\qquad\qquad \mathcal{C}_\rho[p \Rightarrow r(\ldots)] = \mathcal{C}_\rho[p]$$
$$\mathcal{C}_\rho[p, g] = \mathcal{C}_\rho[p] + |\mathcal{T}_\rho[p, g]| \qquad \mathcal{C}_\rho[c_1 \wedge \ldots \wedge c_n] = \sum_{j=1}^{n} \mathcal{C}_\rho[c_j]$$

---

[1] Assume that the implication is not bottom-up bound, and X occurs in the conclusion but not in p. Then we simply add the goal $X = X$ to the list of assumptions.

We conclude that, in order to determine the asymptotic behavior of the number of prefix firings, we must find a description for possible asymptotic behaviors of sets of variable assignments which allows us:

1. to get a (hopefully tight) description for the intersection of sets;
2. to extract a safe cardinality estimate for the sets from their descriptions.

We will now proceed in two steps. First, we abstract relations and sets of variable assignments to a description of their quantitative behavior. The latter then is used to obtain the asymptotic description.

4   Abstract Calculation of Runtimes

Our key idea is to use $(k \times k)$-matrices to describe the quantitative dependencies between the components of k-ary relations.

4.1   Sparsity Matrices

For a k-tuple $t = (a_1, \ldots, a_k)$ and j in the range $1, \ldots, k$, let $[t]_j = a_j$ denote the j-th component of t. Let r denote a relation of arity k over some universe $\mathcal{U}$ of cardinality $N \in \mathbb{N}$. To r, we assign the $(k \times k)$-$sparsity\ matrix$ $\beta[r]$ whose coefficients $\beta[r]_{ij} \in \mathbb{N}$ are given by:

$$
\begin{aligned}
\beta[r]_{ij} &= \bigvee\{|S_j(i,a)| \mid a \in \mathcal{U}\} \qquad \text{where} \\
S_j(i,a) &= \{[t]_j \mid t \in r, [t]_i = a\}
\end{aligned}
$$

Here, $\bigvee$ denotes $maximum$ on integers. Please note that the value $\beta[r]_{ij}$, i.e., the maximal cardinality of one of the sets $S_j(i,a)$, depends on j in a rather subtle way: for each j we first collect the j-th components from the tuples in the relation r in which a appears on the i-th place (call each such an element an j-witness) and then compute the cardinality, i.e., how many $different$ such j-witnesses at most exist. So, for different j's these values can be quite different.

As an example, consider the edge relation e of a directed graph. Then $\beta[e]_{12}$ equals the maximal out-degree of nodes of the graph, $\beta[e]_{21}$ equals the maximal in-degree. The values $\beta[e]_{ii}$ count the maximal number of i-witnesses given a fixed i-th component: thus, they trivially equal 1 (for all non-empty relations). In particular for a binary tree, we obtain the matrix:

$$
\begin{pmatrix} 1 & 2 \\ 1 & 1 \end{pmatrix}
$$

Every sparsity matrix m for a non-empty relation satisfies the following three $metric$ properties:

$$
\begin{aligned}
m_{ii} &= 1 && \text{for all } i \\
m_{ij} &\leq N && \text{for all } i, j \\
m_{ij} &\leq m_{il} \cdot m_{lj} && \text{for all } i, j, l \qquad (triangular\ inequality)
\end{aligned}
$$

Let $\mathcal{M}(N)_k$ denote the set of all $(k \times k)$ sparsity matrices which satisfy the three metric properties above. We have:

Proposition 1. $\mathcal{M}(N)_k$ *is a complete lattice with the following properties:*

1. *The least upper bound operation is computed componentwise, i.e.,*
   $(a \sqcup b)_{ij} = a_{ij} \vee b_{ij}$ *for* $a, b \in \mathcal{M}(N)_k$ *and all* $i, j = 1, \ldots, k$.
2. *The function β is monotonic, i.e.,*
   $R_1 \subseteq R_2 \subseteq \mathcal{U}^k$ *implies* $\beta[R_1] \sqsubseteq \beta[R_2]$ *in* $\mathcal{M}(N)_k$.   □

The mapping β induces a Galois connection between (sets of) k-ary relations and sparsity matrices. Instead of giving a concretization function γ (returning downward closed sets of relations), we here prefer to introduce a description relation $\Delta^{(N)}$ between relations and matrices where for $r \subseteq \mathcal{U}^k$ and $m \in \mathcal{M}(N)_k$,

$$r \ \Delta^{(N)} \ m \qquad \text{iff} \qquad \beta[r] \sqsubseteq m$$

Our next step consists in giving abstract versions of necessary operations on relations. First we define for $a, b \in \mathcal{M}(N)_k$, the $(k \times k)$-matrix $a \oplus b$ by:

$$(a \oplus b)_{ij} = \begin{cases} 1 & \text{if } i = j \\ (a_{ij} + b_{ij}) \wedge N & \text{if } i \neq j \end{cases}$$

where "$\wedge$" denotes minimum. We have:

Proposition 2. 1. *The operation $\oplus$ is monotonic;*
2. *If* $r_i \ \Delta^{(N)} \ a_i$ *for* $i = 1, 2$, *then also* $(r_1 \cup r_2) \ \Delta^{(N)} \ (a_1 \oplus a_2)$.   □

Next, we consider the greatest lower-bound operation which is going to abstract the intersection operation on relations. Opposed to the least upper bound, the greatest lower bound cannot be computed componentwise. As a counterexample consider the two matrices (for $N = 100$):

$$a = \begin{pmatrix} 1 & 2 & 100 \\ 100 & 1 & 100 \\ 100 & 100 & 1 \end{pmatrix} \qquad b = \begin{pmatrix} 1 & 100 & 100 \\ 100 & 1 & 3 \\ 100 & 100 & 1 \end{pmatrix}$$

The componentwise greatest lower bound is given by:

$$a \wedge b = \begin{pmatrix} 1 & 2 & 100 \\ 100 & 1 & 3 \\ 100 & 100 & 1 \end{pmatrix}$$

In particular, $(a \wedge b)_{13} = 100 > 6 = 2 \cdot 3 = (a \wedge b)_{12} \cdot (a \wedge b)_{23}$.

In order to obtain the greatest lower bound of two matrices we additionally have to perform a (reflexive and) *transitive closure* (rt closure for short).

Let m denote a $(k \times k)$-matrix with entries in $\{1, \ldots, N\}$. Then the rt closure $\nu\,m$ is defined by $(\nu\,m)_{ii} = 1$ and:

$$(\nu\,m)_{ij} = \bigwedge \{ m_{ij_1} \cdot m_{j_1 j_2} \cdot \ldots \cdot m_{j_{g-1} j_g} \cdot m_{j_g j} \mid g \geq 0, j_\gamma \in \{1, \ldots, k\} \}$$

for $i \neq j$. In our example, the rt closure of $a \wedge b$ is given by:

$$\nu(a \wedge b) = \begin{pmatrix} 1 & 2 & 6 \\ 100 & 1 & 3 \\ 100 & 100 & 1 \end{pmatrix}$$

It is well-known that the rt closure of a matrix can be computed efficiently. For the greatest lower bound we find:

Proposition 3.   *1. The greatest lower bound of $a, b \in \mathcal{M}(N)_k$ is given by*

$$\begin{aligned} a \sqcap b \quad &= \nu(a \wedge b) \qquad where \\ (a \wedge b)_{ij} &= a_{ij} \wedge b_{ij} \qquad for\ i, j = 1, \dots, k \end{aligned}$$

2. Whenever $r_i\ \varDelta^{(N)}\ a_i,\ i = 1, 2,$ then also $(r_1 \sqcap r_2)\ \varDelta^{(N)}\ (a_1 \sqcap a_2)$.   □

Our domain $\mathcal{M}(N)_k$ is related to the domain of *difference bound matrices* as used, e.g., for the verification of finite state systems with clock variables [5] and for analyzing simple forms of linear dependencies between program variables [14]. In contrast to these applications, we here use positive integers from a bounded range only and also treat this coefficient domain both additively (namely, for abstracting union) and multiplicatively (namely, for abstracting intersection). The key property of our abstraction of relations is that sparsity matrices allow to estimate cardinalities. For $m \in \mathcal{M}(N)_k$ we define:

$$\operatorname{card} m = N \cdot \prod \{ m_{xy} \mid (x, y) \in T \}$$

where $(\{1, \dots, k\}, T)$ is a minimal cost spanning tree of the complete directed graph over $\{1, \dots, k\}$ with edge weights $(i, j) \mapsto m_{ij}$. Consider, e.g., the matrix:

$$c = \begin{pmatrix} 1 & 2\,6 \\ 100 & 1\,3 \\ 100\ 100 & 1 \end{pmatrix}$$

The weighted graph for c is depicted in fig. 1 (self loops and edges with weight 100 are omitted). A minimal spanning tree of this graph is given by the edges

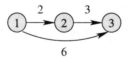

Fig. 1. The weighted graph for the matrix c.

$(1, 2)$ and $(2, 3)$. Therefore, we obtain: $\operatorname{card} c = 100 \cdot 2 \cdot 3 = 600$.   We have:

Proposition 4. *Assume $r \subseteq \mathcal{U}^k$ and $m \in \mathcal{M}(N)_k$ such that $r\ \varDelta^{(N)}\ m$. Then also* $|r| \leq \operatorname{card} m$.   □

4.2   Computing with Sparsities

In a similar way as to relations, we can assign sparsity matrices to sets $\mathcal{E}$ of variable assignments $\sigma : A \to \mathcal{U}$ for some set A of variables. Here, we deliberately allow to index the entries of sparsity matrices by the Cartesian product $A \times A$. The sparsity matrix of the non-empty set $\mathcal{E}$ of variable assignments then is given by:

$$\beta[\mathcal{E}]_{xy} = \bigvee\{ |\{\sigma\, y \mid \sigma \in \mathcal{E}, \sigma\, x = a\}| \mid a \in \mathcal{U}\}$$

Let $\mathcal{M}(N)_A$ denote the complete lattice which consists of all matrices with entries from $\{1, \ldots, N\}$ which are indexed with $A \times A$ and satisfy the three metric properties. We introduce an abstract version of the operator $\text{ext}_{A,V}$ by padding the corresponding matrix with the maximally possible value for the so far missing entries. For $A \subseteq V$, we define $\text{ext}^{\sharp}_{A,V} : \mathcal{M}(N)_A \to \mathcal{M}(N)_V$ by:

$$(\text{ext}^{\sharp}_{A,V}\, m)_{xy} = \begin{cases} 1 & \text{if } x = y \\ m_{xy} & \text{if } x, y \in A,\ x \neq y \\ N & \text{otherwise} \end{cases}$$

Accordingly, we define for $a \in \mathcal{M}(N)_A$, $b \in \mathcal{M}(N)_B$ and $V = A \cup B$:

$$a \sqcap_{A,B} b = (\text{ext}^{\sharp}_{A,V}\, a) \sqcap (\text{ext}^{\sharp}_{B,V}\, b)$$

For convenience, we subsequently drop the subscripts "A, B" at "$\sqcap$". We have:

Proposition 5. 1. If $\quad r\ \Delta^{(N)}\ a \quad$ then also $\quad (\text{ext}_{A,V}\, r)\ \Delta^{(N)}\ (\text{ext}^{\sharp}_{A,V} a)$.

2. If for $\quad i = 1, 2, \quad r_i\ \Delta^{(N)}\ a_i \quad$ then also $\quad (r_1 \sqcap r_2)\ \Delta^{(N)}\ (a_1 \sqcap a_2)$. $\quad\square$

The greatest matrix $\top_A \in \mathcal{M}(N)_A$ maps the pair (X, Y) to 1 if $X = Y$ and to N otherwise. In order to shorten the presentation, we feel free to specify matrices just by enumerating those entries which deviate from the greatest matrix. Thus for $A = \{X, Y\}$ and $N = 100$, we write $\quad \{(X, Y) \mapsto 5\}_A \quad$ to denote the matrix:

$$\{ (X, X) \mapsto 1, \quad (X, Y) \mapsto 5, \\ (Y, X) \mapsto 100, (Y, Y) \mapsto 1\ \}$$

Every abstract interpretation $\rho^{\sharp}$ mapping predicate symbols to corresponding sparsity matrices, gives rise to an abstract description of sets of firings by:

$$T^{\sharp}_{\rho^{\sharp}}[] = \{\}_{\emptyset} \qquad\qquad T^{\sharp}_{\rho^{\sharp}}[p, g] = T^{\sharp}_{\rho^{\sharp}}[p] \sqcap T^{\sharp}_{\rho^{\sharp}}[g]$$

where for individual goals,

$$\begin{aligned} T^{\sharp}_{\rho^{\sharp}}[r(X_1, \ldots, X_k)] &= \{(X_i, X_j) \mapsto (\rho^{\sharp}\, r)_{ij} \mid i \neq j\}_{\{X_1, \ldots, X_k\}} \\ T^{\sharp}_{\rho^{\sharp}}[X = Y] &= \{(X, Y) \mapsto 1, (Y, X) \mapsto 1\}_{\{X, Y\}} \\ T^{\sharp}_{\rho^{\sharp}}[X = a] &= \{\}_{\{X\}} \end{aligned}$$

The treatment of goals $\quad X = a \quad$ as outlined above would record no information about X at all! In order to obtain a better precision here, we consider equalities with constants always together with the preceding goals. We define:

$$T^{\sharp}_{\rho^{\sharp}}[p\ ,\ X = a] = T^{\sharp}_{\rho^{\sharp}}[p] \sqcap \{(Y, X) \mapsto 1 \mid Y \in A\}_{A \cup \{X\}}$$

where A equals the set of variables occurring in the list p. By taking the subsequent extension to the set $A \cup \{X\}$ into account we record that for each value of another variable Y there always can be at most one value of X (namely, a).

Right along the lines of the complexity estimation based on concrete relations and concrete sets of firings, we use abstract descriptions of sets of firings to translate the concrete cost calculation into an abstract one:

$$
\begin{aligned}
\mathcal{C}^{\sharp}_{\rho^{\sharp}}[\,] &= 1 & \mathcal{C}^{\sharp}_{\rho^{\sharp}}[p \Rightarrow r(\ldots)] &= \mathcal{C}^{\sharp}_{\rho^{\sharp}}[p] \\
\mathcal{C}^{\sharp}_{\rho^{\sharp}}[p, g] &= \mathcal{C}^{\sharp}_{\rho^{\sharp}}[p] + \mathsf{card}\,(\mathcal{T}^{\sharp}_{\rho^{\sharp}}[p, g]) & \mathcal{C}^{\sharp}_{\rho^{\sharp}}[c_1 \wedge \ldots \wedge c_n] &= \textstyle\sum_{j=1}^{n} \mathcal{C}^{\sharp}_{\rho^{\sharp}}[c_j]
\end{aligned}
$$

Using the estimation of cardinalities of relations according to proposition 4, we can thus calculate an abstract number $\mathcal{C}^{\sharp}_{\rho^{\sharp}}[c]$ of prefix firings of a clause c given an assignment $\rho^{\sharp}$ of predicate symbols to abstract sparsity matrices:

Theorem 2. *Assume c is a Horn clause and ρ an interpretation of the predicate symbols occurring in c. Then we have:*

1. The number of prefix firings of c (relative to ρ) can be estimated by:

$$
\mathcal{C}_{\rho}[c] \quad \leq \quad \mathcal{C}^{\sharp}_{\rho^{\sharp}}[c]
$$

whenever the universe has cardinality at most N and

$$
(\rho\, r) \;\; \Delta^{(N)} \;\; (\rho^{\sharp}\, r)
$$

for all predicate symbols r occurring in c.
2. The value $\mathcal{C}^{\sharp}_{\rho^{\sharp}}[c]$ can be computed in time polynomial in the size of c. $\qquad\square$

In other words, our abstraction allows to obtain a safe approximation to the number of prefix firings of clauses — given that the solution complies with the assumed sparsity assignment.

5   Asymptotic Calculation of Runtimes

Estimating the runtime of the solver on inputs adhering to a single pre-specified sparsity information, gives us no information on how the runtime scales up when the clause is run on larger relations. The crucial step therefore consists in replacing the abstract calculation from the last section by an asymptotic one. For this, we first introduce the domain of our asymptotic complexity measures. Then we derive the asymptotic runtime calculation and prove its correctness.

5.1   Asymptotic Values

For measuring asymptotic sparsity and complexity we use the abstract value n to refer to the size of the universe. In the application of a program analyzer workbench, the universe typically comprises the set of program points, the names of variables etc. Thus, its cardinality roughly corresponds to the size of the program to be analyzed. Expressing complexities in terms of powers of the cardinality of the universe, however, often is too coarse. Therefore, we introduce a second value $s \ll n$ which is accounted for in the analysis. The parameter s could, e.g., measure the maximal number of successors/predecessors of a node in a graph. Accordingly, we are aiming at complexity expressions of the form $\mathcal{O}(n \cdot s^2)$. In order to be able to compare such expressions, we must fix (an estimation of) the asymptotic functional relationship between s and n. In particular, we may assume that $s^\eta \sim n$ for some $\eta \in \mathbb{N}$ or even $s \sim \log(n)$ implying that $s^\eta < n$ for all η (at least asymptotically). Let us call η the *dependency exponent* of our analysis. For the following, let $\mathcal{N}$ denote the set of non-negative integers extended by a greatest element ∞. Thus for every exponent $\eta \in \mathcal{N}$, we obtain a linearly ordered lattice $\mathbb{D}_\eta$ of asymptotic complexity measures:

$$\mathbb{D}_\eta = \{n^i \cdot s^j \mid 0 \le i, 0 \le j < \eta\}$$

The least element of $\mathbb{D}_\eta$ is given by $n^0 \cdot s^0 = 1$. On $\mathbb{D}_\eta$ we have the binary operations "$\cdot$" (multiplication), "$\sqcup$" (least upper bound) and "$\sqcap$" (greatest lower bound) which are defined in the obvious way. Note that $\mathbb{D}_\eta$ has infinite ascending chains. Also, the lengths of descending chains, though finite, cannot be uniformly bounded.

The set $\mathcal{P}_k(\eta)$ of all asymptotic $(k \times k)$-matrices consists of all $(k \times k)$-matrices a with entries $a_{ij} \in \mathbb{D}_\eta$ such that the following holds:

$$
\begin{aligned}
a_{ii} &= 1 && \text{for all } i \\
a_{ij} &\sqsubseteq n && \text{for all } i, j \\
a_{ij} &\sqsubseteq a_{il} \cdot a_{lj} && \text{for all } i, j, l
\end{aligned}
$$

Similar to $\mathcal{M}(N)_k$, $\mathcal{P}_k(\eta)$ forms a complete lattice where the binary least upper bound "$\sqcup$" and greatest lower bound "$\sqcap$" are defined analogously as for $\mathcal{M}(N)_k$. In particular, we can use a completely analogous definition for the card function.

The elements in $\mathbb{D}_\eta$ should be considered as *functions*. Thus, given a concrete argument $N \in \mathbb{N}$, an element p can be evaluated to a natural $[p]_\eta N$ by:

$$[n^i \cdot s^j]_\eta \, N = \begin{cases} N^i \cdot \log(N)^j & \text{if } \eta = \infty \\ N^i \cdot N^{j/\eta} & \text{if } \eta < \infty \end{cases}$$

Evaluation at a certain point commutes with the operations "$\cdot$", "$\sqcup$" and "$\sqcap$". Asymptotic statements do not speak about individual elements. Instead, they speak about *sequences* of elements. Let $\underline{x} = (x^{(N)})_{N \in \mathbb{N}}$ denote a sequence of integers $x^{(N)} \in \mathbb{N}$ and $p \in \mathbb{D}_\eta$. Then we write:

$$\underline{x} \, \Delta_\eta \, p \quad \text{iff} \quad \exists d \in \mathbb{N} : \forall N \in \mathbb{N} : x^{(N)} \le d \cdot ([p]_\eta \, N)$$

This formalization captures what we mean when we say that $\underline{x}$ is of order $\mathcal{O}(p)$.

5.2 Computing with Asymptotic Values

In order to analyze the asymptotic runtime complexity of the solver, we not only have to consider sequences of numbers. Besides these, we consider sequences of other objects (all marked by underlining). We introduce:

- sequences of relations $\underline{r} = (r^{(N)})_{N \in \mathbb{N}}$ where $r^{(N)} \subseteq (\mathcal{U}^{(N)})^k$ for universes $\mathcal{U}^{(N)}$ of cardinalities at most N;
- sequences of matrices $\underline{m} = (m^{(N)})_{N \in \mathbb{N}}$ where $m^{(N)} \in \mathcal{M}(N)_k$;
- sequences of interpretations $\underline{\rho} = (\rho^{(N)})_{N \in \mathbb{N}}$ and abstract interpretations $\underline{\rho}^{\sharp} = (\rho^{\sharp(N)})_{N \in \mathbb{N}}$ of predicate symbols.

Also, we establish a description relation between sequences of matrices $\underline{m}$ and asymptotic matrices:

$$\underline{m} \ \Delta_\eta \ a \ \text{iff} \ (m_{ij}^{(N)})_{N \in \mathbb{N}} \ \Delta_\eta \ a_{ij} \quad \text{for all } i, j$$

In particular, we have:

Proposition 6.   *1. Assume $\underline{a}, \underline{b}$ are sequences of sparsity matrices which are asymptotically described by a^* and b^*. Then the following holds:*

$$\begin{aligned} (a^{(N)} \sqcup b^{(N)})_{N \in \mathbb{N}} &\ \Delta_\eta &\ a^* \sqcup b^* \\ (a^{(N)} \oplus b^{(N)})_{N \in \mathbb{N}} &\ \Delta_\eta &\ a^* \sqcup b^* \\ (a^{(N)} \sqcap b^{(N)})_{N \in \mathbb{N}} &\ \Delta_\eta &\ a^* \sqcap b^* \end{aligned}$$

2. If $\underline{a}$ is a sequence of sparsity matrices and $\underline{a} \ \Delta_\eta \ a^*$ then also

$$(\mathsf{card}\,(a^{(N)}))_{N \in \mathbb{N}} \ \Delta_\eta \ \mathsf{card}\,(a^*)$$

□

Similarly to section 4, we now can use the operations on asymptotic sparsity matrices to obtain asymptotic complexity expressions for the runtime of the solver – given an asymptotic description of the sparsities of the computed relations. Thus, for an assignment ρ^* of predicate symbols to asymptotic sparsity matrices, we first infer asymptotic sparsity matrices $\mathcal{T}_{\rho^*}^*[p]$ for sequences of sets of firings of pre-conditions and then calculate the corresponding asymptotic cost functions $\mathcal{C}_{\rho^*}^*[t]$ for the pre-conditions and clauses t. We proceed along the lines for sparsity matrices. The main difference is that we now compute over $\mathbb{D}_\eta$ (instead of $\mathbb{N}$) and that we replace the matrix operation "$\oplus$" with "$\sqcup$".

Example.   In [12], we considered a control-flow analysis M_0 for the ambient calculus [3] and showed how to derive an optimized clause M_1 which can be solved in cubic time. For convenience, we described these analyses by using *Horn clauses* extended with explicit quantification and sharing of conclusions — the same analyses, however, can also be described by pure Horn clauses only. In order to illustrate our complexity estimation technique, we take the optimized clause M_1 and pick the abstract description of the In action for ambients. Translating the Flow Logic specification from [12] into plain Horn clauses, we obtain:

$$\mathsf{in}(X, A), \mathsf{father}(X, Y), \mathsf{sibling}(Y, Z), \mathsf{name}(Z, A) \Rightarrow \mathsf{father}(Y, Z)$$

Here, the binary relation in records all pairs (X, A) where A is the label of an In capability of ambients with name A. The binary relation father describes all pairs (X, Y) of labels where Y is a potential enclosing environment of X. The binary relation sibling collects all pairs (Y, Z) which potentially have the same father. Finally, the binary relation name records all pairs (Z, A) where Z is the label of an ambient with name A. Thus, the universe $\mathcal{U}$ consists of the labels given to ambient expressions and capabilities occurring in the program together with all occurring names. Therefore, the size n of the universe asymptotically equals the size of the ambient program. By definition, capabilities and ambients are uniquely related to names. Therefore, the relations in and name are asymptotically described by:

$$\rho^* \text{ in } = \rho^* \text{ name} = \begin{pmatrix} 1 & 1 \\ n & 1 \end{pmatrix}$$

The binary relation father represents the result of the analysis, i.e., describes all places where an ambient may move to. Let us assume that this relation is "sparse", meaning that each label has only few sons and few fathers. Bounding the numbers of fathers and sons, implies upper bounds for the number of siblings as well. Therefore, we set:

$$\rho^* \text{ father} = \begin{pmatrix} 1 & s \\ s & 1 \end{pmatrix} \qquad \rho^* \text{ sibling} = \begin{pmatrix} 1 & s^2 \\ s^2 & 1 \end{pmatrix}$$

Let us assume that the exponent η equals ∞. By varying the exponent η from ∞ (very sparse) down to 1 (dense), we instead could track the impact also of other grades of sparseness onto the complexity of the clause. For the complexity estimation, we first compute the asymptotic descriptions $T^*_{\rho^*}[p_i]$ for the sets of firings for the prefixes $p_1, \ldots, p_4$ of the pre-condition. The corresponding weighted graphs are shown in fig. 2 (self loops and edges with weight n are omitted). Then we calculate their cardinalities. Starting with $p_1 \equiv \text{in}(X, A)$, we find:

$$T^*_{\rho^*}[p_1] = \{(X, A) \mapsto 1\}_{\{A, X\}}$$

(see the leftmost graph in fig. 2). A minimal cost spanning tree is given by the edge (X, A). Therefore, $\text{card}(T^*_{\rho^*}[p_1]) = n \cdot 1 = n$.

Next, consider the prefix $p_2 \equiv \text{in}(X, A), \text{hasFather}(X, Y)$. Here, we have:

$$\begin{aligned} T^*_{\rho^*}[p_2] &= \{(X, A) \mapsto 1\}_{\{A, X\}} \sqcap \{(X, Y) \mapsto s, (Y, X) \mapsto s\}_{\{X, Y\}} \\ &= \nu \{(X, A) \mapsto 1, (X, Y) \mapsto s, (Y, X) \mapsto s\}_{\{A, X, Y\}} \\ &= \{(X, A) \mapsto 1, (X, Y) \mapsto s, (Y, A) \mapsto s, (Y, X) \mapsto s\}_{\{A, X, Y\}} \end{aligned}$$

(see the second graph in fig. 2). A minimal spanning tree of this graph consists of the edges (X, A) and (X, Y) which results in the cardinality estimation: $\text{card}(T^*_{\rho^*}[p_2]) = n \cdot 1 \cdot s = n \cdot s$.

Accordingly, we obtain for p_3:

$$\begin{aligned} T^*_{\rho^*}[p_3] = \{ \ &(X, A) \mapsto 1, \ (X, Y) \mapsto s, \ (X, Z) \mapsto s^3 \\ &(Y, A) \mapsto s, \ (Y, X) \mapsto s, \ (Y, Z) \mapsto s^2 \\ &(Z, A) \mapsto s^3, (Z, X) \mapsto s^3, (Z, Y) \mapsto s^2 \ \}_{\{A, X, Y, Z\}} \end{aligned}$$

where a minimal spanning tree is given by the edges (X, A), (X, Y) and (Y, Z) (see the third graph in fig. 2). Therefore, $\text{card}(T^*_{\rho^*}[p_3]) = n \cdot 1 \cdot s \cdot s^2 = n \cdot s^3$.

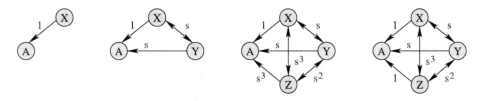

Fig. 2. The weighted graphs for $\mathcal{T}_{\rho^*}^*[p_1]$, $\mathcal{T}_{\rho^*}^*[p_2]$, $\mathcal{T}_{\rho^*}^*[p_3]$ and $\mathcal{T}_{\rho^*}^*[p_4]$.

The asymptotic sparsity matrix for p_4 differs from $\mathcal{T}_{\rho^*}^*[p_3]$ only in the entry for (Z, A) where it has value 1 (instead of s^3) (see fig. 2 to the right), and the asymptotic cardinality stays the same. Summarizing, the contribution of the example clause to the overall complexity is determined as:

$$\mathcal{C}_{\rho^*}^*[p_4] = \bigsqcup_{i=1}^4 \mathsf{card}\,(\mathcal{T}_{\rho^*}^*[p_i])$$
$$= n \sqcup n \cdot s \sqcup n \cdot s^3 \sqcup n \cdot s^3 = n \cdot s^3$$

$\square$

For an asymptotic sparsity assignment ρ^*, let $\mathsf{card}\,\rho^*$ equal the least upper bound of all values $\mathsf{card}\,(\rho^*\,r)$, $r \in \mathcal{R}$. We obtain our main theorem:

Theorem 3. *For a Horn clause c of size $\mathcal{O}(1)$, let ρ^* denote an asymptotic sparsity assignment for the predicates occurring in c. Then the following holds:*

1. *The solutions ρ of c can be computed in time*
$$\mathcal{O}(\mathsf{card}\,\rho^* + \mathcal{C}_{\rho^*}^*[c])$$
provided that the sequence of interpretations ρ is asymptotically described by ρ^* (via β and Δ_η), i.e., for every occurring predicate r,
$$(\beta[\rho^{(N)}\,r])_{N \in \mathbb{N}}\,\Delta_\eta\,(\rho^*\,r)$$
2. *Asymptotic runtime estimates can be computed in time polynomial in the size of clauses.* $\square$

In other words, the runtime analysis predicts correctly the complexity of Horn clause solving for solutions whose sparsity matrices are asymptotically described by ρ^*. Moreover, the estimate itself can be computed efficiently.

6   Asymptotic Sparsity Analysis

Horn clauses will update certain relations by means of assertions. In a general application, we might have knowledge of the (asymptotic) sparsities of some relations whereas others are unknown beforehand or introduced a posteriori during clause tuning. In the control-flow analysis M_1 for Mobile Ambients, this is the case, e.g., for the relation sibling which is defined by the clause:

$$\mathsf{father}(Y, T), \mathsf{father}(Z, T) \Rightarrow \mathsf{sibling}(Y, Z)$$

Clearly, it is both annoying and error-prone if the user has to provide information also for such auxiliary relations – in particular, if these are introduced by some fully automatic clause optimizer.

Therefore, we design a sparsity analysis which takes the partial information provided by the user and tries to infer safe and reasonably precise (asymptotic) sparsity information also for the remaining predicates. We proceed in two steps. First, we infer sparsity matrices and then explain how to do that asymptotically.

6.1   Inferring Sparsity Matrices

For a set $\mathcal{E} \subseteq A \to \mathcal{U}$ of variable assignments and a sequence $args = X_1, \ldots, X_k$ of pairwise distinct variables $X_i \in A$, we define

$$\mathsf{assert}\,(\mathcal{E}, args) \quad = \quad \{(\sigma\,X_1, \ldots, \sigma\,X_k) \mid \sigma \in \mathcal{E}\}$$

Each implication $p \Rightarrow r(args)$ gives rise to the following constraint on ρ:

$$\mathsf{assert}\,(\mathcal{T}_\rho[p], args) \quad \subseteq \quad \rho\,r$$

Thus, the function assert extracts from the firings of the list of assumptions the tuples for the predicate on the right-hand side.

Abstracting this constraint system for solutions of c, we obtain an equation system for the sparsity matrices $(\rho^\sharp\,r), r \in \mathcal{R}$ as follows. For each predicate r in $\mathcal{R}$ of arity k, we accumulate the contributions of assertions onto the sparsity matrix of r where the impact of every implication with matching right-hand side is obtained by abstracting the corresponding concrete constraint. Accordingly, we define an abstract function $\mathsf{assert}^\sharp$ which for $m \in \mathcal{M}(N)_A$ and a list $args = X_1, \ldots, X_k$ of pairwise distinct variables X_i from A, collects the entries from m according to the variable list $args$ to build a $(k \times k)$-matrix from $\mathcal{M}(N)_k$:

$$\mathsf{assert}^\sharp\,(m, args) \quad = \quad \{ij \mapsto m_{X_i,X_j} \mid i,j = 1, \ldots, k\}$$

For $r \in \mathcal{R}$, let $\mathcal{I}[r]$ denote the set of implications in c where r occurs on the right-hand side. Let us furthermore fix an initial interpretation $\rho_0^\sharp$ and a (possibly trivial) upper bound $\rho_1^\sharp$ to the sparsity matrices of occurring predicate symbols. Then we obtain an equation system $\mathcal{S}^\sharp$ for the values $\rho^\sharp\,r, r \in \mathcal{R}$, by:

$$\rho_1^\sharp\,r \sqcap \left(\rho_0^\sharp\,r \oplus \bigoplus_{p \Rightarrow r(args)\,\in\,\mathcal{I}[r]} \mathsf{assert}\,(\mathcal{T}_{\rho^\sharp}^\sharp[p], args)\right) \quad = \quad \rho^\sharp\,r$$

Computing the least model of the clause c is abstractly simulated by the least fixpoint iteration for $\mathcal{S}^\sharp$. This was the easy part. It remains to proceed to asymptotic sparsities.

6.2   Inferring Asymptotic Sparsity Matrices

We define a function assert^* which, given an asymptotic sparsity matrix m and a list $args = X_1, \ldots, X_k$ of pairwise distinct variables X_i, returns

$$\mathsf{assert}^*\,(m, args) \quad = \quad \{ij \mapsto m_{X_i,X_j} \mid i,j = 1, \ldots, k\}$$

Thus, the call assert* $(m, args)$ collects the entries from m according to the variable list $args$ to build a $(k \times k)$-matrix from $\mathcal{P}_k(\eta)$. For a given initial asymptotic assignment ρ_0^* and an upper bound ρ_1^*, we obtain an equation system $\mathcal{S}^*$ for the values $\rho^* r, r \in \mathcal{R}$, by:

$$\rho_1^* r \sqcap \left(\rho_0^* r \sqcup \bigsqcup_{p \Rightarrow r(args) \,\in\, \mathcal{I}[r]} \mathsf{assert}\left(\mathcal{T}_{\rho^*}^*[p], args\right)\right) \;=\; \rho^* r$$

The contributions to $\rho^* r$ from different implications are now combined by the least-upper-bound operator. Since the left-hand sides of $\mathcal{S}^*$ are monotonic in the asymptotic sparsity assignment, the least as well as the greatest solution of $\mathcal{S}^*$ are well defined. Choosing the least solution, though, is no longer *safe*. Intuitively, this is due to the fact that although $\mathcal{O}(1) + \mathcal{O}(1) = \mathcal{O}(1)$, an arbitrary sum

$$\mathcal{O}(1) + \ldots + \mathcal{O}(1)$$

may return any value. This is reflected in proposition 6.1 (line 2) which speaks about asymptotic descriptions of sequences of *binary* "$\oplus$"-applications only. The incorrectness of the least solution becomes apparent when looking at the Horn clause defining the transitive closure t of an input edge relation e:

$$e(X,Y) \Rightarrow t(X,Y) \qquad \wedge \qquad e(X,Y),\, t(Y,Z) \Rightarrow t(X,Z)$$

If we break down the corresponding system $\mathcal{S}^*$ for the value $(\rho^* t)$ to equations for the components $t_{ij} = (\rho^* t)_{ij}$, we obtain the following equation for t_{12}:

$$b_{12} \sqcap (e_{12} \sqcup e_{12} \cdot t_{12}) \;=\; t_{12}$$

Here, $b_{12} = (\rho_1^* t)_{12}$ is the upper bound for t_{12} specified by the user, and $e_{12} = (\rho^* e)_{12}$ is the asymptotic maximal out-degree of the input graph. Let us assume that $e_{12} = 1$, i.e., the input graph has asymptotically constant out-degree. Then the equation for t_{12} can be simplified to:

$$b_{12} \sqcap t_{12} \;=\; t_{12}$$

The least solution of this equation is $t_{12} = 1$ — implying that the transitive closure of e necessarily has constant out-degree as well: which is *wrong*. In contrast, the *greatest* solution gives us $t_{12} = b_{12}$ — which is reasonable, as it is the upper bound provided by the user.   Sparsity inference, however, through the greatest solution of $\mathcal{S}^*$ will not always infer such trivial results.

Example (continued).   Consider the definition of the auxiliary predicate sibling and assume that the matrix:

$$\rho_1^* \,\mathsf{father} = \begin{pmatrix} 1 & s \\ s & 1 \end{pmatrix}$$

has been provided as the asymptotic sparsity matrix of the predicate father. Then we calculate for $p \equiv \mathsf{father}(Y,T), \mathsf{father}(Z,T)$ (see fig. 3):

$$\begin{aligned}
\mathcal{T}_{\rho^*}^*[p] &= \{(Y,T) \mapsto s, (T,Y) \mapsto s\}_{\{Y,T\}} \sqcap \{(Z,T) \mapsto s, (T,Z) \mapsto s\}_{\{Z,T\}} \\
&= \{\ (Y,T) \mapsto s, (T,Y) \mapsto s, (Y,Z) \mapsto s^2, \\
&\qquad (Z,T) \mapsto s, (T,Z) \mapsto s, (Z,Y) \mapsto s^2 \ \}_{\{Y,Z,T\}}
\end{aligned}$$

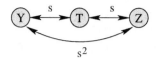

Fig. 3. The weighted graph for $\mathcal{T}_{\rho^*}^*[p]$.

This gives us the value for left-hand side of the equation of $\mathcal{S}^*$ for ρ^* sibling :

$$\mathsf{assert}^*(\mathcal{T}_{\rho^*}^*[p], (Y, Z)) = \begin{pmatrix} 1 & s^2 \\ s^2 & 1 \end{pmatrix}$$

Since this matrix is constant, it provides us with the final value of the greatest solution of $\mathcal{S}^*$ for sibling. Indeed, this was precisely the matrix which we had to assert manually in the complexity computation of section 5.   □

In summary, we prove:

Theorem 4. *Let c denote a Horn clause of size $\mathcal{O}(1)$ and ρ^* the greatest solution of the equation system $\mathcal{S}^*$. Let $\underline{\rho}_0$ denote a sequence of initial interpretations which is asymptotically described by ρ_0^* (via β and Δ_η) and $\underline{\rho}$ the sequence of least solutions of c exceeding $\underline{\rho}_0$. Then the following holds:*

1. *Whenever the sequence $\underline{\rho}$ is asymptotically described by ρ_1^* (via β and Δ_η), then it is also asymptotically described by ρ^*. This means that, whenever*

   $$(\beta[\rho^{(N)} r])_{N \in \mathbb{N}} \; \Delta_\eta \; (\rho_1^* r)$$

   for every predicate r, then also

   $$(\beta[\rho^{(N)} r])_{N \in \mathbb{N}} \; \Delta_\eta \; (\rho^* r)$$

   for every predicate r.
2. *Greatest asymptotic sparsity assignments can be computed in time polynomial in the size of the respective clauses.*

In other words, given a safe assertion about the asymptotic sparsities of (some) predicates, our asymptotic sparsity analysis will provide a possibly better but still safe assertion about the asymptotic sparsities. Thus, it can be seen as a *narrowing* procedure to improve on a given safe information. Theorem 4 holds since, opposed to the least fixpoint, the greatest fixpoint of the system $\mathcal{S}^*$ is reached after a uniformly bounded number of iterations.

Proof. The equation system $\mathcal{S}^*$ can be written as $F \rho^* = \rho^*$ where F is the joint function of left-hand sides in $\mathcal{S}^*$. Then we argue as follows.

(1) We safely may apply *one single* fixpoint iteration, i.e., given that ρ^* is a correct asymptotic sparsity assignment, $F \rho^*$ is still correct.
(2) We safely may apply any *constant* number of fixpoint iterations, i.e., given that ρ^* is a correct asymptotic sparsity assignment, $F^h \rho^*$ is still a correct asymptotic sparsity assignment for any h which may depend on the constraint system – but is independent of the universe and the predicates.
(3) The greatest fixpoint is reached after a finite number of iterations. More precisely, the greatest fixpoint of F is given by $F^h \rho_1^*$, with $h \leq |\mathcal{R}| \cdot a^2$ where a is the maximal arity of a predicate from $\mathcal{R}$.

Assertion (1) follows by induction on the structure of pre-conditions. Assertion (2) follows accordingly. Therefore, it remains to prove assertion (3). First, we observe that each component of F defining an entry (i, j) of the asymptotic sparsity matrix for some predicate r is composed of a bounded number of basic operations on $\mathbb{D}_\eta$. Then we rely on the following observation:

Let $\mathbb{D}$ denote a complete lattice. A function $f : \mathbb{D}^m \to \mathbb{D}$ is called *nice* iff f is monotonic and for all pairs of m-tuples $(x_1, \ldots, x_m), (y_1, \ldots, y_m) \in \mathbb{D}^m$, with $x_i \sqsubseteq y_i$ for all i, the following holds:

$$\text{If } f(x_1, \ldots, x_m) \sqsubset f(y_1, \ldots, y_m) \text{ then } \bigsqcap \{x_i \mid x_i \neq y_i\} \sqsubseteq f(x_1, \ldots, x_m).$$

Niceness of functions is a semantical property which generalizes the (partly syntactically defined) property considered by Knuth in [9]. In contrast to Knuth's property, niceness is preserved under composition, and least upper bounds:

Proposition 7. *1. Constant functions $\lambda x_1, \ldots, x_m.c$, $c \in \mathbb{D}$, the identity $\lambda x.x$ as well as the binary operation $\sqcup$ are nice.*
2. In case of linear orderings $\mathbb{D}$, also $\sqcap$ is nice.
3. Nice functions are closed under composition, greatest and least fixpoints. $\square$

A proof of the following theorem is included in the full version of the paper:

Theorem 5. *Consider a system of equations $f_i(x_1, \ldots, x_m) = x_i$, $i = 1, \ldots, m$, where all left-hand sides $f_i : \mathbb{D}^m \to \mathbb{D}$ are nice. Let $F : \mathbb{D}^m \to \mathbb{D}^m$ denote the function $F = (f_1, \ldots, f_m)$. If $\mathbb{D}$ is a linear ordering, then the greatest fixpoint νF of F is reached after m iterations, i.e., $\nu F = F^m(\top, \ldots, \top)$.* $\square$

Let $\mathcal{S}$ denote the constraint system over $\mathbb{D}_\eta$ which is obtained from $\mathcal{S}^*$ by writing the equations componentwise. Thus, the set of variables of $\mathcal{S}$ are given by all $(\rho^* r)_{ij}$, $r \in \mathcal{R}$, where each left-hand side is an expression built up from constants and these variables by means of applications of the operators "$\sqcup$", "$\sqcap$", and "$\cdot$". Since our operation "$\cdot$" is also nice, we conclude from proposition 7 that all left-hand side expressions in $\mathcal{S}$ represent nice functions. Thus, theorem 5 is applicable. As $\mathcal{S}$ has at most $|\mathcal{R}| \cdot a^2$ many variables (a the maximal arity of a predicate in $\mathcal{R}$), our assertion (3) follows. This completes the proof. $\square$

7   Practical Implementation and Experimental Results

The key idea of McAllester's Horn clause solver is to bring clauses into a specific canonical form which then is easy to solve. In order to do so, he introduces auxiliary predicates for prefixes of pre-conditions and employs constructor applications for collecting instantiated variables.

In our applications, we found it rather restrictive to deal with Horn clauses only. Therefore, we extended the Horn clause framework by explicit quantification, conditional clauses and stratified negation. The Horn clause for transitive closure, e.g., could be written in our logic as:

$$\forall X, Y : e(X, Y) \Rightarrow (t(X, Y) \wedge (\forall Z : t(Y, Z) \Rightarrow t(X, Z)))$$

The logic which we have implemented is known to Logicians as *alternation-free least fixpoint logic* in clausal form [8]. It is more expressive than "Horn clauses with sharing" [12] or Datalog – even with stratified negation [4, 10].

For this richer logic, McAllester's solving method does not suffice any longer. Therefore, we developed and implemented an alternative solving algorithm. In contrast to McAllester's method, our solving procedure does not rely on pre-processing. It also abandons special worklist-like data-structures as are typical for most classical fixpoint algorithms [6]. Still, it meets the same complexity estimation for Horn clauses as McAllester's. For details about this solver algorithm, see [13]. Accordingly, we extended and implemented the complexity estimator described in the preceding sections to this stronger logic and our solver.

Applying the automatic complexity analyzer to the two formulations M_0 and M_1 of control-flow analysis for the Ambient calculus, we succeed in refining the rough complexity estimations from [12] — provided that further assumptions about the resulting control-flow are met.

Besides these refinements for the ambient analyses, we report here also on the results of the complexity estimator on the following benchmarks:

> TC: transitive closure of some edge relation;
> FL: control-flow analysis of a functional language;
> P: control-flow analysis for the pi calculus from [12].

For transitive closure, the results are reported depending on the asymptotic sparsity of the edge relation e. In the sparse case, we use the asymptotic sparsity matrix:

$$\begin{pmatrix} 1 & s \\ s & 1 \end{pmatrix}$$

For all control-flow analyses, we investigate the impact of different assumptions on the asymptotic sparsity of the result relation. The clause M_1 is obtained from the clause M_0 by introduction of various auxiliary predicates [12]. No information has been provided to the complexity analyzer for these — meaning that their asymptotic sparsities are inferred by the system. The following table collects the estimations computed by our analysis:

	dense	sparse
TC	n^3	$n^2 \cdot s$
FL	n^3	$n \cdot s^2$
P	n^3	$n^2 \cdot s$
M_0	n^4	$n \cdot s^3$
M_1	n^3	$n \cdot s^3$

The simplest clause is the one for transitive closure where the tool returns the expected complexities. On CFA for functional languages, it nicely assures that the complexity is low if only few values are found for each expression into which it may develop. The same holds true for the mobile ambients. Interestingly, here both the unoptimized and the optimized analysis give the same asymptotic complexity – provided that the computed relation is sparse.

8 Conclusion

The complexity analysis has benefitted from the pioneering ideas of McAllester [11] and Basin and Ganzinger [2] on the complexity of solving Horn clauses. The contribution of our paper is to *fully automate the necessary calculations*. In particular, the idea of asymptotic sparsity matrices for describing the asymptotic sparseness of relations as well as our narrowing algorithm for inferring asymptotic sparsity matrices for predicates seems to be new.

McAllester himself [11] and together with Ganzinger [7] have provided further complexity meta-theorems for interesting deductive systems which are also candidates for integration into a program analyzer workbench. A challenging open question is whether the necessary complexity calculations for these can be automated as well.

References

1. A. Aiken. Introduction to set constraint-based program analysis. *Science of Computer Programming (SCP)*, 35(2):79–111, 1999.
2. D.A. Basin and H. Ganzinger. Complexity Analysis Based on Ordered Resolution. In *11th IEEE Symposium on Logic in Computer Science (LICS)*, 456–465, 1996. Long version to appear in JACM.
3. L. Cardelli and A.D. Gordon. Mobile ambients. In *Proceedings of FoSSaCS'98*, volume 1378 of *LNCS*, 140–155. Springer-Verlag, 1998.
4. E. Dahlhaus. Skolem normal forms concerning the least fixpoint. In *Computation Theory and Logic*, 101–106. LNCS 270, Springer Verlag, 1987.
5. D. L. Dill. Timing assumptions and verification of finite state concurrent systems. In *Automatic Verification Methods for Finite State Systems*, 197–212. LNCS 407, Springer Verlag, 1989.
6. C. Fecht and H. Seidl. A faster solver for general systems of equations. *Science of Computer Programming (SCP)*, 35(2-3):137–162, 1999.
7. H. Ganzinger and D.A. McAllester. A new meta-complexity theorem for bottom-up logic programs. In *First Int. Joint Conference on Automated Reasoning (IJCAR)*, 514–528. LNCS 2083, Springer Verlag, 2001.
8. G. Gottlob, E. Grädel, and H. Veith. Datalog LITE: A deductive query language with linear time model checking. *ACM Transactions on Computational Logic*, 2001. To appear.
9. D. E. Knuth. On a generalization of Dijkstra's algorithm. *Information Processing Letters (IPL)*, 6(1):1–5, 1977.
10. P.G. Kolaitis. Implicit definability on finite structures and unambiguous computations (preliminary report). In *5th Annual IEEE Symposium on Logic in Computer Science (LICS)*, 168–180, 1990.
11. D. McAllester. On the complexity analysis of static analyses. In *6th Static Analysis Symposium (SAS)*, 312–329. LNCS 1694, Springer Verlag, 1999.
12. F. Nielson and H. Seidl. Control-flow analysis in cubic time. In *European Symposium on Programming (ESOP)*, 252–268. LNCS 2028, Springer Verlag, 2001.
13. F. Nielson and H. Seidl. Succinct solvers. Technical Report 01-12, University of Trier, Germany, 2001.
14. R. Shaham, K. Kordner, and S. Sagiv. Automatic removal of array memory leaks in Java. In *Compiler Construction (CC)*, 50–66. LNCS 1781, Springer Verlag, 2000.

Thread-Modular Verification
for Shared-Memory Programs

Cormac Flanagan, Stephen N. Freund, and Shaz Qadeer

Compaq Systems Research Center, 130 Lytton Ave., Palo Alto, CA 94301

Abstract. Ensuring the reliability of multithreaded software systems is difficult due to the interaction between threads. This paper describes the design and implementation of a static checker for such systems. To avoid considering all possible thread interleavings, the checker uses assume-guarantee reasoning, and relies on the programmer to specify an *environment assumption* that constrains the interaction between threads. Using this environment assumption, the checker reduces the verification of the original multithreaded program to the verification of several sequential programs, one for each thread. These sequential programs are subsequently analyzed using extended static checking techniques (based on verification conditions and automatic theorem proving). Experience indicates that the checker is capable of handling a range of synchronization disciplines. In addition, the required environment assumptions are simple and intuitive for common synchronization idioms.

1 Introduction

Ensuring the reliability of critical software systems is an important but extremely difficult task. A number of useful tools and techniques have been developed for reasoning about sequential systems. Unfortunately, these sequential analysis tools are not applicable to many critical software systems because such systems are often multithreaded. The presence of multiple threads significantly complicates the analysis because of the potential for interference between threads; each atomic step of a thread can influence the subsequent behavior of other threads.

For multithreaded programs, more complex analysis techniques are necessary. The classical assertional approach [Ash75,OG76,Lam77,Lam88] requires control predicates at each program point to specify the reachable program states, but the annotation burden for using this approach is high. Some promising tools [DHJ+01,Yah01] use model checking and abstract interpretation to infer the reachable state set automatically, but the need to consider all possible thread interleavings may hinder scaling to large programs.

A more modular and scalable approach is assume-guarantee reasoning, in which each component is verified separately using a specification of the other components [MC81,Jon83a]. Several researchers have presented assume-guarantee proof rules (see Section 2), and some verification tools that support assume-guarantee reasoning on hardware have recently appeared [McM97,AHM+98].

D. Le Métayer (Ed.): ESOP 2002, LNCS 2305, pp. 262–277, 2002.

However, tools for assume-guarantee reasoning on realistic software systems do not exist.

In this paper, we describe the design and implementation of a static checker for multithreaded programs, based on an assume-guarantee decomposition. This checker is targeted to the verification of actual implementations of software systems, as opposed to logical models or abstractions of these systems. The checker relies on the programmer to specify, for each thread, an *environment assumption* that models the interference caused by other threads. This environment assumption is an action, or two-store relation, that constrains the updates to the shared store by interleaved atomic steps of other threads. The atomic steps of each thread are also required to satisfy a corresponding guarantee condition that implies the assumption of every other thread.

Using these assumptions and guarantees, our checker translates each thread into a sequential program that models the behavior of that thread precisely and uses the environment assumption to model the behavior of other threads. Thus, our assume-guarantee decomposition reduces the verification of a program with n threads to the verification of n sequential programs. This *thread-modular* decomposition allows our tool to leverage extended static checking techniques [DLNS98] (based on verification conditions and automatic theorem proving) to check the resulting sequential programs.

We have implemented our checker for multithreaded programs written in the Java programming language [AG96], and we have successfully applied this checker to a number of programs. These programs use a variety of synchronization mechanisms, ranging from simple mutual exclusion locks to more complex idioms found in systems code, including a subtle synchronization idiom used in the distributed file system Frangipani [TML97].

Experience with this implementation indicates that our analysis has the following useful features:

1. It naturally scales to programs with many threads since each thread is analyzed separately.
2. For programs using common synchronization idioms, such as mutexes or reader-writer locks, the necessary annotations are simple and intuitive.
3. Control predicates can be expressed in our analysis by explicating the program counter of each thread as an auxiliary variable. Therefore, theoretically our method is as expressive as the Owicki-Gries method. However, for many common cases, such as those appearing in Section 6, our method requires significantly fewer annotations.

The remainder of the paper proceeds as follows. The following section describes related work on assume-guarantee reasoning and other tools for detecting synchronization errors. Section 3 introduces *Plato*, an idealized language for parallel programs that we use as the basis for our development. Section 4 provides a formal definition of thread-modular verification. Section 5 applies thread-modular reasoning to the problem of invariant verification. Section 6 describes our implementation and its application to a number of example programs. We conclude in Section 7.

2   Background

One of the earliest assume-guarantee proof rules was developed by Misra and Chandy [MC81] for message-passing systems, and later refined by others (see, for example, [Jon89,MM93]). However, their message-passing formulation is not directly applicable to shared-memory software.

Jones [Jon83a,Jon83b] gave a proof rule for multithreaded shared-memory programs and used it to manually refine an assume-guarantee specification down to a program. We extend his work to allow the proof obligations for each thread to be checked mechanically by an automatic theorem prover. Stark [Sta85] also presented a rule for shared-memory programs to deduce that a conjunction of assume-guarantee specifications hold on a system provided each specification holds individually, but his work did not allow the decomposition of the implementation.

Abadi and Lamport [AL95] view the composition of components as a conjunction of temporal logic formulas [Lam94] describing them, and they present a rule to decompose such systems. Since threads modifying shared variables cannot be viewed as components in their framework, their work is not directly applicable to our problem. Collette and Knapp [CK95] extended the rule of Abadi and Lamport to the more operational setting of Unity [CM88] specifications.

Alur and Henzinger [AH96] and McMillan [McM97] present assume-guarantee proof rules for hardware components. A number of other compositional proof rules not based on assume-guarantee reasoning have also been proposed, such as [BKP84,CM88,MP95].

Yahav [Yah01] describes a method to model check multithreaded programs using a 3-valued logic [SRW99,LAS00] to abstract the store. This technique can verify interesting properties of small programs. Păsăreanu et al. [PDH99] also describe a model checking tool for compositional checking of finite-state message passing systems. Abraham-Mumm and deBoer [AMdB00] sketch a logic for verifying multi-threaded Java programs indirectly via a translation to communicating sequential programs.

A number of tools have been developed for identifying specific synchronization errors in multithreaded programs. These approaches are less general than thread-modular verification and use specific analysis techniques to locate specific errors, such as data races and deadlocks. For example, RCC/Java [FF00] is an annotation-based checker for Java that uses a type system to identify data races [FA99]. While this tool is successful at finding errors in large programs, the inability to specify subtle synchronization patterns results in many false alarms [FF01]. ESC/Java [LSS99], Warlock [Ste93], and the dynamic testing tool Eraser [SBN+97] are other tools in this category, and are discussed in an earlier paper [FF00].

3   The Parallel Language Plato

We present thread-modular verification in terms of the idealized language *Plato* (parallel language of atomic operations). A Plato program P is a parallel composition $S_1 \mid \cdots \mid S_n$ of several statements, or *threads*. The program executes by interleaving atomic steps of its various threads. The threads interact through a shared store σ, which maps program variables to values. The sets of variables and values are left intentionally unspecified, as they are mostly orthogonal to our development.

Statements in the Plato language include the empty statement **skip**, sequential composition $S_1; S_2$, the nondeterministic choice construct $S_1 \square S_2$, which executes either S_1 or S_2, and the iteration statement S^*, which executes S some arbitrary number of times.

Plato syntax

$S \in Stmt ::=$	**skip**	no operation	$P \in Program ::= S_1 \mid \cdots \mid S_n$
	$\mid X \downarrow Y$	atomic operation	$\sigma \in \quad Store \quad = Var \rightarrow Value$
	$\mid S \square S$	nondeterministic choice	$X, Y \in \quad Action \quad \subseteq Store \times Store$
	$\mid S; S$	composition	
	$\mid S^*$	nondeterministic iteration	

Perhaps the most notable aspect of Plato is that it does not contain constructs for conventional primitive operations such as assignment and lock acquire and release operations. Instead, such primitive operations are combined into a general mechanism called an *atomic operation* $X \downarrow Y$, where X and Y are *actions*, or two-store predicates. The action X is a constraint on the transition from the pre-store σ to the post-store σ', and Y is an assertion about this transition.

To execute the atomic operation $X \downarrow Y$, an arbitrary post-store σ' is chosen that satisfies the constraint $X(\sigma, \sigma')$. There are two possible outcomes:

1. If the assertion $Y(\sigma, \sigma')$ holds, then the atomic operation terminates normally, and the execution of the program continues with the new store σ'.
2. If the assertion $Y(\sigma, \sigma')$ does not hold, then the execution *goes wrong*.

If no post-store σ' satisfies the constraint $X(\sigma, \sigma')$, then the thread is blocked, and the execution can proceed only on the other threads.

In an atomic operation, we write each action as a formula in which primed variables refer to their value in the post-store σ', and unprimed variables refer to their value in the pre-store σ. In addition, for any action X and set of variables $V \subseteq Var$, we use the notation $\langle X \rangle_V$ to mean the action that satisfies X and only allows changes to variables in V between the pre-store and the post-store. We abbreviate the common case $\langle X \rangle_\emptyset$ to $\langle X \rangle$ and also abbreviate $\langle X \rangle_{\{a\}}$ to $\langle X \rangle_a$.

Atomic operations can express many conventional primitives, such as assignment, assert, and assume statements (see below). Atomic operations can also express other primitives, in particular lock acquire and release operations. We assume that each lock is represented by a variable and that each thread has a unique nonzero thread identifier. If a thread holds a lock, then the lock variable contains the corresponding thread identifier; if the lock is not held, then the variable contains zero. Under this representation, acquire and release operations for lock **mx** and thread i are shown below. Finally, Plato can also express traditional control constructs, such as **if** and **while** statements.

Expressing conventional constructs in Plato

$$\texttt{x} := e \;\overset{\text{def}}{=}\; \langle x' = e \rangle_x \downarrow \texttt{true} \qquad\qquad \texttt{acq(mx)} \;\overset{\text{def}}{=}\; \langle \texttt{mx} = 0 \wedge \texttt{mx}' = \texttt{i} \rangle_{\texttt{mx}} \downarrow \texttt{true}$$

$$\texttt{assert } e \;\overset{\text{def}}{=}\; \langle \texttt{true} \rangle \downarrow e \qquad\qquad\quad \texttt{rel(mx)} \;\overset{\text{def}}{=}\; \langle \texttt{mx}' = 0 \rangle_{\texttt{mx}} \downarrow (\texttt{mx} = \texttt{i})$$

$$\texttt{assume } e \;\overset{\text{def}}{=}\; \langle e \rangle \downarrow \texttt{true} \qquad\qquad \texttt{if } (e) \texttt{ \{ } S \texttt{ \}} \;\overset{\text{def}}{=}\; (\texttt{assume } e; S) \square (\texttt{assume } \neg e)$$

$$\texttt{while } (e) \texttt{ \{ } S \texttt{ \}} \;\overset{\text{def}}{=}\; (\texttt{assume } e; S)^*; (\texttt{assume } \neg e)$$

3.1   Formal Semantics

The execution of a program is defined as an interleaving of the executions of its individual, sequential threads. A *sequential state* Φ is either a pair of a store and a statement, or the special state **wrong** (indicating that the execution went wrong by failing an assertion). The semantics of individual threads is defined via the transition relation $\Phi \rightarrow_s \Phi$, defined in the figure below.

A *parallel state* Θ is either a pair of a store and a program (representing the threads being executed), or the special state **wrong**. The transition relation $\Theta \rightarrow_p \Theta$ on parallel states executes a single sequential step of an arbitrarily chosen thread. If that sequential step terminates normally, then execution continues with the resulting post-state. If the sequential step goes wrong, then so does the entire execution.

Formal semantics of Plato

$$\Phi \in SeqState ::= (\sigma, S) \mid \textbf{wrong} \qquad\qquad \Theta \in ParState ::= (\sigma, P) \mid \textbf{wrong}$$

[ACTION OK]
$$\frac{X(\sigma, \sigma') \qquad Y(\sigma, \sigma')}{(\sigma, X \downarrow Y) \rightarrow_s (\sigma', \textbf{skip})}$$

[ACTION WRONG]
$$\frac{X(\sigma, \sigma') \qquad \neg Y(\sigma, \sigma')}{(\sigma, X \downarrow Y) \rightarrow_s \textbf{wrong}}$$

[CHOICE]
$$\frac{i \in \{1, 2\}}{(\sigma, S_1 \square S_2) \rightarrow_s (\sigma, S_i)}$$

[LOOP DONE]
$$\frac{}{(\sigma, S^*) \rightarrow_s (\sigma, \textbf{skip})}$$

[LOOP UNROLL]
$$\frac{}{(\sigma, S^*) \rightarrow_s (\sigma, S; S^*)}$$

[ASSOC]
$$\frac{}{(\sigma, (S_1; S_2); S_3) \rightarrow_s (\sigma, S_1; (S_2; S_3))}$$

[SEQ STEP]
$$\frac{(\sigma, S_1) \rightarrow_s (\sigma', S_1')}{(\sigma, S_1; S_2) \rightarrow_s (\sigma', S_1'; S_2)}$$

[SEQ SKIP]
$$\frac{}{(\sigma, \textbf{skip}; S) \rightarrow_s (\sigma, S)}$$

[SEQ WRONG]
$$\frac{(\sigma, S_1) \rightarrow_s \textbf{wrong}}{(\sigma, S_1; S_2) \rightarrow_s \textbf{wrong}}$$

[PARALLEL]
$$\frac{(\sigma, S_i) \rightarrow_s (\sigma', S_i')}{(\sigma, S_1 \mid \cdots \mid S_i \mid \cdots \mid S_n) \rightarrow_p (\sigma', S_1 \mid \cdots \mid S_i' \mid \cdots \mid S_n)}$$

[PARALLEL WRONG]
$$\frac{(\sigma, S_i) \rightarrow_s \textbf{wrong}}{(\sigma, S_1 \mid \cdots \mid S_i \mid \cdots \mid S_n) \rightarrow_p \textbf{wrong}}$$

4   Thread-Modular Verification

We reason about a parallel program $P = S_1 \mid \cdots \mid S_n$ by reasoning about each thread in P separately. For each thread i, we specify two actions — an environment assumption A_i and a guarantee G_i. The assumption of a thread is a specification of what transitions may be performed by other threads in the program. The guarantee of a thread is required to hold on every action performed by the thread itself. To ensure the correctness of the assumptions, we require that the guarantee of each thread be stronger than the assumption of every other thread. In addition, to accommodate effect-free transitions, we require each assumption and guarantee to be reflexive. The precise statement of these requirements is as follows:

1. A_i and G_i are reflexive for all $i \in 1..n$.
2. $G_i \subseteq A_j$ for all $i, j \in 1..n$ such that $i \neq j$.

If these requirements are satisfied, then $\langle A_1, G_1 \rangle, \ldots, \langle A_n, G_n \rangle$ is an *assume-guarantee decomposition* for P.

We next define the translation $[\![S]\!]_G^A$ of a statement S with respect to an assumption A and a guarantee G. This translation verifies that each atomic operation of S satisfies the guarantee G. In addition, the translation inserts the iterated environment assumption A^* as appropriate to model atomic steps of other threads.

$$[\![\bullet]\!]_\bullet^\bullet : Stmt \times Action \times Action \to Stmt$$

$$
\begin{aligned}
[\![\mathbf{skip}]\!]_G^A &= A^* \\
[\![X \downarrow Y]\!]_G^A &= A^*; X \downarrow (Y \wedge G); A^* \\
[\![S_1 \square S_2]\!]_G^A &= A^*; ([\![S_1]\!]_G^A \square [\![S_2]\!]_G^A) \\
[\![S_1; S_2]\!]_G^A &= [\![S_1]\!]_G^A; [\![S_2]\!]_G^A \\
[\![S^*]\!]_G^A &= A^*; (([\![S]\!]_G^A; A^*)^*; A^*)
\end{aligned}
$$

We use this translation and the assume-guarantee decomposition to abstract each thread i of the parallel program P into the sequential program $[\![S_i]\!]_{G_i}^{A_i}$, called the *i-abstraction* of P. For any thread i, if A_i models the environment of thread i and the sequential i-abstraction of P does not go wrong, then we conclude that the corresponding thread S_i in P does not go wrong and also satisfies the guarantee G_i. Thus, if none of the i-abstractions go wrong, then none of the threads in P go wrong. This property is formalized by the following theorem; its correctness proof avoids circular reasoning by using induction over time. (An extended report containing the proof of theorems in this paper is in available at http://www.research.compaq.com/SRC/personal/freund/tmv-draft.ps.)

Theorem 1 (Thread-Modular Verification). *Let $P = S_1 \mid \cdots \mid S_n$ be a parallel program with assume-guarantee decomposition $\langle A_1, G_1 \rangle, \ldots, \langle A_n, G_n \rangle$. For all $\sigma \in Store$, if $\forall i \in 1..n.\ (\sigma, [\![S_i]\!]_{G_i}^{A_i}) \not\to_s^* \mathbf{wrong}$, then $(\sigma, P) \not\to_p^* \mathbf{wrong}$.*

This theorem allows us to decompose the analysis of a parallel program $S_1 \mid \cdots \mid S_n$ into analyses of individual threads by providing an assume-guarantee decomposition $\langle A_1, G_1 \rangle, \ldots, \langle A_n, G_n \rangle$. In practice, we only require the programmer to specify reflexive assumptions $A_1, \ldots, A_n$, and we derive the corresponding reflexive guarantees by

$$G_i = (\forall j \in 1..n.\ j \neq i \Rightarrow A_j).$$

For all examples we have considered, the natural assumptions are transitive in addition to being reflexive. This allows us to optimize the iterations A_i^* in each i-abstraction to simply the action A_i. In addition, the n environment assumptions $A_1, \ldots, A_n$ for a program with n threads can typically be conveniently expressed as a single action parameterized by thread identifier, as shown below.

4.1   Example

To illustrate Theorem 1, consider the following program SimpleLock. The program manipulates two shared variables, an integer x and a lock mx. To synchronize accesses to x, each thread acquires the lock mx before manipulating x. The correctness condition we would like to verify is that Thread$_1$ never goes wrong by failing the assertion x > 1.

SimpleLock program, desugared Thread$_1$, and $[\![\text{Thread}_1]\!]_{G_1}^{A_1}$

Thread$_1$:	Thread$_2$:	Desugared Thread$_1$:	$[\![\text{Thread}_1]\!]_{G_1}^{A_1}$:
acq(mx);	acq(mx);	$\langle \text{mx} = 0 \wedge \text{mx}' = 1 \rangle_{\text{mx}};$	$A_1; \langle \text{mx} = 0 \wedge \text{mx}' = 1 \rangle_{\text{mx}} \downarrow G_1;$
x := x * x;	x := 0;	$\langle \text{x}' = \text{x} * \text{x} \rangle_{\text{x}};$	$A_1; \langle \text{x}' = \text{x} * \text{x} \rangle_{\text{x}} \downarrow G_1;$
x := x + 2;	rel(mx);	$\langle \text{x}' = \text{x} + 2 \rangle_{\text{x}};$	$A_1; \langle \text{x}' = \text{x} + 2 \rangle_{\text{x}} \downarrow G_1;$
assert x > 1;		$\langle \text{true} \rangle \downarrow (\text{x} > 1);$	$A_1; \langle \text{true} \rangle \downarrow (\text{x} > 1 \wedge G_1);$
rel(mx);		$\langle \text{mx}' = 0 \rangle_{\text{mx}} \downarrow (\text{mx} = 1);$	$A_1; \langle \text{mx}' = 0 \rangle_{\text{mx}} \downarrow (\text{mx} = 1 \wedge G_1);$
			A_1

The synchronization discipline in this program is that if a thread holds the lock mx, then the other thread cannot modify either the variable x or the lock variable mx. This discipline is formalized by the following environment assumption for thread identifier $i \in 1..2$:

$$A_i = (\text{mx} = i \Rightarrow \text{mx}' = i \wedge \text{x}' = \text{x})$$

The corresponding guarantees are $G_1 = A_2$ and $G_2 = A_1$. Since A_1 is reflexive and transitive, we can optimize both A_1^* and $A_1^*; A_1^*$ to A_1 in the 1-abstraction of SimpleLock, shown above.

Verifying the two i-abstractions of SimpleLock is straightforward, using existing analysis techniques for sequential programs. In particular, our checker uses extended static checking to verify that the two sequential i-abstractions of SimpleLock do not go wrong. Thus, the hypotheses of Theorem 1 are satisfied, and we conclude that the parallel program SimpleLock does not fail its assertion.

5 Invariant Verification

In the previous section, we showed that the SimpleLock program does not fail its assertion. In many cases, we would also like to show that a program preserves certain data invariants. This section extends thread-modular verification to check data invariants on a parallel program $P = S_1 \mid \ldots \mid S_n$. We use $Init \subseteq Store$ to describe the possible initial states of P, and we say that a set of states I is an *invariant* of P with respect to *Init* if for each $\sigma \in Init$, if $(\sigma, P) \to_p^* (\sigma', P')$, then $\sigma' \in I$.

To show that I is an invariant of P, it suffices to show that I holds initially (i.e., $Init \subseteq I$), and that I is preserved by each transition of P. We prove the latter property using thread-modular verification, where the guarantee G_i of each thread satisfies the property

$$G_i \;\Rightarrow\; (I \Rightarrow I').$$

In this formula, the predicate I denotes the action where I holds in the pre-state, and the post-state is unconstrained; similarly, I' denotes the action where the pre-state is unconstrained, and I holds in the post-state. Thus, $I \Rightarrow I'$ is the action stating that I is preserved.

The following theorem formalizes the application of thread-modular reasoning to invariant verification.

Theorem 2 (Invariant Verification). *Let* $P = S_1 \mid \cdots \mid S_n$ *be a parallel program with assume-guarantee decomposition* $\langle A_1, G_1 \rangle, \ldots, \langle A_n, G_n \rangle$, *and let Init and I be sets of stores. Suppose:*

1. *$Init \subseteq I$*
2. *$\forall i \in 1..n.\ G_i \Rightarrow (I \Rightarrow I')$*
3. *$\forall i \in 1..n.\ \forall \sigma \in Init.\ (\sigma, [\![S_i]\!]_{G_i}^{A_i}) \not\to_s^*$ **wrong***

Then I is an invariant of P with respect to Init.

In practice, we apply this theorem by requiring the programmer to supply the invariant I and the parameterized environment assumption A_i. We derive the corresponding parameterized guarantee:

$$G_i = (\forall j \in 1..n.\ j \neq i \Rightarrow A_j) \wedge (I \Rightarrow I')$$

The guarantee states that each atomic step of a thread satisfies the assumptions of the other threads and also preserves the invariant. Since each step preserves the invariant, we can strengthen the environment assumption to:

$$B_i = A_i \wedge (I \Rightarrow I')$$

The resulting assume-guarantee decomposition $\langle B_1, G_1 \rangle, \ldots, \langle B_n, G_n \rangle$ is then used in the application of Theorem 2. The first condition of that theorem, that $Init \subseteq I$, can be checked using a theorem prover [Nel81]. The second condition, that $\forall i \in 1..n.\ G_i \Rightarrow (I \Rightarrow I')$, follows directly from the definition of G_i. The final condition (similar to the condition of Theorem 1), that each sequential i-abstraction $[\![S_i]\!]_{G_i}^{B_i}$ does not go wrong from any initial store in *Init*, can be checked using extended static checking. The following section describes our implementation of an automatic checking tool for parallel programs that supports thread modular and invariant verification.

6   Implementation and Applications

We have implemented an automatic checking tool for parallel, shared-memory programs. This checker takes as input a Java program, together with annotations describing appropriate environment assumptions, invariants, and asserted correctness properties. The input program is first translated into an intermediate representation language similar to Plato, and then the techniques of this paper are applied to generate an i-abstraction, which is parameterized by the thread identifier i.

This i-abstraction is then converted into a verification condition [Dij75,FS01]. When generating this verification condition, procedure calls are handled by inlining, and loops are translated either using a programmer-supplied loop invariant, or in an unsound but useful manner by unrolling loops some finite number of times [LSS99]. The automatic theorem prover Simplify [Nel81] is then invoked to check the validity of this verification condition.

If the verification condition is valid, then the parameterized i-abstraction does not go wrong, and hence the original Java program preserves the stated invariants and assertions. Alternatively, if the verification condition is invalid, then the theorem prover generates a counterexample, which is then post-processed into an appropriate error message in terms of the original Java program. Typically, the error message either identifies an atomic step that may violate one of the stated invariants or environment assumptions, or identifies an assertion that may go wrong. This assertion may either be explicit, as in the example programs, or may be an implicit assertion, for example, that a dereferenced pointer is never null.

The implementation of our checker leverages extensively off the Extended Static Checker for Java, which is a powerful checking tool for sequential Java programs. For more information regarding ESC/Java, we refer the interested reader to related documents [DLNS98,LSS99,FLL+02].

In the next three subsections, we describe the application of our checker to parallel programs using various kinds of synchronization. Due to space restrictions, these examples are necessarily small, but our checker has also been applied to significantly larger programs. In each of the presented examples, we state the necessary annotations: the assumptions A_i for each thread i and the invariant I to be proved. Given these annotations, our tool can automatically verify each of the example programs. For consistency with our earlier development, these programs are presented using Plato syntax.

6.1   Dekker's Mutual Exclusion Algorithm

Our first example is Dekker's algorithm, a classic algorithm for mutual exclusion that uses subtle synchronization.

Dekker's mutual exclusion algorithm

```
Variables:          Thread₁:                      Thread₂:
  boolean a₁;         while (true) {                while (true) {
  boolean a₂;           a₁ := true;                   a₂ := true;
  boolean cs₁;          cs₁ := ¬a₂;                   cs₂ := ¬a₁;
  boolean cs₂;          if (cs₁) {                    if (cs₂) {
                          // critical section           // critical section
Initially:                cs₁ := false;                 cs₂ := false;
  ¬cs₁ ∧ ¬cs₂           }                             }
                        a₁ := false;                  a₂ := false;
                      }                             }
```

The algorithm uses two boolean variables a_1 and a_2. We introduce two variables cs_1 and cs_2, where cs_i is true if thread i is in its critical section. Each $Thread_i$ expects that the other thread will not modify a_i and cs_i. We formalize this expectation as the assumption:

$$A_i \;\; = \;\; (a_i = a_i' \wedge cs_i = cs_i')$$

We would like to verify that the algorithm achieves mutual exclusion, which is expressed as the invariant $\neg(cs_1 \wedge cs_2)$. Unfortunately, this invariant cannot be verified directly. The final step is to strengthen the invariant to

$$I \;\; = \;\; \neg(cs_1 \wedge cs_2) \wedge (cs_1 \Rightarrow a_1) \wedge (cs_2 \Rightarrow a_2).$$

Using the assumptions A_1 and A_2 and the strengthened invariant I, our checker verifies that Dekker's algorithm achieves mutual exclusion.

In this example, the environment assumptions are quite simple. The subtlety of the algorithm is reflected in the invariant which had to be strengthened by two conjuncts. In general, the complexity of the assertions needed by our checker reflects the complexity of the synchronization patterns used in program being checked.

6.2   Reader-Writer Locks

The next example applies thread-modular reasoning to a *reader-writer lock*, which can be held in two different modes, *read mode* and *write mode*. Read mode is non-exclusive, and multiple threads may hold the lock in that mode. On the other hand, holding the lock in write mode means that no other threads hold the lock in either mode. Acquire operations block when these guarantees cannot be satisfied.

We implement a reader-writer lock using two variables: an integer w, which identifies the thread holding the lock in write mode (or 0 if no such thread exists), and an integer set r, which contains the identifiers of all threads holding the lock in read mode. The following atomic operations express acquire and release in read and write mode for thread i:

$$
\begin{aligned}
\texttt{acq\_write(w,r)} &\overset{\text{def}}{=} \langle \texttt{w} = 0 \wedge \texttt{r} = \emptyset \wedge \texttt{w}' = i \rangle_\texttt{w} \\
\texttt{acq\_read(w,r)} &\overset{\text{def}}{=} \langle \texttt{w} = 0 \wedge \texttt{r}' = \texttt{r} \cup \{i\} \rangle_\texttt{r} \\
\texttt{rel\_write(w,r)} &\overset{\text{def}}{=} \langle \texttt{w}' = 0 \rangle_\texttt{w} \downarrow (\texttt{w} = i) \\
\texttt{rel\_read(w,r)} &\overset{\text{def}}{=} \langle \texttt{r}' = \texttt{r} \setminus \{i\} \rangle_\texttt{r} \downarrow (i \in \texttt{r})
\end{aligned}
$$

For a thread to acquire the lock in write mode, there must be no writer and no readers. Similarly, to acquire the lock in read mode, there must be no writer, but there may be other readers, and the result of the acquire operation is to put the thread identifier into the set r. The release operations are straightforward. All of these lock operations respect the following data invariant RWI and the environment assumption RWA_i:

$$
\begin{aligned}
RWI &= (\texttt{r} = \emptyset \vee \texttt{w} = 0) \\
RWA_i &= (\texttt{w} = i \Leftrightarrow \texttt{w}' = i) \wedge (i \in \texttt{r} \Leftrightarrow i \in \texttt{r}')
\end{aligned}
$$

We illustrate the analysis of reader-writer locks by verifying the following program, in which the variable x is guarded by the reader-writer lock. Thread_2 asserts that the value of x is stable while the lock is held in read mode, even though Thread_1 mutates x while the lock is held in write mode.

Reader-writer lock example

Variables:	Thread_1 :	Thread_2 :
int w, x, y;	acq_write(w, r);	acq_read(w, r);
int_set r;	x := 3;	y := x;
	rel_write(w, r);	assert y = x;
Initially:		rel_read(w, r);
w = 0 ∧ r = ∅;		

The appropriate environment assumption for this program

$$
A_i = RWA_i \wedge (i \in \texttt{r} \Rightarrow \texttt{x} = \texttt{x}') \wedge (i = 2 \Rightarrow \texttt{y} = \texttt{y}')
$$

states that (1) each thread i can assume the reader-writer assumption RWA_i, (2) if thread i holds the lock in read mode, then x cannot be changed by another thread, and (3) the variable y is modified only by Thread_2. This environment assumption, together with the data invariant RWI, is sufficient to verify this program using our checker.

Although the reader-writer lock is more complex than the mutual-exclusion lock described earlier, the additional complexity of the reader-writer lock is localized to the annotations RWA_i and RWI that specify the lock implementation. Given these annotations, it is encouraging to note that the additional annotations required to verify reader-writer lock clients are still straightforward.

6.3   Time-Varying Mutex Synchronization

We now present a more complex example to show the power of our checker. The example is derived from a synchronization idiom found in the Frangipani file system [TML97].

For each file, Frangipani keeps a data structure called an *inode* that contains pointers to disk blocks that hold the file data. Each block has a busy bit indicating whether the block has been allocated to an inode. Since the file system is multithreaded, these data structures are guarded by mutexes. In particular, distinct mutexes protect each inode and each busy bit. However, the mutex protecting a disk block depends on the block's allocation status. If a block is unallocated (its busy bit is false), the mutex for its busy bit protects it. If the block is allocated (its busy bit is true), the mutex for the owning inode protects it. The following figure shows a highly simplified version of this situation.

Time-varying mutex program

Variables:	Thread$_1$:	Thread$_2$:
int block;	acq(m_inode);	acq(m_busy);
boolean busy;	if (¬inode) {	if (¬busy) {
boolean inode;	acq(m_busy);	block := 0;
int m_inode;	busy := true;	assert block = 0;
int m_busy;	rel(m_busy);	}
	inode := true;	rel(m_busy);
Initially:	}	
inode = busy	block := 1;	
	assert block = 1;	
	rel(m_inode);	

The program contains a single disk block, represented by the integer variable block, and uses a single bit busy to store the block's allocation status. There is a single inode whose contents have been abstracted to a bit indicating whether the inode has allocated the block. The two mutexes m_inode and m_busy protect the variables inode and busy, respectively.

The program contains two threads. Thread$_1$ acquires the mutex m_inode, allocates the block if it is not allocated already, and sets block to 1. Since Thread$_1$ is holding the lock on the inode that has allocated the block, the thread has exclusive access to the block contents. Thus, the subsequent assertion that the block value remains 1 should never fail.

Thread$_2$ acquires the mutex m_busy. If busy is false, the thread sets block to 0 and asserts that the value of block is 0. Since Thread$_2$ holds the lock on busy when the block is unallocated, the thread should have exclusive access to block, and the assertion should never fail.

We now describe annotations necessary to prove that the assertions always hold. First, the lock m_inode protects inode, and the lock m_busy protects busy:

$$J_i = (\text{m\_inode} = i \Rightarrow (\text{m\_inode}' = i \wedge \text{inode}' = \text{inode})) \wedge$$
$$(\text{m\_busy} = i \Rightarrow (\text{m\_busy}' = i \wedge \text{busy}' = \text{busy}))$$

In addition, if busy is true, then block is protected by m_inode; otherwise, block is protected by m_busy:

$$K_i = (\text{busy} \wedge \text{m\_inode} = i \Rightarrow \text{block} = \text{block}') \wedge$$
$$(\neg\text{busy} \wedge \text{m\_busy} = i \Rightarrow \text{block} = \text{block}')$$

Finally, the busy bit must be set when the inode has allocated the block. Moreover, the busy bit can be reset only by the thread that holds the lock on the inode. We formalize these requirements as the invariant I and the assumption L_i respectively.

$$I = (\text{m\_inode} = 0 \wedge \text{inode}) \Rightarrow \text{busy}$$
$$L_i = (\text{m\_inode} = i \wedge \text{busy}) \Rightarrow \text{busy}'$$

With these definitions, the complete environment assumption for each thread i is:

$$A_i = J_i \wedge K_i \wedge L_i$$

Given A_i and I, our checker is able to verify that the assertions in this program never fail.

This example illustrates the expressiveness of our checker. By comparison, previous tools for detecting synchronization errors [Ste93,SBN+97,FF00] have been mostly limited to finding races in programs that only use simple mutexes (and, in some cases, reader-writer locks). However, operating systems and other large-scale systems tend to use a variety of additional synchronization mechanisms, some of which we have described in the last few sections. Other synchronization idioms include binary and counting semaphores, producer-consumer synchronization, fork-join parallelism, and wait-free non-blocking algorithms. Our experience to date indicates that our checker has the potential to handle many of these synchronization disciplines. Of course, the more subtle synchronization disciplines may require more complex annotations, and it may be difficult to check the verification conditions resulting from particularly complex programs or synchronization disciplines.

7   Conclusions

The ability to reason about the correctness of large, multithreaded programs is essential to ensure the reliability of such systems. One natural strategy for decomposing such verification problems is procedure-modular verification, which has enjoyed widespread use in a variety of program analysis techniques for many years. Instead of reasoning about a call-site by inlining the corresponding procedure body, procedure-modular verification uses some specification of that procedure, for example, a type signature or a precondition/postcondition pair.

A second, complementary decomposition strategy is assume-guarantee decomposition [Jon83a], which avoids the need to consider all possible interleavings of the various threads explicitly. Instead, each thread is analyzed separately, with an environment assumption providing a specification of the behavior of the other program threads.

This paper presents an automatic checker for multithreaded programs, based on an assume-guarantee decomposition. The checker relies on the programmer to provide annotations describing the environment assumption of each thread. A potential concern with any annotation-based analysis technique is the overhead of providing such annotations. Our experience applying our checker to a number of example programs indicates that this annotation overhead is moderate. In particular, for many common synchronization idioms, the necessary environment assumptions are simple and intuitive. The environment assumption may also function as useful documentation for multithreaded programs, providing benefits similar to (formal or informal) procedure specifications.

We believe that verification of large, multithreaded programs requires the combination of both thread-modular and procedure-modular reasoning. However, specifying a procedure in a multithreaded program is not straightforward. In particular, because other threads can observe intermediate states of the procedure's computation, a procedure cannot be considered to execute atomically and cannot be specified as a simple precondition/postcondition pair. Combining thread-modular and procedure-modular reasoning appropriately is an important area for future work. Some preliminary steps in this direction are described in a related technical report [FQS02].

Acknowledgements We would like to thank Leslie Lamport, Rustan Leino, and Jim Saxe for valuable feedback on an early version of these ideas; the ESC/Java team who provided the infrastructure on which our checker is based; and Sanjit Seshia for helping with the implementation of the checker.

References

[AG96]   K. Arnold and J. Gosling. *The Java Programming Language*. Addison-Wesley, 1996.

[AH96]   R. Alur and T.A. Henzinger. Reactive modules. In *Proceedings of the 11th Annual Symposium on Logic in Computer Science*, pages 207–218. IEEE Computer Society Press, 1996.

[AHM+98] R. Alur, T.A. Henzinger, F.Y.C. Mang, S. Qadeer, S.K. Rajamani, and S. Tasiran. MOCHA: Modularity in model checking. In A. Hu and M. Vardi, editors, *CAV 98: Computer Aided Verification*, LNCS 1427, pages 521–525. Springer-Verlag, 1998.

[AL95]   M. Abadi and L. Lamport. Conjoining specifications. *ACM Transactions on Programming Languages and Systems*, 17(3):507–534, 1995.

[AMdB00] E. Abraham-Mumm and F. S. de Boer. Proof-outlines for threads in java. In *CONCUR 2000: Theories of Concurrency*, 2000.

[Ash75] E.A. Ashcroft. Proving assertions about parallel programs. *Journal of Computer and System Sciences*, 10:110–135, January 1975.

[BKP84] H. Barringer, R. Kuiper, and A. Pnueli. Now you may compose temporal-logic specifications. In *Proceedings of the 16th Annual Symposium on Theory of Computing*, pages 51–63. ACM Press, 1984.

[CK95]   P. Collette and E. Knapp. Logical foundations for compositional verification and development of concurrent programs in Unity. In *Algebraic Methodology and Software Technology*, LNCS 936, pages 353–367. Springer-Verlag, 1995.

[CM88]   K.M. Chandy and J. Misra. *Parallel Program Design: A Foundation.* Addison-Wesley Publishing Company, 1988.

[DHJ+01]   M. Dwyer, J. Hatcliff, R. Joehanes, S. Laubach, C. Pasareanu, Robby, W. Visser, and H. Zheng. Tool-supported program abstraction for finite-state verification. In *Proceedings of the 23rd International Conference on Software Engineering*, 2001.

[Dij75]   E.W. Dijkstra. Guarded commands, nondeterminacy, and formal derivation of programs. *Communications of the ACM*, 18(8):453–457, 1975.

[DLNS98]   D. L. Detlefs, K. R. M. Leino, C. G. Nelson, and J. B. Saxe. Extended static checking. Research Report 159, Compaq Systems Research Center, December 1998.

[FA99]   C. Flanagan and M. Abadi. Types for safe locking. In *Proceedings of European Symposium on Programming*, pages 91–108, March 1999.

[FF00]   C. Flanagan and S.N. Freund. Type-based race detection for Java. In *Proceedings of the SIGPLAN Conference on Programming Language Design and Implementation*, pages 219–232, 2000.

[FF01]   C. Flanagan and S.N. Freund. Detecting race conditions in large programs. In *Workshop on Program Analysis for Software Tools and Engineering*, pages 90–96, June 2001.

[FLL+02]   C. Flanagan, K.R.M. Leino, M. Lillibridge, C.G. Nelson, J.B. Saxe, and R. Stata. Extended static checking for Java. Research Report 178, Compaq Systems Research Center, February 2002.

[FQS02]   C. Flanagan, S. Qadeer, and S. Seshia. A modular checker for multithreaded programs. Technical Note 02-001, Compaq Systems Research Center, 2002.

[FS01]   C. Flanagan and J.B. Saxe. Avoiding exponential explosion: Generating compact verification conditions. In *Conference Record of the 28th Annual ACM Symposium on Principles of Programming Languages*, pages 193–205. ACM, January 2001.

[Jon83a]   C. B. Jones. Tentative steps toward a development method for interfering programs. *ACM Transactions on Programming Languages and Systems*, 5(4):596–619, 1983.

[Jon83b]   C.B. Jones. Specification and design of (parallel) programs. In R. Mason, editor, *Information Processing*, pages 321–332. Elsevier Science Publishers B. V. (North-Holland), 1983.

[Jon89]   B. Jonsson. On decomposing and refining specifications of distributed systems. In J.W. de Bakker, W.-P. de Roever, and G. Rozenberg, editors, *Stepwise Refinement of Distributed Systems: Models, Formalisms, Correctness*, Lecture Notes in Computer Science 430, pages 361–385. Springer-Verlag, 1989.

[Lam77]   L. Lamport. Proving the correctness of multiprocess programs. *IEEE Transactions on Software Engineering*, SE-3(2):125–143, 1977.

[Lam88]   L. Lamport. Control predicates are better than dummy variables. *ACM Transactions on Programming Languages and Systems*, 10(2):267–281, April 1988.

[Lam94]   L. Lamport. The Temporal Logic of Actions. *ACM Transactions on Programming Languages and Systems*, 16(3):872–923, 1994.

[LAS00]   T. Lev-Ami and M. Sagiv. TVLA: A system for implementing static analyses. In *Proceedings of the Static Analysis Symposium*, pages 280–301, 2000.

[LSS99]   K. R. M. Leino, J. B. Saxe, and R. Stata. Checking Java programs
            via guarded commands. In Bart Jacobs, Gary T. Leavens, Peter Müller,
            and Arnd Poetzsch-Heffter, editors, *Formal Techniques for Java Programs*,
            Technical Report 251. Fernuniversität Hagen, May 1999.

[MC81]   J. Misra and K.M. Chandy. Proofs of networks of processes. *IEEE Trans-
            actions on Software Engineering*, SE-7(4):417–426, 1981.

[McM97]   K.L. McMillan. A compositional rule for hardware design refinement. In
            O. Grumberg, editor, *CAV 97: Computer Aided Verification*, Lecture Notes
            in Computer Science 1254, pages 24–35. Springer-Verlag, 1997.

[MM93]   A. Mokkedem and D. Mery. On using a composition principle to design
            parallel programs. In *Algebraic Methodology and Software Technology*, pages
            315–324, 1993.

[MP95]   Z. Manna and A. Pnueli. *Temporal Verification of Reactive Systems: Safety*.
            Springer-Verlag, 1995.

[Nel81]   C. G. Nelson. Techniques for program verification. Technical Report CSL-
            81-10, Xerox Palo Alto Research Center, 1981.

[OG76]   S. Owicki and D. Gries. An axiomatic proof technique for parallel programs.
            Acta Informatica, 6(4):319–340, 1976.

[PDH99]   C.S. Păsăreanu, M.B. Dwyer, and M. Huth. Assume-guarantee model check-
            ing of software: A comparative case study. In *Theoretical and Practical As-
            pects of SPIN Model Checking*, Lecture Notes in Computer Science 1680,
            1999.

[SBN+97]   S. Savage, M. Burrows, C.G. Nelson, P. Sobalvarro, and T.A. Anderson.
            Eraser: A dynamic data race detector for multithreaded programs. *ACM
            Transactions on Computer Systems*, 15(4):391–411, 1997.

[SRW99]   M. Sagiv, T. Reps, and R. Wilhelm. Parametric shape analysis via 3-
            valued logic. In *Conference Record of the Twenty-Sixth ACM Symposium
            on Principles of Programming Languages*, pages 105–118, 1999.

[Sta85]   E.W. Stark. A proof technique for rely/guarantee properties. In *Proceed-
            ings of the 5th Conference on Foundations of Software Technology and The-
            oretical Computer Science*, Lecture Notes in Computer Science 206, pages
            369–391. Springer-Verlag, 1985.

[Ste93]   N. Sterling. WARLOCK — a static data race analysis tool. In *USENIX
            Technical Conference Proceedings*, pages 97–106, Winter 1993.

[TML97]   C.A. Thekkath, T. Mann, and E.K. Lee. Frangipani: A scalable distributed
            file system. In *Proceedings of the 16th ACM Symposium on Operating Sys-
            tems Principles*, pages 224–237, October 1997.

[Yah01]   E. Yahav. Verifying safety properties of concurrent Java programs using
            3-valued logic. In *Proceedings of the 28th Symposium on Principles of Pro-
            gramming Languages*, pages 27–40, January 2001.

Timing UDP: Mechanized Semantics
for Sockets, Threads, and Failures

Keith Wansbrough, Michael Norrish, Peter Sewell, and Andrei Serjantov

Computer Laboratory, University of Cambridge

{First.Last}@cl.cam.ac.uk
www.cl.cam.ac.uk/users/pes20/Netsem

Abstract. This paper studies the semantics of failure in distributed programming. We present a semantic model for distributed programs that use the standard sockets interface; it covers message loss, host failure and temporary disconnection, and supports reasoning about distributed infrastructure. We consider interaction via the UDP and ICMP protocols. To do this, it has been necessary to: • construct an experimentally-validated post-hoc specification of the UDP/ICMP sockets interface; • develop a timed operational semantics with threads, as such programs are typically multithreaded and depend on timeouts; • model the behaviour of partial systems, making explicit the interactions that the infrastructure offers to applications; • integrate the above with semantics for an executable fragment of a programming language (OCaml) with OS library primitives; and • use tool support to manage complexity, mechanizing the model with the HOL theorem prover. We illustrate the whole with a module providing naïve heartbeat failure detection.

1 Introduction

Distributed systems are – almost by definition – concurrent and subject to partial failure; many are also subject to malicious attack. This complexity makes it hard to achieve a clear understanding of their behaviour based only on informal descriptions, in turn making it hard to build robust systems. This paper reports on work towards a rigorous treatment of distributed programming. We have constructed a operational semantics which makes it possible to reason about distributed programs, written in general-purpose programming languages, using standard communication primitives, and in the presence of failure. Developing a model that covers enough of the distributed phenomena (sufficiently accurately) to do this has required a number of problems to be addressed; we introduce them below, sketching our contribution to each.

As a preliminary, we must select the communication abstractions to consider. Interactions between machines can be viewed at many levels. We are primarily interested in the abstractions provided by the standard TCP, UDP and ICMP protocols above IP, for two reasons. Firstly, they are ubiquitous: almost all distributed interaction is ultimately mediated by them. More particularly, we want

D. Le Métayer (Ed.): ESOP 2002, LNCS 2305, pp. 278–294, 2002.

a model that accurately reflects the information about failure that is available to the application programmer – at the level of these protocols, the failure behaviour can be seen clearly. This should provide a solid basis for the design, verification and implementation of higher-level distributed abstractions. To investigate feasibility and techniques, we consider unicast UDP (providing unreliable asynchronous messages) and the associated ICMP messages (providing various error reporting); we do not touch on the more complex TCP (providing reliable streams). The protocols themselves are defined in RFCs [Pos80,Pos81,Bra89].

1.1 Sockets and Experimental Semantics An application programmer must understand not only the protocols, which for UDP and ICMP are relatively simple, but also the *sockets interface* [CSR83,IEE00,Ste98] to the operating system code that implements them. The behaviour of this interface is complex and not well documented (to the best of our knowledge there exist only informal natural-language documents, covering common behaviour but not precise, complete or correct). It is not feasible to analyse the sockets code and hence derive a semantics, nor is it feasible to alter the widely-deployed implementations. We must therefore produce a post-hoc specification with an *experimental semantics* approach: experimentally determining the behaviour of particular implementations.

1.2 Failure and Time Addressing failure requires two things. Firstly, we must model the actual failures – in this paper, we consider message loss and duplication, crash failure of hosts, and connection/disconnection of hosts from the network. More interestingly, we must be able to reason about the behaviour of programs that cope with failure. UDP communication is asynchronous, so these programs typically use timeouts, *e.g.* in calls to select. To model these accurately we use a *timed* operational semantics, involving time bounds for certain operations. Some operations have both a lower and upper bound (message propagation); some must happen immediately (recvfrom must return as soon as a message arrives); and some have an upper bound but may occur arbitrarily quickly (an OS return). For some of these requirements time is essential, and for others time conditions are simpler and more tractable than the corresponding fairness conditions [LV96, §2.2.2]. We draw on earlier work on timed automata [SGSAL98] and process calculi here, but have kept the semantics as lightweight as possible – in part, by building in a *local receptiveness* property.

1.3 Infrastructure Properties: Partial Systems and Threads We are particularly interested in implementations of distributed infrastructure (or middleware), rather than complete distributed systems, as a rigorous approach should be more fruitful in the former. This means that the semantics must be able to describe the behaviour of *partial* systems, consisting of a module that provides some abstraction to higher-level application code (*e.g.* a library for 'reliable' communication), instantiated on many machines. Interesting infrastructure usually also requires intra-machine concurrency in the form of *threads* (at minimum, one for the infrastructure and one for the application). Our model includes threads and simple modules, making explicit the possible interactions offered to a distributed application by per-machine instances of an infrastructure module.

1.4   Executable Code: Language Independence and MiniCaml We aim to reason
about executable code, written in general-purpose programming languages. This
contrasts with work on distributed algorithm verification, in which algorithms are
usually described in pseudocode or in automata or calculi tuned for verification;
it should reduce the 'semantic gap' between verified algorithm and actual system.
Most of what we model, however, is language-independent. We therefore factor
the semantics, regarding infrastructure modules as labelled transition systems
(LTSs) of a certain form. The standard operational semantics of a variety of
languages can be extended to give such LTSs. We do so for *MiniCaml*, a fragment
of OCaml [L+01]. MiniCaml's *types* include the standard built-in bool, int, string,
tuples, lists, references, exceptions, and functions, together with types required
for networking (e.g., fd, ip, port, *etc.*) The constructors, values, expressions and
patterns are as one might expect, as are the typing rules. The dynamic semantics
extends a standard operational semantics with labelled transitions for system
calls, and by specifying the behaviour of modules. We have implemented an
OCaml module that provides exactly the system calls of the model, so MiniCaml
programs can be compiled with the standard `ocamlopt` compiler.

1.5   Semantic Complexity and HOL Mechanization As one can imagine, the
need to deal simultaneously with sockets, failure, time, modules and threads has
led to large definitions. The most complex part, for sockets, has been validated
experimentally. To keep the whole internally consistent, we resort to automated
tools. The entire definition (except for the MiniCaml semantics) has been expressed in the HOL theorem proving system [GM93], which we are using to check
various sanity properties. The HOL and MiniCaml code in this paper has been
automatically typeset from the sources using special-purpose tools. Mechanization identified a number of errors in earlier drafts of the semantics. The process
has also been a useful stress-test of the HOL implementation.

1.6   Overview The remainder of this paper contains a brief introduction to
UDP sockets, outlines the static and dynamic structure of the model, discusses
its experimental validation and HOL mechanization, and analyses a simple heartbeat example in MiniCaml. Most details are perforce omitted; they will be in
a forthcoming technical report. The HOL definitions are available electronically
[WNSS01]. This work is a continuation of that reported in [SSW01a,SSW01b],
which did not address time, threads, modules or mechanization.

2   Background

2.1   The Protocols At the level of abstraction of our model, a network consists
of a number of machines connected by a combination of LANs (*e.g.* ethernets)
and routers. Each machine has one or more *IP addresses* i, which are 32-bit
values such as 192.168.0.11. The *Internet Protocol* (IP) allows one machine to
send messages (*IP datagrams*) to another, specifying the destination by one of
its IP addresses. IP datagrams have the form $IP(i_1, i_2, body)$, where i_1 and i_2 are

the source and destination addresses. The implementation of IP is responsible for delivering the datagram to the correct machine; it abstracts from routing and network topology. Delivery is asynchronous and unreliable – IP does not provide acknowledgments that datagrams are received, or retransmit lost messages. Messages may be duplicated.

The *User Datagram Protocol* (UDP) is a thin layer above IP that provides multiplexing. It associates a set $\{1, .., 65535\}$ of *ports* with each machine; a UDP datagram is an IP datagram with body $UDP(ps_1, ps_2, data)$, containing a source and destination port and a short sequence of bytes of *data*.

The *Internet Control Message Protocol* (ICMP) is another thin layer above IP dealing with some control and error messages. Here we are concerned only with two, relating to UDP, with bodies: $ICMP\_PORT\_UNREACH(is_3, ps_3, is_4, ps_4)$ and $ICMP\_HOST\_UNREACH(is_3, ps_3, is_4, ps_4)$. The first may be generated by a machine receiving a UDP datagram for an unexpected port; the second is sometimes generated by routers on receiving unroutable datagrams. They contain the IP addresses and ports of the original datagram.

2.2 Sockets The OS protocol endpoint code in each host maintains a collection of *sockets*: data structures that we write

$$SOCK(fd, is_1, ps_1, is_2, ps_2, es, f, mq)$$

which mediate between application threads and the asynchronous message delivery activities. The file descriptor fd uniquely identifies this socket within the host. The IP addresses and ports is_1, ps_1 and is_2, ps_2 are a pair of 'local' and 'remote' pairs, some elements of which may be wildcards; the 4-tuple is used for addressing outgoing datagrams and matching incoming datagrams. The flag es stores any pending error condition, while the flags f hold an assortment of socket options. Finally, the message queue mq holds incoming messages that have been delivered by the OS to this socket but not yet received by the application.

The standard *sockets interface* [CSR83,IEE00,Ste98] is the library interface made available to applications. It includes calls **socket** and **close** for creating and closing sockets; **bind** and **connect**, for manipulating the local and remote pairs of IP addresses and ports; **sendto** and **recvfrom**, for sending and receiving messages; and **select**, allowing an application to block until either a timeout occurs or a file descriptor is ready for reading or writing. To avoid dealing with the uninteresting complexities of the standard C sockets interface, we introduce a thin abstraction layer that provides a clean strongly-typed view of the C sockets interface without sacrificing useful functionality. The model is expressed in terms of this interface, which we call LIB and present in Appendix A. To allow MiniCaml programs to be executed, we also implement the interface as a thin layer above the OCaml socket and thread libraries.

There are many behavioural subtleties which the model covers but which we cannot describe here, including: wildcard and loopback IP addresses; wildcard, privileged and ephemeral ports; blocking and non-blocking **sendto**, **recvfrom** and **select**; local errors; and multiple interfaces. These are discussed in detail in

```
val start_heartbeat_k : () → ()
val start_heartbeat_a : () → int ref
val get_status : int ref → int
```

```
(* code for player Kurt *)                      (* code for player Alan *)
let start_heartbeat_k() =                        let start_heartbeat_a() =
  let sender_thread() =                            let status_ref = ref 0 in
    let p = port_of_int (7658) in                  let receiver_thread() =
    let i_a = ip_of_string ("192.168.0.14") in       let p = port_of_int (7658) in
    let fd = socket() in                             let i_k = ip_of_string ("192.168.0.11") in
    let _ = bind(fd, *, *) in                        let fd = socket() in
    let _ = connect(fd, i_a, ↑p) in                  let _ = bind(fd, *, ↑p) in
    while TRUE do                                    let _ = connect(fd, i_k, *) in
      try                                            while TRUE do
        sendto(fd, *, "ping", FALSE);                  let (fds, _) = select([fd], [], ↑2500000) in
        delay1000000;                                  if fds = [] then
      with                                               status_ref := 0
        UDP(ECONNREFUSED) → ()                         else
    done in                                              let (_, _, _) = recvfrom(fd, FALSE) in
  let t = create sender_thread() in ()                   status_ref := 1
                                                   done in
                                                   let t = create receiver_thread() in
                                                   status_ref

                                                 let get_status status_ref =
                                                   !status_ref
```

Fig. 1. `rhbeat2.mli` and `rhbeat2.ml`. The * and ↑ are constructors of option types
$T\uparrow$; `unit` is typeset as ().

[SSW01a]. Here, we shall highlight only the existence of asynchronous errors:
a machine receiving a UDP datagram addressed to a port that does not have
an associated socket may send back an ICMP_PORT_UNREACH message
to the sender. This error message is received *asynchronously*—the sendto that
nominally caused the error has (in general) long since returned to the application,
and so some means of notification must be found. The sockets interface solves this
problem by storing the last such error in the socket, returning it to the application
whenever a subsequent communication operation (which may be quite unrelated)
is attempted on that socket. The operation will fail but the error will be cleared,
allowing subsequent operations to succeed.

2.3 Example Figure 1 gives a simple example of the kind of program which
our model allows us to reason about. It is a MiniCaml module that provides
a failure-detection service for two machines, using a naïve heartbeat algorithm.
The *start_heartbeat_k* function should be called by an application running on
machine KURT. It spawns a thread that creates a socket, sets its remote address
to that of the other machine (192.168.0.14) and its remote port to an agreed
value (7658), and then repeatedly sends "ping" messages, with a 1-second delay

between each. The *start_heartbeat_a* function, to be called by an application on machine ALAN, creates a reference cell *status_ref* to hold its current guess of the status of KURT. It then spawns a *receiver_thread* and returns the reference cell. The thread creates a socket, sets its local port to the agreed 7658, and repeatedly waits for up to 2.5 seconds for a "ping" message. If it receives one, it sets the status to 1 to indicate that KURT is believed to be up (running and connected to the network), otherwise it sets it to 0. The application on machine ALAN can check the status of KURT by calling *get_status*, passing it *status_ref*. We are using OCaml's safe shared-memory communication between the ALAN threads.

3   The Model

This section outlines the main design choices and the static structure of the model. Discussion of the host semantics, which captures the behaviour of the library calls and UDP-related part of the operating system, is deferred to §4.

3.1   Overall Structure A network N is a parallel composition of UDP and ICMP messages in transit (on the wire, or buffered in routers) and of machines. Each machine comprises several *host components* hc – the OS state, a module, the states of threads, the store, *etc.* To simplify reasoning we bring all these components into the top-level parallel composition, maintaining the association between the components of a particular machine by tagging them with *host names* n (not to be confused with IP addresses or DNS names). Networks terms are therefore:

$$
\begin{array}{lll}
N ::= & 0 & \text{empty network} \\
& N \mid N & \text{parallel composition} \\
& msg_d & \text{IP datagram in transit} \\
& n{\cdot}hc & \text{component of machine } n
\end{array}
$$

while host components, to be explained below, are of the forms:

$$
\begin{array}{lll}
hc ::= & \text{HOST}(conn, h) & \text{OS state} \\
& \text{MODULE}(t) & \text{module code} \\
& \text{THREAD}(tid, org, t)_d & \text{running thread snippet} \\
& \text{THREADCREATE}(tid, org, t, t')_d & \text{pending create} \\
& \text{STORE}(st) & \text{shared store} \\
& \text{STORERET}(tid, tlty, v)_d & \text{pending return}
\end{array}
$$

Networks are subject to a well-formedness condition, network_ok N, which requires that no two machines share a host name n or non-loopback IP address, that each machine has exactly one store, and that each host component satisfies its own well-formedness condition, written host_ok h *etc.* We omit the details.

The semantics of a network is defined as a labelled transition system of a certain form. It uses three kinds of labels: labels that engage in binary CCS-style synchronisations, *e.g.* for a call of a host LIB routine by a thread; labels that do not synchronise, *e.g.* for τ actions resulting from binary synchronisations; and labels on which all terms must synchronise, used for time passing, hosts crashing and programs terminating. Parallel composition is defined using a single synchronisation algebra to deal with all of these, and we also use a non-standard restriction on the visible traces of the entire system, to force certain synchronisations to occur. The model is in some respects a nondeterministic loose specification, abstracting from some details, such as the relative precedence of competing errors, that should not be depended upon.

In contrast to standard process calculi we have a *local receptiveness* property: in any reachable state, if one component can do an output on a binary-sync label then there will be a unique possible counterpart, which is guaranteed to offer an input on that label. This means the model has no local deadlocks (though obviously threads can block waiting for a slow system call to return).

3.2 Threads and Modules In order to express and reason about the semantics of infrastructure code, such as the rhbeat2 module, we must define the semantics of a partial system, exposing the interactions that an application program could have with such a module (and with the OS and store). Threads complicate the problem, as we must deal with *external thread snippets*, executing some module routine that has been called by an application thread, and with *internal* thread snippets, spawned by a module routine calling **create** directly. External snippets may return a value or exception to the application, whereas internal snippets do not return.

Thread snippets are written THREAD(tid, org, t)$_d$, with a thread id tid, org either EXTERN or INTERN, state t, and timer d (see §3.4). During thread creation there is a transient state THREADCREATE(tid, org, t, t')$_d$.

To keep as much as possible of the model language-independent, the behaviours of modules MODULE(t), and the resulting states t of thread snippets, are taken to be arbitrary labelled transition systems satisfying various sanity conditions, *e.g.* that a thread cannot simultaneously call two OS routines. This permits automata-theoretic descriptions of infrastructure algorithms, when convenient. To allow reasoning about executable code, though, we can use our Mini-Caml semantics to derive such an LTS from any MiniCaml source program.

3.3 Interactions In more detail, the interactions between network terms are as follows. The external application can call a routine provided by the module. A thread snippet will then be spawned off; ultimately this may return a value or an exception. Thread snippets (and the external application) can call host LIB routines, which may later return. A special case is a call to **create**, which will both create a new thread ID and spawn off a thread snippet with that ID. Another special case is a call to **exit**, which will terminate all the threads of the host and close any sockets they have opened. Thread snippets (and the external application) can call the store operations **new**, **set** and **get**, which will quickly return. Hosts can send and receive IP datagrams. Hosts and thread snippets can perform internal computation. Hosts can crash, whereupon all their components are removed, can be disconnected from the network, and can be reconnected. Hosts can output strings on their console. Time can pass.

3.4   Time Time passage is modelled by transitions labelled $d \in \mathbb{R}_{>0}$ interleaved with other transitions. These labels uses multiway synchronisation, modelling global time which passes uniformly for all participants (although it cannot be accurately observed by them).

Our semantics is built using *timers*, variables containing elements of $\mathbb{R}_{\geq 0} \cup \{\infty\}$ that decrement uniformly as time passes (until zero); the state becomes *urgent* as soon as any timer in it reaches zero. Speaking loosely, only binary-synchronising output actions are constrained by timers. Urgent states are those in which there is a discrete action which should occur immediately. This is modelled by prohibiting time passage steps d from (or through) an urgent state. We have carefully arranged the model to avoid pathological timestops by ensuring the local receptiveness property holds.

Our model has a number of timing parameters: the minimum message propagation delay *dpropmin* and the maximum scheduling delay *dsch*, outqueue scheduling delay doq, store access delay *dstore*, thread evaluation step duration *dthread*, and message propagation delay *dpropmax*.

Many timed process algebras enforce a *maximal progress* property [Yi91], requiring that any action must be performed immediately it becomes enabled. We choose instead to ensure timeliness properties by means of timers and urgency. Our reasoning using the model so far involves only finite trace properties, so we do not need to impose Zeno conditions.

3.5   Messages/Networks Message propagation through the network is defined by the rules below.

$$0 \xrightarrow{n \cdot msg} msg_d \qquad d \in [dpropmin,\ dpropmax] \qquad net\_accept\_single$$

$$msg_{d+d'} \xrightarrow{d'} msg_d \qquad d' > 0 \qquad\qquad net\_msg\_time$$

$$msg_0 \xrightarrow{n \cdot msg} 0 \qquad\qquad\qquad\qquad net\_emit$$

$$0 \xrightarrow{n \cdot msg} 0 \qquad\qquad\qquad\qquad net\_accept\_drop$$

A message sent by a host is accepted by the network with one of three rules. The normal case is *net_accept_single*, which places the message on the network with a timer d attached. The timer is initialised with the propagation delay, chosen nondeterministically. Message propagation is modelled simply by time passage: the rule *net_msg_time* decrements the timer until it reaches zero, making the state urgent. The delivery rule *net_emit* is thus forced to fire at exactly the instant the message arrives. Once the message arrives, it may be emitted by the network to a listening host by *net_emit*. This rule is only enabled at the instant the timer reaches zero, modelling the fact that the host has no choice over when it receives the message. Note that the network rules do not examine the message in any way – it is the host LTS that checks whether the IP address is one of its own. Time aside, this treatment of asynchrony is similar to Honda and Tokoro's asynchronous π-calculus [HT91]. Messages in the network may be reordered, and this is modelled simply by the nondeterministic propagation times. They may also be finitely duplicated, or lost. Rule *net_accept_dup* (not shown) is similar to *net_accept_single* above except that it yields $k \geq 2$ copies of the message, each with an independently-chosen propagation delay; rule *net_accept_drop* simply absorbs the message.

3.6 Stores A store STORE(*st*) has a state *st* which is simply a finite map from (typed) locations to values. It can receive new, set and get labels, spawning off a STORERET(*tid, tlty, v*)$_{dstore}$ which will return the value *v* (of type *tlty*) to thread *tid* within time *dstore*. For simplicity, as the MiniCaml types are not all embedded into the HOL model, the store is restricted to first-order values.

3.7 Hosts A host HOST(*conn, h*) has a boolean *conn*, indicating whether it is currently connected to the network, and a host state *h*, a record modelling the relevant aspects of the OS state. The *h.ifds* field is a set of interfaces, each with a set of IP addresses and other data. We assume all hosts have at least a loopback interface and one other. We sometimes write $i \in h.ifds$ for $\exists ifd.i \in ifd.ipset \wedge ifd \in h.ifds$. The operating system's view of the state of each thread is stored in a finite map *h.ts* from thread identifiers *tid* to host thread states. Each thread may be running (RUN), exiting (EXIT), or waiting for the OS to return from a call. In the last case, the OS may be about to return a value (RET*v*) or the thread may be blocked waiting for a slow system call to complete (SENDTO2*v*, RECVFROM2*v*, SELECT2*v*, DELAY2, PRINT2*v*, ZOMBIE). The host's current list of sockets is stored in *h.s*. The *outqueue*, a queue of outbound IP messages, is given by *h.oq* and *h.oqf*, where *h.oq* is the list of messages (with a timer) and *h.oqf* is set when the queue is full. In HOL syntax, the record $(h \text{ with } \langle\!\langle ts := ts \rangle\!\rangle)$ is the record *h* with the *ts* field replaced by the value *ts*.

4   The Model Continued: Host Dynamics

The host semantics is defined by 78 host transition axioms, encoding the precise behaviour of each of the library calls in Figure 2 and of the UDP subsystem of the operating system. To give a flavour, we examine some of the behaviour of the heartbeat example program of §2.3, explaining the main points of a few rules.

We first consider KURT's execution of *sender_thread*(). Once the thread has converted the port and IP address, it calls socket() to allocate a new socket. The thread performs the call by making an output transition $\cdot \xrightarrow{\overline{tid \cdot \text{socket}()}} \cdot$, where *tid* is the thread ID of the sender thread, and the host synchronises by making the corresponding input transition according to rule *socket_1*:

---

socket_1   **succeed**

h with $ts := ts \oplus (tid \mapsto \text{RUN}_d)$

$\xrightarrow{tid \cdot (\text{socket}())}$

h with $\langle\!\langle ts := ts \oplus (tid \mapsto \text{RET}(\text{OK}fd)_{dsch});$
$\quad\quad s := (\text{SOCK}(fd, *, *, *, *, *, \text{FLAGS}(\mathbf{F}, \mathbf{F}), [\,]) :: h.s)\rangle\!\rangle$

$fd \notin \text{sockfds}\, h.s$

Each rule is of the form "$h \xrightarrow{l} h'$ where *cond*", where h, h' are host states and l is a host transition label. The rules have been automatically typeset from the HOL source (see §6). In *socket_1* the initial host state (above the arrow) requires only that the host thread state for the thread is RUN_d for some d; RUN means the host is waiting for a call from the thread (in reachable states, the timer on a RUN will always be ∞). The side condition (given below the transition itself) states that *fd* is some file descriptor not in the set of file descriptors already used in $h.s$. The final host state (below the arrow) updates $h.s$ by adding a freshly initialised socket with the chosen *fd* to the list, and sets the host thread state for the thread to $\text{RET}(\text{OK}fd)_{dsch}$. This will cause the host to return the value $\text{OK}fd$ to the thread within delay *dsch*, by rule *ret_1* (not shown). Unlike *net_emit* above, this may occur at any time from 0 up until *dsch*; this models a nondeterministic scheduler. The rules are partitioned into several classes; the **succeed** indicates which class *socket_1* belongs to.

We omit the **bind** and **connect** calls, and proceed to the top of the while loop, where the application invokes **sendto**$(fd, *, \text{"ping"}, \mathbf{F})$. Assuming there is room on the outqueue for the message, rule *sendto_1* fires:

---

sendto_1   **succeed** **autobinding**

h with $\langle\!\langle ts := ts \oplus (tid \mapsto \text{RUN}_d);$
$\qquad\qquad s := SC(s \text{ with } es := *)\rangle\!\rangle$

$\overline{\quad tid\text{·sendto}(s.fd, ips, data, nb) \quad}\!\!\rightarrow$

h with $\langle\!\langle ts := ts \oplus (tid \mapsto \text{RET}(\text{OK}())_{dsch});$
$\qquad\qquad s := SC(s \text{ with } \langle\!\langle es := *; ps_1 := \uparrow p_1' \rangle\!\rangle);$
$\qquad\qquad oq := oq'; oqf := oqf'\rangle\!\rangle$

socklist_context $SC \wedge$
$p_1' \in \text{autobind}(s.ps_1, SC) \wedge$
$(oq', oqf', \mathbf{T}) \in \text{dosend}(h.ifds, (ips, data),$
$\qquad\qquad\qquad\qquad\qquad (s.is_1, \uparrow p_1', s.is_2, s.ps_2),$
$\qquad\qquad\qquad\qquad\qquad h.oq, h.oqf) \wedge$
string_size $data \leq \text{UDPpayloadMax} \wedge$
$((ips \neq *) \vee (s.is_2 \neq *))$

The auxiliary function dosend builds the message IP $(i\_k, i\_a, \text{UDP}(\uparrow p_1, \uparrow p_2, \text{"ping"}))$ and places it on the output queue, ready to be delivered to the network; the flag $\mathbf{T}$ indicates that it succeeded. The remaining side conditions check that the payload is not too large for a UDP message, check that a destination IP address is specified either explicitly or implicitly, and automatically provide a local port if none is specified (autobind).

Once the message is on the outqueue, it will eventually be emitted onto the network by rule *delivery_out_1*:

---

delivery_out_1   **misc**   **put UDP or ICMP to the network from** *oq*

h

$$\xrightarrow{\overline{\mathrm{IP}(i_1, i_2, body)}}$$

h with $(\!|oq := oq'; oqf := oqf'|\!)$

$(\mathrm{IP}(i_1, i_2, body), oq', oqf') \in \mathrm{dequeue}(h.oq, h.oqf) \wedge$
$i_2 \notin \mathrm{LOOPBACK} \cup \mathrm{MARTIAN} \wedge$
$i_1 \notin \mathrm{MARTIAN}$

The auxiliary function dequeue takes the top message (if present) from the out-queue and resets the outqueue timer to doq if oq' is nonempty, or ∞ otherwise. We also check that the source and destination addresses are valid for the network; martian [Bak95, §5.3.7] and loopback addresses are handled by other rules.

Once the message is placed on the network (and if it is not lost) it will eventually be delivered to the remote host, where it will either be delivered to a waiting socket, rejected with an ICMP_PORT_UNREACH, or dropped.

In the meantime, ALAN is running *receiver_thread*(). ALAN begins listening for a heartbeat by invoking **select**([*fd*], [ ], ↑2500000), giving a timeout of 2.5 seconds. Rule *select_1* fires:

---

select_1   **enter2**   **entering Select2 state**

h with $ts := ts \oplus (tid \mapsto \mathrm{RUN}_d)$

$$\xrightarrow{tid \cdot \mathrm{select}(readseq, writeseq, tms)}$$

h with $ts := ts \oplus (tid \mapsto \mathrm{SELECT2}(readseq, writeseq)_{d'})$

list_to_set(*readseq* @ *writeseq*) $\subseteq$ sockfds $h.s \wedge$
$(\forall i.(tms = \uparrow i) \implies 0 \le i) \wedge$
$(d' = $ **case** *tms* **of**
     $* \to \infty \parallel$
     $\uparrow i \to \mathrm{time}(\mathrm{real\_of\_int}\ i/1000000))$

---

select is a *slow* call [Ste98, p124], meaning that it may block rather than returning immediately to the caller. Here the host transitions into a special blocked SELECT2([*fd*], [ ])$_{2.5}$ state, recording the lists of file descriptors on which it is waiting. The timer on this state is set to the timeout specified; this forces us to leave the state at or before the end of the timeout. The other side conditions state that all the file descriptors must be valid, and that the timeout must be nonnegative.

If the heartbeat fails to arrive within 2.5 seconds, the blocked state becomes urgent and rule *select_4* will fire, returning OK([ ], [ ]) and leading ALAN to suspect that KURT is down. If the message *does* arrive, however, it is accepted asynchronously into the listening socket's message queue by *delivery_in_udp_1*, which matches the addressing fields of an incoming message to the address quadruples of the host sockets. (Of course, if there were no matching socket, rule *delivery_in_udp_2* might send an ICMP_PORT_UNREACH message back to the sender.) With a message in the queue, the blocked SELECT2 state becomes urgent, forcing rule *select_3* to fire, informing *receiver_thread* of the waiting message by returning OK($[fd],[\,]$). The thread then invokes recvfrom to read the message.

5 Experimental Validation

Our model is based on the existing natural-language documentation [Ste98,Ste94] and [IEE00], inspection of the sources of the Linux implementation (kernel version 2.2.16-22), and a combination of *ad hoc* and automated testing. Our test network comprised a non-routed subnet with three Linux (RedHat 7.0) and two Windows 2000 machines (in a few cases we ran tests further afield). Tests were written in C, using the glibc 2.1.92 sockets library on Linux. Our *ad hoc* tests used C programs to display the results of short sequences of socket calls, using tcpdump to observe the network traffic. Later, we wrote an automatic tool, udpautotest, that simulates the model (hand-translated into C) in parallel with the real socket calls. This tests representatives of most cases of the host transition semantics, giving us a high level of confidence in our model. It helped us greatly in correctly stating the more subtle corners of the semantics. We also tested some aspects of OCaml thread handling. The limitations of our closed-box testing are discussed in [SSW01b].

Having based the semantics on the Linux implementation, we are now using a combination of udpautotest and ad-hoc testing to compare it against the Win2K implementation (v. 5.0, build 2195, no service packs, Winsock2, WS2_32.DLL). The most substantial difference observed so far is that sendto calls are unaffected by earlier ICMP_PORT_UNREACH messages – they successfully send, and do not return the pending error. In contrast, the behaviour of recvfrom and select appears to be as in Linux.

6 HOL Mechanization

We were driven to use mechanized tool support by experience with the model of our earlier work, expressed in conventional non-mechanized mathematics. It was substantially simpler than the model presented here, but its size and complexity already made it hard to keep internally consistent. By expressing the current semantics in HOL we know that its auxiliary functions and semantic rules are all well-typed. We are also using HOL to prove some "sanity" theorems about the model, showing that various invariants on host and network states are maintained, and that the semantic rules cover all possible cases (and overlap only where intended). These results are not especially deep, but proving them has brought up further important points. At the time of writing our most significant result is the following:

Theorem 1 (host _ok **preservation**). *If* host_ok h_0 *and* $h_0 \xrightarrow{l} h$, *then* host_ok h.
The proof (some 2800 lines of script) proceeds by rule category (e.g., **fail**, **succeed**, **slowsucceed**). For each category we prove additional statements that embody type correctness. The host_ok predicate is quite complicated, embodying constraints such as: if a thread is blocking on a **recvfrom** call on a file-descriptor fd, then there must be a socket with that descriptor, and it must have a non-null ps_1 field. (This requirement is maintained in the face of the possibility that some other thread may call **close** on the fd-socket.) Higher order logic seems well-suited to our task. It is quite an expressive logic, and Hindley-Milner type-inference ensures that terms can be written concisely, without excessive type annotation. The mechanization has not required any treatment of binders, simplifying matters.

The HOL system has been used to define operational semantics for various programming languages in the past, including SML and C [Van96,Nor98], so we were confident that the various tools needed for our own definitions and proofs would be present. The implementation of HOL continues to develop (see [NS02]), and our experience has been a substantial prompt to further development.

To make the semantics readable (for ourselves as well as others) we depend on automatic typesetting tools – special-purpose tools we have written to take HOL source and render it into LATEX, applying the various notational conventions seen in the remainder of the paper.

7   Example: Repeated Heartbeat

At this point, we have (finally) set up enough semantic technology to analyse the example of §2.3. Casual examination of the code may convince the reader that it 'works'; we are now in a position to state this more precisely, and to prove it. We have been able to state a key property of the heartbeat failure detector in HOL, and have carried out a hand proof. The interest is not so much in the specific property, but in the fact that we can express it formally, and the various preconditions which it requires.

Obviously we must assume reasonably fast message delivery, and not too many messages dropped by the network; less obviously, we assume that the threads on ALAN and KURT run fast enough to clear backlogs. For an example case of the proof, suppose KURT is started first, and the receiver on ALAN is not yet listening. The first "ping" may be duplicated by the network, with each arriving message potentially generating an ICMP. In turn, the ICMPs may be duplicated and each duplicate arrive immediately before each call to **sendto**, causing it to return immediately with an error (*sendto_5*) and forcing *sender_thread* to retry. (This is why the try .. with must enclose the **delay** as well as the **sendto**.) A similar situation applies to the receiving end, and there are many other possibilities to be considered. We also prove that no uncaught exceptions arise.

The precise statement of the theorem is in HOL, and is quite elaborate; we here translate it into English.

Consider traces of a network N consisting of ALAN and KURT, quiescent, each with a store and an identical copy of the module in Figure 1. For brevity, we first make some simplifying assumptions, restricting the traces of N which we consider: no incoming messages from outside; rule *net_accept_dup* never creates more than 3 duplicates; rule *net_accept_drop* never drops more than one successive message from each host; the application calls the rhbeat2 module, but does not call the host or store directly; neither ALAN nor KURT crash; ALAN does not become disconnected, while KURT may become disconnected and reconnected at any point; and the kernel does not run out of memory, nor does any slow system call get interrupted. These assumptions are severe, but are appropriate for the algorithm we consider. A less naïve algorithm would allow them to be relaxed.

Further (trace) assumptions state that the application uses the module correctly: ALAN and KURT each make a single call to the associated start function; and calls to *get_status* occur only on ALAN, after *start_heartbeat_a*(), with the reference returned by it.

Finally, some model timing parameter assumptions. We impose some crude bounds, supposing that *dthread*, *dsch*, doq, and *dstore* are all less than say 1ms, and *dpropmax* is at most 200ms, to obtain a theorem with a simple statement. These ensure: $2\,dpropmax + 3\,doq < 1.0$, and hence receipt of an ICMP generated from one "ping" cannot be delayed beyond the sending of the next; and $(2.0 + 120\,dthread + 22\,dsch + 2\,doq + dpropmax - dpropmin) < 2.5$, hence a single message being lost cannot cause a timeout leading to a false failure report.

Given all this, we can identify certain intervals during which a reply to *get_status* is guaranteed to be correct:

Theorem 2 (Correct within reasonable time). *For any trace of N under the above assumptions, if get_status is called at time t and returns a value v, then v is the correct result if t is at least 2.6 seconds after the latest of* KURT*'s last status change and* ALAN*'s call to start_heartbeat_a().*

Of course, this is only one desirable property amongst many [ACT99]. It also does not state that *get_status* returns quickly (or at all). Further, we would like to be able to relax some of the conditions (possibly with a more general algorithm), *e.g.*, to allow the applications to perform other communication operations, and inhabit a larger network. This would require a more elaborate proof, but no changes to the semantics.

8   Conclusion

8.1   Contribution We have given a mathematically precise and experimentally validated model of an interesting class of distributed systems, covering UDP sockets programming, threads, message loss and duplication, host failure and disconnection, timeouts, and rudimentary modules. It is expressed in the HOL theorem prover, and illustrated with a simple heartbeat example. This demonstrates that it is feasible to address the combination of features above, though the experimental approach and tool support (for mechanization, testing and typesetting) have been essential. Our work is a step towards a rigorous understanding of distributed systems – such models can: (1) improve our informal understanding and system-building, (2) underpin proofs of robustness and security properties of particular programs, and (3) support the design, proof and implementation of higher-level distributed abstractions.

8.2 Related work The literature contains a great deal of work on the verification of protocols and distributed algorithms. This includes models of TCP using IO automata and LOTOS [Smi96,Sch96], and work on monitoring TCP implementations from outside the hosts [BCMG01]. To the best of our knowledge, however, there is no other work that accurately models the detailed behaviour of the sockets interface, an understanding of which is critical for actually programming with these protocols. At a higher level of abstraction, Arts and Dam [AD99] have a similar goal to ours – they prove properties of executable concurrent programs, written in Erlang – and the IOA language [GLV00] allows certain forms of IO automata to be executed.

Turning to failure detection, the literature contains sophisticated algorithms and their applications, *e.g.* to consensus problems [ACT99]. Such algorithms satisfy more useful (and more subtle) properties than our naive Theorem 2, but are expressed in informal psuedocode. We have begun to consider how they might be expressed in an extended MiniCaml.

8.3 Future Directions To date, our work on the semantics has been mostly descriptive, focussing on developing an accurate model. This addresses (1) above, but for (2) and (3) we must consider more substantial examples, which will require proof techniques to be adapted from the theories of process calculi and distributed algorithm verification. Extending the coverage of the model would also be valuable, in many directions: UDP multicast, PPP connections, TCP, network partition, other OS socket implementations (especially Win2K and BSD), a larger fragment of OCaml, or other language bindings. Finally, we would like to automatically generate tests from the HOL model.

The work also raises some more general problems. Perhaps surprisingly, even the non-distributed part of the semantics is not routine – to reason about properties of infrastructure implementations we need a semantics for modules with multiple threads that is truly compositional, not dependent on substituting out the module expressions. Our model embodies an *ad hoc* solution to the special case of a single infrastructure module that provides only first-order functions; a more general solution is required, perhaps using game-theoretic techniques. Dealing with module initialisation and separate compilation is also important. From the process-calculus point of view, our parallel composition and restriction are non-standard, both in combining binary and multi-way synchronisation, and in having the local receptiveness property. While timed finite trace equivalence is relatively straightforward in this setting, one might expect interesting differences in the theory of finer observational congruences.

Wansbrough and Serjantov are funded by EPSRC research grant GRN24872 Wide-area programming. Norrish is funded by a St Catharine's College Heller Research Fellowship. Sewell is funded by a Royal Society University Research Fellowship.

References

[ACT99]   M. K. Aguilera, W. Chen, and S. Toueg. Using the heartbeat failure detector for quiescent reliable communication and consensus in partitionable networks. *Theoretical Computer Science*, 220(1):3-30, June 1999.

[AD99]   T. Arts and M. Dam. Verifying a distributed database lookup manager
            written in Erlang. In *World Congress on Formal Methods (1)*, 1999.
[Bak95]   F. Baker. Requirements for IP version 4 routers, RFC 1812. Internet
            Engineering Task Force, June 1995. http://www.ietf.org/rfc.html.
[BCMG01]   K. Bhargavan, S. Chandra, P. J. McCann, and C. A. Gunter. What packets
            may come: Automata for network monitoring. In *Proc. POPL 2001*.
[Bra89]   R. Braden. Requirements for internet hosts – communication layers, STD
            3, RFC 1122. Internet Engineering Task Force, October 1989.
[CSR83]   University of California at Berkeley CSRG. 4.2BSD, 1983.
[GLV00]   S. J. Garland, N. Lynch, and M. Vaziri. IOA reference guide, December
            2000. http://nms.lcs.mit.edu/~garland/IOA/.
[GM93]   M. J. C. Gordon and T. Melham, editors. *Introduction to HOL: a theorem
            proving environment*. Cambridge University Press, 1993.
[HT91]   K. Honda and M. Tokoro. An object calculus for asynchronous communi-
            cation. In *Proceedings of ECOOP '91, LNCS 512*, pages 133–147, 1991.
[IEE00]   IEEE. *Portable Operating System Interface (POSIX)—Part xx: Protocol
            Independent Interfaces (PII), P1003.1g*. March 2000.
[L+01]   X. Leroy et al. *The Objective-Caml System, Release 3.02*. INRIA, July 30
            2001. Available http://caml.inria.fr/ocaml/.
[LV96]   N. Lynch and F. Vaandrager. Forward and backward simulations – Part II:
            Timing-based systems. *Information and Computation*, 128(1):1–25, 1996.
[Nor98]   M. Norrish. *C formalised in HOL*. PhD thesis, Computer Laboratory,
            University of Cambridge, 1998.
[NS02]   M. Norrish and K. Slind. A thread of HOL development. *Computer Journal*,
            2002. To appear.
[Pos80]   J. Postel. User Datagram Protocol, STD 6, RFC 768. Internet Engineering
            Task Force, August 1980. http://www.ietf.org/rfc.html.
[Pos81]   J. Postel. Internet Protocol, STD 5, RFC 791. Internet Engineering Task
            Force, September 1981. http://www.ietf.org/rfc.html.
[Sch96]   I. Schieferdecker. Abruptly terminated connections in TCP – a verification
            example. In *Proc. COST 247 International Workshop on Applied Formal
            Methods in System Design*, pages 136–145, 1996.
[SGSAL98]   R. Segala, R. Gawlick, J. Søgaard-Andersen, and N. Lynch. Liveness in
            timed and untimed systems. *Inf. and Comp.*, 141:119–171, 1998.
[Smi96]   M. Smith. Formal verification of communication protocols. In
            FORTE/PSTV'96, pages 129–144, 1996.
[SSW01a]   A. Serjantov, P. Sewell, and K. Wansbrough. The UDP calculus: Rigorous
            semantics for real networking. In *Proc TACS2001, Sendai*, October 2001.
[SSW01b]   A. Serjantov, P. Sewell, and K. Wansbrough. The UDP calculus: Rigorous
            semantics for real networking. TR 515, Computer Laboratory, University of
            Cambridge, July 2001. http://www.cl.cam.ac.uk/users/pes20/Netsem/.
[Ste94]   W. R. Stevens. *TCP/IP Illustrated Vol. 1: The Protocols*. Addison–Wesley,
            1994.
[Ste98]   W. R. Stevens. *UNIX Network Programming Vol. 1: Networking APIs:
            Sockets and XTI*. Prentice Hall, second edition, 1998.
[Van96]   M. VanInwegen. *The machine-assisted proof of programming language prop-
            erties*. PhD thesis, University of Pennsylvania, December 1996.
[WNSS01]   K. Wansbrough, M. Norrish, P. Sewell, and A. Serjantov. Timing UDP:
            the HOL model, 2001. http://www.cl.cam.ac.uk/users/pes20/Netsem/.
[Yi91]   W. Yi. CCS + time = an interleaving model for real time systems. In *Proc.
            ICALP 1991, LNCS 510*, pages 217–228, 1991.

A   The LIB interface

```
The sockets interface
socket        : ()                           → fd
bind          : fd ∗ ip↑ ∗ port↑             → ()
connect       : fd ∗ ip ∗ port↑              → ()
disconnect    : fd                           → ()
getsockname : fd                             → ip↑ ∗ port↑
getpeername : fd                             → ip↑ ∗ port↑
sendto        : fd ∗ (ip ∗ port)↑ ∗ string ∗ bool → ()
recvfrom      : fd ∗ bool                    → ip ∗ port↑ ∗ string
geterr        : fd                           → error↑
getsockopt    : fd ∗ sockopt                 → bool
setsockopt    : fd ∗ sockopt ∗ bool → ()
close         : fd                           → ()
select        : fd list ∗ fd list ∗ int↑ → fd list ∗ fd list
port_of_int   : int                          → port
ip_of_string  : string                       → ip
getifaddrs    : () → (ifid ∗ ip ∗ ip list ∗ netmask) list

Thread operations
create        : (T → T') → T                 → tid
delay         : int                          → ()

Basic operating system operations
print_endline_flush : string                 → ()
exit          : ()                           → void

Exceptions
UDP           : error                        → exn

Here error is a type of UDP-related Unix errors.
```

Fig. 2. The LIB interface, with MiniCaml types

Finite-Control Mobile Ambients

Witold Charatonik[1,2], Andrew D. Gordon[3], and Jean-Marc Talbot[4]

[1] Max-Planck-Institut für Informatik, Germany.
[2] University of Wrocław, Poland.
[3] Microsoft Research, United Kingdom.
[4] Laboratoire d'Informatique Fondamentale de Lille, France.

Abstract. We define a finite-control fragment of the ambient calculus, a formalism for describing distributed and mobile computations. A series of examples demonstrates the expressiveness of our fragment. In particular, we encode the choice-free, finite-control, synchronous π-calculus. We present an algorithm for model checking this fragment against the ambient logic (without composition adjunct). This is the first proposal of a model checking algorithm for ambients to deal with recursively-defined, possibly nonterminating, processes. Moreover, we show that the problem is PSPACE-complete, like other fragments considered in the literature. Finite-control versions of other process calculi are obtained via various syntactic restrictions. Instead, we rely on a novel type system that bounds the number of active ambients and outputs in a process; any typable process has only a finite number of derivatives.

1 Introduction

The ambient calculus [6] is a formalism for describing distributed and mobile computation in terms of *ambients*, named collections of running processes and nested subambients. A state of computation has a tree structure induced by ambient nesting. Mobility is represented by re-arrangement of this tree (an ambient may move inside or outside other ambients) or by deletion of a part of this tree (a process may dissolve the boundary of some ambient, revealing its content).

There are proposals for analysing systems expressed in the ambient calculus and its variants [2,14] via several techniques, such as equational reasoning [3], type systems [8], control flow analysis [16], and abstract interpretation [13]. Still, the ambient calculus is Turing-complete, and little attention has been paid to finding expressive finite-state fragments that admit automatic verification via state-space exploration. The goal of this work is to identity such a fragment, and to develop a model checking algorithm for verifying properties expressible in the ambient logic [5,7]. The long term intention is that automatic verification tools for a finite-state ambient calculus will be useful either by themselves or in conjunction with methods for obtaining finite-state abstractions of infinite-state systems. Similar abstractions [9] are being developed for the π-calculus [15], the formalism from which the ambient calculus derives.

A finite-state version of π exists [12]. It is described as a finite-control calculus because its control structure is finite. Starting in any state, the number of states reachable via internal reduction steps is finite. However, if we allow inputs of external data, the number of reachable states may be infinite. We define in this paper a

D. Le Métayer (Ed.): ESOP 2002, LNCS 2305, pp. 295–313, 2002.
© Springer-Verlag Berlin Heidelberg 2002

finite-control ambient calculus. It is a substantial extension of the replication-free fragment [5,10,11] (sometimes referred to as the "finite-state ambient calculus"). In particular, in the replication-free fragment every process can make only a finite number of computation steps—no recursion or iteration is possible.

We begin, in Section 2, by presenting a variant of the ambient calculus in which recursion is defined by means of an explicit recursive definition instead of replication. We specify standard spatial rearrangements via a structural congruence relation on processes, and specify the operational semantics as a reduction relation on processes. This variant is easily seen to simulate the original one. Then, in Section 3, we design a type system for ambient processes and show that typability of a process guarantees finitary behaviour. The basic idea of the type system is to count the number of active outputs and ambients in a process. Theorem 1 asserts that the number of processes, up to structural congruence, reachable from any typable process is finite. We define the finite-control fragment as those processes that are typable. In contrast, finite-control fragments of the π-calculus are defined via simple syntactic restrictions. In Section 4, we explore the expressivity of our calculus by presenting and developing some standard examples, including an encoding of a finite-control π-calculus.

Turning to the verification problem, Section 5 reviews the syntax and semantics of the ambient logic we use to specify process properties. We prove that the verification problem—model checking against the ambient logic without composition adjunct—is decidable for the finite-control fragment. To achieve this, we adapt the model checking algorithm from [11]. Theorem 2 states that the algorithm is correct with respect to the semantics of the logic. Moreover, our final result is Theorem 3, that the verification problem remains PSPACE-complete, which is the same complexity as verifying the replication-free fragment against the same logic.

A difficulty in designing a finite-control fragment of a process calculus is striking a balance between the expressivity of the fragment and the complexity of the verification problem. The general goal is to make the calculus as expressive as possible while keeping the verification problem decidable. The methods we use differ substantially from the methods used to define finite-control π-calculi. Therefore, for the sake of a simple exposition we omit several possible features from our finite-control ambient calculus while including enough to model interesting iterative computations. Section 6 discusses some of these additional features. Section 7 concludes the paper.

2   An Ambient Calculus with Recursion

We present in this section an ambient calculus with recursive definitions instead of replication. We give examples of the calculus in Section 4; see [6] for more elementary examples.

The following table defines the syntax of *capabilities* and *processes* of our calculus. We assume countably many *names* ranging over by $n, m, a, b, c, \ldots$ and countably many *identifiers* ranging over by $A, B, C, \ldots$. For the sake of a simple presentation we allow only names to be communicated whereas the original calculus allows also the transmission of sequences of capabilities.

Processes and Capabilities:

$\alpha ::=$	capabilities		
in n	can enter n	out n	can exit n
open n	can open n		
$P, Q, R ::=$	processes		
$\mathbf{0}$	inactivity	$P \mid Q$	composition
$n[P]$	ambient	$\alpha.P$	action prefix
$(n).P$	input	$\langle n \rangle$	output
$(\nu n)P$	name restriction	A	identifier
$(\text{fix } A{=}P)$	recursion		

We consider input (n), name restriction (νn) to be binders for the name n and fix A to be a binder for the identifier A. A name n or an identifier A occurring in the scope of respectively (n),(νn) and fix A is *bound*. Otherwise it is *free*. We write $fn(P)$ for the set of free names in P. We say that a process is *closed* if it contains no free identifier. We identify processes up-to capture-avoiding α-renaming of both bound names and bound identifiers. For instance, $(\text{fix } A{=}(\nu n)open\ n.A)$ and $(\text{fix } B{=}(\nu m)open\ m.B)$ are identical processes. Slightly abusing the notation, we write $bn(P)$ for the bound names in an implicitly given syntactic representation of P. We write $P\{m{\leftarrow}n\}$ for the outcome of substituting n for each free occurrence of m in P. Similarly, $P\{A{\leftarrow}Q\}$ is the outcome of substituting Q for each free occurrence of A in P. We will assume without loss of generality that two distinct bound identifiers are different as well as being distinct from any free identifier.

The semantics of our calculus is given by two relations. The *reduction relation* $P \rightarrow Q$ describes the evolution of ambient processes over time. We write $\rightarrow^*$ for the reflexive and transitive closure of $\rightarrow$. The *structural congruence* relation $P \equiv Q$ relates different syntactic representations of the same process; it is used to define the reduction relation.

Structural Congruence $P \equiv Q$:

$P \equiv P$	(Str Refl)	$P \equiv Q \Rightarrow (\nu n)P \equiv (\nu n)Q$	(Str Res)
$P \equiv Q \Rightarrow Q \equiv P$	(Str Symm)	$P \equiv Q \Rightarrow P \mid R \equiv Q \mid R$	(Str Par)
$P \equiv Q, Q \equiv R \Rightarrow P \equiv R$	(Str Trans)	$P \equiv Q \Rightarrow n[P] \equiv n[Q]$	(Str Amb)
$P \mid \mathbf{0} \equiv P$	(Str Par Zero)	$P \equiv Q \Rightarrow \alpha.P \equiv \alpha.Q$	(Str Action)
$P \mid Q \equiv Q \mid P$	(Str Par Comm)	$P \equiv Q \Rightarrow (n).P \equiv (n).Q$	(Str Input)
$(P \mid Q) \mid R \equiv P \mid (Q \mid R)$	(Str Par Assoc)	$P \equiv Q \Rightarrow (\text{fix } A{=}P) \equiv (\text{fix } A{=}Q)$	(Str Fix)
$(\nu n)\mathbf{0} \equiv \mathbf{0}$	(Str Res Zero)	$(\text{fix } A{=}A) \equiv \mathbf{0}$	(Str Fix Id)
$(\nu n)(\nu m)P \equiv (\nu m)(\nu n)P$	(Str Res Res)	$(\text{fix } A{=}P) \equiv P\{A{\leftarrow}(\text{fix } A{=}P)\}$	(Str Fix Rec)
$(\nu n)(P \mid Q) \equiv P \mid (\nu n)Q$ if $n \notin fn(P)$	(Str Res Par)		
$(\nu n)(m[P]) \equiv m[(\nu n)P]$ if $n \neq m$	(Str Res Amb)		

Reduction: $P \rightarrow Q$

$n[\text{in } m.P \mid Q] \mid m[R] \rightarrow m[n[P \mid Q] \mid R]$	(Red In)
$m[n[\text{out } m.P \mid Q] \mid R] \rightarrow n[P \mid Q] \mid m[R]$	(Red Out)
$\text{open } n.P \mid n[Q] \rightarrow P \mid Q$	(Red Open)
$\langle m \rangle \mid (n).P \rightarrow P\{n{\leftarrow}m\}$	(Red I/O)

$P \to Q \Rightarrow P \mid R \to Q \mid R$	(Red Par)
$P \to Q \Rightarrow n[P] \to n[Q]$	(Red Amb)
$P \to Q \Rightarrow (\nu n)P \to (\nu n)Q$	(Red Res)
$P' \equiv P, P \to Q, Q \equiv Q' \Rightarrow P' \to Q'$	(Red $\equiv$)

As in other process calculi with recursion, it is convenient to regard certain unwanted recursive processes as ill-formed, and to disregard them. An example is $(\text{fix } A{=}A \mid A)$. We define a well-formed process as follows.

Definition 1. *A process P is said to be* well-formed *if every recursive subprocess $(\text{fix } A{=}Q)$ of P satisfies the following two requirements: (i) A is the only free identifier in Q, and (ii) A occurs at most once in Q.*

From now on, we only consider well-formed processes. These processes are stable with respect to structural congruence and reduction: if P is well-formed and either $P \equiv P'$ or $P \to P'$ then P' is well-formed.

As in the π-calculus [15], we can easily simulate replication with recursion. To simulate $!P$, which behaves like an unbounded number of replicas of P running in parallel, we introduce a new identifier A_P and replace $!P$ by $(\text{fix } A_P{=}P \mid A_P)$. The resulting process is well-formed. This encoding of replication fulfils the axioms of structural congruence for replication $!P \equiv P \mid !P$ and $!0 \equiv 0$ given in [6]. It does not obey the two additional axioms $!P \equiv !!P$ and $!(P \mid Q) \equiv !P \mid !Q$ from [5], but these axioms are unnecessary for computing reduction steps.

Sangiorgi [17] also considers an ambient calculus with recursion. A difference is that our formulation allows recursively defined ambient structures. In a recursion $(\text{fix } A{=}P)$, the identifier A can appear in P within an ambient construct; for example, the processes $(\text{fix } A{=}m[A])$ and $(\text{fix } A{=}\text{open } n.m[A])$ are well-formed. The latter but not the former belongs to the finite-control fragment defined next.

3   A Finite-Control Ambient Calculus

The finite-control (synchronous) π-calculus [12] is obtained by disallowing parallel composition through recursion. So, a finite-control π-calculus process is a finite parallel composition of threads each of which is a recursive process without parallel composition. This ensures that there is only finitely many pairwise non-congruent configurations reachable from such a process. In the ambient calculus this restriction is both too strong and too weak. It is too strong because it limits the admissible computation too much. In particular, due to the asynchronous communication mechanism in the ambient calculus, it completely excludes communication in recursive programs. On the other hand, it is too weak, as exemplified below, because it does not ensure finitary behaviour of processes. The example shows that in the ambient calculus a bound on the number of parallel threads gives neither a bound on the size of reachable processes nor a bound on the number of possible interactions between threads. This is in contrast to the situation in the π-calculus, and seems to arise from the spatial characteristics of the ambient calculus.

Example 1. Consider the two ambient processes P_A and P_B defined respectively by (fix $A=n[\text{open } m.A]$) and (fix $B=m[\text{in } n.B]$). Neither process contains parallel composition. However, the process $P_A \mid P_B$ reduces in $2k$ steps to $\underbrace{n[\cdots n[P_A \mid P_B]\cdots]}_{k}$,

denoted $(P_A \mid P_B)_k$. Since for $k \neq k'$, $(P_A \mid P_B)_k \not\equiv (P_A \mid P_B)_{k'}$, there are infinitely many non-congruent processes reachable from $P_A \mid P_B$.

Now, if we place another process $m[(\text{fix } C=\text{in } n.C) \mid (\text{fix } D=\text{out } n.D)]$ in parallel with $P_A \mid P_B$, this process can traverse the structure of $(P_A \mid P_B)_k$ in an arbitrary way. Thus, although there are only four recursively defined processes and none of them contains parallel composition, they may create an arbitrary number of locations and interact in any of these locations.

This example shows that directly adopting the syntactic restriction from the finite-control synchronous π-calculus is problematic, but it does not show undecidability of the verification problem. However, if we adopt a more liberal condition from the finite-control asynchronous π-calculus [1] (which ensures that there is only a bounded number of active threads and seems more appropriate here due to the asynchronous communication used in ambient calculus), we obtain undecidability even for the reachability problem. One can adapt the encoding of the Post correspondence problem from [11], in which only finitely many active threads are used.

Thus, one may consider a more severe syntactic restriction, to forbid both parallel composition and ambient construction within recursion. We will see later on that this restriction indeed ensures finite-control. Still, we can see at once that it is too drastic. In such a restricted process only sequences of action prefixes, each invoking a capability, could be defined recursively. Moreover, those sequences would operate on a process whose spatial structure has a bounded size. Inspecting the individual effect of such sequences, one sees that the open capability is somehow the more powerful as it changes the spatial structure of the process by deleting part of it whereas both capabilities in and out only re-arrange this structure. As a consequence, only finitely many occurrences of the powerful capability open can be executed by such a restricted process.

Instead of defining finite-control by means of syntactic restrictions over processes, we adopt a semantic point of view based on a type system. Intuitively, a type of a process P is a natural number that bounds the number of active outputs and ambients in any process reachable from P. We present the type system in Section 3.1. In Section 3.2 we show that typability ensures finitary computation.

3.1   The Type System FC

A *type environment* Γ is a finite set of pairs $\{(A_1, \tau_1), \ldots, (A_n, \tau_n)\}$ such that each A_i is an identifier, τ_i is a natural number and for any two pairs (A_i, τ_i) and (A_j, τ_j), $i \neq j$ implies $A_i \neq A_j$. We say that an environment Γ is defined for A if Γ contains a pair (A, τ). Whenever Γ is defined for no identifier, we simply write $\varnothing$.

Definition 2. *Given a type environment Γ, a type judgment $\Gamma \vdash Q : \tau$ holds for a process Q and a natural number τ if there exists a finite proof tree built with the inference rules from the table below such that its root is labelled by $\Gamma \vdash Q : \tau$ and none of its leaves contains a type judgment.*

Process Typing : $\Gamma \vdash P : \tau$

(Identifier)	(Zero)	(Par)	(Res)

$$\frac{A \text{ is identifier}, (A, \tau) \in \Gamma}{\Gamma \vdash A : \tau} \qquad \frac{}{\Gamma \vdash \mathbf{0} : 0} \qquad \frac{\Gamma \vdash P : \tau, \Gamma \vdash Q : \theta}{\Gamma \vdash P \mid Q : \tau + \theta} \qquad \frac{\Gamma \vdash P : \tau}{\Gamma \vdash (\nu n)P : \tau}$$

(Output)   (Input)   (In/Out)

$$\frac{}{\Gamma \vdash \langle n \rangle : 1} \qquad \frac{\Gamma \vdash P : \tau}{\Gamma \vdash (n).P : \max(\tau - 1, 1)} \qquad \frac{\Gamma \vdash P : \tau, \text{ cap} \in \{\text{in}, \text{out}\}}{\Gamma \vdash \text{cap } n.P : \max(\tau, 1)}$$

(Amb)   (Open)   (Fix)

$$\frac{\Gamma \vdash P : \tau}{\Gamma \vdash n[P] : \tau + 1} \qquad \frac{\Gamma \vdash P : \tau}{\Gamma \vdash \text{open } n.P : \max(\tau - 1, 1)} \qquad \frac{\Gamma \cup \{(A, \tau)\} \vdash P : \theta, \ \theta \leq \tau}{\Gamma \vdash (\text{fix } A = P) : \tau}$$

The basic idea of the type system is to bound the number of active outputs and ambients in all processes reachable from a given one. In the rules (Input) and (Open) the process P is guarded and thus not active. These rules express that P may become active only after dissolving some active output or ambient. The function $\max(\cdot, 1)$ is used to avoid negative types. Without it some processes of unbounded (or even infinite) size like $(\text{fix } A = \text{open } n.\mathbf{0} \mid m[] \mid A)$ could be still typable. We take maximum with 1 and not 0 to obtain a property—used in some proofs—that $\mathbf{0}$ is the only process of type 0.

Example 2. The proof tree stating that the type judgment $\varnothing \vdash (\text{fix } A = \text{open } n.m[A]) \mid n[0] : 2$ holds is given below. In a similar way we can build a proof tree for $\varnothing \vdash (\text{fix } A = \text{open } n.m[A]) \mid n[0] : 3$.

$$\frac{\dfrac{\dfrac{\dfrac{\dfrac{(A, 1) \in \{(A, 1)\}}{\{(A, 1)\} \vdash A : 1}}{\{(A, 1)\} \vdash m[A] : 2}}{\dfrac{\{(A, 1)\} \vdash \text{open } n.m[A] : 1, \ 1 \leq 1}{\varnothing \vdash (\text{fix } A = \text{open } n.m[A]) : 1} \qquad \dfrac{\dfrac{}{\varnothing \vdash \mathbf{0} : 0}}{\varnothing \vdash n[0] : 1}}}{\varnothing \vdash (\text{fix } A = \text{open } n.m[A]) \mid n[0] : 2}$$

Recall Example 1. The process $(\text{fix } A = n[\text{open } m.A]) \mid (\text{fix } B = m[\text{in } n.B])$ is not typable because $(\text{fix } B = m[\text{in } n.B])$ is not typable.

Definition 3. *A type environment Γ well-types a process P if there exists some natural number τ_P such that the type judgment $\Gamma \vdash P : \tau_P$ holds. A process P is typable if there exists a type environment Γ that well-types P.*

If P is typable and does not contain free identifiers, then $\varnothing$ well-types P.

We say that a process P is *balanced* if the number of occurrences of ambients and outputs in P is equal to the number of occurrences of open capabilities and inputs in P. We say that a recursive process $(\text{fix } A = P)$ has a balanced type if for every type environment $\Gamma \cup \{(A : \tau)\}$ such that $\Gamma \cup \{(A, \tau)\} \vdash P : \theta$ and $\theta \leq \tau$ we have $\theta = \tau$. In most natural examples, like in $(\text{fix } A = n[\text{open } n.A])$, if P is balanced then $(\text{fix } A = P)$ is typable. But there are exceptions like $(\text{fix } A = A \mid \text{open} n.n.n[0])$ which is balanced but not typable. If P is not balanced because it contains more outputs and ambients than inputs and opens (like in $(\text{fix } A = n[A])$) then $(\text{fix } A = P)$ is not typable. Finally, note that not all typable processes have balanced types. For example (fix A=open $n.A$) is typable but it does not have a balanced type (the environment $\{(A, 2)\}$ being a counter-example).

In most examples of typable recursive processes that are considered in this paper we will want the types to be balanced. This is because if such a process does not have a balanced type then in each execution it consumes some (strictly more than it creates) messages or ambients in the global context in which it is placed, and thus it can be executed only finitely many times.

For a given type environment Γ and a given process P there may be many natural numbers τ such that the type judgment $\Gamma \vdash P : \tau$ holds. For example, $\varnothing \vdash$ (fix A=A) : τ holds for any natural τ. However, since every set of natural numbers has a least element, we may define a least type.

Definition 4 (Least Type). *For any process P and any type environment Γ that well-types P, the* least *type of P with respect to Γ, denoted $\mathcal{L}^{FC}(P, \Gamma)$, is the least natural number τ such that $\Gamma \vdash P : \tau$ holds.*

Proposition 1 (Type Stability). *Let P and P' be typable processes and let Γ be a type environment that well-types P and P'. Then $P \equiv P'$ implies $\mathcal{L}^{FC}(P, \Gamma) = \mathcal{L}^{FC}(P', \Gamma)$.*

Proof. The proof goes by induction over the proof tree for $P \equiv P'$. The only difficult case is for the axiom (fix A=Q) $\equiv Q\{A \leftarrow ($fix A=$Q)\}$ (Str Fix Rec) which requires an induction over the structure of Q. □

Proposition 2 (Type Checking - Type Inference). *Type checking (that is, deciding, given Γ, P and τ, whether the type judgment $\Gamma \vdash P : \tau$ holds) is decidable. For any process P and type environment Γ, we can decide whether Γ well-types P and compute $\mathcal{L}^{FC}(P, \Gamma)$.*

Proof. Both type checking and type inference amount to solving easy systems of inequalities with addition, subtraction of a constant, and max as the only arithmetic operations. □

Proposition 3 (Subject Reduction). *Let P be a process and Γ an environment that well-types P. Then for all processes P' such that $P \rightarrow P'$, Γ well-types P' and $\mathcal{L}^{FC}(P', \Gamma) \leq \mathcal{L}^{FC}(P, \Gamma)$.*

Sketch of proof. The reductions (Red In) and (Red Out) do not change the type of a process at all. The reductions (Red Open) and (Red I/O) reducing processes of the form open $n.Q$ or $(n).Q$, respectively, do not change the type if $\mathcal{L}^{FC}(Q, \Gamma) > 1$. Otherwise, they strictly decrease the type by removing the ambient n or consuming a message. For the other reductions (Red Par), (Red Amb), (Red Res), and (Red $\equiv$), it follows from induction over P, using Proposition 1 in case of (Red $\equiv$). □

Due to Proposition 1, the least type of any process congruent to **0** is 0. Conversely, we have:

Proposition 4. *For all closed and typable processes P, if $\mathcal{L}^{FC}(P, \varnothing) = 0$ then $P \equiv \mathbf{0}$.*

Proof. It is easy to see that if a closed process P contains either an ambient construct, a capability, an input or an output, then its least type is greater or equal to one. Therefore, it is enough to show that closed and well-formed processes built up with identifiers, **0**, parallel composition, name restriction, and fix are congruent to **0**. The proof goes by induction on the structure of P. □

Additionally, we can prove some other properties. All recursion-free processes are typable. The encoding of replication $!P$ given earlier is not typable for any P non-congruent to $\mathbf{0}$. Processes built without parallel composition and ambient construct are typable. This last property implies that processes are typable if they satisfy the syntactic restriction—to forbid both composition and ambients within recursion—considered in Section 3. As we see in the next section, it follows that processes obeying this syntactic restriction are finite-state.

3.2   Typability and Finite-Control

The goal of this section is to prove that for a typable and closed process, there exist finitely many $\equiv$-congruence classes $\mathcal{K}_1, \ldots, \mathcal{K}_n$ such that for all processes P' with $P \to^* P'$, there exists i for which $P' \in \mathcal{K}_i$. Instead of proving this directly, we show that for any typable and closed process P and any process P' reachable from P, there exists a *representative* P'' of P' (that is, $P' \equiv P''$) such that:

– the size of P'' is bounded and depends only on P;
– the set of free names of P'' is a subset of the free names of P.

Here, by the size $|P|$ of a process P we mean the number of nodes in the tree representation of P. The two statements above imply that there exist only finitely many pairwise non-congruent processes reachable from P. Simply showing the size is bounded is insufficient as there are infinitely many different names. For example, processes from the set $\{n[0] \mid n \text{ being a name}\}$ have a bounded size, but being non-congruent with each other, they represent infinitely many $\equiv$-congruence classes.

The second requirement about free names is straightforward and actually does not rely on typability.

Proposition 5. *For all processes P, P', if $P \equiv P'$ or $P \to P'$ then $fn(P') \subseteq fn(P)$.*

The first requirement is much more involved for various reasons. We need to characterize representatives of structural congruence classes of reachable processes; this requires to consider a process split into several parts.

First, we define pre-normalized processes. Let a process P be *pre-normalized* if it takes the form $(\nu n_1) \ldots (\nu n_k)Q$ and, (i) every n_j occurs free in Q, (ii) $n_1, \ldots, n_k$ are pairwise distinct, and (iii) any other name restriction occurring in Q appears in the scope of some input or of some action prefix. Intuitively, pre-normalization is rewriting a process using the scope extrusion rules (Str Res Par) and (Str Res Amb) to a kind of prenex normal form.

The second part of processes consists in *outermost guarded* subprocesses. A process P is *guarded* if either $P \equiv \mathbf{0}$, $P \equiv \langle M \rangle$, $P \equiv \alpha.P'$ for some P' and some α, $P \equiv (x).P'$ for some P', or recursively $P \equiv (\nu n)Q$ for some guarded Q. This property is clearly stable with respect to structural congruence, that is, if P is guarded and $P \equiv P'$ then P' is guarded as well. Let a subprocess P' be *outermost guarded* in a process P if P' is guarded and for any subprocess P'' of P enclosing P', P'' is not guarded. For instance, out $m.0$ is outermost guarded in $n[\text{out } m.0]$ and as a consequence, $\mathbf{0}$ is guarded but not outermost guarded. In $n[\text{out} m.0 \mid 0]$, out$m.0 \mid 0$ is outermost guarded (because out $m.0 \mid 0$ is congruent to a process of the form $\alpha.P$, namely out $m.0$) and thus, out $m.0$ is not outermost guarded. This last example shows that outermost guardedness is a pure syntactic condition and is not stable with respect to structural congruence.

Finally, the remaining part of the process is captured by a context. A *context* C with l holes (or, for short, an l-context) is a process where exactly l subprocesses have been replaced by a hole $\star_i$ occurring exactly once in C. We write $C[P_1, \ldots, P_l]$ for the process obtained by filling each hole $\star_i$ in C with P_i.

A context is *active* if it consists only of holes, ambients, parallel compositions, and void processes 0 and furthermore if each process 0 occurs as a child node of an ambient in the tree representation of the context.

A process is *normalized* if this process is either 0 or a pre-normalized process of the form $(\nu n_1) \ldots (\nu n_k)Q$, where Q is of the form $C[P_1, \ldots, P_l]$ such that:

- C is an active l-context,
- $P_1, \ldots, P_l$ are the outermost guarded subprocesses from Q that are not congruent to 0.

By the *one-step unfolding* of a process P we mean the process obtained from P by replacing every subprocess of the form $(\text{fix } A = Q)$ by $Q\{A \leftarrow (\text{fix } A = Q)\}$. If Q is obtained by one-step unfolding from P then $|Q| \leq |P|^2$.

Lemma 1. *Any typable and closed process P admits a congruent normalized process Q such that $|Q| \leq |P|^2$.*

Sketch of proof. First, by structural induction we prove that in any recursive process $(\text{fix } A = Q)$ either A is guarded in Q or $(\text{fix } A = Q)$ is congruent to 0. We obtain a normalized version of a pre-normalized process by replacing all recursive definitions congruent to 0 by 0, applying a one-step unfolding to the result, and then removing all 0's from the context that are not child nodes of an ambient. □

We say that a process Q is a *subprocess up to renaming* of a process P if Q can be obtained from some subprocess of P by renaming its free names.

Proposition 6. *Let P be a closed, typable, normalized and non-congruent to 0 process and P' be its one-step unfolding. Then for all processes Q reachable from P (that is, such that $P \to^* Q$), there exists a normalized process $(\nu n_1) \ldots (\nu n_k)C[P_1, \ldots, P_l]$ structurally congruent to Q and such that*

- *k is bounded by the size of C,*
- *the size of C is bounded by $3 \cdot \mathcal{L}^{\mathsf{FC}}(P, \varnothing)$,*
- *each Q_j is a subprocess up to renaming of some outermost guarded part from P'.*

Sketch of proof. Since $(\nu n_1) \ldots (\nu n_k)C[P_1, \ldots, P_l]$ is pre-normalized, every restricted name from the set $\{n_1, \ldots, n_k\}$ must occur freely in C. Thus k is bounded by the size of C.

Since the process is normalized, the subprocesses $P_1, \ldots, P_l$ are not congruent to 0 and thus have strictly positive types. C is an active context, so its tree representation consists of four kinds of nodes:

- leaves representing a hole, whose number is smaller than $\mathcal{L}^{FC}(P_1, \varnothing) + \ldots + \mathcal{L}^{FC}(P_l, \varnothing)$,
- leaves representing 0, whose number is smaller than the number of unary nodes,
- binary nodes representing parallel compositions whose number is smaller than the number of leaves,
- unary nodes representing ambients; the number of such nodes summed with $\mathcal{L}^{FC}(P_1, \varnothing) + \ldots + \mathcal{L}^{FC}(P_l, \varnothing)$ gives $\mathcal{L}^{FC}(Q, \varnothing)$.

This together with the subject reduction theorem (Proposition 3) gives that the size of $\mathcal{C}$ is bounded by $3 \cdot \mathcal{L}^{FC}(P, \varnothing)$.

Finally, the processes Q_j are either directly subprocesses up to renaming of the initial process P or of unfoldings of the recursive definitions, which are already unfolded in P'. This is because the only possibility (apart from using the structural congruence) to modify a process below a guard is to substitute some of its free names with other names coming from communication.   □

The following theorem is a direct corollary from Propositions 5 and 6.

Theorem 1 (Finite-State). *For any closed and typable process P, there exist only finitely many pairwise non-congruent processes reachable from P.*

4   Examples

The model checking algorithm from [5] is limited to replication-free processes. We want to have at least some restricted version of recursion that would help us in modelling mobile computations while keeping model checking decidable. This section gives examples of programs that are typable and that therefore, by Theorem 1, are finite-state.

4.1   Simple Examples with Infinite Behaviour

Probably the simplest possible example with infinite behaviour is $n[P_A] \mid m[]$ where P_A is the process (fix A=in m.out $m.A$). It is typable with the type of P_A equal to 1 and the type of the whole process being 3. We have $n[P_A] \mid m[] \rightarrow m[n[\text{out } m.P_A]] \rightarrow n[P_A] \mid m[]$, which creates an infinite loop.

Another simple example is $P_A \mid P_B$ where P_A is (fix A=a[open $b.A$]) and P_B is (fix B=open $a.b[B]$). Here the least type of P_A is 2 and the least type of P_B is 1. One can see it as a simple synchronization mechanism—we will use such a mechanism later in the encoding of the (synchronous) finite-control π-calculus. We have $P_A \mid P_B \equiv a[\text{open } b.P_A] \mid \text{open } a.b[P_B] \rightarrow \text{open } b.P_A \mid b[P_B] \rightarrow P_A \mid P_B$.

A similar behaviour can be obtained from a simpler process (fix A=open $a.A$) | (fix B=$a[B]$), but we cannot use it since it is not typable.

Our last example in this section shows that we can obtain not only infinite computation paths, but also infinitely many syntactically different processes along these paths. Consider the process $P_A \mid P_B$ where P_A is (fix A=(νa)open n.open $m.(\langle a \rangle \mid a[A])$) and P_B is (fix B=$n[m[(x).\text{open } x.B]]$). The process is typable with the least types of P_A and P_B being respectively 1 and 3. Here, in every iteration, the process P_A creates a new fresh name and sends it to P_B.

4.2   Objective Moves

The only iterative definition in the encoding of objective moves in [6] is $\texttt{allow}\ n \triangleq$ $!\texttt{open}\ n$. This can be directly translated to $(\texttt{fix}\ A{=}\texttt{open}\ n.A)$, but such a translation leads to a definition of $\texttt{mv}\ \texttt{in}\ n.P$ where the type of $\texttt{mv}\ \texttt{in}\ n.P$ is one greater than the type of P, and so does not allow the use of objective moves inside recursion. Therefore we propose an alternative definition.

$$\texttt{allow}\ n \triangleq (\texttt{fix}\ A{=}\texttt{open}\ n.n[A])$$
$$n^\downarrow[P] \triangleq n[P \mid \texttt{allow}\ in]$$
$$n^\uparrow[P] \triangleq n[P] \mid \texttt{allow}\ out$$
$$n^{\downarrow\uparrow}[P] \triangleq n[P \mid \texttt{allow}\ in] \mid \texttt{allow}\ out$$
$$\texttt{mv}\ \texttt{in}\ n.P \triangleq (\nu k)k[\texttt{in}\ n.in[\texttt{out}\ k.\texttt{open}\ k.\texttt{open}\ in.P]]$$
$$\texttt{mv}\ \texttt{out}\ n.P \triangleq (\nu k)k[\texttt{out}\ n.out[\texttt{out}\ k.\texttt{open}\ k.\texttt{open}\ out.P]]$$

It is easy to see that all these processes are typable and are balanced; the least type of $\texttt{allow}\ n$ is 1, the least type of $\texttt{mv}\ \texttt{in}\ n.P$ and $\texttt{mv}\ \texttt{out}\ n.P$ is the maximum of the type of P and 2. One can check that $n^\downarrow[Q] \mid \texttt{mv}\ \texttt{in}\ n.P \rightarrow^* n^\downarrow[P \mid Q]$ and $n^\uparrow[\texttt{mv}\ \texttt{out}\ n.P \mid Q] \rightarrow^* n^\uparrow[Q] \mid P$.

4.3   Firewalls

Consider the firewall from [6]. This is a replication-free process

$$firewall = (\nu w)k[\texttt{in}\ k.\texttt{in}\ w] \mid w[\texttt{open}\ k.P],$$

but it allows only one agent to enter the firewall. Let us first extend this example to allow for more agents. To avoid some confusion we replace one of the two occurrences of the name k with k': $firewall = (\nu w)!k[\texttt{in}\ k'.\texttt{in}\ w] \mid w[!\texttt{open}\ k' \mid P]$. Then we have $k'[\texttt{open}\ k.Q] \mid firewall \rightarrow^* (\nu w)!k[\texttt{in}\ k'.\texttt{in}\ w] \mid w[!\texttt{open}\ k' \mid P \mid Q]$ and the firewall is still ready to allow more agents that are aware of the password (k, k').

We still have a little problem with modelling this firewall as a typable program. The process $k[\texttt{in}\ k'.in\ w]$ is at the beginning outside the ambient w, but at the end (after the agent enters the firewall) it is inside w. In typable programs we need to always start a recursion in the same place that we end it. Therefore we first modify the firewall: $firewall = (\nu w)w[!k[\texttt{out}\ w.\texttt{in}\ k'.in\ w] \mid !\texttt{open}\ k' \mid P]$.

Now it is easy to see that this process behaves in the same way as the following program $firewall$ where

$$firewall = (\nu w)w[hook \mid initiator \mid P]$$
$$hook = (\texttt{fix}\ A{=}k[\texttt{out}\ w.in\ k.\texttt{in}\ w.\texttt{open}\ b.A])$$
$$initiator = (\texttt{fix}\ B{=}\texttt{open}\ k.b[B])$$

We use the additional ambient b to balance the bodies of the procedures $hook$ and $initiator$.

4.4   Routable Packets

Following [6] we define *packet pkt* as an empty packet named *pkt* that can be routed repeatedly to various destinations. Contrary to [6], we do not model routing as communicating the path to be followed (we restricted the calculus not to contain communication of compound messages), but by sending it another ambient containing the path.

$$packet\ pkt \triangleq pkt[(\text{fix } R=\text{open } route.route[R])]$$
$$route\ pkt\ with\ P\ to\ M \triangleq route[\text{in } pkt.\text{open } route.M \mid P]$$
$$forward\ pkt\ to\ M \triangleq route\ pkt\ with\ \mathbf{0}\ to\ M$$

Then there is an execution $packet\ pkt \mid route\ pkt\ with\ P\ to\ M \to^* pkt[M \mid P \mid P_R]$ where P_R is the process $(\text{fix } R=\text{open } route.route[R])$. Similarly, $pkt[P \mid P_R] \mid forward\ pkt\ to\ M \to^* pkt[M \mid P \mid P_R]$.

4.5   A Finite-Control π-Calculus

Here we encode a version of the finite-control π-calculus [12] without name passing in recursive procedures (that is, with parameterless recursive definitions) and without non-deterministic choice. An encoding of the full finite-control π-calculus seems possible using the extensions of our calculus discussed in Section 6.

Processes of the finite-control π-calculus

$P ::=$		process		
$(\nu n)P$		name restriction		
$T_1 \mid \ldots \mid T_k$		parallel threads		
$T ::=$		thread		
$\mathbf{0}$		inactivity	$(\nu n)T$	name restriction
$\alpha.T$		action	A	identifier
$(\text{fix } A=T)$		recursion		
$\alpha ::=$		action		
$n(x)$		input on channel n		
$n\langle x \rangle$		output on channel n		

The encoding of the (asynchronous) π-calculus given in [6] cannot be used here for at least two reasons. First, the finite-control π-calculus uses synchronous communication while the communication in the ambient calculus is asynchronous. In order to simulate synchronous communication we have to run a synchronisation protocol. Second, dynamic generation of new channels strictly increases the size of the encoding and thus cannot be typable. Instead of this, we create new channels for every single communication and we destroy this channel immediately after the communication is finished.

To synchronize the communication, for every thread T_i we introduce an ambient $sync_i[]$ that avoids mixing the order of actions taken by this thread: every thread can send or receive at most one message at a time. Additionally we introduce one ambient $lock[]$ that allows processing only one communication at a time. These ambients are present at the beginning, but they disappear (that is, they get opened) when the respective action starts and they reappear when the action is finished.

In the encoding given below we use an ambient named ch as a place where communication happens. The idea of this encoding is as follows. If two processes $n\langle M\rangle.P$ and $n(x).Q$ in threads T_i and T_j are willing to communicate, they start by opening the respective ambients $sync_i$ and $sync_j$ (if some of these ambients are not present, it means that the thread is busy with some other action, and the process has to wait). Then the output process leaves an ambient $n[]$ (this is the information that there is a message sent over the channel n) and moves inside the ambient ch. There it sends the message $\langle M\rangle$ within another ambient n. The input process opens the ambient $n[]$ (if there is no such ambient, it means that there is no message sent over channel n and the process has to wait), then it opens $lock[]$ (again, if there is no $lock[]$ ambient, it means that there is another communication just taking place and the process has to wait until it is finished) and goes inside ch and inside n where it reads the message M. The rest of the encoding is just to clean up afterwards: both processes go out of ch and together with the auxiliary processes $Sync_i$ and $Sync_j$ they synchronize the two threads and release the lock on communication, and remove all auxiliary ambients used in the meantime (more precisely, after the communication the ambient b gets opened, $done_i$ goes out of n and n goes inside $done_i$ where it gets opened; then $done_i$ moves outside ch, c gets opened, and the two $Sync$ processes open $done_i$ and $done_j$; at this moment the ambients $sync_i[]$, $sync_j[]$ and $lock[]$ appear again at the top level). The ambients a, b, c are used to balance the process and to move inside ch.

Formally, the encoding is defined by the function $[\![\cdot]\!]$ from processes of the finite-control π-calculus to the finite-control ambient calculus. Except from communication, the encoding is quite straightforward: we have $[\![(\nu n)P]\!] \triangleq (\nu n)[\![P]\!]$,

$$[\![T_1 \mid \ldots \mid T_k]\!] \triangleq [\![T_1]\!]_1 \mid Sync_1 \mid \ldots \mid [\![T_k]\!]_k \mid Sync_k \mid ch^{\lceil\rceil}[] \mid lock[]$$

$$[\![0]\!]_i \triangleq 0, \quad [\![(\nu n)T]\!]_i \triangleq (\nu n)[\![T]\!]_i, \quad [\![A]\!]_i \triangleq A, \quad [\![(\text{fix } A{=}T)]\!]_i \triangleq (\text{fix } A{=}[\![T]\!]_i),$$

$$[\![n\langle M\rangle.P]\!]_i \triangleq \text{open } sync_i.(n[] \mid \text{mv in } ch.n[\langle M\rangle] \mid \text{open } a.PostOut_i(P))$$
$$[\![n(x).Q]\!]_j \triangleq \text{open } sync_j.\text{open } n.\text{open } lock.\text{mv in } ch.a[\text{in } n.(x).PostIn_j(Q)]$$

where
$$Sync_i \triangleq sync_i[] \mid (\text{fix } S_i{=}\text{open } done_i.(sync_i[] \mid S_i))$$
$$PostOut_i(P) \triangleq \text{open } b.(\text{in } done_i.lock[] \mid done_i[\text{out } n.\text{open } n.\text{out } ch.\text{open } c.[\![P]\!]_i])$$
$$PostIn_j(Q) \triangleq b[c[done_j[[\![Q]\!]_j]]]$$

5 Ambient Logic and Model Checking

To reason about distributed and mobile computations programmed in the ambient calculus, Cardelli and Gordon [5] introduce a modal logic that apart from standard temporal modalities for describing the evolution of processes includes novel spatial modalities for describing the tree structure of ambient processes. In a recent paper, Cardelli and Gordon extend the logic with the constructs for describing private names [7].

The *model checking* problem is to decide whether a given object (in our case, an ambient process) satisfies (that is, is a model of) a given formula. Cardelli and Gordon [5] give a model checking algorithm for the fragment of the calculus in which the processes contain no replications and no dynamic name generation against a fragment of the logic in which formulas contain no composition adjunct. It was then proved in [10] that model checking this fragment of the calculus against this fragment of the logic is PSPACE-complete. Recently, in [11] it has been shown that on the one hand, extending the calculus with name restriction and the logic with corresponding logical operators is harmless for the complexity of model checking—it remains PSPACE—and on the other hand that either considering replication in the calculus or composition adjunct in the logic makes the model checking problem undecidable.

5.1   Ambient Logic

We recall in this section definitions concerning this logic (omitting the composition adjunct).

In addition to the reduction relation and the structural congruence, we introduce an additional relation called *location* and denoted $\downarrow$ to reason about the shape of ambients (that is, space). The location relation is defined as $P \downarrow Q$ if there exists Q', n such that $P \equiv n[Q] \mid Q'$. We write $\downarrow^*$ for the reflexive and transitive closure of $\downarrow$.

We describe the syntax of the ambient logic and its satisfaction relation in the following tables.

Logical Formulas:

η	a name n or a variable x		
$A, B ::=$	formula	$\eta[A]$	location
T	true	$A@\eta$	location adjunct
$\neg A$	negation	$\eta \circledR A$	revelation
$A \vee B$	disjunction	$A \oslash \eta$	revelation adjunct
0	void	$\Diamond A$	sometime modality
$A \mid B$	composition match	$\diamondsuit A$	somewhere modality
		$\exists x.A$	existential quantification

We assume that names and variables belong to two disjoint vocabularies. We write $A\{x \leftarrow m\}$ for the outcome of substituting each free occurrence of the variable x in the formula A with the name m. We say a formula A is closed if and only if it has no free variables (though it may contain free names).

The *satisfaction relation* $P \models A$ provides the semantics of our logic. It is stable with respect to structural congruence, that is, if $P \models A$ and $P \equiv P'$ then $P' \models A$.

Satisfaction $P \models A$ (for A closed):

$P \models \mathbf{T}$	$P \models n[A] \overset{\triangle}{=} \exists P'.P \equiv n[P'] \wedge P' \models A$
$P \models \neg A \overset{\triangle}{=} \neg(P \models A)$	$P \models A@n \overset{\triangle}{=} n[P] \models A$
$P \models A \vee B \overset{\triangle}{=} P \models A \vee P \models B$	$P \models n \circledR A \overset{\triangle}{=} \exists P'.P \equiv (\nu n)P' \wedge P' \models A$
$P \models \mathbf{0} \overset{\triangle}{=} P \equiv \mathbf{0}$	$P \models A \oslash n \overset{\triangle}{=} (\nu n)P \models A$
$P \models A \mid B \overset{\triangle}{=} \exists P', P''. P \equiv P' \mid P'' \wedge$	$P \models \Diamond A \overset{\triangle}{=} \exists P'.P \rightarrow^* P' \wedge P' \models A$
$\quad P' \models A \wedge P'' \models B$	$P \models \diamondsuit A \overset{\triangle}{=} \exists P'.P \downarrow^* P' \wedge P' \models A$
	$P \models \exists x.A \overset{\triangle}{=} \exists m.P \models A\{x \leftarrow m\}$

5.2   Model Checking Finite-Control Mobile Ambients

In this section we show how closed and typable processes can be model checked against formulas of the ambient logic. We assume that in any process bound identifiers are pairwise distinct and that bound names are pairwise distinct and different from free names (not only free names from the process itself, but also free names occurring in formulas).

We consider here normalized processes as introduced in Section 3.2. To single out name restrictions, we write a normalized process $(\nu n_1) \ldots (\nu n_k)\mathcal{C}[P_1, \ldots, P_l]$ as a pair $\langle \{n_1, \ldots, n_k\}, \mathcal{C}[P_1, \ldots, P_l] \rangle$, separating name restriction prefix from the rest of the process and considering these name restrictions as a set of names. [1]

In a normalized process, only the active-context part is addressed by spatial modalities from the logic, that is, the modalities $\mathcal{A} \mid \mathcal{B}$, $n[\mathcal{A}]$, $\Diamond \mathcal{A}$ and 0. This allows us to control the size and the number of normalized processes considered for model checking these spatial modalities.

The following propositions (Propositions 7–10) express that in polynomial space we can test whether a process is congruent to 0, we can decompose it in all possible ways to a parallel composition of two other processes, we can remove the given leading ambient (if it exists), and we can compute all sublocations of the process. This is possible because it requires examining only the active context of the given process. The proof of these propositions is based on the following lemma.

Lemma 2 (Inversion). *Let P, Q, Q' be normalized processes.*

1. $(\nu n)P \equiv 0$ *if and only if $P \equiv 0$.*
2. *If n and m are different names, then $(\nu n)P \equiv m[Q]$ if and only if there exists a normalized process R such that $P \equiv m[R]$ and $Q \equiv (\nu n)R$.*
3. $(\nu n)P \equiv Q \mid Q'$ *if and only if there exist normalized processes R, R' such that $P \equiv R \mid R'$ and either $Q \equiv (\nu n)R$ and $Q' \equiv R'$ and $n \notin fn(Q')$ or $Q \equiv R$ and $Q' \equiv (\nu n)R'$ and $n \notin fn(Q)$.*

Proof. The proof is the same as for the replication-free fragment of the ambient calculus (Proposition 5.1 in [11]), observing that we have to examine only the active context of a normalized process.   □

Proposition 7. *For any normalized process $\langle N, \tilde{P} \rangle$, $\langle N, \tilde{P} \rangle \equiv 0$ if and only if $\tilde{P} \equiv 0$. Furthermore, we can test whether $\tilde{P}$ is congruent to 0 in polynomial-time.*

Proposition 8. *For any normalized process $\langle N, \tilde{P} \rangle$, we can compute in polynomial space a finite set of pairs of normalized processes that we denote $Decomp(\langle N, \tilde{P} \rangle)$ and defined as $\{ ((\langle N_1, \tilde{Q}_1 \rangle, \langle N_1', \tilde{R}_1 \rangle), \ldots, (\langle N_p, \tilde{Q}_p \rangle, \langle N_p', \tilde{R}_p \rangle)) \}$ satisfying:*

- *for all Q, R satisfying $\langle N, \tilde{P} \rangle \equiv Q \mid R$, there exists i such that $\langle N_i, \tilde{Q}_i \rangle \equiv Q$ and $\langle N_i', \tilde{R}_i \rangle \equiv R$.*
- *for all i in $1 \ldots p$, $N_i \cup N_i' = N$ and $N_i \cap N_i' = \varnothing$, $fn(\tilde{Q}_i) \cap N_i' = \varnothing$ and $fn(\tilde{R}_i) \cap N_i = \varnothing$ and $|\tilde{Q}_i|, |\tilde{R}_i| \leq |\tilde{P}|$.*

---

[1] Whenever two different normalized processes P and P' have the same pair-representation, then $P \equiv P'$ by the axiom (Str Res Res) from the structural congruence.

Proposition 9. *For any normalized process* $\langle N, \tilde{P} \rangle$ *and any name* n, *we can test in polynomial time if there exists* Q *such that* $\langle N, \tilde{P} \rangle \equiv n[Q]$. *Moreover, if such a* Q *exists, then* $n \notin N$ *and we can compute in polynomial time the normalized version* $\langle N, \tilde{Q} \rangle$ *of* Q *such that* $|\tilde{Q}| \leq |\tilde{P}|$.

Combining the two previous propositions, we obtain:

Proposition 10. *For any normalized process* $\langle N, \tilde{P} \rangle$, *we can compute a finite set of normalized processes* $Sublocations(\langle N, \tilde{P} \rangle) = \{\langle N_1, \tilde{Q}_1 \rangle, \dots, \langle N_p, \tilde{Q}_p \rangle\}$ *such that* (i) *for all* Q *such that* $\langle N, \tilde{P} \rangle \downarrow^* Q$, *there exists* i *satisfying that* $Q \equiv \langle N_i, \tilde{Q}_i \rangle$ *and* (ii) *for all* i *in* $1 \dots p$, $N_i \subseteq N$ *and* $|\tilde{Q}_i| \leq |\tilde{P}|$.

Moreover, using results from Section 3.2, we obtain:

Proposition 11. *For any typable and normalized process* $\langle N, \tilde{P} \rangle$, *we can compute a finite set of normalized processes* $Reachable(\langle N, \tilde{P} \rangle) = \{\langle N_1, \tilde{Q}_1 \rangle, \dots, \langle N_p, \tilde{Q}_p \rangle\}$ *such that* (i) *for all* Q *such that* $\langle N, \tilde{P} \rangle \rightarrow^* Q$, *there exists* i *satisfying that* $Q \equiv \langle N_i, \tilde{Q}_i \rangle$ *and* (ii) *for all* i *in* $1 \dots p$, $N_i \subseteq N$ *and* $|\tilde{Q}_i| \leq |\tilde{P}|^2$.

The algorithm presented here is very close to the one given in [11].

Model Checking Algorithm: $Check(\langle N, \tilde{P} \rangle, \mathcal{A})$ **where** $N \cap fn(\mathcal{A}) = \varnothing$, **by convention**

$Check(\langle N, \tilde{P} \rangle, \mathbf{T}) \triangleq \mathbf{T}$

$Check(\langle N, \tilde{P} \rangle, \neg \mathcal{A}) \triangleq \neg Check(\langle N, \tilde{P} \rangle, \mathcal{A})$

$Check(\langle N, \tilde{P} \rangle, \mathcal{A} \vee \mathcal{B}) \triangleq Check(\langle N, \tilde{P} \rangle, \mathcal{A}) \vee Check(\langle N, \tilde{P} \rangle, \mathcal{B})$

$Check(\langle N, \tilde{P} \rangle, \mathbf{0}) \triangleq \begin{cases} \mathbf{T} \text{ if } \tilde{P} \equiv \mathbf{0} \\ \mathbf{F} \text{ otherwise} \end{cases}$

$Check(\langle N, \tilde{P} \rangle, \mathcal{A} \mid \mathcal{B}) \triangleq \bigvee_{(P_1, P_2) \in Decomp(\langle N, \tilde{P} \rangle)} Check(P_1, \mathcal{A}) \wedge Check(P_2, \mathcal{B})$
$\qquad\qquad P_1, P_2$ being respectively $\langle N_1, \tilde{P}_1 \rangle$ and $\langle N_2, \tilde{P}_2 \rangle$

$Check(\langle N, \tilde{P} \rangle, n[\mathcal{A}]) \triangleq \tilde{P} \equiv n[\tilde{Q}] \wedge Check(\langle N, \tilde{Q} \rangle, \mathcal{A})$

$Check(\langle N, \tilde{P} \rangle, \mathcal{A}@n) \triangleq Check(\langle N, n[\tilde{P}] \rangle, \mathcal{A})$

$Check(\langle N, \tilde{P} \rangle, n \circledR \mathcal{A}) \triangleq \bigvee_{m \in N} Check(\langle N - \{m\}, \tilde{P}\{m \leftarrow n\} \rangle, \mathcal{A})$
$\qquad\qquad \vee(n \notin fn(\tilde{P}) \wedge Check(\langle N, \tilde{P} \rangle, \mathcal{A}))$

$Check(\langle N, \tilde{P} \rangle, \mathcal{A} \oslash n) \triangleq Check(\langle N \cup \{n\}, \tilde{P} \rangle, \mathcal{A})$

$Check(\langle N, \tilde{P} \rangle, \Diamond \mathcal{A}) \triangleq \bigvee_{\langle N', \tilde{P}' \rangle \in Reachable(\langle N, \tilde{P} \rangle)} Check(\langle N', \tilde{P}' \rangle, \mathcal{A})$

$Check(\langle N, \tilde{P} \rangle, \diamondsuit \mathcal{A}) \triangleq \bigvee_{\langle N, \tilde{P}' \rangle \in Sublocations(N, P)} Check(\langle N, \tilde{P}' \rangle, \mathcal{A})$

$Check(\langle N, \tilde{P} \rangle, \exists x.\mathcal{A}) \triangleq$ let $n_0 \notin N \cup fn(\tilde{P}) \cup bn(\tilde{P}) \cup fn(\mathcal{A})$ be a fresh name in
$\qquad\qquad \bigvee_{n \in fn(N, \tilde{P}) \cup fn(\mathcal{A}) \cup \{n_0\}} Check(\langle N, \tilde{P} \rangle, \mathcal{A}\{x \leftarrow n\})$

Theorem 2 (Correctness). *For all normalized and typable processes* $\langle N, \tilde{P} \rangle$ *and all closed formulas* $\mathcal{A}$, *we have* $\langle N, \tilde{P} \rangle \models \mathcal{A}$ *if and only if* $Check(\langle N, \tilde{P} \rangle, \mathcal{A}) = \mathbf{T}$.

Sketch of proof. The proof follows the lines of the proof of Theorem 5.1 in [11] and goes by induction on the formula $\mathcal{A}$. In the cases of $\mathbf{T}$, $\neg \mathcal{A}$, $\mathcal{A} \vee \mathcal{B}$, $\mathcal{A}@n$, $\mathcal{A} \oslash n$ the result follows directly from the definition of the satisfaction relation. In the case of $\mathbf{0}$ and $n[\mathcal{A}]$ it follows from Propositions 7 and 9, and in the case of $\mathcal{A} \mid \mathcal{B}$ from Proposition 8. The cases of $\diamondsuit \mathcal{A}$ and $\Diamond \mathcal{A}$ follow from Propositions 10 and 11. The case of $\exists x.\mathcal{A}$ follows the lines of the proof of Proposition 4.11 in [4]. Finally, the case of $n \circledR \mathcal{A}$ reflects the two possibilities that either n is one of the bounded names occurring in the process or it does not occur there (in the latter case observe that for all processes Q, $n \notin fn(Q)$ implies $(\nu n)Q \equiv Q$). □

Theorem 3 (PSPACE-complete). *The model checking problem for finite-control processes against the ambient logic is decidable. Moreover, it is PSPACE-complete.*

Sketch of proof. Decidability follows from Theorem 2. One obtains the PSPACE upper bound by implementing disjunction in polynomial space, as is done in [10]. The PSPACE lower bound is proved in [10]. □

6 Extensions of the System

In this section we discuss some extensions that are possible to the calculus without affecting decidability or complexity of the model checking problem. We did not introduce these extensions before because we want to keep our formal presentation of a finite-control ambient calculus as simple as possible.

Parameters in recursive definitions. In the system we defined the identifiers used in recursive definitions do not carry any name parameters. It is however quite straightforward to allow definitions of the form (fix $A(\boldsymbol{x}){=}P[A\langle\boldsymbol{y}\rangle]$) — one has to clearly distinguish between definitions (λ-abstractions) and calls (λ-application) of such functions and then respectively handle the renaming of parameters.

Nondeterministic choice. In the ambient calculus one may encode an internal nondeterministic choice $P + Q$ (see [6] for an encoding of an external choice) as the process $(\nu n)(n[\mathbf{0}] \mid \text{open } n.P \mid \text{open } n.Q)$.

Then reducing $P + Q$ leads to either $P \mid (\nu n)\text{open } n.Q$ or to $Q \mid (\nu n)\text{open } n.P$. As $(\nu n)\text{open } n.R$ is bisimilar to $\mathbf{0}$, this is a good approximation of nondeterministic choice. However, even this simple encoding is no longer possible in recursive processes of the finite-control fragment, since it goes beyond well-formed processes. But even if we ignore the well-formedness restriction, such an encoding does not work because $(\nu n)\text{open } n.R$ is not congruent (it is only bisimilar) to $\mathbf{0}$, which means that its type must be strictly positive, so it is not possible to balance the type of $P + Q$ if P and Q are balanced (and thus $P + Q$ is not typable). In the encoding of the finite-control π-calculus in Section 4.5 all recursive processes have balanced types and thus to extend the encoding to accommodate nondeterministic choice we need a balanced encoding of choice.

A possible solution is to add nondeterministic choice as a primitive construct in the calculus. To do so, we need to relax the definition of well-formed processes from one occurrence of identifier in a recursive definition to one occurrence per option of a nondeterministic choice. The reduction rules for processes can be then extended in a straightforward way, and an appropriate typing rule is:

(Choice)
$$\frac{\Gamma \vdash P : \tau,\ \Gamma \vdash Q : \theta}{\Gamma \vdash P + Q : \max(\tau, \theta)}$$

Replication-free fragment of the ambient calculus. Our initial motivation was to find a fragment of the ambient calculus that extends the replication-free fragment (for which the decidability and complexity of the model checking problem was known [5,10]) to allow some infinite computation, while retaining a decidable model checking problem. The calculus of this paper does not extend the replication-free fragment because it does not allow for sending capabilities inside messages. It is however quite obvious that a typable finite-control process can be put in a replication-free context without any change to the model checking algorithm. The only subtle point is that if one wants to achieve a PSPACE algorithm one should apply the data structure from [10] only to the replication-free context; otherwise storing an explicit substitution for every communication might lead (in the case of recursive communications) to infinitely growing substitutions.

Sending capabilities in communication. In the current version of the calculus we allow for sending only names. The extension to sending single capabilities is however not difficult. The problem with sending single capabilities is probably best shown in the following process : $\langle \text{in } n \rangle \mid (\text{fix } A=(x).((\langle \text{in } x \rangle \mid A))$. After the first iteration the process sends the message in (in n), then in (in (in n)), and so on, growing infinitely. Probably the simplest solution is to observe that in x cannot be executed if x is not a name, so it is enough to introduce a special deadlock capability and replace these complex capabilities with the deadlock capability.

An intriguing alternative possibility to solve the problem would be to combine the calculus with the type system of [8], where in (in n) cannot be well-typed.

Sending sequences of capabilities. In the original definition of the ambient calculus [6] it is possible to send not only single capabilities but also sequences of capabilities. We do not see a very easy solution to this problem. Consider as an example the following process: $\langle \text{in } n \rangle \mid (\text{fix } A=(x).((\langle x.x \rangle \mid A))$. Here, after k iterations we obtain a sequence of capabilities in $n \ldots$ in n of length 2^k. Thus the process grows infinitely. A possible solution is to distinguish between simple communications (sending a name or a single capability) and complex communications (sending a sequence of length ≥ 2), and to give a simple output type 1 (as in the current version of the system) while a complex output is typed 2 (that is, to introduce an additional typing rule $\Gamma \vdash \langle M \rangle \; : \; 2$ for complex M). Then the above process is not typable, but for example the process $(\text{fix } A=(x).(y).((\langle x.y \rangle \mid A))$ is typable. The decidability of model checking relies then on the observation that such a process cannot be executed infinitely many times (roughly, it can be executed as many times as many outputs are present in the context around).

Again, to achieve PSPACE complexity one has to be careful about substitutions—one should apply the substitution in the case of simple communication but one should store the substitution in the data structure (as is done in [10]) in the case of complex communication.

7   Conclusion

Previous work on model checking the spatial and temporal logic of the ambient calculus is limited to processes lacking any form of recursion or iteration. This work shows the possibility of model checking a richer, more expressive class of mobile behaviours. We hope it will lead to the discovery of further applications of the ambient logic.

References

1. R.M. Amadio and Ch. Meyssonnier. On the decidability of fragments of the asynchronous pi-calculus. In *Electronic Notes in Theoretical Computer Science, Proceedings EXPRESS 2001*, 2001.
2. M. Bugliesi and G. Castagna. Secure safe ambients. In *28th ACM Symposium on Principles of Programming Languages (POPL'01)*, pages 222–235, 2001.
3. L. Cardelli and A. D. Gordon. Equational properties of mobile ambients. In *Proceedings FoSSaCS'99*, volume 1578 of *LNCS*, pages 212–226. Springer, 1999.
4. L. Cardelli and A. D. Gordon. Modal logics for mobile ambients: Semantic reasoning. Unpublished annex to [5], 1999.
5. L. Cardelli and A. D. Gordon. Anytime, anywhere: Modal logics for mobile ambients. In *Proceedings POPL'00*, pages 365–377. ACM, January 2000.
6. L. Cardelli and A. D. Gordon. Mobile ambients. *Theoretical Computer Science*, 240(1):177–213, 2000.
7. L. Cardelli and A. D. Gordon. Logical properties of name restriction. In *Proceedings of the 5th International Conference on Typed Lambda Calculi and Applications (TLCA'01)*, volume 2044 of *LNCS*, pages 46–60. Springer, 2001.
8. L. Cardelli and A.D. Gordon. Types for mobile ambients. In *26th ACM Symposium on Principles of Programming Languages (POPL'99)*, pages 79–92, 1999.
9. S. Chaki, S.K. Rajamani, and J.Rehof. Types as models: Model checking message-passing programs. In *29th ACM Symposium on Principles of Programming Languages (POPL'02)*, 2002. To appear.
10. W. Charatonik, S. Dal Zilio, A. D. Gordon, S. Mukhopadhyay, and J.-M. Talbot. The complexity of model checking mobile ambients. In *Proceedings FoSSaCS'01*, volume 2030 of *LNCS*, pages 152–167. Springer, 2001. An extended version appearas as Technical Report MSR–TR–2001–03, Microsoft Research, 2001.
11. W. Charatonik and J.-M. Talbot. The decidability of model checking mobile ambients. In *Proceedings of the 15th Annual Conference of the European Association for Computer Science Logic*, volume 2142 of *LNCS*, pages 339–354. Springer, 2001.
12. M. Dam. Model checking mobile processes. *Information and Computation*, 121(1):35–51, 1996.
13. R.R. Hansen, J.G. Jensen, F. Nielson, and H. Riis Nielson. Abstract interpretation of mobile ambients. In *Static Analysis (SAS'99)*, volume 1694 of *Lecture Notes in Computer Science*, pages 134–148. Springer, 1999.
14. F. Levi and D. Sangiorgi. Controlling interference in ambients. In *27th ACM Symposium on Principles of Programming Languages (POPL'00)*, pages 352–364, 2000.
15. R. Milner. *Communicating and Mobile Systems: the π-Calculus*. Cambridge University Press, 1999.
16. F. Nielson, H. Riis Nielson, R.R. Hansen, and J.G. Jensen. Validating firewalls in mobile ambients. In *Concurrency Theory (Concur'99)*, volume 1664 of *Lecture Notes in Computer Science*, pages 463–477. Springer, 1999.
17. D. Sangiorgi. Extensionality and intensionality of the ambient logics. In *Proceedings POPL'01*, pages 4–13. ACM, January 2001.

Dependency Analysis of Mobile Systems*

Jérôme Feret

Département d'Informatique de l'École Normale Supérieure
ENS-DI, 45, rue d'Ulm, 75230 PARIS Cedex 5, FRANCE
`jerome.feret@ens.fr`
http://www.di.ens.fr/~feret

Abstract. We propose an Abstract Interpretation-based static analysis for automatically detecting the dependencies between the names linked to the agents of a mobile system. We focus our study on the mobile systems written in the π-calculus. We first refine the standard semantics in order to restore the relation between the names and the agents that have declared them. We then abstract the dependency relations that are always satisfied by the names of the agents of a mobile system. That is to say we will detect which names are always pair-wisely equal, and which names have necessarily been declared by the same recursive instance of an agent.

1 Introduction

We are interested in analyzing automatically the behaviour of mobile systems of agents. Agent distribution in such systems may dynamically change during the computation sequences, which makes their analysis difficult. We address the problem of proving *non-uniform properties* about the interactions between the agents of a mobile system; such properties allow distinguishing between several recursive instances of a same agent. We especially intend to infer the *dependency relations* between the names communicated to each agent. This means that we will calculate whether they are pair-wisely equal (and / or) whether they have been pair-wisely declared by the same recursive instance of an agent.

Previous works. In previous articles [7, 8], we proposed several analyses for mobile systems expressed in the π-calculus. In [7], we already proposed a non-uniform abstraction of the interactions between the agents of a mobile system. This analysis takes into account the dynamic creation of both names and agents, which is an inherent feature of mobility: it assigns a unique marker to each agent instance and stamps each channel with the marker of the agent instance which has declared it. Group creation [3] allows proving that a channel name is confined inside the scope of a given recursive instance, but it can only infer equality or disequality constraints between the groups, and cannot prove any equality constraint by composing disequality constraints. In [7], the algebraic

---

* This work was supported by the RTD project IST-1999-20527 "DAEDALUS" of the European FP5 programme.

D. Le Métayer (Ed.): ESOP 2002, LNCS 2305, pp. 314–329, 2002.

properties of markers allow handling more complex properties: we can prove that a channel name is first sent to the next instance and then returned to the previous one; thus, we prove it is returned to the instance which has declared it.

Contribution. The main two drawbacks of [7] are that the properties it captures are very low level and are not easily understandable, and that the only calculated properties are those which involve a comparison between the marker of a channel name and the marker of the agent it is communicated to.

We propose here a more abstract parametric analysis which handles a wider class of properties. It can especially express some relations between names, even if there is no relation between their markers and the marker of the agent instance they are communicated to. Nevertheless, this raises some complexity problems we propose to solve by designing several domains: there is then a trade-off between information partitioning, and the accuracy of information propagation. Reduced product makes these domains collaborate. At this point, [7] can be seen as a particular instantiation of the parametric domain. We also propose two particular domains that aim at discovering and propagating explicit equality and disequality relations among channel names and among markers.

We briefly present, in Sect. 2, the standard semantics of the π-calculus. We recall the non-standard semantics of [7] in Sect. 3 and derive a new generic abstraction of it in Sect. 4. We design some domains in Sect. 5 and describe outlines for reduction in Sect. 6.

2 π-Calculus

The π-calculus is a formalism well-fitted for describing the behaviour of mobile systems. It is based on the notion of name passing. We use a lazy synchronous version of the π-calculus which is inspired from [11, 1]. Let $\mathcal{N}$ be an infinite set of channel names; agents are built according to the following syntax:

$$P, Q ::= \mathbf{0} \mid \text{action}.P \mid (P \mid Q) \mid (P + Q) \mid (\nu\, x)P \mid [x \diamond y]P$$
$$\text{action} ::= c![\overline{x}] \mid c?[\overline{x}] \mid * c?[\overline{x}]$$

where $c, x, y \in \mathcal{N}$, $\overline{x}$ is a tuple of channel names, and $\diamond \in \{=; \neq\}$. Input guards, replication guards and name restrictions are the only *name binders*, i.e, in $c?[x_1, ..., x_n]P$, $*d?[y_1, ..., y_n]Q$ and $(\nu\, x)R$, occurrences of $x_1, ..., x_n$ in P, $y_1, ..., y_p$ in Q and x in R are said to be bound. Usual rules about scoping, substitution and α-conversion apply. We denote by $fn(P)$ the set of the free names of P, i.e, the names which are not under the scope of any binder, and by $bn(P)$ the set of the bound names of P. The agent $P \mid Q$ denotes the parallel composition of two agents P and Q which performs P and Q simultaneously. The agent $P + Q$ denotes a non-deterministic choice between two agents P and Q which performs either P or Q: the choice is internal and does not depend on the other agents. $[x \diamond y]P$ denotes a matching guard: the agent P can be activated if the guard $[x \diamond y]$ is satisfied and it does not require that the agent P interacts with another agent of the system. We use a lazy version of replication: the agent $*c?[\overline{x}].P$ duplicates itself each time it communicates with another agent.

Example 1. We use, as an illustration, the following system $\mathcal{S}$ [12] throughout the paper:[1]

> **Next** ::= *make?^{0}[*last*](ν *next*)(edge!^{1}[*last; next*] | make!^{2}[*next*])
> **Last** ::= make?^{3}[*last*].edge!^{4}[*last;* first]
> **Test** ::= edge?^{5}[*x; y*].[*x* =^{6} *y*][*x* ≠^{7} first]ok!^{8}[]

$\mathcal{S}$ ::= (ν make)(ν edge)(ν first)(ν ok)(**Next** | **Last** | **Test** | make!^{9}[first]).

The system $\mathcal{S}$ creates a communication ring between several monitors. Each channel name created by the restrictions (ν **first**) and (ν **next**) denotes a monitor. The message **edge!**[**x; y**] represents a connection between the monitors respectively denoted by **x** and **y**. The first monitor is created by the restriction (ν **first**). The resource **Next** can then be used to connect the last created monitor with a newly created one. The thread **Last** is used to connect the last created monitor with the first one. The thread **Test** is used to test whether a monitor is linked with itself and, in such a case, whether it is not the first monitor. We intend to prove that the first matching pattern of **Test** may be satisfied, although the second matching pattern can never be satisfied. This result is out of the range of any uniform analysis [2] which can give no more accurate result than the fact that monitors can be linked to each other.   □

3   Non-standard Semantics

We refine the standard semantics in order to explicitly specify the link between channel names and the agent recursive instances that have declared them: we assign to each instance of an agent an unambiguous marker, and stamp each channel name with the marker of the instance of the agent which has declared it. We consider a closed mobile system $\mathcal{S}$ in the π-calculus, we may assume, without any loss of generality, that no one name occurs twice as an argument of an input guard, a replication guard or a name restriction. Let $\mathcal{L}$ be an infinite set of *labels*. We locate each syntactic component of $\mathcal{S}$ by labeling each action and each matching pattern with a distinct label. We describe each *configuration* of $\mathcal{S}$ by a set of *thread instances*. Each thread instance is a triplet composed of a *syntactic component* which, for the sake of simplicity, will often be denoted by its label, an unambiguous *marker* and an *environment* which specifies the semantic values of the syntactic channel names of the thread. An environment assigns to each syntactic channel name a pair composed of a channel name a and a thread marker id, meaning that the channel name has been declared by the name restriction (ν a) of a thread the marker of which was id.

Thread instances are created at the beginning of the system computation and when agents interact. In both cases, several threads are spawned, in accordance to which non-deterministic choices are made. The function β, defined below, applied to a labeled agent, its marker and its environment, returns the set of all possible combination sets of spawned thread instances:

---

[1] We have labeled each syntactic component, as explained in Sect. 3.

$$\beta((\nu\, n)P, id, E) = \beta\,(P, id, (E[n \mapsto (n, id)]))$$
$$\beta(\mathbf{0}, id, E) = \{\emptyset\}$$
$$\beta(P + Q, id, E) = \beta(P, id, E) \cup \beta(Q, id, E)$$
$$\beta(P \mid Q, id, E) = \{A \cup B \mid A \in \beta(P, id, E),\ B \in \beta(Q, id, E)\}$$
$$\beta(action.P, id, E) = \{\{(action.P, id, E_{\mid fn(action.P)})\}\}$$
$$\beta([x \diamond^i y]P, id, E) = \{\{([x \diamond^i y]P, id, E_{\mid fn([x \diamond^i y]P)})\}\}$$

Markers are the history of the resource duplications which have led to the creation of the agent instances: they are binary trees the nodes of which are labeled with a pair of labels, and the leaves of which are unlabeled (ε). The markers of initial threads are ε, while new thread markers are calculated as follows: when a computation step does not involve fetching a resource, markers of computed threads are just passed to the threads of their continuations; when a resource is fetched, the marker of the new threads created from the continuation of the resource is $N((i, j), id_*, id_!)$ where i and id_* are the label and the marker of the resource, j and $id_!$ are the label and the marker of the message sender.

The set of initial configurations and the computation rules are given in Fig. 2. Standard and non-standard semantics are in *bisimulation*, provided that we restrict ourselves to the set of standard computations where all non-deterministic choices are made before other computation steps.

Example 2. Here is the non-standard configuration for our mobile system $\mathcal{S}$, reached after having replicated the resource **Next** twice, and after having made the last spawned agent labeled by 1 communicated with the thread **Test**:

$$
\left\{
\begin{array}{l}
\left(0, \varepsilon, \left\{ \begin{array}{l} \text{make} \to (\text{make}, \varepsilon) \\ \text{edge} \to (\text{edge}, \varepsilon) \end{array} \right. \right) \\[2ex]
\left(1, id_1, \left\{ \begin{array}{l} \text{edge} \to (\text{edge}, \varepsilon) \\ \text{last} \to (\text{first}, \varepsilon) \\ \text{next} \to (\text{next}, id_1) \end{array} \right. \right) \\[3ex]
\left(2, id_2, \left\{ \begin{array}{l} \text{make} \to (\text{make}, \varepsilon) \\ \text{next} \to (\text{next}, id_2) \end{array} \right. \right) \\[2ex]
\left(3, \varepsilon, \left\{ \begin{array}{l} \text{make} \to (\text{make}, \varepsilon) \\ \text{edge} \to (\text{edge}, \varepsilon) \\ \text{first} \to (\text{first}, \varepsilon) \end{array} \right. \right) \\[3ex]
\left(6, \varepsilon, \left\{ \begin{array}{l} x \to (\text{next}, id_1) \\ y \to (\text{next}, id_2) \\ \text{first} \to (\text{first}, \varepsilon) \\ \text{ok} \to (\text{ok}, \varepsilon) \end{array} \right. \right)
\end{array}
\right\}
\qquad \text{where} \left\{ \begin{array}{l} id_1 = N((0, 9), \varepsilon, \varepsilon) \\ id_2 = N((0, 2), \varepsilon, id_1) \end{array} \right.
$$

It turns out that there is no generic relation between the marker of the agent **6** and the markers of the names linked to the variables **x** and **y**, so both [12, 7] will fail to prove that the second matching pattern is not satisfiable.   □

Moreover, in accordance with the following proposition, we can simplify the shape of the markers without losing marker allocation *consistency* which ensures

$$\mathcal{C}_0(\mathcal{S}) = \beta(\mathcal{S}, \varepsilon, \emptyset)$$

(a) Non-standard initial configurations.

$$\frac{E_?(y) = E_!(x),\ Cont_P \in \beta(P, id_?, E_{?[y_i \mapsto E_!(x_i)]}),\ Cont_Q \in \beta(Q, id_!, E_!)}{C \cup \{(y?^i[\overline{y}]P, id_?, E_?); (x!^j[\overline{x}]Q, id_!, E_!)\} \longrightarrow (C \cup Cont_P \cup Cont_Q)}$$

$$\frac{E_*(y) = E_!(x),\ Cont_P \in \beta(P, N((i,j), id_*, id_!), E_{*[y_i \mapsto E_!(x_i)]}),\ Cont_Q \in \beta(Q, id_!, E_!)}{C \cup \left\{ \begin{array}{l} (*y?^i[\overline{y}]P, id_*, E_*); \\ (x!^j[\overline{x}]Q, id_!, E_!) \end{array} \right\} \longrightarrow \left(C \cup \{(*y?^i[\overline{y}]P, id_*, E_*)\} \cup Cont_P \cup Cont_Q \right)}$$

$$\frac{E(x) \diamond E(y),\ Cont_P \in \beta(P, id, E)}{C \cup \{([x \diamond^i y]P, id, E)\} \longrightarrow C \cup Cont_P}$$

(b) Non-standard transition system.

Fig. 2. Non-standard semantics.

that no one marker can be assigned twice to the same syntactic agent during a computation sequence.

Proposition 1. *Let ϕ_1 and ϕ_2 be the two following functions:*

$$\phi_1 : \left\{ \begin{array}{ccc} Id & \to & (\mathcal{L}^2)^\star \\ N(a,b,c) & \mapsto & \phi_1(c).a \\ \varepsilon & \mapsto & \varepsilon \end{array} \right. \qquad \phi_2 : \left\{ \begin{array}{ccc} Id & \to & \mathcal{L}^\star \\ N((i,j),b,c) & \mapsto & \phi_2(c).j \\ \varepsilon & \mapsto & \varepsilon. \end{array} \right.$$

Marker allocation remains consistent when replacing each marker with its image by ϕ_1 or ϕ_2.

Such simplifications allow us to reduce the cost of our analysis, but also lead to a loss of accuracy since they merge information related to distinct computation sequences of the system.

4   Abstract Semantics

We denote by Id the set of all markers, by $\mathcal{E}(V)$ the set of all environments over the set of syntactic names V, by Σ the set $\mathcal{L}^2$ and by $\mathcal{C}$ the set of all non-standard configurations. We are actually interested in $C(\mathcal{S})$, the set of all the configurations a system $\mathcal{S}$ may take during any finite sequence of computation steps. This is the *collecting semantics* [4], which can be expressed as the least fix point of the following $\sqcup$-complete endomorphism $\mathbb{F}$ on the complete lattice $\wp(\mathcal{C})$:

$$\mathbb{F}(X) = \beta(\mathcal{S}, \varepsilon, \emptyset) \cup \{\overline{C} \in \mathcal{C} \mid \exists C \in X, \ C \longrightarrow \overline{C}\}.$$

The least fix point of such an endomorphism is usually not decidable, so we use a relaxed version of the Abstract Interpretation framework [5] to compute a sound—but not necessary complete—approximation of it.

We assume we are given a family $(\mathcal{G}_V, \sqsubseteq_V, \bigsqcup_V, \perp_V)_{V \subseteq bn(\mathcal{S})}$ of abstract domains of properties. For each $V \subseteq bn(\mathcal{S})$, $\mathcal{G}_V$ is used for globally abstracting the marker and the environment of a thread instance that uses the set of free names V. The relation $\sqsubseteq_V$ is a pre-order which describes the relative amount of information between those properties. Each abstract property is related to $\wp(Id \times \mathcal{E}(V))$ by a monotonic concretization function γ_V. The operator $\bigsqcup_V$ maps each finite set of properties to a weaker property: for each finite $A \subseteq \mathcal{G}_V$, $\forall a \in A$, $a \sqsubseteq_V (\bigsqcup_V A)$. $\perp_V$ is the least element in $\mathcal{G}_V$ with respect to $\sqsubseteq_V$. We assume that γ_V is strict, that is to say, $\gamma_V(\perp_V) = \emptyset$. Then, our main abstract domain $(\mathcal{C}^\sharp, \sqsubseteq^\sharp, \bigsqcup^\sharp, \perp^\sharp)$ is the set of functions mapping each syntactic component P of $\mathcal{S}$ to an element of $\mathcal{G}_{fn(P)}$. The domain structure $(\sqsubseteq^\sharp, \bigsqcup^\sharp$ and $\perp^\sharp)$ is defined pointwise. The abstract domain $\mathcal{C}^\sharp$ is related to $\wp(\mathcal{C})$ by the concretization function γ that maps each abstract property $f \in \mathcal{C}^\sharp$ to the set of configurations $C \in \mathcal{C}$ such that $\forall (p, id, E) \in C$, $(id, E) \in \gamma_{fn(p)}(f(p))$.

During a communication or resource fetching step, we have to describe the relations among the markers and the environments of two threads: a message receiver and a message sender. For that purpose, we also assume that we are given a family $(\mathcal{G}_{V_?}^{V_!})$ of abstract properties[2]. For any $V_?, V_! \in \wp(bn(\mathcal{S}))$, each property in $\mathcal{G}_{V_?}^{V_!}$ is related by a concretization function $\gamma_{V_?}^{V_!}$ to the elements of $\wp((Id \times \mathcal{E}(V_?)) \times (Id \times \mathcal{E}(V_!)))$ which satisfy this property.

Let V, $V_?$ and $V_!$ be three parts of $bn(\mathcal{S})$. We now introduce some primitives to handle elements in $\mathcal{G}_V$ and $\mathcal{G}_{V_?}^{V_!}$, and to relate $\mathcal{G}_{V_?}$ and $\mathcal{G}_{V_!}$ to $\mathcal{G}_{V_?}^{V_!}$:

- *initial environment abstraction*: $\varepsilon_\emptyset \in \mathcal{G}_\emptyset$ satisfies $\{(\varepsilon, \emptyset)\} \subseteq \gamma_\emptyset(\varepsilon_\emptyset)$;
- *abstract restriction*: $\forall x \in bn(\mathcal{S}) \setminus V$, $\nu_x : \mathcal{G}_V \to \mathcal{G}_{V \cup \{x\}}$ satisfies:

$$\left\{ (id, E) \in Id \times \mathcal{E}(V \cup \{x\}) \ \middle| \ \begin{matrix} (id, E_{|V}) \in \gamma_V(A), \\ E(x) = (x, id) \end{matrix} \right\} \subseteq \gamma_{V \cup \{x\}}(\nu_x(A));$$

- *abstract extension*: $\forall X \subseteq bn(\mathcal{S}) \setminus V$, $new_X^\top : \mathcal{G}_V \to \mathcal{G}_{V \cup X}$ satisfies:

$\{(id, E) \in Id \times \mathcal{E}(V \cup X) \mid (id, E_{|V}) \in \gamma_V(A)\} \subseteq \gamma_{V \cup X}(new_X^\top(A));$

- *abstract garbage collection*: $\forall X \subseteq V$, $gc_X : \mathcal{G}_V \to \mathcal{G}_X$ satisfies:

$\{(id, E_{|X}) \in Id \times \mathcal{E}(X) \mid (id, E) \in \gamma_V(A)\} \subseteq \gamma_X(gc_X(A));$

- *abstract matching*: $match : ((V \times \{=; \neq\} \times V) \times \mathcal{G}_V) \to \mathcal{G}_V$ satisfies:

$\{(id, E) \in Id \times \mathcal{E}(V) \mid (id, E) \in \gamma_V(A), \ E(x) \diamond E(y)\} \subseteq \gamma_V(match(x \diamond y, A)).$

- *abstract product*: $\bullet : \mathcal{G}_{V_?} \times \mathcal{G}_{V_!} \to \mathcal{G}_{V_?}^{V_!}$ satisfies:

$\gamma_{V_?}(A_?) \times \gamma_{V_!}(A_!) \subseteq \gamma_{V_?}^{V_!}(A_? \bullet A_!);$

---

[2] The abstract domain $\mathcal{G}_{V_?}^{V_!}$ is not assumed to be a pre-order, because it is only used to make intermediary calculi, and not to make iterations.

- *abstract projections:* $fst^\sharp : \mathcal{G}_{V_?}^{V_!} \to \mathcal{G}_{V_?}$ and $snd^\sharp : \mathcal{G}_{V_?}^{V_!} \to V_!$ satisfy:
  $$fst\left(\gamma_{V_?}^{V_!}(A)\right) \subseteq \gamma_{V_?}(fst^\sharp(A)) \text{ and } snd\left(\gamma_{V_?}^{V_!}(A)\right) \subseteq \gamma_{V_!}(snd^\sharp(A));$$
- *abstract synchronization:* $sync : \wp(V_? \times V_!) \times \mathcal{G}_{V_?}^{V_!} \to \mathcal{G}_{V_?}^{V_!}$ satisfies:
  $$\{((id_?, E_?), (id_!, E_!)) \in \gamma_{V_?}^{V_!}(A) \mid \forall (a, b) \in S,\ E_?(a) = E_!(b)\} \subseteq \gamma_{V_?}^{V_!}(sync(S, A));$$
- *abstract marker allocation:* $fetch : \mathcal{L}^2 \times \mathcal{G}_{V_?}^{V_!} \to \mathcal{G}_{V_?}^{V_!}$ satisfies:
  $$\left\{((id_*, E_?), (id_!, E_!)) \,\middle|\, \begin{array}{l} ((id_?, E_?), (id_!, E_!)) \in \gamma_{V_?}^{V_!}(A) \\ id_* = N((i, j), id_?, id_!) \end{array}\right\} \subseteq \gamma_{V_?}^{V_!}(fetch((i, j), A)).$$

The abstract semantics is then given by an initial abstract element $\mathcal{C}_0^\sharp(\mathcal{S}) \in \mathcal{C}^\sharp$ and an abstract transition relation $\longrightarrow_\sharp$ in Fig. 4. Their definitions use the following abstract extraction function:

$$\begin{aligned}
\beta^\sharp((\nu\, n)P, A) &= \beta^\sharp(P, \nu_n(A)) \\
\beta^\sharp(\mathbf{0}, A) &= \perp^\sharp \\
\beta^\sharp(P + Q, A) &= \bigsqcup^\sharp\{\beta^\sharp(P, A); \beta^\sharp(Q, A)\} \\
\beta^\sharp(P \mid Q, A) &= \bigsqcup^\sharp\{\beta^\sharp(P, A); \beta^\sharp(Q, A)\} \\
\beta^\sharp(action.P, A) &= \{action.P \mapsto gc_{fn(action.P)}(A)\} \\
\beta^\sharp([x \diamond^i y]P, A) &= \{[x \diamond^i y]P \mapsto gc_{fn([x \diamond^i y]P)}(A)\}
\end{aligned}$$

Furthermore, abstract communication and resource fetching require the following synchronization function, which merges the abstract environments of two communicating syntactic components, and mimics the communication of a part of the sender environment.

$$syn_x^y\left(\frac{A_? \leftarrow A_!}{\overline{y} \leftarrow \overline{x}}\right) = sync\left(\{(y; x)\} \cup \left(\bigcup\{(y_i; x_i)\}\right), (new_{\{y_1;\ldots;y_n\}}^\top(A_?)) \bullet A_!\right)$$

Theorem 1. $\mathcal{C}_0^\sharp$ *and* $\longrightarrow_\sharp$ *satisfy the following soundness property:*

1. $\mathcal{C}_0(\mathcal{S}) \subseteq \gamma(\mathcal{C}_0^\sharp(\mathcal{S}));$

2. $\forall C^\sharp \in \mathcal{C}^\sharp,\ \forall C \in \gamma(C^\sharp),\ \forall \overline{C} \in \mathcal{C},\ C \longrightarrow \overline{C} \implies \exists \overline{C}^\sharp \in \mathcal{C}^\sharp, \begin{cases} C^\sharp \longrightarrow_\sharp \overline{C}^\sharp \\ \overline{C} \in \gamma(\overline{C}^\sharp). \end{cases}$

So, the abstract counterpart $\mathbb{F}^\sharp$ to $\mathbb{F}$ defined by :

$$\mathbb{F}^\sharp(C^\sharp) = \bigsqcup^\sharp \left(\{\mathcal{C}_0^\sharp(\mathcal{S})\} \cup \{\overline{C}^\sharp \mid C^\sharp \longrightarrow_\sharp \overline{C}^\sharp\}\right)$$

satisfies the soundness condition $\forall C^\sharp \in \mathcal{C}^\sharp,\ \mathbb{F} \circ \gamma(C^\sharp) \subseteq \gamma \circ \mathbb{F}^\sharp(C^\sharp)$. Using Kleene's theorem, we obtain the soundness of our analysis:

Theorem 2. $lfp_\emptyset \mathbb{F} \subseteq \bigcup_{n \in \mathbb{N}} [\gamma \circ \mathbb{F}^{\sharp\,n}] (\mathcal{C}_0^\sharp(\mathcal{S})).$

A widening operator [6] may be then used to compute a sound and decidable approximation of the abstract semantics.

$$\mathcal{C}_0^\sharp(\mathcal{S}) = \beta^\sharp(\mathcal{S}, \varepsilon_\emptyset)$$

(a) Abstract initial configuration.

$$\frac{\left\{\begin{array}{l} \lambda = y?^i[\overline{y}]P, \; \mu = x!^j[\overline{x}]Q, \\[4pt] E_s = syn_x^y\left(\begin{array}{ccc} C^\sharp(\lambda) & \leftarrow & C^\sharp(\mu) \\ \overline{y} & \leftarrow & \overline{x} \end{array}\right) \end{array}\right.}{C^\sharp \longrightarrow_\sharp \bigsqcup^\sharp\{C^\sharp; \beta^\sharp(P, fst^\sharp(E_s)); \beta^\sharp(Q, snd^\sharp(E_s))\}}$$

$$\frac{\left\{\begin{array}{l} \lambda = *y?^i[\overline{y}]P, \; \mu = x!^j[\overline{x}]Q, \\[4pt] E_s = fetch\left((i,j), \left(syn_x^y\left(\begin{array}{ccc} C^\sharp(\lambda) & \leftarrow & C^\sharp(\mu) \\ \overline{y} & \leftarrow & \overline{x} \end{array}\right)\right)\right) \end{array}\right.}{C^\sharp \longrightarrow_\sharp \bigsqcup^\sharp\{C^\sharp; \beta^\sharp(P, fst^\sharp(E_s)); \beta^\sharp(Q, snd^\sharp(E_s))\}}$$

$$\frac{\diamond \in \{=; \neq\}, \; \lambda = [x \diamond^i y]P}{C^\sharp \longrightarrow_\sharp \bigsqcup^\sharp\{C^\sharp; \beta^\sharp(P, match(x \diamond y, C^\sharp))\}}$$

(b) Abstract transition system.

Fig. 4. Abstract semantics.

5   Analyses

We propose in this section five abstract domains of properties. The first two domains describe properties of interest which can directly be understood by the user. The last three domains represent complex properties which are used to complete the two first domains by reduction.

5.1   Dependencies Among Agent Names

Abstract Domain of Equality and Disequality Relations We introduce an abstract domain for describing equality and disequality relations among a finite set of variables. Let $\mathcal{V}$ be a set of variables, we introduce for all finite subsets of $V \subseteq \mathcal{V}$ the abstract domain T_V of all non-oriented graphs (G, R) such that G is a partition of V. Given a finite subset V of $\mathcal{V}$ and $X = (G, R) \in T_V$, we introduce two binary relations over V as follows:

- $a =_X b \overset{\Delta}{\Longleftrightarrow} \exists \mathcal{X} \in G, \{a, b\} \subseteq \mathcal{X}$,
- $a \neq_X b \overset{\Delta}{\Longleftrightarrow} \exists \mathcal{X} \in G, \exists \mathcal{Y} \in G, a \in \mathcal{X}, b \in \mathcal{Y}, (\mathcal{X}, \mathcal{Y}) \in R$.

The domain T_V is partially ordered by the $\leqslant_V$ relation defined as follows:

$$\forall X, Y \in T_V, \ X \leqslant_V Y \stackrel{\Delta}{\Longleftrightarrow} \begin{cases} \forall x, y \in V, \ x =_Y y \Rightarrow x =_X y \\ \forall x, y \in V, \ x \neq_Y y \Rightarrow x \neq_X y. \end{cases}$$

For every set I, each element A in T_V is related to the set of functions $\gamma_V^I(A)$, defined as follows:

$$\gamma_V^I(A) = \left\{ f \in \mathcal{F}(V, I) \ \middle| \ \forall x, \ y \in V, \ \begin{cases} x =_A y \implies f(x) = f(y) \\ x \neq_A y \implies f(x) \neq f(y) \end{cases} \right\}.$$

We also define some primitives over our abstract domain as follows:
let (G_X, R_X) be an element in T_V,

- given $(G_Y, R_Y) \in T_V$, $(G_X, R_X) \uplus (G_Y, R_Y) = (G', R') \in T_V$ where
  - $G' = \{x \cap y \mid x \in G_X, \ y \in G_Y, \ x \cap y \neq \emptyset\}$
  - $R' = \{(x_1 \cap y_1, x_2 \cap y_2) \in (G')^2 \mid (x_1, x_2) \in R_X \ and \ (y_1, y_2) \in R_Y\}$
- given $V' \subseteq \mathcal{V} \setminus V$, and $(G_Y, A_Y) \in T_{V'}$, $(G_X, A_X) \cap (G_Y, A_Y) \in T_{V \cup V'}$, and $((G_X, A_X) \cap (G_Y, A_Y)) = (G_X \cup G_Y, A_X \cup A_Y)$;
- given $V' \subseteq V$, $proj_{V'}(G_X, R_X) = (G', R') \in T_{V'}$ where
  - $G' = \{A \cap V' \mid A \in G_X, \ A \cap V' \neq \emptyset\}$,
  - $R' = \{(A \cap V', A' \cap V') \in (G')^2 \mid (A, A') \in R\}$;
- given $x \in bn(\mathcal{S}) \setminus V$, $fresh_x(G_X, R_X) \in T_{V \cup \{x\}}$ and $fresh_x(G_X, R_X) = (G_X \cup \{\{x\}\}, R_X \cup (\{\{x\}\} \times G_X) \cup (G_X \times \{\{x\}\}))$;
- given $V' \subseteq bn(\mathcal{S}) \setminus V$, $new_{V'}(G_X, R_X) \in T_{V \cup V'}$ and $new_{V'}(G_X, R_X) = (G_X \cup \{\{v'\} \mid v' \in V'\}, R_X) \in T_{V \cup V'}$;
- given $x, y \in V$, and $\diamond \in \{=; \neq\}$, $set(x \diamond y, (G_X, R_X)) \in T_V$ and:
  - $set(x = y, (G_X, R_X)) = ((G_X)_{/\sim}, (R_X)_{/\sim})$, if not $x \neq_{(G_X, R_X)} y$,
    where $\forall X, Y \in G_X, \ X \sim Y \stackrel{\Delta}{\Longleftrightarrow} X = Y$ or $(x, y) \in (X \times Y) \cup (Y \times X)$,
  - $set(x \neq y, (G_X, R_X)) = (G_X, R_X \cup \{(A, B); (B, A)\})$, if not $x =_{(G_X, R_X)} y$,
    where $A, B \in G_X$ such that $x \in A$ and $y \in B$,
  - $set(x \diamond y, (G_X, R_X))$ is undefined, otherwise.

The union $\uplus$ gives the lowest upper bound of two properties; the intersection $\cap$ gathers the description of two disjoint sets of variables; the projection $proj$ restricts the set of the variables; the operator $fresh$ adds a new variable the value of which is assumed to be distinct from the value of the other variables; the operator new adds a set of variables without any assumption about their values; the operator set simply adds a new constraint.

Then, we lift T_V by adding an extra element $\perp_V$. Its concretization $\gamma_V^I(\perp_V)$ is the empty set of functions. Abstract union is lifted by $A \uplus \perp_V = \perp_V \uplus A = A$, abstract intersection by $A \cap \perp_{V'} = \perp_V \cap A = \perp_{V \cup V'}$. Other primitives are defined to be strict, that is to say:

$$fresh\_(\perp_V) = proj\_(\perp_V) = set(\_, \perp_V) = \perp_V$$

Furthermore, undefined images in set are identified with $\perp_V$.

Equality and Disequality Relations among Channel Names We first abstract the equality and the disequality relations between the channel names of each agent. We set, for that purpose, $\mathcal{V} = bn(\mathcal{S})$ and we introduce, for each $V \subseteq bn(\mathcal{S})$, the abstract domain $\mathcal{G}_V = T_V \cup \{\perp_V\}$. $\mathcal{G}_V$ is related to $\wp(Id \times \mathcal{E}(V))$ by the following concretization function:

$$\gamma_V(A) = \{(id, E) \mid E \in \gamma_V^{(bn(\mathcal{S}) \times Id)}(A)\}, \text{ when } A \neq \perp_V.$$

The same way, we describe relations between the names of two agents: we introduce $\mathcal{V}' = \{x_i \mid x \in bn(\mathcal{S}),\ i \in \{?, !\}\}$, and we define for each subset pair $(V_?, V_!)$ of $bn(\mathcal{S})^2$, $\mathcal{G}_{V_?}^{V_!}$ as being the set $T_{V'} \cup \{\perp_{V'}\}$ where $V' = \{x_i \mid i \in \{?, !\},\ x \in V_i\}$.

We now give primitive definitions: we set $\varepsilon_\emptyset = (\emptyset, \emptyset)$; we set $\nu x = \mathit{fresh}_x$ since, at its creation, a fresh name cannot have been communicated to any other variables; we define the extension $new_X^\top$ (resp. the garbage collection gc_X) by new_X (resp. $proj_X$); we set $match(x \diamond y, A) = set(x \diamond y, A)$; product $A_? \bullet A_!$ is obtained by first renaming the variable x into $x_?$ (resp. $x_!$) in $A_?$ (resp. in $A_!$) and then intersecting the two results using $\sqcap$; projection $fst^\sharp(A)$ (resp. $snd^\sharp(A)$) is obtained by first using the projection $proj_{V_?}$ (resp. $proj_{V_!}$) and then renaming the variable $x_?$ (resp. $x_!$) into x; synchronization is defined by $sync(\{x = y\} \cup X, A) = sync(X, set(x = y, A))$ and $sync(\emptyset, A) = A^3$; we set $fetch((i, j), A) = A$ since the allocation of new markers does not change the marker of channel names.

Equality and Disequality Relations among Markers We then abstract the equality and the disequality relations between the marker of an agent and the markers of its names. We set $\mathcal{V} = bn(\mathcal{S}) \uplus \{\text{agent}\}^4$, and we introduce, for each $V \subseteq bn(\mathcal{S})$, the abstract domain $\mathcal{G}_V = T_{V'} \cup \{\perp_{V'}\}$ where $V' = V \cup \{\text{agent}\}$. $\mathcal{G}_V$ is related to $\wp(Id \times \mathcal{E}(V))$ by the following concretization function:

$$\gamma_V(A) = \left\{ (id, E) \;\middle|\; \left(\begin{cases} V \cup \{\text{agent}\} & \to Id \\ v \in V & \mapsto snd(E(v)) \\ \text{agent} & \mapsto id \end{cases} \right) \in \gamma_{V \cup \{\text{agent}\}}^{Id}(A) \right\},$$

when $A \neq \perp_V$.

The same way, we describe relations between the markers of two agents: we introduce $\mathcal{V}' = \{x_i \mid x \in bn(\mathcal{S}) \uplus \{\text{agent}\},\ i \in \{?, !\}\}$, and define, for each subset pair $(V_?, V_!)$ of $bn(\mathcal{S})^2$, $\mathcal{G}_{V_?}^{V_!}$ as being the set $T_{V'} \cup \{\perp_{V'}\}$ where $V' = \{x_i \mid i \in \{?, !\},\ x \in V_i \uplus \{\text{agent}\}\}$.

Primitives are all defined as in the previous domain, except for the primitives $\varepsilon_\emptyset, \nu, match$ and $fetch$: we set $\varepsilon_\emptyset = (\{\text{agent}\}, \emptyset)$ since it describes an agent with an empty environment; we set $\nu x(A) = match(\text{agent} = x, new_{\{x\}}(A))$ because the marker of a newly created name is the marker of the thread which has declared it; we define $match(x = y, A) = set(x = y, A)$ and $match(x \neq y, A) = A$, since two different names do not necessarily have distinct markers; we set $fetch((i, j), A) = \mathit{fresh}_{\text{agent}_?}(proj_{V' \setminus \{\text{agent}_?\}}(A))$ since, when duplicating a resource, the marker is fresh and distinct from any other existing marker.

---

^{3} This primitive is well-define due to an associativity criterion.

^{4} $A \uplus B$ denotes the disjoint union of A and B.

5.2   Marker Analysis

We aim at describing the markers associated with an agent and its channel names. For the sake of simplicity, we use Prop. 1 and approximate every tree marker id by the word $\phi_1(id)$ of Σ^* written along its right comb. Then, we want to compute, for each agent P, an approximation of the set $Int(P)$, defined as follows:

$$\left\{ \left(id, \begin{cases} fn(P) & \to (\Sigma \cup bn(\mathcal{S}))^* \\ y & \to (a_y.\phi_1(b_y)) \end{cases} \right) \;\middle|\; \begin{array}{l} \exists C \in C(\mathcal{S}),\ \exists id \in Id,\ \exists E \in \mathcal{E}(fn(P)), \\ \begin{cases} (P, id, E) \in C \\ \forall y \in fn(P),\ E(y) = (a_y, b_y) \end{cases} \end{array} \right\}.$$

We will first describe the general shape of markers, and then infer some relational algebraic properties on them. By reduction, we will use this information to synthesize equality and disequality relations between channel names and between markers.

Shape Analysis Shape analysis consists in distinctly abstracting, for each agent P, the set of markers which can be associated to an instance of P and to each of its channel name. Our abstraction is built upon the lattice Reg of regular languages over the alphabet $(bn(\mathcal{S}) \cup \Sigma)$. For each $V \subseteq bn(\mathcal{S})$, we define $\mathcal{G}_V = Reg \times \mathcal{F}(V, Reg)$. For all (A, f) in $\mathcal{G}_V$, $\gamma_V(A, f) \subseteq Id \times \mathcal{E}(V)$ is the set of all the elements (id, E) which satisfy: $\phi_1(id) \in A$ and $\forall x \in V, y.\phi_1(id_x) \in f(x)$ where $(y, id_x) = E(x)$.

Abstract union is defined point-wisely. Since the domain is not relational, we define, for each $V_?$, $V_!$ in $bn(\mathcal{S})$, the domain $\mathcal{G}_{V_?}^{V_!}$ as the Cartesian product $\mathcal{G}_{V_?} \times \mathcal{G}_{V_!}$, and the primitives $\bullet$, $first^\sharp$, $second^\sharp$ as the canonical pair construction and projection functions. Other abstract primitives are defined as follows:

- $\varepsilon_\emptyset = (\varepsilon, \emptyset)$;
- $\nu x(id^\sharp, f^\sharp) = \left(id^\sharp, f^\sharp[x \mapsto x.id^\sharp] \right)$;
- $new_X^\top(id^\sharp, f^\sharp) = \left(id^\sharp, f^\sharp[x \mapsto bn(\mathcal{S}).\Sigma^*,\ \forall x \in X] \right)$;
- $gc_X(id^\sharp, f^\sharp) = \left(id^\sharp, f_{|X}^\sharp \right)$;
- $match(x = y, (id^\sharp, f)) = \begin{cases} [\_ \to \emptyset] & \text{if } f(x) \cap f(y) = \emptyset \\ f[x, y \mapsto f(x) \cap f(y)] & \text{otherwise}; \end{cases}$
- $match(x \neq y, A) = A$;
- $sync(\{x = y\} \cup X, A) = sync(X, match(x = y, A))$ and $sync(\emptyset, A) = A$;
- $fetch((i, j), ((id_?, f_?), (id_!, f_!))) = ((id_!.(i, j), f_?), (id_!, f_!))$.

There can be infinite increasing sequences in Reg, so we need a widening operator to ensure the convergence of our analysis in a finite amount of time.

Global Numerical Abstraction Numerical abstraction captures the relations between the markers which are associated to an agent and to its channel names. This abstraction is built upon the lattice of the affine relations among a set of numerical variables [9]. Each word is first approximated by its Parikh vector [10], then we abstract the relations between occurrence numbers of letters in markers. For each $V \subseteq bn(\mathcal{S})$, we denote by $\mathcal{X}_V$ the set of variables $\{p^\lambda \mid \lambda \in \Sigma\} \cup \{c^{(\lambda,v)} \mid \lambda \in \Sigma \cup bn(\mathcal{S}), \, v \in V\}$. The variable p^λ is used to describe the number of occurrences of λ in the right comb of the markers of the instances of the agent p, while $c^{(\lambda,v)}$ is used to count the number of occurrences of λ in the marker associated to the syntactic name v when $\lambda \in \Sigma$, or in determining whether v is bound to a channel created by an instance of the restriction $(\nu \, \lambda)$ when $\lambda \in bn(\mathcal{S})$. $\mathcal{G}_V$ is the set of affine equality relations among the variables of $\mathcal{X}_V$. For all $\mathcal{K}$ in $\mathcal{G}_V$, $\gamma_V(\mathcal{K}) \subseteq Id \times \mathcal{E}(V)$ is the set of the elements (id, E) such that the assignment

$$\{p^\lambda \to |id|_\lambda, \, c^{(\lambda,v)} \to |y.id_c|_\lambda \text{ where } (y, id_c) = E(c)\}$$

is a solution of $\mathcal{K}$.

In the same manner, for each $V_?, V_! \subseteq bn(\mathcal{S})$, we denote by $\mathcal{X}_{V_?}^{V_!}$ the set of variables $\{p_i^\lambda \mid \lambda \in \Sigma, \, i \in \{?, !\}\} \cup \{c_i^{(\lambda,v)} \mid \lambda \in \Sigma, i \in \{?, !\}, v \in V_i\}$. We also define $\mathcal{G}_{V_?}^{V_!}$ as the set of affine equality relations among the variables of $\mathcal{X}_{V_?}^{V_!}$. For all $\mathcal{K}$ in $\mathcal{G}_{V_?}^{V_!}$, $\gamma_{V_?}^{V_!}(\mathcal{K}) \subseteq Id \times \mathcal{E}(V)$ is the set of elements $((id_?, E_?), (id_!, E_!))$ such that the assignment:

$$\{p_i^\lambda \to |id_i|_\lambda, \, c_i^{(\lambda,v)} \to |y.id_c|_\lambda \text{ where } (y, id_c) = E_i(c)\}$$

is a solution of $\mathcal{K}$.

Most primitives can be encoded using affine operators described in [9]. Positive abstract matching and synchronization are simply defined by adding new affine constraints in the system. These constraints specify that the Parikh vectors coordinates of the synchronized channel names are pair-wisely equal; negative abstract matching is the identity function. Abstract resource fetching $fetch((i, j), \mathcal{K})$ is obtained using an affine projection to keep only constraints not involving variables of the form $p_!^\lambda$, then adding the constraints $p_?^\lambda = p_!^\lambda$ for all $\lambda \in \Sigma$, and last replacing each occurrence of the variable $p_?^{(i,j)}$ by the expression $p_?^{(i,j)} - 1$.

Example 3. In our example, the analysis detects that:

- in each agent labeled **1**, the variable ***next*** is linked to a name created by the $(\nu \; \textbf{\textit{next}})$ restriction, while the variable ***last*** is linked to a name, either created by an instance of the $(\nu \; \textbf{\textit{next}})$ restriction, or by an instance of the $(\nu \; \textbf{first})$ restriction. We also detect that, in the case where the variable ***last*** is linked to a name created by the $(\nu \; \textbf{\textit{next}})$ restriction, this variable is linked to the name created by the previous recursive instance of the one which has created the name communicated to the variable ***next***;
- in each agent labeled **4**, the variable **first** is linked to a name created by the $(\nu \; \textbf{first})$ restriction, while the variable ***last*** is linked to a name either

created by an instance of the (ν **right**) restriction or by an instance of the (ν **first**) restriction.

These properties are deduced from the following invariants:

$$
\begin{cases}
f(1) \text{ satisfies} \begin{cases}
c^{next,next} = 1 \\
c^{first,last} + c^{next,last} = 1 \\
c^{(0,2),next} = c^{(0,2),last} + c^{next,last}
\end{cases} \\
f(4) \text{ satisfies} \begin{cases}
c^{next,last} + c^{first,last} = 1 \\
c^{first,first} = 1
\end{cases}
\end{cases}
$$

where f denotes the result of the analysis.

Nevertheless, our abstract domain is not expressive enough to merge these two environments, and detects no insightful information for the agent labeled **6**. That is why we introduce a partitioned domain.   □

Partitioned Numerical Abstraction We propose to partition the set of the interactions between names and agents in order to get more accurate results. To avoid complexity explosion, we do not globally abstract environments, we only compare pair-wisely the right comb of the markers. Let ψ^5 be a linear form defined on $\mathbb{Q}^\Sigma$. We introduce the set $\mathcal{G}_V$ of functions which map $(V \times bn(\mathcal{S})) \uplus ((V \times bn(\mathcal{S}))^2)$ onto the set of affine subspaces of $\mathbb{Q}^2$. For all $f \in \mathcal{G}_V$, $\gamma_V(f) \subseteq Id \times \mathcal{E}(V)$ is the set of the elements (id, E) such that:

- $\forall x \in V$, such that $E(x) = (c_x, id_x)$.
  $(\psi([\lambda \to |\phi_1(id)|_\lambda]), \psi([\lambda \to |\phi_1(id_x)|_\lambda])) \in f(x, c_x)$;
- $\forall x \in V, \forall y \in V$, such that $E(x) = (c_x, id_x)$ and $E(y) = (c_y, id_y)$,
  $(\psi([\lambda \to |\phi_1(id_x)|_\lambda]), \psi([\lambda \to |\phi_1(id_y)|_\lambda])) \in f((x, c_x), (y, c_y))$.

Because of the precision of the partitioning, we cannot afford much calculi in this domain. This domain will only be used to propagate information we got from the global numerical abstraction.

We now give primitive definitions. For $V_?, V_! \subseteq bn(\mathcal{S})$, we define $\mathcal{G}_{V_?}^{V_!}$ as the Cartesian product $\mathcal{G}_{V_?} \times \mathcal{G}_{V_!}$. The concretization $\gamma_{V_?}^{V_!}$ is defined pair-wise. Pair construction and projection functions are the canonical ones. Other abstract primitives are defined as follows:

- abstract union is defined by applying the affine union component-wise;
- we define $\nu_x(f)$ to be the following element:

$$f[(x,x) \to \{(n,n) \mid n \in \mathbb{Q}\}, ((x,x),(\_,\_)) \to \mathbb{Q}^2, ((\_,\_),(x,x)) \to \mathbb{Q}^2];$$

- $match(x = y, f) = f\left[\begin{matrix} ((x,c),(y,c)) \to f((x,y),(c,y)) \cap \{(n,n) \mid n \in \mathbb{Q}\} \\ ((x,c),(y,d)) \to \emptyset, \text{ if } c \neq d \end{matrix}\right]$;

---

[5] This abstraction must be done with several linear forms chosen according to a pre-analysis and Thm. 3.

- $match(x \neq y, f) = f$;
- $gc_X(f) = f_{|(\{(x,\_) \mid x \in X\} \uplus \{((x,\_),(y,\_)) \mid x,y \in X\})}$;
- $new_X^\top(f) = f \begin{bmatrix} (x,c) \to \mathbb{Q}^2, x \in X \\ ((x,c),(\_,\_)) \to \mathbb{Q}^2, x \in X \\ ((\_,\_),(x,c)) \to \mathbb{Q}^2, x \in X \end{bmatrix}$;
- $sync(\{y_k = x_k \mid k \in K\}, (f,g)) = (f', g)$ where
  $f' = f[((y_i, c),(y_j, d)) \to f((y_i, c),(y_j, d)) \cap g((x_i, c),(x_j, d)), \forall i, j \in K]$;
- $fetch((i, j), (f, g)) = (f[(y, c) \to \mathbb{Q}^2, \forall y \in V, c \in bn(\mathcal{S})], g)$.

We shall notice that no information is calculated by abstract name creation and abstract marker allocation. Nevertheless, during synchronization, the description of the communicated names is copied to the description of the receiver environment. A complete reduction of properties would lead to a time complexity explosion. Thus, we only use a partial reduction. On the first hand, we use thread markers as pivots and replace each abstract element f with the following element:

$$f \left[((x,c),(y,d)) \to f((x,c),(y,d)) \cap \left\{ (x,y) \; \middle| \; \exists z, \begin{cases} (z,y) \in f(y,d), \\ (z,x) \in f(x,c) \end{cases} \right\} \right],$$

and on the other hand, we always perform reductions between the global numerical abstraction and the partitioned numerical abstraction: the global numerical analysis is used to collect all the information, which is then projected onto each case of the partition.

Example 4. For ψ, we choose the linear form which maps each vector of $\mathbb{Q}^\Sigma$ to the sum of its components. Our analysis succeeds in proving that the second pattern matching, in the example, is not satisfiable. Along the abstract iteration, the analyzer proves that, in agent **6**, the names linked to the variables **x** and **y** have been respectively declared:

1. by the restriction (ν **first**) of a thread with a **0** marker length and the restriction (ν **first**) of a thread with a **0** marker length;
2. or by the restriction (ν **first**) of a thread with a **0** marker length and by the restriction (ν **next**) with a **1** marker length;
3. or by the restriction (ν **next**) of a thread t_1 and by the restriction (ν **next**) of a thread t_2 such that the length of the marker of t_2 is equal to the length of the marker of t_1 plus **1**;
4. or by the restriction (ν **next**) of a thread with a marker of arbitrary length and by the restriction (ν **first**) of a thread with a **0** marker length.

Then, it detects that the matching pattern ([**x** = **y**]) can only be satisfied for the case 1 and it discovers that, in agent **7**, the syntactic channel names **x**, **y** and **first** are bound to a channel created by the instance of the restriction (ν **first**) the thread marker of which is ε and concludes that the second pattern matching ([**x** $\neq$ **first**]) cannot be satisfied. □

6   Reduced Product

We run our analysis with a reduced product of these five domains. There are several kinds of reductions: we use the information about equality of channel names and equality of markers to refine marker analysis; conversely, we use the information obtained in marker analysis to infer information about disequalities of channel names and disequalities of markers; we also make reductions between the global and partitioned numerical abstractions; we use the results obtained in marker analysis to prove equality relations between name markers. For the sake of brevity, we only describe this last kind of reduction, which is the most difficult one. Marker analysis may discover that two markers are recognized by the same automaton $\mathcal{A}$ and have the same Parikh vector, but these two conditions do not ensure that these two markers are the same. We give, in Thm. 3, a decidable sufficient condition on the automaton $\mathcal{A}$ to ensure the equality of such markers.

Let Σ be a finite alphabet, ϕ a linear function from the vector space $\mathbb{Q}^\Sigma$ into the vector space $\mathbb{Q}^m$, and $\mathcal{A}$ an automaton $(Q, \rightarrow, I, F)$ such that the set Q is finite, the relation $\rightarrow$ is a part of $Q \times \Sigma \times Q$ and I and F are parts of Q.

Definition 1. *We define the set $Path(\mathcal{A})$ of acyclic derivation sequences in $\mathcal{A}$ as the set of sequences $q_0 \overset{\lambda_1}{\rightarrow} \dots \overset{\lambda_n}{\rightarrow} q_n$ such that $q_0 \in I$, $q_n \in F$, for all $i, j \in [\![0; n]\!]$, $i \neq j \implies q_i \neq q_j$, and for all $i \in [\![1; n]\!], (q_{i-1}, \lambda_i, q_i) \in \rightarrow$.*

Definition 2. *For $q \in Q$, we define the set $Cycle(\mathcal{A}, q)$ of cycles of $\mathcal{A}$ stemming from the state q, as the set of sequences $q = q_0 \overset{\lambda_0}{\rightarrow} q_1 \dots q_n \overset{\lambda_n}{\rightarrow} q_{n+1} = q$ such that for all $i \in [\![1; n]\!]$, $q_i \neq q$, and for all $i \in [\![0; n]\!]$, $(q_i, \lambda_i, q_{i+1}) \in \rightarrow$.*

Definition 3. *Let $q_0 \overset{\lambda_1}{\rightarrow} \dots \overset{\lambda_n}{\rightarrow} q_n$ be a sequence in $\mathcal{A}$, we define its affine description $\mathcal{P}(q_0 \overset{\lambda_1}{\rightarrow} \dots \overset{\lambda_n}{\rightarrow} q_n)$ as the vector $\phi([\lambda \rightarrow |\lambda_1 \dots \lambda_n|_\lambda])$.*

Definition 4. *Let $a = q_0 \overset{\lambda_1}{\rightarrow} \dots \overset{\lambda_n}{\rightarrow} q_n$ be an acyclic derivation sequence in $Path(\mathcal{A})$, we define the family $\mathcal{F}(a)$ of affine descriptions of the cycles stemming from a state of the derivation a as the family $(\mathcal{P}(c))_{c \in \bigcup \{Cycle(q_i) \mid i \in [\![0;n]\!]\}}$.*

Theorem 3. *If*

1. *for all $q \in Q$, $Card(Cycle(\mathcal{A}, q)) \leqslant 1$,*
2. *for all $a \in Path(\mathcal{A})$, $\mathcal{F}(a)$ is linearly independent in $\mathbb{Q}^m$,*
3. *for all distinct acyclic derivations $a, a' \in Path(\mathcal{A})$, the two affine sets $\mathcal{P}(a) + Vect(\mathcal{F}(a))$ and $\mathcal{P}(a') + Vect(\mathcal{F}(a'))$ are disjoint,*

then

$$\forall u, v \in \Sigma^*, [u, v \text{ recognized by } \mathcal{A} \text{ and } \phi[\lambda \rightarrow |u|_\lambda] = \phi[\lambda \rightarrow |v|_\lambda]] \implies u = v.$$

Roughtly speaking, the first condition ensures that the automaton $\mathcal{A}$ contains no embedded cycle. Then, from the description of the Parikh vector of a word, we can deduce which main acyclic derivation is to be used to recognize this word (third condition), and how many times each cycle is to be used (second condition).

7   Conclusion

We have proposed a new parametric framework for automatically inferring the description of the dependency between the channel names used by the agents of a mobile system. We claim that this framework is very generic since $[2, 12, 7, 3]$ may all be seen as a particular use of it.

We have proposed several abstract domains to deal with this framework. They allowed us to prove some properties which cannot be obtained with $[2, 12, 7, 3]$.

Acknowledgments. We deeply thank the anonymous referees for their significant comments on an early version of this paper. We wish also to thank Patrick and Radhia Cousot, Arnaud Venet, Antoine Miné, Francesco Logozzo and Xavier Rival for their comments and discussions.

References

1. G. Berry and G. Boudol. The chemical abstract machine. *Theoretical Computer Science*, 96:217–248, 1992.
2. C. Bodei, P. Degano, F. Nielson, and H.R Nielson. Control flow analysis for the π-calculus. In *Proc. CONCUR'98*, LNCS. Springer-Verlag, 1998.
3. L. Cardelli, G. Ghelli, and A. D. Gordon. Secrecy and group creation. In *Proc. CONCUR'00*, LNCS. Springer-Verlag, 2000.
4. P. Cousot. Semantic foundations of program analysis. In S.S. Muchnick and N.D. Jones, editors, *Program Flow Analysis: Theory and Applications*, chapter 10, pages 303–342. Prentice-Hall, Inc., Englewood Cliffs, 1981.
5. P. Cousot and R. Cousot. Abstract interpretation frameworks. *Journal of logic and computation*, 2(4):511–547, August 1992.
6. P. Cousot and R. Cousot. Comparing the Galois connection and widening-- narrowing approaches to abstract interpretation. In *Proc. PLILP'92*, LNCS. Springer-Verlag, 1992.
7. J. Feret. Confidentiality analysis for mobiles systems. In *Proc. SAS'00*, LNCS. Springer-Verlag, 2000.
8. J. Feret. Occurrence counting analysis for the π-calculus. *ENTCS*, 39.2, 2001. Workshop on GEometry and Topology in COncurrency theory, PennState, USA, August 21, 2000.
9. M. Karr. Affine relationships among variables of a program. *Acta Informatica*, pages 133–151, 1976.
10. R. J. Parikh. On context-free languages. *Journal of the ACM*, 13:570–581, 1966.
11. D. N. Turner. *The Polymorphic Pi-Calculus: Theory and Implementation*. PhD thesis, Edinburgh University, 1995.
12. A. Venet. Automatic determination of communication topologies in mobile systems. In *Proc. SAS'98*, LNCS. Springer-Verlag, 1998.

Author Index

Aspinall, David   36

Bistarelli, Stefano   53

Charatonik, Witold   295

Feret, Jérôme   314
Flanagan, Cormac   262
Freund, Stephen N.   262

Glew, Neal   147
Gordon, Andrew D.   295
Goubault, Eric   209
Grossman, Dan   21

Haack, Christian   115
Hirschowitz, Tom   6
Hofmann, Martin   36
Horwitz, Susan   162
Hu, Zhenjiang   83
Hughes, John F.   68

Iwasaki, Hideya   83

Kandemir, Mahmut   178
Krishnamurthi, Shriram   68

Laird, James   133
Leroy, Xavier   6

Martel, Matthieu   194, 209
McGuire, Morgan   68
Montanari, Ugo   53
Morrisett, Greg   1

Nielson, Flemming   243
Nielson, Hanne Riis   243
Norrish, Michael   278

Putot, Sylvie   209

Qadeer, Shaz   262

Rossi, Francesca   53

Seidl, Helmut   243
Serjantov, Andrei   278
Sewell, Peter   278

Takeichi, Masato   83
Talbot, Jean-Marc   295
Thiemann, Peter   228

Wand, Mitchell   213
Wansbrough, Keith   278
Weirich, Stephanie   98
Wells, Joe   115
Williamson, Galen B.   213

Lecture Notes in Computer Science

For information about Vols. 1–2214
please contact your bookseller or Springer-Verlag

Vol. 1859: M. Jürgens, Index Structures for Data Warehouses. X, 132 pages. 2002.

Vol. 2215: N. Kobayashi, B.C. Pierce (Eds.), Theoretical Aspects of Computer Software. Proceedings, 2001. XV, 561 pages. 2001.

Vol. 2216: E.S. Al-Shaer, G. Pacifici (Eds.), Management of Multimedia on the Internet. Proceedings, 2001. XIV, 373 pages. 2001.

Vol. 2217: T. Gomi (Ed.), Evolutionary Robotics. Proceedings, 2001. XI, 139 pages. 2001.

Vol. 2218: R. Guerraoui (Ed.), Middleware 2001. Proceedings, 2001. XIII, 395 pages. 2001.

Vol. 2219: S.T. Taft, R.A. Duff, R.L. Brukardt, E. Ploedereder (Eds.), Consolidated Ada Reference Manual. XXV, 560 pages. 2001.

Vol. 2220: C. Johnson (Ed.), Interactive Systems. Proceedings, 2001. XII, 219 pages. 2001.

Vol. 2221: D.G. Feitelson, L. Rudolph (Eds.), Job Scheduling Strategies for Parallel Processing. Proceedings, 2001. VII, 207 pages. 2001.

Vol. 2222: M.J. Wooldridge, G. Weiß, P. Ciancarini (Eds.) Agent-Oriented Software Engineering II. Proceedings, 2001. X, 319 pages. 2002.

Vol. 2223: P. Eades, T. Takaoka (Eds.), Algorithms and Computation. Proceedings, 2001. XIV, 780 pages. 2001.

Vol. 2224: H.S. Kunii, S. Jajodia, A. Sølvberg (Eds.), Conceptual Modeling – ER 2001. Proceedings, 2001. XIX, 614 pages. 2001.

Vol. 2225: N. Abe, R. Khardon, T. Zeugmann (Eds.), Algorithmic Learning Theory. Proceedings, 2001. XI, 379 pages. 2001. (Subseries LNAI).

Vol. 2226: K.P. Jantke, A. Shinohara (Eds.), Discovery Science. Proceedings, 2001. XII, 494 pages. 2001. (Subseries LNAI).

Vol. 2227: S. Boztaş, I.E. Shparlinski (Eds.), Applied Algebra, Algebraic Algorithms and Error-Correcting Codes. Proceedings, 2001. XII, 398 pages. 2001.

Vol. 2228: B. Monien, V.K. Prasanna, S. Vajapeyam (Eds.), High Performance Computing – HiPC 2001. Proceedings, 2001. XVIII, 438 pages. 2001.

Vol. 2229: S. Qing, T. Okamoto, J. Zhou (Eds.), Information and Communications Security. Proceedings, 2001. XIV, 504 pages. 2001.

Vol. 2230: T. Katila, I.E. Magnin, P. Clarysse, J. Montagnat, J. Nenonen (Eds.), Functional Imaging and Modeling of the Heart. Proceedings, 2001. XI, 158 pages. 2001.

Vol. 2231: A. Pasetti, Software Frameworks and Embedded Control Systems. XIV, 293 pages. 2002.

Vol. 2232: L. Fiege, G. Mühl, U. Wilhelm (Eds.), Electronic Commerce. Proceedings, 2001. X, 233 pages. 2001.

Vol. 2233: J. Crowcroft, M. Hofmann (Eds.), Networked Group Communication. Proceedings, 2001. X, 205 pages. 2001.

Vol. 2234: L. Pacholski, P. Ružička (Eds.), SOFSEM 2001: Theory and Practice of Informatics. Proceedings, 2001. XI, 347 pages. 2001.

Vol. 2235: C.S. Calude, G. Păun, G. Rozenberg, A. Salomaa (Eds.), Multiset Processing. VIII, 359 pages. 2001.

Vol. 2236: K. Drira, A. Martelli, T. Villemur (Eds.), Cooperative Environments for Distributed Systems Engineering. IX, 281 pages. 2001.

Vol. 2237: P. Codognet (Ed.), Logic Programming. Proceedings, 2001. XI, 365 pages. 2001.

Vol. 2239: T. Walsh (Ed.), Principles and Practice of Constraint Programming – CP 2001. Proceedings, 2001. XIV, 788 pages. 2001.

Vol. 2240: G.P. Picco (Ed.), Mobile Agents. Proceedings, 2001. XIII, 277 pages. 2001.

Vol. 2241: M. Jünger, D. Naddef (Eds.), Computational Combinatorial Optimization. IX, 305 pages. 2001.

Vol. 2242: C.A. Lee (Ed.), Grid Computing – GRID 2001. Proceedings, 2001. XII, 185 pages. 2001.

Vol. 2243: G. Bertrand, A. Imiya, R. Klette (Eds.), Digital and Image Geometry. VII, 455 pages. 2001.

Vol. 2244: D. Bjørner, M. Broy, A.V. Zamulin (Eds.), Perspectives of System Informatics. Proceedings, 2001. XIII, 548 pages. 2001.

Vol. 2245: R. Hariharan, M. Mukund, V. Vinay (Eds.), FST TCS 2001: Foundations of Software Technology and Theoretical Computer Science. Proceedings, 2001. XI, 347 pages. 2001.

Vol. 2246: R. Falcone, M. Singh, Y.-H. Tan (Eds.), Trust in Cyber-societies. VIII, 195 pages. 2001. (Subseries LNAI).

Vol. 2247: C. P. Rangan, C. Ding (Eds.), Progress in Cryptology – INDOCRYPT 2001. Proceedings, 2001. XIII, 351 pages. 2001.

Vol. 2248: C. Boyd (Ed.), Advances in Cryptology – ASIACRYPT 2001. Proceedings, 2001. XI, 603 pages. 2001.

Vol. 2249: K. Nagi, Transactional Agents. XVI, 205 pages. 2001.

Vol. 2250: R. Nieuwenhuis, A. Voronkov (Eds.), Logic for Programming, Artificial Intelligence, and Reasoning. Proceedings, 2001. XV, 738 pages. 2001. (Subseries LNAI).

Vol. 2251: Y.Y. Tang, V. Wickerhauser, P.C. Yuen, C.Li (Eds.), Wavelet Analysis and Its Applications. Proceedings, 2001. XIII, 450 pages. 2001.

Vol. 2252: J. Liu, P.C. Yuen, C. Li, J. Ng, T. Ishida (Eds.), Active Media Technology. Proceedings, 2001. XII, 402 pages. 2001.

Vol. 2253: T. Terano, T. Nishida, A. Namatame, S. Tsumoto, Y. Ohsawa, T. Washio (Eds.), New Frontiers in Artificial Intelligence. Proceedings, 2001. XXVII, 553 pages. 2001. (Subseries LNAI).

Vol. 2254: M.R. Little, L. Nigay (Eds.), Engineering for Human-Computer Interaction. Proceedings, 2001. XI, 359 pages. 2001.

Vol. 2255: J. Dean, A. Gravel (Eds.), COTS-Based Software Systems. Proceedings, 2002. XIV, 257 pages. 2002.

Vol. 2256: M. Stumptner, D. Corbett, M. Brooks (Eds.), AI 2001: Advances in Artificial Intelligence. Proceedings, 2001. XII, 666 pages. 2001. (Subseries LNAI).

Vol. 2257: S. Krishnamurthi, C.R. Ramakrishnan (Eds.), Practical Aspects of Declarative Languages. Proceedings, 2002. VIII, 351 pages. 2002.

Vol. 2258: P. Brazdil, A. Jorge (Eds.), Progress in Artificial Intelligence. Proceedings, 2001. XII, 418 pages. 2001. (Subseries LNAI).

Vol. 2259: S. Vaudenay, A.M. Youssef (Eds.), Selected Areas in Cryptography. Proceedings, 2001. XI, 359 pages. 2001.

Vol. 2260: B. Honary (Ed.), Cryptography and Coding. Proceedings, 2001. IX, 416 pages. 2001.

Vol. 2261: F. Naumann, Quality-Driven Query Answering for Integrated Information Systems. X, 166 pages. 2002.

Vol. 2262: P. Müller, Modular Specification and Verification of Object-Oriented Programs. XIV, 292 pages. 2002.

Vol. 2263: T. Clark, J. Warmer (Eds.), Object Modeling with the OCL. VIII, 281 pages. 2002.

Vol. 2264: K. Steinhöfel (Ed.), Stochastic Algorithms: Foundations and Applications. Proceedings, 2001. VIII, 203 pages. 2001.

Vol. 2265: P. Mutzel, M. Jünger, S. Leipert (Eds.), Graph Drawing. Proceedings, 2001. XV, 524 pages. 2002.

Vol. 2266: S. Reich, M.T. Tzagarakis, P.M.E. De Bra (Eds.), Hypermedia: Openness, Structural Awareness, and Adaptivity. Proceedings, 2001. X, 335 pages. 2002.

Vol. 2267: M. Cerioli, G. Reggio (Eds.), Recent Trends in Algebraic Development Techniques. Proceedings, 2001. X, 345 pages. 2001.

Vol. 2268: E.F. Deprettere, J. Teich, S. Vassiliadis (Eds.), Embedded Processor Design Challenges. VIII, 327 pages. 2002.

Vol. 2270: M. Pflanz, On-line Error Detection and Fast Recover Techniques for Dependable Embedded Processors. XII, 126 pages. 2002.

Vol. 2271: B. Preneel (Ed.), Topics in Cryptology – CT-RSA 2002. Proceedings, 2002. X, 311 pages. 2002.

Vol. 2272: D. Bert, J.P. Bowen, M.C. Henson, K. Robinson (Eds.), ZB 2002: Formal Specification and Development in Z and B. Proceedings, 2002. XII, 535 pages. 2002.

Vol. 2273: A.R. Coden, E.W. Brown, S. Srinivasan (Eds.), Information Retrieval Techniques for Speech Applications. XI, 109 pages. 2002.

Vol. 2274: D. Naccache, P. Paillier (Eds.), Public Key Cryptography. Proceedings, 2002. XI, 385 pages. 2002.

Vol. 2275: N.R. Pal, M. Sugeno (Eds.), Advances in Soft Computing – AFSS 2002. Proceedings, 2002. XVI, 536 pages. 2002. (Subseries LNAI).

Vol. 2276: A. Gelbukh (Ed.), Computational Linguistics and Intelligent Text Processing. Proceedings, 2002. XIII, 444 pages. 2002.

Vol. 2277: P. Callaghan, Z. Luo, J. McKinna, R. Pollack (Eds.), Types for Proofs and Programs. Proceedings, 2000. VIII, 243 pages. 2002.

Vol. 2281: S. Arikawa, A. Shinohara (Eds.), Progress in Discovery Science. XIV, 684 pages. 2002. (Subseries LNAI).

Vol. 2282: D. Ursino, Extraction and Exploitation of Intensional Knowledge from Heterogeneous Information Sources. XXVI, 289 pages. 2002.

Vol. 2284: T. Eiter, K.-D. Schewe (Eds.), Foundations of Information and Knowledge Systems. Proceedings, 2002. X, 289 pages. 2002.

Vol. 2285: H. Alt, A. Ferreira (Eds.), STACS 2002. Proceedings, 2002. XIV, 660 pages. 2002.

Vol. 2287: C.S. Jensen, K.G. Jeffery, J. Pokorny, Saltenis, E. Bertino, K. Böhm, M. Jarke (Eds.), Advances in Database Technology – EDBT 2002. Proceedings, 2002. XVI, 776 pages. 2002.

Vol. 2288: K. Kim (Ed.), Information Security and Cryptology – ICISC 2001. Proceedings, 2001. XIII, 457 pages. 2002.

Vol. 2289: C.J. Tomlin, M.R. Greenstreet (Eds.), Hybrid Systems: Computation and Control. Proceedings, 2002. XIII, 480 pages. 2002.

Vol. 2291: F. Crestani, M. Girolami, C.J. van Rijsbergen (Eds.), Advances in Information Retrieval. Proceedings, 2002. XIII, 363 pages. 2002.

Vol. 2292: G.B. Khosrovshahi, A. Shokoufandeh, A. Shokrollahi (Eds.), Theoretical Aspects of Computer Science. IX, 221 pages. 2002.

Vol. 2293: J. Renz, Qualitative Spatial Reasoning with Topological Information. XVI, 207 pages. 2002. (Subseries LNAI).

Vol. 2296: B. Dunin-Kęplicz, E. Nawarecki (Eds.), From Theory to Practice in Multi-Agent Systems. Proceedings, 2001. IX, 341 pages. 2002. (Subseries LNAI).

Vol. 2300: W. Brauer, H. Ehrig, J. Karhumäki, A. Salomaa (Eds.), Formal and Natural Computing. XXXVI, 431 pages. 2002.

Vol. 2301: A. Braquelaire, J.-O. Lachaud, A. Vialard (Eds.), Discrete Geometry for Computer Imagery. Proceedings, 2002. XI, 439 pages. 2002.

Vol. 2305: D. Le Métayer (Ed.), Programming Languages and Systems. Proceedings, 2002. XII, 331 pages. 2002.

Vol. 2309: A. Armando (Ed.), Frontiers of Combining Systems. Proceedings, 2002. VIII, 255 pages. 2002. (Subseries LNAI).

Vol. 2314: S.-K. Chang, Z. Chen, S.-Y. Lee (Eds.), Recent Advances in Visual Information Systems. Proceedings, 2002. XI, 323 pages. 2002.